EPOCH

We have seen the fall of the Christian West. . . Kevin Swanson has written a marvel-ous book called *Epoch*. Highly recommend it.

Epoch is a stunning achievement. It is extremely well-researched and is so accessibly written that it easily stands with the finest secular texts. But what makes *Epoch* stand out is the intelligent way the material is selected, presented, and understood from within a thoroughly Christian worldview. I am so excited about this book, and I highly recommend it.

Here is a thoughtful, well-documented and researched analysis of the rise and fall of Western culture from the first Century to the present, and the crucial place of the Christian faith in those events and epochs. Presently faced with Western civilization lying in ashes as it turns away from God, the author challenges believers not to lose heart but, surrounded by ashes, to offer to King Jesus and to the world around us a full-orbed reformation of education, science and technology, media, culture, family life, business, and church life, a reformation which God will bless in His good time according to His sovereign plan for human history.

In times of crisis, we desperately need those who raise the prophetic alarms as well as those who mobilize us for the hard work ahead. In this powerfully incisive book, Kevin Swanson undertakes both roles. He alerts us to the full dimensions of this present darkness, but he also penetrates that darkness with the light of truth so that we may journey onward toward a hope-filled future. This is essential worldview training for the days in which we now live.

GEORGE GRANT

Pastor, Parish Presbyterian Church, Franklin, Tennesse

This book views history through the lens of Scripture, showing that blessing comes through obedience, and judgment comes through disobedience. This survey reminds us that if we don't learn from history we will be doomed to repeat it!

DR. ERWIN LUTZER

Pastor Emeritus, The Moody Church, Chicago

No one will ever fault *Epoch* for being too milquetoast. Some will attempt to dismiss Kevin's magnum opus as too severe. Compromisers with the world in the Old Covenant said the same about Jeremiah and the prophets. Either way, *Epoch* is a history of redemption to be reckoned with.

DOUGLAS BOND

Author, Numerous Books on Christian History

Suppose someone gave you the task of writing the history of Western civilization, detailing its rise and decline, and outlining a strategy of where to go from here. Would that feel daunting? The word "epic" might come to mind. Well, Kevin Swanson has done just that in *Epoch*, a new history course that helps us to understand how we got here and how we should then live; all through the lens of a Biblical worldview. Get the 30,000-foot view of history from the Cross to contemporary culture in this "Epoch" curriculum for adults and their students. I am truly amazed at the size and scope of this undertaking!

ISRAEL WAYNE

Author, Founder of Family Renewal Ministries

I just finished reading Kevin Swanson's new book, *Epoch*. I highly recommend this book. It has become my favorite history of Western civilization. Kevin Swanson acts as a tour guide through the complicated twists and turns of church history, showing key points which had lasting influence for good or evil. But this book is far more than a history. Kevin Swanson has masterfully woven together history, theology, worldview, cultural critique, apologetics, philosophy, presuppositional analysis, futurology, and practical theology into a powerful call to the church to repent for its failure to ground every area of life in the Bible. There is no other book like it.

Though this is a sobering book, I also found it encouraging. Unlike the ten spies of Numbers 14 who accurately described the giants in the land but did so in a way that killed everyone's faith, Kevin Swanson's book showcases giant-slaying heroes of the past who point the way for us to live by faith and not by sight. This book avoids the extremes of false optimism and faith-killing pessimism. It is one of the best interpretations of history that I have read in my lifetime. I recommend it.

DR. PHILLIP KAYSER
President, Biblical Blueprints

Friends, I simply cannot recommend this work enough. In fact, I have an ongoing practice of referring families who are passionate about passing on a biblical worldview to their children to the Generations website. By God's grace, Kevin Swanson and his team have been raised up by God for such a time as this. The work they are doing is exceptional. *Epoch* is no different. Not only is this work an excellent resource for 12th graders, but it is needful for churches as well! Buy this book. Use it. Pass it on. If the LORD tarries, we must "strengthen the things which remain!" (Rev 3:2) Solus Christus!

CARLTON C. MCLEOD
Senior Pastor, Calvary Reformation Church, Chesapeake, VA

Every civilization rests on a creed, a confession of faith. Every civilization rests on a concept of life and law and represents a religion in action. Culture, or the way people live, expresses that people's religion. Any attack on civilization is an attack on its religion. The life of a civilization is its creed. Any civilization with a dying creed is ripe for subversion and destruction. Every creed, even the healthiest, is under continual attack. The civilization which does not defend and further its creedal base is exposing its heart to the enemy's attack. Western civilization is facing death in a life and death struggle with humanism.

When a civilization begins to crumble, it is because its faith, its creed, has been undermined. Conservatives attempt to retain the political forms of the Christian West with no belief in Biblical Christianity. Ultimately, they cannot defend their position. Subversion succeeds by attacking the creed and replacing it with a new creed. When a new creed is accepted, the civilization follows. Western civilization cannot be restored except on the foundation of the Christian faith which God has revealed in the Bible.

ARCHIBALD A. ALLISON
Pastor, Emmaus Orthodox Presbyterian Church, Fort Collins, Colorado

As the Church goes, so goes society. Ideas have their consequences, and the impact on all aspects of society is significant when the Church succumbs to humanistic ideas. While tracing the epistemologies of thought since the ascension of Christ that spawned various ideas, the author identifies their resulting historical consequences throughout the world, showing not only the rise of the West through the power of the gospel, but also its decline and fall as a result of problems within the Church. One of the strengths of this book is not merely explaining *what* the problems are, but *how* we got here and *why*. Swanson provides many cited examples and facts that support his thesis well. This work is valuable to awaken the Church to the vast infiltration of humanism in its many forms and to drive us back to the power of the Gospel and all-encompassing God-centered way of life.

MARION LOVETT
Pastor, Heritage Church, Centerville, Tennessee

EPOCH

*The Rise and Fall
of the West*

KEVIN SWANSON

Generations

PASSING ON THE FAITH

Printed in the United States of America
1st Edition, 2021
2nd Edition, 2022

ISBN: 978-1-954745-09-4

All blockquote Scripture quotations, unless otherwise noted, are taken from the King James Version (KJV). All other Scripture quotations are taken from the New King James Version (NKJV). Copyright © 1982 by Thomas Nelson. Used by permission. All rights reserved.

Cover Design: Kent Jensen
Cover Artwork: Getty Images, Notre Dame Cathedral, Paris, France
Interior Layout Design: Sarah Lee Bryant

Published by:
Generations
19039 Plaza Drive Ste 210
Parker, Colorado 80134
www.generations.org

For more information on this and
other titles from Generations,
visit www.generations.org or call 888-389-9080.

CONTENTS

PREFACE 13

INTRODUCTION 17

CHAPTER I
The Fall 25

CHAPTER II
The Rise & Fall of the Christian Ethos 75

CHAPTER III
The Rise of the Western Church 129

CHAPTER IV
The Decline of the Medieval Church 171

CHAPTER V
The Reformation of the Western Church 203

CHAPTER VI
The Diaspora & Fall of the Western Church 227

CHAPTER VII
The Rise & Fall of a Christian Civilization 301

CHAPTER VIII
The Rise & Fall of Humanity and Charity in the West 377

CHAPTER IX
The Rise & Fall of Science in the West.. 413

CHAPTER X
The Rise & Fall of the Western Economy.. 471

CHAPTER XI
The Rise & Fall of Western Culture 527

CHAPTER XII
The Rise & Fall of Western Liberties 579

CHAPTER XIII
The Rise & Fall of Education in the West.. 627

CHAPTER XIV
The Rise & Fall of the West... 667

NOTES.. 707
IMAGE CREDITS.. 739
GENERAL INDEX 741
SCRIPTURE INDEX... 763

PREFACE

This a simple story, but one that needs be told. The Fall will stand out in world history as paradigmatic as the Fall of Jerusalem or the Fall of Rome. The lesson is a simple one—just one more iteration of the Proverbs 16:18 principle: "Pride goes before destruction, and a haughty spirit before a fall." It is hardly worth defending the truism by historical example, for this divinely-ordained law stands as true and obvious as the force of gravity. The Apostle Paul issued the clarion warning to the early European church while describing the spiritual downfall of his fellow Jews in Romans 11:18-20: "Do not boast against the branches. . . Do not be haughty, but fear."

In the course of history, the Western Gentiles boasted. They were high-minded and they did not fear God. That is the story of the Christian West, and there isn't much more to add to it.

Nevertheless, this was a tragedy of biblical proportions. Such stories must yield "sorrow and continual grief " (Rom. 9:2), or there would be no heart left in us. Not unlike the Jewish experience of AD 70, the tragic nature of what happened defies all description. The consequences are severe—a prominent example of the severity of

God (Rom. 11:22). It is appropriate to feel the heart of the Apostle Paul communicated with such pathos in the 9th through the 11th chapters of Romans 11. Mourning and sorrow indicates what spiritual feeling is left in the heart. Yet, still another response is called for as the remnant grapples with the sadness and horror of it all. God still shows mercy on all (Rom. 11:32), and with Paul we exalt in the perfection of His wisdom and purpose in all things. "Oh, the depth of the riches both of the wisdom and knowledge of God! How unsearchable are His judgments and His ways past finding out!" (Rom. 11:33)

The severity of this book reflects the severity of God. Of course, the proud heart would reject the message out of hand. "Too pessimistic! Too severe! Too depressing!," comes the charge. The other set of prophets are always crying, "Peace, peace!" when there is no peace (Jer. 6:14). To pretend the fall didn't happen or to manufacture an eschatology which would distort the picture is of no benefit to the people of God. Humility, confession, and faith are the right responses. The purpose of this survey of the Rise and Fall of the West is simply this—to encourage the remnant to humility. The message is the same as Paul's admonition to the Roman Gentiles. Be humble. Humble yourself before the mighty hand of God (1 Pet. 5:6).

> Be afflicted, and mourn, and weep: let your laughter be turned to mourning, and your joy to heaviness. Humble yourselves in the sight of the Lord, and he shall lift you up. (James 4:9-10)

Yet we must not conclude that the word of God has failed to take effect (Rom. 9:6). Certainly, the purposes of God will not be thwarted (Rom. 11:31-36). By the Fall of the West, the riches of the kingdom have fallen upon the whole world (Rom. 11:12). The last two hundred years have seen the largest expansion of the Christian faith in the history of the church. Christianity has fanned out into the Global South: Africa, Asia, and Latin America. All praise be to God!

The story is also worth telling because these things are examples, "for our admonition, upon whom the ends of the ages have come" (1 Cor. 10:11). Should our Lord's return delay for a thousand years or a hundred years, here is a story for Africans, Asians, South Americans, and all other Christians. These things are written for their admonition.

To be clear from the outset, real people are held to account for the fall of the West. Real mistakes were made and real sins were committed. The human agents in the decline have real names. While not overlooking the powerful spiritual influences at work, appropriate fault must still lie with the likes of Judas Iscariot, Simon the Sorcerer, Alexander the Coppersmith, and Demas. The villains are people with real faces in the dismantling of the West, and these men and their various organizations must take responsibility for the part they played in the Fall. History has her heroes and villains, and these are to be recorded. As this survey of the Rise and the Fall of the West will bear out, the list of principal defectors, at key moments along the way, must include Paschasius Radbertus, Hincmar of Rheins, Peter Abelard, Innocent III, Fausto Sozzini, Christian Wolff, Immanuel Kant, John Goodwin, Benjamin Whichcote, Charles II of England, William Brattle, and John Leverett. Outside of the Christian church, the self-described apostates and criminal provocateurs, such as Rousseau, Marx, Bentham, Keynes, Dewey, and Sartre, must take their due culpa for the enormous contributions they made to the destruction of Western civilization. Less conspicuous, but included in the list of those who surrendered important ground in the battle for the faith, are Peter Lombard, Thomas Aquinas, Rene Descartes, John Locke, Thomas Hobbes, and George Berkeley.

The many prophetic voices from the last Century warned of the Fall in rather severe apocalyptic tones, offering ample analysis of the putrefying corpse of Western thought. It is not our primary intention to perform more extensive autopsies of the stinking rot of death produced by a thousand post-Christian philosophers. We will only perform a brief postmortem examination to certify the cause of death. Our goal is to edify the reader and to "strengthen the things which remain." Whenever the dead and dying Sardis is encountered in the course of kingdom history, the remnant would do well to apply all energies to heeding the Lord's admonition:

> Be watchful, and strengthen the things which remain, that are ready to die: for I have not found thy works perfect before God. Remember therefore how thou hast received and heard, and hold fast, and repent. If therefore thou shalt not watch, I will come on thee as a thief, and thou shalt not know what hour I will come upon thee. (Revelation 3:2-3)

INTRODUCTION

The thing that hath been, it is that which shall be; and that which is done is that which shall be done: and there is no new thing under the sun. Is there any thing whereof it may be said, See, this is new? it hath been already of old time, which was before us. There is no remembrance of former things; neither shall there be any remembrance of things that are to come with those that shall come after...Let us hear the conclusion of the whole matter: Fear God, and keep his commandments: for this is the whole duty of man. For God shall bring every work into judgment, with every secret thing, whether it be good, or whether it be evil. (Ecclesiastes 1:9-11; 12:13-14)

Augustine's classic work *City of God*, issued in AD 426, was a Christian apologetic intended to absolve Christ and His people of the charge that Christianity was responsible for Rome's fall. The treatise set forth a Christian understanding of history, and it would serve as a blueprint for Christian civilization during the fall of a civilization. At the close of an era, after the collapse of the city of humanist man, the wise would take heed and take a moment to consider what happened. What were the virtues which brought God's blessings upon a civilization at first? And why did it fall? What precipitated this monumental decline and fall? The fall of Rome was blamed on the Christians, but actually came by suicidal paganism. Once again, the fall of the West cannot be blamed on Christians, for the ideology that brought it about was anti-Christian, post-Christian, and apostate Christian. There is hardly any need for a Christian "apology." Beyond any doubt whatsoever, the fall of Western civilization came by "enlightened" humanist philosophy and suicidal social and cultural revolutions. This great epoch in human history resoundingly confirms the blessing of Jesus Christ upon the whole world, as well as the bad fruit produced by the anti-Christian, apostate worldview of the secular atheists and materialists. Here is a grand story of the spectacular rise of a Christian civilization, and the breakdown of that civilization at the hands of those who turned against the faith.

There is yet another reason for looking at historical cataclysms. In Luke's Gospel, chapter 13, the Lord Himself provides us with an interpretive device with which to consider the disaster or the destruction which might visit a human society. The message is the same for all of us—another call for repentance, sackcloth and ashes, here and now.

> There were present at that season some that told him of the Galilaeans, whose blood Pilate had mingled with their sacrifices. And Jesus answering said unto them, "Suppose ye that these Galilaeans were sinners above all the Galilaeans, because they suffered such things? I tell you, Nay: but, except ye repent, ye shall all likewise perish. Or those eighteen, upon whom the tower in Siloam fell, and slew them, think ye that they were sinners above all men that dwelt in Jerusalem? I tell you, Nay: but, except ye repent, ye shall all likewise perish." (Luke 13:1-5)

HOW TO READ HISTORY

And of the children of Issachar, which were men that had understanding of the times, to know what Israel ought to do. (1 Chronicles 12:32)

Where are we? That is a relevant question, especially for every Christian who wishes to know what to do. Of course, all of us would like to know what we ought to do today, tomorrow, and next year. How might we best deny ourselves, take up the cross, and follow Christ today? What shall we do next? Where shall we invest our money? How shall we minister? The men of Issachar knew what they should do because they were able to discern the times. That is a major objective for this study: to discern the times, so that we should know what to do.

Think of an amnesiac who jerks awake in a business meeting and finds himself surrounded by 25 department heads. All heads are looking to him, and he quickly realizes he is in charge of a company. But he knows nothing of the history of the company. He doesn't know what challenges were faced previously, or those to address in the present. How does he lead? What is the next thing to do? His position is completely untenable. He is doomed to failure. The question therefore is relevant: Where are we in history? And, what are the lessons to be learned?

When considering the human experience, there are highly significant, determinative events, actions, and persons which establish trajectories for the rise and fall of world civilizations. Some events or developments may be considered a thousand times more significant, both in their causal influence and historical interpretive import. There are trends to analyze which better illustrate effects of worldview shifts among the nations. Some sins are more heinous and more aggravating in the sight of God than others, evincing the true state of the heart for all to see. History has its "Waterloos" and "Rubicons"—direction-setting moments of the highest importance.

Picking and choosing the newsworthy or history-worthy reports is what every journalist and historian does every day. (The news is merely the chronicling of more recent history, taking place over the previous 24-hour period). It would be practically impossible to record every human event, taking place over a certain period of time, while including every particular detail of that event to an infinite level of precision. Such comprehensive coverage would require millions of pages, and the historian and the reader would still be left with the task of separating gnats and camels—the significant from the insignificant. All historical knowledge requires interpretative work. Yet, the task of separating between the gnats and camels is not easy. First, one must apply the right worldview filter to the historical data. Without applying a biblical worldview rooted in divine revelation, how could anyone determine with any degree of certainty the truth value, the ethical value, the meaningfulness, the purpose, and the significance of any historical data? How could any historian weigh the historicity of the data itself without applying a worldview filter known to be absolutely, infallibly, and impeccably trustworthy for its fundamental truth value? This survey begins with the assumption that "Thy [God's] Word is truth" (John 17:17).

History is vitally important to us. Christ comes in history, for our redemption. But, historical reporting as well as news reports are infamous for creating diversions. When a smoke bomb goes off in the post office, the wise police officer refuses to investigate the post office. Instead, he immediately attends to the bank, where the robbery is happening. Much of history and news reporting then is diversionary—directing the reader to the post office to consider more smoke bombs, while the bank is robbed over and over again. Godly, thoughtful, and wise teachers will apply a biblical ethic and theology to history so as to identify the data that matters most.

Given that the worldview applied to the historical record of events will always determine their significance, will the Supreme Court *Obergefell* decision prove more devastating than *Marbury* or *Dred Scott*? Could the removal of J. Gresham Machen from the Presbyterian Church have been of greater import than the formation of the League of Nations? Do the scandalous sins that came to mark the leadership of so many Christian denominations between 1980 and 2020 signify anything at all in the flow of ecclesiastical history? Does the selling of doves and the exchange of money in the temple mean anything in the scheme of things? In the final analysis, there is only one question that matters when recording the history of the actions of men; and that is, "What does God think of this?" For a review of the rise and fall of the West all attempts will be made for a self-consciously biblical and consistent interpretation of events. Would that we could all think as God thinks, love as God loves, and hate as Christ hates!

There are historical landmarks more significant than others along the way—some appearing as small hills on the landscape, and others towering like Mount Everest. The seismographs of Western culture hit 9.0 on the Richter scale with such things as the loss of Harvard College to the Latitudinarians, the French Revolution, the publication of *The Origin of Species*, Friedrich Nietzsche's insanity, J. Gresham Machen's defrocking, the publication of the *Humanist Manifesto* (1933), the eugenics of Adolf Hitler (1930s), the publication of *Playboy* magazine (1953), FDA approval of the abortifacient conception control pill (1960), *Engle v. Vitale* (1962), The Beatles "invasion" (1964), the California no-fault divorce law signed by Ronald Reagan (1969), *Roe v. Wade* (1973), Kurt Cobain's suicide (1994), the ordination of Gene Robinson (2003), the election of Barack Obama (2008), *Obergefell v. Hodges* (2011), the homosexualization and transgendering of schools in California (2011), the CCCU Utah Compromise (2019), and the worldwide Coronavirus crisis (2020). Not all registered significant as a cause or fundamental force in the decline, but such occurrences are highly revelatory and symptomatic of the Western apostate cultural demise. These represented a marked shift, a sharp angling downwards, and a decided move in the wrong direction—all part of the ongoing saga of a revolution against God.

HISTORY—ESSENTIAL, COMPULSORY, CORE FOR CHRISTIANS

Psalm 78 instructs the people of God to tell their children of the "wonderful works that He has done." Christian parents should teach their children the Word of God and the works of God in history, beginning with the work of Christ in redemption. Failure to do so, Asaph says, produces a generational apostasy—a people who forget God's works, who turn back in the day of battle, and refuse to walk in His law (Ps. 78:8-11). Thus, nobody takes history more seriously than the Christian, because it is a record of true reality—God's reality. It is a record of His salvation visiting this world. These are the outworking of God's providence. More than this, the Christian cannot help but be encouraged by a study of history. For all of history testifies to the truths of Scripture, the sovereign hand of God, the judgment of God, the mercies of God, and the inevitable success of the church.

> Give ear, O my people, to my law: incline your ears to the words of my mouth. I will open my mouth in a parable: I will utter dark sayings of old: Which we have heard and known, and our fathers have told us. We will not hide them from their children, shewing to the generation to come the praises of the Lord, and his strength, and his wonderful works that he hath done. For he established a testimony in Jacob, and appointed a law in Israel, which he commanded our fathers, that they should make them known to their children: That the generation to come might know them, even the children which should be born; who should arise and declare them to their children:

That they might set their hope in God, and not forget the works of God, but keep his commandments: And might not be as their fathers, a stubborn and rebellious generation; a generation that set not their heart aright, and whose spirit was not stedfast with God. (Psalm 78:1-8)

I

_____

THE FALL

The crown is fallen from our head: woe unto us, that we have sinned!
For this our heart is faint; for these things our eyes are dim.
Because of the mountain of Zion, which is desolate,
The foxes walk upon it.
Thou, O Lord, remainest for ever;
Thy throne from generation to generation.
Wherefore dost thou forget us for ever, and forsake us so long time?
Turn thou us unto thee, O Lord, and we shall be turned;
Renew our days as of old.
But thou hast utterly rejected us; thou art very wroth against us.
(Lamentations 5:16-22)

The lamentations of Jeremiah were appropriate for the fall of Jerusalem and the impending judgment facing the people of God. But should we apply such lamentations to the present condition of the Western church and associated nations? Those who have witnessed the Fall firsthand and its effects upon friends, family, churches, schools, cities, villages, and cultures resonate to these words. Grieving and lamenting, pining for the days of visitation, and crying out for spiritual revitalization is the everyday position of the remnant. The plaintive cry goes up, "Will You not revive us again, that Your people may rejoice in You?" (Ps. 85:6). Surely we would not wish to emulate the Old Testament prophet Jonah—watching dispassionately from the outside for the judgment of God upon Nineveh, more concerned about the worm in his gourd. When the body suffers, "all the members suffer with it"(1 Cor. 12:26). These are our people. These were our churches. With the Apostle, it is quite right to feel "great sorrow and continual grief" in our hearts for the tragic loss. (Rom. 9:2).

Since the West was blessed with the very best heritage of Christian faith and ready access to the oracles of God (Rom. 3:2), could Jesus's warning given in Matthew 11 apply? Will it be more tolerable for Sodom and Tyre in the day of judgement than for America?

> Woe to you, Chorazin! Woe to you, Bethsaida! For if the mighty works which were done in you had been done in Tyre and Sidon, they would have repented long ago in sackcloth and ashes. But I say to you, it will be more tolerable for Tyre and Sidon in the day of judgment than for you. And you, Capernaum, who are exalted to heaven, will be brought down to Hades; for if the mighty works which were done in you had been done in Sodom, it would have remained until this day. But I say to you that it shall be more tolerable for the land of Sodom in the day of judgment than for you. (Matthew 11:21-24)

Central to the thesis of this book is the proposition that the decline of the Western Christian church (both Catholic and Protestant) contributed to a much-reduced Christian influence in every aspect of the macro culture. The Christian worldview underpinnings of the culture were eventually replaced by a predominately anti-Christian worldview. These corrupted footers in the foundation were too flimsy to hold up the superstructure leading to the decline and fall of Western civilization.

At the present, only slight disagreement remains over the extent of the Fall of the West, but no serious historian would question the Fall itself. The easiest and most obvious metric is economic. Until the year 2000, Europe and North America produced over half of the Gross World Product, peaking out at 66% in 1960, while these nations constituted only 10% of the world population. This economic index collapsed to 37% in 2015, and continued to contract in following years.[1] Definitively, the West has fallen—first realized by the loss of a position of worldwide economic supremacy. The implications were manifold. The East was on the rise, economically and militarily. And, the whole world was on notice that two-thirds of the entire globe's socio-economic systems were shrinking fast. The economic dominoes were stacked closer in the international markets, and this would most certainly have a profound impact on the whole world for at least a century. The entire world's political power structures were shifting.

PRIMA FACIE EVIDENCE FOR THE FALL

The last two worldwide recessions were the worst—first with the 2008 banking crisis, spurred on by greedy sub-prime lending, followed by the 2020s recession. America celebrated the recovery from the 2008 recession by almost doubling its debt-to-GDP ratio. By 2020, the United States made up 52% of the gross world government debt while contributing only 25% of the gross world product. The United States' federal government debt-to-GDP ratio was trailing not far behind the world's most volatile and debt-ridden economies—Japan, Greece, Portugal, Lebanon, and Italy.[2] Of 200 countries, these have been labeled as the worst economies in the world. By another metric, the International Monetary Fund put the United States as the fourth worst nation in the world for its debt-to-GDP ratio, behind Japan, Greece, and Italy.[3] By the metric of Net Lending/Borrowing, the United States was the third worst nation in the world, following the crippled nations of Oman and Sudan.[4] The index registered in the negative, meaning that America was now the biggest borrower in the world. *Between 1980 and 2020, the United States became the largest and most unstable domino in the train of stacked dominoes representing the world economy.* Although touted as the largest, richest economy in the world, in truth the United States was at the bottom—the tail (in the words of Deuteronomy 28).

> The stranger that is within thee shall get up above thee very high; and thou shalt come down very low. He shall lend to thee, and thou shalt not lend to him: he shall be the head, and thou shalt be the tail. Moreover all these curses shall come upon thee, and shall pursue thee, and overtake thee, till thou be destroyed; because thou hearkenedst not unto the voice of the Lord thy God, to keep his commandments and his statutes which he commanded thee: And they shall be upon thee for a sign and for a wonder, and upon thy seed for ever. Because thou servedst not the Lord thy God with joyfulness, and with gladness of heart, for the abundance of all things. (Deuteronomy 28:43-47)

Nothing portrays the Western worldview shift and its destructive effects better (on a societal level) than debt and birth rates. This shift in worldview is evident by the following chart:

Year	Total US Debt to GDP[5]	US Birth Rate (per woman)
1950 - 1980	140% - 160%	3.0 - 1.8
1980 - 2021	160% - 417%	1.8 - 1.5 est.

While the US total public and private debt moved from 140% to 417% of the GDP, the UK and the Eurozone increased their total debt about the same amount.[6] Between 1970 and 2020, the fertility rate for European Union nations dropped from 2.7 to 1.5 children per woman, and closer to 1.4 for non-immigrant women.[7] Trend charts following birth rates show all twenty-one Western European nations sinking below the replacement level of 2.1 between 1970 and 1993.

Meanwhile, the world fertility rate dropped from 4.6 to 2.4 between 1950 and 2020, largely due to the influence of Margaret Sanger and the conception control/abortion revolution. The only continents maintaining a reproducible social system by the 2020s were Africa and Oceania. North America and Europe came up last for reproductive strength.

The above table reveals the bankruptcy of a dying Western culture, and the worldview shift bringing it about. Ideas have consequences, and the consequences are clearly visualized on the trendcharts. Why then did the West implode its birth rates, consume all the capital of previous generations, and mortgage the future of its grandchildren by unprecedented debt between 1970 and 2020? This generation was living out the hopeless and hapless ideas of the existentialist Jean-Paul Sartre and the homosexual economist, John Maynard Keynes. This data speaks to a loss of the will to continue a civilization. This was the point at which the self-centered, myopic existentialists crossed over the line of despair, and the toxic, corrupting worldview had gone mainstream in the West by AD 1980.

THE FALL

Why should ye be stricken any more? ye will revolt more and more: the whole head is sick, and the whole heart faint. From the sole of the foot even unto the head there is no soundness in it; but wounds, and bruises, and putrifying sores: they have not been closed, neither bound up, neither mollified with ointment. Your country is desolate, your cities are burned with fire: your land, strangers devour it in your presence, and it is desolate, as overthrown by strangers. And the daughter of Zion is left as a cottage in a vineyard, as a lodge in a garden of cucumbers, as a besieged city. Except the Lord of hosts had left unto us a very small remnant, we should have been as Sodom, and we should have been like unto Gomorrah. (Isaiah 1:5-9)

But what describes the very essence of the "Fall of the West?" The symptoms and effects of the breakdown of a civilization are hard to miss, but what is the root of it? Externally, the Fall is easily represented by every social and economic indexes—all of which appear to be ten times worse than they were 50-100 years ago when the warning sirens sounded. Isaiah 1 describes the heart of the spiritual condition: "The whole head is sick, and the whole heart faint," and "ye will revolt more and more." The post-Christian condition is worse than the pre-Christian condition. The disposition is a vehement, self-conscious hatred towards Christ, and continual revolt against God and all that is good. As common grace that sustains pagan, pre-Christian nations through the centuries is withheld from the apostate civilization, imminent destruction must necessarily follow. The de-Christianization of Western culture has resulted in the breakdown of Western civilization itself; and the de-Christianization of culture is most evident in the widespread institutionalized acceptance of the worst forms of social sin and public immorality. A universal rejection of God and His law must inevitably result in the breakdown of civilization on a broad scale. The effects are obvious in the socio-economic sphere. But the prevalent, public sins contributing to the decline are also unmistakable. Repeatedly throughout history, primitive tribes and pagan empires have disintegrated and disappeared when they countenance the breakdown of the family, the widespread practice of infanticide, human sacrifice, and the open acceptance of sodomy. Such was the story of the demise of the Persians, Greeks, Romans, Mayas, Aztecs, the Calusa tribe, etc. Inevitably, this demise is brought about by the idealization of man, the pride of man, moral decay, and the futility of a man-oriented philosophy. But the more rapid and severe demise of any civilization must occur upon Christian apostasy, as is discovered in the present milieu. "To whom much is given, much will be required" (Luke 12:48).

At this point, the sheer quantity of peoples in the West—both inside and outside the organized church—espousing and celebrating infanticide, moral perversions, and the breakdown of the family cannot be ignored. Faced with such a crisis, God's people should respond with a rising, holy, moral sensitivity to the condition of the Western world and the Western church. As always, the warnings of Christ apply:

> And take heed to yourselves, lest at any time your hearts be overcharged with surfeiting, and drunkenness, and cares of this life, and so that day come upon you unawares. For as a snare shall it come on all them that dwell on the face of the whole earth. Watch ye therefore, and pray always, that ye may be accounted worthy to escape all these things that shall come to pass, and to stand before the Son of Man. (Luke 21:34-36)

REAL DEATH

> For the wages of sin is death; but the gift of God is eternal life through Jesus Christ our Lord. (Romans 6:23)

Humanist man is caught in tension between an unrealistic optimism and pessimism in reference to himself. On the one hand, he attempts to displace God with self for determining his own ethics, truth, gender, etc. He would be as "god" determining good and evil. But then, on the other hand, he would insist that he is cosmic dust, alone in the universe with God, without a transcendent purpose and essential value. God or mere cosmic dust, neither is realistic. He makes a poor god and he cannot live as though he were cosmic dust. Gradually, optimism gives way to pessimism, and man crosses the line of despair.

On February 10, 2011, *Time* Magazine featured a front-page article headlined: "2045: The Year Man Becomes Immortal." Still hoping technology would save him, modern man marked out the year of "singularity" in which computers would transform man's reality. In what appeared a divine irony of ironies, 2011 also marked the year at which life expectancy peaked in America and started on the decline—

largely due to the increase in despair deaths attributed to alcohol, drugs, and suicide.

The death of the West was realized most noticeably in the increase in despair deaths. The rate of drug-overdose deaths increased by 400% between 2000 and 2020. The suicide rate increased 38% over the same period. The rate of alcoholic liver disease deaths rose 40%, the rate of liver cancer deaths rose 60%, and the rate of alcoholic poisoning deaths increased 400%. Between 1965 and 2018, drug overdose deaths increased from 1 per 100,000 to 20 per 100,000—a twenty-fold increase. These were the social consequences of nihilist ideas, a world of pessimism. These statistics represented a people fully committed to escaping reality and repudiating life in the real world. Despair had gone mainstream. This is what the end of a civilization looks like.

> And even as they did not like to retain God in their knowledge, God gave them over to a reprobate mind, to do those things which are not convenient... (Romans 1:28)

Insanity turned into a mainstream phenomenon in the 2010s. Between 1991 and 2017, the medical administration of opioids increased from 76 million to 259 million legal prescriptions per year, amounting to almost two prescriptions for every adult in America. Per capita use of the legally-dispensed drugs increased fifty-fold between 1980 and 2020.[8] Neither were children exempted from the sad demise of the American psyche, with Psychotropic drug prescriptions for children increasing sixty-fold between the 1980s and 2020.[9]

Whether the society would opt towards slow individual suicides or mass institutional suicide, it was all the consequence of postmodern thinking. Man was evermore self-consistent with his nihilism—the worldview of meaninglessness.

More often, this death revealed itself in ever-increasing levels of disconnection from reality and isolation. It was the death of personality and the death of human relationship. It was a slow, torturous death of addiction to drugs, internet/electronic games, pornography, social media, and all forms of electronic stimulation. To watch the process and to witness the mass of victims was itself a terrifying ordeal.

> Be not over much wicked, neither be thou foolish: why shouldest thou die before thy time? (Ecclesiastes 7:17)

ABORTION

> And thou shalt eat the fruit of thine own body, the flesh of thy sons and of thy daughters, which the LORD thy God hath given thee, in the siege, and in the straitness, wherewith thine enemies shall distress thee. (Deuteronomy 28:53)

The final and ultimate horror and curse attending a society, as described in Deuteronomy 28, arrives when women consume their own children. Nothing manifests a civilization's commitment to death more than mothers killing their infants—the squelching of the natural instinct of maternal love. Humans descend lower than the animal kingdom when the natural love of a mother for her children disappears. What utter devastation was visited upon the West by this cursed plague, beginning in the 1960s and 1970s!

During the decline of faith and the rise of transcendentalism and unitarianism in the 1830s and 1840s, abortion appeared on the scene in America (especially in New York, Boston, Philadelphia, and Newark). Mainly facilitated through the clandestine work of Madame Restell and her competitor Madame Costello, at an estimated rate of 0.5% of live births met the abortionist's knife and apothecary's abortifacient drug. This was virtually eliminated during the Christian revivals following the civil war. A century later, the rate of child killing had increased a thousand-fold. After a thousand years of the Christian era, infanticide or abortion had returned to the West with a vengeance.

The complete deception of the nations, as political, educational, and medical institutions, was finally completed when New Zealand officially legalized the killing of infants on March 19th, 2020. Northern Ireland followed suit on April 9th, as the last of the Western nations to do so. It was a fatal reversal of a thousand years of Christian influence in the West.

The whole aggregation of pagan tribes could never compete with the Western world with its mass production of death, aided by modern technology. Between 1950 and 2020, the West championed a holocaust resulting in the elimination of one-third to one-half of the world population—*between two and four billion* babies. This mass killing was at least thirty times worse than the devastation of World War II, and twenty times worse than the bloody work of the communists. The sheer quantities of children killed by abortion doctors and the abortifacient effects of the IUD and the conception control pill are beyond anything the world had ever seen. The destruction appeared less obtrusive than the torture chambers of the inquisitions, the Nazi death camps, and the cruel coliseums of Rome, but far exceeded all these atrocities in sheer quantity of lives lost. Moreover, the egregiousness of this modern evil was heightened by the helplessness and innocence of the victims, the dissolution of natural maternal love, and the hypocrisy of the "liberals" who advocated for the killing.

> Who being past feeling have given themselves over unto lasciviousness, to work all uncleanness with greediness. (Ephesians 4:19)

The mass distribution of the death spirit came by extremely powerful, rich governments enabled by an advanced science and technology. This phenomenon was unlike anything human society had ever achieved in history—an unleashing of evil at levels never contemplated by the cruelest tyrants of the past.

But he that sinneth against me wrongeth his own soul: all they that hate me love death. (Proverbs 8:36)

EUTHANASIA

The death march continued. Between 1994 and 2019, ten US states adopted doctor-assisted suicide laws. Legal euthanasia or doctor-assisted suicide was introduced into the Netherlands, Belgium, Columbia, Luxembourg, Canada, Switzerland, and Germany around the same time.

The year 2011 was a highly symbolic year in the history of the West, as the year the US Social Security Fund dipped into the red for the first time and the Baby Boom generation entered retirement. First conceived as a sophisticated Ponzi Scheme at a time when Americans were still having babies, the system assumed a minimum birth replacement rate and a strong worker-to-retiree ratio. The timing for the bust of Social Security could not have been worse, because 2011 was also the year that the first of 80 million Baby Boomers entered their retirement years. For the following thirty-five years, these retirees would require more medical and economic support from the younger generation. But, this was the same generation that initiated an abortion holocaust which resulted in at least 80 million dead babies (by surgical abortion and various abortifacient conception control devices). Who would support the retirees in most of the developed countries around the world through the 2050s? Because of the imploding birth rate in 80 countries around the world, the worker-to-retiree ratio in 2030 would amount to one third of what it was in 1950 (when the social security systems were first implemented).

But what about the character of the younger generation? Would the few young people left be prepared to support the heavy load of elderly retirees and a bankrupt social security system? Alas, the timing could not have been worse for this either. The character of the nation was in free fall. Over 50% of Americans were supported by state and federal governments, mostly by welfare programs. And, over 50% of children born to millennials were born out of wedlock—an increase from 5% in 1960.[10] If young men were disinterested in fathering their own children, why would they care for the elderly?

Not surprisingly, *Time Magazine* concluded that the Millennial generation was the laziest, the unluckiest, and the most narcissistic generation ever.[11] This younger generation, on average, started out with less capital than any previous generation, and they were saddled with three hundred times more college debt than the Baby Boomers carried in the 1970s. Meanwhile, the Baby Boomers retired with far more debt than the Silent Generation and very little if any inheritance to pass along to future generations. *What was the lesson the Baby Boomer generation passed on to their progeny when they aborted 80 million of their siblings?* What would the most narcissistic generation do to the 80 million Baby Boomers who aborted 80 million children between 1970 and 2010—in the year 2040? Mass euthanasia appeared to be the only possible answer to the question given the socio-economic degrade and the moral conditions dominant in Western nations. Parricide would be the inevitable consequence of the mass infanticide committed by the previous generation.

THE "END OF MEN" & THE "DEMISE OF GUYS"

As for my people, children are their oppressors, and women rule over them. O my people, they which lead thee cause thee to err, and destroy the way of thy paths. (Isaiah 3:12)

Books and articles poured out of publishing houses through the opening decades of the 21st Century announcing the "end of men" and the "demise of guys." The first indication of social disintegration was that men went AWOL—"absent without leave"—in respect to family and community.

The 20th Century novelist, John Steinbeck could not help but signal the real problem with a society given up to despair in his award-winning classic, *The Grapes of Wrath* (1939). Although the author would have rather blamed the hopeless conditions on the dust bowl and environmental causes, the root of despair is found in the human heart. When the going got tough for the family, the men would disappear, walk down the river—never to be seen again. The last painful scene perfectly portrays the death of manhood and modern society as Joad absconds with the child's last few drops milk from its mother's breast.

In the year 2000, the suicide rate for men was 4.5 times that of women.[12] The number of nations in the world led by a female increased from two to seventy between 1950 and 2020, thirty-five before the year 2000 and another thirty-five between 2000 and 2020. Nations capitulating to female leadership included most of Europe, most of South America, Canada, South Africa, and Australia.[13] The United States increased its female leadership from 2% to 21% between 1960 and 2020.[14] Between 1950 and 2020, women delayed having children, and upon birth, remanded them to professional daycare. Access to abortion and abortifacients also enabled more "freedom" to enter the workforce and thereby temporarily maintain something of a national economy. The women's share of the national workforce increased from 28% to 47% during those years, while the men's share dropped from 72% to 53%.[15] Fatherhood was disappearing quickly. By 2018, 71% of children born to women under 24 years of age were born out of wedlock. Only one third of the country lived in a household with two parents.[16] As men disappeared, the nuclear family declined.

The death of nations followed. Seven Western nations boasting the highest levels of male abdication in leadership, with over 50% of legislative or cabinet-level female involvement, averaged an increase of only 23% of the GDP/Capita between 2010 and 2020. Nations with greater than 80% male involvement witnessed an average increase of

39% on GDP/Capita over the same timeframe.[17]

THE DEATH OF TRUTH & REALITY

> But the path of the just is as the shining light, that shineth more and
> more unto the perfect day. The way of the wicked is as darkness: they
> know not at what they stumble. (Proverbs 4:18-19)

Well into the 21st Century, the millennial generation and others
were busy playing computer games while empires burned to the ground
(a pattern seen in the fall of Rome in the 4th and 5th centuries). Video
gaming, a $40 billion industry at the turn of the century, ballooned
into a $160 billion industry by 2020, surpassing the music and movie
industries by fifteen-fold (and the entire sports industry by more than
double).

Sports had always offered something of a metaphor for real
battles in real life. But, as the post-modern man painted his meta-
narrative with new layers of pretend unrealities, an entire genre of
sports competitions developed around sports video games. Incredibly,
modern sports fans were left watching fake sports heroes playing fake
sports games. National playoff and championship events were held
in which "the world's best Madden competitors face-off for a piece
of the $220,000 prize purse and to claim the title of Madden NFL 20
Champion."[18] Some three million viewers crowded in to watch the
"games" on electronic devices, adding another layer to the pretend
narrative.[19]

The movie industry abandoned itself to pure escapism in the
early 21st Century. By 2019, five of the top grossing blockbusters
were of the Science Fiction/Fantasy genre: *Star Wars: Episode VII - The
Force Awakens* (2015), *Avengers: Endgame* (2019), *Avatar* (2009), *Black
Panther* (2018), and *Avengers: Infinity War* (2018). Previous generations
preferred *Gone with the Wind*, *Titanic*, *The Sound of Music*, and *The Ten*

Commandments. In 2019, nine out of the top thirteen highest-grossing motion pictures represented the Science Fiction/Fantasy genre. In 2008, only three out of the thirteen highest-grossing films represented the Science Fiction/Fantasy genre, and two decades earlier, none of the top thirteen highest-grossing films could have been classified under the Science Fiction/Fantasy genre.

At this time, first world nations and those most influenced by Western culture, showed little interest in reality. Post-modern relativism moved from the rejection of absolute truth value to the abandonment of reality itself. That philosophy propounded by John Dewey, Jean-Paul Sartre, Friedrich Nietzsche, and G.W.F. Hegel was running in the mainstream. By nature, man runs from God and Western society had paved the highways for the escape route. The final escape must necessarily include the denial of all existence, which can only end with insanity and other forms of suicide. Symptomatic of this escape from reality was a wholesale rejection of sobriety and maturity at all levels of society. In the fading of human civilization, nobody really cares much about anything, at least for more than ten minutes at a time.

THE DEATH OF PERSONALITY

The death of humanness must involve the depersonalization of man as made in the image of God, a phenomenon which appeared mainly after the development of the personal computer and the internet. Face-to-face relationships were replaced with face-to-screen. Portable computers (laptops, i-Pads, and i-Phones) enabled a 7-day, 24-hour escape into the electronic universe of avatars, social media relationships, fake news/narratives, and entertainment. Ever-increasing levels of isolation destroyed relationships as man wandered with Cain in the wildernesses further east of Eden.

Sexuality, as the highest form of human intimacy, suffocated by the loss of relationship. Modern man was left as void of the image of God as he had ever been—a hollow shell absent of personality or relationship with other personalities. Most tragically, the ultimate depersonalization of sexuality came by the mass proliferation and accessibility of pornography. All social barriers were removed when Apple launched the iPhone in 2007, and smartphones spread around the world. Access to pornography and the isolation of media was widespread for children as well as adults. In 2019, 95% of teens 13 to 17 years of age had constant access to a smartphone (and pornography), and almost half of those surveyed admitted to "constantly" being on the internet.[20] By the end, eighty percent of American men 18 to 30 years of age were addicted to pornography, admitting to at least monthly use.[21] Such was the prevalence of this social corruption. Overall, Americans had increased their participation in pornography from 20% to 65% between 1970 and 2019.[22]

THE DEATH OF SEXUALITY, HUMANNESS, & GENDER IDENTITY

Removing sexuality from the context of God's order of marriage would inevitably lead to social burnout. Sexual sin is ever present in a fallen world, but sexual chaos and mass corruption is only witnessed with civilizations in their death throes. Based on US legal records and public surveys, persons involved in homosexuality increased from 57 identifiable cases between 1865 and 1880 to 7% of the population in 2022 (with 70% public support for it)—an increase of 120,0000-fold.[23] The corruption was total. Between the years 2000 and 2022, the whole Western world moved towards encouraging and approving all forms of perverted sexuality—and persecuting any who might disagree.

This wholesale embrace of sexual sin has introduced devastating effects upon the human body in the form of sexually-transmitted diseases. Between 2007 and 2018, incidents of chlamydia increased

149%, gonorrhea 126%, and syphilis 80%.[24] The US Centers for Disease Control estimated 110 million cases of STD's in the country, with an additional 20 million new cases occurring each year.[25] The worldwide AIDS epidemic—which is mainly transmitted sexually—killed more people than the Spanish flu of 1918-1920. By 2020, the Center for Disease Control set the death toll from HIV / AIDS related illnesses at 32 million.[26] In the providence of God, this turned out to be the largest sexually-transmitted disease killer in history.

Considered the worst of the Roman emperors by pagan and Christian historians alike, Emperor Nero is the historical prototype for the present malaise. His agenda was defined by three crucial elements—the introduction of homosexual marriage, the initiation of major Christian persecution, and the incineration of Rome. At the turn of the 20th Century, all three of these elements were replicated across the Western world. It was a return to the "Neronic agenda."

In the final rejection of God's creation order, modern man attempted total self-definition and ultimate autonomy by surrendering his birth gender. Thereby he lost all remnants of identity and humanity in his own mind. Gender dysphoria was institutionalized at the highest echelons of power. Public schools and other institutions were required by law to accommodate children and adults attempting to change their gender, and those refusing to participate in the insanity were persecuted. The suicidal nature of such desperate attempts to self-definition was manifest, in that 42% of those dissatisfied with their God-given gender would attempt suicide.[27]

THE NATURE OF THE FALL

Now all these things happened unto them for ensamples: and they are written for our admonition, upon whom the ends of the world are come. Wherefore let him that thinketh he standeth take heed lest he fall. There hath no temptation taken you but such as is common to man: but God is faithful, who will not suffer you to be tempted above that ye are able; but will with the temptation also make a way to escape, that ye may be able to bear it. (1 Corinthians 10:11-13)

Paul's words to the European Gentile world (Corinth) are very relevant to Christians in the present extremity. Something very dramatic and very awful has occurred here in the West. But what is this shift, basically? Some may wish to discount the influence of Christianity in the age of Constantine, or during the age of missions, or in the period of the Reformation, etc., but even the most cursory review of history would find such a position untenable. Over the course of many centuries, God most certainly poured out His blessings upon the European Gentile world. The Lord Jesus Christ has made His mark on history, and the purpose of this book is to further substantiate this.

No question, a great fall has occurred—but a fall from what? This entire civilization must have fallen from somewhere to arrive at the current state of affairs. Clearly from a Christian perspective, the West has fallen from God's grace, from first Christian foundations laid down over a thousand years. Such a fall involves many complexities, but Scripture provides more than adequate explanations, allowing for a clear understanding of the cause and nature of this demise.

Even when Christians do not make up the majority of a population, several mitigating factors attend a fallen world to prevent complete moral ruin, anarchy, tyranny, and self-destruction. The first of these is God's common mercy and grace, as described in Matthew 5 and Acts 14.

But I say unto you, Love your enemies, bless them that curse you, do good to them that hate you, and pray for them which despitefully use you, and persecute you; That ye may be the children of your Father which is in heaven: for he maketh his sun to rise on the evil and on the good, and sendeth rain on the just and on the unjust. (Matthew 5:44-45)

And saying, Sirs, why do ye these things? We also are men of like passions with you, and preach unto you that ye should turn from these vanities unto the living God, which made heaven, and earth, and the sea, and all things that are therein: Who in times past suffered all nations to walk in their own ways. Nevertheless he left not himself without witness, in that he did good, and gave us rain from heaven, and fruitful seasons, filling our hearts with food and gladness. (Acts 14:15-17)

This passage speaks of God's common grace and goodness shared with the entire race of mankind. Also, the Apostle points out in Romans 2, that "Gentiles, who do not have the law, by nature do the things in the law" (vs. 14). The common grace of God bears a preserving influence upon human societies. But when God withholds this grace, the destructive influences of sin take immediate effect upon that civilization.

For centuries, all the Western nations (unbelievers included), borrowed heavily from a Christian world and life view, and they enjoyed the fruits of Christian thinking in science, economics, and culture. Yet Paul warned of "perilous times" to come when "evil men and impostors will grow worse and worse, deceiving and being deceived" (2 Tim. 3:1, 13). These times are now upon us. The zeitgeist bears a heightened "epistemological self-consciousness," what Dr. Cornelius Van Til described as "God allow[ing] men to follow the path of their self-chosen rejection of Him more rapidly than ever."[28] This is especially applicable to a civilization turned against its Christian roots. As descendants of a hundred generations of Christians, Reformers, Pilgrims, Covenanters, and Huguenots, the Western apostates hasten their end. The downgrade is steep, and as promised in 2 Peter 2:20, "the latter end will be worse with them than the beginning."

THE SALT LOSES ITS SAVOR

The other root cause for the present fall is explained by the Lord's words in Luke 14.

> So likewise, whosoever he be of you that forsaketh not all that he hath, he cannot be my disciple. Salt is good: but if the salt have lost his savour, wherewith shall it be seasoned? It is neither fit for the land, nor yet for the dunghill; but men cast it out. He that hath ears to hear, let him hear. (Luke 14:33-35)

Christ referred to His followers as "the salt of the earth"—preserving and blessing their communities with spiritual, moral, and economic benefits. However, He said, when the salt loses its saltiness, it is good for nothing but "the dunghill." Such prophetic proclamations exactly describe what happened to the organized, mainline churches in Europe and North America beginning in AD 1700. Although church attendance in the United States remained consistent during the breakdown of faith and morality in the 20th Century, the salt was steadily losing its enhancing and preserving qualities. Both the mainline and evangelical churches had little to no influence on the wider culture during the social revolutions, the cultural and musical revolutions, and the sexual revolution, which brought the widespread increase of divorce and cohabitation, the abortion plague, and the normalization of sexual perversion. Church attendance fell off after 2007, and the salt was discarded into the dunghill.

US Christians touted a decreased surgical abortion rate between 1995 and 2020, while they themselves continued to use abortifacient forms of conception control at roughly the same rates as the unbelieving world. Some claimed the abortion numbers had dropped to 1.2 million in America over the 2000s. However, the Stanford Study ("Mechanisms of action of intrauterine devices") found that an average of 0.8 post-fertilization babies were lost per woman by the IUD per annum on five different IUDs tested.[29] That equated to 12,300,000 babies killed per year by the use of this single form of contraceptive—an increased rate from 960,000 babies in 2000. Surgical abortions were only a drop in the bucket compared to the number of children killed by the use of these abortifacients. Christian opposition to these forms of conception control was non-existent during these years, except for a few obscure protests here and there. As of 2008, 32% of sexually-active evangelical women, 39% of women aligned with mainline denominations, and 36% of Catholic women employed highly effective forms of conception control, compared to the national average of 36%.[30] The salt had lost its savor.

Attempts at cultural influence through politics on the part of Christians during the decline of the West were mostly symbolic and superficial, especially in the United States. The fundamental problem was not to be found in politics or solved there. The problem was rooted deep in the culture, the schools, the churches, and the hearts of the people. The problem was the absence of faith and life in the evangelical church. Judgement begins in the household of God, and so does repentance (1 Pet. 4:17). Before addressing politics, the Christian church should first have busied itself with true faith and repentance, and the fulfillment of its own obedience.

> (For the weapons of our warfare are not carnal, but mighty through God to the pulling down of strong holds;) Casting down imaginations, and every high thing that exalteth itself against the knowledge of God, and bringing into captivity every thought to the obedience of Christ; And having in a readiness to revenge all disobedience, when your obedience is fulfilled. (2 Corinthians 10:4-6)

Between 2006 and 2017, the percentage of evangelical young people supportive of homosexual "marriage" increased from 16% to 47% while support from the general evangelical population moved from 10% to 35%.[31] This was the great "evangelical disaster" spoken of by that evangelical prophet of the 1960s, Francis Schaeffer. It was a house divided—salt without savor.

The Christian political efforts by the Moral Majority, the Christian Coalition, and other groups produced no lasting good, because the problem was in the pulpits and the pews. Women were using abortifacients, their children were in schools that rejected the fear of God, Christian family media habits were essentially the same as the world, and churches had rejected God's laws. There was great need for a change of heart.

The raw humiliation of the dunghill was fully experienced by American evangelicals in December, 2019, when the National Association of Evangelicals adopted the "Fairness for All" compromise. This policy statement, first advocated by the Mormon church, targeted Christian businessmen with legal sanctions upon refusal to support homosexual "weddings" and other pagan practices. The "evangelical Christian" board endorsed legislation to add sexual orientation and gender identity (SOGI) to federal nondiscrimination laws. Member churches of the National Association of Evangelicals included the Evangelical Free Church, the Presbyterian Church of America,[32] the Evangelical Presbyterian Church, the Christian Reformed Churches of North America, Church of the Nazarene, Assemblies of God, Foursquare Church, the Vineyard, and others. The policy would have subjected Christian businessmen to fines and imprisonment, while at the same time preserving Christian churches from similar persecution. By this time the salt was pretty well scattered over the dunghill.

This pathetic capitulation to the Neronic agenda by evangelical leadership and Christian Colleges signaled the cultural irrelevance of a dying church. The faith had lost its power. The salt had lost its savor. Proverbs 25:26 was relevant: "A righteous man who falters before the wicked is like a murky spring and a polluted well."

BEFORE THE FALL—PRIDE 2019

Pride goeth before destruction, and an haughty spirit before a fall. (Proverbs 16:18)

The Fall came in 2020, but first pride came in 2019. Actually, pride was on the rise well before that. Beginning in 1969, various groups advocating open sexual perversion began organizing "pride marches" in the United States and elsewhere. On the fiftieth anniversary of such pride events in the summer of 2019, New York City's pride event attracted five million participants. Record-breaking crowds also appeared in New Orleans, Denver, Madrid (Spain), Brussels (Belgium), Cologne (Germany), London (UK), Amsterdam (Netherlands), Tel-Aviv (Israel), Belgrade (Serbia), Singapore, Santiago (Chile), Montreal (Canada), Kiev (Ukraine), Tokyo (Japan), and Taipei (Taiwan). Tens of millions of people showed up for the largest international pride celebration in the history of the world. The goal of these marches was to flaunt sexual license and public bald-faced opposition to God's laws. The announcement went forth: "Let us break His bands in pieces and cast His cords away from us." But "He who sits in the heavens shall laugh; the LORD shall hold them in derision. Then He shall speak to them in His wrath, and distress them in His deep displeasure" (Ps. 2:4-5).

First, there was pride, then came the fall. The year 2020 followed "Pride 2019," bringing with it a worldwide depression, disease, and death (ie. destruction). Dread fear gripped the whole world. The highest deaths per capita came upon the Western states—where the Pride marches were held—Belgium, Spain, Italy, France, the UK, the Netherlands, and the United States. Over three hundred pride marches were cancelled in the summer of 2020.

THE WORDS OF THE "PROPHETS"

Yet he sent prophets to them, to bring them again unto the LORD; and they testified against them: but they would not give ear. (2 Chronicles 24:19)

Ye stiffnecked and uncircumcised in heart and ears, ye do always resist the Holy Ghost: as your fathers did, so do ye. Which of the prophets have not your fathers persecuted? (Acts 7:51-52a)

The fall of the West was anticipated for at least a hundred years—two hundred years for those who were watching more closely. God sent a sufficient supply of prophets and preachers to warn the West. Their words were never inspired and inerrant as in the case of the Scriptures. But all along they spoke the word in season. Usually disquieting, the word came pungent, timely, lucid, and unambiguous. Prominent minds, pens, and voices—both unbelievers and believers spoke to the demise. The intensity with which the cultural, social, economic, and political suicide occurred was apparent to the prophets. What stood out in the prophetic statements was their vehemence, the horror and the dead earnestness in their voices—as it were, the ghastly ardor characterizing the last gasps of a dying man.

Writing in 1940, the famous author George Orwell surmised that the soul of modern man had been hacked to pieces over the previous 200 years. The destroyers and the saboteurs, he said, were Gibbon, Voltaire, Rousseau, Shelley, Byron, Dickens, Stendhal, Samuel Butler, Ibsen, Zola, Flaubert, Shaw, and Joyce. Orwell drew the very unhappy conclusion, that, "There is no wisdom except in the fear of God; but nobody fears God; therefore there is no wisdom. Man's history reduces itself to the rise and fall of material civilizations, one Tower of Babel after another...and so downwards into abysses which are horrible to contemplate."[33] Between 1940 and 2020, this cultural and societal suicide was to worsen by orders of magnitude.

Another prophet of sorts, C.S. Lewis, was himself plucked like a brand from the fire. The most well-known Christian author of the 20th Century reserved his most prophetic warnings for *The Abolition of Man,* first published in 1944. His concern centered on modern education and the influx of relativism—the rejection of "the doctrine of objective value, the belief that certain attitudes are really true, and others really false, to the kind of thing the universe is, and the kind of things we are."[34] Lewis warned that the acceptance of this worldview in education must result "in the destruction of the society that accepts it."

That was eighty years ago. The warning was not well taken. C.S. Lewis was not the only thinker or writer who eyed modern secular education with deep mistrust and concern. Indeed, many Christian leaders recognized the academy as the very essence of the dangerous zeitgeist and juggernaut, which would bowl the whole Western world over in the 20th Century.

Most remarkable of all was the prophetic voice of A. A. Hodge, principal of Princeton Theological Seminary (1878–1886). Here are words still resonating through the empty chambers of a hollowed-out civilization:

> I am as sure as I am of Christ's reign that a comprehensive and centralized system of national education, separated from religion, as is now commonly proposed, will prove the most appalling enginery for the propagation of anti-Christian and atheistic unbelief, and of anti-social nihilistic ethics, individual, social and political, which this sin-rent world has ever seen.[35]

Prophetic. Prescient. Amazing.

That was said 140 years ago. The world is now very far down the river and has just passed over the falls.

The first of the pulpit prophets as it were, Charles Spurgeon (1834-1892), sounded the warning in 1885, while the sin of Sodom was still in the closet, but crawling out into the streets of London during the dark hours of the night. Speaking to the destruction of Jerusalem in AD 70, Spurgeon cautioned, "I am growingly fearful lest our own country should furnish a parallel to all this." In the good pastor's view, already the civil state had declined to countenancing a frightening degree of sexual sin:

> Worse still, if worse can be: those who dare walk our streets after sundown tell us that Sodom, in its most putrid days, could scarce exceed this metropolis for open vice. To our infinite disgust and horror, the names of certain of the greatest in the land are at this hour openly mentioned in connection with the filthiest debauchery . . . What horrible clouds are darkening our skies? There were judges once who would not have suffered the laws to be trampled on by the great, but would have dealt out equal justice to rich and poor: I cannot persuade myself that it will be otherwise now, and yet I fear the worst. O God, have mercy upon the land whose judgment-seats and palaces are defiled with vice.[36]

The churches in England were already in poor shape, as would be witnessed by the Downgrade Controversy, and which would prove to bring about the downfall for Spurgeon's ministry. This sad development occurred about the same time Spurgeon brought out this prophetic word:

> The modern pulpit has taught men to be infidels. What truth is there which has not been doubted by divines, questioned by doctors of divinity, and at length been denounced by the priests of "modern thought"? Nothing remains upon which a certain school of preachers have not spit their skepticism. The experience of the unbelief of Germany is being repeated here. Among those who are ordained to be the preachers of the gospel of Christ, there are many who preach not faith but doubt, and hence they are servants of the devil rather than of the Lord.[37]

What to do if apostasy, homosexuality, and sophistry were to prevail? The good pastor encouraged stalwart commitment to the standards of God's law and the power of a pure Gospel message.

> Does this nation really intend to cast off the fear of God and the doctrines of Holy Scripture to follow the vain imaginings of the sophists and the fashionable follies of the great? Are we to see again unbelief and luxurious sin walking hand in hand? If so, there be some of us who mean to take up our sorrowful parable, and speak as plainly as we can for truth and holiness, whether we offend or please. Be it ours still to thunder out the law of God, and proclaim with trumpet clearness the gospel of Jesus, not bating one jot of firm belief in the revelation of God, nor winking at sin, nor toning down truth, even though we fear that the only result will be to make this people's hearts gross, and their ears heavy, and their eyes blind.[38]

Skepticism, unbelief, and luxurious sin had the upper hand in the churches by the 1920s. A refugee from academia himself, J. Gresham Machen (1881-1937) studied first at Princeton University, and for a while was thrown into confusion while studying at the University of Marburg in Germany under the tutelage of liberal Lutheran theologian, Professor Wilhelm Herrmann. By the grace of God, Machen returned to his right mind, embraced a reformed Christian orthodoxy, and later wrote extensively on the extreme danger of secular education. His warnings rang with an ominous tone:

> Place the lives of children in their formative years, despite the convictions of their parents, under the intimate control of experts appointed by the state...where the mind is filled with the materialism of the day, and it is difficult to see how even the remnants of liberty can subsist. Such a tyranny, supported as it is by a perverse technique used as the instrument in destroying human souls, is certainly far more dangerous than the crude tyrannies of the past.[39]

Did he underestimate the soul-killing influence of socialist education in 1924? Accepted by the arch-skeptic, H.L. Mencken, as the most worthy opponent of modernism, and commended for his "remarkable clarity and cogency as an apologist," Machen was without peer in his fight against liberalism. He warned that "humanity is standing over an abyss."[40] In his view, "Russia and Germany are already in the abyss. But how shall it be with our country?" As for America, Machen said, "We are witnessing today in America the decay of free institutions, and that decay is proceeding quite in the well worn track which it followed, for example, when the Roman Republic gave place to the Roman Empire."[41] Not exactly a prophet in the formal sense, of foretelling the future, yet Machen ventured, "There are many things that are uncertain about the future; but of one thing we can be sure—a nation that tramples thus upon the law of God, that tramples upon the basic principles of integrity, is headed for destruction unless it repents in time."[42] His immediate concern, in writing these words (in 1934), was a few divorces that took place in Reno, Nevada. The clarion warning comes a century before the social collapse occurred.

Another well-known Christian writer/thinker, Dr. Gordon Clark, speaking on the topic of education in 1935, told Christian families:

> In public schools, children receive pagan education...Any Christian should have sense enough to see that subjection to pagan influences works an injustice to the child...Just because a young man survives pagan instruction is no reason for subjecting him to it...Only if they reject the godless view of the world, will our Christian families be prepared to face the ensuing dark ages.[43]

Such severe admonitions were issued almost ninety years ago. Yet most contemporary Christian leaders were far less concerned about the godless, homosexualized schools, a hundred times worse in 2020 than it was then. Anti-social nihilistic ethics have become the order of the day.

The Lutheran, Dietrich Bonhoeffer (1906-1945), placed hopes for the perpetuation of Christian civilization upon England and America during the great war. Germany was already post-Christian under the Nazi's. Little did Bonhoeffer know that the rest of the West would follow in the footsteps of Germany, as apparent in these words:

> Christians in Germany will have to face the terrible alternative of either willing the defeat of their nation in order that Christian civilization may survive or willing the victory of their nation and thereby destroying civilization. I know which of these alternatives I must choose but I cannot make that choice from security.[44]

During his last days in the German prison, preparing for his execution, Boenhoeffer confidently asserted, that we are "approaching a completely religionless age. People as they are simply cannot be religious anymore."[45] The movement towards human autonomy (where man becomes a law to himself), he said, had finally achieved "a certain completeness."[46] The defeat tempted the quivering soul to capitulation to the enemy. The assassination plot had failed, and civilization was a sinking ship from which something might be salvaged.

> [W]hat we have built up is destroyed overnight. Our lives, unlike our parents' lives, have become formless or even fragmentary. . . . It will be the task of our generation, not to "'seek great things," but to save and preserve our souls out of the chaos, and to realise that this is the only thing we can carry as "booty" out of the burning house.

Although leading-evangelical, Billy Graham (1918-2018) may have been less attendant to the social conditions of the nation in the 1970s, he took up the prophetic mantle on July 19, 2012. Quoting his wife, Ruth, the 94 year-old evangelist wrote,

> "'If God doesn't punish America, He'll have to apologize to Sodom and Gomorrah.' Millions of babies have been aborted and our nation seems largely unconcerned. Self-centered indulgence, pride, and a lack

of shame over sin are now emblems of the American lifestyle. My heart aches for America and its deceived people. The wonderful news is that our Lord is a God of mercy, and He responds to repentance."[47]

Peter Marshall (1902-1949), serving as chaplain of the US Senate, preached a sermon on March 11, 1944 while America faced the tragedy of a World War. The prophetic tone reappeared:

There are evil forces plotting within the nation as well…Our moral standards have been lowered. Our national moral standards—and no nation makes progress in a downward direction…Illustrations could be multiplied, both of the decay of morals and of the activity of evil forces in our midst. The old time evangelists used to express the tragedy of men and women individually going to hell. But we don't hear much about that nowadays. Because they say people don't believe in hell. But I notice that they talk a lot about it in their conversations…We must decide and decide quickly who is chief—whom we will serve. Millions of people in America live in moral fog. The issues are not clear to them. They cannot face the light that makes them black or white. They want grays and neutral picks. They move in sort of a spiritual twilight. Modified morality on the basis of cleverness guides millions of people. Modified dishonesty within the letter of the law is the practice of millions more. Surely the time has come—because the hour is late—when we must decide. The choice before us is plain: Jehovah or Baal? Christ or chaos? Conviction or compromise? Discipline or disintegration? I have not stated the matter too strongly. You may agree mildly or you may disagree violently, but the time has come to face the duties and obligations of our citizenship and be willing to assume the disciplines imposed by the things we believe in before we are forced to accept the disciplines of tyranny.[48]

An evangelical prophet of the post-Christian age, Francis Schaeffer, poured tears over his last book, *The Great Evangelical Disaster* (issued in 1984).[49] The zeitgeist, he said, has crushed "all that we cherish in its path," and then he announced the end of Christian civilization in the past tense:

> The Christian influence upon the whole of culture has been lost...Do not take this lightly! It is a horrible thing for a man like myself to look back and see my country and my culture go down the drain in my lifetime.[50]

Schaeffer put the decline of the US Christian church as taking place between 1900 and 1936. "It was this drift which laid the base for the cultural, social, moral, legal, and governmental changes from that time to the present."[51] The cultural shift was completed by 1969: "In four decades," Francis Schaeffer wrote, "The change came in every portion and in every part of life."[52] He identified the worldview replacing the Christian outlook in the West as "the idea that the final reality is impersonal matter or energy shaped into its present form by impersonal chance."[53] He saw this alternate worldview leading to a world of chaos or slavery to the state, or both.

Schaeffer summed up the sixty-year span between 1924 and 1984 as one royal "moral disaster," and the evangelical response to it as one more catastrophe. The problem for the church, he said, was "accommodation" and a refusal to confront the world with the Word. There was, in his words, "no clear voice speaking to the crucial issues of the day with instinctively biblical, Christian answers." There was no turning back now, and no hope for Western society to be found in evangelicalism. Schaeffer concluded that "a large segment of the evangelical world has become seduced by the world spirit of this present age...For the evangelical accommodation to the world of our age represented the removal of the last barrier opposing the breakdown of our culture."[54] Though seen as a reformer in his own right, Francis Schaeffer's last assessment of evangelicalism's progress under his watch was less than optimistic—actually, a miserable failure. And, that was forty years ago.

The breakdown of Western civilization is attributed to more fundamental causes lodged in the foundations of Western thought. According to Schaeffer, the epistemological root of the collapse is found in the philosophy of Georg Wilhelm Friedrich Hegel (1770-1831). When this Western philosopher gave up on the possibility of distinguishing between truth and untruth, he stepped over what Schaeffer called "the line of despair." Hegel's capitulation to irrationalism set the direction for the destruction of everything—rationality at all levels, education, wise governance, culture, science, the family, and economics. Schaeffer goes on: "What is this despair? It arises from the abandonment of any hope of a unified answer for knowledge and life."[55] Mainstreaming this hopelessness requires at least 200 years, for it to saturate into the masses of the common people. This came about through the popularized existentialism of Jean-Paul Sartre and the pragmatism of John Dewey. By 1970, Schaeffer referred to his generation as "The generation of anti-philosophy people caught in an uncertainty of knowing."[56]

Hopelessness prevailed, and cynicism reigned. Fifty years later, the problem was a hundred times worse and the despair was thorough-going in the mainstream.

Coming to the same basic diagnosis as Schaeffer, Christian thinker and writer, R.J. Rushdoony concluded that "the modern age gives every evidence that it is approaching death."[57] He called the 1990's the "end of an era," and, without apologies, assessed the Western world as "a society that deserves to die."[58] Shortly before his death in 2001, the "prophet" issued a last warning: "The problem now is more serious. A powerful element in the modern world has no intention of defending its civilization, because, while murderous towards Christianity, it is suicidal with regard to itself."[59]

About the same time, Jacques Ellul (1912-1994) defined the post-Christian era where "Christianity no longer supplies a set of shared values, a norm of judgment, and a frame of reference to which men spontaneously relate all their thoughts and actions."[60] Atheistic humanism replaced this worldview, resting on and legitimizing "unlimited growth of power, technology, and the economy."[61] A voice crying in the middle of the Sahara desert, Ellul pointed to technology as replacing culture. Technology enabled diversion and destroyed all reflection, and, he said this breakdown of culture itself must "rupture." His concluding words in his final writings declared: "Even without nuclear war or an exceptional crisis, we may thus expect enormous global disorder which will be the expression of all the contradictions and disarray."[62]

Another refugee from the materialist, atheist camp during the modern age, Malcolm Muggeridge (1903-1990), left this warning... with some hope:

> Let us then as Christians rejoice that we see around us on every hand the decay of the institutions and instruments of power, see intimations of empires falling to pieces, money in total disarray, dictators and parliamentarians alike nonplussed by the confusion and conflicts which encompass them. For it is precisely when every earthly hope has been explored and found wanting, when every possibility of help from earthly sources has been sought and is not forthcoming, when every recourse this world offers, moral as well as material, has been explored to no effect, when in the shivering cold the last twig has been thrown onto the fire and in the gathering darkness every glimmer of light has finally flickered out; it is then that Christ's hand reaches out sure and firm.[63]

The prophets wandered in from other ecclesiastical traditions. Eugene David Rose represented the Eastern Orthodox when he wrote *Nihilism: The Root of the Revolution of the Modern Age* prior to his death in 1982. Here he defined the prevailing spirit of the age as "Nihilism."

> ...we shall characterize as "Nihilists" men of, as it seems, widely divergent views: humanists, skeptics, revolutionaries of all hues, artists and philosophers of various schools; but they are united in a

common task. Whether in positivist "criticism" of Christian truths and institutions, revolutionary violence against the Old Order, apocalyptic visions of universal destruction and the advent of a paradise on earth, or objective scientific labors in the interests of a "better life" in this world—the tacit assumption being that there is no other world— their aim is the same: the annihilation of Divine Revelation and the preparation of a new order in which there shall be no trace of the "old" view of things, in which Man shall be the only god there is.[64]

The editor for Rose's book, a man named Hieromonk Damascene of the Saint Herman Monastery, added this comment in the same source: "It is obvious to any Orthodox Christian who is aware of what is going on around him today, that the world is coming to its end. The signs of the times are so obvious that one might say that the world is crashing to its end."

After chronicling the nightmare of the Soviet communist experiment, that prophet of Russia, Aleksandr Isayevich Solzhenitsyn, gave the most succinct description of the root cause for the Fall— and he could hardly detect much difference between the east and the west. Both had imbibed deeply of the 18th Century enlightenment philosophies. Three times, the Nobel Prize laureate repeated his point in the famous Templeton Address given in 1983:

> Over a half Century ago, while I was still a child, I recall hearing a number of old people offer the following explanation for the great disasters that had befallen Russia: *"Men have forgotten God; that's why all this has happened."* Since then I have spent well-nigh 50 years working on the history of our revolution; in the process I have read hundreds of books, collected hundreds of personal testimonies, and have already contributed eight volumes of my own toward the effort of clearing away the rubble left by that upheaval. But if I were asked today to formulate as concisely as possible the main cause of the ruinous revolution that swallowed up some 60 million of our people, I could

not put it more accurately than to repeat: *"Men have forgotten God; that's why all this has happened."* What is more, the events of the Russian Revolution can only be understood now, at the end of the Century, against the background of what has since occurred in the rest of the world. What emerges here is a process of universal significance. And if I were called upon to identify briefly the principal trait of the *entire* 20th Century, here too, I would be unable to find anything more precise and pithy than to repeat once again: *"Men have forgotten God."* The failings of human consciousness, deprived of its divine dimension, have been a determining factor in all the major crimes of this Century.[65]

Solzhenitsyn left us with that epithet for the Western world almost forty years ago. But the most incisive prophetic assessments left a chill in the room: "Today's world has reached a stage which, if it had been described to preceding centuries, would have called forth the cry: 'This is the Apocalypse!' Yet we have grown used to this kind of world; we even feel at home in it."[66]

The Russian dissident, exiled in the West, spoke as a prophet to a wayward people on June 8, 1978, in his address to the Harvard University's graduating class. Since the enlightenment of the 1700s, Solzhenitsyn said, "a total liberation occurred from the moral heritage of Christian centuries with their great reserves of mercy and sacrifice." State systems were becoming increasingly and totally materialistic.[67] His conclusion held little hope or promise for the Western world:

Even if we are spared destruction by war, our lives will have to change if we want to save life from self-destruction.[68]

"The prophets" warned again and again of the depersonalization, dehumanization, and barrenness of modern life—a reality ten times worse today than it was in their own time.

G.K. Chesterton spoke prophetically of the onslaught of homosexuality, which he described as "the very powerful and very desolate philosophy of Oscar Wilde. It is the *carpe diem* religion, but the *carpe diem* religion is not the religion of happy people, but of very unhappy people."[69] He offered descriptions of the modern world, using insightful nuggets, as in: "full of lawless little men and mad movements,"[70] "insincere about their sincerity,"[71] "a strange indifference," and the "loneliness of millions in a crowd."[72] Chesterton quickly recognized the insanity of a world that knew God and then forsook Him.

Conservatives of the Roman Catholic ecclesiastical tradition occasionally offered their prophetic reflections. Paul Johnson detected a shift "from utopianism to hedonism" following the wars. His summary of the great intellectuals of the 19th and 20th Centuries described madmen who *en masse* "create climates of opinions and prevailing orthodoxies, which themselves often generate irrational destructive courses of action.[73] And Benjamin Wiker wraps up his book on *10 Books that Screwed up the World (And 5 Others Didn't Help)*, gazing over "the smoking rubble of the twentieth Century…[where] we see a strange sight: humanity devouring itself."[74]

The nationally renown Pentecostal evangelist David Wilkerson was soundly rejected by the Christian population in 1974 when he issued his controversial book, *The Vision*.[75] Speaking with the ardor of John the Baptist as with grasshopper legs caught between his teeth, Wilkerson projected calamity on America because of her "rampant sin." Especially far-fetched were his predictions concerning the easy accessibility of pornography via television for children to watch in their homes, and ordination of homosexuals in "Christian" churches. He also stated, "Divorce and immorality will become more and more commonplace among ministers."[76] He was right. In 1993, Wilkerson was speaking of the corruption and destruction of America more in the present tense:

What God is more concerned about—and what is bringing God's

judgment on America—is the growing number of homosexual defenders! They number in the millions! When Colorado voted against special rights for gays, the entire Hollywood establishment went into action, boycotting that state in defense of homosexual rights. God's wrath is upon us because the majority of Americans have lost their values! There are masses of people who would not move an inch to defend America against an enemy aggressor—yet they would gladly lay down their lives to defend abortion rights. The last election showed that 40 million Americans defended the right to kill babies! America was once renowned as a defender of truth and justice. Now, we have become defenders of baby killers, pornographers, and perverts…All are being withered and made dry! We are no longer the most productive country—but instead have been helpless to stop the withering and decay of our once-great institutions and corporations. We have lost our influence. America is now the tail and not the head!… What lies ahead for America? A withering of all things! God's wind is now blowing, and He is doing what He said He would do—spoiling our treasures.[77]

David Wilkerson is gone now, and the presidential election he referenced happened thirty years ago.

Another evangelical revivalist of the 1960s and 1970s, Leonard Ravenhill, looked for spiritual revival as the only hope left for the West. For over forty years, Ravenhill spoke with jarring urgency, and a prophetic zeal unmatched by anyone else in his day. He seemed to see something others couldn't see. In his classic little book entitled *Why Revival Tarries*, Ravenhill wrote,

America cannot fall—because she is already fallen! This goes for Britain, too. She cannot go into slavery—because her people are fettered at the moment in the chains of self-forged, self-chosen moral anarchy. Here are millions, diseased morally, with no longing for healing. Here are men paying for shadows the price of their immortal souls, men who not only reject the Substance, but who openly sneer at and caricature it. An unprecedented tidal wave of commandment-breaking, God-defying, soul-destroying iniquity sweeps the ocean of human affairs. Never before have men in the masses sold their souls to the devil at such bargain prices…What hell-born mesmerism holds them? How does the spell bind? Who brainwashed them?[78]

And that was sixty years ago. A very great amount of water has flowed under the bridge since then.

After fifteen years of persecution at the hands of the homosexual community in San Francisco, pastor and author, Chuck McIlheny, summarized the matter in 1991 as follows: "The homosexual issue is a secondary issue. The real fundamental issue is a secular humanism which rejects Christ and the Scripture as the basis to society. And the ultimate end is always death—death to a society."[79]

That was thirty years ago, well before *Obergefell* (2015) and *Bostock* (2020).

Among the litany of prophets who came and went, the nations were visited by a line of poets and lyricists too. The 20th-Century poet T.S. Eliot (1888-1965) described modern life—or rather death—in "The Waste Land." What better epithet was written for the 20th Century?

April is the cruelest month, breeding
Lilacs out of the dead land, mixing
Memory and desire, stirring
Dull roots with spring rain.
Winter kept us warm, covering
Earth in forgetful snow, feeding
A little life with dried tubers…
What are the roots that clutch, what branches grow
Out of this stony rubbish? Son of man,
You cannot say, or guess, for you know only
A heap of broken images, where the sun beats,
And the dead tree gives no shelter, the cricket no relief,

And the dry stone no sound of water.[80]

Elliot suggested in "The Hollow Man" that the world would end not with a bang but "a whimper." In Elliot's view, the breakdown of Christianity would mean the breakdown of Western culture itself: "I do not believe that the culture of Europe could survive the complete disappearance of the Christian Faith...If Christianity goes, the whole of our culture goes."[81]

Among the "sons of the prophets" one could hardly find a better description of the 20th Century as Rudyard Kipling's final poetic word, "The Gods of the Copybook Headings." It was something of an epitaph for the British Empire. He could see it coming better than anyone. The copybook headings were Scriptural quotations and proverbs adorning the headings of children's copybooks in the 19th Century.

> As I pass through my incarnations in every age and race,
> I make my proper prostrations to the Gods of the Market Place.
> Peering through reverent fingers I watch them flourish and fall,
> And the Gods of the Copybook Headings, I notice, outlast them all.
>
> We were living in trees when they met us. They showed us each in turn
> That Water would certainly wet us, as Fire would certainly burn:
> But we found them lacking in Uplift, Vision and Breadth of Mind,
> So we left them to teach the Gorillas while we followed the March of Mankind.
>
> We moved as the Spirit listed. They never altered their pace,
> Being neither cloud nor wind-borne like the Gods of the Market Place,
> But they always caught up with our progress, and presently word would come
> That a tribe had been wiped off its icefield, or the lights had gone out in Rome.
>
> With the Hopes that our World is built on they were utterly out of touch,
> They denied that the Moon was Stilton; they denied she was even Dutch;
> They denied that Wishes were Horses; they denied that a Pig had Wings;
> So we worshipped the Gods of the Market who promised these beautiful
>   things.

When the Cambrian measures were forming, they promised perpetual peace.

They swore, if we gave them our weapons, that the wars of the tribes would cease.

But when we disarmed they sold us and delivered us bound to our foe,

And the Gods of the Copybook Headings said: "Stick to the Devil you know."

On the first Feminian Sandstones we were promised the Fuller Life

(Which started by loving our neighbour and ended by loving his wife)

Till our women had no more children and the men lost reason and faith,

And the Gods of the Copybook Headings said: "The Wages of Sin is Death."

In the Carboniferous Epoch we were promised abundance for all,

By robbing selected Peter to pay for collective Paul;

But, though we had plenty of money, there was nothing our money could buy,

And the Gods of the Copybook Headings said: "If you don't work you die."

Then the Gods of the Market tumbled, and their smooth-tongued wizards withdrew

And the hearts of the meanest were humbled and began to believe it was true

That All is not Gold that Glitters, and Two and Two make Four

And the Gods of the Copybook Headings limped up to explain it once more.

As it will be in the future, it was at the birth of Man

There are only four things certain since Social Progress began.

That the Dog returns to his Vomit and the Sow returns to her Mire,

And the burnt Fool's bandaged finger goes wobbling back to the Fire;

And that after this is accomplished, and the brave new world begins

When all men are paid for existing and no man must pay for his sins,

As surely as Water will wet us, as surely as Fire will burn,

The Gods of the Copybook Headings with terror and slaughter return![82]

As he approached the end of his life, Kipling's poems took on an increasingly foreboding feel, as in "The Storm Cone" from 1932: "This is the tempest long foretold—slow to make head but sure to hold... Only the darkness hides the shape, of further peril to escape.[83]

Still another unconventional prophet stood at the very center of the cultural revolution, this time for the benefit of the popular audience. Don McLean had a very unusual hit in 1971, securing the top position on the charts—"American Pie." Commenting later on the hit, McLean confessed he was only fiddling "while Rome burned."[84] He knew the country was "headed in the wrong direction" when he penned the piece. He further lamented, "there is no poetry and very little romance anymore, so it is really like the last phrase of 'American Pie.'"[85] By 2020, McLean said he had pretty much given up on all modern music. "The music doesn't mean anything," he said. "The music reflects the spiritual nature of the society. We have a kind of a nihilistic society now. No one believes in anything, no one likes anything, no one has any respect for anything much. The music shows that."[86]

At the end of his magnum opus, the songwriter watches the "Father, the Son, and the Holy Ghost, [catch] the last train to the coast..." singing "Bye, Bye American Pie." In God's providence, the song held first place on the charts for four weeks—long enough to let everyone know that "the music died." That was, after all, the point of the song.

And that was fifty years ago.

Representing the folk minstrels of the American heartland, Merle Haggard wished "that a buck was still silver...back when the country was strong...when a man could still work and still would." He kept asking, "Are we rolling downhill like a snowball headed for hell, with no kinda chance for the flag or the liberty bell?" and "Are the good times really over for good?"[87]

And, that was forty years ago.

The conservative politicians, hanging on for dear life to what used to be, issued their warnings. Pat Buchanan released his prophecy in 2001: *The Death of the West*. The old conservative bitterly kicked a tombstone over the grave: "To its acolytes the cultural revolution has been a glorious revolution. But to millions, they have replaced the good country we grew up in with a cultural wasteland and a moral sewer that are not worth living in and not worth fighting for—their country, not ours."[88] It was the gods of the new cultural marketplace who had shouldered aside the God of the Old and New Testaments, he said. Buchanan advised the few who were still reading his stuff in 2001, "Societies organized to ensure the maximum pleasure, freedom, and happiness for all their members are at the same time, advancing the date of their own funerals...Americans who look on this cultural revolution as politics-as-usual do not understand it. It means to make an end of the country we love."[89]

Sensible economists tried to figure out how to get out of the vicious, suicidal cycle instigated by John Maynard Keynes. Friedrich Hayek wrote in 1981:

> It should surprise no one that the last generation of British economists who had succumbed to the teachings of Lord Keynes should form a panicky mob when a reversal of the policies they had inspired reveals the damage they have done...Following their advice has induced a structure of employment that can be maintained only by accelerating inflation but will collapse only when it becomes a gallop and destroys any possibility of a rational use of resources. Nobody has ever claimed that so long as it is necessary to reduce inflation to get out of this vicious circle the effect can be anything but to destroy the particular employments created by past inflation. Only after inflation has been brought to a full stop can the market be expected to guide workers to jobs which can be maintained without accelerating inflation. All those who plead for 'mild' inflation and oppose 'too much' inflation are merely preparing the ground for a later depression.[90]

That was written a generation ago. Hayek is dead now. And, that depression is now.

In his classic work, *The Road to Serfdom*, Hayek spoke of the "impending dangers," and complained of the willful ignorance and utter disregard of the warnings, "The number of dangerous mistakes we have made before and since the outbreak of the war because we do not understand the opponent with whom we are faced is appalling. It seems almost as if we did not want to understand the development which has produced totalitarianism because such an understanding might destroy some of the dearest illusions to which we are determined to cling."[91] His rebuke comes with much heightened relevance 75 years later.

Several of the aging economist-prophets were still issuing their warnings as the end approached. After the 2020 elections, an 81-year-old Paul Craig Roberts, President Ronald Reagan's Assistant Secretary of the Treasury for Economic Policy, announced, "The West has thrown itself into the waste basket of history," and, "We can begin by writing the obituary."[92] Reagan's Director of Office of Management and Budget (1981-1985), David Stockman, was dubbed "the prophet of doom" when he said America was "doomed" in 2013—"The United States is broke—fiscally, morally, intellectually..."[93] As 2020 rolled around, Stockman figured the 30-year experiment in "Keynesian Central Banking...is over."[94] We are, he said, "in a demographic and fiscal dead end. It's a very dangerous prospect and one with no obvious answer on how to escape."[95]

As the end approached, pastors in the church spoke a word in season for the people of God. Preaching in the very heart of the Western world at the center of London, Dr. Martyn Loyd-Jones described the 20th Century as a time in which "God allowed man to have his own way...Man has turned his back upon God...God deliberately turns from man...Now, you are seeing the world as it is without the restraints of God. God is no longer keeping evil in check." Lloyd-Jones pointed out that, earlier in the 1800s, Western academics and cultural leaders worked hard to establish "the dignity of man," the autonomy, and the "capability of man" without God. But now the modern world fit the description given in Romans 1, where God has given man up to ultimately undignified "sexual perversions," and the rest.[96]

Shortly before he died, Dr. Lloyd-Jones delivered a heavy sermon, himself traumatized by the contemplation of the contemporary situation as he saw it in 1980: "It's an age of vileness, an age of raging. It's an age in which men and women are breaking every rule and every law, and the whole world is in a state of confusion...I'm even weary with this...things seem to be going from bad to worse...a break-down of the home, of marriage, and of all the sanctities of everything that is holy."[97] "The state of the world is," he said, "organized insanity."[98]

That was 35 years before *Obergefell*.

The potential for the self-immolation of a culture approached the realm of probability for those who read Neil Postman's 1985 tome: *Amusing Ourselves to Death*. By nature man has an infatuation with distraction, but modern technology put this infatuation on steroids. Postman (1931-2003) forecasted cultural death:

> When a population becomes distracted by trivia, when cultural life is redefined as a perpetual round of entertainments, when serious public conversation becomes a form of baby-talk, when, in short, a people become an audience, and their public business a vaudeville act, then a nation finds itself at risk; culture-death is a clear possibility.[99]

That was thirty-five years ago—before all the inanities of the internet, iPhones, social media, texting, sophisticated computer gaming, and the omnipresent and perpetual accessibility of a thousand more diversions.

The last of the prophets, Herbert Schlossberg, issued his magnum opus in 1990, *Idols for Destruction*, prefaced by the failed Supreme Court Justice nominee, Robert Bork. Schlossberg attacked the idols of History (revolutionary thinkers), Humanity (antinomians, autonomists, egalitarians), Mammon (John Maynard Keynes, Karl Marx), Greed, Corruption, Inflation, Debt, Nature (Naturalism, Charles Darwin), Power (the Leviathan State), and Religion (false Christian gods). This last of the sages ended his gloomier outlook with this prediction: "Judgment that issues in catastrophe is the only way for good to come, inasmuch as it entails the erasure of evil."[100] He noted that, by 1958, Aldous Huxley's dystopian *Brave New World* was "already upon us," as was admitted by the author himself.[101] "The judgment," said Schlossberg "[embraces] almost every branch of human affairs: economic, medical, military, psychological, domestic, political, religious." He emphasized the Keynesian debt model, greed, consumption of capital, increase in strife and lawlessness, dehumanization, torture, and euthanasia as consequences that flow from a society that embraces idolatry and rejects the true and living God.

That was thirty years ago.

Joel Belz, founder of *WORLD* magazine, produced an editorial on December 9, 2017 harking back to an editorial he wrote on January 25, 1992. He warned of a "wobbly economy" back then, "vulnerabilities of our political structure and its attendant freedoms."[102] Belz had considered the collapse imminent twenty-five years earlier, but he said he was only "wrong in my timing." By the socio-economic indexes, the problem was five times worse in 2017, and the nations were far less concerned than they were in 1992 when Belz's warning was first issued.

The prophets were dead. Francis Schaeffer died in 1984, Lloyd-Jones in 1981, C. S. Lewis died in 1963, Ellul in 1994, Postman in 2003, Solzhenitsyn in 2008, and Herbert Schlossberg in 2019. Christian publishing houses once publishing the "hard stuff" rarely considered such eccentric "screeds" for public distribution. Nobody would listen to the prophets anyway. Their books wouldn't sell. Besides, it was all old news. What they said already happened, and it was difficult to find anyone who cared.

WHERE IS THIS GOING?

Jerusalem fell. Rome fell. Now, the Western world was falling. A thousand-year Western ascendance in the world was coming to an end. The story will be highly significant in the chronicles of world history for a thousand years hence, should God permit the world to continue that long.

The long reign and worldwide spreading of European and Western culture was over. The Christian influence lasted for a thousand years, and waned. Afterwards, the post-Christian, apostate, materialistic, atheistic, utterly destructive philosophies exported by Western nations corrupted the rest of the world for a hundred painful years. At the end of the West, the most revealing and significant socio-economic reports monitored the highest debt load and corresponding low birth rates. Incredibly, the worst nations in the world by these indexes were Italy, Greece, France, Spain, Portugal, the UK, and the United States— all once great Western empires of world renown. They had ruled the world (the Romans, the Greeks, the Spanish Empire, the French Empire, the British Empire, and the United States). Not anymore. As another prophet put it, the mills of God grind slowly but very fine.

How would the world recover from the Fall of the West? Would a world war be a suitable "reset" button? What would bring about the due humbling of the nations (like what occurred during World War II)? What could possibly salvage a civilization so far gone? Was there anything that could revive and remotivate dead and dying culture? Given that the nation is blessed whose God is the Lord (Ps. 33:12), which nations in the world would most likely acknowledge the true and living God? Considering that some degree of integrity, honesty, and Christian character is necessary to assemble the spiritual or moral capital to rebuild a culture, where would this happen? Either there must be revival in the West, or the Spirit moves elsewhere—Africa, South America, Asia, or anywhere not already perverted by the West.

By the turn of the 21st Century, the Christian worldview had failed as the primary cultural influence and basis for Western civilization. Western institutions worked overtime for a hundred years to destroy every last remnant of their Christian foundations upon which the superstructure of the civilization was built. At the heart of it, the faith lapsed which each successive generation, and Christian churches failed. Following hard on the heels of the Christian apostasy in the churches came the breakdown of the civilization itself, with its educational, cultural, political, social, and economic systems. For the humanist worldview proved itself incapable of producing a sustainable civilization.

In the waning years of the civilization, this author traveled to eighteen nations around the world, addressing assemblies of political, economic, ecclesiastical, and educational leaders concerning the end of Western civilization. The same dry rot destroying America was infecting these other countries as well. But, to the end much of the world was still dependent on the West for economic, educational, and political leadership. With the foreign aid came the "secular" educational, cultural, and social programs imposed on the nations by the corrupted Western world.

The message for these national leaders was simple. Western civilization is collapsing because the foundations are corrupted, but the same corruption has been exported everywhere else around the world. The United States and the Western nations were built upon strong Christian foundations over a period of a thousand years. Given such substantial 10-yard-deep footers, a great amount of force would be required for their dismantlement. Very large wrecking balls were set to the footers of these great institutions, and the destructive process would take a concerted period of time. Yet, other foreign nations have not received such rich Christian heritage, and the foundations lack the depth and strength of that which was laid in the West. Their foundations and superstructures of economy are more vulnerable to this destructive force and the corrupting toxins channeled in from the US and Europe. For that reason, the sooner the nations rid themselves of Western funding and influence, the better.

Given the tightly-integrated world economy and the recent dominance of the Western world, it would be hard to believe that the rest of the nations of the world could exempt themselves from the social, economic, and cultural destruction of the West. Most developing nations and their governments were too closely intertwined with these destructive institutions through access to western media, international funding, and ideologies. Their leaders were trained in Western universities.

Does all this mean that Christ is coming back or that some antichrist is about to arise? Such questions often surface when empires fall and civilizations collapse. Though some may be tempted to interpret the present events according to some preconceived eschatological construct, such thinking has proved disastrous for believers in the past. God works His purposes in the world, and it isn't for us to know the time of Christ's return. Nonetheless, general Scripturally-oriented lessons may be drawn from world events, and a word in season is appropriate for the remnant who have the "ears to hear."

Let us be content to know that Christ is still on His throne, bringing all of His enemies under His feet (1 Cor. 15:25). His kingdom must come. His will must be done on earth as it is in heaven. He is above all things for the church, His church must prevail, and the gates of hell cannot possibly prevail against it.

So shall they fear the name of the Lord from the west, and his glory from the rising of the sun. When the enemy shall come in like a flood, the Spirit of the Lord shall lift up a standard against him. And the Redeemer shall come to Zion, and unto them that turn from transgression in Jacob, saith the Lord. As for me, this is my covenant with them, saith the Lord; My spirit that is upon thee, and my words which I have put in thy mouth, shall not depart out of thy mouth, nor out of the mouth of thy seed, nor out of the mouth of thy seed's seed, saith the Lord, from henceforth and for ever. (Isaiah 59:19-21)

II

THE RISE & FALL
OF THE CHRISTIAN ETHOS

This Jesus hath God raised up, whereof we all are witnesses. Therefore
being by the right hand of God exalted, and having received of the
Father the promise of the Holy Ghost, he hath shed forth this, which
ye now see and hear. For David is not ascended into the heavens: but
he saith himself, The Lord said unto my Lord, Sit thou on my right
hand. Until I make thy foes thy footstool. Therefore let all the house
of Israel know assuredly, that God hath made the same Jesus, whom
ye have crucified, both Lord and Christ. (Acts 2:32-36)

These words from the Apostle Peter, preached at Pentecost around
AD 33, set the governing context for world history thereafter.
It is the metaphysical reality of all realities. Either men would
acknowledge this, or they would ignore it at great peril to their own
souls. Any treatment of history must assign due credit to the Lord
and His reign. Wherever Christ's kingdom would be realized in
the world, demonstrated by real transformation of life and culture,
these contributions need to be noted, appreciated, and praised by His
followers.

The fact remains that Jesus Christ rules. This historical fact is more certain than the reign of Queen Elizabeth. Christ's presence has been made known, and the world will never be the same. There is no reversing the impress that Jesus and His followers have made upon the world. While the spiritual influence does ebb and flow, and the Spirit may shift somewhat from one continent to another, the overall growth and success of His rule cannot be denied.

Some explanation is in order for the mere fact that 38.4% of the world's professing Christians still live in the West by 2010, while constituting only 16% of the world population. The same land mass made up 81% of the world's Christians in AD 1800, and almost 100% of Protestant missionaries in the 19th Century hailed from the English isles and America. To deny that God had performed significant work to build a church in the West over a thousand years would verge on pure dishonor to Christ, and a rejection of the most obvious historical reality.

The Rise of the West is a most remarkable story in the annals of world history that must be told to have a right view of history and Christ's church. Never in history was so much progress made for the Christian faith. Never was so much transformation of culture and development of a Christian ethos visible as it was in the Western world. During the first centuries, the gross darkness of paganism gave way to the light—the light of Christ. The missionary accounts at the outset of the Christian West are most thrilling and amazing. This survey will only briefly touch on the progress of Christian civilization, focusing mainly on the ideas that made it all possible. The progress comes, but never without an enormous cosmic struggle between the forces of darkness and the forces of truth and light. This saga will be traced in this chapter.

THE WEST AT ITS BEGINNING

This I say therefore, and testify in the Lord, that ye henceforth walk not as other Gentiles walk, in the vanity of their mind, having the understanding darkened, being alienated from the life of God through the ignorance that is in them, because of the blindness of their heart...
(Ephesians 4:17-18)

Before the light of the Gospel appeared, all ancient lands were sunk in abject ignorance, gross immorality, blinding fear, and inescapable futility of mind. We all started out as pagans and barbarians. Civilized man with a bit of wealth and power thought himself to be better than the barbarians who dwelt beyond the boundaries of the empires, but he could never shed himself of the practices of the barbarians. Pagan Romans and Greeks sacrificed to their gods, both human and animal. The Carthaginians were known for their mass sacrifices of infants to their gods in hopes of material blessings. As the Christian influence spread across Europe, the West was freed from this terrible pagan ritual. The last recorded human sacrifice in Europe occurred on November 10, AD 1066—to the Radigast god who had been cast down from Mount Radhost by Cyril and Methodius two hundred years earlier. And Iceland gave up infanticide around the same time.

Slavery was universally practiced in the pre-Christian world. Parricide and infanticide were legal in Rome. Homosexuality appeared occasionally, though usually in the closet, and was generally kept in check even by pagans.

Powerful empires inevitably deified the state—whether the Pharaoh or the Caesar. Polytheistic worship usually translated into humanism—the worship of man. This was called "civilization," but every civilization that would deify man was destined to fall.

The pagan gods were nothing more than "amplified humanity"[1] as Schaeffer put it. Men invented the gods for their own purposes, and

77

they looked a lot like the persons who invented them. When humanism (man-worship) gained ascendance, the gods were typically set aside in Greece and Rome. After the Roman Republic died, Julius Caesar sought deification, and his nephew Octavius perpetuated the myth of the emperor cult. When Christ came, His followers were persecuted because they did not worship Caesar. Millions were killed over a period of three hundred years—tortured, torn apart by beasts, skinned alive, dipped in boiling oil, burned at stakes, and crucified for refusing to worship the state. But theirs was the faith and the civilization which emerged out of the ashes upon the fall of that great empire, full of vitality and sustaining grace.

Although appearing more intelligent, and certainly more labyrinthine and convoluted in presentation, Greek philosophy was just one more attempt to "suppress the truth in unrighteousness" (Rom. 1:18). Though some conception of an ultimate power may have emerged at points, in the case of Aristotle, this god was nothing more than an impersonal force disinterested in man's ethical problem. For the Creator of the universe, Plato conceived a lesser god, or "demiurge," with an ultimate god again too transcendent to be interested in the moral character of the universe. Always, the goal of the philosophers and world religionists was to duck out of moral culpability for man's sin against God.

Thus, the Christian conception of God is fundamentally different from the Greek ideal. The very conception of ultimacy and sovereignty over ethics and reality, the transcendence and immanence of God, and the equal ultimacy of the one and the many in the Godhead, were basic truths completely missed by the Greek thinkers.

THE WORLDVIEW SHIFT IN THE WEST

Although some Christians have pointed to certain pagan holdouts in doctrine and practice among the post-Constantian nations, the shift towards Christian thinking and life was radical and substantial. The cultural transformation was fundamental and foundational. The worldview reformulation from polytheism to Trinitarian monotheism was monumental.

Polytheistic idolatry virtually disappeared over the centuries. Reviewing contemporary history in his *City of God,* Augustine refers to a pagan oracle prophesying something to the effect that Christianity would only last 365 years. Then he goes on to say that, around AD 397, "in the most noted and eminent city, Carthage, in Africa,...officers of the Emperor Honorius,...overthrew the temples and broke the images of the false gods. And from that time to the present, during almost thirty years, who does not see how much the worship of the name of Christ has increased, especially after many of those became Christians who had been kept back from the faith by thinking that [pagan] divination true."[2] So much for the pagan pipedream.

Heliopolis remained one of the last pagan holdouts in Syria in AD 362. During the reign of Julian the Apostate, Cyril the Deacon was martyred and cannibalized by the pagans for his zealous attempts to remove the idols from the city. This was a last-ditch attempt to save the paganism of the empire. Reportedly, Julian died on the battlefield, mouthing the memorable words: "Oh Galilean, thou hast conquered!"

The cultural transformation was radical. Christianity's influence upon Western society penetrated into the worldview foundations, with attendant society-wide cultural effects. In AD 324 the Emperor Constantine issued a law "intended to restrain idolatrous abominations which in time past had been practiced in every city and country, and it provided that no-one should erect images, or practice divination and other false and foolish arts, or offer sacrifice in any way."[3] Historians do not believe that Constantine forcibly executed the law; however, the populace got the message. The practice of animal and human sacrifice faded quickly in the Western world and remained socially reprehensible for 1,500 years. Constantine also ended mandatory sacrifice for his army officers and closed the temples. He introduced laws to limit the exposure of children (infanticide), he banned concubinage for married men, provided strong sanctions for rape, and outlawed gladiatorial shows for the first time in Rome's thousand year history.

As Rome crumbled over the rotten foundations of a bad humanist worldview, the church fathers Augustine and Athanasius testified loudly to the failure of these bad ideas and the success of Christ. The optimism with which Athanasius spoke of the progress of Christ's kingdom in the world comes across as shocking to many Christians living in the current anti-Christian West (especially after experiencing the radical apostasies of the 19th and 20th centuries).

> Since the Savior came to dwell among us, not only does idolatry no longer increase, but it is getting less and gradually ceasing to be. Similarly, not only does the wisdom of the Greeks no longer make any progress, but that which used to be is disappearing. And demons, so far from continuing to impose on people by their deceits and oracle-givings and sorceries, are routed by the sign of the cross if they so much as try. On the other hand, while idolatry and everything else that opposes the faith of Christ is daily dwindling and weakening and falling, see, the Savior's teaching is increasing everywhere! Worship, then, the Savior "Who is above all" and mighty, even God the Word, and condemn those who are being defeated and made to disappear by Him. When the sun has come, darkness prevails no longer; any of it that may be left anywhere is driven away. So also, now that the Divine epiphany of the Word of God has taken place, the darkness of idols prevails no more, and all parts of the world in every direction are enlightened by His teaching.[4]

THE WORLDVIEW OF THE WEST

The modern word "worldview" is best defined as a network of foundational truth propositions. While individuals holding to a particular worldview are not always self-conscious of the propositions, still they will rely on that worldview to interpret their experiences and sensations about truth and reality. These religiously-held commitments include basic beliefs concerning God, man, sin, ethics, and salvation. Both terms "Theology"and "philosophy" are synonyms for worldview. Some would distinguish these fields in an attempt to define philosophy as a neutral area. But this is a ruse and a fatal lie. Theology explains our basic faith commitments concerning what is real, what is true, and what is right and wrong. Philosophy does the same thing, only using different terminology.

The basic worldview embraced by the early church in the West was simply this: Salvation does not come from the state. Man is saved from his sins by Jesus Christ, the Son of God, who took upon Himself human nature. The basic constituents of the Apostles Creed include the Trinitarian God, the Creator, Jesus Christ as Savior and Lord, His incarnation, death, burial, and resurrection, the communion of the church, and the final Judgment.

> I believe in God, the Father Almighty,
> maker of heaven and earth;
> And in Jesus Christ his only Son, our Lord;
> who was conceived by the Holy Spirit,
> born of the Virgin Mary,
> suffered under Pontius Pilate,
> was crucified, dead, and buried;
> the third day he rose from the dead;
> he ascended into heaven,
> and sitteth at the right hand of God the Father Almighty;
> from thence he shall come to judge the quick and the dead.
> I believe in the Holy Spirit,
> the holy catholic church,
> the communion of saints,

the forgiveness of sins,

the resurrection of the body,

and the life everlasting. Amen.

These foundational truths laid down by Christ and His followers are firmly embedded the world over. While they have been largely abandoned by individuals in the West, institutions formed over a thousand years still borrow from this faith heritage. In later centuries, the whole world was to be shaped by Western institutions, receiving some benefit from the Christian worldview (while still not committing to the worldview itself). The Western worldview was constructed on the following foundational footers: the ultimate epistemological authority of Scripture, the Triune God, the sovereignty of God, the law of God, and the salvation of God in Jesus Christ.

SCRIPTURE & KNOWLEDGE

For the church fathers, the basic source of truth was not to be found in the mind of man, but only in the mind of God, communicated through the Scriptures. Athanasius stated that "the holy and inspired Scriptures are fully sufficient for the proclamation of the truth."[5] Chrysostom preached that the "cause of all evils" is "not knowing the Scriptures," when "no man teaches" the oracles of God.[6]

Moreover, the God who speaks to man is capable of conveying a clear and sufficient word of truth, while not granting man a comprehensive understanding of all things (including Himself). "The secret things belong to the LORD our God, but those things which are revealed belong to us and to our children forever, that we may do all the words of this law" (Deut. 29:29). Scripture reveals God and His ways to us, though man (as a finite being) can never fully comprehend an infinite God. Paganism and the early gnostic heresy, however, resorted to vagueness, erring on the side of mystery and uncertainty. Their god was so transcendent as to be wholly unknowable. Yet, others in the early years of the church (including Arius and other anti-Trinitarians) erred on the other side. They removed the mystery of the Trinity, rejected the deity or the humanity of the Son, or denied the three distinct Personalities. Man's pride would overcompensate in teaching—in an attempt to comprehend the incomprehensible. The councils of Nicaea and Chalcedon soundly rejected these early heresies.

GOD & THE WESTERN PERCEPTION OF REALITY

The problem of unity and particularity was never resolved by Greek and Roman philosophers, who always erred on one side or the other. Which is more important: the one or the many? Does the good of the individual take precedence over the needs of society? Or should the individual's desires and rights be sacrificed to achieve the "greater good" of society as a whole? Humanist thinking and man's finite mind can never resolve such a difficult conundrum. However, as humble and trusting children, Christians would submit to the Father's revelation, and human civilization was finally granted a thousand years of meaningful existence upon a right view of reality. God is one, and God is three, both propositions equally ultimate, and never completely comprehended by the finite human mind.

The Council of Nicea of AD 325 rejected Arianism, concluding there is one God but three Persons in the Godhead, equal in essence, power, and glory. Later Christian thinker, Cornelius Van Til explained the powerful implication of this doctrine against the futility of man's philosophy: "It is only in the Christian doctrine of the triune God, as we are bound to believe, that we really have a concrete universal. In God's being there are no particulars not related to the universal and there is nothing universal that is not fully expressed in the particulars."[7]

The implications of this doctrine affect every area of life, every moment of life, and every human institution in every time and place of human existence. As this worldview is accepted and lived out, marriage, art, culture, science, politics, economics, and education experience increased levels of richness, meaning, freedom, and blessing. For instance, human governments maximized political liberties in the West. Humanist thinking devolves into hopeless oscillation between anarchy (the ultimacy of the particulars) on the one hand, and totalitarianism (the ultimacy of the unity) on the other.

What is found with the ancient Greeks and Romans but people forever caught between the anarchy of mobs and the tyranny of the dictators and Caesars? There was no escape from this horrible tension. Their aspirations for successful civilization always settled on hierarchy, tyranny, war, and ever-expanding power centers. This is what Christian civilization countered for a thousand years.

THE WORSHIP OF MAN

The rise of Christianity was not without its challenges over the first six centuries of the church. Errors like Arianism and Nestorianism were popular with kings and emperors. For humanists looking for a path to the deification of man, Christological heresies were attractive. If Christ started out a man, and then achieved deity at some later time, what opportunities might this open up for others?

Nestorianism allowed for the worship of Christ only in His human nature, a position ultimately rejected by the Church. The Council of Ephesus (AD 431) was careful to clarify that whoever teaches that "the assumed man (ἀναληφθέντα) ought to be worshipped together with God the Word... as two different things,...let him be anathema."[8] Nestorius was wont to say, "Let us worship the man." This opened the way for mankind to become God over against the faith and the truth concerning God who became Man without surrendering His deity. Such heresies aligned more perfectly with what kings of the earth had been attempting to achieve for 4,000 years.

Assuming the Son of God to have been created, Arius allowed

for the creation of more demigods like Jesus who might possess equal power and glory to Christ. He would say that, "One equal to the Son the Superior (god) is able to beget." Once again, this doctrine extended hope for human kings who wished to ascend into the old pagan pantheon of gods. Shortly after Nicea, Arianism became the dominant view throughout the empire, largely because of enthusiastic support from emperors like Constantius II (Constantine's son) and Valens. And, Athanasius of Alexandria survived five exiles over twenty years (346-366) for his orthodox stance. Finally, in AD 378, the emperor Theodosius I restored orthodox Christianity in the empire, and persecution of Christians abated, though Arianism continued to thrive on the outer edges of civilization. The Germanic tribes embraced Arianism for centuries, and the Lombards dragged the heresy back into northern Italy in the 590s. In the providence of God, Arianism died out around AD 711 as Muslims conquered Spain and became the next formidable threat to the faith in Europe.

THE ULTIMACY OF GOD

Fundamental to Christian monotheism is the above-all-ness of God—the *ultimacy* or *sovereignty* of God.

Before his martyrdom, Polycarp (AD 69-155) acknowledged that God had foreordained "me as an acceptable sacrifice."[9] Clement (35-99), one of the first bishops of Rome, declared, "When and as He pleases, He will do all things, and none of the things determined by Him shall pass away."[10] Justin Martyr (100-165) also pointed out that "God directs the government of the Universe."[11] Both human responsibility and God's sovereignty are equally accepted in his *First Apology*: "So that what we say about future events being foretold, we do not say it as if they came about by a fatal necessity." Yet, Justin adds, "God foreknowing all that shall be done by all men, and it being His decree that the future actions of men shall all be recompensed according to their several value…"[12]

Thus Justin was careful to avoid the cheap cop-out provided by the pagan doctrine of fate, in which man relieves himself of moral responsibility. Fatalism is the weak attempt to pacify the conscience, claiming that, "If the fates made me do it, why should I be held liable?" While rejecting this pagan doctrine, Justin still acknowledged God's perfect foreknowledge and His immutable decree. God absolutely, sovereignly ordains the free actions of men, while at the same time holding man responsible for his moral choices.

Then it was left to Augustine of Hippo to defend the doctrine of God's sovereignty in both His works of providence and redemption.

A major theme in Augustine's City of God is God's sovereignty over the kingdoms of men: "Even if the demons have any power in these matters, they have only that power which the secret decree of the Almighty allots to them."[13] And, "He alone is the true God, Himself gives earthly kingdoms both to good and bad. Neither does He do this rashly, and, as it were, fortuitously, because He is God, not fortune, but according to the order of things and times."[14]

The adoption of a sovereign, personal God overseeing the free actions of men meant a complete rejection of the pagan doctrine of fate. In his Confessions, we find Augustine repudiating astrology for this reason:

All this wholesome advice [the astrologers] labor to destroy when they say, "The cause of your sin is inevitably fixed in the heavens,"…all this in order that a man, who is only flesh and blood and proud corruption, may regard himself as blameless, while the Creator and Ordainer of heaven and the stars must bear the blame of our ills and misfortunes.[15]

Furthermore, in City of God, Augustine equated fate to atheism and godlessness:

In a word, human kingdoms are established by divine providence. And if any one attributes their existence to fate, because he calls the will or the power of God itself by the name of fate, let him keep his opinion, but correct his language...But those who are of opinion that, apart from the will of God, the stars determine what we shall do, or what good things we shall possess, or what evils we shall suffer, must be refused a hearing by all, not only by those who hold the true religion, but by those who wish to be the worshipers of any gods whatsoever, even false gods. For what does this opinion really amount to but this, that no god whatever is to be worshiped or prayed to?"[16]

Augustine's point is well taken. How could any god be worthy of worship if he can't even control what is ordained by some mechanical fate operating within the universe? The true Sovereign has replaced the pagan deterministic worldview in the minds of Western Christians.

Augustine went on to expound upon God's sovereign election in the salvation of sinners:

God chose us in Christ before the foundation of the world...to the adoption of children, not because we were going to be of ourselves holy and immaculate, but...that we might be so...He did this according to the good pleasure of His will, so that nobody might glory concerning his own will, but about God's will towards himself. He did this according to the riches of His grace...which He purposed in His beloved Son, in whom we have obtained a share...to the purpose, not ours, but His...that He worketh in us to will also. Moreover, He worketh according to the counsel of His will, that we may be to the praise of His glory...for which purpose He called us...[with] that special calling of the elect.[17]

Prominent Christian pastors through the ages, including Bede (672-735), Alcuin (735-804), Isidore of Seville (560-636), and Gottschalk of Orbais (808-867), held to Augustine's doctrine of double predestination—that God purposed the destiny of all peoples, believers and unbelievers. However, the Augustinian position was undermined by the Council of Orange (AD 529) and again with the condemnation of Gottschalk at the councils at Quierzy (849 and 853), Valence (855), and Langres and Savonnieres (859). Augustine's influence was later revived during the Reformation through the writings of John Calvin and others.

By the turn of the 11th Century, the prevailing theological opinion still upheld God's absolute sovereignty, although this commitment weakened quickly with the scholastics and the humanist Renaissance. Anselm of Canterbury clearly advocated the doctrine of God's predestination over the free actions of men (good and evil) in *De Concordia* (AD 1070):

> [God] is, however, more precisely said to foreknow and predestine their good works because in their case he causes both that they exist and that they are good, whereas in the case of the evil ones he is only the cause that they simply exist and not that they are evil...[18]

This conception of the ultimacy of the true and living God wasn't only confined to the theologian's study. It was a faith, vibrant throughout the popular culture of Christian Europe, appearing repeatedly throughout the story of *Beowulf* (8th Century):

> No one was ever permitted to enter the ring-hall unless God Himself, mankind's Keeper, True King of Triumphs, allowed some person pleasing to Him—and in His eyes worthy—to open the hoard.[19]

In fact, Beowulf is only enabled to overcome the enemy "through the power of the Lord," for He is the *Alwealdan*—"the Ruler of All." The protaganists are always aware that "God can easily halt these raids and harrowing attacks"[20] of the evil personage Grendel. Beowulf is convinced that all evil forces in the universe "must await the mighty judgment of God in majesty."[21] Moreover, says Beowulf, "The truth is clear, Almighty God rules over mankind and always has."[22] There is no competition, as it were, between good and evil in the Western worldview. Grendel's real problem was that he failed to consider God. "As he would have killed more, had not mindful God and one man's daring prevented that doom. Past and present, God's will prevails."[23]

Striking to the post-Christian reader in the Western world are the hundreds of references to the sovereignty of God, the almighty power of God, and the judgment of God in this seminal literature.

Caedmon's hymn is the earliest recorded English poem, written around AD 658. References to the true and living God in His power, holiness, and eternality are prominently laid out in language similar to that used by the author of Beowulf:

> Now [we] must honour the guardian of heaven,
>
> the might of the architect, and his purpose,
>
> the work of the father of glory
>
> as he, the eternal lord, established the beginning of wonders;
>
> he first created for the children of men
>
> heaven as a roof, the holy creator
>
> Then the guardian of mankind,
>
> the eternal lord, afterwards appointed the middle earth,
>
> the lands for men, the Lord almighty.[24]

THE SALVATION OF GOD— PERPETUAL VICTORY & HOPE

Bolstered by this view of the sovereignty and power of God, the Christian world maintained a keen sense of victory and hope, the inevitable triumph of good over evil. Beowulf's God is the King of Triumphs, the God who always wins His wars. Indeed, the very essence of Christ's work involves His victory over the devil, sin, and death. Jesus came to defeat the enemy, and His record is one of ongoing, perpetual victory, beginning at the cross.

John Scotus Eriugena contrasted the Greek tragic worldview with the secure and eternal victory of Christ in this poem—a powerful picture of the Christian worldview formed in the consciousness of a converted Christian people.

> Homer once sang of his Hellenes and Trojans
> And Virgil composed verse about the descendants of Romulus;
> Let us sing about the kindly deeds of the king of Heaven
> Whom the world never ceases joyously to praise.
> Homer and Virgil took pleasure in speaking about the flames that brought
> Sudden destruction to Troy and about the struggles of their heroes,
> But our delight is to sing of Christ
> Drenched in blood after vanquishing the prince of this world.
> They [Homer and Virgil] were both learned in how to compose falsehoods
> With an appearance of truth and how to deceive an Arcadian verse;
> We prefer to sing hymns of fine praise
> To the power of the Father and His true wisdom.
> As brilliant stars in our minds.
> Behold the four corners of the world are clasped by the wooden cross.[25]

The Christian world was rooted in a sovereign God, a victorious Christ, and a robust faith. And, above all, this salvation is of God and by God's grace. Although this core message died the death of incalculable qualifications during the Renaissance and following years, the basic gospel message stayed intact through the European missionary age.

The mighty missionary Cuthbert (634-687) preached a gospel message summarized by Bede as simply: "The loving kindness of our Saviour is mighty and abundant. He will give us grace, unworthy though we are, to extinguish the flames of vice in this world, and escape the flames of punishment in the next."[26] Throughout Northumbria, Cuthbert would preach and the people would confess "every sin openly" and "made amends by fruits worthy of repentance as he commanded."[27]

Upon his first missionary journey into Sweden, Anskar (801-

865) was received by the local chieftain Herigar. In the first public assembly, the missionary challenged the people to turn to God. His basic summary of the Christian gospel is remarkable for its simplicity and power: "Alas, wretched people," he said, "ye now understand that it is useless to seek for help from demons who cannot succour those who are in trouble. Accept the faith of my Lord Jesus Christ, whom ye have proved to be the true God and who in His compassion has brought solace to you who have no refuge from sorrow. Seek not any more after superstitious worship, or to appease your idols by useless sacrifice. Worship the true God who rules all things in heaven and earth, submit yourselves to Him, and adore His almighty power."[28]

Jesus Christ is both God and Savior, and there is no other true salvation available to man. As Jonah testified in the belly of the fish, "Salvation is of the Lord" (Jon. 2:9). This is the core message of the Christian faith.

Despite the tendency to drift into merit, a simple medieval faith persisted through the centuries. The Christian faith did not get its start at the door in Wittenberg in 1517; it had existed and flourished since the coming of Christ. Anselm (1033-1109), the pastor at Canterbury, is best known for his development of the doctrine of substitutionary atonement. In his advice to the sick and dying, he would write,

> Dost thou believe that thou canst not be saved but by the death of Christ? Go to, then, and whilst thy soul abideth in thee, put all thy confidence in this death alone—place thy trust in no other thing— commit thyself wholly on this death,—wrap thyself wholly in this death. And if God would judge you, say, "Lord! I place the death of our Lord Jesus Christ between me and Thy judgement: otherwise I will not contend, or enter into judgement, with Thee." And if He shall say unto thee, that thou art a sinner, say unto Him, "I place the death of our Lord Jesus Christ between me and my sins." If He shall say unto thee, that thou hast deserved damnation, say, "Lord! I put the death of

our Lord Jesus Christ between Thee and all my sins; I offer His merits for my own, which I should have, and have not." If He say, that He is angry with thee, say "Lord! I place the death of our Lord Jesus Christ between me and Thy anger."[29]

Early English literature blossomed out of a substantially Christianized culture that had formed between the 8th and 14th centuries. The literature is anything but pagan. An early example, *Piers Plowman*, was a popular allegory presenting the Christian faith and life in living color. Dated about 1370, the story comes to a climax at the scene of the crucifixion of Christ, where the four daughters converse—Peace, Righteousness, Truth, and Mercy.

Peace wants to "welcome all the lost souls, whom I have not seen for many a long day now, because of the darkness of sin."

However, Righteousness contends strongly with her: "Have you gone off your head? Or had you too much to drink? Do you really suppose that this light can unlock hell, and save the souls of men? Don't you believe it! God Himself pronounced this doom in the beginning, that Adam and Eve and all their seed should surely die, and after death live in torment...I am Righteousness, and I tell you this for certain: that their suffering will never cease..."

But then, Christ steps in, having conquered Satan and introduced a ministry of reconciliation. He explains to them, "I can grant them mercy without offending justice, and all my words remain true."

At this point, Peace breaks out in song, "No weather is warmer than after the blackest clouds."

And, Truth turns to Mercy and says, "You are in the right. Let us make our peace together, and seal it with a kiss."[30]

Here was a Christian literature—the beautiful, simple story of salvation that resonated in the hearts of a Christian people in the West, for a millennium.

THE LAW OF GOD

> And it shall come to pass in the last days, that the mountain of the Lord's house shall be established in the top of the mountains, and shall be exalted above the hills; and all nations shall flow unto it. And many people shall go and say, Come ye, and let us go up to the mountain of the Lord, to the house of the God of Jacob; and he will teach us of his ways, and we will walk in his paths: for out of Zion shall go forth the law, and the word of the Lord from Jerusalem. (Isaiah 2:2-3)

The earliest extant Christian documents present the way of life as submission to the commandments of God, contained in both the Old and New Testaments. Primary of these is to, "love the Lord your God with all your heart, soul, mind, and strength, and love your neighbor as yourself." And, in the words of Jesus, "Turn to him the other cheek" and "love those that hate you."[31] The 1st Century *Didache* presented two ways to its readers: the way of life and the way of death. The way of life is the way of keeping the commands of God. The way of death is outlined as murder, adultery, stealing, using magic, procuring abortion, committing infanticide, perjury, speaking evil, covetousness, hypocrisy, pride, and bearing malice.[32] In the single letter still available of the apostolic father and martyr Polycarp, we find the fundamental doctrine of the early church: "Let us teach, first of all, ourselves to walk in the commandments of the Lord. Next, [teach] your wives [to walk] in the faith, loving their own husbands in all truth, and loving all equally in all chastity; and to train up their children in the knowledge and fear of God."[33] Distinguishing between the ceremonial and the moral, Augustine of Hippo also affirmed the abiding relevance of the Old Testament commandments:

> (With the exception of the sacramental ordinances which were the shadow of things to come, such as circumcision, the Sabbath and other observances of days, and the ceremonies of certain meats, and

the complicated ritual of sacrifices and sacred things which suited *"the oldness"* of the carnal law and its slavish yoke) [the Old Testament law] contains such precepts of righteousness as we are even now taught to observe, which were especially expressly drawn out on the two tables without figure or shadow: for instance, *"You shall not commit adultery," "You shall do no murder," "You shall not covet," "and whatsoever other commandment is briefly comprehended in the saying, You shall love your neighbour as yourself."* (Romans 13:9)[34]

More can be said about the development of Christian morality, and this will be treated in a subsequent chapter. Suffice it to say that the early church and the Reformation church was anything but antinomian. Only in a post-Christian world was there to be found the predominance of churches set in opposition to God's laws. Christians, at the most seminal level, have always been defined as those who "keep the faith of Jesus" and "keep the commandments of God" (Rev. 14:12). While exceptions are made for the Old Testament ceremonial laws, circumcision, the food laws, and sabbath laws by the Apostles (Col. 2:16, Acts 15:5,19-20), the rest of it was to be taught in the churches. The commission was in force: "Teach them to observe whatsoever I have commanded you."

A SOUND REJECTION OF PAGAN PHILOSOPHY

A transference from pagan to Christian civilization must necessarily include the shedding of the pagan philosophy, for a biblical epistemology, metaphysic, and ethic. The attraction of worldly philosophies is strong, however, especially for the academic-minded. On the one hand, the legendary preacher from the East, John Chrysostom, held nothing but contempt for Greek philosophy. While preaching a homily on Ephesians 6:4, he addresses the Greek academy:

For if a set of Greeks, men worthless as they are and dogs, by taking up that worthless philosophy of theirs (for such the Grecian philosophy is), or rather not itself but only its mere name, and wearing the threadbare cloaks and letting their hair grow, impress many; how much more will he who is a true philosopher.[35]

The good preacher recommended "lessons from Scripture" rather than this Greek education.

Other Christian educators maintained an uneasy relationship with Greek ideas. Boethius (c. 475-526), for example, was a student of Greek philosophy but finally had to admit that Aristotelian logical categories were insufficient for understanding the doctrine of the Trinity. In his theological treatises, he demonstrates where these categories break down and how understanding is left to analogy.

The main point in his magnum opus, *Consolation of Philosophy*, was to trace the differences between the method of autonomous humanist thinking and Christian thinking. He compares the Greek metaphysical concept of a non-interventionist god and a universe operated by impersonal forces with the true and living God who personally rules the universe at every point as the final cause. Effectively, Boethius abandons all hope of explaining how God predestines the free actions of men, conceding that philosophy is insufficient to answer such metaphysical mysteries. The *Stanford Encyclopedia of Philosophy* wraps up a full analysis of Boethius with this important conclusion: "It is plausible, however, to hold that Boethius wished, whilst acknowledging the value of philosophy—to which he had devoted his life, and for which he presented himself as being about to die—to point out its limitations: limitations which Philosophy herself, who is keen to emphasize that she is not divine, accepts."[36] So, at the last, humility will submit the human mind to the mind of God. If we could boil down the Christian worldview to its most seminal distinction from pagan philosophy, it would be this: The Christian worldview is willing to explain impossibilities by incomprehensibilities and leave it there, for it acknowledges that we have the mind of a child, and God is omniscient.

Bottom line: according to Boethius, the Christian God rules with absolute sovereignty for His foreordained purposes, and this is what marked the most radical shift from a pagan metaphysic to a Christian understanding of reality.

THE REJECTION OF PAGAN LEARNING

To understand the worldview of the early medieval period or the European Christian era, a thorough study of the life and work of Alcuin of York (735-804), the organizer of Charlemagne's Palace School, is very much in order. This central figure in the Carolingian court was trained in England by Ethelbert of York (710-780). As England embraced the Christian faith, these discipleship centers mainly focused on biblical doctrine, the history of the church, apologetics, astronomy, arithmetic, and natural science. The only pagans allowed in these 8th Century English discipleship centers were Pliny and Cicero, for a little zoology and rhetoric. Besides these two, all studies were taken from Christian writers—Isidore, Bede, Gregory the Great, Cassiodorus, and Boethius.

Alcuin is described as a "constant reader of Augustine." In his discussions with students, he leaned heavily on Augustine's *City of God* as a polemic against the pagan worldview and interpretation of history.[37] In his philosophical treatise, *On the Nature of the Soul*, he reminded his readers that wisdom "will not be found in the lies of Virgil, but in abundance within the truth of the Gospel."[38] He insisted that his students be well read in the church fathers and encouraged them to "Preach! Preach in season and out of season! Let your throat be as a trumpet for the Lord!"[39] Although pagan histories were tolerated by the school, they were carefully edited before use. Paul the Deacon was assigned to edit Eutropius' *Roman History* before giving it to the students, making it "suitably Christian."[40]

Alcuin wrote his own grammar and includes Scriptural definitions for wisdom, clarifying that this must be the gift of the Holy Spirit.[41] In his "True Philosophy" essay introducing his studies in grammar, logic, and rhetoric, Alcuin argued that biblical wisdom was superior to the Greeks and urged his students to find the foundation of true philosophy in Proverbs and Ecclesiastes.[42] For Alcuin true philosophy is confined to just two branches—active philosophy, which enables the Christian to actively follow Christ, overcome "worldly ambition," and live for heaven; and the branch of theology. In a distinctively biblical view of education, these Christians understood the vital importance of actively obeying Christ as well as a right biblical theology. Head knowledge without life application is dead knowledge. Also, Alcuin would not tolerate a worldly philosophy built up on human reason, separate from theology.[43] This would come 500 years later.

Yet, the pull towards man-derived wisdom was strong in academia. John Scotus Eriugena (810-877), Alcuin's successor at Charlemagne's Palace School in Aachen, was greatly influenced by Neoplatonic thinking and turned out to be an opponent of the Augustinian view of God's sovereignty. Arguing against Gottschalk, he stated that God cannot be sovereign over certain things like death,[44] in complete disagreement with 1 Samuel 2:6: "The LORD kills and makes alive; He brings down to the grave and brings up." His argument was based on "human reason." *The battle for the soul of the Christian West played out on this field: Is God sovereign? And does human reason trump Scripture?*

The Christian world of the Western missionary age soundly rejected the pagan worldview, whether polytheism or humanist philosophy. Alcuin, concerned that the young men at Lindisfarne were being drawn back to pagan superheroes, wrote to the Bishop Higbald in AD 797:

> What has Ingeld to do with Christ? The house is narrow, it cannot contain both. The king of the heavens will have nothing to do with the heathen and damned so-called kings. For the eternal King rules in the

heavens, the lost heathen repines in hell.[45]

For Christianized Europe, nothing short of a total abandonment of the philosophy and narrative of the old pagan world would do. Aldhelm of Malmesbury, England (639-709) asked the obvious question: "What advantage does it bring to the sacrament of the orthodox faith to sweat over reading and studying the polluted lewdness of Proserpine, or Hermione, the wanton offspring of Menlaus and Helen, or the Lupercalia and the votaries of Priapus [the ancient Roman gods]?"[46] The Venerable Bede agreed. Concerning the poetry of Porphyry (the Neoplatonic philosopher of the 3rd Century), he submits, "Because they were pagan, it was not permitted for us to touch them."[47]

Anselm of Canterbury (1033-1109) represents the last of the early medieval theologians. Like Augustine, he rejected human reason as a means of establishing fundamental truths. He embraced the Augustinian phrase, "I believe that I might understand." The proposition was so important to him that he called his book *Proslogium*, "Faith Seeking Understanding." There is certainly no indication that Anselm is resorting to proud, autonomous, human reason in his thinking as he writes:

> I do not endeavor, O Lord, to penetrate thy sublimity, for in no wise do I compare my understanding with that; but I long to understand in some degree thy truth, which my heart believes and loves. For I do not seek to understand that I may believe, but I believe in order to understand. For this also I believe—that unless I believed, I should not understand.[48]

And so the West was won until the universities and schoolmen entered the scene.

> And I saw heaven opened, and behold a white horse; and he that sat upon him was called Faithful and True, and in righteousness he doth judge and make war. His eyes were as a flame of fire, and on his head

were many crowns; and he had a name written, that no man knew, but he himself. And he was clothed with a vesture dipped in blood: and his name is called The Word of God. And the armies which were in heaven followed him upon white horses, clothed in fine linen, white and clean. And out of his mouth goeth a sharp sword, that with it he should smite the nations: and he shall rule them with a rod of iron: and he treadeth the winepress of the fierceness and wrath of Almighty God. And he hath on his vesture and on his thigh a name written, KING OF KINGS, AND LORD OF LORDS. (Revelation 19:11-16)

There is little to debate of this. The Galilean had conquered and continued to conquer. He conquered the West and the East, from Alexandria to Constantinople. He conquered Eastern Europe and Russia. He conquered Ireland. Over a thousand years, Christ had conquered the Gentile world from Italy to Iceland, and from Spain to Finland. It was a Christian world and life view that won out in the West. Nobody was reading Homer in Malmesbury in AD 800. They were reading the gospels of Christ and Augustine's *City of God*. By the turn of the first millennium, Athens had very little to do with Jerusalem throughout the Christian West. The Christian worldview, emphasizing the ultimacy of the only true and living God, the Trinity, the salvation of God, the resurrection of Jesus Christ, and the law of God, had won out against all pagan worldviews.

> The ancient triumph of Christianity proved to be the single greatest cultural transformation our world has ever seen. Without it the entire history of Late Antiquity would not have happened as it did. We would never have had the Middle Ages, the Reformation, the Renaissance, or modernity as we know it.[49]—Bart D. Ehrman

THE WORLDVIEW SHIFT IN THE WEST

A recent survey from *Christian History Magazine* on the most influential Christian books of all time provides a convenient illustration for understanding what has happened in the West.[50] Augustine takes the place as the most influential writer in history—setting the tone for the Christian West. Aquinas comes in second with his *Summa Theologiae*, representing the major theological decline of the Middle Ages. And, John Calvin's *Institutes of the Christian Religion* comes in third place as one masterful endeavor to restore a Christian worldview in the Western church.

The decline and fall of Western civilization begins with Aquinas. If the conflict is seen as man-centered thinking set against the God-centered worldview, then the Reformation was a mogul on the ski slope of the West. Augustine slipped, Calvin and the Reformers recovered, but Thomas Aquinas won out.

The West began to fall in the 13th Century with the reintroduction of high octane humanist-Greek thinking in the universities. Aquinas is considered the apex of the schoolmen or the "scholastics." These university men were trained in the Aristotelian dialectic or logic to sort through extra-scriptural theological writings, and to systematize Scripture by these categorical methods. Aquinas' formulations then, provided the highest intellectual representation of the epistemology (a view of truth) that would undermine the Christian worldview in the Western world. The very introductory words of the *Summa* is the failure point, as the theologian posits two forms of knowledge differing "in kind."

> Now Scripture, inspired of God, is no part of philosophical science [knowledge], which has been built up by human reason. Therefore it is useful that besides philosophical science, there should be other knowledge, i.e. inspired of God. I answer that, it was necessary for man's salvation that there should be a knowledge revealed by God besides philosophical science [knowledge] built up by human reason... Hence theology included in sacred doctrine differs in kind from that theology which is part of philosophy.[51]

For the Christian worldview to be completely dismantled in the Western world, adequate room would have to be made for a humanist theory of knowledge to infiltrate at the most foundational level. The authority or relevance of Scripture would have to be set aside.

THE RECOVERY OF ARISTOTLE

Fittingly, the long and painful displacement of the Christian worldview began in the new universities with the rediscovery of Aristotle and his perceived "genius." Pride comes before a fall, and the Fall of the West found its roots in the pride of man in academia. A later chapter will detail the blow-by-blow battle whereby Aristotle was introduced into the universities (between AD 1080 and AD 1280). By the time of his death in AD 1274, the Western church was begging for some intellectual justification to bring secular knowledge back into the university. Aquinas is that apologist, himself quite enamored with Aristotle, whom he refers to throughout his work "the Philosopher;" and he makes room for Aristotelian studies in the university—the categories, the ethics, the logic, the epistemology, and his way of thinking. To be clear, Aquinas would not dismiss the authority of Scripture by offering his apologetic for Aristotle. Rather, he invented two forms of knowledge, "differing in kind;" and this sacred-secular distinction on the epistemological level opened up a field of knowledge in which the autonomous mind of man was "free" to operate, independent of God's revealed Word. Passing off his entire life's work as nothing but "straw," at the end, Thomas passed away before seeing magnum opus published.

Aquinas's system of knowledge allowed the Scriptures to speak authoritatively on the subjects of God and salvation, while humanist man and the university philosophy department would take care of the categories of philosophy—specifically the areas of epistemology, metaphysics, and ethics. Where there had been a single department for the training of clerics in the church (under Charlemagne's training centers), henceforth there were two: the theology department and the philosophy department. This would change everything for Western civilization.

Aquinas maintained an overly optimistic view of the reasoning capability of fallen man. He received Romans 1:19 but neglected the premise in verse 18. Aquinas wrote, "The existence of God and other like truths about God, which can be known by natural reason, are not articles of faith, but are preambles to the articles..."[52] So he fails to reckon with the wicked, rebellious, deceitful mind of man is always actively engaged in suppressing the truth in unrighteousness. Thus, natural man is entirely unreliable in his quest towards answering the fundamental questions relating to reality and life.

For the ensuing eight hundred years, Western academia would progressively disconnect the subjects of philosophy, psychology, history, music, mathematics, culture, and physical science from the worldview framework established by Scripture. The domain of "sacred" knowledge would contract, and the field referred to as "philosophical knowledge" would expand in the mind of Western man and his institutions to include every point of human knowledge. When secular philosophy took ownership of epistemology, metaphysics, ethics, law, social theory, political theory, etc., it was not long before sacred doctrine was left with nothing. If philosophy built up on human reason rejected the possibility of the supernatural, then the seminary and the church would follow suit. If the Trinitarian worldview did not work well with a humanist theory of truth and logic, the humanist would revert to a defective metaphysical theory, erring toward the unity or the particulars. If biblical law seemed unreasonable to modern man, humanist ethics—whether Marxist or utilitarian or any other theory— would become the norm.

While Aquinas does retain something of a "veto power" for divine revelation, philosophy is left very much alone to develop its own infrastructure of knowledge independent of sacred doctrine. Christian theologian John Frame recognizes that this became an "enormous problem" for Aquinas and his successors.[53] Frame writes, "For the realm of 'nature' is, for Aquinas, essentially a realm in which autonomous reason (the reason that Aristotle advocated) is relatively unhindered... And since Aquinas even develops his doctrine of God out of natural reason...he is not able to insulate his theology, even his discipline of 'sacred doctrine,' from the effects of would-be autonomous thought."[54] Nancy Pearcey describes Aquinas' "two-tiered" epistemological schema as "unstable." She notes that "the two orders of existence had a tendency to separate and grow increasingly independent...because there was no real interactions or inter-dependence between them... Aristotelian 'nature' remained complete and sufficient in itself, with grace merely an external add-on. No matter how much icing you spread on a cake, it is still a separate substance."[55]

Certain of the Protestant Reformers could already see the bankruptcy of humanist thought creeping into the Western world. Martin Luther described Aquinas as "the fountain and original soup of all heresy, error, and Gospel havoc, as his books bear witness."[56] Luther compared Aquinas with "the star of the book of Revelation which fell from heaven," equating "the empty speculations of Aristotle to the smoke of the bottomless pit, the universities to the locusts, and Aristotle himself to his master Apollyon."[57]

> Beware lest any man spoil you through philosophy and vain deceit, after the tradition of men, after the rudiments of the world, and not after Christ. (Colossians 2:8)

THE SUBSTANCE OF THE WORLDVIEW SHIFT

This means that the mistake must be at the root, at the very basis of human thinking in the past centuries. I refer to the prevailing Western view of the world which was first born during the Renaissance and found its political expression from the period of the Enlightenment. It became the basis for government and social science and could be defined as rationalistic humanism or humanistic autonomy: the proclaimed and enforced autonomy of man from any higher force above him. It could also be called anthropocentricity, with man seen as the center of everything that exists. (Aleksandr Solzhenitsyn, 1978)

When humanist man attempts self-deification (as expressed to the ultimate degree in the recent age), for a time he celebrates the "death of God." He cannot allow for any competition. Reading through the philosophies of Marx or Nietzsche, it is impossible to miss the bitter animus spewing out against God and Christ. Truly, they have very deliberately "set themselves against the Lord and against His anointed" (Ps. 2:1-3). They have protested too loudly—hating that which they say does not exist. Varying descriptions or terms have been offered for the man-centered, man-derived philosophies which have successfully undermined the foundations of the West over the past eight hundred years, including secular humanism, materialism, enlightenment rationalism, romanticism, transcendentalism, existentialism, and nihilism. Going straight to the heart of it, this corrupted worldview of the West is better described as self-consciously anti-Christian, anti-Christ, post-Christian, and apostate. This was something beyond the regurgitated philosophical meanderings of Aristotle, Plato, Parmenides, or Heraclitus. The new philosophers of humanism were post-Christian, this time rebelling against Christ with whom they were quite familiar. Their rebellion was starker, more self-conscious, more self-consistent, more vehement, and more destructive than that of their predecessors.

For when they speak great swelling words of vanity, they allure through the lusts of the flesh, through much wantonness, those that were clean escaped from them who live in error. While they promise them liberty, they themselves are the servants of corruption: for of whom a man is overcome, of the same is he brought in bondage. For if after they have escaped the pollutions of the world through the knowledge of the Lord and Saviour Jesus Christ, they are again entangled therein, and overcome, the latter end is worse with them than the beginning. (2 Peter 2:18-20)

RENAISSANCE

We have also a more sure word of prophecy; whereunto ye do well that ye take heed, as unto a light that shineth in a dark place, until the day dawn, and the day star arise in your hearts: Knowing this first, that no prophecy of the scripture is of any private interpretation. For the prophecy came not in old time by the will of man: but holy men of God spake as they were moved by the Holy Ghost. (2 Peter 1:19-21)

The term "renaissance" is derived from the French word meaning "rebirth." The Renaissance of the 15th and 16th centuries was the rebirth of pagan Greek humanism in a Christian world. As the humanist age progressed, lapsed-Christian intellects began to speak of the Christian age (AD 325-1325) as the "dark age." Christ brought darkness, but Aristotle brought light into the world, according to the post-Christian narrative. After a thousand years of relying upon divine revelation for the basis of human knowledge, lapsed Christians now would dedicate themselves to building up a philosophy, a worldview, a psychology, education, and life built up on human reason. This ideological shift would replace God with man at the center.

Francis Schaeffer famously described two conflicting streams of thought battling for the mind of the Western world—the God-centered and the man-centered. The Renaissance, beginning with Thomas Aquinas (d. 1274) and the advent of the classical, humanist universities, produced the first stream of thought which would come to dominate Western universities almost universally. The Reformation initiated in

Wittenberg on October 31, 1517 ushered in the second stream.

The importance of Aquinas to the Renaissance is best portrayed in Andrea da Firenze's (d. 1377) famous painting hanging in the Spanish Chapel in Florence. "The Triumph of St. Thomas Aquinas" pictures Aquinas elevated above Aristotle, Cicero, Ptolemy, Euclid, and Pythagoras, pagan philosophers and historians. Augustine is placed in the mix as an important theologian. While Aquinas is pictured as the ultimate master philosopher, the others are given their due—pagan and Christian alike important in their contributions to Western thought and life.

The ascendance of humanist, autonomous reason was gradual. Marsilio Ficino (1433-1499) translated and published thirty-six of Plato's works. He spoke of both Plato and Zoroaster as rustic theologians, but he still thought of philosophy as subservient to theology.

To better understand the Renaissance, one should follow the life and thinking of Dante Alighieri (1265-1321), whose *Divine Comedy* (1320) marked the beginning of Italian humanism. The readmission of the classical Greek and Roman worldview is well attested to by the employment of the Roman poet Virgil as Dante's guide through hell. For Dante, Aristotle was "a supreme and chief Authority."[58] and "the master and leader of Human Reason insofar as it aims at its final operation."[59] This archetypal Christian-humanist longed for the "good old days" of ancient pagan Rome, "a most Holy See." As with Lot's wife, Dante looks with longing eyes back to the old pagan world, confessing that, "If the Roman empire was not of right, the sin of Adam was not punished in Christ."[60]

His was an overweening faith in the state as god on earth. In a letter to the emperor, he gushed, "...my hands handled thy feet and my lips paid their debt. Then did my spirit exult in thee, and I spoke silently with myself, 'Behold the Lamb of God! Behold him who hath taken away the sins of the world.'"[61] Visible here in seed form, this doctrine of salvation by the state would come to dominate the world by the 21st Century.

Therefore, the sins which seem to take men to hell in the *Comedy*, are sins against the state (as the highest representation of man as god on earth.) These are not to be considered sins against a holy God—not for the humanist of the 14th Century. Rebels, traitors, barrators, schismatics, and any who would undermine the ultimate unity of the empire deserved the hottest flames in the humanist hell.

Even more troubling was Dante's discontentment with his own wife and an obsession to have the love of another man's wife. The entire *Divine Comedy* is centered around his love for Beatrice, with whom apparently Dante had had something of an infatuation in his younger years. Throughout his career, Dante would dedicate his poetry to this other woman, Beatrice, while snubbing his own wife. In the minds of the Renaissance poet class, an artificial distinction was drawn between the sensual and spiritual love of a woman. But, cutting through these cheap self-justifications and applying a clear biblical consideration of this behavior, one must conclude that this man was coveting his neighbor's wife even after her death. This sinful infatuation with Beatrice returns repeatedly throughout the *Comedy*:

> Then Beatrice looked at me with eyes so full of sparks of love, eyes so divine that my own force of sight was overcome, took flight, and, eyes downcast, I almost lost my senses.[62]

> ...even as I gazed at her, my soul was free from any other need.[63]

As the *Comedy* proceeds, Dante begins to define love for God in terms of his love for Beatrice. It is the love of Beatrice that draws him to heaven, not the love of God. As he approaches heaven, Dante envisions Beatrice coming to meet him and confesses: "I felt the mighty power of old love."[64] And Beatrice admits the same:

Beatrice am I, who do bid thee go;

I come from there, where I would fain return;

Love moved me, which compelleth me to speak.

When I shall be in presence of my Lord,

Full often will I praise thee unto him.[65]

Love, even the love of a woman and for a woman, is framed as the ultimate value in Dante's universe. Scripture, on the other hand, does not elevate one divine attribute above the others in the character of God but instead presents God's goodness, power, wisdom, and holiness on an equal plane. Our ascendance to heaven can only come by God's absolute commitment to love—as well as His commitment to His own holiness and justice.

ERASMUS—THE TRIUMPH
OF RENAISSANCE HUMANISM

Trained for the priesthood, even as a university man, Desiderius Erasmus Roterodamus (1466-1536) is usually regarded as embodying the core thinking of the 16th Century humanist. Although his writing is filled with uncertainties which played a strong part in his theological view of truth, Erasmus believed that man's fall had only lightly affected his will. He would hold it "...probable that there was a will in some way ready for the good but useless for eternal salvation without the addition of grace by faith."[66] Erasmus could not admit that God was absolutely sovereign—especially over the free actions of men. In his view, "God's decree must turn according to man's decision."[67] The theology produced by the scholastics and maintained by the Renaissance men was a definitive shift away from the thinking of Augustine which had reigned for a thousand years in the Western church. According to these men, the human will retained a sovereignty of its own, endowed with the ability to thwart the purposes of God. This gets to the very essence of humanism—the sovereignty of man's will over the sovereignty of God. Martin Luther, John Calvin, John Knox, and others would attempt to refute these ideas and stem the flood of humanism between 1517 and 1700.

The effects of the humanist Renaissance and the revival of Greek classical humanism upon art, culture, the university, and the church were devastating—calling for the Reformation and a less-enthusiastic counter-reformation in the Roman church.

The Reformation's dominant influence on Western civilization lasted about 150 years—a mogul on the ski slope of Western culture. Nonetheless, ripples from this God-centered thinking from the Reformers extended beyond the Western world to influence a major Protestant missionary endeavor of the 19th and 20th centuries. In the providence of God, the influence of a Christian world and life view would have increasing effect upon the whole world, while the West was lost.

FAILURE TO ANSWER THE ULTIMATE QUESTIONS

There is no better picture of the flow of Western apostasy and the futility of a post-Christian humanism than Michelangelo's famous sculpture of a man tearing himself out of a rock. He is the self-defining humanist man. He must create himself and his own reality. He must be the ultimate source of truth and ethics. Therefore, he sets out in the age of new birth and enlightenment, quite excited and greatly optimistic that he is able to replace God as ultimate. However, somewhere along the line, the man tearing himself out of the rock comes to the realization that he can't do this unless he has a pair of hands first. But how can one form a pair of hands unless he first possesses a pair of hands wherewith to sculpture these hands? Thus, at some point it must dawn upon humanist man that he cannot make for himself any knowledge built up on his own reason unless he first has the elementary principles of objective, absolute, and ultimate truth. He cannot be sure of his own existence—let alone determine his own reality—unless he exists first and unless that existence is derived from an Absolute Existence.

This is the point where man gives way to despair and pessimism. He gives up on the possibility of truth, ethics, or his own existence. This is humanist man. He has hands, but not really, according to his own thinking. He has truth, but not really. He has a reality, but not really, because he is incapable of sourcing any of this. He acts as if he can source and define these things. He plays the part of a god, but he doesn't make a very good god. He has deified himself, but the gods are failing him—as they always do. Thus, he is left with nothing but the meaninglessness of modern life. There are no melodies left and no resolution. There is only cacophony, primal screams, and despair streaming through the mediums. It is Psalm 115 all over again.

Not unto us, O Lord, not unto us,
But unto thy name give glory,
For thy mercy, and for thy truth's sake.
Wherefore should the heathen say,
Where is now their God?
But our God is in the heavens:
He hath done whatsoever he hath pleased.
Their idols are silver and gold, the work of men's hands.
They have mouths, but they speak not:
Eyes have they, but they see not:
They have ears, but they hear not:
Noses have they, but they smell not:
They have hands, but they handle not:
Feet have they, but they walk not:
Neither speak they through their throat.
They that make them are like unto them;
So is every one that trusteth in them. (Psalm 115:1-8)

SCIENTIFIC KNOWLEDGE & THE ENLIGHTENMENT

Synthesizing propositional statements in obvious disagreement with each other would never work, so efforts were made to maintain two departments in the university and two separate knowledges—philosophy and theology in university and seminary. The Bible affirms two revelations, both natural and special (Psalm 19), but never two knowledges separate in kind as posited by Thomas Aquinas.

> The heavens declare the glory of God; and the firmament sheweth his handywork. Day unto day uttereth speech, and night unto night sheweth knowledge.... The law of the Lord is perfect, converting the soul: the testimony of the Lord is sure, making wise the simple. (Psalm 19:1, 2, 7)

Moreover, God's system of education for His people does not allow a separation of the Word from any part of life. Deuteronomy 6:7 speaks of the Word as a "frontlet" before the eyes, always thoroughly integrated into every part of life. For the true Christian, no dualism may be countenanced in the business of education or knowledge.

> And these words, which I command thee this day, shall be in thine heart: And thou shalt teach them diligently unto thy children, and shalt talk of them when thou sittest in thine house, and when thou walkest by the way, and when thou liest down, and when thou risest up. And thou shalt bind them for a sign upon thine hand, and they shall be as frontlets between thine eyes. (Deuteronomy 6:6-8)

Even before man's nature was corrupted by the Fall, God provided him with special revelation by which he could know himself, his calling, and his Creator. Following the Fall into sin, man's intellect was badly warped, terribly unreliable, and self-deceptive, especially in regard to the fundamental questions of truth, ethics, and reality.

After Aquinas, the universities more and more treated the

knowledge of God or sacred knowledge as a derivative of that knowledge obtained by human reason. And sacred knowledge was seen as subjective and unscientific, but still given a place, at least temporarily. Then with the Enlightenment, man resorted to scientific knowledge as that philosophy built upon human reason—rational, objective, and ultimate. At this point, human reason was employed to judge the "reasonableness" of Christian doctrine and sacred knowledge.[68] The Christian apologist of the 20th Century, Francis Schaeffer, preferred to call this the upper and lower registers of knowledge—a nature/grace dualism. In the realm of ethics, two forms of knowledge appeared in the form of natural law and revealed, sacred law.

René Descartes (1596-1650) translated this dualism into two separated views of reality—the mind or spirit and matter or machine. The nature of man is reduced to a detached ghost functioning in the machine of the body. Descartes questioned his own existence, and strangely enough, settled on the ultimacy of his mind or his doubting as the starting point for knowledge concerning his existence. Abandoning Augustine's commitment to belief prior to understanding, Descartes relied on autonomous reason (rather than divine revelation) to answer the first questions in his philosophy.

Jean-Jacques Rousseau and other Enlightenment men espoused an unbound, irrational romanticism in tandem with a rational scientism. For these men, religion was to be kept in the category of irrational romanticism, locking up the Christian faith in the realm of uncertainty and rationalism during the apostasy of the European Enlightenment.

After Descartes and Leibnitz, ultimate questions were abandoned and subsequently replaced by scientific observations and technological advancement. Technology was sufficient to assure man's pride with his own genius. However, modern man was not to be honest with himself. He would not face his own failure to address the ultimate questions of knowledge, reality, and ethics, or provide satisfactory answers.

THE GERMAN APOSTASY BEGINS—WOLFF & KANT

Immanuel Kant (1724-1804) was a seminal figure in the Christian apostasy of the Protestant world in the West. He was raised by committed Christian Pietist parents and educated in a "classical" approach by his pastor at a local Christian school. Kant was particularly charmed by the Roman poet and philosopher Lucretius, and his primary influence came under a professor named Christian Wolff (1679-1754), who taught at the University of Konigsburg in the 1740s. Twenty years earlier, Wolff had been expelled from the University of Halle at the insistence of the Christian Pietist and missionary leader August Hermann Francke. His crime? Wolff had concluded that the Chinese philosopher Confucius was an example of pure moral philosophy generated by the autonomous human mind without any reliance upon divine revelation. Wolff was one of the first major apologists for the humanist Enlightenment in Germany.

The newly-formed University of Halle had developed two departments—the department of theology led by Francke and the philosophy department led by Wolff. But then, Professor Wolff called for the philosophy department to operate independently of the department of Christian theology. In his view, the business of developing moral ethics, epistemology, and metaphysics must be left to autonomous human reason without any imposition or influence from divine revelation. Wolff "refused to submit the text of his lecture for subsequent examination by the faculty of theology."[69] By the time Wolff left Halle, two independent departments remained—a phenomenon which would define the very essence of the humanist Enlightenment. The theology department may have won the first battle, but the philosophy department built up on human reason would win the war in the Western mind.

Wolff also took the position that God *possibly* existed as the basis of his proof for His existence, introducing doubt into the Christian academic world. These were the first steps towards total skepticism, agnosticism, and atheism for all major institutions in the West.

Setting out to develop a system of knowledge without any dependence upon God, Descartes and Wolfe managed to crack the door to doubt concerning God and everything else. By pride and independence from God, man surrendered certainty and true knowledge, and reduced himself to doubt concerning the most fundamental truths in the universe. The condemnation of James 1 applies:

> If any of you lack wisdom, let him ask of God, that giveth to all men liberally, and upbraideth not; and it shall be given him. But let him ask in faith, nothing wavering. For he that wavereth is like a wave of the sea driven with the wind and tossed. For let not that man think that he shall receive any thing of the Lord. A double minded man is unstable in all his ways. (James 1:5-8)

Immanuel Kant took the highly immoral Jean-Jacques Rousseau (1712-1778) as his role model, no doubt affecting his ethical philosophy. He kept Rousseau's picture hanging on his study wall. Kant's job was to free man from a biblical morality, something that would come in handy for the humanist revolutions of the next 300 years.

At first, Kant was drawn to the developing scientific work of Isaac Newton and others, proposing a reality in which "everything which takes place should be infallibly determined in accordance with the laws of nature."[70] However, within this deterministic conception of the universe, Kant still wanted to maintain freedom for the human will to determine right or wrong for itself. Moral worth, said Kant, can only be found "in the principle of the [human] will, without regard to the ends that can be effected through such action."[71] The idea for Kant was that everyone should "act externally in such a manner that the free exercise of the will may be able to exist with the freedom of all others."[72] According to this new philosophy, consenting adults were now at liberty to do whatever they wanted to do, released from any obligation to the revealed law of God. How freedom of the will might exist in an otherwise deterministic world was a tension Kant could not resolve. Abandoning a thousand years of Augustinian Christian thinking, Kant outright rejected the biblical doctrine of God's sovereign ordination of the free actions of men.

To rid himself of any sure knowledge of God, Kant divided knowledge into the *phenomenal*—what we can see and the world we describe for ourselves based on the data we collect from our senses, and the *noumenal*—the religious stuff people will believe about God (but what is essentially unknowable). This guaranteed uncertainty and doubt concerning divine revelation, an important component for the undermining of Western faith. Actually, neither Kant's noumenal or phenomenal are knowable because Kant assigned man to define his own reality. He said that the human mind "does not derive its laws from nature, but rather *prescribes* them to nature."[73] Only in man's subjective experience does he encounter some kind of truth.

Basically, Kant provided an "intelligently" written argument for preferring ignorance, doubt, and non-explanations over God's revelation on the big questions of truth and reality. He insisted that reality was unknowable but left it open for autonomous reason to come up with a structure of categories by which to explain the unknowable. Most importantly for this survey, Kant's human reason had relegated sacred doctrine and the knowledge of God to the wastebasket at the turn of the 19th Century.

G.W.F. HEGEL

Immanuel Kant and Georg Wilhelm Friedrich Hegel (1770-1831) would become the most important philosophical influences on Karl Marx, Friedrich Nietzsche, and other post-Christian apostates who wrecked the Western world.

Still maintaining a semblance of optimism, Hegel believed man could attain a higher level of truth by pitting what he thinks to be true (*thesis*) against an opposing thought (*antithesis*). Careful analysis of both positions would reveal partial truths contained in each. By combining these propositions, a *synthesis* appears—ostensibly, a combination of the best of each opposing position. This dialectic, it was supposed, would lead to the improvement of man in history and would usher him into the self-consciousness of his own deity. Of course, such thinking assumes that the mind of man is capable of developing truth by this evolutionary process. It also assumes that first principles of truth are accessible without God's revelation. This messianic view of mankind was attractive to Karl Marx and Adolf Hitler. It is at this point in the development of modern humanist philosophy that man would reach the height of optimism and arrogance in his attempt to achieve the status of godhood.

Importantly, Hegel and Kant still considered themselves Christians, but they made religion the "handmaiden" of reason and philosophy. Kant rejected the proofs for God's existence offered by Anselm and Aquinas. Now, for Kant, religion served the "practical needs" of a philosophy built up on human reason—maybe helping people live up to the moral standard established by man's reason. This was a denial of God's law or God's Word as authoritative for a human conception of reality and truth, and God's plan of salvation in His Son, the Lord Jesus Christ. According to Kant, all truth propositions, including those coming from Scripture, must now be fed through the grid of human reason—what makes sense to a preconceived system of thought created by the mind of man. In his work on "Religion" or the Christian faith, Immanuel Kant put biblical doctrines to the test and rejected Christ's atoning work on the cross as something detestable to what he called "rational religion."[74] This was the spirit of apostasy, autonomy, and rebellion in the age of Enlightenment.

Lo, this only have I found, that God hath made man upright; but they have sought out many inventions. (Ecclesiastes 7:29)

ENGLISH & SCOTTISH ENLIGHTENMENT— THE ROAD TO UNITARIANISM & DEISM

Having traced the German apostasy in the 18th Century, it would be well to touch on the English and Scottish Enlightenment. The endless philosophizing of the Enlightenment made two contributions. It confirmed man's total incapability of determining any solid basis for human knowledge by the philosophical meanderings of proud men, and it introduced doubt concerning biblical truth. Man would surrender all truth certainty in order to reject God's truth.

Continental philosophers like Descartes, Spinoza, and Leibnitz tried to formulate a system of knowledge out of self-evident, innate ideas. They failed, utterly overwhelmed in a sea of internal contradictions and incoherencies. Meanwhile, British thinkers like Locke, Berkeley, and Hume thought they could determine an understanding of everything by sense experience, without the aid of divine revelation. These were more attempts to construct an independent system of thought based on human reason, in accord with Aquinas' epistemological construct. These too ended in failure.

Enlightenment men began to make lists of things that "made sense" to their own reason concerning the revelation of Scripture. Edward, Lord Herbert of Cherbury (1583-1648), listed five fundamental religious truths he believed were innate in the mind of man. John Toland (1670-1722) and Matthew Tindal (1657-1733) went so far as to claim that nature was sufficient to teach fundamental truths, rejecting the necessity of divine special revelation altogether.

Out of these philosophies emerged the Christian apostasy of Deism and Unitarianism in the 1700s. With astonishing rapidity, these heterodoxies received almost universal acceptance in England

and America among leading academics in universities and churches. Pretending to apply a cool, calm, detached, unbiased, imminently reasonable mind to the faith, these apostate philosophers rejected all the fundamental Christian doctrines one by one—the Trinity, God's sovereignty, the gospel of salvation, justification by faith alone, the incarnation, the miracles of Christ, the atonement of Christ, and the law of God revealed in the Old Testament. Doctrines accepted, defended, and contended for over 1,400 years of Western history were abandoned on every side. The coronation of human reason was complete in American institutions by the turn of the 19th Century. Orthodox Christianity was fighting for its life, and only a handful of orthodox pastors—men like Lemuel Haynes, Asahel Nettleton, and Timothy Dwight still held on to the basic Augustinian, biblical faith in America by the year 1815.

In 1693, John Locke defended "the Reasonableness of Christianity" in an important essay, calling the Scriptures to stand in the dock and be judged by human reason. This marked a significant shift in terms of modern man's submission to the authority of God's revelation. The modern Christian apologist, C. S. Lewis noted this worldview shift in his essay, "God in the Dock."

> The ancient man approached God (or even the gods) as the accused person approaches his judge. For the modern man, the roles are quite reversed. He is the judge: God is in the dock. He is quite a kindly judge; if God should have a reasonable defense for being the god who permits war, poverty, and disease, he is ready to listen to it. The trial may even end in God's acquittal. But the important thing is that man is on the bench and God is in the dock.[75]

The Scottish thinker, David Hume (1711-1776), was more consistent in his thinking than other Enlightenment men. Following in the footsteps of the ancient Greeks, Socrates, and Diogenes, this modern philosopher tipped into skepticism. He came to doubt that any certain knowledge was possible at all. Incredibly, Hume still hung on to some profession of faith while denying the biblical record of miracles and every proof relating to the existence of God. Some have called him a "non-dogmatic atheist."[76] At the most basic level, Hume denied the authority of God's revelation in Scripture. Slowly but surely, the great minds and institutions of the Christian West were turning towards Christian apostasy.

The Irish bishop-philosopher George Berkeley (1685-1757) rejected all material existence, treating the material universe as only a perception in the mind. Yet, Berkeley still held to some notion of God, claiming that ideas concerning stuff around us were placed there by God.

However, as a more consistent skeptic, David Hume questioned the existence of everything including God, claiming the world to be a mere projection of man's finite and fallible mind.

This was the dry rot that would destroy the Western world. These seeds, planted primarily in the 18th Century, sprouted into poisonous plants intended by the devil to bring about the destruction of an entire civilization.

THE WHOLESALE ABANDONMENT
OF CHRISTIAN FAITH

Whereas it was fashionable to hang on to remnants of Christianity in the 1700s while rejecting its most foundational truths, the philosophers of the 1800s jettisoned the faith completely—as in the case of Ludwig Feuerbach (1804-1872), Arthur Schopenhauer (1788-1860), and Karl Marx (1818-1883). British ethicists Jeremy Bentham and John Stuart Mill advocated wildly anti-Christian ethics, even to the point of embracing the abomination of homosexuality—a behavior universally condemned in the whole Western world for 1,500 years (with the possible exception of Italy during the Renaissance). These were disciples of Locke, Hegel, and Kant who carried their humanist philosophies to the most self-consistent conclusions.

A close adherent to Hegel's philosophy, Karl Marx developed atheistic ideas, dialectical materialism applied through politics, a humanist morality enforced by the state, and an egalitarian ethic. His ideas would bring about much destruction of human society in the 20th Century.

Meanwhile, American transcendentalists and romanticists like Ralph Waldo Emerson (1803-1882) and Henry David Thoreau (1817-1862) turned towards Eastern monism and pantheism. "I am part or particle of god,"[77] wrote Emerson. By this time, the religious perspectives of many leading academics and literary men and women were as far from Christianity as the most pagan religions this world had ever invented.

While Marx applied this modern autonomy to a new man-centered view of history and social systems, Charles Darwin (1809-1882) set about to radically change the Western view of human origins and reality. Later, John Dewey would exalt in Darwin's work, claiming he had released mankind from "2,000 years...of the fixed and the final."[78] No single philosopher was more influential in mainstreaming a materialistic, godless view of the universe. The entire civilized world with all its universities, schools, museums, media, and governments followed Darwin. More than any other single person in the worldview shift of the last millennium, Charles Darwin successfully deceived "the nations"—with almost no exceptions. Darwin spoke of religion as a mere phase man must pass through as he evolves into higher forms. His science was very flawed, but the ontological and sociological implications of his ideas were far more important, more popular, and more dangerous for modern man. Introducing eugenics to the already arrogant white European, he coyly suggested that future mankind would have to find ways to "exterminate and replace throughout the world the savage races throughout the world."[79] Such language would inspire a century of demagogues, genocides, pogroms, and world wars.

Under the guise of science, Darwin hypothesized that humans had evolved from apes, life from non-life, and so forth. The hypothesis was wrongly characterized as a theory, and almost universally accepted by the world without any meaningful evidence obtained from the fossil record (in transitional forms), without any replication of the process in a laboratory, and without an agreed-upon mechanism for bringing about the miracle of life and advanced life forms. The deception was thorough-going, reaching into every developed nation in the world.

THE LINE OF DESPAIR

The final set of major-impact philosophers to bring down Western civilization were Friedrich Nietzsche (1844-1900), John Dewey (1859-1952) and Jean-Paul Sartre (1905-1980), the latter using Nietzsche's philosophy as the subject of his exit exam at the Sorbonne University of Paris. Without question, these were the definitive humanist philosophers forming the spirit of the age in the 20th Century.

Friedrich Nietzsche is considered the father of modern psychology—he called himself the first psychologist. Though his father and grandfather were Lutheran ministers, this apostate declared war on God, called himself the antichrist, spoke as the mouthpiece of a strange spirit, and suffered mental insanity for the last seven years of his life. It was a fitting irony that the first psychologist was himself insane. He called himself "the most terrible opponent of Christianity," and he was the major influence upon the leading intellects and demagogues of the 20th Century: Sigmund Freud, Martin Heidegger, Jean-Paul Sartre, Carl Jung, Albert Camus, Emma Goldman, Adolf Hitler, Benito Mussolini, and Ayn Rand.

The fool hath said in his heart, There is no God. They are corrupt, they have done abominable works, there is none that doeth good. The Lord looked down from heaven upon the children of men, to see if there were any that did understand, and seek God. They are all gone aside, they are all together become filthy: there is none that doeth good, no, not one. Have all the workers of iniquity no knowledge? who eat up my people as they eat bread, and call not upon the Lord. (Psalm 14:1-4)

Nietzsche was the very embodiment of Psalm 14. He exemplified the Jude apostate, following in the tradition of the antediluvian giants who had raised themselves to the highest and most hostile treason against the Most High. The apostate Lutheran confessed openly:

"Man is evil"—so said to me for consolation, all the wisest ones. Ah, if only it be still true today! For the evil is man's best force.

"Man must become better and eviler"—so do I teach. The evilest is necessary for the Superman's best…

I rejoice in great sin as my great consolation.[80]

Arguably, the most influential philosopher for the 20th Century cultural institutions, Nietzsche went further than Kant, rejecting all attempts to answer the ultimate questions. They were "unanswerable" in Nietzsche's fast-disintegrating mind. Kant admitted that we can have no knowledge of reality—the thing in itself—but only the phenomenon of the thing. But Nietzsche had to admit the impossibility of constructing categories concerning human experience with that phenomenon. While man cannot know anything, he can still exert the will to do this or that. Apparently, Nietzsche still found some purpose for life in the exercise of the human will (especially if that will opposed God's law and God's revealed will for his life). Nietzsche found value in exercising power over the weaker elements of society. He announced to the world the death of God and then resolved that there could be no meaning to life except in the will to power—the exercise of power over others. In the end, this nihilist worldview could not possibly provide purpose, meaning, truth, or even the freedom the philosopher so desperately wanted. If this world was only matter in motion, then man is subject to determinist forces larger than himself which sets all existence on a course over which he has no control.

Nietzsche turned the quest for knowledge into a quest for power and for what was useful to accomplish arbitrary ends. John Dewey held to the same perspective, concluding true knowledge is only resolving to "the doubtful" and the "uncertain." Thus, his philosophy of pragmatism was interested mainly in discovering better ways to accomplish what was uncertain and doubtful at root. By this time, all truth and moral values had turned entirely relativistic. Truth was unattainable for man who had attempted to be god. The man without hands could not possibly tear himself out of the rock.

And so, "although they knew God, they did not glorify Him as God, nor were thankful, but became futile in their thoughts, and their foolish hearts were darkened. Professing to be wise, they became fools" (Rom. 1:21-22). God gave them up to a "debased mind" and utter futility in their thinking.

Finally, the capstone on the tomb of Western thought came in the form of existentialism with Martin Heidegger and Jean-Paul Sartre, both influenced by the nihilism of Nietzsche. Despite their relinquishment of ultimate questions relating to truth and reality, these men still attempted to develop a moral imperative and perhaps even a purpose for life in the purposeless universe they had constructed in their own minds.

Sartre, who lived a completely dissolute life absorbed in fornication and drugs, had more influence on modern motion pictures and popular culture than any single thinker in modern history. He posited that man could establish his own essence and perhaps even a little meaning in life by making free and uninhibited, authentic choices.

The modern "pro-choice" movement, legitimizing every sexual perversion and the killing of billions of children via abortion and abortifacients, was enabled by Sartre's ideology. If man would make these free choices and thereby establish himself as the god of his own ethics, then perhaps he could also claim to be the one defining himself, forming his own essence, and choosing his own sexual orientation and gender identity.

However, Sartre's radical human autonomy could only be achieved by total isolation from other people or competing gods or influences. "Hell is other people" was Sartre's famous line. Thus, modern man increasingly isolated himself from others in what would become the loneliest period of time in human history. Modern life turned into a wasteland of alienation by electronic media, institutionalization, pornography, drugs, and escapism.

Sartre moved God out of the picture entirely. About his ethical theory, he approvingly noted, "Everything is possible if God does not exist."[81] Furthermore, Sartre stated, "If God does not exist, we find no values or commands to turn to which legitimize our conduct. So, in the bright realm of values, we have no excuse behind us, nor justification before us. We are alone, without excuses."[82] Quite opposite to what Scripture tells us, sin (according to Sartre) is obedience to God's commands or submitting one's will to the expectations of others. With that, modern man had finally come full circle, back to the original temptation presented to Eve in the garden:

> Now the serpent was more subtil than any beast of the field which the LORD God had made. And he said unto the woman, Yea, hath God said, Ye shall not eat of every tree of the garden? And the woman said unto the serpent, We may eat of the fruit of the trees of the garden: but of the fruit of the tree which is in the midst of the garden, God hath said, Ye shall not eat of it, neither shall ye touch it, lest ye die. And the serpent said unto the woman, Ye shall not surely die: for God doth

know that in the day ye eat thereof, then your eyes shall be opened, and ye shall be as gods, knowing good and evil. (Genesis 3:1-5)

Thus, the entirety of Western philosophy, from Aquinas forward, is encapsulated in these words: "Yea, hath God said?" First and foremost, the devil inspires doubt. Doubt God, and then doubt everything else. That is the history of Western thought. Doubt God, trust yourself, and then don't trust yourself. From there man gives way to total skepticism, cynicism, and intellectual suicide.

Here again is the "debased mind" of Romans chapter one—looking for meaning in a world without meaning. Sartre and Heidegger were only using sleight of hand, pretending to lend some kind of meaning to life. For one thing, man could never act completely free of the many forces in the universe acting upon him and thereby prove himself a god capable of establishing his own essence. What Sartre suggested was impossible. In the end, existentialist man still found himself with "no hope and without God in the world" (Eph. 2:12). The humanist worldview had already surrendered the possibility of any true reality, ethics, or truth. If the world existed at all, the modern humanist thought it to be nothing but matter in motion, a chance universe with death as the most certain possibility for all mankind. It was a miserable attempt to create meaning in a meaningless universe.

The Christian writer Salvian (400-460), chronicled the end of Rome, with this poignant observation! "It is dying, but continues to laugh."[83] There are no better words to describe the present scenario. As post-modern man loses a grip on his own reality, we watch him laughing at his own laughter. Relativism has metastasized, and modern man has given up on the possibility of truth and ethics, and then, his own existence. Only the faint echoes of empty laughter are still heard at the end.

THE OPTIMISM-PESSIMISM TENSION

At the turn of the 21st Century, postmodern man was still sort of celebrating his successes. Humanists like Steven Pinker boasted of "irrefutable statistics showing human progress: the decline of violence and war, the rise of democracy, the astonishing gains against poverty of the last couple of decades, the rise of tolerance and erosion of cruelty, lengthening lifespans, revolutions in health, huge increases in safety…"[84] Meanwhile, other humanist writers like Patrick Deen, paraphrased by Andrew Sullivan, claim: "There is no going back. For our civilization, God is dead. Meaning is meaningless outside the satisfaction of our material wants and can become, at its very best, merely a form of awe at meaninglessness…it is perfectly possible that this strange diversion in human history—a few centuries at most, compared with 200 millennia—is a massive error that will at some point be mercilessly corrected; that our planet, on present trends, will become close to uninhabitable…that our technology will render us unnecessary for the tasks our species has always defined itself by; and that our era of remarkable peace could end with one catastrophic event, as it did in 1914. We have, after all, imperfectly controlled weapons of mass destruction, and humans have never invented a weapon we haven't used (including nukes, of course)."[85]

Time Magazine announced man would be immortal by 2045, but life expectancy was falling and despair deaths had tripled by percentage. Man makes himself into a god—and then suddenly realizes that he cannot meet the criteria of godhood. To dismiss God, man must reduce himself to cosmic dust in a universe of pure chance, while at the same time making himself out to be a god. Caught in the tension between materialist dehumanization and humanism, disappointment replaces his early optimism. Disappointment turns to despair, and pride comes before a fall. Rather than seek God, he turns to death. "But he who sins against me wrongs his own soul; all those who hate me love death" (Prov. 8:36).

There comes a time at which "men's hearts will fail them for fear," in the words of our Lord (Luke 21:26). The guilt...the irrationalism bordering on insanity...the realization of the precariousness of their position...the growing self-consistent and self-conscious awareness of the meaninglessness of a godless worldview and the sense of God's impending judgment catches up with man. He hears laughter, and then he hears someone speaking to him in His sore displeasure. The piper invoices. And "the gods of the copybook headings with terror and slaughter return."

If man is completely alone, without hope and without God in his mind, then he cannot know anything or be assured of the certainty of anything whatever. But fallen, natural man clutches tightly to the lie.

Yet, we can be certain that God knows all things, and "His understanding is infinite" (Ps. 147:5; 1 John 3:20). Since God knows all things, He alone can give man a starting point of truth about any one thing in the field of knowledge and reality. With one word from God, we have the beginning of truth. With no word from God, we have nothing. Indeed, God is ultimately trustworthy, and He cannot lie (Num. 23:19; Heb. 6:18). To call God a liar is the ultimate blasphemy and is destructive of all true knowledge. "The words of the LORD are pure words, like silver tried in a furnace of earth, purified seven times" (Ps. 12:6).

There are no competitors for divine revelation. The Hindu Gitas did not claim to proceed from a supreme god. These writings were the confused ramblings of mostly demon-inspired humans. The writings of Buddha came from a human philosopher who took credit for seemingly unlimited streams of moralisms. The *Quran* showed up 600 years after God finished writing His book, with the advertised purpose of correcting God's original revelation. That didn't accord with the doctrines of the omniscience, infallibility, omnipotence, and sovereignty of God. He is more competent with His revealing of truth to man than Mohammed made Him out to be. *The Book of Mormon* also came too late—1800 years after God had completed His book.

In a world where man has given up even the pretense of searching for truth, forever wandering about in a snowstorm of relativism, the Christian answer is the only one left. In the ultimate and final sense, God is trustworthy, and immutable. His very nature is truth. "God is light, and in Him is no darkness at all" (1 John 1:4). His promises can be counted on: "Your testimonies, which You have commanded, are righteous and very faithful" (Ps. 119:138). His truth is the same from one generation to the next (Ps. 100:5). In this present malaise of craven doubt and hopeless self-deception, a biblical epistemology expresses itself with unreserved, refreshing clarity, "Let God be true but every man a liar!" (Rom. 3:4)

What light! What mercy! What blessing comes by God's revelation of pure truth to man! What relief floods into the soul of man when he finally comes upon certainty, truth, and light in a world of doubt, deception, and despair! What a lucid contrast between darkness and light! What an absolute variance between the dark labyrinth of post-Christian apostasy and the clear light of the revelation of Christ to the world! Here is the only hope left for apostate nations in a post-Christian age.

> For this cause God shall send them strong delusion, that they should believe a lie: that they all might be damned who believed not the truth, but had pleasure in unrighteousness. But we are bound to give thanks alway to God for you, brethren beloved of the Lord, because God hath from the beginning chosen you to salvation through sanctification of the Spirit and belief of the truth... (2 Thessalonians 2:11-13)

III

THE RISE OF THE WESTERN CHURCH

When Jesus came into the coasts of Caesarea Philippi, he asked his disciples, saying, Whom do men say that I the Son of man am? And they said, Some say that thou art John the Baptist: some, Elias; and others, Jeremias, or one of the prophets. He saith unto them, But whom say ye that I am? And Simon Peter answered and said, Thou art the Christ, the Son of the living God. And Jesus answered and said unto him, Blessed art thou, Simon Barjona: for flesh and blood hath not revealed it unto thee, but my Father which is in heaven. And I say also unto thee, That thou art Peter, and upon this rock I will build my church; and the gates of hell shall not prevail against it. (Matthew 16:13-18)

Plainly stated here, the church of Jesus Christ must be victorious, and the gates of hell cannot prevail against it. From a Christian viewpoint therefore, the worldwide progress of this church is the greatest story in world history. No Christian would want to minimize the accomplishments of Christ in any respect. Always, any historical account of Christ's church must end with, "To God be the glory; great things He has done!"

That said, this doesn't mean that certain segments of the church will not fall. The North African Church fell in the 7th Century. The Nestorian Church fell. The Jews were clipped off the olive tree as spoken of Romans 11, and the Gentiles (to include the Western Gentile church) were cautioned not to boast lest they be cut off. Something truly remarkable happened in the Western world over the next 2,000 years. There was a tremendous, historically unprecedented rise of a mighty church over a thousand years, and after that, a fall. This is how it happened.

THE MOST SUCCESSFUL MISSION
IN CHRISTIAN HISTORY

> And Jesus came and spake unto them, saying, All power is given unto me in heaven and in earth. Go ye therefore, and teach all nations, baptizing them in the name of the Father, and of the Son, and of the Holy Ghost: teaching them to observe all things whatsoever I have commanded you: and, lo, I am with you always, even unto the end of the world. Amen. (Matthew 28:19-20)

As Christ prepared for His ascension to the right hand of the Father in AD 33, He left His apostles with the commission to disciple all the nations in the world. With the Apostle Paul, the mission focus would shift from the Jews to the Gentiles, as chronicled in the Acts of the Apostles. The first European church was formed in Philippi during Paul's second missionary trip (around AD 49), his first convert —a woman named Lydia. Churches were later planted in Thessalonica and Corinth on this missionary journey. It was the beginning of a one-thousand-year mission to disciple the nations of Europe for Jesus Christ. By God's grace, the discipleship of the Western nations would turn out to be the most successful, thorough-going, and sustainable work in the history of the Church.

And from thence to Philippi, which is the chief city of that part of Macedonia, and a colony: and we were in that city abiding certain days. And on the sabbath we went out of the city by a river side, where prayer was wont to be made; and we sat down, and spake unto the women which resorted thither. And a certain woman named Lydia, a seller of purple, of the city of Thyatira, which worshipped God, heard us: whose heart the Lord opened, that she attended unto the things which were spoken of Paul. And when she was baptized, and her household, she besought us, saying, If ye have judged me to be faithful to the Lord, come into my house, and abide there. And she constrained us. (Acts 16:12-15)

The church at Rome was probably planted by Urbanus and Aquila, Paul's co-laborers mentioned in Romans 16. At least twenty-eight believers (and several households) were included in this list of those belonging to the church before Paul arrived there in AD 61.

By AD 1100, the Christian church had found its way into almost every corner of Europe. Dedicated missionary work continued from Polycarp's first sponsorship of missionaries into Gaul in AD 130 until 1155 when Henry of Uppsala carried the Christian Gospel into Finland. Largely accomplished by Scotch-Irish (Culdee) and Rome-based missions, the discipleship of the Western nations took place over a 1,000 year span.

Remnants of pagan thinking and culture still hung on here and there, but faithful missionaries stuck to the task of preaching and teaching for centuries. Sanctification of individual lives, tribes, and nations was the inevitable result. Over time, Christianity really transformed barbarian nations, and longstanding pagan cultural habits were summarily discarded. Human sacrifice, infanticide, polygamy, witchcraft, and assorted superstitions would slowly but surely disappear from Europe as the gospel lights turned on.

In God's amazing providential outworking, many pagan kings

Timeline of European Missions			
Nation	**Lead Missionary**	**Date (AD)**	**Sending Church**
Southern Gaul	Pothinus	130	Smyrna
Paris, France	Denis	250	Gaul
Spain	Hosius	295	Rome
Switzerland	Narcissus	303	Gaul
Gaul	Martin of Tours	360	Rome
Britain	Germanus	429	Gaul/Rome
Ireland	Patrick	460	Culdee
Scotland (Picts)	Columba & Mauricius	563	Culdee
Northumbria	Aidan	590	Culdee
England	Augustine	600	Rome
France	Columbanus	612	Culdee
Northumbria	Paulinus	626	Rome
Belgium	Eloquius	680	Culdee
Germany	Killian	680	Culdee
Netherlands	Wilfrid, Willibrord	692	Culdee
Bavaria, Germany	Rupert	700	Culdee
Germany	Boniface	720	Rome
Denmark/Sweden	Anskar	840	Rome
Moravia	Cyril & Methodius	860	Constantinople
Bohemia	Adalbert	980	Rome
Norway	Tryggvasson	995	Rome
Iceland	Tryggvasson & Team	1000	Rome
Finland	Henry of Uppsala	1155	Rome

throughout Ireland, Scotland, England, Gaul, Bavaria, Moravia, Bohemia, Denmark, and elsewhere embraced the Christian gospel. Resistance to the preaching would sometimes persist for a hundred years or so, but an irrepressible spiritual force would inevitably press through.

This mission work was not without sufferings. The Culdean missionary Trudpert was martyred in the Black Forest (Germany) around AD 620, Killian and two associates were killed in Wurtzberg (Germany) in 689, and Boniface was killed in Frisia (Netherlands) around 754. Henry of Uppsala was martyred in Finland in 1156. Kings resisted the Gospel. Radbod of Frisia said he would rather go to hell than accept Christ in AD 700. Gorm persecuted the churches in Denmark, but his son Harald Bluetooth bowed the knee to Christ (c. 960).

There is only one explanation for the joyous reception of the gospel throughout Gaul and the Anglo-Saxon world. For century after century, with nation upon nation, as God opened the heart of Lydia at the first, He opened the hearts of these Gentile Europeans. It was commonplace for kings to invite missionaries into their lands to bring the good news of Jesus Christ. Kings Harald and Horic invited Anskar into Denmark. King Bjorn invited the same missionary into Sweden, and King Rastislav invited missionaries into Moravia from Constantinople in the 840s.

As early as AD 420, Isidore of Pelusium echoed the "prophetic" words recorded by Athanasius a century earlier:

> The pagan faith made dominant for so many years, by such pains, such expenditure of wealth, such feats of arms, has vanished from the earth.[1]

There are six factors which contributed to a healthy church in Western history, each of which will be carefully examined in this brief survey of the rise and fall of the church in the West:

- the regular preaching and teaching of the Word of God (and the availability of the Scriptures)
- the retention of the basic core scriptural doctrines of God and the gospel
- the rejection of heretical aberrations and worldly philosophies
- missionary zeal
- serious long-term discipleship via full-time discipleship centers
- a resistance to the accumulation and centralization of worldly power

Throughout the ages, the church was never immune from spiritual attacks, internal schism, fatal synthesis with pagan ideas, and gross heresy. Always, the root of pride within the church would seek to grab for secular power over lands and peoples—bodies, bucks, and buildings. Always, that insidious root of pride and man's autonomous reason would press on men to transgress the boundaries of mystery—manhandling the doctrines of the Trinity, the two natures of Christ, the sacraments, the authority of Scripture and God's revealed law, and the sovereignty of God. Yet, a substantial faith grew for more than a millennium, made possible only by the sovereign work of God.

HOW TO DISCIPLE THE NATIONS—WHAT THE MISSIONARIES DID FOR 800 YEARS

The stories of the early missionaries appear to the modern mind as unusual, surreal, and even fantastical. Those who doubt that God will work without, above, and against natural laws would reject the stories out of hand. Miracles are recorded in a great many of the pioneering missionary stories. The faith and courage of these men of God would hardly find a parallel in the present day. Their forthright and bold faith manifest in cutting down sacred groves and burning down heathen temples shocked the pagan communities then. Such behavior would come across even more offensive to the Western mind today. It was a spiritual blitzkrieg impossible for any demonic force to resist. *But how did they do it?* What did these missionaries do to disciple a continent in a millennium? A quick read-through of Bede, Rimbert, and other early historians reveals a clear picture of the strategy. *They preached the Word.* Without question, this was the main method relied upon by these early evangelists in the frontier age of the Western church. They treated Paul's words with dead seriousness: "Preach the word! Be ready in season and out of season. Convince, rebuke, exhort, with all longsuffering and teaching" (2 Tim. 4:2).

We read, for example, of Bishop Felix (AD 630) who "preached the word of life to this nation of the [East] Angles. Nor did he fail in his purpose; for, like a good farmer, he reaped a rich harvest of believers."[2] In Lindsey, Paulinus "preached the word of God...and his first convert was Blaecca, Reeve [magistrate] of the city of Lincoln, with all his family."[3] Further north in Northumbria, the Culdean missionary Aidan and his monks "came to preach."[4] Another holy man, named Fursey, had been "preaching the Word of God among the Irish for many years."[5] Tired of the crowds, he came to the East Angles in AD 633 and "preached the Gospel as he always did. Inspired by the example of his goodness and the effectiveness of his teaching, many unbelievers were converted to Christ, and many who already believed were drawn to greater love and faith in Christ."[6]

After Aidan spent seventeen years as pastor in Northumbria, Finan served as pastor, and then Colman. Bede writes that these pastors would send missionaries throughout the villages, where people gathered "to hear the word of God...for clerics always came to a village solely to preach, baptize, visit the sick, and, in short, to care for the souls of its people."[7] Then, another missionary named Chad was sent to the West Saxons around 665. "After the example of the Apostles, he travelled on footing not on horseback, when he went to preach the Gospel, whether in towns or country, in cottages, villages, or strongholds; for he was one of Aidan's disciples and always sought to instruct his people by the same methods."[8] Chad's success in missions is explained: "In addition to Chad's many virtues of continence, humility, right preaching, prayer,…he was so filled with the fear of God and so mindful of his last need in all he did…that if a gale arose while he was reading or doing anything else, he would at once call upon God for mercy and pray him to show mercy on mankind."[9]

Then there was Oftfor, who had dedicated his life to "reading and applying the Scriptures." In 680 he "preached the word of faith"[10] in the province of Hwiccas (in southwest England), then ruled by King Osric. The missionary Willibrord "preached the Word of God far and wide, recalling many from their errors and establishing several churches" throughout Frisia. Before he died, Willibrord was faithful to "appoint a number of bishops, choosing them from among the brethren who had come with him or after him to preach."[11] Wilfrid initiated the missionary work in Frisia (Netherlands) when the ship in which he was sailing was blown off course and unintentionally arrived at these barbarous lands. He went on to "preach Christ among them, teaching the word of truth to many thousands…he was the first to attempt the work of their evangelization, which was later completed so zealously by Willibrord."[12]

Bede's words to Egbert, written in 734 just before his death, contain the crystal-clear commission given to all pastors during those critical, formative years of the church in England:

> Because the distances between the places which belong to your diocese are too great for you alone to suffice for visiting them all and preaching the word of God in its many hamlets and homesteads within the span of a year, you should certainly appoint several helpers for yourself in this holy work, that is by ordaining priests and appointing teachers who

will zealously preach in each village the word of God and offer the heavenly mysteries and above all perform the sacrament of baptism whenever the opportunity arises. In preaching to the people, this message more than any other should be proclaimed; that the Catholic faith, as contained in the Apostle's Creed and the Lord's Prayer which the reading of the Gospel teaches us, should be deeply memorized by all who are under your rule.[13]

In the same letter, Bede was particularly concerned to warn those church leaders who "take no trouble at all in preaching, exhorting, or reproving for the peoples' eternal salvation."[14]

Later, in 826, the intrepid missionary Anskar committed himself to missionary work, believing he was called to martyrdom. His confession: "I am asked whether I am willing on God's behalf to go to pagan nations in order to preach the gospel. So far from daring to oppose this suggestion I desire, with all my strength, that the opportunity for going may be granted to me, and that no one may be able to divert me from this design."[15]

Alcuin told his trainees, "Preach, preach in season and out of season!"[16] Quite aware of the uselessness of baptism without proper teaching, Alcuin wrote to Charlemagne: "Seek for the new nation preachers of upright conduct, who are well taught in the faith, who follow the example of the Apostles in preaching the Gospel; in the beginning feeding their hearers with the milk of faith."[17] He cautioned the emperor not to saddle the tribes with "the yoke of tithes." He encouraged the office of preaching to be used in the right way, "lest the outward baptism of the body become useless."[18] Referring to the work of Augustine of Canterbury and others among the Saxons, Alcuin warns Arno, pastor of Salzburg: "The unhappy nation of the Saxons has so often abused the sacrament of baptism, because the foundation of faith was not laid in the heart."[19]

The strategic emphasis for the successful missionary work

accomplished in Europe through the early centuries was neither baptism nor the mass. The focus was never miracles, relics, and genuflections, although these accoutrements were not absent from some of the work. The men were thoroughly committed to preaching—in season and out of season.

SERIOUS DISCIPLESHIP CENTERS

Thou therefore, my son, be strong in the grace that is in Christ Jesus. And the things that thou hast heard of me among many witnesses, the same commit thou to faithful men, who shall be able to teach others also. (2 Timothy 2:1-2)

To disciple the nations requires a commitment to teaching and equipping men over many years, repeated again and again through generations. The discipleship must be reproducible, as envisioned by the Apostle in 2 Timothy 2. When missionaries and Christian leaders committed to discipling Europe, they found it necessary to commit their lives to this task—focusing especially on the discipleship of young men.

Benedict of Nursia (480-547) was the first to organize serious, reproducible, thorough-going discipleship in the construction of monasteries (or discipleship centers) in Western Europe. Benedict was born at the end of an era, and at the beginning of the new age of Christendom—four years after the official date of Rome's fall. The empires of men had come to end, and the slate was clear for the discipleship of the nations in the frontier age of the Church. Separating himself far from the city, some forty miles east of Rome, the first Benedictine monks gathered in a makeshift monastery. Towards the end of his life, Benedict built another discipleship center eighty miles southeast of Rome at Monte Cassino.

Benedict's primary theological and pedagogical influence was Augustine of Hippo. He patterned his discipleship approach after

Augustine's *De Opere Monachorum*. Benedict's *Rules* for his school stood for a thousand years, a portion of the prologue of which follows:

> Listen, my son, to your master's precepts, and incline the ear of your heart. Receive willingly and carry out effectively your loving father's advice, that by the labor of obedience you may return to Him from whom you had departed by the sloth of disobedience. To you, therefore, my words are now addressed, whoever you may be, who are renouncing your own will to do battle under the Lord Christ, the true King, and are taking up the strong, bright weapons of obedience. And first of all, whatever good work you begin to do, beg of Him with most earnest prayer to perfect it, that He who has now deigned to count us among His sons may not at any time be grieved by our evil deeds. For we must always so serve Him with the good things He has given us, that He will never as an angry Father disinherit His children, nor ever as a dread Lord, provoked by our evil actions, deliver us to everlasting punishment as wicked servants who would not follow Him to glory.
>
> Let us arise, then, at last, for the Scripture stirs us up, saying, "Now is the hour for us to rise from sleep." Let us open our eyes to the deifying light, let us hear with attentive ears the warning which the divine voice cries daily to us, "Today if you hear His voice, harden not your hearts." And again, "He who has ears to hear, let him hear what the Spirit says to the churches." And what does He say? "Come, My children, listen to Me; I will teach you the fear of the Lord. Run while you have the light of life, lest the darkness of death overtake you."[20]

Although a life of holiness was urged upon the men, Benedict made it clear that the primary motive for obedience must be love for God, not fear of judgment.

> Feeling the guilt of his sins at every moment, he should consider himself already present at the dread Judgment and constantly say in his heart what the publican in the Gospel said with his eyes fixed on the earth: "Lord, I am a sinner and not worthy to lift up my eyes to

heaven"; and again with the Prophet: "I am bowed down and humbled everywhere." Having climbed all these steps of humility, therefore, the monk will presently come to that perfect love of God which casts out fear. And all those precepts which formerly he had not observed without fear, he will now begin to keep by reason of that love, without any effort, as though naturally and by habit. No longer will his motive be the fear of hell, but rather the love of Christ, good habit and delight in the virtues which the Lord will deign to show forth by the Holy Spirit in His servant now cleansed from vice and sin.[21]

Benedict's school offered a distinctively biblical discipleship, generally rejecting the humanist epistemology of the heathen Greeks. Historian Columba Stewart explains:

Whatever form monastic writing of the Middle Ages took, whether discourse...poetic and dramatic...or visionary...it tended to stay close to the Bible and the liturgy, and to be concerned primarily with growth in the spiritual life...monastic theologians were often uneasy with the rise of the Schools [and the scholastic theologians] in major cities during the 12th Century. That different kind of theological exploration, more analytical and speculative, shifted the centre of gravity of Latin theology from lectio divina to academic disputation.[22]

After the fall of the classical world with its man-centered philosophies, the libraries were emptied of pagan books. Even the library of Cassiodorus in Calabria (the "Vivarium") was lost in the "blood and the smoke."[23] For the next half millennium, the content of this Christian discipleship program would focus upon the psalms, various other Scripture readings, conferences (devotionals), and biographies of the church fathers. Sections of both the Old and New Testaments, as well as all 150 psalms, were to be memorized by the disciples. Four hours a day were spent in Scripture readings and prayer, and typically the entire psalter was covered each week. These learning centers eschewed a mere head knowledge, always aiming for a heart understanding of the material under study. The monks read aloud, either in community or individually, and "the focus was conversion of heart rather than intellectual curiosity, though mind and heart obviously have to work together in the project of monastic living."[24]

Between AD 500 and 1100, three thousand of these Benedictine monasteries were erected in France, Belgium, and Britain—about 10% of them for women.[25] Until the Cluniac reform (AD 950-1100), the monastery governance was decentralized, avoiding the always-corrupting hierarchy of the Roman church. Typically, about one hundred men populated a monastery, making up a community of 300,000 monks across Europe by the 11th Century—about 5% of the total populace. That would be akin to 16,000,000 theological students registered in seminaries in the United States today. For comparison purposes, conservative estimates put the current number of seminarians at 100,000.[26] The vast majority of the 19,000,000 students currently registered in American colleges are given a thoroughly secular education at these schools, and the initiates are no longer required to memorize the psalter and much of the Old and New Testaments. Calculating on the basis of the sheer numbers enrolled, medieval youth were 160-times more likely to receive a Christian-based training program compared to youth living in the modern post-Christian world of the 21st Century. That is, the medieval world was 160 times more Christianized than the secular collegiate world.

While the papacy had severely degraded itself in the 10th Century, the monasteries were reformed independently of Rome. A thousand new monasteries were built between AD 950 and 1100. After this, Bernard of Clairvaux, finding the Cluny monasteries lacking in rigor and wanting to return to the Benedictine model, stirred up another reform via the Cistercians. Another 750 or so of these Cistercian abbeys were built between 1112 and 1500.[27] All of these reformations occurred outside of the orbit of the Roman papacy.

CELTIC MONASTICISM

An honest survey of the mission work and the gigantic spiritual transformation brought about in Europe over a thousand years must include full coverage of the work done by Patrick of Ireland and his spiritual progeny. There is no story like this one. Ireland in the fifth Century was the "uttermost parts of the earth," regarded as barbarian lands by the "civilized" world of the empire. Virtually alone, except for the attending presence of the Holy Spirit, Patrick established a beachhead of faith on the island. Initiating the ministry around AD 432, the intrepid missionary to the Irish continued the work until his death in 493.

Patrick's doctrine was robust, a more rustically-expressed Augustinian theology. Though raised in Britain, the homeland of Pelagius, there is not a hint of the Pelagian heresy in Patrick's letters. Historian Philip Freeman sums up his soteriology simply: "Patrick believed with all his heart that if the chasm between God and humanity was to be bridged, it had to be by the grace of God alone."[28]

Patrick's *Confession* is simple, humble, concise, substantial, stuffed with core scriptural truth and teeming with life and faith. His gospel is solid:

> There is no other God—there never was and there never will be. God our father was not born nor did he have any beginning. God himself is the beginning of all things, the very one who holds all things together, as we have been taught.

> And we proclaim that Jesus Christ is his Son, who has been with God in spirit always, from the beginning of time and before the creation of the world—though in a way we cannot put into words. Through him everything in the universe was created, both what we can see and what is invisible. He was born as a human being and he conquered death, rising into the heavens to be with God. And God gave to him power

greater than any creature of the heavens or earth or under the earth, so that someday everyone will declare that Jesus Christ is Lord and God. We believe in him and wait for him to return very soon. He will be the judge of the living and the dead.[29]

If there is a theme to be found in Patrick's doctrinal statements, it is the absolute sovereignty of God.

"God knows everything before it happens..."[30]

"God knew everything that would occur even before the beginning of time."[31]

"I throw myself on the mercy of God, who is in charge of everything."[32]

"Everything I can do comes from Him."[33]

Patrick was particularly bothered by the academic pride characterizing the more educated, and he encouraged the fear of God and humility in his disciples.[34]

Patrick's letter to Coroticus amounts to a pronouncement of excommunication for "Christian" slave traders ravaging the Irish communities. He was one of the first Christian pastors to speak out so strongly against slavery as a violation of God's law. It was a disruption of his mission work, where he says, "God in His great kindness had just recently planted His law in Ireland, where it had been growing by His grace."[35]

"St. Patrick's Breastplate" is to this day recognized as one of the most powerful statements of Christian faith in the history of Christ's church.

St. Patrick's Breastplate

I arise today
Through a mighty strength, the invocation of the Trinity,
Through belief in the Threeness,
Through confession of the Oneness of the Creator of creation.
I arise today

Through the strength of Christ's birth with His baptism,
Through the strength of His crucifixion with His burial,
Through the strength of His resurrection with His ascension,
Through the strength of His descent for the judgment of doom.

I arise today
Through the strength of the love of cherubim,
In the obedience of angels,
In the service of archangels,
In the hope of resurrection to meet with reward,
In the prayers of patriarchs,
In the predictions of prophets,
In the preaching of apostles,
In the faith of confessors,
In the innocence of holy virgins,
In the deeds of righteous men.

I arise today, through
The strength of heaven,
The light of the sun,
The radiance of the moon,
The splendor of fire,
The speed of lightning,
The swiftness of wind,
The depth of the sea,
The stability of the earth,
The firmness of rock.

I arise today, through
God's strength to pilot me,
God's might to uphold me,
God's wisdom to guide me,
God's eye to look before me,
God's ear to hear me,
God's word to speak for me,

God's hand to guard me,
God's shield to protect me,
God's host to save me
From snares of devils,
From temptation of vices,
From everyone who shall wish me ill, afar and near.
I summon today
All these powers between me and those evils,
Against every cruel and merciless power
that may oppose my body and soul,
Against incantations of false prophets,
Against black laws of pagandom,
Against false laws of heretics,
Against craft of idolatry,
Against spells of witches and smiths and wizards,
Against every knowledge that corrupts man's body and soul;
Christ to shield me today
Against poison, against burning,
Against drowning, against wounding,
So that there may come to me an abundance of reward.

Christ with me,
Christ before me,
Christ behind me,
Christ in me,
Christ beneath me,
Christ above me,
Christ on my right,
Christ on my left,
Christ when I lie down,
Christ when I sit down,
Christ when I arise,
Christ in the heart of every man who thinks of me,

Christ in the mouth of everyone who speaks of me,

Christ in every eye that sees me,

Christ in every ear that hears me.

I arise today

Through a mighty strength, the invocation of the Trinity,

Through belief in the Threeness,

Through confession of the Oneness of the Creator of creation.[36]

Salvation is of the Lord,

Salvation is of the Lord,

Salvation is of Christ;

May thy salvation, O Lord, be ever with us.[37]

The postscript at the end of the Breastplate is another strong testimony to the core nature of Patrick's faith. Nothing is more basic to a biblical soteriology than Jonah's testimony in the belly of the fish a thousand feet underwater: "Salvation is of the LORD" (Jon. 2:9).

The combination of Patrick's solid core orthodoxy, a robust faith, and his "emotional grasp on Christian truth…(greater than Augustine's)"[38] produced an enormous kingdom thrust for Christ in Ireland. Its repercussions would be felt throughout Europe for 1,500 years. Patrick's beloved Ireland would be the last Western nation to reinstitute the pagan practices of child sacrifice and sexual perversion when Northern Ireland fell in AD 2020.[39]

By AD 613, the Culdee missionary Columbanus wrote to update Boniface IV on the progress of the faith in Ireland: "We Irish who live at the ends of the earth are followers of Saints Peter and Paul and all those who wrote the Scriptures under the direction of the Holy Spirit. We teach nothing beyond the truth revealed in the Gospels and by the Apostles. There are no heretics living on our island… our adherence to the universal faith is firm."[40]

The first Irish monastery probably began in the 6th Century with Kevin of Glendalough, who more or less allowed a community to form around his humble dwelling. The men built little hovels, and throughout the day and twice at night they gathered to sing the psalms.

The Benedictine order required a commitment to celibacy, which arguably became counterproductive to the development of a Christian population. This was certainly not the way to encourage church growth through generational faithfulness and the covenant family. However, the Celtic (Culdean) church required no such commitment. For example, abbots of monasteries at Claine, Lusca, and Cluain Moccu Nois had families (wives, sons, and daughters). It was customary for abbots to train their sons to succeed them in their offices. Successive generations would lead the monasteries for 300 years.[41] By 725, the Culdees had established 150 monasteries outside of Ireland. Chief among them was the monastery organized in the Alps by Columbanus' greatest spiritual son—Gall. For over forty years, Gall cultivated the faith among the Alemans in Switzerland by the patient and plodding work of discipleship. Gall's spiritual son Leinsterman would continue the work in the next generation. Among Leinsterman's writings are found excerpts from Jerome and Augustine, some Latin hymns, and a poem about his cat, Pangur Ban.

The three largest Irish monasteries—Clonard, founded by Finian (Patrick's successor), Bangor, founded by Comgall, and Clonfert, founded by Brendan—each inducted 3,000 to 4,000 men into a Christian discipleship program. By the 7th Century, the monastery population in Ireland would have reached about 40,000, to the point that about half of Irish young men were educated in Christian monasteries.[42] These discipleship centers also received students from Wales and England. According to Bede: "The Irish welcomed them all, gave them food and lodging without charge (they sometimes had to beg to scrape by), lent them books to read and taught them without fee."[43]

Once again, the Culdean training focused on the psalms, requiring recitation six times per day. In the year 1150, a library of books from an Irish discipleship center at Locklevin was discovered and the inventory included: books of ecclesiastical order, the Acts of the Apostles, the text of the Gospels, the three books of Solomon, glossaries on the Song of Solomon, works of Origen and Bernard, an exposition of Genesis, and a dictionary. Missing from this catalog of books were the Greek and Roman pagan works.[44]

Historian Thomas Cahill claims Roman monasteries were no competition for Irish scholarship. Even Charlemagne in France was forced to draw on Irish learning from the likes of Alcuin of York, Dungal of Saint Denis, Dicuil—the king's geographer—and Sedulius who copied out a Greek psalter, an interlinear Greek/Latin version of the Gospels, and the Codex Boernerianus, an interlinear version of Paul's Epistles.[45] On this basis, Cahill concluded that "the Irish saved civilization." Actually, Patrick's progeny took Christian discipleship seriously as their missionaries spread out across Europe to disciple the nations in obedience to Christ…"teaching them to observe all things that I have commanded you; and lo, I am with you always, even to the end of the age. Amen" (Matt. 28:20).

The golden age of Irish monasteries ended when the Viking invasions began around AD 795. Over the next one hundred years, the marauders destroyed many of these Christian institutions until King Alfred and his grandson beat them out of England by AD 930, and King Brian Boru got them out of Ireland in AD 1014.

A DECENTRALIZED ERA

Without any hierarchical leadership or centralized power center, the Culdean (Scotch-Irish) churches made an indelible mark on Europe by tireless missionary work over 200 years (between AD 450 and 650). At the missionary training island base of Iona, Columba himself trained 115 men for missionary service during his lifetime.[46] Typically, each new mission work was planted with twelve presbyters, without formal oversight from Iona or anywhere else. These churches were scattered in Kuneld, Abernethy, Brechin, and Moniumusk. Under the team leadership of Columbanus, Killian, and others, Culdean churches were planted throughout Germany, each led by twelve presbyters. The Culdees expanded their influence into Wales. Pastor Dionoth served as one of the early preachers, and when he was pressed to acknowledge the supremacy of the pope by Augustine of Canterbury, he refused in love. His response: "We desire to love all men meekly…and what we do for you we will do for him also whom you call the pope. But he is not entitled to call himself the father of fathers and the only submission we can render him is that which we owe to every Christian."[47] Church schisms sometimes ended in military conflict in these early days. Regrettably, with the approval of Augustine of Canterbury and the Roman Christians, the Saxons razed Bangor to the ground, killing thousands of Culdean Christians (c. AD 613).

At the Synod of Whitby (AD 664), Aidan's successor, Pastor Colman from Northumbria, argued valiantly for the independence of the Culdean church but his cause failed when the synod ruled to follow the dictates of the church of Rome. Shortly thereafter, Colman retired from the ministry in Northumbria and retreated to Ireland. The material issues taken up by Whitby were of minor consequence—the date of Easter and the Roman pope's recommended haircut for pastors. Yet, at the heart of it, the problem was pride and power mongering, as is often the case in church fights.

The independence of the Scotch-Irish church continued into the days of William Wallace and Robert the Bruce in the early 1300s. The pope's excommunications of the rightful King of Scotland didn't bother the Scots or the Scottish bishops in their longstanding battle for independence from England. Always resisting the impulse to centralize power on the part of church and state, the Scots stood resolute. Earlier, in AD 1170, Richard, the Archbishop of Canterbury, complained "certain false bishops of Ireland, or pretending the barbarism of the Scottish language, [who] although they have received from no one imposition of hands, discharge episcopal functions to the people."[48] And still concerned with the independent spirit of the Scottish clerics, Pope Adrian IV issued a bull in which he granted King Henry II the right to invade Ireland, "for the purposes of enlarging the borders of the Church."[49]

The healthiest and longest-standing elements of the Western church would remain in the British Isles after the Protestant Reformation. This heritage would make its way into the future United States.

About a century after the synod of Whitby, tension between the Scotch-Irish element of the Western church and Rome surfaced on the mission field with the Irish missionary Clement. History records Clement of the Franks as both "a husband and a father." This missionary worked among peoples of the Lower Rhine, teaching the doctrines of the Trinity, the sovereignty of God, the ultimate authority of the Scriptures over human traditions, and the church as the local assembly of believers. In line with the Irish church tradition, Clement recommended all elders for the church be married.[50] A council was called at Soissons on March 2, 744, and Clement was excommunicated and thrown into prison. The uproar among the local churches was so strong that the minister was eventually released, only to continue his protests against those who refused to submit all truth claims to the Word of God. Shortly afterwards, Clement disappeared—probably murdered. At the Council of Charon, the Roman church complained that "in certain places, Scots, who call themselves 'bishops,'...without the license of their lords or superiors, ordain presbyters and deacons." This, the council said, "ought to be invalidated by all possible means."[51]

Thus, until at least AD 800, the Culdean discipleship of Europe continued to flourish without a thoroughly centralized control of piety, mission work, and pastoring of the flocks.

POWER IN THE PAPACY

And he said unto them, The kings of the Gentiles exercise lordship over them; and they that exercise authority upon them are called benefactors. But ye shall not be so: but he that is greatest among you, let him be as the younger; and he that is chief, as he that doth serve. (Luke 22:25-26)

The cause of the undoing of the Western church may be discerned in this very warning from Christ. Pride and competition for power characterized "the Gentiles." Indeed, that is the very essence of the humanist vision—the inclination towards centralizing and amassing power and control over others. "Come, let us build ourselves a city and a name for ourselves" is the mantra of those out to consolidate power in the fashion of Babel (Gen. 11:4).

Actually, the centralization of ecclesiastical power and authority under a single man had its start more in the East than the West. By AD 595, John IV, patriarch of Constantinople, was already referring to himself as "universal bishop." But Gregory, the bishop or pastor at Rome, was scandalized by such references and demanded a renunciation of what he considered a "wicked" title. When Eulogius of Alexandria tried to ascribe a similar title to Gregory, the bishop's response was: "No more of this! Away with words which inflate pride and wound charity!"[52] Gregory argued that even the Apostle Peter would not have referred to himself as "the universal bishop."

Gregory's major contribution turned out to be his support for the missionary work in Europe. His theology was Trinitarian, he rejected the Augustinian view of God's total sovereignty, and he also avoided the use of classical humanist works. Above all, Gregory was an imminently practical pastor, most interested in providing direction for Christian pastors in his four books of *Pastoral Care,* which were used throughout Europe for a thousand years.

For the Roman church, the power lure came by undue involvement in civil affairs, beginning with Pope Stephen's II anointing of Pepin as king of the Franks in AD 755. The pope crammed another title in with the kingship: "Patrician of the Romans," which committed Pepin to chase the Lombards out of Rome. The conquered territory was then turned over to the ecclesiastical sphere in what became known as the "Donation of Pepin." From henceforth, the pope would control parts of Romagna, the Duchy of Spoleto and Benevento, and the Pentapolis in the Marche. It was the pope's own little secular kingdom, and this would bring no end of trouble to the Western church.

The next concerted step towards the corruption of power was taken when Pope Leo III crowned Charlemagne as "Holy Roman Emperor" on Christmas Day, AD 800. Although an unexpected move (at least from Charlemagne's perspective), the largely symbolic act placed civil powers under the authority of the ecclesiastical. The fruit of such power games was only bad in the following centuries, and the papacy went into a moral tailspin shortly thereafter.

All this politicization of the papacy was rooted in a spirit of avarice, deceit, and fraud—eventually culminating in a fraudulent document known as the "Donation of Constantine." The manuscript, produced in the 9th Century, was ostensibly written by Constantine to the bishop of Rome, Sylvester I around AD 330. Contained within was a wish list of everything human pride would have wanted for itself in the 9th Century—power, prestige, and riches. It was everything Christ and His church wasn't. The Catholic Encyclopedia explains:

> Constantine is made to confer on Sylvester and his successors:… primacy over the four Patriarchs of Antioch, Alexandria, Constantinople, and Jerusalem, also over all the bishops in the world.

The Lateran basilica at Rome, built by Constantine, shall surpass all churches as their head, similarly the churches of St. Peter and St. Paul shall be endowed with rich possessions. The chief Roman ecclesiastics (*clerici cardinales*), among whom senators may also be received, shall obtain the same honours and distinctions as the senators. Like the emperor the Roman Church shall have as functionaries *cubicularii*, *ostiarii*, and *excubitores*. The pope shall enjoy the same honorary rights as the emperor, among them the right to wear an imperial crown, a purple cloak and tunic, and in general all imperial insignia or signs of distinction; but as Sylvester refused to put on his head a golden crown, the emperor invested him with the high white cap (*phrygium*). Constantine, the document continues, rendered to the pope the service of a *strator*, i.e. he led the horse upon which the pope rode. Moreover, the emperor makes a present to the pope and his successors of the Lateran palace, of Rome and the provinces, districts, and towns of Italy and all the Western regions...[53]

The forgery can be traced back to the archbishopric of Rheims, probably to a monastery at Corbie, considered the very center of 9th Century scholarship. Sometime in the 850s, a mysterious book appeared called "the Pseudo-Isidorian Decretals," the first work to include the Donation. The Decretals pretended to be a historical record advocating a papal theocracy, with ample references to the pope as the *episcopus universalis*, a title which Gregory had soundly rejected two centuries earlier. It was the second part of the Decretals that contained the forged Donation of Constantine, by transferring temporal powers over to the church (specifically, to the Lateran palace). In short, the forgery and its advocacy in church courts would contribute greatly towards centralizing power in the papacy itself. No single document or any other illicit action conducted by churchmen would do so much damage to the Western church as this pestiferous piece of work produced in the dark recesses of the Rheims diocese. Historians point to Paschasius Radbertus (785-865), the abbott of Corbie as the most likely author of the mysterious and damaging document—the same cleric who championed the doctrine of transubstantiation in the early medieval period. Could a single influential monk be the root cause of so much destruction to the Western church over the following centuries?

To commence the initial fall of the Western church and to sow the seeds which would yield its ultimate corruption, a key figure enters the scene—Pope Nicholas I (800-867). A touch of irony comes in Schaff's explanation: "By a remarkable coincidence the publication of the Pseudo-Isidorian Decretals synchronized with the appearance of a pope who had the ability and opportunity to carry the principles of the Decretals into practical effect."[54] Pope Nicholas I and the Eastern Patriarch, Photius, assumed the authority for themselves to excommunicate each other; and then, Nicholas proceeded to take control of politicized church discipline cases affecting pastors in France.

Power corrupts, especially when a man exceeds the limits of his divinely-ordained jurisdiction. Rome went downhill quickly after Nicholas. For the bulk of the 10th Century, mostly blackguards and criminals filled the papal seat. Their careers often ended with "deposition, prison and murder."[55] Pope Sergius III (904-911) fathered an illegitimate son who later became pope (John XI). Sergius' paramour Marozia essentially controlled all papal appointments for eight years, assigning her friends and relatives to vacant posts. Marozia's grandson, Pope John XII (955-963), may have been the most depraved of all popes and is referred to by historians as "a monster of iniquity."[56] He was probably killed by a jealous husband. A second wave of very bad popes swept in from 973 to 1046. Inevitably, the lure of power would attract the wrong people into the church hierarchy of Rome. Peter himself warned of this in his second epistle, and the church at Rome should have taken notice.

But there were false prophets also among the people, even as there shall be false teachers among you, who privily shall bring in damnable heresies, even denying the Lord that bought them, and bring upon themselves swift destruction. But these, as natural brute beasts, made to be taken and destroyed, speak evil of the things that they understand not; and shall utterly perish in their own corruption; And shall receive the reward of unrighteousness, as they that count it pleasure to riot in the day time. Spots they are and blemishes, sporting themselves with their own deceivings while they feast with you; Having eyes full of adultery, and that cannot cease from sin; beguiling unstable souls: an heart they have exercised with covetous practices; cursed children: Which have forsaken the right way, and are gone astray, following the way of Balaam the son of Bosor, who loved the wages of unrighteousness; But was rebuked for his iniquity: the dumb ass speaking with man's voice forbad the madness of the prophet. These are wells without water, clouds that are carried with a tempest; to whom the mist of darkness is reserved for ever. For when they speak great swelling words of vanity, they allure through the lusts of the flesh, through much wantonness, those that were clean escaped from them who live in error. While they promise them liberty, they themselves are the servants of corruption: for of whom a man is overcome, of the same is he brought in bondage. For if after they have escaped the pollutions of the world through the knowledge of the Lord and Saviour Jesus Christ, they are again entangled therein, and overcome, the latter end is worse with them than the beginning. For it had been better for them not to have known the way of righteousness, than, after they have known it, to turn from the holy commandment delivered unto them. But it is happened unto them according to the true proverb, The dog is turned to his own vomit again; and the sow that was washed to her wallowing in the mire. (2 Peter 2:1, 12-22)

THE RULE OF FAITH

> Moreover, brethren, I declare unto you the gospel which I preached unto you, which also ye have received, and wherein ye stand; By which also ye are saved, if ye keep in memory what I preached unto you, unless ye have believed in vain. For I delivered unto you first of all that which I also received, how that Christ died for our sins according to the scriptures; And that he was buried, and that he rose again the third day according to the scriptures. (1 Corinthians 15:1-4)

The Christian West formed on a solid theological basis over a period of 600 years. But, at first, that orthodox faith was assailed by powerful heresies of every sort. The church responded by clear definitions of the rule of faith in the form of the Apostle's Creed. The first form of the rule appears in Irenaeus of Lyon, Gaul (AD 130-202), who wrote that the whole church "believes in one God the Father Almighty, maker of heaven and earth and the seas and all that is therein, and in one Christ Jesus the Son of God, who was made flesh for our salvation, and in the Holy Spirit who through the prophets preached the dispensations and the comings and the virgin birth and the passion and the rising from the dead and the assumption into heaven in his flesh of our beloved Lord Jesus Christ, and his coming from heaven in the glory of the Father...to raise up all flesh."[57] The statement was a clear recapitulation of Paul's definition of the gospel in 1 Corinthians 15. This is core faith. What is core in Scripture has to be prioritized in the discipleship of the nations—and, by the Holy Spirit, the church fathers centered on it.

The Nicene Creed (AD 325) and Chalcedonian Creed (AD 451) articulated the doctrines of the deity of Christ, the two natures of Christ, and the Trinity.

Boniface, bishop of Rome, summarized the rule of faith in his letter to Edwin, king of the English (AD 625):

The clemency of the Divine Majesty, who by His Word alone created and established the heavens and the earth, the sea and all that in them is, has ordained the laws by which they subsist; and by the counsel of His co-eternal Word in the unity of the Holy Spirit He has formed man after His own image and likeness from the dust of the earth... This God—Father, Son and Holy Spirit—the undivided Trinity—is adored and worshiped by the human race from east to west, which confesses Him by the faith that brings salvation as Creator of all things and Maker of all men... He has been pleased to warm with His Holy Spirit the frozen hearts of the most distant nations of the world in a most wonderful manner to knowledge of Himself...

In this letter we affectionately urge Your Majesties to renounce idol-worship, reject the mummery of shrines, and the deceitful flattery of omens, and believe in God the Father Almighty, and in His Son Jesus Christ, and in the Holy Spirit. This Faith will free you from Satan's bondage, and through the liberative power of the holy and undivided Trinity you will inherit eternal life...

Therefore accept the knowledge of your Creator, who breathed into your frame the breath of life, and who sent His only-begotten Son for your redemption, that He might deliver you from original Sin and the evil power of the Devil, and grant you the prize of heaven."[58]

Helpful insight into the early missionary faith comes in this short summary of Aidan's remarkable ministry in Northumbria, excerpted from the "Venerable" Bede's History: "He believed, worshiped, and taught exactly what we do, namely the redemption of the human race through the Passion, Resurrection, and Ascension into heaven of the Man Jesus Christ, the Meditator between God and Man."[59] This is the core faith in its most seminal expression. The ministry, as summarized by Bede, included "cultivating peace and love, purity and humility, [keeping] as well as to teach the laws of God...[comforting] the sick, [and relieving and protecting] the poor."[60]

The goal of the ministry, as expressed by Honorius, was always that the church "grow ever stronger in faith and good works, and in reverence and love for God; and that in due time the promises of our Lord Jesus Christ may be fulfilled in you."[61]

Powerful hymns developed during the frontier age of the Western church, communicating a robust, fundamental Christian orthodoxy.

Aeterna Christi Munera[62]

The eternal gifts of Christ the King,
The Martyrs' glorious deeds we sing;
And while due hymns of praise we pay,
Our thankful hearts cast grief away.

The Church in these her princes boasts,
These victor chiefs of warrior hosts;
The soldiers of the heavenly hall,
The lights that rose on earth for all.

The terrors of the world despised,
The body's torments lightly prized,
By one brief space of death and pain
Life everlasting they obtain.

To flames the Martyr Saints are hailed:
By teeth of savage beasts assailed;
Against them, armed with ruthless brand
And hooks of steel, their torturers stand.

The mangled frame is tortured sore,
The holy life-drops freshly pour:
They stand unmoved amidst the strife,
By grace of everlasting life.

'Twas thus the yearning faith of saints,
The unconquered hope that never faints,
The love of Christ that knows not shame,
The Prince of this world overcame.

In these the Father's glory shone;
In these the will of God the Son;
In these exults the Holy Ghost;
Through these rejoice the heavenly host.

Redeemer, hear us of thy love,
That, with the glorious band above,
Hereafter, of thine endless grace,
Thy servants also may have place.

Cantemus cuncti melodum nunc Alleluia[63]
The strain upraise of joy and praise: Alleluia.

To the glory of their King
Shall the ransomed people sing: Alleluia.

And the Choirs that dwell on high
Shall re-echo through the sky: Alleluia.

They through the fields of Paradise that roam,
The blessed ones, repeat that bright home: Alleluia.

The planets glitt'ring on their heavenly way,
The shining constellations, join, and say: Alleluia.

Ye clouds that onward sweep!
Ye winds on pinions light!
Ye thunders, echoing loud and deep!
Ye lightnings, wildly bright!
In sweet consent unite your: Alleluia.

Ye floods and ocean billows!
Ye storms and winter snow!
Ye days of cloudless beauty!
Hoar frost and summer glow!
Ye groves that wave in spring,
And glorious forests, sing: Alleluia.

First let the birds, with painted plumage gay,
Exalt their great Creator's praise, and say: Alleluia.

Then let the beasts of earth, with varying strain,
Join in Creation's Hymn, and cry again: Alleluia.

Here let the mountains thunder forth, sonorous, Alleluia.
There let the valleys sing in gentler chorus, Alleluia.

Thou jubilant abyss of ocean, cry Alleluia.
Ye tracts of earth and continents, reply Alleluia.

To God, Who all Creation made,
The frequent hymn be duly paid: Alleluia.

This is the strain, the eternal strain, the Lord of all things loves: Alleluia.
This is the song, the heav'nly song, that Christ Himself approves:
    Alleluia.

Wherefore we sing, both heart and voice awaking, Alleluia.
And children's voices echo, answer making, Alleluia.

Now from all men be outpour'd,
Alleluia to the Lord;
With Alleluia evermore
The Son and Spirit we adore.

Praise be done to Three in One.
Alleluia! Alleluia! Alleluia! Alleluia!

THE AUGUSTINIAN THEOLOGY—A STAYING FORCE

O the depth of the riches both of the wisdom and knowledge of God! how unsearchable are his judgments, and his ways past finding out! For who hath known the mind of the Lord? or who hath been his counsellor? Or who hath first given to him, and it shall be recompensed unto him again? For of him, and through him, and to him, are all things: to whom be glory for ever. Amen. (Romans 11:33-36)

Wrapping up his final works just as the barbarians were rushing into the empire, breaking down the churches and burning down the cities, Augustine of Hippo, Africa (354-430) was one of the last of the church fathers. The ancient City of Man was being destroyed, and the City of God was just getting started. For a thousand years, Augustine's copious theological work and its biblical philosophy of history held sway in the West. His God-centered view stood against a man-centered approach to philosophy, metaphysics, and ethics. In the providence of God, Augustine's work was helpful for the maintenance of Christian orthodoxy through the missionary-frontier age. His life bridged the major heresies that racked the early church—Arianism, Manichaenism, Pelagianism, and Donatism.

To this day, Christians of all stripes recognize the positive contributions of this church father. The Anglican *Church Times* places Augustine's *Confessions* as the "Best of the Best books in church history."[64] As late as 2017, Newsmax Media put the *Confessions* in first place as the most important Christian book in history.[65]

Augustine's theory of truth did not leave knowledge in the realm of abstract ideas. Because the Son of God is a person, revealed as the "Word" or "Logos" in John 1:1, truth must be personal. Moreover, Augustine did not trust human reason to build up its own system of knowledge. Instead, his maxim was, "I believe that I might understand." Without faith in God and a reception of His revelation, no certain understanding of anything is possible.

Augustine was a uniquely humble theologian. He was willing to correct his earlier thinking with various retractions throughout his career. When it came to God's sovereignty and predestination, four years before he died, the theologian confessed that he had gotten it wrong earlier: "[I] was in a similar error, thinking that faith whereby we believe on God is not God's gift, but that it is in us from ourselves, and that by it we obtain the gifts of God, whereby we may live temperately and righteously and piously in this world."[66] Augustine summarized his view of God's absolute sovereignty over all things in this short statement:

> The omnipotent God, then, whether in mercy He pities whom He will, or in judgment hardens whom He will, is never unjust in what He does, never does anything except of His own free-will, and never wills anything that He does not perform.[67]

As the kingdoms of men fail, they demonstrate their weak philosophical and moral foundations. Thus, Augustine created a formidable apologetic for the Christian faith with his *City of God*, in which he pointed out the failure of Rome—the greatest empire in the history of man. He distinguished between the city of God and the city of man by their two distinct loves. The city of man loves itself, and the city of God loves God and seeks the glory of God.

Though standing as a bulwark of the faith in many areas, Augustine failed to distinguish between justification and sanctification in his theology, thus leaving the door open for the development of merit-based theology. It would be left to the Protestant reformers to define a distinct-but-not-separate relationship between faith and works in the Christian life.

THE FIGHT FOR ORTHODOXY

> But there were false prophets also among the people, even as there shall be false teachers among you, who privily shall bring in damnable heresies, even denying the Lord that bought them, and bring upon themselves swift destruction. And many shall follow their pernicious ways; by reason of whom the way of truth shall be evil spoken of. And through covetousness shall they with feigned words make merchandise of you: whose judgment now of a long time lingereth not, and their damnation slumbereth not. (2 Peter 2:1-3)

The attacks upon orthodoxy during the first five hundred years of the Christian church were fundamental, compromising on the nature of reality and the nature of God and Christ. Typically, heretics refuse to handle the mysteries with reverence and care—using human reason to reduce God to something more comprehensible to the mind of man. The root issue is always pride. They are incapable both of maintaining the substance of the faith and properly discerning the trunk and the leaves, the camels and gnats in doctrine. However, none of these heresies and cults survived. Some disappeared over hundreds of years, but nothing could stand against the predominant orthodoxy of the Western church.

The early heresies were more grotesque aberrations—obvious departures from a biblical metaphysic and system of truth. Gnosticism held a degraded view of the physical world and the physical body and suggested that the world was created by a lesser god. In his epistles, the Apostle John addressed this heresy which ultimately rejected the material incarnation of Christ:

> Beloved, believe not every spirit, but try the spirits whether they are of God: because many false prophets are gone out into the world. Hereby know ye the Spirit of God: Every spirit that confesseth that Jesus Christ is come in the flesh is of God: and every spirit that confesseth not that

Jesus Christ is come in the flesh is not of God: and this is that spirit of antichrist, whereof ye have heard that it should come; and even now already is it in the world. (1 John 4:1-3)

Marcionism rejected the unity of the testaments, suggesting that the Old Testament "god" was of a lesser position and character than that of the New Testament "god." Similar to the Gnostics, the Marcionites believed the world was created by this Old Testament god—a lower-world demiurge. These teachings were an imposition of Neoplatonic and other pagan thinking upon the Biblical faith. Preferring the New Testament Pauline Epistles to the rest of Scripture, Marcion rejected Old Testament law (particularly Christ's teachings affirming the law in the Gospel of Matthew).

Think not that I am come to destroy the law, or the prophets: I am not come to destroy, but to fulfil. For verily I say unto you, Till heaven and earth pass, one jot or one tittle shall in no wise pass from the law, till all be fulfilled. Whosoever therefore shall break one of these least commandments, and shall teach men so, he shall be called the least in the kingdom of heaven: but whosoever shall do and teach them, the same shall be called great in the kingdom of heaven. (Matthew 5:17-19)

Montanism came around AD 160, resorting to extra-scriptural prophecies, and ordaining women as bishops and deacons in the pattern of modern sects in the post-Christian era. Although never formally condemned by the church, this group did not survive long. As explained by Eusebius of Caesarea, "[Montanus] became beside himself, and being suddenly in a sort of frenzy and ecstasy, he raved, and began to babble and utter strange things, prophesying in a manner contrary to the constant custom of the Church handed down by tradition from the beginning."[68]

Since the dragon had failed to destroy the church by Roman persecutions in the first centuries, the demonic strategy shifted to the dissemination of a bewildering array of heresies relating to the most foundational issues—the nature of God and Christ. The entire 4th Century was a knock-down, drag-out fight against Arianism and ten other Trinitarian and Christological heresies. Arius of Alexandria (256-336) taught the essential supremacy of the Father over the Son, and that the Son had a beginning. This doctrine was rejected at Nicea (AD 325); however, later Roman emperors generally endorsed the heresy until 381.

The East was more particularly affected by these early heresies than the developing Western church. For example, Nestorius, the patriarch of Constantinople (428-431), taught that the two natures of Christ were separated, such that Christ appeared as a multi-personality. This sect developed into 15 sees across Persia and Europe, peaking out around AD 900. On the other hand, the Monophysites taught that Christ was a single nature, a sort of mix of human and divine, verging on a demigod. These schisms created ongoing troubles for the Eastern church, weakening the overall cultural influence of Christianity as far east as Russia and China.

The 5th Century witnessed another mammoth struggle against a man-centered, man-dependent salvation in the form of Pelagianism. Pelagius (360-420) denied original sin, held to the perfectibility of man, and taught that man's works proceed entirely from his own ability. In his *Defense of the Freedom of the Will,* he wrote, "That we are able to do good is of God, but that we actually do it is of ourselves."[69] Pelagianism was condemned at the Council of Carthage in AD 418. Its influence continued in Britain for a time, but Germanus of Auxerre (Gaul) redressed this wrong doctrine on his mission to the island around AD 429.

A superficial attachment to symbols and images was also a detriment to the developing Christian church, although less so in the West. The Eastern church wavered back and forth on the use of religious images and icons, banning them first in AD 730 and then bringing them back in AD 787 with the Seventh Ecumenical Council. The concern was idolatry, the tendency of the people to worship these images. However, the Council ended up "permitting kissing, bowing, strewing of incense, burning of lights, saying prayers before the idols; such honor to be intended of the living object in heaven which the images represented."[70]

This decision met resistance in the West. The controversy was addressed by the Charlemagne court in a four-volume series called the *Libri Carolini*, most likely authored by Alcuin of York. Image worship was rejected out of hand as patently unbiblical: "God alone is the object of worship and adoration, saints may be revered, but images can in no way be worshiped. To bow or kneel before them, to salute or kiss them, to strew incense and to light candles before them, is idolatrous and superstitious...the Scriptures know nothing of such practices."[71] About the same time, Agobard (779-840), Archbishop of Lyon, condemned the worship of saints and image worship in the church, concerned particularly that it would draw men away from spiritual worship into the sensual. In his treatise Agobard cited the Council of Elvira (AD 309), canon 36: "There shall be no pictures in the church, lest what is worshipped and adored should be depicted on the walls." Such pushback illustrates the commitment to the Scriptures, the respect for the commandments of God, and the conservative orthodoxy persisting in the West well into the 9th Century. Although some of the reformers discouraged the use of images, by the early 20th Century most of the Protestant churches had returned to their use in the context of worship.

Many of these early heresies ganged up on the Western church again during the 19th and 20th centuries; prominent of which were Unitarianism, semi-Pelagian doctrines, the Arian and Polytheist cults, the Montanist focus on experience and extra-scriptural revelation, and a superficial, sentimental attachment to cultural symbols.

However, by the grace of God, the devil was held at bay and the Western church flourished for a few more centuries. Generally, a God-centered, Scripture-based theology permeated Europe for the length of the Frontier Age, between AD 33 and 1000.

HANDLING THE MYSTERIES IN A PURE CONSCIENCE

Likewise must the deacons be grave, not doubletongued, not given to much wine, not greedy of filthy lucre; holding the mystery of the faith in a pure conscience. (1 Timothy 3:8-9)

For hundreds of years, the doctrine of the Lord's Supper was held in the realm of mystery. Few attempts were made to violate the bounds of mystery or institutionalize a damaging heresy in the church. The *Didache* had referred to the Lord's Supper as "spiritual food and drink."[72] The *Didascalia Apostolorum* spoke of the elements as the "likeness of the royal body of Christ." Eusebius refused to equate the elements to the actual body and blood of Jesus as well: "Christians daily commemorate Jesus's sacrifice with the symbols of His body and saving blood." Ambrose of Milan had spoken of the elements being changed into the body and blood of Christ, but Augustine and others would still speak of these elements as "symbols" and "sacraments." Using language much like that of John Calvin in the 16th Century, Augustine explained the sacramental mysteries as "[bearing] resemblance of the things of which they are sacraments...In most cases, this resemblance results in their receiving the names of those things."[73]

In the 9th Century, discord erupted in Corbie of Picardy. Abbot Paschasius Radbertus (785-865), the same man suspected of forging the Donation of Constantine, strongly advocated the position that the communion bread and wine were *transformed* into the body and blood of Christ at the table. Two other theologians, Rabanus and Ratramnus, opposed Radbertus, holding that the elements operated as the body and blood of Christ *in a spiritual sense* for the believer who partook of the supper. In the end, Archbishop Hincmar of Rheims took the side of Radbertus in the debate. Both views would be tolerated in the Western church, and a measure of mystery was allowed until the Fourth Lateran Council of 1215.

THE EVIL TREATMENT OF GOTTSCHALK

These things have I spoken unto you, that ye should not be offended. They shall put you out of the synagogues: yea, the time cometh, that whosoever killeth you will think that he doeth God service. And these things will they do unto you, because they have not known the Father, nor me. (John 16:1-3)

About the same time that the Donation of Constantine was being forged deep in the archbishopric of Rheims, another controversy arose in connection with a monk named Gottschalk of Bern. Although he had been consigned to monastic life as a child against his will, and had lost his bid to leave the monastery, Gottschalk dedicated his life to studying Augustine's writings and the works of Fulgentius of Ruspe (c. 467-533). The monk was convinced of Augustine's position concerning the absolute sovereignty of God over all things. He maintained in his writings that nothing could happen unintended by God's sovereign purpose, including the ultimate eternal state of all persons—believer and unbeliever. Man's will could in no way confound God's will. Gottschalk's consistent commitment to God's sovereignty was such that he believed Christ died only for those who would be saved.

On October 1, 848, Gottschalk was called before a synod at Mainz in the presence of the German king. He was condemned and sentenced to prison. However, still not satisfied with the verdict and sentence, Archbishop Hincmar of Rheims called the monk before the Synod of Chiersy. In the spring of 849, Gottschalk was convicted, scourged, tortured "most atrociously" until half dead, and his books were thrown into the fire.[74] Even the Archbishop of Lyon remonstrated the archbishopric of Rheims for what he called "unheard-of impiety and cruelty" in these proceedings.[75] Something apparently quite sinister, perhaps an unsavory spiritual power, had descended upon Rheims during Hincmar's term of service (845-882). While languishing in the prison, Gottschalk reiterated his position in writing, confessing the absolute sovereignty of God over the sovereignty of man. His excommunication held, and he died in prison somewhere around 869.

At the end of the controversy, Augustine's doctrine of divine sovereignty lost, and semi-Pelagianism emerged the winner at the National Synod of France held at Toucy in 860. The French church concluded that God does not purpose that any should go to hell. Furthermore, they said God has elected some by His grace to salvation, and Christ died for all men, even those who will not believe and will go into perdition. Having some sympathy for Gottschalk, Pope Nicholas withheld his approval of the Synod's decision, and Augustinian doctrine was still permitted within the rubric of the Western church for succeeding generations. However, the forgeries, the mishandling of doctrinal debates, and the treatment of Gottschalk at Rheims set the path for the breakdown of the French church. No significant reformation of faith would sustain at a national level through the ages; and the center of Western Christianity would shift north to Canterbury by the 11th Century.

THE SUSTAINING OF THE WESTERN CHURCH

For a long time the Western Church grew and flourished, and the gates of hell did not prevail against it. It is well to honor Christ for His accomplishments in history. Indeed, the Western church remained orthodox on matters of the Trinity, the sovereignty of God, the use of images, the authority and supremacy of Scripture, discipleship in the

Word of God, a resistance to pagan Greek philosophy, and the rule of faith and the gospel (the death and resurrection of Jesus Christ). On potentially controversial doctrines and the difficult mysteries, the Church remained careful to avoid unhealthy specificity and institutionalized error. Despite its struggles and the breakdown at Rheims, Western Europe received a Christian discipleship from AD 50 through AD 1050. A vibrant faith and church life developed and paganism receded greatly over these thousand years. This was the definitive, sustained rise of the Christian faith in the Western world, and from here the faith would spread over the whole earth. If the words of Isaiah 60 applied anywhere in the world over two millennia after the coming of Christ, they must have applied to Gentile Europe:

> Arise, shine; for thy light is come, and the glory of the Lord is risen upon thee. For, behold, the darkness shall cover the earth, and gross darkness the people: but the Lord shall arise upon thee, and his glory shall be seen upon thee. And the Gentiles shall come to thy light, and kings to the brightness of thy rising. Lift up thine eyes round about, and see: all they gather themselves together, they come to thee: thy sons shall come from far, and thy daughters shall be nursed at thy side. Then thou shalt see, and flow together, and thine heart shall fear, and be enlarged; because the abundance of the sea shall be converted unto thee, the forces of the Gentiles shall come unto thee. The multitude of camels shall cover thee, the dromedaries of Midian and Ephah; all they from Sheba shall come: they shall bring gold and incense; and they shall shew forth the praises of the Lord. (Isaiah 60:1-6)

IV
___

THE DECLINE OF THE MEDIEVAL CHURCH

Take heed therefore unto yourselves, and to all the flock, over the which the Holy Ghost hath made you overseers, to feed the church of God, which he hath purchased with his own blood. For I know this, that after my departing shall grievous wolves enter in among you, not sparing the flock. Also of your own selves shall men arise, speaking perverse things, to draw away disciples after them. (Acts 20:28-30)

The state of the Western church in AD 1000 was a mixed bag (as it has always been), and the student of history must be careful not to make sweeping generalizations. The corruption of one power-mongering pastorate in Rome did not mean the end of the Christian church, by any means. However, five hundred years later the leaven of bad doctrine, bad discipleship, and bad behavior among the clergy had pretty well spread over the entire continent. The Church had experienced dramatic spiritual decline by all accounts, such that Martin Luther would use the most severe language in his descriptions communicated to Pope Leo X: "Your seat is possessed and oppressed by Satan, the damned seat of Antichrist..."[1] He told the German nobility: "the devilish government of the Romanists...are verily of the fellowship of Antichrist and the Devil and have nothing of Christ but the name."[2] In Luther's view, a very dark spiritual force had descended upon Rome and her churches.

Demographers estimate Europe's population topped 30 million at 1000 AD, including 1.5 million for England, 11 million for the Holy Roman Empire, France with 7.5 million, and Ireland with 630,000. Europe made up about 10% of the world's population and almost all the Christians on earth, (with Byzantium claiming about 3% of the world's population).

ATTEMPTS AT REFORM

Now the Spirit speaketh expressly, that in the latter times some shall depart from the faith, giving heed to seducing spirits, and doctrines of devils; speaking lies in hypocrisy; having their conscience seared with a hot iron; forbidding to marry, and commanding to abstain from meats, which God hath created to be received with thanksgiving of them which believe and know the truth. (1 Timothy 4:1-3)

Pope Nicholas' appeal to the fraudulent Pseudo-Isidorian Decretals in AD 864 was the first major power grab in the medieval church. The leaven spawned in Rome. Surely, as the first pope to reference the forgery, Nicholas must have been complicit in giving the document credence at its beginning. In Schaff's words, "he must have known that a large portion of this forged collection,...did not exist in the papal archives."[3]

Immediately after Nicholas, the popes began quarreling over secular power. Morals degenerated quickly in the papacy, and the careers of most of the popes during this period were marked by murder and dark intrigue. Papal corruption at the top of the ecclesiastical order spread quickly to the lower clerics, at least in Italy. As a consequence, it wasn't long before the worst evils were pervading the monasteries, especially in Italy. Peter Damian (1007-1072) reported that "the cancer of sodomitic impurity…is creeping through the clerical order."[4] The "diabolical tyranny," he said, had come in the "pretense of religion."[5] Damian could hardly tolerate the sheer horror of the sexual perversion which followed apostasy in the church. In his words: "It is shameful to relate such a disgusting scandal to sacred ears!"[6]

Damian's friend Hildebrand, occupied the papacy for twelve years (1073-1085) and implemented church reform between 1049 and 1085. Hildebrand's main concern was simony and the concubinage of the priests. Long into the 10th Century, priests still married despite the decrees and canons forbidding the practice. This kept some of the immorality among the clerics at bay. However, Hildebrand's reform meant more submission to the traditions of men versus the laws of God.

The moral decay of the church was furthered, however inadvertently, when the First Lateran Council (AD 1123) brought the hammer down on clerical marriage in canons 7 and 21:

> We absolutely forbid priests, deacons, and subdeacons to associate with concubines and women, or to live with women other than such as the Nicene Council (canon 3) for reasons of necessity permitted, namely, the mother, sister, or aunt, or any such person concerning whom no suspicion could arise.

> We absolutely forbid priests, deacons, subdeacons, and monks to have concubines or to contract marriage. We decree in accordance with the definitions of the sacred canons, that marriages already contracted by such persons must be dissolved, and that the persons be condemned to do penance.[7]

By the time Hildebrand was elected pope (AD 1073), the moral condition of the church was in desperate straits, as he himself described it:

The Eastern Church fallen from the faith, and attacked by the infidels from without. In the West, South, or North, scarcely any bishops who have obtained their office regularly, or whose life and conduct correspond to their calling, and who are actuated by the love of Christ instead of worldly ambition...And when I look to myself, I feel oppressed by such a burden of sin that no other hope of salvation is left me but in the mercy of Christ alone.[8]

Hildebrand, as Pope Gregory VII, resorted to secular power to "clean up the world." His assiduous enforcement of the prohibition on clergy concubinage was resisted in France, Spain, and England, though William the Conqueror attempted to enforce the rule among the Norman clergy for awhile. Gregory pushed back against state appointments of pastors throughout the empire and claimed sole authority to appoint bishops. He collided with Henry IV, the Holy Roman Emperor, who insisted on controlling the appointment of bishops within his own realm. This dispute became known as the Investiture Controversy. Henry lobbied sufficient bishops to depose Gregory as pope, so Gregory excommunicated Henry calling his own synod of 110 bishops. Henry lost political support in his crusade and ended up begging for mercy from Gregory at the gates of the fortress of Canossa in January 1077. Gregory gave him "absolution," securing the right to depose any king who resisted the pope thereafter. He backed this claim with the threat of excommunication. Troubles didn't subside, however, and the Holy Roman Empire degenerated into a shameful war between two kings teamed up with two popes. In 1083, King Henry chased Gregory out of Rome, replacing him with his own "pope." But the year following, Gregory solicited help from a Norman duke, Robert Guiscard, who reentered Rome with 36,000 men and destroyed about half the city.

By AD 1050, the Holy Roman Empire (comprising parts of Germany, Switzerland, Bohemia, and Italy) had expanded to roughly

400,000 square miles, approaching the magnitude of the pagan empires of previous centuries. The ancient Roman Empire had topped 770,000 square miles. Power-hungry tyrants would not be able to surpass the power of the Holy Roman Empire until the Portuguese Empire secured control of 310,000 square miles in the 16th Century and the Spanish over 1,000,000 square miles of territory in the 17th Century. Moreover, the population of the Holy Roman Empire was almost ten times the size of England and twice the size of France by AD 1000. The lure of secular power put in place by the Donation of Constantine was bearing its bad fruit and further breaking down the spiritual condition of the church. Empire fever had infected the papacy, and its effects would be devastating in the years to come. The unholy alliance of power-hungry popes and emperors resulted in a return to the pagan power state in the form of the Holy Roman Empire. Without the pope's powerful influence, it is doubtful that the Germans, the Swiss, and the Italians would have allowed for the development of this empire between AD 850 and AD 1050. Modern empire-building and the centralization of secular power was envisioned first by the papacy. The Portuguese, Spanish, and French would jump on the power-empire bandwagon, further weakening the church and persecuting true Christian believers through inquisitions in the centuries that followed.

Henceforth, the papacy would invariably choose the wrong side when it came to political liberties—choosing to support King John over the Magna Carta and King Edward I and II over the independence of Scotland and Robert the Bruce. If a proposition included more centralization of power for the state, the pope was generally for it, unless it came at his own expense.

ENGLAND—FAITH DEPOSITORY, FAITH CENTER (AD 1066-1620)

While France's leading pastors fell to a man-centered outlook by AD 850 and the papacy was hardly salvageable by AD 1080, more successful attempts at reform came about in England by two pastors, both of Italian birth.

William the Conqueror's invasion of England in AD 1066, and his subsequent appointment of the Archbishop of Canterbury kicked off a period of state tyranny. But, at the same time, England was granted some autonomy from the papacy. Lanfranc (1004-1089), William's somewhat reluctant choice for archbishop, turned out to be a reformer who allowed rural clergy to marry while cracking down harder on the ordination of unqualified priests. He resisted the pope's claim to temporal authority and refused to obey orders when summoned to appear before the pope in Rome. All this turned out to be for the benefit of the English church. The king cut off communications between the Church of England and the papacy, refusing to allow any pastor to leave the country to visit the pope. Thus, England adopted an arms-length relationship with the pope, a connection which was to be tested by bishop and king alike for the next five hundred years.

Around the same time, Osmund (d. 1099), pastor at Salisbury, developed the *Sarum Use*, a liturgy which would later be used as a basis for the *Book of Common Prayer* during the Protestant Reformation.

Following the Conqueror came his son William Rufus, a tyrant and a reprobate. He confiscated church lands and was best known for his licentiousness and his bold-faced hatred of God. However, in the providence of God, Rufus approved the appointment of Anselm (1033-1109) to the archbishopric of Canterbury. Anselm's only real interaction with the king occurred three years before the monarch's untimely death in a hunting accident. He told the king he would not leave until he had prayed for him, to which the king reluctantly agreed.

The remainder of Anselm's career was filled with a degree of persecution. He was exiled several times for refusing to go along with the derelict king's appointment of pastors to England's churches.

After William Rufus' death, his brother Henry I took the throne and for a while fought for the power of investiture, but finally relented.

FORMING A STRONGER DOCTRINAL & DEVOTIONAL ORTHODOXY

Beloved, when I gave all diligence to write unto you of the common salvation, it was needful for me to write unto you, and exhort you that ye should earnestly contend for the faith which was once delivered unto the saints. (Jude 3)

Anselm of Canterbury may very well be considered the proto-reformer, four hundred years before the fact, advocating the doctrine of the substitutionary atonement and the satisfaction of God's justice at the cross. In his magnum opus, *Cur Deus Homo*, Anselm corrected the longstanding error holding sway in the church that Christ's redemption price was paid to Satan. Defining sin as the violation of God's law, Anselm understood Christ's sacrifice to be a necessary satisfaction of divine justice. Like Augustine, Anselm held to the total sovereignty of God while rejecting fatalism and retaining a non-coercive freedom of the will. He resolves this conundrum by recognizing God as equally existing and personally present everywhere at the same time: "...since no law of space or time prohibits the Supreme Being from being present as a whole in every place at once or from being present as a whole at every time at once."[9] By his commitment to maintain a historical and biblically-robust orthodoxy against the rising humanist trends, Anselm was sometimes referred to as the "Tongue of Augustine" or "the Second Augustine."

About the same time, the Frenchman Peter Abelard (1079-1142) appeared on the scene—one of the first humanist philosophers of the age to usher in a lapse of faith and epistemological autonomy to the West. Serving as Master of the cathedral school at Notre Dame (c.

1115), Abelard made considerable inroads with his new theology in the French Church. Innocent II excommunicated the proto-humanist on July 16, 1141, although the sentence was later lifted.

Anticipating the post-Christian, humanist epistemology, Abelard wrote, "It is by doubting that we come to inquire and by inquiring that we reach truth."[10] He refused to begin his theory of knowledge with the line of Augustine and Anselm, "I believe in order to understand." As with Descartes and other humanists who set out to build up a knowledge based purely on human reason, Abelard began with, "I doubt; therefore I am." These were the epistemological seeds of destruction, for the undermining of the faith in the West.

In clear opposition to his contemporary, Anselm of Canterbury, Abelard argued that Christ's death was not intended to pay any penalty for sin but merely to serve as an example of love. Bernard of Clairvaux refuted Abelard, calling him a "son of perdition." Applying sound biblical arguments from Romans 5, Bernard wrote, "I was made a sinner by deriving my being from Adam; I am made just by being washed in the blood of Christ and not by Christ's 'words and example.'"[11] But more fundamentally, Bernard took issue with Abelard's use of the pagan dialectic to explain the incomprehensibilities of God. In his view, Abelard was obfuscating the plain meaning of biblical doctrine, by pretending he could explain the incomprehensible elements of it using Aristotelian logic. Such attempts to argue out the finer distinctions by human reasoning would produce endless, fruitless debates over future centuries. This human reason, in Bernard's view, had "no place either in grasping the plain meaning (since the very plainness of plain meaning consists in its being grasped immediately without reasoning) or in reaching some more profound understanding (since only the plain meaning is open to us at all)."[12] For these and other reasons, the Protestant reformers held immense respect for Bernard of Clairvaux.

In the later Medieval Period, head religion would displace the heart, and scholastic argument would squelch heart worship, praise, love, and experiential knowledge and enjoyment of God. However, such was not the case for Anselm and Bernard. When men are humbled by the sheer incomprehensibility of God's infinite knowledge and humbled to realize themselves to be recipients of His truth and sovereign grace, the various expressions and writings of these men must be full of love, wonder, and praise. These truths were not mere theoretical ideas for these pastors. It is one thing to theorize that God sovereignly saves. It is quite another to realize that I am the recipient of this ultimately sovereign and gracious action. It is one thing to know of it and argue about it in the head. It is another thing to have received it in the heart. Thus, Anselm combined "lofty speculation" with "pious devotion" and "prayer with logical analysis."[13] In Schaff's words: "The soaring grandeur of Anselm's thoughts may be likened to the mountains of the land of his birth, and the pure abundance of his spiritual feeling to the brooks and meadows of its valleys. He quotes again and again from Scripture, and its language constitutes the chief vehicle of his thoughts."[14]

Likewise, Bernard of Clairvaux is also recognized for his experiential and devotional life and writings. He is best known today for his hymnody.

O Sacred Head, Now Wounded
Translated into English by James W. Alexander

O Sacred Head, now wounded,
With grief and pain weighed down,
How scornfully surrounded,
With thorns Thine only crown!
How pale Thou art with anguish,
With sore abuse and scorn!
How does that visage languish
Which once was bright as morn!

O Lord of Life and Glory,
What bliss till now was Thine!
I read the wondrous story,
I joy to call Thee mine!
Thy grief and Thy compassion
Were all for sinners' gain;
Mine, mine was the transgression,
But Thine the deadly pain.

What language shall I borrow
To praise Thee, heavenly Friend,
For this Thy dying sorrow,
Thy pity without end?
Lord, make me Thine forever,
Nor let me faithless prove;
O let me never, never
Abuse such dying love!

Be near me, Lord, when dying;
O, show Thyself to me;
And for my succour flying,
Come, Lord, to set me free:
These eyes, new faith receiving,
From Jesus shall not move;
For he who dies believing
Dies safely through Thy love.

Anselm died in 1109 and Bernard in 1153. These were the last good years for the Western church, for the decline now was well underway. It had been a thousand years since Lydia first received the Gospel by the river in Philippi; and 800 years since the dragon's persecuting force was quelled in Rome; and 500 years since the faith came into England via Augustine of Canterbury. Decline followed.

AD 1150—FATAL & FUNDAMENTAL CRACKS IN THE FOUNDATIONS

This charge I commit unto thee, son Timothy, according to the prophecies which went before on thee, that thou by them mightest war a good warfare; holding faith, and a good conscience; which some having put away concerning faith have made shipwreck… (1 Timothy 1:18-19)

Throughout the centuries, intramural arguments had always existed over the sovereignty of God and the will of man, Augustinian theology, the real presence of Christ's body and blood at the table, the use of images, and other doctrinal matters. Sometimes, the Augustinian position won out, and at other times the contest would end in a draw. However, the entire theological atmosphere in the West would perceptibly shift between 1150 and 1215 with Peter Lombard's entrance on the scene.

Peter Lombard (1096-1160) is credited with the most influential work of the later medieval period. His contribution of a systematic theology known as *The Sentences* would dominate the church and shape the worldview of the continent between AD 1150 and 1550. It was the official textbook used by the theology department of the medieval universities. Over four centuries, hundreds of scholars would write their commentaries on Lombard's work.

Lombard rejected Anselm's of substitutionary atonement, erring towards Abelard's view—that Christ's death was only an example of love. Anticipating the Fourth Lateran Council of 1215, Lombard's theological manual institutionalized for theological students the "transition" of the elements at the table from wine and bread into the blood and body of Christ. Lombard mainstreamed Radbertus's treatment of the mystery. This early French scholastic was also the first to formalize the idea of merit by including these difficult words in his theological manual: "Without merits, to hope for anything cannot be called hope, but presumption."[15] Such language made it impossible for future Catholic theologians to extricate themselves from a salvation by works motif.

Lombard also vacillated on the doctrine of God's sovereignty, allowing for man a freedom to act outside of God's sovereign control.[16] He would not admit to man's total inability to assist in his own salvation, and he imposed on Christian theology an extra-biblical category he called "cooperating grace."[17] Human logic tends to create new theological categories. Rejecting the Augustinian idea of irresistible grace, Lombard wanted to preserve the right of man to resist God's purpose. In future generations, theologians became increasingly adept at introducing categories to aid in resolving biblical mysteries which did not comport well with man's reason. Also, Lombard minimized the corruption of the soul by limiting it to what he called "the flesh,"[18] implying that the mind was not corrupted by the Fall. In comparison with Augustine and Anselm, this more popular theologian of the later Medieval Period introduced a theology more ennobling to fallen sinful man and more ingratiating to the prideful mind of humanist man. Scripture bears no such encouraging view of the natural mind of fallen man:

> For to be carnally minded is death; but to be spiritually minded is life and peace. Because the carnal mind is enmity against God: for it is not subject to the law of God, neither indeed can be. (Romans 8:6-7)

> Unto the pure all things are pure: but unto them that are defiled and unbelieving is nothing pure; but even their mind and conscience is defiled. (Titus 1:15)

More than Thomas Aquinas, Peter Lombard's work was far and away the most defining theological force in the medieval Church. Therefore, it comes as no surprise that the major theological contributor to the Protestant Reformation, John Calvin, selected Lombard as the prime target in his writings—referring to the medieval theologian (mostly negatively) no less than one hundred times in his *Institutes*.

CENTRALIZATION OF POWERS

> But Jesus called them unto him, and said, Ye know that the princes of the Gentiles exercise dominion over them, and they that are great exercise authority upon them. But it shall not be so among you: but whosoever will be great among you, let him be your minister; and whosoever will be chief among you, let him be your servant: even as the Son of man came not to be ministered unto, but to minister, and to give his life a ransom for many. (Matthew 20:25-28)

Pope Nicholas I was the first to give papal sanction to the forged Pseudo-Decretals around AD 864. Using the forgeries to justify his interference with the church in France, the pope forced reinstatement of a bishop over the protests of local ecclesiastical authorities. Then it was Gregory VII (Hildebrand) who played tug-of-war with Henry IV at the Roman Synod at Lent in 1075 over investiture. Instead of allowing appointment of pastors to be vested within the local churches and presbyters, centralized, powerful interests (i.e. the pope and the emperor) fought over these appointments. Gregory VII insisted on the pope's right to rule over pretty much everything—issuing ultimate judgment in both ecclesiastical and civil affairs. In one particularly arrogant moment of his career, he compared the priestly class to the sun and the kings to the moon. And he informed the king of Aragon that Jesus "had made Peter lord over all the kingdoms of the world."[19] The megalomania was virtually unstoppable at this point, and its fruit was catastrophic. This false conception of a top-down, pyramid-like system of world transformation, borrowed from the Gentile political approach of "lording it over" others, came to dominate in the minds of these proud men.

The culmination of papal power was left to Pope Innocent III (1161-1216). Schaff summarizes Innocent, the youngest pope in the history of the church, thusly:

> He was a born ruler of men, a keen judge of human nature, demanding unconditional submission to his will, yet considerate in the use of power after submission was once given,—an imperial personality towering high above the contemporary sovereigns in moral force and in magnificent aims of worldwide dominion.[20]

Whereas Pope Gregory VII had compared the priestly class to the sun, Innocent went further. He called *himself* the sun, endowed with the absolute right to rule over the whole world. The Scriptures had warned about a person who would try to take the place of God, called "the son of destruction, who opposes and exalts himself against every so-called god or object of worship, so that he takes his seat in the temple of God, proclaiming himself to be God" (2 Thess. 2:3-4, ESV).

Such pride and power mongering of these unrestrained proportions was the undoing of the entire Western church, and the beginning of much terrible tyranny. Innocent's hands were in the affairs of almost every nation in Europe. After the death of Henry VI on September 28, 1197, he took over the empire himself, appointing Otto to rule in 1201. The pope meddled in the state matters of France, Denmark, and Spain. He excommunicated King John and the whole nation of England, once again over the matter of the appointment of an archbishop. When it came to the liberty of the people, however, he took the side of King John against the Magna Carta. With tyrants, birds of a feather flock together. Innocent III condemned "the wicked audacity of the barons"—the men who had laid down the basis for Western liberties in one of the most important documents in all history. Innocent called the charter "a low and base instrument, yea, truly wicked and deserving to be reprobated by all," and pronounced it "null and void."[21] He excommunicated all the English barons who stood for liberty. Nevertheless, the independent spirit of the Church of England prevailed, and Archbishop Stephen Langton refused to publish the pope's writ. For good measure, the pope relieved Langton of his post and fumed at the English pastors, calling them "worse than Saracens, worse than those open enemies of the cross."[22] By God's merciful providence, Innocent died on July 16, 1216, John died three months later, and the Magna Carta survived.

1215—THE BEGINNING OF THE END

The year 1215 marked the beginning of Western civil liberties, but for the Western church it was also the year of the Fourth Lateran Council, referenced by some church historians as the "zenith of the papal theocracy."[23]

The consolidation and corruption of power at the highest levels of the church contributed to serious downgrade of its doctrine and practice. The notorious Fourth Lateran revealed the heart of a church in apostasy. It was the best attended Western church council up to that time, involving 412 bishops, 800 abbots or priors, and others. But the actions taken would be most devastating to the health of the Western church; these included the institutionalizing of the doctrine of transubstantiation, the forceable removal of Raymond VI's lands in Toulouse, and the sanctioning of the notorious Inquisition.

THE FATEFUL CANON ONE

Likewise deacons must be reverent, not double-tongued, not given to much wine, not greedy for money, holding the mystery of the faith with a pure conscience. (1 Timothy 3:8-9)

For centuries, the Western church dared not tread on the mysteries of the faith. Though men would debate these matters and suggest this or that, the church was careful not to cinch up the debate into one categorical statement. The church had allowed for a range of perspectives on difficult soteriological, ecclesiological, and sacramental doctrines. At some point, however, proud men will mangle the mysteries, subjecting them to man-made categories and exceeding the bounds of Scripture. Such was the case when the Western church resorted to the pagan Aristotle's distinction between the substance and the accidents of things to explain away the mystery of Christ's presence in the communion elements.

At the Fourth Lateran Council of 1215, the first fateful canon formalized the doctrine that Christ's "body and blood are truly contained in the sacrament of the altar under the forms of bread and wine; the bread being changed (*transsubstantiatio*) by divine power into the body, and the wine into the blood."[24]

Indeed, at the first supper Christ had told His disciples that "this is My body given for you." However, He did not say the bread *"turns into My body."* Such redacting would tread upon the mystery, something the Apostolic and early church fathers dared not do. The Apostle Paul acknowledged a *koinonia,* or fellowship, with the body and blood of Christ at the table, but once again he would not elucidate further. This was more than a memorial of Christ's death, but the matter of *how* the fellowship or the participation in the sacrifice happened was left a mystery (1 Cor. 10:16-17).

In the contest for retaining orthodoxy on the matter of the table, the one who is best at retaining the mystery in the supper wins. Some wished to reduce it to a mere memorial, and others concluded that the elements were transformed into the physical body and blood of Christ. Both opinions stripped away the mystery, sacrificing the doctrine to the pride of men. Lateran IV institutionalized a particular interpretation of the sacrament—to the detriment of the whole church.

THE DREADED CANON THREE

Another parable put he forth unto them, saying, The kingdom of heaven is likened unto a man which sowed good seed in his field; but while men slept, his enemy came and sowed tares among the wheat, and went his way. But when the blade was sprung up, and brought forth fruit, then appeared the tares also. So the servants of the householder came and said unto him, Sir, didst not thou sow good seed in thy field? from whence then hath it tares? He said unto them, An enemy hath done this. The servants said unto him, Wilt thou then that we go and gather them up? But he said, Nay; lest while ye gather up the tares, ye root up also the wheat with them. Let both grow together until the harvest: and in the time of harvest I will say to the reapers, Gather ye together first the tares, and bind them in bundles to burn them: but gather the wheat into my barn. (Matthew 13:24-30)

The Fourth Lateran Council wreaked yet more damage upon the church and the entire socio-political order of Europe. Powerful religious leaders armed with a misplaced zeal, a confused view of Scripture, and a commitment to use civil power to eradicate all that is wrong in the world are really dangerous people. Such turned out to be the case with popes Innocent III and Gregory VII. They had a moral agenda. They were reformers. However, they turned to the power of the state to perform a task that can only be accomplished by the preaching of the Word and the power of the Holy Spirit working in the hearts of people.

In the Wheat and Tares parable, our Lord clearly laid out the field as the world, where both believer and unbeliever find themselves in the same context. There must be no holy war, no attempt to root out unbelievers, and no civil penalty for unbelief. The parable does not address the church or the matter of excommunication. It is simply a reminder to the Christian world that there must be no attempt to use civil power to sort out unbelievers from believers. Both must "grow together until the harvest." This does not forbid the civil power to prosecute crime according to God's law. But, at the least, it forbids the church from prosecuting crimes or relying upon the magistrate to weed out those teachers who "offend" (Matt. 13:41; Rom. 16:17; Rev. 2:14). While the church must teach against error and sin, and make proper use of the "keys" in church discipline, the power of the state is limited by God's ordinance. Only power-hungry tyrants and control mongers transgress these boundaries and initiate inquisitions and unwarranted persecutions.

What a tragedy that Innocent III and the bishops attending the Fourth Lateran Council would introduce the Inquisition in direct defiance of Christ's words in Matthew 13! Incredibly, canon 3 of the Council also threatened excommunication for any civil magistrate who refused to exterminate heretics:

> Secular authorities, whatever office they may hold, shall be admonished and induced and if necessary compelled by ecclesiastical censure, that as they wish to be esteemed and numbered among the faithful, so for the defense of the faith they ought publicly to take an oath that they will strive in good faith and to the best of their ability to exterminate in the territories subject to their jurisdiction all heretics pointed out by the Church; so that whenever anyone shall have assumed authority, whether spiritual or temporal, let him be bound to confirm this decree by oath. But if a temporal ruler, after having been requested and admonished by the Church, should neglect to cleanse his territory of this heretical foulness, let him be excommunicated by the metropolitan and the other bishops of the province.[25]

This edict was a culmination of Innocent's heresy-hunting and his tireless efforts to exterminate the Cathari and Albigenses beginning in AD 1208.

HERETICAL CULTS—CREEPING IN FROM THE EAST

> For such are false apostles, deceitful workers, transforming themselves into the apostles of Christ. And no marvel; for Satan himself is transformed into an angel of light. Therefore it is no great thing if his ministers also be transformed as the ministers of righteousness; whose end shall be according to their works. (2 Corinthians 11:13-15)

Any consideration of the breakdown of the Western Church must trace the problem to its roots. Inevitably, that turns out to be the sin, pride, and rebellion always lurking in the hearts of men and the malefic spiritual influences upon them. Pride is behind every scandal, every heresy, every untruth, every schism, and every autonomous human opinion that corrupts the church.

The Eastern church was more infected by pagan humanist thinking than the West. The anti-Trinitarian heresies gained more traction in the East. At first, idolatry took hold in the East more than in the West. The East confounded church and state institutions and gave way more quickly to the deification of the state.

For about 800 years (after Pelagius), the Western world was largely free of wild sects, weird cults, and anti-trinitarian doctrines. The ancient dualistic worldview of Manicheanism reappeared in Bulgaria around AD 930 via a priest by the name of Bogomil. Not much is known of this mysterious character except that he taught his followers that the material world was evil. Consistent with this dualist perspective, Bogomil rejected eating meat, drinking wine, marriage, and baptism. He condemned all secular power and riches and encouraged servants not to obey their masters. From this bad seed emerges the spirit of rebellion or revolution, later replicated in the secular humanist world of the West and East. As commonly practiced among early heretical groups, women were also encouraged to take on spiritual leadership in the assemblies. The Bogomils kept some elements of the Christian faith while rejecting its essence. The initiates would repeat the Lord's Prayer four times throughout the day and four times at night.[26]

The Paulicians also came from the East, first forming in Armenia in the 650s. Theirs was a recapitulation of the Marcionite heresy rejecting the Old Testament, the book of Matthew, and any other Scripture allowing for the preservation of God's moral law. Like Marcion, this group posited two gods—the god of this world (found in the Old Testament) and the supreme god of the New Testament. Determining the material world as evil, the sect would reject the incarnation of Christ and His atonement for sin on the cross.[27]

From these two sects came most of the aberrant cults and anarchical brands of heresy that plagued the West for at least five hundred years: the Cathari, the Albigenses, the Patarenes, the Benguines, and the Arnoldists. The first of the Manicheans appeared in Mainz, Germany in 1012. Persecutions began almost immediately, and the first thirteen adherents were burned at the stake in 1022. By 1195, some reports estimated the members of these aberrant cults at 4,000,000—at least 10% of the population of Europe.[28]

The spirit of lawlessness or antinomianism had come alive in Europe (2 Thess. 2:3, 7). Tyranny always seems to inspire more anarchy in its ranks. As man seeks to centralize power at the top, the marginalized individual will then seek illegitimate power for himself at the bottom. As tyrannical governments and powers trample over God's law and become a law to themselves, the same spirit of autonomy will infect individuals. Thus, the tyrant plays off the anarchist, and vice versa. With the rise of church tyranny, initiated upon the persecution of Gottschalk in AD 850, came the rise of the autonomist sects willing to oppose the Word of God at a different level. Thus, tyranny proliferated, and so did the anarchical elements. This is the pattern that continued during the period of the Inquisition until the Reformers entered the scene; and William Tyndale insisted that God's law must trump the pope's law, and Samuel Rutherford averred that God's law must trump the king's law.

TORTURE & INQUISITIONS

> These things have I spoken unto you, that ye should not be offended. They shall put you out of the synagogues: yea, the time cometh, that whosoever killeth you will think that he doeth God service. And these things will they do unto you, because they have not known the Father, nor me. (John 16:1-3)

The consolidation and corruption of power, as well as the intoxicating influence of temporal power upon church officials, would subject the church and all of Europe to a very dark, nightmarish evil. At root it was a doctrinal problem. The idea of the sovereignty of man and the sovereignty of the state played into the false notion that torture could save a man's soul. The road to hell is paved with good intentions, as the saying goes, and the Roman church was bound and determined to "save men's souls" by the force of tyranny. To that end, on May 15, 1252, Pope Innocent IV issued a bull allowing for the torture of heretics. Paragraph 26 of the *Ad extirpanda* reads:

> The head of state or ruler must force all the heretics whom he has in custody, provided he does so without killing them or breaking their arms or legs, as actual robbers and murderers of souls and thieves of the sacraments of God and Christian faith, to confess their errors and accuse other heretics whom they know, and specify their motives, and those whom they have seduced, and those who have lodged them and defended them, as thieves and robbers of material goods are made to accuse their accomplices and confess the crimes they have committed.[29]

A careful review of God's law would discover that there is no allowance for torture, forced confessions, or anything of the like. The corrupted papacy had become a seedbed of tyranny, rejecting Christian morality—Old and New Testament. Mostly, these churchmen were led to trust in the absolute and ultimate "sovereignty" of man's governments. One of the most instructive and important ironies in all Christian history is seen with Gottschalk of Orbais—the man who most defended the sovereignty of God, was the first to be subjected to torture at the hands of the sovereign god-wannabe state.

The god-state first seeks omniscience and thereby curtails all rights to privacy, turning the community into a network of spies and snitches. More regulations for the Inquisition came at the Synod of Toulouse in 1229, including a mandate that all men over fourteen years of age and women over twelve years of age be required to turn in all known heretics. Such edicts became the forerunners of the humanist, communist states of the 20th Century.

For three hundred years, heretics were burned at the stake, while others had their tongues and other parts of their anatomy torn out. The torture involved such exquisite, devilish devices and processes as the strappado, the rack, the toca waterboarding, the Brazen Bull, the Judas Cradle, Saint Elmo's Belt, Cat's Paw, Brodequins, Heretic's Fork, the Scold's Bridle, and the Drunkard's Cloak.

A spirit of vengeance plays out in the screeds against Catholicism through the ages, and the death count estimates from the inquisitions have sometimes reached the tens of millions. Truth told, the death counts were probably in the tens of thousands. While questions remain concerning the relative severity of these inquisitions from 1100 through 1600, the quantity of victims is not the primary concern. It is enough to say that "something wicked this way came," following the edicts of Innocents III and IV. After a thousand years of discipleship in the West, something shifted. A bad theology from Rheims in 850 produced a bad result. A man-centered theology introduced the tyrannical state, with its accompanying tortures and terrors.

Most Western European nations cooperated with the Inquisition.

Only England held out on the burning of heretics until 1401. All of this served to undermine the reputation of the Western church, the spiritual power of the church, and the influence of the church upon Western society to the present day.

INNOCENT III & THE ALBIGENSIAN CRUSADE

The blackest mark upon the medieval church came by the direct order of Innocent III. The Albigensian Crusade began with the siege of Beziers on July 9, 1209. Practically all of Europe had submitted to the pope's political control—except Raymond VI, count of Toulouse. A more tolerant ruler, Raymond VI pushed for exemptions from taxes for his people and tried to stave off persecution of the Cathari and Albigenses living in his territory. The pope was not at all happy with the Count and called for a crusade against the wayward sects. Raymond offered his apologies and himself submitted to flagellation at the hand of the pope's legate, but nothing could appease the wrath of Innocent III.

In the massacres that filled up the twenty years from 1209 to 1229, there was no meaningful distinction maintained between Catholic and Cathari. It was a political power move, more than anything else. Upon breaching the walls at the siege of Beziers, the pope's legate and self-styled military captain, Arnaud-Amalric, proceeded to massacre all the citizenry. His orders remain the most infamous and shameful in the annals of Christian history: "Kill them all. God will know His own." Writing to the pope, Arnaud reported: "Our men spared no one, irrespective of rank, sex, or age, and put to the sword almost 20,000 people."[30] Hundreds more were burned alive in Minerve, Lavaur, and Casses. Ten years later, the French army captured Marmande and proceeded to massacre 5,000 victims, including women and children. This slaughter was personally handled by Prince Louis, son of Philippe Auguste, king of France. Three attempts to take Toulouse were thwarted over the length of the extermination; however, at one point the defenders made clear they were faithful Christians. In their communication, the residents of Toulouse underscored their faith in Jesus Christ who, they said, "endured martyrdom in His flesh to save sinners..." Clearly distinguishing themselves from Manichean doctrine, the southern patriots confessed openly to their assailants: "We believe in the God who delivers us from evil, the God who made heaven and earth with its fruits and flowers, who created the sun and the moon for the beauty of the world, who made men and women and endowed them with souls."[31]

Despite Raymond's ingratiating appeals to the pope and council, nothing could persuade the ecclesiastical leaders to return his rightful lands to him. The entire Albigensian Crusade was a pretense, effectively an excuse for the king of France to secure control over the lands of Occitania (on the southwest corner of France). Finally, with the Treaty of Meaux, signed on April 12, 1229, King Louis IX of France received dominion over the entirety of the southern lands, with the agreement that Raymond's daughter be wed to Louis' brother. Ahab had finally secured full control over Naboth's vineyards. Make no mistake about it. These shenanigans were merely a continuation of the vision cast by King Louis' grandfather Philip to build an empire. Here was the opportunity to turn France from a small feudal state into the most prosperous and powerful country in Europe—which came about between 1180 and 1223. Historian Jacques Madaule summarizes the whole shameful affair as a "pretext covering totally unjustified ambitions...the struggle was primarily political" and not religious.[32] The tragic massacre of the Cathari came as collateral damage in a political power struggle involving Pope Innocent III and the rising French power. There was no real interest in defending biblical orthodoxy in these conflicts. Catholic bishops supported the crusade only to see the southern lords dispossessed and power turned over to the king of France. All along, Raymond VI would have much rather reconciled with the pope, but he failed at every attempt. What he eventually came to realize was that he could not reconcile with the church until he had first submitted himself to the king of France and surrendered southern independence. The Albigensian and Cathari crusade was only a ruse—an excuse for increasing the power of the northern kingdom of France by power politics and the pope's political maneuverings. It was the "inauguration" of the modern, powerful nation state.[33]

The pride of political position and that Gentile power principle had thoroughly infiltrated the papacy by 1215.

THE PAPACY HITS ROCK BOTTOM

Pope Boniface VIII (1294-1303) was even more involved in the political affairs of England, France, Sicily, and Italy. He was a flagrant fornicator, to the point of publicly excusing homosexual pedophilia. After excommunicating French leaders on political grounds, Boniface was captured by a French army, beaten, and released. He went insane and, as some traditional accounts relate it, he chewed on himself until he died.

The involvement of the papacy in the Holy Roman Empire and the French wars against the southern kingdom (and the extermination of the Cathari) backfired in the 14th Century. After popes Innocent III and Honorius III built up the power of the king of France, power shifted quickly from the papacy to the secular kings. Megalomaniacs do not submit well one to another, and the pope came out with the shorter end of the stick at the end of the power struggle. The period from AD 1309 to AD 1376 is referred to as the Avignon Babylonian Captivity of the Church. During this time, the popes ruled from Avignon, France under the auspices of the French power center instead of Rome. To further disgrace the entire Western church, political struggles ensued between rival popes for a forty year period (1376-1417), both claiming to be legitimate. The embarrassment of the "mother church" with its gross religious hypocrisies and insincerities was such that a line of social critics or satirists arose, including the likes of Francisco Petrarch (1304-1374). This opened the way for the humanist Renaissance and the first major Western apostasy. Petrarch referred to the Avignon papacy as "the sink of every vice, the haunt of all iniquities, a third Babylon, the Babylon of the West."[34] The curia gained a notorious reputation for its extravagance and sensuality—a mockery, a living satire of everything Christ wasn't.

The 15th Century marked the most severe decline in the history of the Christian church to that point, as the papacy and the institutional church degenerated to unprecedented levels of immorality, ignorance, and corruption. Rome had become a center of worldly power utterly unqualified to represent the true Christ. Far from innocent, Innocent VIII (elected 1484) admitted to fathering eight illegitimate children. Sixtus IV (elected 1471) was claimed as the father of six illegitimate children, including one by his own sister. Alexander VI (elected 1492) had at least nine illegitimate children, and he is known for organizing ecclesiastical events for the purpose of facilitating mass sexual sin. Although probably not referring to this particular historical situation, the Lord's reference to the "abomination of desolations" was very much applicable to the 15th Century Roman Church.

> And this gospel of the kingdom shall be preached in all the world for a witness unto all nations; and then shall the end come. When ye therefore shall see the abomination of desolation, spoken of by Daniel the prophet, stand in the holy place, (whoso readeth, let him understand:) (Matthew 24:14-15)

WITCHCRAFT—A SELF-FULFILLING PROPHECY

Then certain of the vagabond Jews, exorcists, took upon them to call over them which had evil spirits the name of the Lord Jesus, saying, We adjure you by Jesus whom Paul preacheth. And there were seven sons of one Sceva, a Jew, and chief of the priests, which did so. And the evil spirit answered and said, Jesus I know, and Paul I know; but who are ye? And the man in whom the evil spirit was leaped on them, and overcame them, and prevailed against them, so that they fled out of that house naked and wounded. (Acts 19:13-16)

Since the days when Patrick "drove the snakes out of Ireland" and the power of the gospel penetrated pagan Gentile nations of Europe, the West was more-or-less cleansed of Satanism, witchcraft, and human sacrifice. This was to change in the late Medieval Period. Although a few cases of witchcraft were reported in the 1200s, the papacy would obsess over Satanic activity during the spiritual decline of the next two centuries. Superstitious beliefs, over-reporting of Satan's works, and fear-mongering would play into the hands of the demonic powers—especially as the popes fueled the fires. Popes would espouse a "wild witch mania" to stir up the fires of the Inquisition. The more they talked about it, the more the business increased for the "Sons of Sceva Deliverance Ministries" and their inquisitors. It is impossible to know the degree to which the devil was influencing the obsessions and fear-mongering, and the degree to which he was inspiring true witches and the dark arts. Most likely, the devil was working both ends and sifting the nations like wheat, especially during the 15th Century. Thousands died at the hands of the inquisitors with this purposeless charade. Nothing short of a severe demonic incursion into the highest echelons of the Roman church could have brought about the fear, confusion, torment, and tyranny of this period in Western history.

The burgomaster of Bamberg serves as one example of a poor soul forced to confess sins of witchcraft under torture by the inquisitors. Before his death, Johannes Junius wrote a letter to his daughter:

> Many hundred good nights, dearly beloved daughter, Veronica. Innocent have I come into prison, innocent must I die. For whoever comes into a witch prison must become a witch or be tortured till he invents something out of his head and—God pity him—bethinks himself of something. I will tell you how it has gone with me...Then came the executioner and put the thumbscrews on me, both hands bound together, so that the blood ran out at the nails and everywhere, so that for four weeks I could not use my hands, as you can see from the writing...Then they stripped me, bound my hands behind my back and drew me up. I thought heaven and earth were at an end. Eight times did they do this and let me drop again so that I suffered terrible agony...[After rehearsing the mock confessions, he continues:] Now, dear child, you have all my confessions for which I must die. They are sheer lies made up. All this I was forced to say through fear of the rack, for they never leave off the torture till one confesses something...Dear child, keep this letter secret so that people may not find it or else I shall be tortured most piteously and the jailers be beheaded...I have taken several days to write this for my hands are both lame. Good night, for your father, Johannes Junius will never see you more.[35]

DOCTRINAL NOVELTIES

Ye shall not add unto the word which I command you, neither shall ye diminish ought from it, that ye may keep the commandments of the Lord your God which I command you. Your eyes have seen what the Lord did because of Baalpeor: for all the men that followed Baalpeor, the Lord thy God hath destroyed them from among you. But ye that did cleave unto the Lord your God are alive every one of you this day. (Deuteronomy 4:2-4)

As is often the case, the corruption of fleshly pride precipitated more theological degeneration in the church. Cultic Mary worship took to the mainstream in the 11th and 12th centuries. Thomas Aquinas had affirmed the doctrine of the Immaculate Conception of Mary in his commentary on *The Sentences*. Besides making room for a humanist epistemology, Thomas institutionalized the doctrine of condign merit—the fallacy that catalyzed the Protestant Reformation of the 16th Century. This new soteriological theory proposed that God binds himself to reward a person with salvation for a minimal work accomplished, only because of His own promise to that effect. The catch in the deal, however, was that nobody could quantify the "minimal work," and such systems would be employed by the church to tyrannize the souls of men for centuries. The reformers saw condign merit as a contradiction of plain Scriptures like Romans 11:6, "And if by grace, then it is no longer of works; otherwise grace is no longer grace. But if it is of works, it is no longer grace; otherwise work is no longer work."

The doctrine of the Treasury of Merit came in 1230, logically followed up by the sale of indulgences—enthusiastically promoted by an increasingly avaricious papacy. By this time, the Church was well into a moral and theological decline which would continue for three hundred years.

Speculation on the intermediate state after death lent some credence to the idea of purgatory in the Western Church, as early as Augustine. He had written that "temporary punishments are suffered by some in this life only, by others after death...before that last and strictest judgment."[36] However, it was left to the 12th and 13th centuries to codify these speculations in a complex extra-biblical scheme involving the treasury of merit, purgatory, and indulgences. Finally, the Council of Florence in 1439 formulated this aberrant teaching in detail.

SCRIPTURE BANNED

Hear, O Israel: The LORD our God is one LORD: and thou shalt love the LORD thy God with all thine heart, and with all thy soul, and with all thy might. And these words, which I command thee this day, shall be in thine heart: and thou shalt teach them diligently unto thy children, and shalt talk of them when thou sittest in thine house, and when thou walkest by the way, and when thou liest down, and when thou risest up. And thou shalt bind them for a sign upon thine hand, and they shall be as frontlets between thine eyes. And thou shalt write them upon the posts of thy house, and on thy gates. (Deuteronomy 6:4-9)

From the moment that the first divine communication was taken down in written form by Moses (around 1400 BC), the Word of God was to be immediately accessible to every home among the people of God. Over and over again in the ministry of Christ, He rebukes the Pharisees for their failure to know Scripture, and their tendency to displace God's law with their own traditions (Matt. 15:1-8, Matt. 19:4, Luke 10:26, etc.). The expectation was that all God's people would know the Bible.

The final coup de grace for the medieval Church came with the banning of the Scriptures for popular consumption, the refusal on the part of the church to make the Bible accessible in the common languages. Translations of Scripture into the languages of the common people was clearly permitted, especially during the frontier mission age of the Church. The Venerable Bede translated the Gospel of John into old English (AD 735), and Ælfric of Eynsham (955-1010) translated the Gospels into the West Saxon (Wessex) dialect around AD 990.

Pope John VIII had reluctantly allowed for the translation of the Bible into the Cyrillic language by Cyril and Methodius (c. 870). But this was no longer tolerated by the time of Gregory VII in 1079 when the Duke of Bohemia requested that his people receive the liturgy in the common tongue. Gregory's terse and condescending response spoke volumes:

> We cannot in any way grant this petition...It is evident to those who consider the matter carefully that it pleased God to make Holy Scripture obscure in certain places lest, if it were perfectly clear to all, it might be vulgarized and subjected to disrespect or be so misunderstood by people of limited intelligence as to lead them into error...We forbid this practice and command you to oppose this foolish rashness by every possible means.[37]

Henceforth, God's Word would be shut out from the peoples of Europe. The Bible ban came to northeastern Spain in AD 1234 when King James I of Aragon disallowed the Scriptures in the common tongue. The lack of scriptural literacy resulted in the retrograde of faith, the failure to disciple the man of God in every good work, and the loss of Christian culture. For the next three hundred years, the authentic faith would be relegated into the nooks and crannies of Christian Europe. Yet still, God was not finished with His work in the Western world.

> Thus saith the LORD of hosts, Hearken not unto the words of the prophets that prophesy unto you: they make you vain: they speak a vision of their own heart, and not out of the mouth of the LORD. (Jeremiah 23:16)

V

THE REFORMATION
OF THE WESTERN CHURCH

Repent ye therefore, and be converted, that your sins may be blotted out, when the times of refreshing shall come from the presence of the Lord. And he shall send Jesus Christ, which before was preached unto you: Whom the heaven must receive until the times of restitution of all things, which God hath spoken by the mouth of all his holy prophets since the world began. (Acts 3:19-21)

As He promised in the Gospels, the Lord will never abandon His church, or allow the Great Commission to fail. When the Western church was at its very lowest point, following the Avignon Babylonian Captivity and the moral catastrophe attending the curia of the 15th Century, God brought a powerful Reformation. This "Protestant" movement was to have a worldwide effect, providing for an effective continuance of the Lord's commission to disciple the nations.

After the Reformation, Protestantism spread to Asia and Africa, collecting some 432 million self-professing adherents by 2011. That compares to a count of 308 million professing Roman Catholics on the same continents. The missionary zeal of the Protestants was crucial to the extension of the Christian faith in these far-off regions. Meanwhile, Western nations were still home to 800 million Roman Catholics, but only 368 million Protestants.[1] Thus, the major effect of Protestantism was seen as missionaries took the gospel message to "the uttermost parts of the earth." In God's providence, the major contribution of the Reformation would be lost to Europe, but rediscovered in a worldwide diaspora. Where the Roman Church failed, Protestants would pick up the slack in missions. All the while, the purposes of the Lord in the increase of His kingdom to every tribe and nation could not be thwarted.

> The people that walked in darkness have seen a great light: they that dwell in the land of the shadow of death, upon them hath the light shined. Thou hast multiplied the nation, and increased the joy: they joy before thee according to the joy in harvest, and as men rejoice when they divide the spoil...For unto us a child is born, unto us a son is given: and the government shall be upon his shoulder: and his name shall be called Wonderful, Counsellor, The mighty God, The everlasting Father, The Prince of Peace. Of the increase of his government and peace there shall be no end, upon the throne of David, and upon his kingdom, to order it, and to establish it with judgment and with justice from henceforth even for ever. The zeal of the LORD of hosts will perform this. (Isaiah 9:1-2, 6-7)

A FLOURISHING REMNANT

I say then, Hath God cast away his people? God forbid. For I also am an Israelite, of the seed of Abraham, of the tribe of Benjamin. God hath not cast away his people which he foreknew. Wot ye not what the scripture saith of Elias? how he maketh intercession to God against Israel saying, Lord, they have killed thy prophets, and digged down thine altars; and I am left alone, and they seek my life. But what saith the answer of God unto him? I have reserved to myself seven thousand men, who have not bowed the knee to the image of Baal. Even so then at this present time also there is a remnant according to the election of grace. (Romans 11:1-5)

The tale of the Western Church was not all bad news following the Fourth Lateran Council. Faithful, humble pastors were still leading their flocks here and there throughout the rising nation states of Europe. Not all dissidents were of the Manichean sort. Peter de Bruys and Henry of Lausanne appear in history as the world's first Baptists, in the modern sense of the term. Peter was burned to death in AD 1105. From the scant evidence available, it appears these preachers rejected transubstantiation, infant baptism, the mass, prayers for the dead, and all music in worship.

Peter and Henry's followers disappeared, but the Lord would use another evangelical preacher by the name of Peter Waldo to sustain the faith through the dark centuries from the 1200s through the 1500s. Waldo was a wealthy cloth merchant from Lyons, France. Converted around 1170, he went on to preach in the highways and byways throughout southern France and Switzerland. One of his first accomplishments was a translation of the Gospels, certain other portions of Scripture, and important writings of the church fathers into the vernacular. Over time, the entire New Testament, Psalms, Proverbs, Song of Solomon, and Ecclesiastes were translated into the Provençal dialect of southern France. The entire Scriptures were finally translated into the French language by a Waldensian cousin of John Calvin, named Pierre Olivetan—published in 1535. Calvin provided the preface for the translation, but only after Olivetan had convinced him of the reformed faith.

Waldo's followers were mockingly referred to as the *Humiliati*, and several of their leading brethren showed up at the Third Lateran Council in 1179. They were laughed out of the council for their apparent poverty and ignorance. Although their intent was to remain in communion with the Roman Church, they were forthwith expelled and went on to establish independent churches throughout Europe. Waldo taught that the Scriptures were ultimately authoritative in matters of faith and life. As witnessed by the Dominican Inquisitor Stephanus de Borbone at Lyons (c. 1225), "[Peter's] one desire was to have a fuller knowledge of Holy Scripture than he could obtain from hearing the lessons read in church, and to regulate his life by the example and precepts of Christ and His Apostles."[2] Both faith and the fear of God were foundational emphases, as witnessed in an early letter authored by a Waldensee elder: "Dear brethren, the divine sacraments are not so properly matters of investigation, as of faith, and not only of faith, but also of fear, for no one can receive the discipline of faith, unless we have for a foundation, the fear of the Lord."[3]

Almost every modern separatist sect in the Christian church through the ages has attempted to fashion Waldo's beliefs according to their own preferential doctrines. In such cases, the honest historian will rely entirely upon original writings for a true account of these peoples. The earliest confession of the Waldenses (dated around AD 1200), clearly accepted the doctrine of the Trinity. The people were instructed to fear God and love God above all else. The confession pointed out that Christ "renewed" the Old Testament law that it may be better kept, referring to Matthew 5, sidestepping the Marcion heresy.[4] The document further enjoined "watching and reading" the Scriptures to know the teaching of Christ. Their main complaint with the pastors in the Roman church was that they "persecute and kill those who are better than themselves…they love not the sheep except for their fleeces."[5]

The document further condemned the church for the cheap end-of-life auricular confessions and the last minute absolutions provided upon donations made to the church. Those who trusted in these arrangements, they said, would not be saved, for they had never repented. And besides this, only God has the power to forgive sin. The simple confession of faith ended with these summary statements:

> [Pastors] should preach to the people, and pray with them; Feed them often with divine doctrine, And punish sinners with discipline, and admonish them to repent. And chiefly, that they should confess their sins to God without reserve;
>
> And repent in this life; fast, give alms, and pray with a fervent heart;— For by these things the soul finds salvation.
>
> Wherefore we Christians who have sinned, and forsaken the commands of Jesus Christ, because we have no fear, faith, or love, We should acknowledge our sins without delay; We should weep tears of penitence for the offences we have committed, particularly for these three mortal sins, the lust of the flesh,—the lust of the eye,—and the pride of life; by which we have done evil.
>
> We must keep in this way, if we will love and follow Jesus Christ: We must be poor in spirit and heart: Love chastity, and serve God humbly. Then we follow the way of Jesus Christ, and thus overcome our enemies.[6]

Emulating Innocent III in his passion to exterminate heresy 300 years earlier, Pope Innocent VIII initiated a crusade against the Waldensians in AD 1487. Three thousand of these faithful Christians were killed by fire in a cave in the French Alps, and in 1545 some twenty-two villages were burned to the ground in southern France.

THE BRETHREN OF THE COMMON LIFE

> Abide in me, and I in you. As the branch cannot bear fruit of itself, except it abide in the vine; no more can ye, except ye abide in me. I am the vine, ye are the branches: He that abideth in me, and I in him, the same bringeth forth much fruit: for without me ye can do nothing...

As the Father hath loved me, so have I loved you: continue ye in my love. If ye keep my commandments, ye shall abide in my love; even as I have kept my Father's commandments, and abide in his love. (John 15:4-5, 9-10)

The dry academic scholasticism and lifeless, dialectical theology produced by the university and seminary men of the 13th and 14th centuries met a spiritual reaction from a reforming movement, preferring a more experiential, practical, and relational faith. The Christian faith involves both truth and relationships, both loving God and keeping His commandments. Over-stress on doctrine and over-infatuation with legal casuistry can fail to ascertain the "spirit of the law," and end with the abandonment of the other half of the faith— love, prayer, hymn-singing, discipleship, obedience, care for the poor, walking by faith, experiencing joy in suffering, Holy Spirit filling, and a recognition of God's mighty works. Right doctrine and authentic spiritual life are both necessary to the Christian experience, and every Christian sect risks losing one or the other along the way.

The 14th and 15th centuries were not "all bad." It was during these years God raised up the Dutch and German spiritual experimentalists, who helped to prepare the way for the German Reformation of the 16th Century. Initially, Geert Groote (1340-1384) formed a pre-Reformation discipleship center called "The Brethren of the Common Life" in Zwolle, Netherlands. He influenced Thomas à Kempis, author of the classic work, *Imitation of Christ*, as well as Martin Luther, John Calvin, and Martin Bucer.[7]

JOHN WYCLIFF (1324-1384)

And what more shall I say? For the time would fail me to tell of Gideon and Barak and Samson and Jephthah, also of David and Samuel and the prophets: who through faith subdued kingdoms, worked righteousness, obtained promises, stopped the mouths of lions, quenched the violence of fire, escaped the edge of the sword, out of weakness were made strong, became valiant in battle, turned to flight the armies of the aliens... Still others had trial of mockings and scourgings, yes, and of chains and imprisonment. They were stoned, they were sawn in two, were tempted, were slain with the sword. They wandered about in sheepskins and goatskins, being destitute, afflicted, tormented—of whom the world was not worthy. They wandered in deserts and mountains, in dens and caves of the earth. . . (Hebrews 11:32-38 NKJV)

From the days of the Magna Carta (AD 1215), the English spirit had soured towards the Roman pope and his attempts to control the politics of their nation. To make matters worse, King John had obligated the English to an ecclesiastical tax levied by the pope who was at that time under the oversight of the French crown. John Wycliff first appeared on the geopolitical scene in 1374 as a member of the commission seeking a peace treaty with France and a relaxation of papal control over the nation. Evidently, something about his interactions with the curia in Bruges must have boiled his blood because Wycliff returned with a condemnation of the bishop of Rome, whom he referred to as "the anti-Christ, the proud, worldly, priest of Rome, and the most cursed of clippers and cut-purses."[8] He wasn't the only Englishman of this opinion. About the same time, *Piers Plowman* took up the same banner, calling the pope "the anti-Christ, that treacherous fiend, reigning over all the people." If any king dared to favor "mild and holy men," the followers of anti-Christ and his "clerics" would curse him, the Plowman helpfully pointed out.[9]

By 1377, Wycliff was the subject of rebuke in some five bulls issued by Pope Gregory XI, who called on the English archbishop to imprison the proto-reformer. The University of Oxford stepped in to defend their professor, and mercifully Gregory died weeks later and the Avignon papacy collapsed. This allowed breathing room for the reforming agenda under the stifling, inquisitional conditions predominating throughout the continent.

John Wycliff spoke and wrote with forthright vigor and crystal clarity. His political opposition to the tyranny of the pope appealed strongly to ordinary persons and segments of the English monarchy and nobility. He was refreshingly biblical, theologically true, and eminently practical in ministry. He preached. He discipled. His followers discipled others.

However, Wycliff's political connections in the university and the monarchy quickly dissolved when he took issue with the doctrine of transubstantiation. After all, since the Fourth Lateran Council of 1215, the doctrine had become the very cornerstone of Roman theology, and every cleric had been taught to defend it to the death. Only one major theological leader in 350 years dared to take a stand against it—alone. Here again was another Athanasius, *contra mundum*—standing by himself against the whole world. The archbishop of Canterbury called a synod in 1382, condemning Wycliff in twenty-four articles. At issue were Wycliff's position on transubstantiation, his call for a national church independent of Rome, and his rejection of the requirement of an oral confession before dying. The King of England stood by the archbishop's condemnation, and many of Wycliff's followers recanted. Wycliff continued with his translation of the Scriptures and a steady stream of pamphleteering. Two years before he died, he was cited to appear before the pope. He refused, but sent the Roman bishop a letter in which he laid bare the root of the corruption in the Church from the Donation of Constantine. "Renounce all right to worldly authority over kings and princes," Wycliff wrote. The reformer described the Donation as "the beginning of all evils" for the Western church.[10]

Thirty years after Wycliff's death, the Council of Constance of 1415 declared "John Wycliff a notorious heretic, and excommunicat[ed] him and condemn[ed] his memory as one who died an obstinate heretic."[11] His body was exhumed and burned. As one historian put it, "They burnt his bones to ashes and cast them into Swift, a neighboring brook running hard by. Thus this brook hath conveyed his ashes into Avon, Avon into Severn, Severn into the narrow seas, they into the main ocean. And thus the ashes of Wicliffe are the emblem of his doctrine, which now is dispersed the world over."[12]

Like Peter Waldo, John Wycliff also saw the fundamental need for the Scriptures to be made available in the common tongue. At the heart of his work stood his writing, *Truth of Scripture*, a 1,000-page defense of the value and authority of the enscripturated Word of God. While the Aristotelian (man-based) logic taught at Oxford and other universities was flawed, only the Scripture could be the standard and measure of all good logic as well as philosophy and ethics.[13] Though Wycliff had never learned Hebrew or Greek, his English translation was made from the Latin Vulgate. It was hand copied hundreds of times, giving Christians in England and Scotland access to the Word of God for 150 years. Owning a Wycliff translation warranted the death penalty in 15th Century England. Nonetheless, 250 copies of Wycliff Bible may still be found in museums and libraries around the world. Wycliff's followers, known as the Lollards, continued to minister across England. Some recanted, while others were burnt alive for their faith.

THE REFORMATION IN MORAVIA—JAN HUS

From the early days when the faith first took root in Bohemia, the people had the Bible in their own language—first translated by Cyril and Methodius in the 870s. According to the purposes of divine providence, the Reformation on the continent found its roots in the same soil. The Protestant Reformation on the continent began with the preaching of the Word of God in the common language in Prague, Bohemia.

Born in AD 1369, pre-reformer Jan Hus would refer to himself as "the Goose," after his last name. Jan attended the University of Prague (established in 1347), and he graduated with a bachelor in divinity in 1393. He was invited to teach at the university in 1398. In 1402, he began preaching at the Chapel of the Holy Innocents of Bethlehem. Two wealthy church members had built the church eleven years earlier on the condition that the Word of God be preached there in the Bohemian language each Lord's Day and on special festival days. Such expectations were part of the Bohemian faith since the days of Cyril and Methodius.

By this time, Hus was already well recognized as the main advocate of Wycliff's views at the university. He opposed the Crusades, especially papal fundraising for the wars by way of the sale of indulgences. He took issue with the Catholic system of penance and taught that remission of sins comes instead through repentance. And he agreed with Wycliff in rejecting the doctrine of transubstantiation.

In 1409, Pope Alexander V issued a bull excommunicating the preacher, but no one paid much attention to it, mostly because of the papal schism. Alexander came up with the short end of the stick in the conflict, and he was declared the antipope in 1410. Hus responded to the excommunication by burning the papal order. He continued preaching, pointing out that Christ Himself had been excommunicated by the religious authorities of His day. However, these were not safe times for reformers. Piece by piece, the whole world turned against him—the university, the priests, and the archbishop, although the people remained enthusiastic in their reception of his preaching. After he was removed from the pulpit in Prague, Hus moved to the countryside and continued preaching in the fields and woodlands.

In the fall of 1414, Hus was invited to the Council of Constance in southern Germany. He was offered safe conduct by German emperor Sigismund, who later reneged on his promise. Arrested and held in prison for nine months, Hus was sentenced to be burned at the stake. The Council disagreed with Hus when he said that the church is made up of the totality of the elect. They were especially upset with his view that popes who were guilty of sexual sin, simony, and murder should not possess any spiritual authority over the people.

On July 6, 1415, Hus was taken to the place of execution, professing to his friends that, "I shall die with joy today in the faith of the gospel which I have preached." As the flames arose, he sang out with a strong voice, "Christ, thou Son of the living God, have mercy upon me."

> And you will be hated by all for My name's sake. But he who endures to the end shall be saved. (Mark 13:13)

After Jan Hus' death, someone penned a prophetic statement, pointing toward another day and another reformer: "Today you roast a goose—Hus—but a hundred years from now a swan will arise out of my ashes which you shall not roast." Clearly, Jan Hus was the stimulus behind the German Reformation a century later. Before he was converted, Martin Luther came upon Hus' sermons in a chapel library, later remarking, "I was overwhelmed with astonishment. I could not understand for what cause they had burnt so great a man, who explained the Scriptures with so much gravity and skill."[14]

Three groups emerged out of the Bohemian Reformation, though only one survived: the Moravian Brethren. After three hundred years of persecution in their native land, God would use the Moravians to spawn the missionary movement of the 18th Century. The Moravian Brethren were also very much to be credited for their influence upon John Wesley, George Whitefield, and the Great Awakening in England and America. Thus, in God's providential order of events, Jan Hus would become the seminal stimulus behind all three major works of God in the last half millennium: the Protestant Reformation, the modern Protestant missionary movement, and the 18th Century Great Awakening in the West.

During these years, the consistent ill-treatment of the Hussites

(Moravian Brethren), the Waldensians, and the Lollards by the Roman Church was further indication of the moral degradation, the spiritual blindness, and a dominant demonic force controlling and characterizing the institutionalized Western church.

THE PROTESTANT REFORMATION

Return, we beseech thee, O God of hosts: look down from heaven, and behold, and visit this vine; And the vineyard which thy right hand hath planted, and the branch that thou madest strong for thyself. It is burned with fire, it is cut down: they perish at the rebuke of thy countenance. Let thy hand be upon the man of thy right hand, upon the son of man whom thou madest strong for thyself. So will not we go back from thee: quicken us, and we will call upon thy name. Turn us again, O Lord God of hosts, cause thy face to shine; and we shall be saved. (Psalm 80:14-19)

Martin Luther's family hailed from Thuringia, the ancient land first visited by Culdean missionaries, where Killian and Colman had ministered 800 years earlier. However, the reformer was born on November 10, 1483 in Eisleben in eastern Germany. His parents were hard-working peasants, and, (as in the case of most children raised up a Christian civilization), Luther memorized the Apostles Creed, the Lord's Prayer, and the Ten Commandments as a youth. At eighteen years of age, Luther attended the University of Erfurt, where he studied the new humanist philosophies, logic, and rhetoric. It was at the college library, however, that he found his first copy of the Latin Bible and began to meditate on the Scriptures. He received his bachelors and masters degrees in 1505 and at the age of twenty-one joined the Augustinian monastery in the university town of Erfurt. There he was discipled by John von Staupitz, who "first caused the light of the gospel to shine in the darkness of Luther's heart."[15]

There was no more enthusiastic monk than Martin Luther. But, no matter how hard he worked, he could find no peace of heart and mind. Two years after entering the monastery, he was ordained a priest with the intent of serving as pastor in a local congregation. However, before he graduated from Erfurt University, Frederick III (Frederick the Wise), prince of Saxony, moved him to the recently established university in Wittenberg. After spending a year teaching at the college (1508), Luther traveled to Rome, where he witnessed firsthand the theological and moral bankruptcy of a church badly in need of reformation.

Upon his return to Wittenberg in 1511, Luther began to teach the Scriptures in earnest, first expositing the book of Psalms. Then in October 1516, the young reformer started a study through the book of Galatians with his students, at which time he began to define and defend the doctrine of justification by faith alone apart from works.

Meanwhile, the pope was making plans to rebuild Saint Peter's Basilica in Rome, funding the project with the sale of indulgences. These charitable offerings, as it was explained, were supposed to reduce purgatorial punishment in the afterlife for purchasers and their relatives. In 1515, the German archbishop of Mainz sent a Dominican monk named Johann Tetzel into Saxony to raise money for Pope Leo X's project. Frederick the Wise objected to the sale, so Tetzel set up shop just outside of the district. Incensed by the greed, the pomposity of the church, the extortion of the poor, and the wrong theological basis for these sales, Martin Luther issued his 95 theses, posting them at noon on October 31, 1517 on the door of the Wittenberg Castle Church. Luther's first point drilled into the heart of the matter relating to penance and contrition: these indulgences represented a highly superficial and pretended demonstration of repentance—nothing from the heart. Luther's first thesis then, reads: "Our Lord and Master Jesus Christ in saying: 'Repent ye' intended that the whole life of believers should be penitence."

Such was the beginning of the Protestant Reformation. It was an attempt to revive genuine faith, genuine repentance, a genuine gospel, a genuine Christian worldview, and a genuine Christian life.

Most importantly, the Word of God was made available everywhere in the language of the people. Luther translated the Bible into German. William Tyndale introduced a very competent English translation before he was burned at the stake near Brussels in 1536. Miles Coverdale successfully completed the work Tyndale began and issued his first printing of the entire Bible in 1535.

When a cleric told him he would rather have the laws of the pope than the law of God, Tyndale told him: "I defie the Pope and all his lawes. If God spare my life, ere many yeares I will cause a boy that driveth the plough to know more of the Scripture, than thou dost."[16]

The Reformation only took hold in Northern and Western Europe. Southern Europe remained Roman Catholic while Eastern Europe remained mostly Eastern Orthodox. Whether the Counter-Reformation or other small revivals ever transformed the Catholic and Orthodox churches is open for debate. A careful look at the moral indexes, the Corruption Perception Index, birth rates, abortion rates, influence of homosexuality, etc., still put the Protestant nations well ahead of most Catholic nations in later centuries.

The ironclad hold the pope maintained over the civil governments of Europe melted away quickly during and after the years of the Avignon exile. The humanist quest for godlike powers among the rising empires would quickly shift from pope to prince to the people (by the 19th Century). As secular power shifted, the attendant corruptions of the papacy lessened from the 16th through the 19th Century.

Nonetheless, the spiritual decline of the Protestant Church was more precipitous than the decline experienced in the Church of Rome during the medieval period. There were only 150 years between the "Wittenberg Door" and the Great Ejection of 1662. There were only 180 years between the "Wittenberg Door" and the Latitudinarian victory at that great American Protestant institution—Harvard College. Protestantism did not long survive as a dominant force before the humanism of the Renaissance and the Enlightenment took over.

Although the Bible was made available and mass-produced for nations around the world, so were 1,000,000 other books with a man-centered, humanist philosophy undergirding them. Diversions soon drowned out the influence of the Bible in the schools, universities, libraries, homes, and even the churches in the West.

THE REFORMING AGENDA

O the depth of the riches both of the wisdom and knowledge of God! how unsearchable are his judgments, and his ways past finding out! For who hath known the mind of the Lord? or who hath been his counsellor? Or who hath first given to him, and it shall be recompensed unto him again? For of him, and through him, and to him, are all things: to whom be glory for ever. Amen. (Romans 11:33-36)

Beyond any doubt, the Reformation left an indelible mark on Western nations—and the whole world. Cultures were impacted for centuries because of these men and their reforming agenda. Luther mainly impacted Germany and Scandinavia. But Calvin placed a long and lasting mark upon Switzerland, the Netherlands, England, Scotland, and America by his influence on John Knox, the Puritans and Pilgrims, the Dutch Reformed, and the French Huguenots. France later expelled most of its Reformed Christians by relentless persecutions and so received little of the Reformation heritage.

Though much has been said of Reformation ideology, it is best to let the reformers themselves speak to the true nature of their reforming agenda rather than leave it to the Monday morning quarterbacks and commentators who came later. Much of the reformation agenda was practical in nature, involving church worship and function. Yet, in his book *Of the Bondage of the Will*, Martin Luther confessed that the question of God's sovereignty versus the will of man was indeed "the grand turning point" of the cause. In his exchange with Erasmus, Luther wrote, "You, and you alone saw, what was the grand hinge upon which the whole turned."[17] Erasmus had rejected the idea that God was sovereign over the free actions of men, stating that "God's decree must turn according to man's decision."[18] Luther, however, held nothing back in his commitment to the doctrine of the sovereignty of God. He unleashed the "thunderbolt," as he calls it, when he wrote: "This, therefore, is also essentially necessary and wholesome for Christians to know: That God foreknows nothing by contingency, but that He foresees, purposes, and does all things according to His immutable, eternal, and infallible will."[19] Luther also maintained God as first cause in man's salvation: "But a man cannot be thoroughly humbled, until he comes to know that his salvation is utterly beyond his own powers, counsel, endeavours, will, and works, and absolutely depending on the will, counsel, pleasure, and work of another, that is, of God only."[20] Thus, Luther took his place in line after Augustine, Gottschalk, and Anselm, holding steadfastly to the doctrine of God's absolute sovereignty over all.

Martin Luther laid out a more specific reforming agenda in his *Letter to the Christian Nobility of the German Nation* issued in 1520. Agreeing with Wycliff, he pressed for the church to get out of the business of usurping jurisdiction over "temporal powers." He also argued against the pope's right to monopolize all reading and interpretation of Scripture.[21] To this, Luther added the great need for a reformation of education in the schools and universities. Especially problematic, he noted, was the advocacy of the teachings of Aristotle. In Article 25 of his reforming agenda, this reformer struck at the heart of what would destroy Protestantism over the next 500 years:

> The universities need a sound and thorough reformation. I must
> say so no matter who takes offence. Everything that the papacy has

instituted or ordered is directed solely towards the multiplication of sin and error. Loose living is practiced there; little is taught of the Holy Scriptures or the Christian faith; the blind pagan teacher, Aristotle, is of more consequence than Christ. Yet this defunct pagan has attained supremacy; impeded, and almost suppressed, the Scriptures of the living God. When I think of this lamentable state of affairs, I cannot avoid believing that the Evil One introduced the study of Aristotle, that dead, blind, accursed, proud, knavish heathen teacher…His book on Ethics is worse than any other book, being the direct opposite of God's grace, and the Christian virtues; yet it is accounted among the best of his works…

Nothing is more devilish than an unreformed university…The number of books on theology must also be reduced, only the best being retained. For neither many books nor much reading make a man learned; but a good book, often read, no matter how short, will give Scriptural scholarship plus religious-mindedness. Even the writings of any one of the holy Fathers or, indeed, all of them, should only be read for a while, and in order that they might lead us to the Bible. Today, however, we read them alone, and get no further; we never enter on the Bible. Thus we are like those who look at the sign-posts, but never set out on the journey. The intention of the early Fathers in their writing was to introduce us to the Bible; but we use them only to find a way of avoiding it. Nevertheless, the Bible is our vineyard, and there we should all labour and toil. Above all, the most important and most usual teaching, in both the universities and the lower schools, ought to be concerned with the Holy Scriptures; beginning with the gospels for the young boys. Would it not be reasonable for every Christian person on reaching his ninth or tenth year to know the holy gospel in its entirety, since his name and standing as a Christian are based on it?[22]

In his tract *The Babylonian Captivity of the Church*, released in October 1520, Luther stated his opposition to Rome's codification of transubstantiation. Yet his most succinct presentation of Christian doctrine against the obfuscations and deceptions of an unreformed church came with *Christian Freedom*, his last letter to the pope, issued in the same month. Here, Luther presents an elegant knitting together of faith and love in the life of the Christian, carefully avoiding the bondage of works and merit as well as a spiritually powerless license. He explains that, by faith, the Christian receives maximum freedom from guilt and the power of sin in his life. The Christian enjoys liberty *in* Christ, not liberty *from* Christ and His law. By faith, he is subject to none. And by love he is made the servant of all.

John Calvin defended the Reformation in the form of a personal confession of faith produced in response to the accusations of Jacopo Sadoleto (1477-1547), a bishop from Carpentras (located in southeastern France). Calvin claimed that the Roman Church didn't really care about the Scriptures; but instead, "they only drove people to and fro with strange doctrines, and deluded them with I know not what follies."[23] Calvin noted also that the religious authorities "were not at all instructed of righteousness by Thy law, [but also] they had fabricated for themselves many useless frivolities, as a means of procuring Thy favor."[24] Although Calvin said he always professed the Christian faith from childhood, what he had been taught could never "pave the way for me to a sure hope of salvation, nor train me aright for the duties of the Christian life."[25] Thus, the church had failed on two accounts—in the matter of faith and obedience, as well as in the presentation of both the grace of God and the law of God to the people.

In his work *The Necessity of Reforming the Church*, issued to Holy Roman Emperor Charles V prior to the Diet of 1544, John Calvin explained more of the reforming agenda as he saw it. Among Calvin's chief concerns was the church's abandonment of a biblical view of worship as submitted to the law of God. Calvin complained that "the whole form of divine worship in general use in the present day is nothing but mere corruption."[26] Human autonomy and rebellion was especially palpable in this abandonment of biblical worship. Secondly, Calvin pointed to the doctrine of justification by faith alone as absolutely necessary for the integrity of the church. Indeed, because of a works-based salvation, the church had come to "the very brink of destruction."[27] Getting to the very heart of a biblical view of the salvation and life of the Christian, Calvin wrote:

> ...by convincing man of his poverty and powerlessness, we train him more effectually to true humility, leading him to renounce all self-confidence, and throw himself entirely upon God; and that, in like manner, we train him more effectually to gratitude, by leading him to ascribe, as in truth he ought, every good thing which he possesses to the kindness of God.[28]

In the vein of Peter Waldo, Wycliff, Hus, and Luther, Calvin also pointed to the abuse of the mysteries of the sacrament by an overly-systematized doctrine of transubstantiation. Finally, Calvin was concerned with the terrible bondage and the diminishment of Christian liberty resulting from the doctrine, the tyrannical ecclesiastical controls, and the system of church government which had developed over the centuries. As well, he was concerned with the failure of pastors to preach the Word and exemplify and teach biblical holiness in the church. In a nutshell, Calvin was concerned with a failure to teach justification by faith alone and a failure to exhort people to true holiness according to God's standards, not according to the laws of men. This was the true Reformation agenda in the 16th Century, as well as for all future reformations in the Western Church.

THE BATTLE FOR THE FAITH IN ENGLAND

> And unto the angel of the church in Sardis write; These things saith he that hath the seven Spirits of God, and the seven stars; I know thy works, that thou hast a name that thou livest, and art dead. Be

watchful, and strengthen the things which remain, that are ready to die: for I have not found thy works perfect before God. Remember therefore how thou hast received and heard, and hold fast, and repent. If therefore thou shalt not watch, I will come on thee as a thief, and thou shalt not know what hour I will come upon thee. Thou hast a few names even in Sardis which have not defiled their garments; and they shall walk with me in white: for they are worthy. He that overcometh, the same shall be clothed in white raiment; and I will not blot out his name out of the book of life, but I will confess his name before my Father, and before his angels. (Revelation 3:1-5)

England's Reformation occurred in fits and starts, largely because of the politicization of the church from the 11th Century onwards. King Henry VIII (1491-1547) was determined to secure complete state control over the church, a move which would prove to be a detriment to any attempts for further reformation through the centuries following. His son Edward VI was a Protestant and made a little ground with the Reformation. But he ruled for only six years, dying at a tender fifteen years of age. Following Edward came Bloody Mary and Elizabeth I.

The Puritan and Separatist movements formed during Elizabeth's reign, seeking a more complete reformation of the church in England. Whereas the Puritans set about to purify the established church during the 16th and 17th centuries, the Separatists separated themselves from the established church to form their own denominations. John Knox and other reforming leaders had been exiled to Geneva in the early years, coming under John Calvin's influence which defined Puritanism.

Mary was responsible for the martyrdoms of at least 300 English pastors and laymen during her short reign of six years. Her sister and successor Elizabeth I offered some respite to the reforming Protestants. However, the ill-begotten Star Chamber was used to condemn many an innocent man to imprisonment and death during her reign. Archbishop Whitgift created this tyrannical tribunal—eerily familiar to those who still remembered the horror of the Spanish Inquisition. This kangaroo court was vested with the power to apprehend a person without a charge and without an accuser. If the individual would not answer the questions directed to him, he would be remanded to the jailhouse until he was willing to do so. Between 1583 and 1593, twenty-five pastors were confined to the jails in London, many of whom were cruelly beaten. At least three died while in prison. On May 29, 1593, three Christian men dropped from the scaffolds on St. Thomas-a-Watering in Central London, just south of the river Thames. John Penry, Henry Barrow, and John Greenwood were sentenced to death by hanging for authoring books on the subject of church discipline. The rising influence of Puritans and Separatists in England had become an irritant to the state-regulated church.

Joel Beeke and Randall Pederson summarize English Puritanism by five characteristics:

1. The Puritans sought to search the Scriptures, collate their findings, and apply them to all areas of life.

2. The Puritans were passionately committed to focusing on the Trinitarian character of theology. They never tired of proclaiming the electing grace of God, the dying love of Jesus Christ, and the applicatory work of the Holy Spirit in the lives of sinners.

3. The Puritans believed in the significance of the church in the purposes of Christ...Puritanism was a movement that focused on plain and earnest preaching, liturgical reform, and spiritual brotherhood.

4. The Puritans looked to Scripture for light on the duties, powers, and rights of king, Parliament, and citizen-subjects.

5. The Puritans focused on personal, comprehensive conversion... They excelled at preaching the gospel, probing the conscience, awakening the sinner, calling him to repentance and faith, leading

him to Christ, and schooling him in the way of Christ.[29]

Under Elizabeth I and James I, the Separatists and Baptists were subjected to worse persecutions than the more mainstream Puritans. However, the almost-Puritans Nicholas Ridley, Hugh Latimer, and Thomas Cranmer were all burned at the stake during the reign of Bloody Mary; first Ridley and Latimer on October 16, 1555, then Cranmer on March 21, 1556. The persecuting forces pressed the Separatists first into the Netherlands for political protection in 1606; then, in 1620, the little group of Pilgrims made their way to America, carrying with them some of the most ardent adherents to the Protestant Reformation. Nine years later, a ship laden with Puritans led by John Winthrop landed in Massachusetts, where these reforming Christians set out to build what the governor called a "City on a Hill."

Cambridge University, or more specifically, Emmanuel College, became a hotbed for Puritanism in Elizabethan England, where Reformed doctrine combined with practical disciplines and a devotional piety to produce a robust faith. Routine persecution throughout the reign of the Stuarts helped to polish out what might have become a purely academic scholasticism. William Perkins is sometimes considered the father of Puritanism, passing on a more biblical faith to the likes of William Ames (1576-1633), Richard Sibbes (1577-1635), and John Cotton (1585-1652). Ten years after Perkins' death, Thomas Goodwin reported that Cambridge was still "filled with the discourse of the power of Mr. William Perkins' ministry." Beeke summarizes the influence of the first Puritan, "Nearly one hundred Cambridge men who grew up in Perkins's shadow led early migrations to New England, including William Brewster of Plymouth, Thomas Hooker of Connecticut, John Winthrop of Massachusetts Bay, and Roger Williams of Rhode Island. Richard Mather was converted while reading Perkins, and Jonathan Edwards was fond of reading Perkins more than a century later."[30]

The Stuart Dynasty took the throne in 1603 beginning with James I (1566-1625), and the battle for the soul of England's Reformation continued in earnest. A Protestant and increasingly Puritan parliament was almost constantly at odds with the monarchy, eventually resulting in the English Civil War, the beheading of Charles I (the son of James), and the short administration of Oliver Cromwell as Lord Protector. The Westminster Assembly was called into session during the civil war, and the Westminster Confession of Faith was drawn up. This document is sometimes regarded as the highest achievement of the Protestant Reformation in England. Although the English Church continued under the Thirty-Nine Articles, the Church of Scotland and the Presbyterian churches in America have upheld the Westminster Confession (with very few revisions) until the present. The London Baptists formed around 1590, in theology a mixture of the English-Calvinist Puritans and the Dutch-Anabaptists. The early Baptists retained a strong commitment to the centrality and sovereignty of God over reality and ethics.

The Reformation's influence upon the Western church and nations was enormous. Its benefits to the whole world were still felt well into the 21st Century. Those who have never studied the doctrine, the life, and the testimony of the Reformers will fail to understand the next five hundred years of world history and the history of Christ's church. There is only one explanation for the long-standing, worldwide spiritual impact, the massive transformation of cultures and nations, and the restoration of robust faith and holiness among the Protestant churches and clergy. The 16th Century Reformation must have been another Pentecost—one more gracious visitation of the Holy Spirit of God upon the Christian world.

> And it shall come to pass afterward, that I will pour out my spirit upon all flesh; and your sons and your daughters shall prophesy, your old men shall dream dreams, your young men shall see visions: and also

upon the servants and upon the handmaids in those days will I pour out my spirit. and I will shew wonders in the heavens and in the earth, blood, and fire, and pillars of smoke. The sun shall be turned into darkness, and the moon into blood, before the great and terrible day of the LORD come. And it shall come to pass, that whosoever shall call on the name of the LORD shall be delivered: for in mount Zion and in Jerusalem shall be deliverance, as the LORD hath said, and in the remnant whom the LORD shall call. (Joel 2:28-32)

VI

THE DIASPORA & FALL
OF THE WESTERN
CHURCH

O LORD God of hosts, how long wilt thou be angry against the prayer of thy people? Thou feedest them with the bread of tears; and givest them tears to drink in great measure. Thou makest us a strife unto our neighbours: and our enemies laugh among themselves. Turn us again, O God of hosts, and cause thy face to shine; and we shall be saved. (Psalm 80:4-7)

The spreading yeast in the loaf of the Kingdom of God becomes harder to keep track of as the gospel is unleashed through a worldwide Protestant missionary campaign. Protestantism in the form of Lutherans, Reformed, Presbyterians, Baptists, and the "radical" reformation or Anabaptists further splintered over succeeding centuries, making it almost impossible to monitor the progress of the church. Truly there can be no single organizational head of this gigantic organism, the true Church, except the Lord Jesus Christ Himself. There is no statistical clearinghouse monitoring every denomination and independent work in the world. We may gather anecdotal information and make rough estimates as to the state of the

Church in every tribe and nation, but the decentralization following the Reformation removed institutionalized control and monitoring of the worldwide activity of the body of Christ. Certainly, the Chief Shepherd of the Church keeps everything well in hand despite the informal arrangements, as well as the almost constant rise of new heterodoxies (or false teachings).

The shift of power and control over the church from the pope to the king (or the civil magistrate) in England, Germany, and Sweden proved unhealthy for the Protestant church. In retrospect, this political control at the hands of the state was not much better than the pope, especially in Germany and Sweden. Where independence from state control was permitted, such as in the Netherlands, Switzerland, Scotland, and America, a greater spiritual improvement resulted.

Two ideological forces emerged during the 15th and 16th centuries—the humanist Renaissance and the biblical Reformation. These forces battled it out through the 18th Century Enlightenment, and the cultural war for the heart of the Western world was essentially lost by the 20th Century. A man-centered view of truth, ethics, and reality took the driver's seat in Europe and America. God's Word was set aside as the chief rule of faith and life. As far as churches adopted this humanist thinking, apostasy was sure to follow. First it came by the German higher critics, virtually destroying German Lutheranism in the 19th Century, preparing the way for Adolf Hitler and the Third Reich. Subsequently, this man-centered, faithless skepticism crept into England and America by way of Deism, Unitarianism, higher criticism, modernism, and neo-orthodoxy.

Finally, an evangelical church emerged out of the revivals of Dwight L. Moody and others around the turn of the 20th Century. It wasn't a reformation. Modern evangelicalism was a reformed halfway house, retaining basic Christian orthodoxy, but always veering towards a man-centered doctrine of salvation and subjective experientialism.

Still, something of the biblical faith was discernible well into the 21st Century. A bump for reformation theology and evangelicalism occurred again in the 1970s and 1980s with the Jesus movement, followed by another serious spiritual decline after 2010.

By the 21st Century, the major institutions controlling almost every nation in the Western world were consumed by this humanist vision, most significantly recognized in the international approval of homosexual marriage. The fall only occurred after a titanic battle was waged over centuries between the ideas of humanism and the faithful God-centered truths which had defined the Protestant Reformation.

THE GREATEST GIFT TO THE WORLD

And the scripture, foreseeing that God would justify the heathen through faith, preached before the gospel unto Abraham, saying, In thee shall all nations be blessed...Christ hath redeemed us from the curse of the law, being made a curse for us: for it is written, Cursed is every one that hangeth on a tree: that the blessing of Abraham might come on the Gentiles through Jesus Christ; that we might receive the promise of the Spirit through faith. (Galatians 3:8, 13-14)

The greatest gift the West gave to the world was the Christian missionary outreach of the last four centuries.

Prior to AD 1600 there were very few efforts to take the Gospel around the world. Leif Ericson of Norway took the Gospel into Greenland and planted Christian colonies in Newfoundland for a short time. China had received serious Christian mission initiatives through the centuries via the Nestorians and the Roman church.

Technically, the first successful Protestant mission work in the world began with Thomas Mayhew (1593-1682), on Martha's Vineyard, Massachusetts Bay, and John Eliot (1604-1690), "the apostle to the Indians" in Roxbury, Massachusetts. The Mayhew mission work continued for 140 years, from 1642 to 1782, through four generations.

The first widespread Christian Protestant mission to the world came by way of August Hermann Francke (1663-1727) and his protege, Nicolaus von Zinzendorf (1700-1760). Having received the Moravian Brethren to his Saxony holdings, Zinzendorf inspired them to take the Gospel into the Caribbean, North America, and South Africa. The story is legendary.

Pioneering missionaries came largely from England (William Carey, Hudson Taylor, Thomas Thompson, Henry Martyn, Robert Morrison, John Horden, Henry Williams, John Williams, John Hunt, Allen Gardiner, C.T. Studd), Scotland (David Livingstone, Robert Moffat, William Chalmers Burns, Alexander Duff, William Milne, Samuel Duff, James Maxwell, Frederick Stanley Arnot, Alexander Mackay, John G. Paton, Robert Reid Kalley), and America (Hiram Bingham, Adoniram Judson, John Eliot, David Brainerd, Samuel Kirkland, Justus Nelson). Germans and Danes contributed to pioneering work in India (Bartholomaus Ziegenbalg), Angola (Johann Schmelen), and Newfoundland (Jens Haven).

How did the rest of the world get the Gospel? How do we find 500 million adherents to the evangelical faith in Asia, Africa, and South America? By ratios, the Western countries contributed close to 100% of pioneering missions since AD 1600. Over 70% of these Holy Spirit-filled missionaries were sent from England and Scotland, and 20% originated from the United States. At the turn of the 21st Century, the chief missionary-sending Protestant nations were the United States (127,000), South Korea (20,000), Britain (15,000), Germany (14,000), and Canada (8,500).[1] Even during the decline of faith in the West, 90% of the world's Protestant missionaries were still coming out of Western nations.

All the nations of the world are blessed because of David's Son and Abraham's Seed. Following the reformation of the biblical faith in the 16th and 17th centuries, this blessing reached the other 87% of the world's land mass through European and American missionaries. Before the humanist Enlightenment could completely destroy Western institutions, by God's grace, the Reformation faith and the Holy Scriptures would spread out far and wide over the whole earth.

DIASPORA—THE CHRISTIAN FAITH
MOVES TO AMERICA

And Saul was consenting unto [Stephen's] death. And at that time there was a great persecution against the church which was at Jerusalem; and they were all scattered abroad throughout the regions of Judaea and Samaria, except the apostles. And devout men carried Stephen to his burial, and made great lamentation over him. As for Saul, he made havock of the church, entering into every house, and haling men and women committed them to prison. Therefore they that were scattered abroad went every where preaching the word. (Acts 8:1-4)

The geographical center of the Christian faith has moved continuously throughout history. Initially, the missionary sending churches began in Jerusalem and Antioch (in Syria). For several hundred years, the center remained in Rome with an occasional shift northward. Ireland and Scotland contributed greatly to the faith during the 6th, 7th, and 8th centuries until Charlemagne and the school of Alcuin of York. By the turn of the first millennium, the geographical center reached Canterbury of England, and there it would remain until the 19th Century. During the Reformation, the continental reformers contributed to the spiritual transformation of Switzerland, Germany, and the Netherlands. But, the long term effects were seen in England and America. The Great Awakening originated in England. The outpouring of the Holy Spirit upon the St. Andrews Seven and others occurred in the 1820s, spurring on tremendous missionary action in India and China. Finally, by the end of the 19th Century, the center of the Christian faith shifted to the United States. This country would become the most prolific missionary-sending agency for the next century of kingdom work. At the turn of the second millennium, the center would move to. . . everywhere, accommodating the rise of an indigenous, international evangelistic and church planting movement in Africa, Asia, South America, and elsewhere.

The modus operandi for the health and growth of this church was always the combination of missionary exertion, persecution, and diaspora. Such was the spiritual energy propelling the church from one century to the next, and from one nation to another. These factors played in strongly with the Pilgrims, Puritans, and Scottish Presbyterians who fled to the wilderness of America in the 17th Century.

The Christian faith moved into North America in 1620, as Calvinistic-congregationalist Pilgrims found their way into Massachusetts Bay where they organized the first colony at Plymouth. Following the Reformation, the move to the state-controlled church in England and Scotland did not necessarily reduce persecution of the godly. Reforming pastors and churches suffered under the Stuarts especially. Between 1620 and 1700, England and Scotland would lose many of their best Reformed pastors and congregants to the American colonies. Initially, these colonies were settled by denominational preference—the Baptists in Rhode Island, the Congregationalists in Massachusetts, the Dutch Reformed in New York, and the Quakers in Pennsylvania.

For several generations, the predominant worldview in New England was largely set by the continual preaching of the Word of God. Though not all would profess faith, the average New Englander heard seven thousand sermons in his lifetime, each averaging nearly two hours long.[2] Even convicted murderers in the colony would hear several lengthy sermons before being hanged on the gallows. For the Pilgrim colony, church attendance was required by law.[3] Church historian, Mark Noll estimates that as much as 75% of New Englanders were regular church attenders at the turn of the 18th Century.[4] Full membership in the churches however was quite a bit lower in New England largely due to the high bar Puritan pastors set for those who wished to partake of the Communion table. The effects of religion on the social and moral conditions in the colonies were admirable—Plymouth Colony enjoyed a 0.1% divorce rate, and only 1-2% of its inhabitants engaged in sexual activity before marriage.[5] The influence of the Enlightenment would do its damage, however. By 1776, sexual activity outside of the bounds of marriage increased to something above 30%[6]—still, this is hardly comparable to the current rate of 95%.[7]

The downside to the American experiment in congregationalism and church independence was the ever-increasing fracturing of church unity. Whereas Europe's churches were largely based on national boundaries, American churches formed around minor doctrinal distinctions and a spirit of exclusivity. Scores of Protestant denominations would separate from brethren in the towns and cities, constructing high walls and wide moats about their castles and kingdoms. Strife, prideful competition, schism, and divisions prevailed. Add to that an incipient inability to distinguish between majors and minors in the faith, and an improper handling of the mysteries of the faith, and there was no stopping the confusion. 19th Century revivals created more divisions—usually in an attempt to bring some particular emphasis to the forefront—in hopes that these new divisions would revive the faith and provide a haven for the "true church." Or, some may have hoped the Holy Spirit would favor this denomination over that one. Some divisions were necessitated by gross heterodoxies and apostasy among certain churches. Wave after wave of humanist thinking swept into the colleges and seminaries, weakening the doctrine and breaking down almost every church communion, generation after generation. Regrettably, the Protestant heterodoxies, competitions, and divisions were very often dragged into the international mission field. Denominational exclusivism would hamper both foreign and domestic mission work (with immigrants) and weakened the effect of the American faith. Such conditions were quite antithetical to Christ's vision and heart for His church.

> Neither pray I for these alone, but for them also which shall believe on me through their word; that they all may be one; as thou, Father, art in me, and I in thee, that they also may be one in us: that the world may believe that thou hast sent me. And the glory which thou gavest me I have given them; that they may be one, even as we are one: I in them, and thou in me, that they may be made perfect in one; and that the world may know that thou hast sent me, and hast loved them, as thou hast loved me. (John 17:20-23)

THE EROSION OF AMERICAN FAITH

> For the Jews require a sign, and the Greeks seek after wisdom: but we preach Christ crucified, unto the Jews a stumblingblock, and unto the Greeks foolishness. . . (1 Corinthians 1:22-23)

The crisis of faith among American Puritans began in Harvard College with the Latitudinarian conflict between "the last Puritan," Increase Mather (1639-1723), and the college tutors - William Brattle (1662-1717) and John Leverett (1662-1724), the latter of which served as president in 1708. At issue were "Pelagian principles,"[8] and the "reconciliation of Christian and Platonic ethics,"[9] worked out by Henry More and championed at the college by Brattle and Leverett.

The epistemological crisis among Christian leaders came with the rise of enlightenment empiricism, which gave way to "seeking a sign," or a fixation on "spectral evidence" of either demonic activity or angelic visitations. How would you prove the supernatural but by natural manifestations? Increase Mather wrote books on the subject, and his son Cotton said he was visited by angels, and recorded his conversations. Qualitative, visible evidences became increasingly important to certify real conversions and faith. This produced the half-way covenant, in which grandchildren were baptized into the churches without their parents taking communion. Church membership was based on subjective experiences over objective limits provided in 1 Corinthians 5 or 2 Thessalonians 3:6-13. Like the Jews mentioned by the Apostle in 1 Corinthians 1, the experientialists would seek after signs, dreams, visions, trances, and spirit journeys. This impulse continued well into the Great Awakening of the 1740s. Such extravagances would motivate the more moderate Jonathan Edwards to write, "The Distinguishing Marks of a Work of the Spirit of God." Jesus and the apostles had warned about the tendency to "seek signs," as an indication of a lapse in faith, not an evidence of faith. (Matt. 16:4, 1 Cor. 1:22). The American puritans were demonstrating a tendency towards walking by sight, and not by faith at the turn of the 18th Century.

Among the American religionists, one-time conversion experiences, revival meetings, signs, and visions replaced the patient and plodding discipleship work intended for the local churches by the original commission (Matt. 28:18-20).

Moreover, a divide occurred in the mind of the enlightened Christians of the early 18th Century, between Sunday piety and Monday life. Herbert Schneider describes the dichotomy slowly forming between the secular and sacred in the mind of the lapsed Puritan: "On Sunday the Puritan as wholeheartedly lost himself in God, as on Monday he devoted himself to business."[10] The preacher, Thomas Prince summarized the Puritan decline this way in 1730, on the centennial of the founding of Massachusetts Bay:

> Though 'tis true we still maintain in general the same religious
> principles and profession with our pious fathers, yet how greatly is the

spirit of piety declined among us, how sadly is religion turning more and more into a mere form of godliness, as the apostle speaks, without the power, and how dreadfully is the love of the world prevailing more and more upon this professing people.[11]

Without question, the Enlightenment was the primary ideological fountain of all Western apostasy in the 1700s. The exaltation of man's reason and the preeminence of empirical science displaced the authority of God speaking in His Word. Breakthroughs in science introduced increased levels of pride and new prosperity heretofore never enjoyed by human society—especially in America. Average annual household incomes had doubled between 1600 and 1800 in England and America, and they were pretty sure that "the might of mine hand hath gotten me this wealth" (Deut. 8:17). Isn't that why every materially blessed people, or their children and grandchildren forgets God?

Though properly considered a conservative, and still holding on to the Calvinism of the Puritans, Jonathan Edwards (1703-1758) was overly enamored by the empirical epistemology of John Locke. As a young man, Edwards read John Locke as what he called a "newly discovered treasure."[12] Instead of accepting the revelation of God given in words, Edwards set out to "extricate all questions from the least confusion of the ambiguity of words, so that the ideas will be left naked."[13] Words for Edwards were useful to elicit a visceral, emotional response, noting that "I should think myself in the way of duty to raise the affections of my hearers as high as I possibly can."[14]

Diagnosing the problem a century later, the Presbyterian, Charles Hodge suggested that "inward impressions" were preferred among the 18th Century revivalists over the Word of God.[15] Doctrine (even fundamental propositions) were seen to introduce useless divisions, while subjective spiritual experience and outward signs of enthusiasm became the metrics for authentic faith. Thus, the American lapse of faith in the 18th Century came by a misunderstanding of faith itself. If anything, experience and emotion were mistaken for faith, and the object of Christian faith in the Person of Christ, the Work of Christ, the visible body of Christ in the Church, and the Doctrines of the Word of Christ were all deemphasized and diluted; and, covenant faithfulness in the local church and the living faith of daily obedience were little valued.

Moreover, the Enlightenment like the Renaissance three hundred years earlier, revived that philosophy built up on human reason by the ancient Greeks. The worldly "wisdom of the Greeks" mentioned by the Apostle (1 Cor. 1:22) was a powerful lure to the rising humanism in the academy and political society. The tension within John Adams, the second president of the United States, in his formative years (during the 1750s) is also not to be missed. As a young man, he set out to "study Scriptures on Thursday, Friday, Saturday, and Sunday mornings," and he said he had committed himself to "conquer my natural pride and conceit."[16] But just four years later, he admitted, "I have a strong desire for distinction."[17] For he had read in Cicero that, "The first way for a young man to set himself on the road towards glorious reputation is to win renown."[18]

The severance of the church from state in the colonies occurred quicker in the north than the south where the Church of England had more sway. The state-supported college, however, would then maintain more control over the mind of the nation. The tug-of-war over the English-issued charter for Harvard College continued well into the 1700s.

Moreover, the Christian church in America became known for its constant denominational fracturing, especially with the Baptists and the Presbyterians—continuing into the 19th and 20th centuries. Increase Mather exerted meager efforts to a union with Presbyterians in 1691, and the church in Connecticut attempted a union under the Saybrook

Platform in 1710. For the Church in New England, independence and congregationalism broke down quickly.

THE SLIP IN FAMILY PIETY

Usually missed out in the analysis made of the failure of faith in the Western church is the matter of family piety. Without the Deuteronomy 6:7-9 mandate worked into the social fabric of a Christian culture, the faith must inevitably languish. When the Scriptures were provided in the common language and made available to each cottage in every Christian community throughout Europe, for the first time in centuries a vibrant familial piety revived in the hearts and homes of millions.

The Presbyterians provided a "Directory for Family Worship" and required a twice-a-day regimen for their congregants. The Puritan, Richard Baxter (1615-1691) recommended excommunication to those fathers who refused to nurture their children in God's Word. Phillip Doddridge (1702-1751) warned his congregation that God would "pour his fury upon the families that call not on His name."[19] Doddridge preached to his congregation: "If after all you will not be persuaded, but will hearken to the voice of cowardice, and sloth, and irreligion, in defiance of so many awakening and affecting reasons… if your children raise profane and profligate families; if they prove the curse of their country, as well as the torment and ruin of those most intimately related to them; the guilt is in part yours and (I repeat it again) you must answer it to God at the great Day!"[20]

Son of another Puritan, and best known for his Bible commentary, Matthew Henry (1662-1714) testified that his work was largely drawn from his father's daily sessions at the "family altar." Henry exhorted his congregants: "You are unjust to your God, unkind to your children, and unfaithful to your truth, if having by baptism, entered your children in Christ's school, and lifted them under his banner, you do not make conscience of training them up in the learning of Christ's scholars, and under the discipline of his soldiers."[21]

This commitment to family worship and generational continuity of faith was a primary emphasis in the early American colonies. Massachusetts' first governor, John Winthrop was insistent that children be "brought up in the knowledge and fear of God." For the first generation of American puritans, Massachusetts's first legal code of 1648 required that parents teach their children "some short catechism" and the law of God, including the Old Testament civil law codes on penalty of a fine. Parents were directed by law to teach children to read "at least to be able duely to read the Scriptures," to include, "the Capital Laws. . . and the Main Ground and Principles of the Christian Religion."

That generational vision came on the first vessels arriving in the New World with Richard Mather—the archetypal Puritan patriarch. The vision coalesced at a Puritan home in Toxteth England in 1611 where 15-year-old Richard boarded while assuming an apprenticeship. The family would meet twice a day for prayers and scripture reading, and the singing of psalms. The older children were given responsibility in the reading, leading the prayers, and catechizing the younger ones. As the first of New England's pastors, Richard Mather continued the legacy of family discipleship with his own five sons; exhorting his own congregation: "You must not leave your children to themselves, neglecting to instruct them in the ways of God, but as you love yourselves and your own comfort, you must be careful of this duty."

Richard's youngest son, Increase frequently recorded prayers for his nine children in his diary:

"After I had prayed, as I was in my garden, and had this soliloquy 'God has heard my prayer for this child, God will answer me, and the child shall live to do service for the Lord his God and God of his father. . . My heart was melted before the Lord, and therefore I am not altogether with out hope that this child shall be blessed and made a blessing in his generation. Amen! O God in Christ Jesus, Amen. . . Tears gushed from me before the Lord. I trust prayer and Faith shall not be in vain. Oh! I have prevailed and obtained mercy for my poor children. Amen! Lord Jesus!"[22]

Increase's eldest son, Cotton had 14 children for which he penned "A Father's Resolutions."

1. At the birth of my children, I will resolve to do all I can that they may be the Lord's. I will now actually give them up by faith to God; entreating that each child may be a child of God the Father, a subject of God the Son, a temple of God the Spirit—and be rescued from the condition of a child of wrath, and be possessed and employed by the Lord as an everlasting instrument of His glory.

2. As soon as my children are capable of minding my admonitions, I will often, often admonish them, saying, "Child, God has sent His Son to die, to save sinners from death and hell. You must not sin against Him. You must every day cry to God that He would be your Father, and your Saviour, and your Leader. You must renounce the service of Satan, you must not follow the vanities of this world, you must lead a life of serious religion."

3. Let me daily pray for my children with constancy, with fervency, with agony. Yea, by name let me mention each one of them every day before the Lord. I will importunately beg for all suitable blessings to be bestowed upon them: that God would give them grace, and give them glory, and withhold no good thing from them. . .

The first three generations of American Puritans fought hard to retain a generational component to the "kingdom vision" on earth as it is in heaven. Increase Mather produced a biography of his father, in an effort to honor the vision and the mission of the first generation. Sermons reprinted for "the Rising Generation" were the most popular theme for New England churchgoers between 1679 and 1685.

Nevertheless, the zeal for generational faith waned quickly at the turn of the 18th Century. The reasons for the failure are hard to pinpoint, but Edmund Morgan may have struck close to home when he attributes it to "religious elitism." "God refused to become a respecter of persons. He refused to grant a monopoly on salvation to a religious elite."[23]

This wasn't the first time in history that diaspora or apostasy interrupted an ingrown church. Reaching out to the unsaved and missions must always play a significant role in the church vision—and this was too much missing with the Puritans of the 17th Century. Eventually, the Moravians would carry out the vision for missions, with men like David Brainard and Jonathan Edwards following on.

But why did the children fail to carry on the faith, or participate as members in the church? Certain set requirements for the religious experience and expectations of piety may have been too restrictive. The New England Puritans were known for promoting a regulative civil society, placing more weight on the sovereignty of man's controls over trust in the sovereignty of God. Persecution of Baptists in the colonies, as well as civic regulations on clothing and dancing revealed this commitment to top-down control. As the 17th Century came to a close, threats from the pulpits intensified, jeremiads warned of God's temporal judgments upon listeners who appeared not repentant enough. Was this an indication of men relying more on the words than the power of God to do the spiritual work? Whatever the case, in the providence of God, membership in the churches (and church attendance) had waned greatly by 1720.

As the Great Awakening was gathering steam in 1741, Jonathan Edwards exhorted parents that, "After a dead time in religion, 'tis very requisite that religion should revive in heads of families and those that have the care of children."[24] When expelled from his church in 1750, Edwards' final sermon focused mainly on the failure of family-based discipleship of the children. "If these [means of grace] fail," he said, "All other means are like to prove ineffectual."[25] The pastor's final exhortation came as the last words of a dying man to a dying church: "Let me now, therefore, once more, before I finally cease to speak to this congregation, repeat and earnestly press the counsel which I have often urged on heads of families here, while I was their pastor, to great painfulness in teaching, warning and directing their children; bringing them up in the nurture and admonition of the Lord; beginning early, where there is yet opportunity, and maintaining a constant diligence in labors of this kind. . ."[26]

A century later, in 1847, the Presbyterian, J.A. Alexander recorded his concerns that the world had "invaded the household," "family worship had lost ground," and "heads of households. . . ruling elders, deacons. . . maintain no daily service to God in their dwellings."[27] He lamented "the decay of family worship in the original seats of the Reformation."[28] This "neglect of family worship as springing from lukewarmness and worldliness in religion and as a portentous evil of our day," he further attributed to "the hurry of our great cities. . . the preference given to Mammon over God."[29] These all, Alexander wrote, indicate "the tepid languors of our American condition in divine things."[30]

Whether by religious pride, academic pride, national pride, the pride of economic success, science, or technology, the Reformation faith died out quickly in America. The glory had pretty much departed, and "Ichabod" was written over the colonies by the turn of the 19th Century. As God would have it, the ideal of the founders for a continuous generational faith and a Christian "city on a hill" was not to materialize. Nonetheless, the roots of faith die hard, and some remnants of the Christian cultural heritage in America's founding would remain for another century or two.

THE END OF PURITANISM

> Now the Spirit expressly says that in latter times some will depart from the faith, giving heed to deceiving spirits and doctrines of demons, speaking lies in hypocrisy, having their own conscience seared with a hot iron. (1 Timothy 4:1-2)

The vehemence with which Satan attacked the Reformation churches in England and America, and the blinding speed of the apostasy was truly remarkable—exceeding the rate of breakdown occurring in the Western Church during the Medieval Period. The deceitfulness of the devil, the frailty of the human situation, and the powerful influence of institutional forces were all-important factors in the corruption of faith in the Western world. The force of autonomous thinking in the universities and the budding pride of Enlightenment men during the "Age of Reason" would capsize Protestantism by the turn of the 19th Century.

First came the politically-oriented purge. Following the restoration of the monarchy with Charles II, thousands of Puritan pastors in England were imprisoned or exiled between 1662 and 1688 in what was known as the Great Ejection. These were the best of England's pastors. At the same time, thousands of Scottish Covenanters, including women and children, were hunted down and executed in the cruelest manner. These stories chronicle some of the most heart-wrenching martyrdoms in the history of the church. Dr. W. H. Carslaw summarizes the historical research he conducted on the Killing Time in Scotland in these words:

> While during the twenty-eight miserable years between the Restoration and the Revolution, apart from untold hardships and sufferings, the slain on the scaffold and in the fields cannot have fallen much short of two thousand, including 360 executed after some form of examination had been perfunctorily and summarily hurried through. Moreover, it is

impossible to count the men and women and children who succumbed to rain and frost and fatigue and hunger in their wanderings across mosses and mountains.[31]

These persecutions solidified faith and sealed a commitment to the Reformation church among a remnant for generations to come, inspiring missionaries, revivals, and small reformations here and there. However, the persecutions also initiated another diaspora and weakened the Christian faith in both England and Scotland.

This period also marked an end of Puritan influence in England. These were among the last persecutions in the era of the Reformation, for the devil now would implement other schemes to strip back the influence of the church. By 1676, leading Puritan theologian-pastor, John Owen, had become extremely disillusioned with the state of the Christian faith in the West. In one of his final books, *On the Nature and Causes of Apostasy*, Owen wrote, "The state of religion is at this day deplorable in most parts of the Christian world."[32] The aged Puritan even despaired of the survival of Reformation faith:

> The reformed religion is by not a few so taken off from its old foundations, so unhinged from those pillars of important truths which it did depend upon, and so sullied by a confused medley of noisome opinions, as that its loss in reputation of stability and usefulness seems almost irreparable.[33]

In a prophetic moment of sorts, John Owen could see that this explosion of heresies and man-derived ideas emerging from the developing humanist Enlightenment would overwhelm the Christian church in Europe. From Owen's point of view, the Reformation heritage of the 16th Century was now insufficient to salvage the faith in Europe: "Is it nothing unto us that so many nations in the world, where the profession of the gospel and an avowed subjection of soul and conscience unto Jesus Christ did flourish for some ages, are now utterly overrun with Mohammedanism, paganism, and atheism?"[34] He could have been writing in the 21st Century.

DOCTRINAL RETROGRADE

> But though we, or an angel from heaven, preach any other gospel unto you than that which we have preached unto you, let him be accursed. As we said before, so say I now again, if any man preach any other gospel unto you than that ye have received, let him be accursed. (Galatians 1:8-9)

As it turned out, the controversies which precipitated the apostasy of the Protestant church were the same ancient heresies addressed by the church in the 4th-11th centuries, and the same corrupting the Western church in the 12th-15th centuries. These included:

1. The Doctrine of the Trinity and the Divinity of Christ

2. The Doctrine of God's Sovereignty

3. The Doctrine of Biblical Ethics and the Relationship of Old Testament to the New Testament

Eight hundred years earlier, Hincmar of Rheims had subjected Gottschalk to torture over the matter of the sovereignty of man versus the sovereignty of God. What happened on a micro-scale in Rheims was only repeated on the macro-scale in the Protestant West. As the doctrine of God's sovereignty erodes, replaced by the doctrine of the sovereignty of man, what follows is the deification of the state—the introduction of torture, inquisitions, and various attempts to exercise absolute control.

In the 1660s, two English pastors, John Goodwin and Benjamin Whichcote, led the departure from the more robust Reformed faith, introducing new humanist, latitudinarian thinking into the Anglican church. In his magnum opus *Redemption Redeemed*, Goodwin tried to retain foreknowledge for God while at the same time stripping Him of His sovereign control of the world. He called this "foreseeing without fore-determining."[35] Plainly stating that "All things cannot be determined by God,"[36] John Goodwin goes so far as to say that God does not determine the sparrow that falls to the ground.[37] When a person's house or goods are consumed, he says, "There is no competent ground to say these are determined by God." Job would have disagreed. After all the evils that befell him, the man of God cried out, "The LORD gave, and the LORD has taken away; blessed be the name of the LORD" (Job 1:21).

The abandonment of the biblical doctrine of God's sovereignty was central to the English Puritan apostasy. Yet, the apostasy went deeper. The departure was epistemological. The biblical doctrine was subjected to the mind of man and found wanting. As humanist rationalism is applied to the complex discussion of the relationship of God's will to man's will, God's sovereignty must fall victim to the Procrustean bed. Proud, intellectual men cannot tolerate the possibility of knowability and incomprehensibility in peaceful co-existence. They would not allow for any incomprehensible elements relating to the knowledge of God and His works. How could God sovereignly ordain the free actions of men, to include sinful actions or actions bearing evil consequences? None of this makes sense to the puny, sinful, and corrupted mind of man. And so, sacred knowledge must always be subjected to humanist philosophical knowledge built up on human reason, and then it is debased in the process.

Historical battles for the faith have always aided with identifying and certifying the fundamentals. The doctrine of the Trinity surfaced as one essential footer in the foundation of the entire Christian faith. Over centuries of battle with humanist metaphysical constructs, the doctrine of the sovereignty of God over all reality was shown to be essential to the conception of God's very "godness." The person of Jesus Christ and the nature of God distinguishes Christian theology from false religions and demonic falsities. As humanists within the church chipped away at the fundamental doctrine of God, the true faith died the death of a thousand qualifications in the minds of men. Aberrant cults and humanist thinkers have continued this work from the beginning until now.

The 16th and 17th centuries were not all rosy and reforming. This period also introduced strange aberrant cults, radical reformers, and humanist skepticism into the world. With humanism, two strains always develop—tyranny and anarchy, institutional rebellion against God and individual and factionalized rebellion against authority. Certain Anabaptist strains endorsed polygamy, such as that led by Jan van Battenberg; and the Anabaptist community at Munster was one of the first experiments in communism (an inspiration for Friedrich Engels in the 19th Century). While Oliver Cromwell was pressing for more religious liberty in England, a rogue Quaker by the name of James Naylor came into town impersonating Jesus Christ. Antitrinitarians like Fausto Sozzini (1539-1604) burst onto the scene, attracting followers among the Polish Reformed. Sozzini, an Italian theologian, rejected the doctrine of the foreknowledge of God (called "open theism") and also denied the pre-existence of Christ. Socinianism made inroads into England in the 1600s and paved the way for the Unitarian and Deist apostasy of the 1700s in America. These ideas were attractive to the enlightened minds of 18th Century humanists and rationalists who could not tolerate the apparent paradox contained in the sacred doctrine of God. These were the roots of further apostasy that came to England and America in the 18th Century.

Two groups developed in the early Protestant apostasy of the Enlightenment—the blatantly anti-orthodox Unitarians and the Latitudinarians. The latter wouldn't have embraced the heretical views of the Unitarians, but they argued for a wider range of doctrines within the scope of orthodoxy. The English Latitudinarians were more of a politically-minded movement at the beginning, intent on incorporating various religious flavors under the rubric of the state church. The English church was still fighting off the influence of the Catholics and worked off the theory—"The enemy of my enemy is my friend." While still opposing the Catholics, Latitudinarians would ally themselves with just about everybody else.

The leading philosopher in the English Enlightenment, John Locke, joined the Latitudinarians in 1668—a movement largely spearheaded by his pastor, Benjamin Whichcote. This rogue Puritan rejected the doctrines of total depravity, hell, God's omnipotence, God's eternality, and God's omnipresence. He called human reason "the divine governor of man's life" and the very "voice of God" in his book *Moral and Religious Aphorisms*. Whichcote formed a group called the Cambridge Platonists in an effort to "reconcile Christian ethics with the humanist Renaissance."[38] The doctrine they espoused was humanist to the core, abandoning God's sovereignty and embracing humanist autonomy to determine what is good for man's own self.

In the latter half of the 17th Century, Oxford and Cambridge universities churned out graduates well schooled in Enlightenment philosophies "built up on human reason." Now sacred doctrine was subjected to the bar of human reason, giving the new academics reason to reject it. This was the cauldron in which Protestant apostasy was produced. Close associates of John Locke included John Tillotson and Ralph Cudworth, who began to reject God's interaction with the universe in favor of what was called "an inward natural governing principle." These were shades of humanist rationalism that would lead to Deism and Unitarianism in the 18th Century. The doctrine of Deism offers a minimalist view of monotheism, rejecting most of what is revealed about God in the Scriptures. Famous Deists of the 17th and 18th centuries include Matthew Tindal (1653-1733), John Toland (1670-1722), Thomas Woolston (1670-1733), Bernard de Mandeville (1670-

1733), Lord Shaftesbury (1671-1713), Anthony Collins (1671-1729), and Lord Bolingbroke (1678-1751).

The first Unitarian denomination formed in England in 1774 under the leadership of Theophilus Lindsey. Jonathan Mayhew became one of the first Unitarian pastors in America when he took Boston's Old West Church pulpit in 1747. Another Unitarian, Charles Chauncy, pastored the First Church in Boston from 1727 through 1787.

The universities which had provided a defensive guard for reformers like Wycliff and Hus in earlier centuries turned hard against the Christian faith in subsequent centuries. Their distaste for the control of the Roman Church may have led to temporary support of the Reformers in the early days. However, once the secular universities gained complete autonomy with the sole commission to build up human knowledge on human reason (absent the authoritative revelation of Holy Scripture), the university took on the role of leading the Western Protestant apostasy. After Harvard College turned over to the Latitudinarians in 1707, Unitarianism filtered in quickly. By 1805, Reverend Henry Ware, a self-professed Unitarian, was appointed the Hollis Professor of Divinity at the college. Then Yale College and Princeton University abandoned their Christian heritage in the 19th Century. The battle for orthodoxy against apostasy was fought vigorously at the universities and seminaries, and generally it was a losing battle for orthodox Protestants. The synthesis of Greek thought and method in education was nothing less than devastating to the Church over the centuries. Where control of seminary training was decentralized and placed closer to the local church with local pastors, orthodoxy had a better chance at survival.

It was the Deism, the doubts, and the humanist rationalism of the 17th and 18th centuries that produced the great humanists who would change the entire world in the 19th and 20th centuries—Charles Darwin, Ralph Waldo Emerson, Jeremy Bentham, John Stuart Mill,

John Dewey, Karl Marx, and others.

THE GERMAN APOSTASY

> Take heed therefore unto yourselves, and to all the flock, over the
> which the Holy Ghost hath made you overseers, to feed the church
> of God, which he hath purchased with his own blood. For I know this,
> that after my departing shall grievous wolves enter in among you, not
> sparing the flock. Also of your own selves shall men arise, speaking
> perverse things, to draw away disciples after them. (Acts 20:28-30)

Paul's words to the Ephesian elders were especially apropos for
the exceedingly dangerous years following the Reformation age.
During the 17th and 18th centuries, German Protestantism played
tug-of-war between what some thought to be cold rationalism (and a
compromised orthodoxy) and pietism, which emphasized obedience,
personal devotion, emotions, and Scripture reading. Throughout
Christian history, one finds the "heart people" often set against "the
head people," to the impoverishment of both sides. The disagreement
resolves quickly with the understanding that God would have His
people love Him with all their heart, soul, mind, and strength—*every
part and parcel of their being.* When German Protestants in both camps
surrendered essential Christian doctrine for the pietist experience or for
academic pride's sake, apostasy was well underway on the continent.

The apostasy of the Gentiles came to full fruition in the 21st
Century, but its roots can be traced back to the Enlightenment and
the higher-criticism movement of 18th Century Germany. Higher
criticism purportedly set out to determine the original authors of the
biblical text as well as the original meaning in its historical context and
its literal sense. These "objective" scholars hailing from the universities
developed theories based on obscurantist guess-work. In the end, the
higher criticism movement was just another expression of human
autonomy and faithlessness. The higher critics did not believe God

was capable of communicating His Word with perfect precision and accuracy for faith and life. They could not believe He was able to preserve His Word and maintain its authority and infallibility over the millennia. At root, the higher critics had already rejected a supernatural metaphysic, the authority of God speaking through His Word, and the biblical ethic. Natural man is repulsed by God's Word. Either he will reject it outright or he will pick and choose what he will accept from God's revelation. The higher critics set out to do this under the cloak of intellectualism and a false pretense of seeking the truth.

This major breach in the Christian faith began in Germany with Johann Gottfried Eichhorn (1752-1827), generally recognized as the father of this new religious skepticism. Eichhorn denied the supernatural events recorded in the Old Testament, rejecting the authenticity of most of the Old Testament books, as well as the Pauline authorship of the pastoral epistles (1 Timothy, 2 Timothy, and Titus), along with 1 Peter, 2 Peter, and Jude.

Another liberal theologian, Ludwig Andreas von Feuerbach (1804-1872), had a profound influence upon some of the formidable humanist thinkers of the 19th Century, including Karl Marx and Friedrich Engels. Although starting out as a student of theology, Feuerbach's skepticism reached its apex with the publication of *The Essence of Christianity*. He hypothesized an anthropological reason for the existence of human religions, an idea that caught on quickly in a world looking for an excuse not to believe in God. Another German biblical scholar, Julius Wellhausen, developed the documentary hypothesis in the 1870s, denying the Mosaic authorship of the Pentateuch. Wellhausen's theory identified four independent texts which were purportedly written over several centuries and eventually redacted into the five books of Moses. Such wild theorizing worked wonders, casting many a spell and doubt over the minds of seminary students, pastors, church laity, and entire denominations throughout the following Century.

By the 1930s, about 40 million German Protestants were united under the German Evangelical Church. However, this was the group which enabled the election of Adolf Hitler and put the Nazi Party in power. Worst of all, the church's general synod assembled on September 5, 1933, adopted the infamous "Aryan Paragraph" espousing evolutionary racism and forbidding men with Jewish background from ministry. Such actions taken by the Protestant church dramatically demonstrate the severity of the apostasy taking place—a very precipitous departure from a biblical view of origins and biblical ethics.

> Anyone not of Aryan descent or who is married to a person of non-Aryan descent may not be appointed as minister or official. Ministers or officials who marry non-Aryans are to be dismissed. The State Law decides who is to be reckoned non-Aryan. Ministers of non-Aryan descent or married to non-Aryans are to be retired. The exceptions are the same as those laid down in the State Law.[39]

In 1934, the German Confessing Church formed under the leadership of Karl Barth and Martin Niemoller. It was hardly a bastion of reformational orthodoxy given that Barthian theology barely aligned with the faith of the Church Fathers. The Barthians conceded that the Bible was fallible, but that God would somehow use the words contained there to facilitate a personal encounter with Himself. It was a half-way house away from heterodoxy. . . a further demonstration of the impoverishment of the German faith in the 20th Century.

A hundred years later, the secularization of Germany was complete. During the 2010s, several Christian families attempted to exempt themselves from a thoroughly anti-Christian public education by homeschooling their children. Following multiple arrests, imprisonments, and court battles, these families lost the battle at the high courts, and some were forced to flee the country.[40] When the West fell only 0.8% of Germans regularly attend Protestant churches, and

Luther's legacy of faith had all but disappeared from his homeland.[41]

OCCASIONAL TIMES OF REFRESHING— REVIVALS & REFORMATIONS

Repent ye therefore, and be converted, that your sins may be blotted out, when the times of refreshing shall come from the presence of the Lord. (Acts 3:19)

20th Century Christian author J. I. Packer defined revival as "the visitation of God which brings to life Christians who have been sleeping and restores a deep sense of God's near presence and holiness. Thence springs a vivid sense of sin and a profound exercise of heart in repentance, praise, and love, with an evangelistic outflow."[42] Thankfully, amidst the constant tendency to spiritual slackness, compromise, and decay, the Spirit of the living God does return and has returned with renewed power to enliven the Church of God even during the recent centuries.

By the early 1700s, that loyal opposition facing off the liberal Deists and Unitarians in England was weak—"timid, polite, and reticent to controversy." What opposition existed in the face of the aggressive skepticism and apostasy of the day appealed to some of the same standards of humanist rationalism and cold logic employed by the enemy in the debates. Almost every teacher in the church lacked the warmth of biblical Christianity, and genuine religious fervor or love for God with full heart, soul, mind, and strength was almost universally condemned. If anyone revealed an earnestness in prayer or preaching, such "enthusiasm" was perceived as a "threat to the peace of the realm."[43] Religion in England had descended into an empty formalism. Non-conformist congregations were legitimized after the Glorious Revolution of 1690, but instead of multiplying, these denominations chose division instead. By 1700, there were four Independent denominations, six Baptist and three Presbyterian. The populace was taken by drunkenness. Prisons were filled to the brim. *The Weekly Miscellany* newspaper summarized the conditions in London in 1732:

> The people were engulfed in voluptuousness and business; and...a zeal for godliness looked as odd upon a man as would the antiquated dress of his great grandfather...freethinkers were formed into clubs, to propagate their tenets, and to make the nation a race of profligates; and that atheism was scattered broadcast throughout the kingdom... it was publicly avowed that vice was profitable to the state; that the country would be benefited by the establishment of public stews [houses of prostitution]; and that polygamy, concubinage, and even sodomy were not sinful.[44]

The condition of religion in England looked a lot like the description of the Laodicean church in Revelation 3. In the Lord Jesus Christ's words:

> I know thy works, that thou art neither cold nor hot: I would thou wert cold or hot. So then because thou art lukewarm, and neither cold nor hot, I will spue thee out of my mouth. Because thou sayest, I am rich and increased with goods, and have need of nothing: and knoweth not that thou art wretched, and miserable, and poor, and blind, and naked: I counsel thee to buy of me gold tried in the fire, that thou mayest be rich. (Revelation 3:15-18)

GEORGE WHITEFIELD

Turn us, O God of our salvation, and cause thine anger toward us to cease. Wilt thou be angry with us for ever? wilt thou draw out thine anger to all generations? Wilt thou not revive us again: that thy people may rejoice in thee? (Psalm 85:4-6)

If revivals should bring about discernible improvements of life and culture in communities and nations, then it would be hard to find many true revivals since the period of the Reformation. The Great Awakening or Evangelical Revival of the 1730s and 1740s, however, distinguishes itself more than any other. The Western nations of England, Scotland, Wales, and America were very much impacted by this work of God through men like George Whitefield, John Wesley, and Jonathan Edwards.

George Whitefield (1714-1770) is generally considered the greatest evangelist of the modern age. Influenced in his early years by the works of Thomas à Kempis, Henry Scougal, Joseph Alleine, and Richard Baxter, as well as John and Charles Wesley and the Moravian Brethren, Whitefield described in his journals something of a conversion or "new birth" occurring in his nineteenth year. He confessed that he was set free from the deadly paralysis of "sect religion" or denominationalism and he repented of frequenting stage plays. Right away, the young evangelist began a prison ministry, reading the Scriptures to prisoners, which helped him prepare for a more public ministry.

Ordained to the pastorate at twenty-one years of age, Whitefield began working in a small country parish called Dummer. There he maintained a rigorous daily schedule of eight hours in study and prayer, eight hours in visitation, and eight hours of sleep. Upon the encouragement of John Wesley, Whitefield considered mission work to Georgia in America. However, before leaving England, he spent a year (1737) engaged in an itinerant preaching ministry in various churches and meetinghouses. Instantly, a fire was lit which would continue burning throughout England and America for the remaining years of his life. Whitefield writes:

> Neither church nor house could contain the people that came. I found uncommon manifestations granted me from above. Early in the morning, at noonday, evening, and midnight, nay, all the day long, did the blessed Jesus visit and refresh my heart.[45]

Weeks later, we again read in his journals:

The congregations continually increased, and generally, on a Lord's Day, I used to preach four times to very large and very affected auditories...Henceforward, for near three months successively, there was no end of the people flocking to hear the Word of God...I now preached generally nine times a week...On Sunday mornings, long before day, you might see streets filled with people going to church with their lanterns in their hands, and hear them conversing about the things of God. [46]

Whitefield's crowds increased to as many as 20,000 per venue. His preaching aroused controversy, especially among the clergy. The doctrine of the new birth bothered clergymen the most because his preaching called into question the faith of nominal church members. Whitefield did not push for immediate conversions or public professions of faith in his meetings, but clearly thousands were impacted with every message he preached. Charles Wesley reported that "The whole nation is in an uproar," and James Hervey wrote that "All London and the whole nation ring of the great things of God done by his ministry."[47]

George Whitefield's work in America was even more extensive. By the end of Whitefield's life, biographer Dallimore claims there is "little doubt that far more than half of the total population of the Colonies had heard him preach."[48] His ministry extended beyond evangelistic preaching. He raised funds to build orphanages in Georgia, and he advocated for American liberties—at one point, attending a parliamentary meeting with Benjamin Franklin.

In the early 1740s, Whitefield's preaching enjoyed great success throughout Scotland. Tens of thousands gathered to hear him. In a letter to his wife Elizabeth, the evangelist recorded the unusual response he witnessed: "I preached at two to a vast body of people, and at six in the evening and again at nine at night. Such a commotion surely never was heard of, especially at eleven at night. It far outdid all that I ever saw in America. For about an hour and a half there was such weeping, so many falling into deep distress and expressing it in various ways, as is inexpressible. . . Their cries and agonies are exceedingly affecting. . . All night in the fields could be heard the voice of prayer."[49] For weeks he continued to preach to the Scottish crowd—in one place 40,000 willingly stood in the rain to hear the man of God.

George Whitefield died on September 30, 1770 in Newburyport, Massachusetts while on a preaching tour in America. No doubt, millions of lives and every Protestant denomination in England and America were impacted by his ministry.

Most of America's important founding fathers commended Whitefield, including Benjamin Franklin, George Washington, John Adams, and Patrick Henry. A certain ten-year-old boy named William Wilberforce was also deeply impacted by Whitefield's preaching in England. With his fellow Clapham evangelicals, Wilberforce would become an important leader in England's evangelical revival, as well as the major force behind ending England's participation in the African slave trade.

If England ever saw another revival of true faith it was only brief and non-consequential, yielding little lasting effect on the wider culture. The evangelical movement following the Great Awakening and the evangelistic ministry of Charles Spurgeon of the 1870s faded quickly. Liberalism, socialism, and the social gospel masqueraded as Christian morality. Church attendance in England would fall off to 4.7% by the 21st Century, when apostasy had completely matured.

What were the effects of the Great Awakening upon England twenty years following Whitefield's death? John Newton, rector at St. Mary Woolnoth in London and author of the famous hymn "Amazing Grace," made the grim assessment of England's spiritual condition. Referring to the contemporary times as a "dark and declining day, when iniquity abounds,"[50] Newton asked, "Can those who reverence the name of God be easy and unconcerned when they hear it blasphemed? No! Their ears are wounded, and their hearts are pained. Can those who are followers of peace and purity, behold unmoved the riots, licentiousness, and daring wickedness of those who have cast off both shame and fear?"[51] Newton said, "Almost everyone [is] in a conspiracy against [God], despising him to his face, trampling upon his laws, rejecting his authority, and abusing his patience; their eyes affect their hearts."[52] The national debt had "swelled to an enormous greatness, to form a tolerable idea of accumulated millions."[53] But the spiritual debt, Newton said, was much worse. In Newton's view, the worst description of pagan Roman days "would hardly be found exaggerated if compared with our own."[54]

As for the churches, Newton said, "The formality, conformity to the world, the lack of Christian love, the intemperate and unprofitable contentions, which prevail among us, show how faintly the power of the Gospel is felt, even by many who profess to have embraced it." He recommended that the church should unite in earnest prayer and, with deep remorse of heart, to "bemoan those evils which, unless repented of and forsaken, may bring upon us as a people such distress as neither we nor our fathers have known! If [God] is pleased thus to give us a heart to seek Him, He will yet be found of us; but if, when His hand is lifted up, we cannot or will not see, nor regard the signs of the times—there is great reason to fear that our case is deplorable indeed."[55]

SCOTLAND'S 19TH CENTURY REVIVALS

By the 21st Century, Scotland's church attendance would drop to 7% (in 2016), of which only about 35% were evangelical Christians.[56] In 2018 Scotland became the first national government mandating that primary school children be taught the sexual license of Sodom and Gomorrah. Concerning the new law, one news correspondent noted,

"There will be no exemptions or opt-outs to the policy, which will embed LGBTI inclusive education across the curriculum and across subjects."[57]

However, in God's good providence, the reformation zeal of John Knox and the to-the-death faith commitment of the Covenanters played a part in the worldwide campaign for Christ's gospel. Scotland's spiritual revivals were particularly significant in stirring up the most aggressive Protestant missions work to date. A surprisingly large proportion of 19th Century missionaries originated from this small rugged country, strong on faith—David Livingstone, Robert Moffat, John G. Paton, Alexander Duff, Alexander Mackay, Mary Slessor, William C. Burns, Frederick Arnot, etc.

The 17th Century "Killing Time" which took place during the reinstatement of Charles II and James II provided more healthy seed for the church. The stories concerning the martyrdoms of James Guthrie, James Renwick, the two Margarets, and others were not to be soon forgotten. Church father Tertullian's *Apologeticus* first offered the profound statement, "The blood of the martyrs is the seed of the church," and surely, the faith of John G. Paton, David Livingstone, Patrick Henry, and others could be traced back to these Covenanter martyrs.

Toward the end of his life, the great reformer, John Knox warned future generations of Scottish Christians: "Above all things, preserve the Kirk [church] from the bondage of the Universities. . . Subject never the pulpit to their Judgment."[58] By the turn of the 19th Century, these universities and seminaries had done their damage, and the Enlightenment had fairly well infiltrated the Church of Scotland. Iain Murray explained the condition of the Scottish church at that time: "The Moderates preached morality, with almost nothing of the supernaturalism of true Christianity. They ignored the Fall of man, sneered at the idea of a new birth and said nothing of the perfection and power of the work of the Son of God."[59] Preacher and missionary

Alexander Duff wrote of the situation, "The savor and unction of divine grace was gone; the peculiarities of the gospel were despised as offensive to classic taste and culture, and devotion scorned as fanatical and contemptible."[60] No less than the Catholics, Protestant civilization was often enamored with the proud learning of the Greeks—the mind and works of man over that of the living God.

Thomas Chalmers (1780-1847) matriculated at the University of St. Andrews at twelve years of age, where he quickly abandoned the beliefs of his godly father for the new-fangled ideas of modern academia. It was a story repeated a million times between the 18th and the 21st centuries for many a child who apostatized from their parents' faith through the influence of progressive seminaries and universities.

About the year 1808, Chalmers took a break from his pitiful apostate ministry in the church after he witnessed the death of his sister and his uncle. He nearly died of illness himself. But, by God's mercy, the man was arrested from his spiritual malaise and became a mighty pulpit reformer in Scotland thereafter. In his readings, he turned with great interest to the writings of Jonathan Edwards, John Owen, John Calvin, John Newton—and the Scriptures, of course, "which he began to read and memorize with an intensity which astonished those who had known his former interests."[61] As others had in times past, Chalmers recovered the foundational doctrines of the centrality and sovereignty of God, the work of God in salvation, and the absolute authority of Scripture. He reintroduced the Puritan writers to his classes at the University of St. Andrews when he was offered the professorship of divinity in 1827. Above all, he taught his ministerial students to preach the Word, visit their congregants, and engage in evangelistic outreach. Chalmers released into the world students aflame with a passion to preach the gospel "to every creature." Murray summarizes the work of the seminary revival: "Few professors of divinity have had such students that crowded Chalmers' classroom in the 1830s. Many of them—as their subsequent biographies reveal—were to become men of outstanding usefulness... By 1843, Chalmers was able to say that he could travel from one end of Scotland to the other and spend each night in the manse of one of his former pupils."[62] His students included such luminaries as Robert Murray M'Cheyne, Andrew Bonar, Horatius Bonar, George Smeaton, and James Hamilton, as well as the famous St. Andrews Seven, whose missionary zeal inspired another wave of worldwide Gospel impact. Between 1839 and 1843, revivals broke out in Kilsyth and Perth under the ministry of Robert M'Cheyne, William C. Burns, and John Milne.

Every genuine pentecostal outpouring of the Holy Spirit in Christian history would burgeon into fruitful cross-cultural evangelism and church planting, and this one was no different. The revivalist preacher William C. Burns (1815-1868) received the call to China and left the mother country to plant seeds that would grow into the largest Christian church in the world by AD 2020. While in China, Burns served as a mentor for a young Englishman struggling in his spiritual life but interested in pursuing missions—Hudson Taylor (1832-1905). Taylor's biographer made the connection between the two pioneering missionaries to China: "William Burns was better to [Taylor] than a college course with all its advantages, because he lived out before him right there in China the reality of all he most needed to be and know."[63] Under Hudson Taylor's leadership, the China Inland Mission was formed in 1865, and the influence of the Christian Gospel in the Far East increased a hundred fold.

> And when the day of Pentecost was fully come, they were all with one accord in one place. And suddenly there came a sound from heaven as of a rushing mighty wind, and it filled all the house where they were sitting. And there appeared unto them cloven tongues like as of fire, and it sat upon each of them. And they were all filled with the Holy Ghost, and began to speak with other tongues, as the Spirit gave them

utterance. And there were dwelling at Jerusalem Jews, devout men, out of every nation under heaven. Now when this was noised abroad, the multitude came together, and were confounded, because that every man heard them speak in his own language. And they were all amazed and marvelled, saying one to another, Behold, are not all these which speak Galilaeans? And how hear we every man in our own tongue, wherein we were born? Parthians, and Medes, and Elamites, and the dwellers in Mesopotamia, and in Judaea, and Cappadocia, in Pontus, and Asia, Phrygia, and Pamphylia, in Egypt, and in the parts of Libya about Cyrene, and strangers of Rome, Jews and proselytes, Cretes and Arabians, we do hear them speak in our tongues the wonderful works of God. (Acts 2:1-11)

THE WELSH REVIVAL OF 1859

The Welsh revival of the 19th Century began with a meeting of two preachers, one a Wesleyan and the other a Calvinistic Methodist—pastors Humphrey Jones and David Morgan. The two men united their churches for prayer in 1859, two things being their chief concern: "the deadness of the church" and the lack of "earnest prayer."[64] This corporate prayer continued daily until "old backsliders began to return." As one pastor recounted: "Men came in crowds from the mountains, and all the country round, to our meetings, until we were afraid the chapel would come down—men who were never seen in any place of worship, except in church at a christening or a funeral, and knew nothing of worshipping God!"[65] The revival beginning in David Morgan's home turf of Llangeitho spread to the College at Trevecca. Then the fire swept into Merionethshire, Bala, Dolgelly, Barmouth, Harlech, Talsarnau, Maentwrog, Festiniog, Carmarthen, Pembroke, Glamorgan, Breakneck, Radnor, and the Welsh part of Monmouth. Reports of revival also surfaced in Montgomeryshire, Flintshire, Denbighshire, Caernarvonshire, Beddgelert, Snowdonia, etc. The impact was national, multi-generational, and cross-denominational, affecting the Baptists, Congregationalists, Wesleyans, and Calvinist Methodists. This latter denomination maintained the stronger revival impetus well into the 20th Century.

According to Thomas Phillips' eyewitness account of the revival, its principal features included:

1. Unified, fervent prayer of the church body

2. Great numbers of people renouncing sin, leading godly lives, and discipling their own children in the gospel of Christ, and,

3. An aggressive evangelistic outreach, pressing beyond comfort zones, beyond geographical boundaries, always seeking to reach the lost in the highways and byways.[66]

This remarkable revival yielded more fruit through the ministry of the Welsh evangelist-pastor D. Martyn Lloyd-Jones (1899-1981), of Calvinistic Methodist extraction. While England and America were experiencing severe faith retrograde through the 20th Century, a few evangelical leaders still resisted the Protestant apostasy and carried a God-centered, biblical message to the West. Among leading evangelicals like Billy Graham, John Stott, J. Vernon McGee, A. W. Tozer, G. Campbell Morgan, and Donald Barnhouse, Dr. Lloyd-Jones was most committed to the Reformed worldview, and his preaching stood out for doctrinal balance, revivalist passion, trenchant clarity, and cross-denominational influence. Once more, interest in the Puritans and the Reformation revived in the 1960s and 1970s, as influential pastors including John MacArthur, J. I. Packer, John Piper, R. C. Sproul, Joel Beeke, and others would point to Lloyd-Jones as a primary influence on their own ministries.

THE FAILURE OF REVIVALISM

Beginning in the early 1800s, revivalism largely failed in America due to a softening of the doctrine of God's sovereignty. The question raised by Pelagius, Hincmar, and John Goodwin had returned once more. The battles are always the same. Will God be God, or will man attempt to take His place? Attempting to salvage the faith from skepticism and atheism, the 19th Century revivalists leaned heavily on man's will to "get it done." Man's actions, man's decisions, and man's works (vs. God's works) became the primary emphasis. Charles Finney preached, "Sinners, change your own heart!"[67] For men to be converted, Finney said, "It is necessary to raise an excitement among them."[68] Following Peter Lombard's lead in the decline of the Catholic Church beginning in AD 1150, Finney also rejected the doctrine of substitutionary atonement, holding instead to the moral influence theory. In his words, "It is true, that the atonement, of itself, does not secure the salvation of any one."[69] And, he said, "The atonement would present to creatures the highest possible motives to virtue."[70]

If the faith was to be salvaged in America, Christian leaders increasingly looked to themselves to make it happen. The major evangelist of the 20th Century, Billy Graham, tried to explain to dead people "How to be Born Again" in his most famous book. He left his parent's Associate Reformed Presbyterian denomination, claiming that one's own repentance and faith would somehow produce new life. Graham expressed a doctrinal minimalism and a wide-sweeping ecumenicity when he would say, "I feel I belong to all the churches. I am equally at home in an Anglican or Baptist or a Brethren assembly or a Roman Catholic Church."[71] Such teaching would not form solid foundations for the Western faith in its waning years.

With the possible exception of Dwight L. Moody (1837-1899), the revivals of the 19th and 20th centuries veered away from a God-centered view of salvation and an emphasis on the sovereignty of God. Consequently, the fruit of these revivals turned out to be more wood, hay, and stubble than gold, silver, and precious stones. After the

Jesus movement and the revivals of the 1960s and 1970s, evangelical professions of faith in America hit 28% by 1990 (up from 20%).[72] However, this ratio dropped back to 21% by 2019,[73] of which 30% advocated homosexual marriage.[74]

THE CULTS

Man-centered theologies and fake revivals produced very bad fruit for the American church of the early 19th Century, especially in upstate New York. This area turned into a breeding ground for several cults and wayward sects of Christianity which would continue distracting, diverting, and deceiving millions of Christians and non-Christians in America for the next two centuries. The devastation characterizing the "burned-over districts" and the longevity of the fallout is truly a remarkable historical phenomenon.

The cults focused on man's works and man's choices over God's powerful work of salvation. Thus, faith in God's accomplished work in Christ Jesus was minimized. As with all proud humanists before and after the demonically-inspired Enlightenment, these wayward sects refused to accept the incomprehensible elements of the knowledge of God. If a Scriptural doctrine did not comport with a human philosophy built up on human reason, it was forthwith rejected. Also, a fascination with Adventism or the imminent return of Christ arose. An inordinate emphasis on imminently-occurring eschatological events became a distraction from more essential truths. Finally, the cults always seemed to gravitate towards the most external elements or characteristics of God's law and the Christian life—reducing the full import of God's law to something more "doable" by human effort. Emphasis on the resurrection of Christ, the incarnation of Christ, the effectual atoning work of Christ, the sovereignty of God, and other key doctrines always moved to the back burner with these schismatics, and the focus turned towards questionable matters (1 Tim. 6:4), controversies over words (1

Tim. 6:4), controversial speculations (1 Tim. 1:4), fables (1 Tim. 1:4), miscellaneous myths and commands of men (Tit. 1:14), arguments about the law (Tit. 3:9), and almost everything else the Apostle warned about.

These Protestant spin-off cults increased in numbers to about 35,000,000-56,000,000 adherents worldwide by 2010, which amounts to 4-6% of Protestantism.[75] The anti-trinitarian cults which had roots in New York included Mormons and Jehovah's Witnesses. Mormons would bear their strongest influence in the United States, Canada, Japan, Brazil, and the Philippines. Jehovah's Witnesses would infiltrate strongly into the United States, Italy, Mexico, Brazil, and Japan.

THE BAPTISTS & THE BATTLE
FOR A BIBLICAL FAITH

Beloved, while I was very diligent to write to you concerning our common salvation, I found it necessary to write to you exhorting you to contend earnestly for the faith which was once for all delivered to the saints. (Jude 3)

Worldwide Protestantism in the 21st Century broke out roughly into the following statistical assessment (obtained from Pew Forum):[76]

- Pentecostal—300 million
- Baptist—100 million
- Anglican—85 million
- Nondenominational—80 million
- Lutheran—80 million
- Reformed/Presbyterian—60 million
- Methodist—60 million

Of the Pentecostals, evangelicals, and nondenominational groups formed in the 19th and 20th centuries, most of them found their roots in the English Baptists of the 1600s. A full 63% of modern-day

Protestant Christians and at least 90% of evangelicals traced their theological beginnings to Thomas Helwys and John Spilsbury. The primary distinctive of Baptists was their rejection of infant baptism or household baptisms in favor of baptism on profession of faith. The Baptists sought a thoroughly regenerate church membership based on a "credible" profession of faith on the part of individuals baptized into the church.

Influenced somewhat by the Dutch Anabaptists, Thomas Helwys moved from Holland to England and planted a church at Spitalfields, London in 1612. These first English Baptist churches became known as General Baptists, rejecting the Calvinistic doctrine of "particular atonement." Several church splits in the 1630s resulted in the formation of the Particular Baptists, John Spilsbury taking the Calvinistic view that Christ died for His elect. The Baptists found more fertile soil in America, where individualism was more cherished and radical conversion experiences more encouraged (in the early Puritan years). The First London Baptist Confession of 1644 has a "particular" flavor to it, as evident in Article 21: "Jesus Christ by His death did purchase salvation for the elect that God gave unto Him: These only have interest in Him, and fellowship with Him, for whom He makes intercession to His Father in their behalf, and to them alone doth God by His Spirit apply this redemption; as also the free gift of eternal life is given to them, and none else." The Second London Baptist Confession of 1689 more closely followed the Westminster Confession of Faith produced in 1647.

Benjamin Keach was a prolific Baptist writer and a signer of the 1689 Confession. His son immigrated to America in 1686, organized the first Baptist church in Pennepek, Pennsylvania, and planted churches throughout Pennsylvania and New Jersey. The Philadelphia Baptist Association was formed in 1707, slightly modifying the 1689 London Confession in 1742 to create the Philadelphia Baptist Confession.

Meanwhile, the General Baptists formed in New England under the leadership of Roger Williams of Rhode Island. By 1780, there were 457 Baptist churches in America (up from 33 in 1700).[77] By 1850, the Baptists were the second largest denomination in America behind the Methodists. By 1906, they had overtaken the Methodists as the largest Protestant communion. The health of the Baptists may have been partly due to the persecution they received in New England in the 17th Century and in the Southern states through the American War for Independence. It was the Virginia Declaration of Rights, written by George Mason and adopted on June 12, 1776, that finally guaranteed liberty to the Baptists (and Presbyterians) in Virginia. Article 16 of the declaration contains the critical clause: "All men are equally entitled to the free exercise of religion, according to the dictates of conscience."

However, the 19th Century marked a period in which revivalism downplayed the importance of doctrine, creeds, and confessions. Some American Baptists were given to hyper-Calvinist doctrine as in the case of the Primitive Baptists or Hardshell Baptists, under the leadership of Daniel Parker (1781-1844). This anti-evangelistic doctrine was fatal to a segment of evangelical Christianity which relied heavily on evangelism to bring about conversions and church growth.

Modernism took the American Baptists by storm in the late 19th and 20th centuries, while the old Reformation heritage was barely salvaged by some Southern Baptists. The Northern Baptists (and Northern Presbyterians) were more prone to capitulate to the rationalist thinking of modernism than their Southern cousins. Meanwhile, the more conservative Baptists were heavily influenced by John Nelson Darby and C. I. Scofield's theology, which tended towards Dispensationalism and semi-Pelagianism. Also, the higher life and Keswick movements took up a superficial, sentimental, or unrealistic view of sin, holiness, and moral perfection, and had a strong influence on American "conservative" evangelicalism in the 20th Century.

BAPTIST APOSTASY—
THE DOWNGRADE CONTROVERSY

Meanwhile, the renowned Baptist preacher, Charles Spurgeon (1834-1892), appeared to be making some headway, reforming the church in England for a time. However, the extent of England's apostasy was realized when the Downgrade Controversy exploded in 1887. The conflict surfaced at the publication of two articles in Spurgeon's monthly magazine *The Sword and the Trowel*. The articles, written by Robert Shindler, helpfully traced the historical roots of the Protestant apostasy in England over the two preceding centuries. Shindler uncovered the faith drift in the Puritan era beginning in 1662, noting that the nonconformist's downgrade pretty much paralleled the Anglicans. Hundreds of churches, he said, had abandoned Christian orthodoxy for Socinianism, Unitarianism, and the sovereignty of man (against the doctrine of the sovereignty of God). Some of these nonconformist spiritual leaders went so far as to deny the deity of Christ, embracing a full-bore Arianism. Schindler noted that "The Presbyterians were the first to get on the down line," favoring academic pride and humanist classical education over the humble discipleship of Jesus that would take place in the boats on the Sea of Galilee.

> "They paid more attention to classical attainments and other branches of learning…It [was therefore] an easy step in the wrong direction to pay increased attention to academical attainments in their ministers, and less to spiritual qualifications; and to set a higher value on scholarship and oratory, than on evangelical zeal and ability to rightly divide the word of truth."[78]

Instead of leaving the church altogether and professing open atheism, Schindler said these leaders stayed in the church to wreak the havoc of doubt and heterodoxy. "These men deepened their own condemnation, and promoted the everlasting ruin of many of their followers by their hypocrisy and deceit; professing to be the ambassadors of Christ, and the heralds of his glorious gospel, their aim was to ignore his claims, deny him his rights, lower his character, rend the glorious vesture of his salvation, and trample his crown in the dust."[79] At first, this teaching was brought in by "assistants or occasional preachers" in the Presbyterian congregations in the city of Exeter.[80]

Moving on to 19th-Century England, Shindler pointed out that the "tadpole of Darwinism was hatched...[in a pew] of the old chapel in High Street, Shrewsbury."[81] Apparently, this was where Charles Darwin attended church in his early years and where he was personally tutored by the Reverend George Case in the confusion of Socinianism. Moreover, Shindler noted that the chapel previously pastored by the famous Puritan commentator Matthew Henry also fell prey to the Socinian heresy.

With his second article issued in *The Sword and the Trowel,* Shindler drilled into the heart of the contemporary retrograde taking place in England's nonconformist churches:

> The first step astray is a want of adequate faith in the divine inspiration of the sacred Scriptures. All the while a man bows to the authority of God's Word, he will not entertain any sentiment contrary to its teaching. "To the law and to the testimony," is his appeal concerning every doctrine. He esteems that holy Book, concerning all things, to be right, and therefore he hates every false way. But let a man question, or entertain low views of the inspiration and authority of the Bible, and he is without chart to guide him, and without anchor to hold him.

> In looking carefully over the history of the times, and the movement of the times, of which we have written briefly, this fact is apparent: that where ministers and Christian churches have held fast to the truth that the Holy Scriptures have been given by God as an authoritative and infallible rule of faith and practice, they have never wandered very seriously out of the right way. But when, on the other hand, reason has been exalted above revelation, and made the exponent of revelation, all

kinds of errors and mischiefs have been the result.[82]

Charles Spurgeon added several of his own notes to the *Sword and Trowel* articles, sparking a controversy which eventually led to his withdrawal from the Baptist Union, and ecclesiastical censure. Central to Spurgeon's concerns was the doctrine of the sovereignty of God, which he said, "has in it a conservative force which helps to hold men to the vital truth."[83] Man's attempts to sovereignly ordain his own salvation will devolve into the use of manipulative methods and contrivances to gain an audience, usually involving various amusements and theatrical devices. Spurgeon lamented a general lack of interest in prayer meetings and a rejection of the basic gospel message: "Alas! many are returning to the poisoned cups which drugged that declining generation. . . Too many ministers are toying with the deadly cobra of 'another gospel,' in the form of 'modern thought.'"[84] The source of the problem in 1887, he noted, was the leaven seeping into England from a full-on German apostasy. Spurgeon continues: "The case is mournful. Certain ministers are making infidels. Avowed atheists are not a tenth as dangerous as those preachers who scatter doubt and stab at faith...Germany was made unbelieving by her preachers, and England is following in her tracks."[85] He summarized the central matter of the Downgrade: "Our warfare is with men who are giving up the atoning sacrifice, denying the inspiration of Holy Scripture, and casting slurs upon justification by faith."[86]

The fallout from the articles was akin to the martyrdom of Polycarp and the public opposition to John Wycliff and Athanasius. Though he may have been the most famous preacher in the world at the time, that made no difference. At the height of his career, Spurgeon had fallen over the sword, with the publication of these articles in *The Sword and the Trowel*. The voice of the Prince of Preachers in the Metropolitan Tabernacle had been reduced to a voice crying in the wilderness. Pastor and author John MacArthur described the backlash as something akin to a tsunami: "The article rocked the evangelical world. Spurgeon, who for decades had been almost universally revered by evangelicals, was suddenly besieged with critics from within the camp. What he was proposing was diametrically opposed to the consensus of evangelical thought. All the trends were toward unification, harmony, amalgamation, and brotherhood. Suddenly here was a lone voice—but the most influential voice of all—urging true believers to become separatists. The church was neither prepared nor willing to receive such counsel—not even from the Prince of Preachers."[87]

What had seemed to be something of a revival of evangelical faith under the ministry of Charles Spurgeon dissipated quickly after his death. His wife Susannah believed that the Downgrade had become "his fight for the faith" and that it had "cost him his life."[88]

Still afterwards, Charles Spurgeon's worldwide ministry of books and sermons published in newspapers and magazines continued to strengthen evangelicalism and render life support to the Reformation faith well into the 21st Century. His evangelical teachings, rooted in a strong commitment to God's sovereignty, spurred on church leaders and writers like A. W. Pink, John Piper, John MacArthur, and other pastors associated with the Reformed Baptists and the Founders Movement of the Southern Baptist Convention.

The strengths of evangelical Baptists included their steadfast commitment to the authority of Scripture, preaching, evangelism, and an insistence on Christian commitment (and being doers of the Word). Weaknesses would include tendencies towards individualism, church splits and disunity, devaluation of the church body, baptism, and the Lord's Supper, and a lack of submission and accountability among pastors. Modern fundamentalist Baptists were also prone to gravitate towards external forms of sanctification, legalism (replacing God's laws with man's laws), antinomianism (rejecting God's laws altogether), hero worship (via charismatic leaders), and humanism (strongly emphasizing man's will and man's choice as ultimately determinative).

At the end of Spurgeon's life, weekly church attendance in England was still hovering around 40%.[89] This decreased to 12% by 1970,[90] and then bottomed out at 3% in 2020.[91] By this time, Church of England weekly attendance was a mere 854,000 persons, or just 1.5% of the population. There were more Christians in Japan than people attending the English Church, and Japan was among the most resistant to Christianity of all the nations in the world. Baptist church attendance in England stood at 226,000 individuals or 0.4% of the population, a drop-off from 287,000 thirty years earlier.[92] Evangelicalism was barely surviving in the UK. Between 1990 and 2020, the evangelical population within the Church of England dropped from 320,000 to 220,000 (amounting to only 0.4% of the population).[93] Over the same thirty year period, overall evangelical church attendance dropped from 1.4 million to 1.2 million (or just 2% of the population).

No doubt church attendance in England in earlier centuries was an empty formality for many. While the genuineness of the faith may have been better reflected in faithful church attendance in the year 2020, it was clear that now Christianity in England had lost its cultural influence upon its national institutions and the Western world.

PRESBYTERIAN LIBERALISM IN AMERICA

American Presbyterian minister Charles Briggs was brought to ecclesiastical trial and defrocked in 1893 for his views concerning the evolutionary origins of man, higher criticism, and the errancy of Scripture. The actions taken were a little too late, however, in that Briggs had already infected pastors-in-training with his ideas for two decades at Union Seminary in New York City. Briggs turned Episcopalian, and Union Seminary cut off ties with the Northern Presbyterian church

(PCUSA), retaining Briggs on its faculty. The seminary continued educating Presbyterian pastors, who in turn passed their liberal views on to local congregations for generations to come.

Nobody epitomized American liberal apostasy so well as Woodrow Wilson, the 28th President of the United States. Following the pattern of apostasy set by most 19th Century Western ideological leaders, Wilson was raised in the Presbyterian tradition and turned away from it. His father, Joseph Ruggles Wilson, had served as a pastor and stated clerk of the Southern Presbyterian church for 37 years. In 1902, Woodrow Wilson became president of Princeton University, and right away discontinued Bible instruction classes in the school. He would consult a ouija board on matters relating to Princeton politics, and in his writings, recommended Darwinist and secular humanist philosophies for modern political governance. His own leadership at the nation's helm marked the most radical departure from Christian principle—racist segregation in government offices, evolutionary eugenics, graduated taxation, monopolized and debauched currency, big government socialism, and internationalism.

Liberalism came to a head in the Northern Presbyterian church (PCUSA) in 1924. The Darwinist, materialist, anti-supernaturalist worldview had dug in hard by this time, and Protestantism was overwhelmed by this juggernaut. Five fundamental doctrines were at stake: 1) the inerrancy of Scripture, 2) the virgin birth and the deity of Christ, 3) the doctrine of substitutionary atonement, 4) the bodily resurrection of Jesus Christ, and 5) the authenticity of Christ's miracles. At least two of these doctrines were present in the Apostles Creed as early as the 2nd Century of the Church. All five doctrines had been stridently defended by the Reformers and their confessions of faith. Yet, in 1924, a petition was circulated just prior to the PCUSA General Assembly, garnering the support of 1,274 liberal ministers. The Auburn Affirmation rejected the inerrancy of Scripture and recommended against using the five "essential" doctrines as a test for ordination. From that point forward, new denominations splintered off from the PCUSA. These included the Orthodox Presbyterian Church (formed in 1936), and the Evangelical Presbyterian Church (formed in 1981). The Southern Presbyterian church (PCUS) followed the same liberal path more slowly. In 1973, conservatives pulled away from the union of the PCUS/PCUSA to form the PCA.

THE PENTECOSTALS OF THE 20TH CENTURY

And when they had prayed, the place was shaken where they were assembled together; and they were all filled with the Holy Ghost, and they spake the word of God with boldness. And the multitude of them that believed were of one heart and of one soul: neither said any of them that ought of the things which he possessed was his own; but they had all things common. And with great power gave the apostles witness of the resurrection of the Lord Jesus: and great grace was upon them all. (Acts 4:32-34)

Arguably, the Pentecostal and Charismatic movements of the 20th Century constitute the fastest-growing branch of Christianity in history—an extraordinary 300 million adherents collected in just one hundred years. In 1980, Charismatics and Pentecostals made up about 6% of the world's Christian population. Forty years later, the ratio was closer to 25% by some estimates.

The movement is thought to have begun in Los Angeles at the Azusa Street Mission, where a one-eyed black preacher by the name of William J. Seymour came to minister in 1905. Seymour had been discipled by Charles Fox Parham in Houston, Texas, a follower of Keswick holiness teachings. Parham believed miraculous healings could be a norm in modern Christian ministry, and he advocated xenoglossia—the supernatural gift of speaking in a foreign tongue. He added a third work of the Holy Spirit to regeneration and sanctification (or perfectionism), which he called empowerment for spiritual service.

For three years the Azusa Street Revival continued. It was racially integrated. Services were absent of any particular order, and multitudes spoke and sang in tongues. From the outset, the cross-cultural impact of Pentecostalism was probably its greatest strength. Female leadership was common among the Pentecostals, similar to the Montanists of the 3rd Century. These included such names as Florence Crawford, Ida Robinson, Kathryn Kuhlman, and Aimee Semple McPherson. Because of its strong cross-cultural attraction, Pentecostalism quickly spread into foreign nations. Between 1907 and 1910, mission works were established in Argentina, Brazil, South Africa, Russia, and Italy.

Pentecostals held to the ultimate authority and sufficiency of Scripture for faith and life, but sometimes negated the doctrine by claiming to receive extra-scriptural, authoritative revelation from God. Theologians Duffield and van Cleave offered this explanation for the Pentecostal use of prophecy: "Normally, in the operation of the gift of prophecy, the Spirit heavily anoints the believer to speak forth to the body not premeditated words, but words the Spirit supplies spontaneously in order to uplift and encourage, incite to faithful obedience and service, and to bring comfort and consolation."[94] To the extent that these "encouragements" lacked a basis in Scriptural revelation, the teaching veered wildly, and the "standard deviation" or range of perspective within Pentecostalism was huge.

During the 20th Century, Pentecostals and Charismatics came to be known for their boldness in evangelism and robustness under persecution. Casting aside concern for their own safety, many of these brethren demonstrated steadfast faith under fire, especially in the Soviet Bloc nations and the Islamic states. Our God wants us to love Him with heart, soul, and mind; the charismatics sometimes demonstrated a heart love for God in worship and service. They also emphasized the doctrine of the Holy Spirit, accepting Him as active, omnipresent, powerful, and personal. For some Christian denominations, God becomes very distant to the individual through excessive focus on dogma and doctrinal contentions, or by constant immersion into an anti-supernatural zeitgeist. Institutions, liturgies that have lost meaning, rote worship, and so forth can get in the way of true spiritual worship. Thereby, God becomes distant, depersonalized, less real, and less sovereign over the sparrow that falls and the hairs on our heads. When the Charismatic begins to realize God's hand in his life and by faith responds in heart-felt gratitude and praise, he demonstrates faith.

On the other hand, Pentecostals sometimes traded faith for presumption, falling into the trap of manipulating God through prayer. The Word of Faith movement hinged everything on the faith of the one who seeks health and wealth—not necessarily the will of Christ for believers. Thus the Word of Faith teacher lost sight of God's ultimate sovereignty and neglected to include the phrase "nevertheless not my will, but thine be done" (Luke 22:42) in his prayers.

Moreover, the use of prophecy as the conveyance of one's own ideas, the endless seeking after miracles and personal experiences would often trump the authority of God's Word in the mind of the Pentecostal. The Jews sought continually for signs but lacked faith, and this same faithlessness infected many modern Christians (1 Cor. 1:22). Faith must believe even when it has not witnessed a miraculous healing or resurrection of late. "Faith is the substance of things hoped for, the evidence of things not seen" (Heb. 11:1). And, "Blessed are those who have not seen, and yet believe" (John 20:29).

The Pentecostal and Charismatic movements also tended towards moral scandal. Aimee Semple McPherson was twice divorced; healing evangelist A. A. Allen was arrested for drunk driving while conducting revival meetings and then skipped bail. Charles Fox Parham was arrested on charges of sodomy, although the case was later dismissed. Kathryn Kuhlman became involved with a married man, another evangelist by the name of Burroughs Waltrip. The scandals continued into the 1980s with the televangelists and mega-church leaders, including Jim Bakker, Jimmy Swaggart, Peter Popoff, Earl Paulk, Paul Crouch, Paul Cain, Ted Haggard, Randy and Paula White, Benny Hinn, and Frank Houston (Hillsong Church and the Australian Pentecostal movement); and the list goes on. At the least, the lengthy catalog of shameful scandals among the leadership demonstrated a basic weakness or immaturity within these 20th Century sects.

The line between a life of humble confession and repentance and ostentatious programs promising a "higher life" or a "second blessing" is sometimes a little thin and gray. While Christians should never resist the encouragement to sanctification, holiness, Spirit-filling, mortification of sin, dedication to Christ, and the gifts of the Spirit, there are many false pretenses of all of the above. Charlatans are a dime-a-dozen in the religion business, and have been since the days of Simon the Sorcerer. Well did our Lord remind us, "You will know them by their fruits" (Matt. 7:16). To this day with modern evangelicalism, Christ's warnings concerning false prophets remain critically relevant.

Since the 19th Century, various Christian sects and movements had formed around the impulse to find singular spiritual experiences or to delineate discrete spiritual levels (whether it be a "second" work of the Spirit or some "higher" life). For some groups, this offered a stronger sense of exclusivity to the membership, or a stronger allegiance to a charismatic leader. Nonetheless, all of these teachings required an unnatural, forced, or mechanical imposition on Scripture. The Holy Spirit of God should never be limited to just two or three discrete works or outpourings. His sanctifying work in the life of the believer appears as an ongoing process and a growth over time, rather than an immediate one-time experience (Phil. 1:9-11). Indeed,

Scripture urges that every Christian should seek the "filling" of the Spirit (Eph. 5:18). The interpersonal relationship with the Spirit of God may involve a grieving or a quenching from time to time, and every Christian is always and constantly reliant on the Holy Spirit for every spiritual gift and work.

Where Christianity spreads rapidly, the resultant effect over communities and nations may at first turn out to be painfully superficial, as the saying goes, "a mile wide and an inch deep." Nonetheless, every believer is still thankful for every inch of depth, always grateful for whatever work the Spirit of God has accomplished. Regrettably, the Pentecostal church rated worse than Roman Catholics, Muslims, and Hindus in surveys assessing the moral condition of 21st Century Christianity (at least when considering divorce and cohabitation rates).[95] One worldview survey found that Pentecostals were the most likely among American evangelicals to approve of abortion—54% rejected the proposition that life in the womb is sacred and 69% rejected ethical absolutes (revealed by God in Scripture).[96] The failure to "disciple the nations" by teaching all things Jesus commanded (Matt. 28:18-20) was one root cause for the ensuing apostasy in the West.

MAINLINE DENOMINATIONAL APOSTASY

Therefore take heed to yourselves and to all the flock, among which the Holy Spirit has made you overseers, to shepherd the church of God which He purchased with His own blood. For I know this, that after my departure savage wolves will come in among you, not sparing the flock. Also from among yourselves men will rise up, speaking perverse things, to draw away the disciples after themselves. Therefore watch, and remember that for three years I did not cease to warn everyone night and day with tears. So now, brethren, I commend you to God and to the word of His grace, which is able to build you up and give you an inheritance among all those who are sanctified. (Paul's last words to the Ephesian elders, Acts 20:28-32)

The Western Protestant apostasy sank to depths never before witnessed in church history, even exceeding the wickedness of the ancient pagan world, at points. After the Western nations had corrupted themselves with the leaven of evolutionary materialism, atheism, Marxism, sexual autonomy, gender confusion, and all the other elements of Christian apostasy, they proceeded to export the toxins into second and third world countries. Not willing to participate in the Fall of the Western church, African and South American churches would break communion with Western denominations. For instance, in 2005, Nigeria's Anglican Church cut ties with the Anglican communion of England and North America over the matter of homosexuality.[97] Finally, the glory had departed from Canterbury—it was the end of a 1,400 year legacy.

Twentieth Century Western apostasy capitulated to feminism, homosexuality, and transgenderism. Both ideologies of gender role confusion and gender confusion were highly corrupting and destructive influences for human society at large. That which was destroying society would eventually destroy the mainline church as well as large segments of the evangelical church.

Radical changes came about in the 20th Century among US mainline Protestant churches. In the 1930s, the Northern Presbyterian church (PCUSA) ordained its first female elders, and put the first women in ministerial office in 1956. The Church of Scotland opened the pulpit to women in 1949, and the first women ministers appeared in 1968. The Evangelical Lutheran Church of America began ordaining women in 1973 with the ordination of "Rev. Elizabeth Platz." Then the Christian Reformed Church (of Dutch derivation) began ordaining women in 1995. Between 1980 and 2012, at least thirty-two Protestant denominations (in New Zealand, Norway, Canada, Denmark, Sweden, the Philippines, Guatemala, Australia, Germany, Finland, Iceland,

South Africa, and Ireland) initiated the ordination of female pastors.

In 2012 (according to its executive commission), the Presbyterian Church of Brazil (IPB) announced that there was "no biblical impediment that, in special occasions or situations, women preach under the authority of a pastor."[98] This confusion of gender roles and the breakdown of the family in apostate Western countries between 1960 and 2000 prepared the Western world for its final stage of corruption.

Coming on the heels of feminism and egalitarianism in the churches was the acceptance of homosexuality among mainline denominations. In 2003, the United States Episcopal Church ordained Gene Robinson as the first openly practicing homosexual bishop in the Western world. He was "legally joined" to his "partner" in 2008 and subsequently "divorced" in 2014. In 2005, the United Church of Christ as a denomination issued a statement encouraging congregations to affirm "equal marriage rights for all" and to consider "wedding policies that do not discriminate based on the gender of the couple." On August 21, 2009, the Evangelical Lutheran Church in America approved the ordination of non-celibate homosexuals to the office of minister by a vote of 559 to 451. This was the largest Lutheran denomination in America, boasting 4 million members. Following suit, the Presbyterian Church (USA), representing 1.9 million members, approved a constitutional change on May 10, 2011, to allow the ministerial ordination of non-celibate homosexuals. Then, on June 19, 2014 the PCUSA General Assembly approved ministers officiating same-sex "weddings" in states where the practice had been legalized in the civil courts or legislatures.

During its annual gathering in 2011, Church of Scotland commissioners voted to accept homosexual clergy, "on the condition they had declared their sexuality and were ordained before 2009." Following the lead of these apostate churches, almost every Western nation proceeded to offer government sanction of homosexual unions and "marriages."

Not to be outdone by the Protestants, the Roman Catholic Pope Francis endorsed the homosexual orientation in 2020, announcing to members of the church, "God loves [homosexuals] as they are" and "the church loves [them] as they are because they are children of God."[99] Such public endorsements of scandalous sin finds no pattern in church history—even during the worst, most morally degraded papacies of John XII, Julius II, or Innocent VIII.

The battles for the faith continued in the 21st Century, especially as education and cultural systems became thoroughly post-Christian, apostate, and humanist. Since much of the Christian family and the Christian church gave up on daily discipleship for children and turned this function over to the secular humanist state, the faith largely failed across Western nations. It should be no surprise that church attendance dropped off with the millennial generation in England, Scotland, Canada, and America. This was the inevitable result of the failure to disciple successive generations and the synthesis of humanism with the Christian faith. The rejection of biblical authority came surreptitiously at first. The modern church more and more rejected the worldwide flood, six-day creation, the immediate creation of man out of the dust, and the historical fall of man into sin. Gradualistic, naturalistic evolutionary theories eroded the faith in the young people, generation by generation. But the fundamental erosion happened when individuals gave up on the authority of God speaking through His revealed Word. "The words of the LORD are pure words, like silver tried in a furnace of earth, purified seven times" (Ps. 12:6).

Post-modern relativism came to infect the preaching of the Word, where less and less could be said with certainty and force in the modern pulpit. Increasingly, the music program replaced the centrality of preaching in many assemblies for the first time in the history of the church. Paul's pastoral epistles contain nothing about music programs, but he did insist that pastors focus on preaching the Word in season and out of season, exhorting, rebuking, and admonishing (2 Tim. 4:1-3). Singing also was assigned to the churches as one more means by which men and women were to be admonished in the truth (Col. 3:16).

Ethical capitulation to the autonomy of a post-Christian culture occurred as the church embraced feminism, abortion, conception control, in vitro fertilization, gender confusion, deviant forms of sexuality, and the education of children in all of that. The forces now destroying family and sexuality in the modern world were almost equally active inside as outside evangelical and Protestant churches in the West.

Pornography was infecting young men in the church at equal or higher rates as those outside of the church. Illegitimate divorce and remarriage had become commonplace within the Christian church. The sins of fornication, pedophilia, and homosexuality were named over and over again in the churches. Some sects argued over the benefits of polygamy. All of this pointed to the weakness of faith, the absence of the Spirit's work, and the failure to preach both the Gospel and the law. It was the failure to disciple the nations.

> Let no man deceive you by any means: for that day shall not come, except there come a falling away first, and that man of sin be revealed, the son of perdition; Who opposeth and exalteth himself above all that is called God, or that is worshipped; so that he as God sitteth in the temple of God, shewing himself that he is God. (2 Thessalonians 2:3-4)

The deification of man came by way of the *Humanist Manifesto*, infecting all major institutions in the West. Yet, humanism also infiltrated the church, situating itself in the temple of God, like the man of sin of 2 Thessalonians 2. Humanism is self-consciously man-centered, placing man as the source and sovereign over reality, truth, and ethics. The "man of sin" or "lawlessness" (*anomia* in Greek) is against the law of God. The rejection of God's law in the church was blatant, boldfaced, and arrogant. Autonomy as an ethical ideology was deeply imbedded and institutionalized in every aspect of American life, and much of church life. Antinomianism restructured theology, the soteriology, and the methodology of the church.

Wrong theological systems disallowed much of the ethical force of Scripture and discouraged the instruction of God's people in the law of God. Whereas the Old Testament was intended to "equip the man of God for every good work" (2 Tim. 3:16-17), it was hardly used that way anymore. The great contentions in the church were over the uses of the law of God, the applicability and relevance of Old Testament law, and whether the law ought to be taught at all within the Church. Jettisoning the law of God also meant jettisoning the Gospel. If by the law comes the knowledge of sin (Rom. 3:20), and if Jesus Christ came to save us from sin (Matt. 1:21), then the Church should have salvaged the Gospel message by defending the sanctity and authority of God's law. The Gospel was rendered meaningless as the law of God was discarded by both evangelicals and modernists.

The roles of family, church, and state were also increasingly confounded in this modern age. Christians could not tell whether God's law should bind back the hand of the tyrant as the state expanded its purview over every area of life (mostly by democratic vote). State control of the church was the battle in the 17th Century, but state control over education, family, medicine, business, and the rest of life was the battlefield for liberty in the 21st Century. Does God's law speak to this? Would Christians stand in opposition to a rising, persecuting state or merely capitulate to it? These questions became increasingly important in a post-Christian age when the Western world has reverted to paganism, raw humanism, socialism, statism, and a self-consciously anti-Christian worldview.

SCANDALS AMONG THE CONSERVATIVES— THE CATHOLICS & THE EVANGELICALS

For first of all, when ye come together in the church, I hear that there
be divisions among you; and I partly believe it. For there must be
also heresies among you, that they which are approved may be made
manifest among you. (1 Corinthians 10:18-19)

While liberal Protestant churches were openly embracing
sexual perversion and abortion, conservative Roman Catholics and
evangelicals were swamped in scandals.

The moral effects of the Reformation had pretty well worn off by
1960, and the scandals of the late 20th Century far exceeded the terrible
conditions of the 16th Century Western Church. In 1531, Martin Luther
chastised Pope Leo X for vetoing a measure that would have limited
pedophilia among the clergy. Luther wrote, "otherwise it would have
been spread throughout the world how openly and shamelessly the
pope and the cardinals in Rome practice sodomy."[100] Yet, following
the sexual revolution of the 1960s, heart-sickening reports of child
abuse committed by clergymen churned out continuously for fifty
years via the major media, utterly desecrating the reputation of the
Christian church in the eyes of the world. The John Jay report, covering
churches in the United States, concluded 5,000 clergy were accused
in 11,000 cases—constituting an unconscionable ratio of 1 in 15 of
Roman Catholic ecclesiastics. By 2020, twenty-one Catholic dioceses
were forced to declare bankruptcy due to sexual abuse lawsuits.[101]

The presence of this devilish evil seemed to exempt none of
the Western nations. A study conducted by three German Catholic
Universities alleged 3,677 cases of sexual abuse, mostly homosexual
in nature. Ireland was the worst, with some 1,300 clergy accused

of abuse and tens of thousands of complainants.[102] Australia also was dealing with thousands of cases. Of some orders, like the St. John of God and the Benedictine Priests, 20-40% of clergy and lay brothers were alleged perpetrators.[103] The vast majority of the cases were homosexual (81%).[104] Around the same time (dating from 1950 to 2010), the Australian Anglican Church registered about one third of the number of alleged perpetrators as found among the Catholic churches.[105] Although the media coverage was far less and the number of pastors accused much smaller, the fundamentalist Baptists[106] and Southern Baptists[107] were caught in the same types of scandals. Evidently, the modern sexual revolution and the post-Christian zeitgeist had swept the mainstream churches into the rushing stream. More than ever before, these effects demonstrated the rot in the theological foundations of Western churches. The latter part of the 20th Century was a shameful, nightmarish time for the organized church—both Catholic and Protestant.

THE 20TH CENTURY—
STRENGTHENING THE THINGS THAT REMAIN

As Western civilization collapsed, a small remnant of the Western church was determined to "strengthen the things that remain, that are ready to die" (Rev. 3:3). Indeed, the West had entered a post-Christian age. At the turn of the 21st Century, the academic world had changed the designation of the year from "AD" (the year of our Lord) to "CE" (common era). It was a symbolic move, representing the high-handed apostasy in the Western world and the humanist deception of this world's major institutions.

Throughout the 19th and 20th centuries, atheists and anti-Christian thinkers such as Friedrich Nietzsche, Sigmund Freud, and B. F. Skinner developed the "scientific" field of psychology, and much of Christianity integrated the new religion into the church. Beginning in

1965, a Reformed Presbyterian pastor named Jay Adams reintroduced biblical counseling to the Christian world. Adams' "nouthetic counseling" work produced a worldwide movement of biblical counseling led by the Association of Certified Biblical Counselors.

A thoroughly secular education espoused by John Dewey and other prominent humanists in the early 20th Century prevailed for awhile and was even promoted by Christian pastors and teachers for several generations. Constituting a loyal opposition to this anti-Christian, naturalist-materialist worldview in the macro culture, a steady stream of conservative Presbyterian theologians emerged. Francis Schaeffer, Gordon Clark, R. J. Rushdoony, Cornelius Van Til, and J. Gresham Machen advocated a distinctively Christian theory of knowledge and education. The impact was slight however, as no major church denomination would officially oppose the secular zeitgeist advanced in the public schools. A small Christian school movement formed in the 1960s and 1970s, maxing out at 1 million students and then tapering off. Between 1980 and 2022, the American homeschool movement grew to about 5 million students, of which just over 50% were evangelical.[108] An estimated 3.5% of the population of school-aged children in the United States received a Christian education in the year 2020.

In 1960, a diminutive, conservative publishing house (Presbyterian and Reformed Publishers) released a book that shook the Christian world to its foundations. Authored by two scientists, *The Genesis Flood* reintroduced a creationist paradigm to a world where very few Christian scientists and pastors would have agreed with the universal opinion of the church fathers and reformers regarding the age of the earth and *ex nihilo* creation. In most of the Western church, the opinions of scientists who produced far-fetched hypotheses concerning the evolution of the species were far more respected than the authority of divine revelation. The evolutionary paradigm for the origins of the sentient creation was thoroughly engrained in every educational, scientific, and political institution. No wonder this published work came as a seismic event upon Western churches and academic institutions! Of most significance however, as the worldview implications are considered, was that this reformation began with scientists. Henry Morris and John C. Whitcomb had bowed the epistemological knee to the authority of God's Word—interpreting the evidence of rock layers and fossils by the Word of God and the testimony of a worldwide flood, instead of reinterpreting the Genesis narrative by the evolutionary hypothesis. The resultant controversy raged for half a century. Large parachurch ministries formed around the doctrine of creation, including the Institute for Creation Research (founded by Dr. Henry Morris), Creation Ministries International, and Answers in Genesis (founded by Ken Ham). Christian apologetics ministries and worldview training organizations also formed, equipping thousands of students to combat an increasingly, aggressive anti-Christian world. Yet, once again, none of the major Christian seminaries or major denominations (with the exception of the Lutheran Church-Missouri Synod)[109] would endorse these attempts to reform or join the resistance to the zeitgeist at the most critical point. Over and over again, the loyal opposition was remanded to the Cave of Adullam (see 1 Samuel 22:1-2) and the parachurch backwoods.

At the same time, pro-life ministries formed to address the rising tide of abortion in a post-Christian culture. Also, Christian media gained tremendous momentum during the 1970s and 1980s, and most radio broadcasters were on the more biblical, evangelical, or conservative end of the scale. In the 2000s, Christian film producers like Stephen Kendrick and Rich Christiano began to introduce films with Christian themes to theaters, some of which reached short-term first position in box office sales.

During the 1970s, the United States experienced a brief revival called "the Jesus movement." A sincere interest in the study of the

Word of God arose amongst young people, and evangelicalism received a boost from 20% to 30% of the US population (between 1972 and 1985). A Pentecostal preacher named David Wilkerson contributed strongly to the rise of this fresh breath of evangelicalism. Throughout his life, Wilkerson was increasingly influenced by Leonard Ravenhill and the writings of the Puritans and reformers, including John Owen, Thomas Brooks, William Gurnall, and John Calvin. Chuck Smith, a pastor from Southern California, formed Calvary Chapel out of this revivalist movement, and his method of teaching through the entire Bible offered a discipleship program that seemed to bear fruit beyond the boundaries of his own denomination. College ministries, including Campus Crusade for Christ, Inter-Varsity Christian Fellowship, and The Navigators, also offered serious discipleship opportunities for college students. Prison ministries formed out of the 1970s, offering discipleship to the world's largest prison population (in the United States). These discipleship ministries also provided some impetus to an albeit brief recovery of fatherhood, family discipleship, and the practice of family worship in the 1990s and 2000s.

Nonetheless, this reviving work had no measurable effect upon the wider culture in the West. It was only of temporary benefit to the evangelical church. It was remnant work and offered islands of culture and generational faith for biblical churches and Christian families.

THE 21ST CENTURY—THE FINAL DECLINE FOR THE WESTERN CHRISTIAN CHURCH

At the turn of the 3rd millennium, the largest evangelical churches in the West were still located in England and the United States. In 2010, the United States claimed 160 million professing Protestant Christians. Nigeria came in second with 60 million, China third with 58 million, Brazil fourth with 41 million, South Africa with 37 million, and the UK with 34 million.[110] Yet, in Western nations, these numbers didn't mean much after two hundred years of apostasies and fundamental compromises within the churches.

As the last bastion of the Western church, American evangelicalism began its fall at the turn of the 21st Century. Those calling themselves evangelicals in America dropped from roughly 30% in 1980 to 20% in 2019.[111] Church membership across the board reduced from 71% to as low as 50% for the first time in the nation's history.[112] And weekly church attendance dropped from 34% to 23% between 1990 and 2018. The proportion of those who believed that the Bible was God's actual Word dropped from 40% to 24% of the population between 1980 and 2017.[113] Although church attendance did not diminish as quickly among American evangelicals, the worldview or fundamental belief system of these professing Christians proved to be a more precise barometer of the Christian faith in America. The pollster George Barna discovered a precipitous decline in a commitment to the most basic and essential Christian doctrines— over a twenty-five year period. Barna's worldview survey included questions relating to the existence of God, the omnipotence and omniscience of God, the sovereignty of God, justification by faith alone, absolute ethics communicated through divine revelation, and the inspiration and authority of the Word of God. By 2020, only 6% of Americans held to a Christian worldview, down from 12% in 1995.[114] While 61% of American millennials (19-29 years of age) still professed Christianity, only 2% held to a biblical worldview—a strong indication of the tremendous humanist grip which public schools and popular media had achieved over the minds of the younger generation. Once again, the rock of stumbling for these millennials in the survey turned out to be the proposition that "absolute ethics are communicated through the Scriptures." Only 20% of American evangelicals and 1% of Catholics held to the most basic rudiments of a biblical worldview for an estimated 4% of all Americans.[115]

METASTASIS

In terms of church attendance, a metastasis of rank apostasy in the United States occurred between 2011 and 2014. For a hundred years plus, American "regular" church attendance continued above forty percent...until 2011. Within just nine years, 54% of the professing Christian population abandoned the church. Arguably, the year 2020 was the worst per-year bloodletting for the Christian church in recorded history.

The Final Downgrade

Year	Regular Church Attendance [116]
2011	48%
2017	38%
2020 (January)	29%
2020 (December)	22%

Explanations for the abrupt decline following 2011 included a stream of scandals in the American evangelical and reformed churches as well as an accelerated exit on the part of the millennial generation. However, some particular catalyst must have precipitated the sharp decline, producing the sudden wind shift coming about in the macro-culture. Social observers witnessed Western culture moving from a positive view of Christian values and culture to a negative view sometime between 2011 and 2014. After 400 years of general reception on the part of political and cultural institutions, Christians would henceforth be victims of persecution. The first instance came in 2006, when a Christian photographer in New Mexico was fined for refusing to participate in a homosexual "wedding" ceremony. The case was finally adjudicated in 2012, and the New Mexico Court of Appeals ruled in favor of the homosexual plaintiff—a ruling sustained by the US Supreme Court two years later.[117] A Christian florist found herself in a similar situation in December of 2012,[118] and a Christian family running a bakery shop in Oregon was similarly charged in January, 2013.[119] The zeitgeist had shifted in 2012. The gauntlet was set down before the Christian population, and the majority of churchgoers would have nothing to do with it. Faced with a choice of accommodation or confrontation with the macro-culture, the majority chose rather to accommodate—compromise the message or just leave the church.

> And unto the angel of the church in Thyatira write; These things saith the Son of God, who hath his eyes like unto a flame of fire, and his feet are like fine brass...Notwithstanding I have a few things against thee, because thou sufferest that woman Jezebel, which calleth herself a prophetess, to teach and to seduce my servants to commit fornication, and to eat things sacrificed unto idols. And I gave her space to repent of her fornication; and she repented not. Behold, I will cast her into a bed, and them that commit adultery with her into great tribulation, except they repent of their deeds. (Revelation 2:18-22)

One of the most telling marks of a weakening church was the disappearance of men from church leadership. A 2017 survey found that women comprised 21% of American clergy, with liberal denominations claiming a ten-fold increase in female leadership over the previous forty years. At this time, women made up 25% of the enrollment in the ten largest evangelical seminaries in the nation.[120] In 2020, eight out of ten of the best-selling nonfiction books listed on the Evangelical Christian Book Publishers list were written by women.[121] Fifteen years earlier, ten out of the top ten nonfiction bestsellers were written by men—pastors and leaders like John MacArthur, Larry Burkett, and Rick Warren.[122] The feminist-driven evangelical church leaned towards accepting homosexuality. Leading authors in "Christendom" like Jen Hatmaker announced in 2018 that Jesus came "to affirm the LGBT community," and celebrated her daughter's lesbianism in 2020. And, evangelicalism's favorite author in 2019, Rachel Hollis, told everybody in her bestselling book, there is no "one right way to be," and it's okay to be "gay."[123]

At the Fall, American Christianity (at least for the younger generation) had descended into the murky depths of England's religious situation by 2020. The discipleship of the Western nations had faded substantially by this point. The salt had lost its savor.

THE CHURCH GROWTH PHENOMENON

About half of evangelicalism moved into large megachurches between 1970 and 2014. The number of churches boasting more than 2,000 attendees increased from 10 to 1,600 in forty-four years.[124] Large expensive buildings and music programs were accommodated. Yet none of this benefited the overall quality or quantity of evangelicalism. To the contrary, the overall number of adherents dropped off through the 1990s and 2000s. These large ministries multiplied the effect of scandals when high-profile pastors and church growth gurus like Ted Haggard, James MacDonald, Bill Hybels, Joshua Harris, Perry Noble, Darrin Patrick, Tullian Tchividjian, and Mark Driscoll "fell from grace," or at least from high-profile spiritual leadership. All of this played a part in the disillusionment and collapse of the church growth methodologies and movements of the latter 20th Century.

> O my people, they which lead thee cause thee to err, and destroy the way of thy paths. (Isaiah 3:12)

Youthful leadership served as a temporary phenomenon and a weakening element in the breakdown of evangelicalism in America. Many of the megachurch pastors were in their early or mid-twenties when they formed their movements and evangelical denominations. Although revolutionary culture was attracted to the youth element, young leadership did not add to the strengthening of faith and life in the church.

CRISIS IN EVANGELICALISM

What is it then? I will pray with the spirit, and I will pray with the understanding also: I will sing with the spirit, and I will sing with the understanding also. (1 Corinthians 14:15)

Neither give heed to fables and endless genealogies, which minister questions, rather than godly edifying which is in faith. Now the end of the commandment is charity out of a pure heart, and of a good conscience, and of faith unfeigned... (1 Timothy 1:4-5)

Experientialism affected the evangelical church greatly at this time—the subjective experience became more-or-less the sole test of true belief. The worldview of irrationalism in the form of Romanticism came to dominate in much of what was left of 21st-Century evangelicalism. Both subjective feelings and the primacy of the individual was the outlook. Reality faded in the arts, and truth faded in the mind of the postmodern. Mainly through music and art forms, the worldview of Romanticism was eroding the very notion of truth itself in the consciousness of the West. Thus, the term "I feel" became the essential confession of faith. The term was ubiquitous, and increasingly the epistemology of "I feel" undermined faith in "God said," especially in the churches.

The German composer Richard Wagner (1813-1883) best incarnated the worldview of Romanticism in music for the *avant-garde* of Europe. He intentionally designed the force of emotion in his music to overwhelm the organization of melody and content. This "Dionysian Revolution" became mainstream in the 1960s and virtually took control of church music in the 1990s and 2000s.

Thus, the genuineness of religious experience came to be measured by the emotional intensity of the music or the sheer volume of the primal scream. At this point it didn't seem to matter that the Christian musician or worship leader was living with her boyfriend.

The experientialist takeover was complete.

We were supposed to be impressed by pietistic language, emotional tones, and passionate music, but this cheap spirituality cannot withstand malevolent spiritual forces and sexual temptation. The first impression was a lie. To express a truth with mere exaggerated emotion could not be equated to the quality of faith. Wearing a "Patrick's Breastplate" amulet to protect one from evil spirits is futile—superstitious externalities do no good. However, believing the rich content of truth contained on the Breastplate and praying in true faith actually contributes to the victory in the spiritual war.

Fifty years of focus upon music, concerts, drama, youth groups, and high-production worship performance, capitalizing on emotionalism and Romanticism, produced little discernible benefit for the health of the Christian church. When the fire burned, there turned out to be quite a bit of wood, hay, and stubble in the mix (1 Cor. 3:12). What was needed was real faith, steadfast faith, intrepid faith, active faith, and substantial faith in the true and living God, the resurrected Christ, and the substance of His Word. The goal of ministry is always true faith, love that endures all things, church unity without endless denominationalism, Christian maturity, obedience, sanctification, and (as John puts it) not sinning (1 John 2:1; Eph. 2:10-14; 1 Thess. 4:10).

> This know also, that in the last days perilous times shall come. For men shall be lovers of their own selves, covetous, boasters, proud, blasphemers, disobedient to parents, unthankful, unholy, without natural affection, trucebreakers, false accusers, incontinent, fierce, despisers of those that are good, traitors, heady, highminded, lovers of pleasures more than lovers of God; having a form of godliness, but denying the power thereof: from such turn away. (2 Timothy 3:1-5)

What had served as a half-way house for Protestant orthodoxy in the 20th Century was now in crisis. Evangelicalism was a house divided against itself. Egalitarianism, Marxism, and feminism pulled hard at the heartstrings of the churches. The world's view of gender, "race," and economic inequalities introduced discontentment, misplaced guilt, hatred, competition, strife, power struggles, and gross disunity into the churches. Worldly ideas like Critical Race Theory, Social Justice, and Wokism plagued American evangelical seminaries largely because God's law, which defines right and wrong, was displaced by humanist categories.

Ethnic division was furthered by worldly thinking inside the church. Sometimes nationalist pride, ethnic pride, denominational pride, and superficial cultural divisions lay at the root of the schisms and divisions. Environmental causes and systems were blamed for racism or hatred of other peoples. Vindictive, unforgiving spirits blamed children for the sins of their great, great, great, great, great-grandparents in clear contradiction of the gospel spirit and God's law (Ezek. 18:20). Where there is no gospel and no cross of Christ to which to flee for refuge, there is no forgiveness and no unity of the church.

Most striking of all was the powerlessness and spiritual paralysis characterizing Western churches. It didn't matter whether it was a weak, antinomian, humanist evangelicalism or a legalistic, man-oriented fundamentalism. These were different expressions of the same powerless faith.

A powerless gospel message prevailed which promised some kind of forgiveness but never a cleansing or release from the power of sin. The Methodist church split down the middle in the year 2020 over homosexual "marriage." Doctrines of homosexual orientation and gender confusion swept into mainline evangelical denominations like the Southern Baptist Convention and the Presbyterian Church in America. The Revoice Conference, organized in 2018 and 2019, where homosexuals gathered to affirm their "gay" identity and "gay" orientation, was led by PCA and Southern Baptist pastors.

This religion had "a form of godliness" but promoted a powerless gospel void of Holy Spirit transforming work, such that none could say, "Such were some of you" (1 Cor. 6:11). There was no hope to be found for the sinner locked into the humanist categories of "identity" and "orientation" in the modern church. Previous generations of Westerners were blessed with true revivals, "Repent" conferences, and "Rejoice" conferences—life-changing, culture-changing, world-changing transformation. But the 21st Century American evangelical church had nothing but a "Revoice" conference to offer—no hope for a supernatural transformation of heart, mind, life, body, identity, and orientation.

> Know ye not that the unrighteous shall not inherit the kingdom of God? Be not deceived: neither fornicators, nor idolaters, nor adulterers, nor effeminate, nor abusers of themselves with mankind, nor thieves, nor covetous, nor drunkards, nor revilers, nor extortioners, shall inherit the kingdom of God. And such were some of you: but ye are washed, but ye are sanctified, but ye are justified in the name of the Lord Jesus, and by the Spirit of our God. (1 Corinthians 6:9-11)

Thus, faith in the power of the Holy Spirit, the mighty work of Christ, and the sovereign, effectual salvation of God languished in the mainline evangelical denominations. Moreover, a general abandonment of the law of God as the ethical standard left evangelicalism in a mass of confusion and capitulation to worldly standards.

An unwieldy, confused separation of faith and works in evangelical theology left churches with perpetual discomfort or antipathy towards holiness and the law of God. Among the conservative fundamentalist Baptists and others was to be found a pharisaical tendency to replace God's law with superficial standards, while at the same time, minimizing the power of the sovereign grace of God to work in His people "both to will and to do for His good pleasure" (Phil. 2:12-13).

A traditional, externalized faith clung hard to 19th-Century Britain and barely lasted into the 21st Century in America, while true faith and love for God were fast disappearing. Consequently, the cultural effects of this tradition in the life of the nation gradually faded decade by decade. Jesus said, "By their fruits you will know them" (Matt. 7:16). And His brother James offered, "Thus also faith by itself, if it does not have works, is dead" (Jas. 2:17). Where there was no true faith, the fruit withered.

> And unto the angel of the church in Sardis write; These things saith he that hath the seven Spirits of God, and the seven stars; I know thy works, that thou hast a name that thou livest, and art dead. Be watchful, and strengthen the things which remain, that are ready to die: for I have not found thy works perfect before God. Remember therefore how thou hast received and heard, and hold fast, and repent. If therefore thou shalt not watch, I will come on thee as a thief, and thou shalt not know what hour I will come upon thee. (Revelation 3:1-3)

The olive branches formed during the Protestant Reformation were now dead and dying—little fruit, no leaves, or just dried out and crusty leaves barely hanging to the olive tree. Whether it was the Revoice conference, a Dionysian worship session, or a decrepit, proud, and dying reformed and revivalist faith, the Western church was primarily characterized by a lapse in faith in the year 2020. Where was the faith that could move mountains? Where were the greater works that Jesus had promised His disciples would perform? For so many, there was little anticipating or seeking of divine power to transform. The prayer meeting had disappeared from the churches. Here and there, remnants of orthodoxy and shades of right doctrine were still visible. But, for too many it was only a head knowledge and a hypothetical faith. By the year 2020, the life-changing, culture-transforming power of the Holy Spirit had greatly diminished in the West.

Evangelicalism turned into a ginned up, man-centered religion—

more concerned with the works of man than the works of God. On the one hand, some gave up on any hope of miracles and the supernatural work of God in the hearts of men. Yet, others were more focused circus tricks, laughing revivals, and physical healings (vs. spiritual healing). Religious men were more concerned with their own works—yet all the while talking of some kind of supernatural power bringing about a superficial life transformation. Once more, faith in man trumped faith in God.

Where was the man once paralyzed from birth, now walking and leaping and praising God? Where were the lepers cleansed from the inside out? Where was the man who could honestly say, "One thing I know. Once I was blind, but now I can see" (John 9:25)? Where was Lazarus, gone for four days and then walking out of the tomb? Where were the true demonstrations of divine power in the life of the soul?

What will future generations find when looking back at the 21st Century? Will they see a reformation of faith in the West, substantial and long-lasting? Or will they discover a worldwide reformation of the biblical faith this time, unprecedented in all human history? Will the Spirit of God sustain the life of the Church in the West, or will it fade away as the Chinese Nestorian church did in the 14th Century? The life of the Church will always and ever be entirely dependent upon the work of God and the direction of the Chief Shepherd of the Church, the Lord Jesus Christ.

Mid toil and tribulation,
And tumult of her war,
She waits the consummation
Of peace forevermore;
Till, with the vision glorious,
Her longing eyes are blest,
And the great Church victorious
Shall be the Church at rest.
(*The Church's One Foundation*, Samuel J. Stone)

VII

THE RISE & FALL OF A
CHRISTIAN CIVILIZATION

For if after they have escaped the pollutions of the world through
the knowledge of the Lord and Saviour Jesus Christ, they are again
entangled therein, and overcome, the latter end is worse with them
than the beginning. For it had been better for them not to have known
the way of righteousness, than, after they have known it, to turn from
the holy commandment delivered unto them. But it is happened unto
them according to the true proverb, The dog is turned to his own vomit
again; and the sow that was washed to her wallowing in the mire. (2
Peter 2:20-22)

The world that fell back into abject paganism in the modern age was
much different than pre-Christian, pagan civilizations sustained
by common grace and holding to a more-or-less steady state for 4,000
years. The post-Christian breakdown in the West was an agonizingly
painful process, radically disrupting social constructs— with its nations
more self-conscious of their radical rebellion and apostasy, and left
more culpable for their gross iniquity.

The difference between a pagan culture and an apostate culture is comparable to the difference between a prostitute and an adulterous wife. The latter is more culpable and her treachery more shameful. What played out then between the 1960s and the 2020s jarred the Christian psyche unlike anything that came before it. For those with the mind of Christ, the radical moral, social, and cultural revolutions appeared as something more than the end of a civilization, but what very well could have been the end of the world.

The cultural shift was radical and the disappointment crushing for those who still appreciated a Western heritage. Over a thousand years, a Christian epistemology, Christian education, Christian charity, Christian socio-economics, a Christian view of liberty, and a Christian view of science coordinated to transform human civilization. More than in any other human society, Christian civilization provided the highest motives to scientific inquiry, medical advancement, and practical technological developments for the betterment of mankind. Christians worked up the most effective definition of science and method for scientific inquiry to bring about technological progress. The foundations of all of it were destroyed, and the fruit corrupted at the end.

This chapter will pay particularly close attention to civil government and law, which usually makes for an accurate reflection of the moral condition of the people. Indeed, the change that came about in the Western world with the message of Christ at the beginning, was as distinguishable as day and night. It was an historical phenomenon more impressive than any and all other happenings in world history— even eclipsing the Western apostasy that came at its fall.

THE SOCIAL DECLINE OF ANCIENT GREECE & ROME

This I say therefore, and testify in the Lord, that ye henceforth walk not as other Gentiles walk, in the vanity of their mind, having the understanding darkened, being alienated from the life of God through the ignorance that is in them, because of the blindness of their heart: who being past feeling have given themselves over unto lasciviousness, to work all uncleanness with greediness. But ye have not so learned Christ; if so be that ye have heard him, and have been taught by him, as the truth is in Jesus; that ye put off concerning the former conversation the old man, which is corrupt according to the deceitful lusts; and be renewed in the spirit of your mind; and that ye put on the new man, which after God is created in righteousness and true holiness. (Ephesians 4:17-24)

Here Paul offers a perfect description of the Greek and Roman world in AD 50. The Apostle states in a rather matter-of-fact tone that the Gentiles were "past feeling" in their complete surrender to lewdness and "all uncleanness." Yet the dawning of the light comes with the word of Christ. The Gospel results in transformation, renewal of mind, and a putting off of the old deceitful lusts characterizing Greek and Roman society for a thousand years. Access to the words of Christ would transform Gentile nations in the most remarkable way. No more dramatic demonstration of this change can be found than in the sexual morality and public laws which came to characterize the Christian West.

By the 200s BC, Greece had given way to an extremely toxic, skeptical atheism much like the 20th Century philosophies following the humanist Renaissance. Popular opinion held that Zeus had died in the Cretan wars. As the kings deified themselves and were deified in the minds of their citizens, the gods became less important to Greek society. Philosophy always disappointed, consistently giving way to skepticism. Weird mystery religions predominated. Effeminacy became the rule of the day. Men shaved their beards. Homosexuality was increasingly normalized. The pursuit of pleasure was all that mattered, especially for the upper class. Women sought emancipation from motherhood, and abortion became socially acceptable. The majority of infants were killed or exposed as the normative practice of Greek families. Centuries earlier, both Plato and Aristotle advocated abortion, favoring state-controlled conception control. Should any "uncertified" woman be found with child, Plato recommended that she "dispose of it on the understanding that we cannot rear such an offspring."[1] Aristotle also advocated state conception controls, and where the woman failed to comply, he said, "abortion must be practiced."[2] As the coming of Christ approached, the birth rate among the ancient Greeks dropped below replacement levels, as low as 1.85 in Miletus. A contemporary historian reported that, "At Eretria only one family in twelve had two sons; hardly any had two daughters."[3]

Around 150 BC, Polybius recorded that "the whole of Greece has been subject to a low birth rate and a general decrease of population, owing to which cities have become deserted and the land has ceased to yield fruit... men had fallen into such a state of luxury, avarice, and indolence that they did not wish to marry, or, if they married to rear the children born to them, or at most but one or two of them..."[4] The Greeks, then, epitomized the pattern for social disintegration— abortion, infanticide, birth implosions, and homosexuality became the familiar marks of a dying humanist culture.

Gibbon places the beginning of the terrible decline in sexual morality and the unravelling of the Roman family at the end of the Punic wars. By the time of Augustus, the sexual behavior of the Romans was out of control. The family, as the basic foundation of civil society, had been decimated. Adultery was rampant, to the point that Seneca referred to the magnitude of the country's sexual sin as "the greatest evil of our time."[5] Considered a "conservative" and a savior of Roman society by his prudent laws, Augustus Caesar issued the *Lex Julia de adulteriis* in 18 BC. The laws themselves offer insight into the dysfunctional, immoral chaos characterizing pagan society.

> In the second chapter of the lex Julia concerning adultery, either an adoptive or a natural father is permitted to kill with his own hands an adulterer caught in the act with his daughter in his own house or in that of his son-in-law, no matter what his rank may be...A husband cannot kill anyone taken in adultery except persons who are infamous, and those who sell their bodies for gain, as well as slaves. His wife, however, is excepted, and he is forbidden to kill her...After having killed the adulterer, the husband should at once dismiss his wife, and publicly declare within the next three days with what adulterer, and in what place he found his wife...Sexual intercourse with female slaves is not considered an injury.[6]

By God's common grace, the Roman family was somewhat preserved and the life of the Roman Empire was extended by Augustus Caesar's more conservative policies. However, government policy alone could not salvage human society from moral degradation and social suicide. A quick review of Roman art reveals the most graphic and degraded forms of pornography painted on everyday household items: lamps, cups, bowls, mosaics, and ceramics, any description of which would only defile the reader. Such displays would have been commonplace in Roman homes for children to view. It was a harsh, abusive, depraved life before the coming of Christ.

> So [the angel] carried me away in the spirit into the wilderness: and I saw a woman sit upon a scarlet coloured beast, full of names of blasphemy, having seven heads and ten horns. And the woman was arrayed in purple and scarlet colour, and decked with gold and precious stones and pearls, having a golden cup in her hand full of abominations and filthiness of her fornication: And upon her forehead was a name written, Mystery, Babylon The Great, The Mother Of Harlots And Abominations Of The Earth. And I saw the woman drunken with the blood of the saints, and with the blood of the martyrs of Jesus: and

when I saw her, I wondered with great admiration. (Revelation 17:3-6)

Exceeding the immoral reputation of the pagan Greeks and Persians, the Roman Caesars excelled in all forms of debauchery, probably best portraying the image of the harlot riding the beast of Revelation 17. Tiberius (AD 14-37) kept live pornography shows going in his dining room. Caligula (37-41) habitually trespassed against the laws of consanguinity in the most egregious manner, with multiple victims. Nero (54-68), Titus (79-81), Hadrian (117-138), Commodus (180-192), and Carus (282-283) were promiscuous in all forms of deviant sexuality, including those listed in Romans 1 and Leviticus 18. Pagan historians look upon Elagabalus (218-222) as the most contemptible of all the Caesars, certainly the most outrageous in his sexual deviance.[7] Nero will forever be remembered for his institutionalization of homosexual "marriage," wedding himself to two separate men in mock ceremonies. A perfect prototype for all that destroys nations and empires, this monster is also known for murdering his mother and wife, burning down his own city, and persecuting Christians. Nero's reign was nightmarish even to the standards of pagan Rome; the historian, Tacitus, described the time (AD 54-68) as "a period rich in disasters... even in peace full of horrors."[8] By His mercies and long suffering, God still delayed the destruction of that wicked culture for a few hundred years.

The form of homosexuality preferred and idealized by the ancient Greeks and Romans involved the corruption of boys; as well, the molestation of children was a common practice. Though this behavior would be considered utterly abhorrent, even criminal and worthy of the death penalty for almost 2,000 years in the Christian West, the Romans tolerated it for centuries. In his classic work *History of the Romans*, Charles Merivale rightly assessed Rome's degraded sexuality as the ultimate disgrace, the very "opprobrium of history."[9] In short, nobody had to come out of the closet in Rome—there was no closet.

For any who would romanticize or idealize the "classical world" with its humanist autonomy and worldview, this witness to the most grotesque forms of sexual abuse and universally immoral conditions should utterly condemn such views.

Persian, Greek, and Chinese emperors dabbled in homosexuality at points, and their sexual perversions quickly stripped their kingdoms of all moral and social integrity. These sins mark the end of empires. At the end of the Aztec Empire, the nation's blood-soaked, human-sacrificing priests were exclusively homosexual. In the 1560s, the native chiefs of the Calusa tribe in Florida were taken by the sin, and the tribe died out quickly. But, in the 2,518 years following the worldwide flood, no great nation or people group so tolerated the nature-corrupting crimes of sexual perversion as the Romans. No powerful leaders in recorded history immersed themselves so thoroughly in the ultimate degradations as was witnessed with the Caesars over hundreds of years. Certainly, the long-suffering of God towards the Romans in their grossest abominations was unprecedented in recorded history. And so, to the Romans the Apostle Paul wrote:

> For this cause God gave them up unto vile affections: for even their women did change the natural use into that which is against nature: and likewise also the men, leaving the natural use of the woman, burned in their lust one toward another; men with men working that which is unseemly, and receiving in themselves that recompence of their error which was meet...Who knowing the judgment of God, that they which commit such things are worthy of death, not only do the same, but have pleasure in them that do them...And thinkest thou this, O man, that judgest them which do such things, and doest the same, that thou shalt escape the judgment of God? Or despisest thou the riches of his goodness and forbearance and longsuffering; not knowing that the goodness of God leadeth thee to repentance? (Romans 1:26, 27, 32, 2:3-4)

Yet, the stage was set for a different world at the turn of the 1st Century. The coming of Christ changed everything. While he visited Athens in AD 50, the Apostle gave the "heads up" to the Greeks on Mars Hill. For a thousand years, the Greeks and Romans had lived in pitch darkness and utter ignorance, but henceforth things would be different.

> Truly, these times of ignorance God overlooked, but now commands all men everywhere to repent, because He has appointed a day on which He will judge the world in righteousness by the Man whom He has ordained. He has given assurance of this to all by raising Him from the dead. (Acts 17:30-31)

VIOLENCE, MURDER, & INFANTICIDE

> The LORD is in his holy temple, the LORD's throne is in heaven: his eyes behold, his eyelids try, the children of men. The LORD trieth the righteous: but the wicked and him that loveth violence his soul hateth. Upon the wicked he shall rain snares, fire and brimstone, and an horrible tempest: this shall be the portion of their cup. For the righteous LORD loveth righteousness; his countenance doth behold the upright. (Psalm 11:4-7)

A study of ancient pagan tribes and empires is one long, tiresome recital of the most cruel and tyrannical violence at the highest echelons of power. One loses count of how many emperors killed their mothers, wives, and children, and how many emperors were killed by their friends and relatives. The history of the Roman Republic and Empire is an uninterrupted series of murders, treacheries, wicked intrigues, bloody pogroms, and revolutions. There is nothing to be seen here that might commend the classical world to our studies. Ancient records of the Assyrian Empire are stuffed with monotonous recounting of feats of cruel violence—the flaying alive of victims, stabbings, body mutilations, burnings, and dismemberments. The last 135 years of the Persian Empire is made up of another long list of murdered emperors, including Xerxes I, Darius, Xerxes II, and Artaxerxes III (after he murdered his entire family).

The worst manifestation of pagan civilization came in the form of the Roman gladiatorial competitions. Although beginning in 520 BC, it was Julius Caesar who mainstreamed the killing events for popular entertainment. The first amphitheater was built in Pompeii around 75 BC, and the Roman Colosseum was constructed in AD 70, where 400,000 human victims were slaughtered.[10]

Practically every pagan culture practiced infanticide and abortion without meaningful restrictions. Child sacrifice was particularly common among the Carthaginians. Remains of children by the tens of thousands have been uncovered in burial grounds in ancient Carthage as well as in Carthaginian territories on Malta, Sardinia, and Sicily. One burial ground recently excavated on Sardinia yielded up the bodies of 3,000 children aged one month to four years old. The Roman historian Plutarch explained in gruesome detail how the Carthaginians would sacrifice their children: they "offered up their own children, and those who had no children would buy little ones from poor people and cut their throats as if they were so many lambs or young birds; meanwhile the mother stood by without a tear or a moan."[11] Infanticide was a way of life for the Romans: Cicero (106-43 BC) agreed with the ancient Twelve Tables of Roman law, recommending death for "deformed infants."[12] And Seneca (d. AD 65) spoke of Roman custom: "We drown children who at birth are weakly and abnormal."[13]

Pagan social morality died hard over five hundred years. The last remnants of official polygamy in Europe were seen with King Harald Harfagre of Norway (ruled AD 852-932). He divorced ten wives at once and had twenty sons by just about as many women. Afterwards, the Gospel entered Norway with King Tryggvason putting an end to the ancient pagan institutions, although of course, sin remained.

Christians stopped the murderous games in the Roman Colosseum. *Christians* stopped abortion and infanticide. *Christians* stopped homosexuality and endemic adultery. *Christians* stopped the murderous intrigue in the courts among political leaders. *Christians* stopped cannibalism and polygamy wherever they found them. Over a thousand years, the transformation came by a constant, steady, and indomitable force. No more powerful moral force has ever been unleashed upon humanity than the work of Christ and His people in the Western world.

THE RISE OF CHRISTIAN MORALITY[14]

And leaving Nazareth, [Jesus] came and dwelt in Capernaum, which is upon the sea coast, in the borders of Zabulon and Nephthalim: That it might be fulfilled which was spoken by Esaias the prophet, saying, The land of Zabulon, and the land of Nephthalim, by the way of the sea, beyond Jordan, Galilee of the Gentiles; The people which sat in darkness saw great light; and to them which sat in the region and shadow of death light is sprung up. (Matthew 4:13-16)

To this world of moral confusion, sexual degradation, categorical devaluation of life, and savage-like family life, came the Son of God, the Savior of the world, the Lord Jesus Christ. After the inauguration of the New Testament Church, Christians immediately began to draw moral lines as witnessed in the writings of the Apostolic Fathers.

The 2nd Century Christian apologist Justin Martyr spoke against polygamy in his *Dialogue with Trypho*: "It is for you to follow God [rather] than your imprudent and blind masters, who even till this time permit each man to have four or five wives."[15] The church father Tertullian also rejected polygamy: "For Adam was the one husband of Eve, and Eve his one wife, one woman, one rib."[16] This church father dedicated an entire book to the subject (*On Monogamy*), drawing from the teaching of Christ and Paul.

Barnabas, writing around AD 74, addressed the social sin of abortion in no uncertain terms: "Thou shalt not slay the child by procuring abortion; nor, again, shalt thou destroy it after it is born." Just prior to this instruction, Barnabas tells his readers, "Thou shalt love thy neighbor more than thy own life."[17] The inescapable conclusion must be that the apostles considered the child in the womb a true neighbor and a person to be loved.

The early church manual known as the *Didache* (AD 110) is brief and succinct but clearly includes abortion in the short list of iniquities characterizing the "Way of Darkness."

> Thou shalt do no murder, thou shalt not commit adultery, thou shalt not corrupt boys, thou shalt not commit fornication, {thou shalt not steal,} thou shalt not deal in magic, thou shalt do no sorcery, thou shalt not murder a child by abortion nor kill them when born...[18]

From the very first, these early documents set forth a pro-life standard for the Christian church, from which the church fathers never deviated.

Justin Martyr (c.100-165) strongly condemned infanticide, taking the position as a basic tenet of the faith passed down in church tradition from the apostles: "But as for us we have been taught that to expose newly-born children is the part of wicked men; and this we have been taught lest we should do any one an injury, and lest we should sin against God."[19]

The church fathers were less concerned about speaking of the civil magistrate's involvement in abortion because first and foremost they feared God, the One who "destroys body and soul in hell" (Matt. 10:28). *The Apocalypse of Peter* dates from the mid-100s AD and is noted in the Muratorian Fragment. The particularly grim reference to abortion attests to quite a deep-seated animus the early church held towards the sin of abortion.

And near by this flame shall be a pit, great and very deep, and into it floweth from above all manner of torment, foulness, and issue. And women are swallowed up therein up to their necks and tormented with great pain. These are they that have caused their children to be born untimely, and have corrupted the work of God that created them. Over against them shall be another place where sit their children [both] alive, and they cry unto God. And flashes (lightnings) go forth from those children and pierce the eyes of them that for fornication's sake have caused their destruction.

Other men and women shall stand above them, naked; and their children stand over against them in a place of delight, and sigh and cry unto God because of their parents, saying: These are they that have despised and cursed and transgressed thy commandments and delivered us unto death: they have cursed the angel that formed us, and have hanged us up, and withheld from us (or, begrudged us) the light which thou hast given unto all creatures. And the milk of their mothers flowing from their breasts shall congeal, and from it shall come beasts devouring flesh, which shall come forth and turn and torment them for ever with their husbands, because they forsook the commandments of God and slew their children. As for their children, they shall be delivered unto the angel Temlakos (i.e., a care-taking angel). And they that slew them shall be tormented eternally, for God willeth it so.[20]

The second and third generation of church fathers did not deviate a single iota from a thoroughly pro-life orthodoxy. What follows is an assembly of quotations easily accessible among Christian historical records:

How, then, when we do not even look on, lest we should contract guilt and pollution, can we put people to death? And when we say that those women who use drugs to bring on abortion commit murder, and will have to give an account to God for the abortion, on what principle should we commit murder? For it does not belong to the same person to regard the very foetus in the womb as a created being, and therefore an object of God's care, and when it has passed into life, to kill it; and not to expose an infant, because those who expose them are chargeable with child-murder, and on the other hand, when it has been reared to destroy it. But we are in all things always alike and the same, submitting ourselves to reason, and not ruling over it. (Athenagoras, AD 170)[21]

In our case, murder being once for all forbidden, we may not destroy even the foetus in the womb, while as yet the human being derives blood from other parts of the body for its sustenance. To hinder a birth is merely a speedier man-killing; nor does it matter whether you take away a life that is born, or destroy one that is coming to the birth. That is a man which is going to be one; you have the fruit already in the seed. (Tertullian, AD 200)[22]

Our whole life can go on in observation of the laws of nature, if we gain dominion over our desires from the beginning and if we do not kill, by various means of a perverse art, the human offspring, born according to the designs of divine providence; for these women who, in order to hide their immorality, use abortive drugs which expel the child completely dead, abort at the same time their own human feelings. (Clement of Alexandria, AD 210)[23]

Some women take medicines to destroy the germ of future life in their own bodies. They commit infanticide before they have given birth to the infant. (Marcus Minucius Felix, AD 215)[24]

The first church councils on record also took a strong position against the crime of child killing. Before Nicea, the Council of Elvira (Spain) issued the harshest church censure for the sin of abortion, forbidding reconciliation even at death. In the eyes of the historical church, abortion was the essence of that which is anti-Christian. Following are the canons of the council:

Elvira Canon 63. If a woman conceives in adultery and then has an abortion, she may not commune again, even as death approaches, because she has sinned twice.

Elvira Canon 68. A catechumen who conceives in adultery and then suffocates the child may be baptized only when death approaches.[25]

Later, the Council of Ancyra (Turkey/Asia) softened the sanction to ten years penance while noting the fact that "ancient" church traditions were more austere.

Ancyra Canon 21: Women who prostitute themselves, and who kill the child thus begotten, or who try to destroy them when in their wombs, are by ancient law excommunicated to the end of their lives. We, however, have softened their punishment and condemned them to the various appointed degrees of penance for ten years.[26]

As the Christian church branched into the East (Constantinople), the West (Rome), the North (Irish-Culdean), and the South (Coptic), a uniform pro-life (anti-abortion) position was maintained everywhere throughout Christendom.

An Irish synod of AD 675 clearly addressed abortion as a grievous sin similar if not equal to the crime of murder.

The penance for homicide is seven years on bread and water...The penance for the destruction of the embryo of a child in the mother's womb [early abortion?] is three and a half years. The penance for the destruction of flesh and spirit [late-term abortion?] is seven and a half years on bread and water...The penance for a mother's destruction of her own child [infanticide?] is twelve years on bread and water.[27]

The Council of Trullo, held in Constantinople (AD 692), addressed the matter of abortion in Canon 91, equating it to murder.

Those who give drugs for procuring abortion, and those who receive poisons to kill the fœtus, are subjected to the penalty of murder.[28]

SEXUAL SINS[29]

While the pagan philosophers and kings tolerated and even participated in the most degraded forms of sexuality, Christians had no reservations about condemning it all. Justin Martyr wrote against infanticide, the prostitution of children, and other "shameful" sexual perversions of the day in his *First Apology*. The Apostle Paul was concerned with homosexuality and effeminacy in his First Epistle to the Corinthians.

> Know ye not that the unrighteous shall not inherit the kingdom of God? Be not deceived: neither fornicators, nor idolaters, nor adulterers, nor effeminate, nor abusers of themselves with mankind,...shall inherit the kingdom of God. (1 Corinthians 6:9-10)

The word Paul chose for effeminate is *malakos* which can be transliterated as, "soft clothing." This refers to men who prefer a feminine bearing or accoutrement. Clement of Alexandria excoriates men who pluck their beard hairs to look womanly: "Out of effeminate desire they enwreath their latches and fringes with leaves of gold... For God wished women to be smooth; but has ordained man, like the lions."[30]

Clement finds androgyny or transgenderism to be a horrendous assault on nature and morality. "Men play the part of women, and women that of men, contrary to nature...Oh miserable spectacle! horrible conduct!"[31] He further commends ancient Roman civil laws addressed to these "crimes:" "I admire the ancient legislators of the Romans: these detested effeminacy of conduct; and the giving of the body to feminine purposes, contrary to the law of nature, they judged worthy of the extremest penalty according to the righteousness of the land."[32] This church father may have allowed for a shave now and then, but the plucking of beard hairs he deemed "unlawful" and rejected clothes for men which were feminine "in feel and dye."[33]

There is a certain shame associated with speaking of the things that make it to the front page of the newspaper almost every day in our society. As with many other church fathers, Clement discouraged speaking in any detail concerning sexual sin: "In accordance with these remarks, conversation about deeds of wickedness is appropriately termed filthy [shameful] speaking, as talk about adultery and pederasty and the like."[34]

Clement also considered the temporal punishment of homosexuality essential to the maintenance of a stable society:

> The fate of the Sodomites was judgment to those who had done wrong, instruction to those who hear. The Sodomites having, through much luxury, fallen into uncleanness, practicing adultery shamelessly, and burning with insane love for boys; the All-seeing Word, whose notice those who commit impieties cannot escape, cast his eye on them. Nor did the sleepless guard of humanity observe their licentiousness in silence; but dissuading us from the imitation of them, and training us up to his own temperance, and falling on some sinners, lest lust being unavenged, should break loose from all the restraints of fear, ordered Sodom to be burned, pouring forth a little of the sagacious fire on licentiousness; lest lust, through want of punishment, should throw wide the gates to those that were rushing into voluptuousness. Accordingly, the just punishment of the Sodomites became to men an image of the salvation which is well calculated for men. For those who have not committed like sins with those who are punished, will never receive a like punishment.[35]

Another passage from Clement's *The Instructor*, refers to Leviticus 18:20 as ethically directive. "The Word, too, commands emphatically, through Moses: 'Thou shalt not lie with mankind as with womankind, for it is an abomination.'"[36]

The *Constitutions of the Holy Apostles* also condemned sodomy and bestiality in no uncertain terms. "For the sin of Sodom is contrary to nature, as is also that with brute beasts."[37] While this early church directory specified certain discontinuities of Old Testament laws touching Sabbaths, circumcision, sacrifices, cleanliness laws, and food laws, it just as clearly endorsed the civil laws addressed to homosexuality and adultery:

> For thus saith the oracles: "Thou shalt not lie with mankind as with womankind." "For such a one is accursed, and ye shall stone them with stones: they have wrought abominations." "Every one that lieth with a beast, slay ye him: he has wrought wickedness in his people." "And if any one defile a married woman, slay ye them both: they have wrought wickedness; they are guilty; let them die." And afterwards: "There shall not be a fornicator among the children of Israel, and there shall not be an whore among the daughters of Israel. Thou shalt not offer the hire of an harlot to the Lord thy God upon the altar, nor the price of a dog." "For the vows arising from the hire of an harlot are not clean." These things the laws have forbidden; but they have honoured marriage, and have called it blessed.[38]

Several church fathers equated homosexuality with a form of frenzy or insanity, as in this reference from Cyprian of Carthage (AD 253):

> [T]urn your looks to the abominations, not less to be deplored, of another kind of spectacle...Men are emasculated, and all the pride and vigor of their sex is effeminated in the disgrace of their enervated body; and he is more pleasing there who has most completely broken down the man into the woman. He grows into praise by virtue of his crime; and the more he is degraded, the more skillful he is considered to be. Such a one is looked upon—oh shame!—and looked upon with pleasure...Nor is there wanting authority for the enticing abomination...that Jupiter of theirs [is] not more supreme in dominion than in vice, inflamed with earthly love in the midst of his own thunders...now breaking forth by the help of birds to violate the

purity of boys. And now put the question: Can he who looks upon such things be healthy-minded or modest? Men imitate the gods whom they adore, and to such miserable beings their crimes become their religion.[39]

No doubt, these church fathers would be arrested in post-Christian Canada or Scotland if they were caught using such inflammatory language to describe these sexual sins. Yet such high moral tones demonstrate the strong ethical force carried by Christian ethics upon the conscience of this new civilization. Cyprian went so far as to call the mere consideration of the "crime" of homosexuality as defiling and sinful: "Oh, if placed on that lofty watchtower, you could gaze into the secret places—if you could open the closed doors of sleeping chambers and recall their dark recesses to the perception of sight— you would behold things done by immodest persons which no chaste eye could look upon; you would see what even to see is a crime; you would see what people embruted with the madness of vice deny that they have done, and yet hasten to do—men with frenzied lusts rushing upon men, doing things which afford no gratification even to those who do them."[40]

> And have no fellowship with the unfruitful works of darkness, but rather reprove them. For it is a shame even to speak of those things which are done of them in secret. But all things that are reproved are made manifest by the light: for whatsoever doth make manifest is light. (Ephesians 5:11-13)

AUGUSTINE

The Western theologian and church father who set the direction of Christianity for a thousand years plainly condemned the common pagan practice of homosexuality. In this excerpt from his *Confessions*,

Augustine endorses the civil penalty for the crime:

[T]hose shameful acts against nature, such as were committed in Sodom, ought everywhere and always to be detested and punished. If all nations were to do such things, they would be held guilty of the same crime by the law of God, which has not made men so that they should use one another in this way.[41]

Augustine refers to the sin of Sodom in *The City of God,* remarking that, "After this promise Lot was delivered out of Sodom, and a fiery rain from heaven turned into ashes that whole region of the impious city, where custom had made sodomy as prevalent as laws have elsewhere made other kinds of wickedness."[42] Also, in his instructions to the community of women in convents, Augustine warned of inappropriate sexual relationships between women: "The love between you...ought not to be earthly but spiritual, for the things which shameless women do even to other women are to be avoided."[43]

FIRST CHURCH COUNCILS

The early church councils provide helpful insight into the sort of discipline issues encountered by the church in the pagan Roman world. The modern church would do well to consider the wisdom afforded here, given that our pagan world is not all that different from the pre-Christian pagan world. Of course, every true church that exercises church discipline is interested in working towards the restoration of the sinner. For better or worse, the early church developed a uniform policy across the board for restoring the wayward member. Though conscientious church leaders would never restore members under discipline without genuine signs of repentance, the details of this restoration process would likely vary from case to case. Most biblical churches today would restore erring members based on demonstrated fruits of repentance, genuineness of confessions, transparency and trust, and willingness to be accountable. Thus, we would find varying probationary periods required for restoration to communion, depending on many factors.

The Council of Elvira assembled nineteen bishops (teaching elders) and twenty-four presbyters (ruling elders) in AD 305 to address immoral behavior among church members. The assembly condemned homosexual activity with boys, assigning the most severe church censure of excommunication for life to those who succumbed to it: "Canon 71. Those who sexually abuse boys may not commune even when death approaches." For comparison's sake, the most egregious sins treated by the Council of Elvira—for which the church would delay communicant status to death—were restricted to murder by sorcery (canon 6), serial unrepentant fornication (canon 7), unlawful divorce and remarriage (canon 8), parents who prostitute their children (canon 12), marrying a daughter to a pagan priest (canon 17), sexual immorality in the case of bishops and elders (canon 18), abortion (canons 63 and 68), incest (canon 67), and false accusations made against bishops, elders, or deacons (canon 77).

The Council of Ancyra in Asia Minor (AD 314) somewhat relaxed these earlier sanctions. Bestial (irrational) sin, which included homosexuality and bestiality, required fifteen years' probation for those who committed the crime while under twenty years of age; a probation of thirty years for those older than twenty years of age; and life probation for those who committed the crime while over fifty years of age (canon 16). The sanctions also specified ten years for abortion (canon 21), seven years for adultery, and life probation for murderers (canon 22).

In his letters, Basil the Great (c. 367) equated the sin of homosexuality to the sin of adultery when considered for church censure: "He who is guilty of unseemliness with males will be under discipline for the same time as adulterers."

As Christianity spread into pagan lands, the church was pressed to deal with the sin of homosexuality along the way. In Wales, the Synod of the Grove of Victory (c. AD 550) reduced the penance to four years, probably due to the pagan background from which the Irish converts were taken. "Whoever commits the male crime as the Sodomites [shall do penance] for four years…"[44]

The Apostle Paul required church discipline for serious sexual sins, such as incest, in 1 Corinthians 5, and then followed up with a list of other sexual sins (including homosexuality), not to characterize the people of God (1 Cor. 6:9,10).

> It is actually reported that there is sexual immorality among you, and such sexual immorality as is not even named among the Gentiles--that a man has his father's wife! And you are puffed up, and have not rather mourned, that he who has done this deed might be taken away from among you. For I indeed, as absent in body but present in spirit, have already judged (as though I were present) him who has so done this deed. In the name of our Lord Jesus Christ, when you are gathered together, along with my spirit, with the power of our Lord Jesus Christ, deliver such a one to Satan for the destruction of the flesh, that his spirit may be saved in the day of the Lord Jesus. (1 Corinthians 5:1-5)

THE MIDDLE AGES—
STEMMING THE FLOW OF GROSS SEXUAL SIN[45]

The 8th Century English church included the sin of sodomy as a matter of church discipline in The Penitential of Egbert (successor of Bede): "If anyone has sinned as the Sodomites, some say ten years penance; if he is in the habit, more must be added; if he has ecclesiastical rank, he is to be degraded and do penance as a lay person."[46] The Penitential of Columban (AD 600) required that a monk "who had committed the sin of murder or sodomy do penance for ten years."[47] The Penitential of Cummean and Finnian required something similar, sometimes distinguishing between varied levels of heinousness or degrees of habituation. A recently-conducted historical survey identified thirty-one penitentials, dating from AD 500 to 1100, assigning disciplinary measures for male homosexuality (as well as an additional fourteen penitentials assigned to lesbianism).[48]

The Council of Toledo's third canon (AD 693) advocated castration for the crime of homosexuality, and the Council of Paris (AD 829) also addressed the civil magistrate's responsibilities relating to egregious sexual sins. Convener of the Paris council, Bishop Wala, introduced the purpose of the council as to "make diligent inquiry into the way in which the rulers and the faithful were observing the law of God." The resultant Canon 34 both endorsed the Old Testament civil law and referred to the Apostle's severe language used in Romans 1:32. "Moreover, the Lord in his law commands that any who commit this infamous crime be punished with death [Lev. 20:13], and the Apostle adds that they are 'worthy of death' [Rom. 1:32]." The Diocesan regulations issued to priests from the 800s through the 1000s presented homosexuality as a most devastating problem for human society and earthly kingdoms:

> Because of homosexuality kingdoms are destroyed and delivered into the hands of pagans. Every Christian should guard himself against this crime and those not polluted by it should beware lest they fall.[49]

While presenting an entire treatise (1007-1072) on the subject (intended as an appeal to Pope Leo IX), Peter Damian insisted that this sin was "never to be compared with any other vice because it surpasses the enormity of all vices."[50] The homosexual, wrote Damian, "is confounded by the authority of the whole church, condemned by the judgment of all the holy fathers."[51] He is "subject to the iron rule of diabolical tyranny" and "possessed by a diabolical spirit,"[52] warnings echoed later in Martin Luther's condemnation.[53]

Although the role of the state is barely noted in Damian's treatise, clearly medieval churchmen were primarily concerned with the eternal souls of men and their repentance and restoration with the church this side of eternity. Damian warned the homosexual: "How miserable it is that because of the present satisfaction of one organ's pleasure, afterwards the whole body together with the soul will be tortured forever by the most atrocious, flaming fires...Those who are now troubled by the ardour of sodomite lust afterwards will also burn along with the author of all iniquity in the flames of perpetual burning."[54] He instructed the sinner to cry out for the mercy of God, repent, and "establish an unremitting contest against the flesh; with weapons always ready, [to] stand against the importunate madness of lust."[55]

Damian distinguished four associated sins in order of increasing egregiousness, beginning with self-stimulation (considered a milder form of homosexuality) and proceeding to the act of sodomy.

Commenting on Pope Gregory's instructions to Bishop Passivus, Damian testified by the Old Testament civil law, that homosexuality is "surely to be punished by death."[56] On this basis, he argued that a sin of this magnitude must permanently disqualify a man from ecclesiastical rank:

> Surely, it is clear that a person who has been degraded by a crime deserving death is not reformed so as to receive an order of ecclesiastical rank by any sort of subsequent religious life.[57]

To promote such a person, to office, Damian added, would be "entirely against the norm of sacred law."[58]

Responding to Damian's treatise by letter, Pope Leo essentially agreed with his recommendation:

> There may be no hope of recovering their rank for those who are tainted with either of the two types of sin you have described—alone or with others—for a long time or with many men even for a short time, or—what is horrible to mention as well as to hear—who have fallen into [the act of sodomy].[59]

323

Finally, the Third Lateran Council (AD 1179), borrowing language from the earlier Council of Paris, required church censures for homosexual sin: "Let all who are found guilty of that unnatural vice for which the wrath of God came down upon the sons of disobedience and destroyed the five cities with fire, if they are clerics be expelled from the clergy or confined in monasteries to do penance; if they are laymen they are to incur excommunication and be completely separated from the society of the faithful."[60]

> But fornication, and all uncleanness, or covetousness, let it not be once named among you, as becometh saints; neither filthiness, nor foolish talking, nor jesting, which are not convenient: but rather giving of thanks. For this ye know, that no whoremonger, nor unclean person, nor covetous man, who is an idolater, hath any inheritance in the kingdom of Christ and of God. (Ephesians 5:3-5)

THE RISE OF CHRISTIAN LAW

> He [Christ] shall have dominion also from sea to sea, and from the river unto the ends of the earth. They that dwell in the wilderness shall bow before him; and his enemies shall lick the dust. The kings of Tarshish and of the isles shall bring presents: the kings of Sheba and Seba shall offer gifts. Yea, all kings shall fall down before him: all nations shall serve him. (Psalm 72:9-11)

While the Christian church discipled the nations upon robust socio-moral standards relating to sexual sin and infanticide, that influence quickly spread into civil government to form a new law and order for the Western world. Augustine had argued that Christian magistrates should legislate Christian laws at the dawn of the Christian age. Although such a suggestion is taken as utterly reprehensible in a post-Christian or anti-Christian age, this made perfect sense for Augustine writing in the 5th Century: "As to the argument of those men who are unwilling that their impious deeds should be checked by the enactment of righteous laws, when they say the Apostles never sought such measures from the kings of the earth, they do not consider the different character of that age, and that everything comes in its own season."[61] The church father went on to endorse laws against both impiety and adultery.

On February 27, 380, Emperor Theodosius I issued an edict defending orthodox Christianity in the clearest possible terms.

> It is our desire that all the various nations which are subject to our Clemency and Moderation should continue to profess that religion which was delivered to the Romans by the divine Apostle Peter as it has been preserved by faithful tradition and which is now professed by the Pontiff Damasus [Bishop of Rome] and by Peter, Bishop of Alexandria, a man of apostolic holiness. According to the apostolic teaching and the doctrine of the Gospel, let us believe in the one deity of the Father, the Son and the Holy Spirit in equal majesty and in a holy Trinity.

Ten years later, the Theodosian Code introduced the first civil penalty for homosexuality, a cultural standard which would continue to hold for over 1,500 years.[62] As Christian influence increased in the empire, the Roman Emperor Justinian I (ruled 527-565) formed the *Corpus Juris Civilis,* a code which became the basis for civil law in the West. Included in this legislation were references to biblical law in relation to sexual crimes.

> In cases of penal suits, public prosecution will be guided by various statutes, including the *Lex Julia de adulteriis*…which punishes with death not only those who violate the marriages of others, but also those who commit acts of vile concupiscence with other men.[63]

> Whereas certain men, overcome by diabolical incitement to practice among themselves the most unworthy lewdness and acts against

nature, we exhort them to be fearful of God and the coming judgment, and to abstain from such illicit and diabolical practices so that the just wrath of God may not fall upon them on account of these heathen acts, with the result that cities perish with all their inhabitants. For Sacred Scriptures teach us that similar impious acts caused the annihilation of cities with all their inhabitants.[64]

By the turn of the 5th Century, the true and living God and His moral law had come to be respected in the Western world. This was a far cry from Nero, Caligula, Commodus, Elagabalus, Diocletian, and the old pagan social disorder.

By the time of the Carolingian era, Christian morality was well ensconced in Western society. Alcuin, Charlemagne's tutor and head teacher for the kingdom, encouraged meditation on the law of God (c. 796): "The old age of those who have trained their youth in honest arts and have meditated in the law of the Lord day and night, becomes more learned with age, more polished by use, wiser by the lapse of time, and reaps the sweetest fruits of studies long grown old."[65]

The Holy Roman Empire was inaugurated in AD 802, with Charlemagne's issuance of the first capitulary—a true effort to govern according to Christian law. The king instructed the realm, that "all should live together according to the precept of God in a just manner and under just judgment, and each one should be admonished to live in unity with the others in his occupation or calling...And thus, altogether and everywhere and in all cases, whether the matter concerns the holy churches of God, or the poor, or wards and widows, or the whole people, let them fully administer law and justice according to the will and to the fear of God. And if there should be any matter such that they themselves, with the counts of the province, could not better it and render justice with regard to it: without any ambiguity they shall refer it, together with their reports, to the emperor's court."[66] Charlemagne required that murder be punished "with the greatest severity," and adultery with "grave severity."[67]

This seminal legal code clearly wielded Christian language and law for the prosecution of criminal murder:

> Or how can any one believe that Christ will be gracious to him who has slain his brother. It is a great and inevitable risk to arouse the hatred of men besides incurring that of God the Father and of Christ the ruler of Heaven. By hiding, one can escape them for a time; but, nevertheless, one falls by some chance into the hands of his enemies. And where can one flee God to whom all secrets are manifest? By what rashness can any one hope to evade His wrath? Therefore we have taken care to avoid, by every possible regulation, that the people committed to us to be ruled over perish by this evil. For he who has not feared that God will be angry with him, will by no means find us gentle and gracious; we wish rather to punish with the greatest severity him who dares to commit the crime of murder.[68]

As the Western nations were discipled in the commandments of God by faithful evangelists and preachers, governments quickly incorporated Christian law for the kingdoms of Europe. Alfred the Great, king of the Anglo-Saxons (849-899), introduced a Christian worldview and legal code into England. His father Æthelwulf, king of Wessex (ruled 839-858), was the first to include Christian pastors in the royal court. From the time he was a child, Alfred kept his own handwritten collection of the psalms of David, which he would read day and night.[69] Later in life, he would seek out other passages of the Scriptures, translating them into English himself, and "like the busy bee, wandering far and wide over the marshes in his quest, eagerly and relentlessly assembles many various flowers of Holy Scripture, with which he crams full the cells of his heart."[70]

In defense of Wessex from the Viking invasions, Alfred won the definitive battle of Edington. Shortly thereafter, he led Guthrum king of the Danes into the Christian faith. He is the only king of the Saxons (or England) who has been given the title "the Great."

In consideration of Alfred's worldview, first and foremost, the king submitted himself to the ultimate sovereignty of God—a remarkable position for any ruler who ever lived in the history of the world. Alfred confesses in his poetry:

> One, only One, made all the heavens and earth;
> Doubtless, to Him all beings owe their birth;
> And guided by His care,
> Are all, who therein dwell unseen of us,
> And these whom we can look at, living thus
> In land and sea and air.
> He is Almighty: Him all things obey,
> That in such bondage know how blest are they,
> Who have so good a king;
> Those also serve, who thereof know not aught;
> Dutiful work, however little thought,
> As bondslaves they must bring…
> By reign and bridle in a hint I teach
> The waywardness of all things each on each;
> For, if the Ruler will'd
> The thongs to slacken, things would soon forsake
> All love and peace, and willful evil make
> Instead of good fulfilled.[71]

In the preface to his legal code, Alfred defended his use of biblical law, explicitly stating that, "These are judgments which Almighty God Himself spoke to Moses and commanded him to keep. Now, since the Lord's only begotten Son our God and healing [Saviour] Christ has come to Middle Earth—He said that He did not come to break nor to forbid these commandments but to approve them well, and to teach them with all mild-heartedness and lowly-mindedness."

Following the Apostles' teaching in Acts 15, Alfred then

appropriately argued for maintaining the non-ceremonial elements of Moses' law—admonishing the Saxons to "refrain from worshipping devil-gilds [or 'idols'], and from tasting blood and stranglings, and from fornication!'"[72] With each legislative code, Alfred referenced Exodus 20-22, as well prefacing the codes with a direct quote from the Ten Commandments.

Such are the beginnings of Western legal history, and the basis for English common law. The impact of Alfred's law over the succeeding thousand years cannot be overstated. Winston Churchill notes, in his *History of the English-Speaking Peoples*, "The laws of Alfred... grew into that body of customary law administered by the shire and hundred courts which, under the name of the Laws of St Edward (the Confessor), the Norman Kings undertook to respect, and out of which, with much manipulation by feudal lawyers, the Common Law was founded."[73]

The Christianization of England was more or less completed in AD 930 under the leadership of Alfred's grandson, Athelstan. He was the first king of England.

Athelstan was conscientiously tutored in the Christian faith by his aunt (King Alfred's daughter), Aethelflaed. Serving as the ruler of the realm and provided the title of "Lady of Mercia," after her husband died, from all reports Aethelflaed was a woman of deep Christian piety. Upon her death and that of Athelstan's father, Edward, in AD 917, Athelstan took advantage of the opportunity to unite the kingdoms of Wessex and Mercia, and then chased the remaining Vikings out of Northumbria. A formidable king in power and piety, Athelstan remained single and celibate his whole life, a marked contrast to his father Edward, who would disavow one wife for another, on several iterations.

Athelstan won a key battle in 937 at Brunanburh against a formidable host collected out of the remaining pagan and apostate kingdoms on the island. These monarchs had united against Christ and against a Christian kingdom, in one final initiative to salvage pagan rule. Like Julian before them, they failed.

In 927, Athelstan held a convocation on the banks of the River Eamont, inviting tribal leaders from the Welsh-speaking Cumbrians, the English-speaking Northumbrians, and Norse-speaking Scandinavians. All participants were required to take an oath "to renounce all idolatry,"[74] and here Athelstan was presented for the first time as *rex totius Britanniae*—"The King of the whole of Britain."

These were the crucial years in the eradication of paganism from England. During Athelstan's reign, the ancient habits of witchcraft, Odin-worship, superstition, sun worship, and pagan rituals were still scattered about the kingdom. Occasionally, some heathen ceremony conducted under cover of night would force women into the most perverse sexual activities. Athelstan set about to squelch the last of this and the Christian faith flourished more than ever across England, Wales, Scotland, and Ireland for the next thousand years. Legislating for all the country of England, Athelstan ordered that "with regard to witchcraft and sorcery, and deadly spells, that if it causes death, and the accused is unable to deny it, then his life shall be forfeit."[75] Athelstan's law code further stated, "Let there be no marketing on Sundays. Let the offender forfeit the value of the goods, and pay thirty shillings."[76] In his judicial dealings, Athelstan was also known for his moderate treatment of children in matters like theft and robbery. "The King thinks it cruel to have such young people put to death, and for such minor offenses, as he has learnt is the common practice everywhere. Therefore, it is the stated opinion both of the King and of those with whom he has discussed the matter that no one should be put to death who is under fifteen years of age."[77]

On Christmas Day 932, the great Athelstan issued a charter requiring all who worked his estates to be sure that no person should ever starve to death. The king announced to all the lords: "My wish it is that you should always provide the destitute with food."[78]

Such was one more amazing instance of the powerful influence which Christ had upon one nation—continuing for a thousand years, only waning badly after the year 1900.

King Ethelred (978-1016) followed Alfred's lead by instituting additional legal precedent in accord with biblical law. The king condemned slavery on Christian principle, and encouraged a love for God's law "in word and deed."

> And the ordinance of our lord and of his witan [king's advisors] is, that Christian men and uncondemned be not sold out of the country, especially into a heathen nation; and be it jealously guarded against, that those souls perish not that Christ bought with his own life.

> And the ordinance of our lord and of his witan is, that Christian men for all too little be not condemned to death; but in general let mild punishments be decreed, for the people's need; and let not, for a little, God's handiwork and His own purchase be destroyed, which He dearly bought.

> But let God's law be henceforth zealously loved, by word and deed, then will God soon be merciful to this nation.[79]

Archenemies of the Anglo-Saxons for centuries, the Vikings eventually found their way to Christ at the turn of the 11th Century. Harald Bluetooth received the Gospel in 965, and his grandson Canute went on to faithfully incorporate Christian law into Denmark, England, Norway, and all throughout his burgeoning empire. Sections of this "doom" is contained below:

> This is further the secular ordinance which, by the advice of my councillors, I desire should be observed over all England.

> 1. The first provision is, that I desire that justice be promoted and

every injustice zealously suppressed, that every illegality be rooted up and eradicated from this land with the utmost diligence, and the law of God promoted. §1. And henceforth all men, both poor and rich shall be regarded as entitled to the benefit of the law, and just decisions shall be pronounced on their behalf.

2. And we enjoin that, even if anyone sins and commits grievous crime, the punishment shall be ordered as shall be justifiable in the sight of God and acceptable in the eyes of men. 2a. And he who has authority to give judgment shall consider very earnestly what he himself desires when he says thus: "And forgive us our trespasses as we forgive [them that trespass against us]." §1. And we forbid the practice of condemning Christian people to death for very trivial offenses. On the contrary, merciful punishments shall be determined upon for the public good, and the handiwork of God and the purchase which he made at a great price shall not be destroyed for trivial offenses.

3. We forbid the all too prevalent practice of selling Christian people out of the country, and especially of conveying them into heathen lands, but care shall be zealously taken that the souls which Christ bought with his life be not destroyed.

4. And we enjoin that the purification of the land in every part shall be diligently undertaken, and that evil deeds shall everywhere be put an end to.[80]

Canute further strengthened the law against adultery, yet stopped short of requiring the death penalty for the crime.

As Christian law and liberty found fertile soil in England, the kings and kingdoms became more grounded in biblical law. John of Salisbury (1115-1180) served as something of an advocate for the English Church in the papal court, and then, was later appointed as Archbishop of Canterbury during the tyrannical years of the Plantagenets. Largely by his writings, John played a major role in the development of medieval

English law, always advocating that princes be held to the standard of God's law. His magnum opus, *Policraticus,* urged all earthly kings to "attend to the law which is imposed upon princes by the Greatest King who is an object of fear over all the earth and who takes away the breath of princes." Quoting from Deuteronomy 17:18, John told the princes of Europe:

> And afterwards he will sit upon the throne of the kingdom and he will write for himself a copy of this law of Deuteronomy in a book, drawing from the exemplar of the priests of the tribe of Levi, and it will be with him and he shall read therein all the days of his life, that he may learn to fear the Lord his God, and to keep all His words and ceremonies which are prescribed by the law. His heart should not be lifted up haughtily above his brethren, nor should he incline in his direction to the right or to the left, in order that he and his children may reign a long time over Israel.

> Need one ask whether anyone whom this law constrains is limited by law? Certainly this is divine and cannot be dismissed with impunity. Each word of this text is thunder in the ears of the prince if he is wise.[81]

John further reasoned that all princes are bound to execute the justice of this law: "Note how diligent in guarding the law of God should be the prince, who is commanded to hold it, to read it and to reflect upon it always, just as the King of Kings—created from woman, created under law—carried out the whole justice of law, to which He was subject not by necessity, but by will because His will is law, and He meditated day and night on the Law of God."[82] Some historians credit John of Salisbury as a seminal influence in the development of the Magna Carta—the first of the great Western codes of constitutional liberties, inaugurated thirty-five years after his death. This respect for God's law would continue with Reformation men like Samuel Rutherford five hundred years later, as evidenced in this excerpt from his masterpiece, *Lex Rex*:

> He who is made a minister of God, not simply, but for the good of the subject, and so he take heed to God's law as a king, and govern according to God's will, he is in so far only made king by God as he fulfilleth the condition; and in so far as he is a minister for evil to the subject, and ruleth not according to that which the book of the law commandeth him as king, in so far he is not by God appointed king and ruler, and so must be made a king by God conditionally...[83]

This was the basic description of a Christian king and government. Here was the culmination of the great experiment with Christian law and liberty in the Western world. What more obvious testimony could there be for a Christian civilization than the biblical legal codes of the most powerful kings in Europe during the early Medieval Age—Charlemagne, Alfred, Athelstan and Canute? In keeping with the old prophecies, here are the clear records that the Servant of the Lord actually brought forth "judgment to the Gentiles" for at least a thousand years.

> Behold my servant, whom I uphold; mine elect, in whom my soul delighteth; I have put my spirit upon him: he shall bring forth judgment to the Gentiles. He shall not cry, nor lift up, nor cause his voice to be heard in the street. A bruised reed shall he not break, and the smoking flax shall he not quench: he shall bring forth judgment unto truth. He shall not fail nor be discouraged, till he have set judgment in the earth: and the isles shall wait for his law. (Isaiah 42:1-4)

A CHRISTIAN EUROPE

That is the story of how the pagan world turned Christian. While there may be some reasonable debate over the *extent* of the cultural transformation, none could deny the night-to-day dramatic change that Christ and His people brought to Europe over a thousand years. Of course, European man still sinned. Pagan habits remained here and there. Pagan symbols died hard. But the contrast between King

Alfred and Emperor Nero stands out as a stark testimony to the most remarkable story in the history of the world.

THE DECLINE BEGINS IN ROME (AD 930)

> For the time is come that judgment must begin at the house of God: and if it first begin at us, what shall the end be of them that obey not the gospel of God? And if the righteous scarcely be saved, where shall the ungodly and the sinner appear? (1 Peter 4:17-18)

Ironically, the breakdown of morals in the West began in Rome with the papacy. The spiritual and moral decline of the curia following the forgery of the Donation of Constantine and the consequent power struggles led to the corruption of the church and the disintegration of public morals, especially in Italy and France.

Not forty years after Pope Nicholas I (820-867) employed the Donation and took the bait of secular power, the papal see turned into a mass of murder, revolutions, wars, sexual confusion, and evil intrigue. It was a recapitulation of pagan Rome.

Theophylact I, count of Tusculum, gained control of Rome by swapping political favors with Pope Sergius III. Theophylact's wicked wife Theodora succeeded in advancing her paramour into the papacy (John X). Theodora's daughter Marozia (890-937) proved to be of worse character than her mother, using her sexual powers to control the political and ecclesiastical hierarchy in Rome. Between AD 931 and 1048, at least six popes descended from Marozia and Theodora (via Theophylact I). Medieval historian Liutprand of Cremona refers to Marozia as a "shameless whore," and historian Gibbon summarized the period thusly: "The influence of two sister prostitutes, Marozia and Theodora, was founded on their wealth and beauty, their political and amorous intrigues: the most strenuous of their lovers were rewarded with the Roman mitre and their reign may have suggested to the darker ages the fable of a female pope. The bastard son, the grandson, and the great-grandson of Marozia, a rare genealogy, were seated in the Chair of St Peter..."[84]

In the year 955, Marozia's grandson became Pope John XII—arguably the worst character in Roman church history. John grappled with Italian secular rulers to retain control of the papal states and allied himself with Otto of the Holy Roman Empire to gain the upper hand in Rome. Then John went to war with Otto over control of central Italy. He double-crossed the Emperor, who proceeded to chase him out of Rome, and he was finally deposed by a synod made up of fifty bishops on December 4, 963.

Power-mongering and sexual sin usually go hand in hand, and John was no exception. His adultery extended to literally hundreds of women—prostitutes, his own sisters, and his father's concubine. At the end, God took his life in the very act of adultery, as the traditional account goes. The Roman pastorate was morally bankrupt by the mid-10th Century. This was the seed that destroyed Western morality, eventually corrupting the very foundations of Western civilization. The papacy never recovered.

By the time Peter Damian published his *Book of Gomorrah* (c. 1051), the corruption and perversion in Rome had evidently crept as far away as Fonte Avellana—150 miles to the north. Damian prefaces his alarming little book on sodomy with the salvo that "a certain abominable and terribly shameful vice has grown up in our region."[85] Around the same time, the Council at Rheims condemned "sodomists."[86] The cancer was already afflicting the Italian church.

The Santo Spirito foundling hospital was established in Rome (in 1204) to care for abandoned children produced by an increasingly immoral populace. The paintings in the halls depicting morally calloused mothers in the act of committing infanticide exceed in grotesqueness the most explicit pro-life placards used by activists in the present century. Translated from the Latin, the inscription on the fresco reads, "... in different ways the cruel mothers butcher their offspring which have come into the light following illicit coitus."[87] Another fresco pictures fishermen in the Tiber River retrieving little babies from their net, and the accompanying inscription reads: "the nefarious women in order to conceal their shame, also undertake to force their offspring, brought forth in clandestine sex, down into the river from the bridge by night…with great stupefaction and disturbance of feeling, fishermen by chance capture and drag out with nets from the Tiber, in place of fish, the castaway infants."[88]

But still, some Christian cultural deposits within the conscience of the West remained. The ancient pagans, Greeks, Romans, and Carthaginians openly fornicated and exposed infants to death, without regret or shame. For a thousand years, some shame regarding perverse sexual sin and abortion was retained within a Christian culture; and some moral restraint was kept in place, with the closet door closed or partially cracked, until the 1960s, that is.

Despite the papal debaucheries in the Roman church (and among its pastor-bishops), Christian civilization carried on. Abortion was far from normative and even farther from receiving any social approval at all throughout the Middle Ages. The only real reference to infant killing in literature is found in the urban legend material of *Malleus Maleficarum (The Hammer of Witches)*. In this 1486 propaganda manual for the encouragement of inquisitors, the author claims a witch midwife of Basel "confessed she had killed more than forty children, by sticking a needle through the crowns of their heads into their brains, as they came out from the womb."[89] Whether these witches or the witch midwives ever existed even in small numbers is difficult to ascertain. These sorts of stories were meant to scare the living daylights out of everybody—fanciful tales on the order of Hansel and Gretel, the production of over-active imaginations.

For about a thousand years, there was little or no mention of lesbianism and only slight reference to homosexuality in the law codes of Europe. Such perversions were unheard of in a Christian society, until 1260. In that year a French legal treatise appeared, called *Li livres de jostice et de plet,* specifying civil punishments for both male and female homosexual behavior.

With the arrival of the Italian Renaissance, the hypocrisy of the papacy was replaced by the more "honest" autonomy of humanism. The downgrade of Christian culture would always start with a first generation marked by scandal and hypocrisy in the church, followed by a second generation openly practicing the sin and seeking social acceptance of it. Thus the sculptor, Donatello (1386-1466), reintroduced nude art in 1440 with a homosexualized David, reminiscent of the depravity of the ancient Romans. By 1432, the city of Florence initiated a special commission to root out homosexuality. In a city of 40,000, a full 3,000 men were convicted of the sin and mostly given a moderate sentence. By 1348, Venice also began to deal with the problem, establishing the Council of Ten and implementing severer sanctions, up to execution. The council continued until 1797, at which point European governments were "throwing in the towel" in their efforts to slow the rise of sexual perversion. The forces of darkness were gathering strength with each proceeding century.

As late as the mid-1500s, sexual perversions more common with the papacy and clergy in Italy were held at bay elsewhere in Europe. Commenting on the Sodom story, Martin Luther wrote, "I for my part do not enjoy dealing with this passage, because so far the ears of the Germans are innocent of and uncontaminated by this monstrous depravity; for even though disgrace, like other sins, has crept in through an ungodly soldier and a lewd merchant, still the rest of the people are unaware of what is being done in secret. The Carthusian monks deserve to be hated because they were the first to bring this terrible pollution into Germany from the monasteries of Italy."[90] The Carthusian monasteries appeared in Germany in the 14th and 15th centuries.

The most degraded forms of pagan sexuality recovered by the Italian Renaissance were practically unheard-of in England. Henry VIII's minister, Thomas Cromwell, introduced England's first modern "buggery" law in 1533, addressing the crimes listed in Leviticus 20:13. However, prosecution of such crimes was extremely rare in Elizabethan England. Only a single conviction is found on record over a period of a hundred years, namely one Mervyn Tuchet, 2nd Earl of Castlehaven (1593-1631).

HENRY VIII (1491-1547)—A LEGACY OF IMMORALITY FOR THE WESTERN WORLD

> As a roaring lion, and a ranging bear; so is a wicked ruler over the poor people. The prince that wanteth understanding is also a great oppressor: but he that hateth covetousness shall prolong his days. A man that doeth violence to the blood of any person shall flee to the pit; let no man stay him. (Proverbs 28:15-17)

Political leaders prepared the way for the demoralization of the Western world, and both Henry VIII and James I of England made their contributions. Without question, the sanctity of marriage in a Christian world was undermined by Henry's marital shenanigans.

That Henry allowed for the shifting of control of the English church from the pope to himself was no cause for celebration. The shift of church government from the pope to king was hardly an improvement. Henry was one of England's most profligate and tyrannical kings. While room was made for reformation of the English Church according to providential workings of God, Henry's support was traded for political advantage and a consolidation of power.

Henry claimed a "divine right"—which, ultimately, turned out to be the right to act autonomously apart from the law of God. Such a position was outrageously contrary to the safety of the people. Although there is some legitimate debate as to the number of executions conducted by

Henry VIII, the conservative estimate is 57,000. Percentage wise, that would equate to the purge of 9,000,000 Americans in a contemporary setting. Worse yet, Henry opted for the worst forms of execution for his victims, including pressing people to death, boiling, burning, and drawing and quartering. Although his daughter Mary would continue this legacy of slaughter, she only reigned for five years vs. Henry's thirty-eight year career. To a lesser extent Mary and Elizabeth would continue this legacy of persecution, particularly with reforming or nonconformist groups. By his treatment of marriage, Henry also championed an immoral standard for England and beyond (divorcing or killing at least five wives). Protestant attitudes towards divorce were at least in part influenced by this legacy. Western Protestants continued to court higher divorce rates than Catholics well into the 21st Century—39% for Protestants vs. 28% for Catholics, according to a recently-conducted study.

THE ELIZABETHAN MORAL REVOLUTION

Following the Reformation, liberal arts schools, artists, and literary culture would repave the way for acceptance of homosexuality in the Western world. Significant to this end were William Shakespeare's Love Sonnets, written for an anonymous man (W.H.). Shakespeare's close associate or alter ego, Christopher Marlowe, is recognized as the first of the English Renaissance literary men. Marlowe's dalliance with homoeroticism in *Hero and Lenader*, and his fixation on the king's homosexual relationship with Piers Gaveston in *Edward II* is well known. Marlowe and others were coming back to glorify the "great men" of the classical world who were renown for their homosexual relationships (to include Alexander the Great, Tully, or Socrates). The literary revolutions aided in priming the pump for the corruption of sexuality in the west. An apostate humanism and a reforming Puritanism were battling it out for the heart of Protestant England at the end of the 17th Century.

JAMES I (1566-1625)

Alas, the Stuarts were just as bad as the Tudors. Mary Stuart, Queen of Scots (1542-1587) murdered her husband in Scotland (and was later executed in England for treason). Her son James proved himself to be of no better character. Historian Otto Scott credits James I with undermining the Reformation.[91] It was under James and his son Charles I that the best of English Puritanism left for America, and this king remained stubbornly resistant to the Reformation doctrines of God's sovereignty and the rule of God's law. Secretly, James lived out the sonnets of Shakespeare and the proclivities of Edward II. History is a little sketchy as to the extent of it. However, the legacy of gross sexual infidelity continued in the Stuart line with Charles II and James II, both of whom fathered a fair number of illegitimate children.

ENGLAND'S STEADY MORAL DOWNFALL (1720-1850)

For a hundred years, the English Puritans fought hard against the moral breakdown of the nation and successfully shut down the indecent Globe Theater in London by 1642. With the reinstatement of the Stuart monarchy came a restoration of popular theater featuring sexually-explicit language - further contributing to the moral degrade of the nation in the late 1600s and early 1700s. Playwrights John Vanbrugh and William Congreve played with themes of adultery and half-hearted repentance scenes, to the delight of morally-compromised London spectators.

Reaction to the loosened morals of the English monarchy and the popular culture, the Society for the Reformation of Manners was formed in 1691. Towards the late 1720s, a "molly-house" in central London (where sexual perversions were encouraged) was raided and three patrons were executed. Four hundred years after Venice encountered the problem, London was experiencing the same thing. What appeared as the fruits of the humanist Renaissance for Italy were the same fruits coming on the heels of the Enlightenment in the north.

The sexual immorality resulting from England's religious lapse led to the establishment of the first "foundling" orphanage for abandoned children in 1741 (500 years after Rome's Santo Spirito). Some were resistant to providing too much support for prostitutes and other irresponsible persons who came to "rely" on orphanages to take care of the children they produced out of wedlock. But sin produces confusion and usually gives birth to increased levels of sin and social evils unless the Gospel of Christ transforms hearts. Thus, society turns to Band-Aids and crutches to take care of the collateral damage created by sinful lifestyles. Between 1728 and the end of the century, historians calculate 500,000 babies were delivered up to workhouses in England.[92]

In his 1859 study *Observations on Illegitimacy*, William Acton records 42,651 children born out of wedlock in England and Wales.[93] Such needs stirred up Christian men like George Mueller to provide shelter and sustenance for some 10,000 orphans in very large institutions. Men as distinct as Daniel Defoe[94] and the missionary John G. Paton[95] would point to the breakdown of the family economy as a major contributor to the disintegration of family, society, and morality. Eventually, the state would step in to fund the "Band-Aids" for the dying family in the West—providing education, school lunches, foster care systems, etc. Such governmental initiatives would only perpetuate the breakdown of the family, beginning in the 1830s and continuing to the Fall.

Following the breakdown of public morals on the heels of the Enlightenment and the disintegration of the Puritan movement, the deterioration of the social condition of England came gradually, with an occasional, temporary reversal. The 1,000-year Christian moral influence hung on tenaciously until the 20th Century. Acton's calculation of illegitimacy amounted to just 5.22% of English and

Welsh births in 1859[96]—hardly comparable to the 40-70% illegitimacy rates present in Western nations today.

The Great Awakening and the Clapham evangelicals slowed the moral breakdown of England for a while. Later evangelical revivals however, did little to harness the moral slide in England and America. The force of Enlightenment ideas, the apostasy of the university, French revolutionary influence, and the inevitable moral compromise attending the public theater was just too strong against the counter force coming from a weakening Protestant church.

Nonetheless, Victorian governments steadfastly opposed the murder of children in the womb, by legislation. Section 58 of the Offences Against the Person Act of 1861 made it a felony, punishable by life imprisonment, to purposefully abort a child, as follows:

> Every woman, being with child, who, with intent to procure her own miscarriage, shall unlawfully administer to herself any poison or other noxious thing, or shall unlawfully use any instrument or other means whatsoever with the like intent, and whosoever, with intent to procure the miscarriage of any woman whether she be or be not with child, shall unlawfully administer to her or cause to be taken by her any poison or other noxious thing, or unlawfully use any instrument or other means whatsoever with the like intent, shall be guilty of felony, and being convicted thereof shall be liable...to be kept in penal servitude for life...[97]

The Victorian social order was intent upon maintaining at least external moral conventions and character in both Great Britain and America. The Offences Against the Person Act of 1828 legislated against pedophilia and homosexuality. Between 1806 and 1861, some 9,000 men were prosecuted under these sexual laws, and fifty-six were executed.

However, the influence of the Utilitarian ethicists, Jeremy Bentham

(1748-1832) and his godson John Stuart Mill (1806-1873) inspired a recast of the English legal system. These highly influential cultural leaders would take primary responsibility for the moral corruption of the modern world. At root, Bentham's utilitarian ethic was an assault on the absolutes of God's law which had held firm for 1,500 years in Western society. Augustine, Theodosius, and Alfred were dead and gone by 1861. Now, man would determine what would produce the most good in the long run without a clue of what *good* is or what might even produce it. Nonetheless, Bentham and Mill's ethical theory and their intellectualism appealed to human autonomy and pride, and captured the heart of the people. Central to Bentham's agenda was the legalization and normalization of homosexuality, as admitted to in a treatise published under a pseudonym. Bentham wrote:

> Among the modern nations [homosexuality and homosexual pedophilia are] comparatively but rare...in Edinburgh or Amsterdam you scarce hear of it two or three times in a century. In Athens and in ancient Rome, in the most flourishing periods of the history of those capitals, regular intercourse between the sexes was scarcely much more common. It was upon the same footing throughout Greece: everybody practiced it; nobody was ashamed of it.[98]

In so many words, Bentham bemoans the influence of 1,600 years of Christianity and lamented the disappearance of the "good old days" of sexual perversion and the "guilt-free autonomy" of the pagan world. This offers insight into the social conditions, and the rarity of homosexuality or pedophilia in the 1790s: only a case or two discoverable in Edinburgh or Amsterdam in a hundred years. By the 21st Century, major cities in the United States like San Francisco contained 6.2% self-described homosexuals, and Seattle, Portland, and Austin boasted of a five percent homosexual population.[99] At the Fall of the West, 30% of young millennials (and 40% of 18-24 year olds) identified as homosexual, as well as 28% of millennial "born again"

Christians, according to a survey conducted by George Barna (released in November, 2021). Never had the world witnessed such widespread acceptance of and participation in sexual perversion, even among the most primitive tribes completely isolated from access to the Christian Gospel. Per another national survey, some 6% of British men confessed to homosexual activity, and 4% of the marriages conducted in the Netherlands were for men or women living in unnatural relations with one another. During the 2010s, 92% of the Dutch accepted homosexuality as a moral value.[100] The same survey found only the Muslim and Hindu populations still opposed to sexual deviance—30% of Turkish immigrants and 25% of Moroccan immigrants approved.[101] By its acceptance of the ultimate abominations of the Canaanites enumerated in Leviticus 18, the post-Christian West had degraded itself to the lowest possible moral position—well below the standards of morality retained by Muslims, Hindus, and other pagan peoples.

Of course, there can be no state of perfection in a sinful, fallen world. Yet, for the maintenance of stable human society, dysfunctional conditions are kept to a minimum where the barest of moral standards are retained. So what could be said of this world where the divorce rate was 500 times higher than four centuries earlier, and homosexuality a million times more prevalent in public high schools than it was five decades earlier? Something happened in Amsterdam between 1810 and 2010. What will be the final results of this awful legacy? When the world finally emerges from this tragic era of human history, then all shall know that surely something wicked this way came.

The ethical presuppositional framework of these Christian nations was completely dismantled in the 19th Century. Literary men and *avant-garde* academics on both sides of the Atlantic such as Walt Whitman, Oscar Wilde, Havelock Ellis, Emma Goldman, and George Bernard Shaw served as the vanguard for homosexuality and "free-love" (fornication) a century before the ideas went mainstream.

First-wave feminists like Mary Wollstonecraft (1759-1797), Victoria Woodhull (1838-1927), and Elizabeth Cady Stanton (1815-1902) were pioneers of the post-Christian era, fighting hard for the legalization of prostitution, convenience divorce, and "free adultery" for women. These were the visionaries, the heroes, the apostles, and prophets of the modern age. What they envisioned came to pass in the 1960s and 1970s. The entire Western and developed world came to embrace this post-Christian humanist amorality—the corrupting dry-rot of a civilization.

The espousal of human evolution as formulated by Charles Darwin and the development of modern psychology provided more justification for ethical autonomy. Psychology reinterpreted the concept of guilt in naturalistic, atheistic terms. These were the ideas which provided modern man with just enough psychological margin to break through the ancient mores, and provide the moral license to do whatever he wanted to do.

The Pilgrims and Puritans left England and Holland disillusioned not just with the compromised theology and church order, but with the sinking moral order of Europe. Perhaps it was a premonition of what would happen with the Netherlands in the 21st Century. In his *Of Plymouth Plantation*, Bradford confided:

> ...many of the children, influenced by these conditions, and the great licentiousness of the young people of the country, and the many temptations of the city, were led by evil example into dangerous courses, getting the reins off their necks and leaving their parents.[102]

Historians reviewing 17th Century public records from the Plymouth Colony calculate the divorce rate at 0.1% and the illegitimacy rate about 1%. In fifty years of the Pilgrim Colony, there were only two prosecutions for Leviticus 20:13-15 crimes—one ended in the death penalty, the other in exile.[103] The Massachusetts Bay

Colony prosecuted only twice for Leviticus 20:13 crimes. In both cases children were involved, and the perpetrators were executed.[104] Given a population of 100,000 over several generations, such numbers are extremely low (.002%). By no means will any human society claim moral perfection, but the blessings of God's common grace and special grace enable civilizations to carry on. Given full rein, sexual sin will always erode the foundations and bring unspeakable misery to pagan and post-Christian nations alike.

By 1676, Increase Mather was concerned that drunkenness had become "a common sin" in New England.[105] A decade later, Puritan pastors were concerned with a dance instructor who showed up in Boston to organize "mixt dances."[106] Matters became more serious towards the end of Mather's ministry and life. The old minister spent his last jeremiads in 1719 pointing out that "many in Boston are guilty of the sins of Sodom."[107] Between 1691 and 1710, Boston increased its tavern count from thirty-two to eighty-one, and "cases of adultery and bastardy steadily increased...prostitution became common."[108]

With the deterioration of theology and the rise of Unitarianism, conditions did not improve for the United States. A demonic spell seemed to have fallen on the nation by the 1830s and 1840s. The rise of spiritism, cults, terrorism, and the continuation of slavery constituted some of the nation's sins. Presidents Pierce and Lincoln introduced seances into the White House—plunging the nation to a new moral low.

Once again, by God's merciful providences, the nation was humbled during the 1860s, after suffering through the Civil War. A degree of sanity and social morality returned to the nation, however briefly. The New York Businessmen Revival of 1857, the bona fide revivals of the Civil War camps, and the Dwight L. Moody revivals offered a slight correction to the nation's downward course.

From 1875 through 1915, Anthony Comstock and others fought

back the forces of darkness in New York and elsewhere, battling against abortionists and pornographers taking advantage of the newly-discovered technology of photography. These moral campaigns constituted something of a losing battle as the nation's worldview was transmuted in academia, government, and popular culture. The heart of this Western nation was corrupted and running towards that which was evil at ever-accelerating speed. The American people were turning away from God culturally, morally, ecclesiastically, and in every other way. Nonetheless, Comstock was successful in confiscating fifteen tons of obscene books and 4,000,000 pornographic pictures. America's first bona fide abortionist worked in New York City for forty-one years (1837-1878) before Anthony Comstock assembled enough evidence to have her arrested. Madame Restell died in her own bathtub (by suicide) before the police could take her into custody.

Popular culture led the way to mainstreaming sexual license in the 1920s and then again in the 1960s. The Roaring Twenties brought a revival of Christopher Marlowe's play *Edward II*, adapted by Bertolt Brecht of Munich in 1924. In America, Mae West (1893-1980) and Cole Porter (1891-1964) produced their vaudeville and musical acts, pushing a loose view of sexual sin (including homosexual forms). Over 300,000 people attended West's plays before the police shut her down. Yet, almost nothing could slow the popular appetite for this revolution.

Only by the merciful providence of God, the moral dissolution of the nations in the West was delayed until the 1960s; no doubt, a byproduct of the Great Depression and World War II.

MORAL COMPROMISE AT THE HIGHEST ECHELONS

America's moral fall came first in the 1920s. Leading the way were presidents, academics, and cultural icons. Initially, America was enamored with Darwinism and the worst kind of racist eugenics. Men as renowned as Woodrow Wilson, Theodore Roosevelt, and Oliver

Wendell Holmes were strong advocates of racist eugenics—a very bad doctrine also embraced by the Germans and Japanese, contributing much to bring about the horrors of World War II.

President Woodrow Wilson, raised a Presbyterian in the South, gave way to an adulterous relationship and set Princeton on the path towards secularism and Darwinism. Warren G. Harding was one of the foulest presidents in history conducting sordid (and now infamous) affairs with Carrie Phillips and Nan Britton. Franklin D. Roosevelt also carried on an affair with Lucy Mercer, and Mrs. Roosevelt was known for her lesbian dalliances dragged into the White House, at least via her letters.

Granted, such "public indiscretions" were almost nothing compared to the Roman Caesars and popes, but this was the Christian Protestant world transgressing boundaries held in place for a thousand years. This was the beginning of the end of the Christian West.

REVOLUTIONIZING LAW (1870-1932)

Charles Darwin's evolutionary construct for origins and the modern conception of a purely naturalistic reality took immediate effect on legal theory. Harvard Law dean, Christopher Columbus Langdell (1826-1906), incorporated Darwin's theory of evolution into law as early as 1870. In his textbook *Cases on the Law of Contracts,* Langdell presented law as a science of discovery, an evolving doctrine.

> Law, considered as a science, consists of certain principles or doctrines...Each of these doctrines has arrived at its present state by slow degrees; in other words, it is a growth, extending in many cases through centuries.[109]

It would be left up to Langdell's student (and a disciple of Ralph Waldo Emerson), Oliver Wendell Holmes Jr., to bring a revolution of law to the Western world. Serving as a US Supreme Court justice from 1902 to 1932, Holmes loudly testified that "The common law is not a brooding omnipresence in the sky."[110] Attorney General Francis Biddle noted: "Holmes's beliefs are...that men make their own laws; that these laws do not flow from some mysterious omnipresence in the sky."[111] Utterly abandoning all concept of natural law or absolute ethics, Holmes wrote to a friend, "You believe in some transcendental sanction, I don't."[112] Holding strictly to a naturalistic evolutionary metaphysic, Holmes called man "an idealizing animal" who happens to express his laws in "conventions."[113] Therefore, for Holmes, constitutions and laws are "living, organic institutions" meant to be changed by political leaders and judges as they see fit.

For Benjamin Cardozo (1870-1938), another influential US Supreme Court justice, government laws must be considered entirely unbound by tradition or God's law, and left to the determination of a democratic majority. Cardozo wrote in his manual *The Nature of the Judicial Process:*

> My duty as judge may be to objectify in law, not my own aspirations and convictions and philosophies, but the aspirations and convictions and philosophies of the men and women of my time. Hardly shall I do this well if my own sympathies and beliefs and passionate devotions are with a time that is past.[114]

Within an article published in 1910, John Dewey, the father of modern humanist education, summarized the impact Darwin exerted upon the field of law and governance:

> That the publication of the "Origin of Species" marked an epoch in the development of the natural sciences is well known to the layman. That the combination of the very words origin and species embodied an intellectual revolt and introduced a new intellectual temper is easily overlooked by the expert. The conceptions that had reigned in the philosophy of nature and knowledge for two thousand years, the conceptions that had become the familiar furniture of the mind, rested on the assumption of the superiority of the fixed and final [God

and His Word]; … In laying hands upon the sacred ark of absolute permanency, in treating the forms that had been regarded as types of fixity and perfection as originating and passing away, the "Origin of Species" introduced a mode of thinking that in the end was bound to transform the logic of knowledge, and hence the treatment of morals, politics, and religion…

The Darwinian principle of natural selection cut straight under this philosophy. If all organic adaptations are due simply to constant variation and the elimination of those variations which are harmful in the struggle for existence that is brought about by excessive reproduction, there is no call for a prior intelligent causal force to plan and preordain them…

"God" [is] a faded piece of metaphysical goods.[115]

President Theodore Roosevelt's appointment of Oliver Wendell Holmes Jr. to the US Supreme Court in 1902 was the first major breach in the hull of Western society. Holmes' endorsement of eugenics in the *Buck v. Bell* decision in 1927 marked an important turn for the worse. His comment, "Three generations of imbeciles is enough," remains a testimony to his evolutionary and eugenics perspectives to this day. The decision resulted in the forced sterilization of Carrie Buck.

After the smoke cleared following World War II, the Warren Court of the 1950s-1970s became the primary mechanism to utterly decimate 1,700 years of Christian influence on Western jurisprudence. Chief Justice Earl Warren enthusiastically embraced evolutionary foundations for law, best put in this famous quote: "The Constitutional Amendment must draw its meaning from the evolving standards of decency that mark the progress of a maturing society."[116] In the words of Dostoyevsky, "If God doesn't exist, everything is possible."[117] After 1950, the American courts unreservedly adopted this viewpoint, opening the door for "evolving standards of decency"—thereby surrendering all limits for moral indecency and sexual perversion, bringing the West to societal ruin.

Winning the Second World War would take a toll on American morals. It was a boost to the pride of a nation at the zenith of its power. President Dwight Eisenhower's appointment of Earl Warren in 1953 was a major setback for Western morals in governance. The Warren Court went to work, legalizing pornography (*Roth v. US,* 1957), and removing prayer (*Engel v. Vitale,* 1962) and Bible reading (*Abington School District v. Schempp,* 1963) from public schools.

Over the succeeding sixty years, the pornography revolution would ruin the American male, modern sexual life, and marriage. Pornography enabled mass isolation, depersonalization of sexuality, and homosexuality (by the accommodation of self-gratification). Once again, it was electronic technology which mass-produced and fast-tracked the dry rot for the corruption of human society in the modern world. Electronic access to pornography was constant and omnipresent after the smartphone (or iPhone) was released in 2011. Children were corrupted by this technology as readily as the Greeks had accomplished the same feat with their own children in pagan homes and gymnasiums. On average, a child first encountered pornography around eleven years of age, and 94% of children were viewing porn at fourteen years of age.[118] By 2019, 95% of teens (13 to 17 years of age) had full access to a smartphone and pornography, and almost half of them admitted to "constantly" being on the internet.[119] Eighty percent of American men 18 to 30 years of age were addicted to pornography, admitting to at least monthly use.[120] Overall, Americans increased their participation in pornography from 20% to 65% between 1970 and 2019.[121] The sheer number of men, boys, and families ruined by this electronic and demonic scourge would be impossible to figure. All that was left to assess was lying in the ashes of Western civilization.

Highly symbolic of the return to paganism was the reopening of the ancient pornographic displays of Pompeii in the 20th Century. During the Enlightenment, the obscenest creations of this perverted city (destroyed in AD 79) were unearthed and placed under wraps. King Francis I of Naples sealed up the "Secret Museum" in 1821, and a brick wall was installed in front of the door in 1849. Yet the exhibit was made available for full public access at the National Archaeological Museum in 2000. *Pandora's box had already been opened.* The Western world had already turned into Pompeii.

THE MASS CORRUPTION OF MEDIA

The mass corruption of mainstream Western society took place over a period of sixty years. The earliest television Emmys were awarded to "family-friendly" productions like *Father Knows Best* and *Huckleberry Hound* in 1960, and nominations were made for programs such as *Lassie*, *Perry Mason*, and *The Twilight Zone*. Sixty years later, *Schitt's Creek* received an unprecedented seven awards—a show dedicated to the normalization of homosexuality and three-some orgies. HBO's *Euphoria* took home the rest of the awards—a program described by major news sources as pornography, featuring every variety of sexual perversion, not to mention ample doses of drug abuse, rape, transgenderism, and suicidal tendencies.

The Grammy Award for Song of the Year in 1959 was awarded to Johnny Horton's historical ballad, "Battle of New Orleans." As the sun set in the West, the Song of the Year Grammy for 2020 was awarded to a dark, mentally-disturbed tribute to sadomasochism—a little number called "Bad Guy" coughed up by some "artist" by the name of Billie Eilish. The rest of the album was dedicated to the themes of hopelessness, suicide, self-mutilation, Lucifer, and cannibalism.

This cultural milieu was worse than the last days of Pompeii in AD 78, in that the Christian apostasy was self-conscious, radical, and deserving of the ultimate judgment of God. In the words of 2 Peter

2:21, it would have been better for the West "not to have known the way of righteousness, than having known it, to turn from the holy commandment delivered to them." The cultural degrade is a story in itself, recounted in full at a later chapter.

THE CORRUPTION OF CHILDREN

The corruption and sexualization of children appeared as the most devastating effect of the sexual revolution on human society. Child abuse, child pornography, and child prostitution were still condemned and prosecuted—albeit half-heartedly. The sexualization of children continued all the while unabated, and the abundance of filth proliferated especially on the internet.

For decades, Disney and other child film-producers sexualized children through their productions. The $80 billion-strong, Disney Corporation had introduced "homosexual days" to its theme parks in the early 1990s, and its first film encouraging transgenderism for children came in 1998. *Mulan* expressed discontentment with her gender, crying out over the theme music: "When will my reflection show who I am inside?" This more sophisticated Pied Piper was to lead hundreds of millions of children down the "primrose" path to hell during the waning decades of the West.

But, even more troubling was the pressures to sexualize the children by government order. The incorrigible obsession to indoctrinate children in homosexual and transgender ideologies was particularly evident when the Biden Administration tied federal monies received by 100,000 public schools in America to the incorporation of homosexual and transgender policies. Thousands of schools adopted "comprehensive" sex education curricula based on "free sex" and homosexual ideologies, and hundreds of public libraries and schools routinely invited men dressed like women ("drag queens") to perform before young primary school students. The insanity was ubiquitous and persisted unabated. Most tragically, the children themselves were not exempted from it.

CONVENIENCE DIVORCE

For over 1,500 years, the sanctity of marriage and the nuclear family maintained strong underpinnings for Western society. From the turn of the 20th Century, the United States led the world in divorce and the breakdown of the family unit. Reno, Nevada was recognized as the divorce capitol of the world in 1909, and California's Governor Ronald Reagan was faulted as the first to sign a no-fault divorce bill into law (in 1969). Australia followed suit in 1975. The United Kingdom passed a law in 1969 permitting divorce in cases where the marriage is "irretrievably broken down."

As the laws loosened and the moral revolution worked its way out, the US divorce rate increased ten-fold between 1900 and 1980 (from 4% to 40%). That's about 400 times the divorce rate of the Puritans and Pilgrims who first populated this Christian nation. Between 1850 and 1990, the divorce rate per 1000 increased from 0.3 per 1,000 to 5 per 1,000, a sixteen-fold increase.[122] As the fall of the social system materialized, young people avoided marriage entirely, preferring to live in fornication with each other—a response to their parents' failed marriages. By the 2020s, the social system was ruined as dysfunctional households outnumbered functional households. A full 9% of young men and women 18 to 24 years of age lived together outside of the bounds of marriage, compared to 7% who were lawfully married.[123] The cohabitation rate was *ninety times* what it was in 1970.[124] And the illegitimacy rate (children born outside of wedlock) increased from 1% in 1900 to 6% in 1960, then to 41% by 2020. Among women giving birth, 26 to 31 years of age, 57% of the children were born out of wedlock—with no father in the home.[125] This was the majority of society. A study issued by the Center for Social Justice in the UK in

2020 found that children living with a cohabiting couple were 4 times worse off than those kids living with married parents. By the time they turned five years old, 53% of those kids living with cohabiting parents would experience parental separation. That only happened 15% of the time for kids living with married parents.[126] This marked the end of a civilization, assuming of course, that the family is fundamental to human society.

As the end approached, Turkey, Greece, Korea, and Japan in the East averaged an illegitimacy rate of only 5%, compared to an average rate of 48% for Sweden, Norway, Netherlands, the UK, France, and the United States. Most of the disintegration of family life occurred after AD 1980.[127] But the social fallout for these children representing the majority population of these nations, suffering the consequences of cohabitation and divorce, would continue for generations.

Something was made of the annual declining divorce rate in the US between 1990 and 2020, but the news was only a diversion from the fuller picture. With the decline in divorces came a sharper decline in marriage. The social attrition ratio, calculated by dividing the divorce rate into the marriage rate, serves as a better barometer of social health. The attrition ratio climbed to 45%—a retention of only a tenth of the social integrity registered at the turn of the 20th Century.[128]

US Social Attrition Ratio

Year	Marriage Rate	Divorce Rate	Social Attrition Ratio
1880	9	0.4	4%
1900	9.3	0.7	7%
1920	12	1.4	12%
1930	10	1.3	13%
1940	12.7	1.9	15%

1950	11.1	2.6	23%
1960	8.5	2.2	26%
1970	10.6	3.5	33%
1980	10.6	4.7	44%
1990	9.7	4.1	43%
2000	8.8	3.6	41%
2018	6.5	2.9	45%

RETURNING TO THE PAGAN WORLD
WITH A VENGEANCE—ABORTION

Fittingly, the grossest manifestation of mass-produced evil in the modern world began in the East with the Soviet Union under the atheistic Bolsheviks—the prime product of the German and French Enlightenment. The great humanist legacy of mass-produced murder began when the Soviets legalized abortion in October 1920 under the "Decree on Women's Healthcare" issued by the Russian Soviet Federative Socialist Republic. The terrible legislation was unleashed upon Ukraine on July 5, 1921. Well into the 21st Century, Russia retained the highest abortion rate in the world, with the possible exception of Greenland.

Once again, it was the *avant-garde* literary crowd leading the way in the United States for the mass murder of children made in the image of God. Novelist F. Scott Fitzgerald's wife aborted their second child in 1922, and Nobel Prize-winning author John Steinbeck forced his wife Carol to abort in 1939—almost killing her.

England came close to legalizing abortion in 1937 following the Roaring Twenties, but by God's mercies, she diverted her attention to a world war. Largely due to the influence of the American eugenics advocate, Margaret Sanger, Japan eagerly adopted the very racist and nasty Eugenics Protection Law in 1948. Thereafter, Japan quickly gained the unenviable position of claiming the highest abortion rate in the world. By 1955, 55% of Japanese babies were aborted.

Finally, "Pandora's box" opened in 1967 when England, California, and Colorado legalized abortion. The world will forever remember that it was Republican governors John Love and Ronald Reagan who introduced this bane to the modern age. Six years later, abortion on demand was legalized in all fifty US states by the Supreme Court decision *Roe v. Wade* (1973). Five of the seven men responsible for this crucial element of the moral fall were appointed by Republican presidents Richard Nixon and Dwight D. Eisenhower.

Over the next fifty years, every major Western country followed suit. With heavy pressure from the US State Department and the United Nations, abortion was legalized and accepted by an additional forty-seven countries after 1994, mostly in the Middle East, South America, Asia, and Africa.[129] To complete the death march of the Western world, the last holdouts of Northern Ireland and New Zealand fell in 2020. New Zealand passed its first bill reading through the legislature on August 8, 2019, legalizing abortion nationwide on March 26, 2020, just as the nation shut down for the Covid-19 pandemic. Northern Ireland was forced by the UK parliament to legalize child killing in October 2019. The policy was implemented on April 9, 2020, and twenty-two children were killed in the first year. At least symbolically, this would mark the end of Christian culture among Western nations, and the end of Western civilization.

The old paganism in the form of infanticide had returned to North America, Europe, and most of Asia by 2019, legitimized and normalized among 60% of the world's population.[130] Only those cultures somewhat insulated from the West (in Africa, South America, and the remote parts of Southeast Asia) would remain opposed to abortion on demand.

THE FINAL GOVERNMENTAL CAPITULATION
IN THE FALL OF THE WEST

The Roman Church at its very worst in the 11th and 15th centuries never descended to the depths of moral degrade achieved in the 20th and 21st Centuries. Despite the only half-hearted commitment to curtail immorality by the Council of Ten in Venice and the Morality Committee of Florence in the 15th Century, there was no widespread social approval for sodomy and child killing in those days. What could have predicted the utter moral degradation which would characterize Europe and the United States in the 21st Century? Dante placed sodomites in the third degree of the seventh hell, below highway robbers, mass murderers, cruel imperialists (like Alexander of Macedonia), and others. The very worst accusations brought against the very worst popes—such as Benedict IX (1012-1056) and anti-pope John XXIII (1370-1419)—was this sin.

Humanist autonomy finds its zenith as man pretends to redefine reality, to reconstruct or recreate himself into an image he would concoct in his own mind. For the Christian Western apostasy, homosexuality and transgenderism became the final and ultimate bastion of humanist autonomy. This was the high castle in the kingdom of humanist autonomy, the final achievement of the humanist revolution "against the Lord and His Anointed." There could be no more fundamental revolt than the attempt to redefine a sexual or gender identity and thereby violate the most basic creation ordinance. There was no higher treachery against God which could be imagined in the minds of rebel man.

This corruption of the natural world could only work unimaginable ruin to modern life. At the point where human society reaches its very lowest level of degradation, the Apostle Paul explains that God has "given them up" to "dishonor their bodies among themselves" (Rom. 1:24). By 2017, 8.2% of young American millennials identified themselves as having a proclivity towards homosexuality, compared to only 2.4% of the baby boomer generation.[131] This metric increased for young millennials to 40% in 2022.

In the epochal Christian degrade in the West, the governments and great powers of this world would commit the final and ultimate act of moral and spiritual treachery—institutionalizing the perversion of homosexual "marriage" into civil codes. For 6,000 years, even pagan governments shied away from such society-destroying inclinations. Never had such a daring act of social revolution ever been attempted on this scale. Never would any Christian have imagined such an evil fate for entire civilizations. Scarcely a single pagan tribe had dared to do what the post-Christian apostate nations had set out to do.

FRENCH ROOTS—THE IMPETUS IN THE BREAKDOWN OF WESTERN SOCIAL MORALITY

> Then the fifth angel sounded: and I saw a star fallen from heaven to the earth. To him was given the key to the bottomless pit. And he opened the bottomless pit, and smoke arose out of the pit like the smoke of a great furnace. So the sun and the air were darkened because of the smoke of the pit. Then out of the smoke locusts came upon the earth. And to them was given power, as the scorpions of the earth have power. (Revelation 9:1-3)

The revolt began in France. The spine-chilling description of demonic evil spilling onto the earth from Revelation 9 points to some horrible eschatological event—perhaps not actually fulfilled in 1792, but at least resembling such an event. This was a defining turning point in history. Indeed, the modern age was birthed out of moral, social, and cultural revolutions—some physically bloody and some spiritually bloody—but all rooted in the French Revolution of 1789-1799. Looking back, one can only conclude that something very wicked this way came via France.

The forgery of Rheims, the Janus-faced Albigensian Crusade, the Avignon Babylonian Exile, the persecution of the Huguenots, and the French rejection of the Reformation produced very rotten fruit for 18th Century France. Nowhere in the world was there found such open hatred for God or such demonic frenzy or rabid apostasy as that seen in 1790s Paris. Here was the cesspool from which arose many secret societies, evil conspiracies, communist revolutions, atheistic ideas, sexual anarchy, and just about every other curse that came down upon the Western world in the 19th and 20th centuries.

The Left Wing Enlightenment philosophers Voltaire and Rousseau were much at fault for the chaos of the French Revolution and all other revolutions following in its wake. Immorality characterized these men from beginning to end—Voltaire took his niece as his mistress, and Rousseau abandoned his five children on the steps of an orphanage. Voltaire was embittered against Christianity, and outright rejected the possibility of an afterlife, preferring a worldview of naturalist materialism. Rousseau favored an autonomist romanticism or irrationalism. Exceedingly proud and seemingly very intelligent men, these were extreme idealists, revolutionaries, and humanists, armed with a budding confidence in autonomous human reason. They were extremely popular and powerful writers for their times, bearing an almost supernatural, irresistible influence over their adherents.

While there may have been controversy over the murder of the king and his wife (Louis XVI and Marie Antoinette) in 1793, the Revolution quickly unified around an unmitigated spite for Christianity. The time had come to shake off the heritage, the moral conscience, the symbols, and the spiritual influence of 1,600 years of Christian faith in Europe. In some places of the country, Christian worship was banned upon pain of death. Christian symbols were torn down everywhere, crosses destroyed, and altars chopped up. The Clermont Cathedral was confiscated and given the name "The Temple of Reason." Men and women exchanged their Christian names for ancient pagan Roman names. The Cathedral of Notre Dame was turned into another "Temple of Reason," and an actress was set on the high altar and given the title "Goddess of Reason" for all to worship.

It seemed as if the dragon himself had been unleashed from the bottomless pit. The Reign of Terror commenced on September 5, 1793 with a call to action from Bertrand Barère: "Let us make terror the order of the day!"[132] President Robespierre pontificated, "Terror is nothing more than speedy, severe and inflexible justice; it is thus an emanation of virtue."[133] Some 17,000 people were executed by the guillotine. The spiritual element was working overtime behind the scenes to produce the mayhem, endless bloodshed, and unrelenting terror. At this time, hundreds of secret cults surfaced and proliferated. Pornography and prostitution were rampant. Satanic orgies, black masses, sexual perversions, and blasphemies were the order of the day around Paris. Nobody was safe, including Robespierre; he was taken to execution on July 24, 1794.

During the Revolution, it was Louis-Michel Le Peletier de Saint-Fargeau (1760-1793) who advocated a socialist education program patterned after Sparta, much encouraged in the writings of both Voltaire and Rousseau. On September 25, 1791 the same Le Peletier presented a new penal code to the assembly, in which he had eliminated what he called the "Phony offenses created by superstition [Christianity]" including such things as blasphemy, witchcraft, sodomy, and incest. This was the end product of the Satanic incursion into the Christian West. The Napoleonic Code merely perpetuated the secular humanist law fomented during the Revolution. Under Napoleon's domination in 1811, the Netherlands also adopted the Napoleonic Code, allowing for homosexual behavior. Later, the Netherlands would become the world leader in sexual license, prostitution, and homosexual marriage (1980-2020).

Following the pattern of France's Revolution, the Soviet Union led the way to the decriminalization of homosexuality in the East when the Bolsheviks repealed Article 995 in 1917. A more explicit approval came in 1922. Poland and Denmark followed in the 1930s. Then came Iceland (1940), Switzerland (1942), Sweden (1944), Hungary (1961), the state of Illinois (1962), England and Wales (1967), Hawaii and Norway (1972), the state of California (1975), and Northern Ireland (1982).

Fifty years of self-imposed sexual sterility by conception control, depersonalized sexuality by pornography, and no-fault divorce prepared the world for the final chapter in the moral decline. Under the leadership of Margaret Sanger (1879-1966), founder of the Conception Control League, the world turned to sexuality without procreation, sexuality without responsibility and meaningful lifelong commitments, and sexuality without moral discipline and restraints. US Supreme Court cases *Lawrence v. Texas* (2003) and *Obergefell v. Hodges* (2015), legitimizing homosexual behavior and sodomic marriage, were inevitable consequences of all that came before them. Austria and Northern Ireland capitulated in 2019. Western Europe, most of North America, two-thirds of South America, Australia, New Zealand, and South Africa adopted the "new" definition of marriage—consummating the Christian apostasy of the Western Gentile world.

Practicing homosexuals took the helm of leadership for many of the Western nation states. Nero's depraved legacy was first realized in Iceland (2009), followed by Belgium (2011), Luxembourg (2013), Oregon (2015), the Republic of Ireland (2017), Serbia (2017), and Colorado (2019). The political leaders of the Western world also embraced childlessness. At the Fall, heads of governments in France, Germany, Holland, Sweden, Scotland, Lithuania, Romania, and the United Kingdom had no natural children. Whether consciously realizing it or not, these leaders were admitting the obvious: There was no future for the West—only a legacy of unprecedented debt, birth implosions, sexual nihilism, and child murder.

> Well; because of unbelief they were broken off, and thou standest by
> faith. Be not highminded, but fear: For if God spared not the natural
> branches, take heed lest he also spare not thee. (Romans 11:20-21)

CROSSING OVER THE MORAL THRESHOLD—AD 2007

Beginning in 2001, the analytics company Gallup began tracing what they termed the American Moral Acceptability poll. This was a measure of the *vox populi* (the voice of the people), or better yet the *lex populi* (the law of the people), monitoring the moral opinions of Americans. Two thousand years of Christian influence in the West and four hundred years of this influence upon America would die hard. Intellectual and political leadership had worked rigorously to destroy every strand of the American moral fiber, beginning in the 1950s. It would take a bit of time to reach the heartland and infect the majority of the population. According to the Gallup research, between 2001 and 2020, America increased in immorality by 32.6% on the major indexes. During this time, the nation moved from 40% to 66% favorability towards homosexuality. Support for the immoral choice to have a baby outside of marriage increased from 45% to 66%. Favorability towards the use of baby tissue for stem cell research increased from 52% to 66%. Opposition to abortion remained about the same, around 47%. America's overall immorality index averaged out at 48.6% in 2001 and 64.4% in 2020.[134] As the last Christian holdout in the Western world, America crossed over to the dark side around the year 2007 (by this metric). From this point on it appeared the West was bound over to the judgment of God. Morality had been rejected by the masses, and common grace influence over the institutions was slipping. The cancerous sin of the nation was metastasizing, and it had already spread into the heart. The reversal of 1,500 years of Christian moral influence in the West was finally accomplished by the year 2020.

To review and summarize the key moments in the unraveling of American morality, the ten most devastating events paving the way for the downfall of the nation are listed as follows:

1. 1957—The US Supreme court decision *Roth v. United States* paved the way for easy access to Playboy Magazine and pornography for millions of American men.

2. 1962—The US Supreme Court decision *Engel v. Vitale* banned prayer, thanksgiving, and the fear of God in public schools.

3. 1965—The use of abortifacient conception control was approved by the US Supreme Court in the *Griswold v. State of Connecticut* case. These first three landmark decisions came through the Earl Warren Court. Many of the justices were appointed by President Dwight Eisenhower.

4. 1967—Republican governors Ronald Reagan of California and John Love of Colorado signed bills legalizing abortion in their respective states.

5. 1969—Governor Ronald Reagan signed the first convenience divorce law for the state of California.

6. 1970—Congressman George H. W. Bush introduced Title X funding to subsidize abortifacient drugs, resulting in $10 billion of government subsidies for conception control over the next fifty years.

7. 1973—The US Supreme Court decision *Roe v. Wade* produced one of the most liberal abortion laws in the world, legalizing abortion in all fifty states.

8. 2003—The US Supreme Court decision *Lawrence v. Texas* legalized sodomy after 1,600 years of Western Christian influence beginning with the Theodosian Code.

9. 2015—The US Supreme Court decision *Obergefell v. Hodges* institutionalized homosexual faux marriage as the apostate

Christian West made the first overt attempt to violate God's creation order in 6,000 years of world history.

10. 2020—The US Supreme Court decision *Bostock v. Clayton County* initiated persecution against Christian ministries and businesses refusing to advertise transvestism and homosexuality in the workplace.

THE FINAL ABANDONMENT OF A CHRISTIAN CULTURAL DENOMINATOR

The erosion of the Christian cultural denominator continued over a long period of time in the United States, but the final remnants were lost during the 1990s. Cultural commentator, Aaron Renn observed a positive view of Christian cultural influences dominant until 1994. This shifted to a neutral view between 1994 and 2014. But, after 2014, Christians became a "social negative, especially in high-status positions. Christianity in many ways was seen as undermining the social good."[135] Point of fact, Senator Gary Hart lost the Democrat presidential nomination in 1987 when the Miami Herald captured a few choice pictures of him with a woman not his wife on a yacht. To the end they insisted the relationship was platonic. However, by 1998, President Bill Clinton achieved his highest approval ratings after impeachment proceedings trotted out his multiple sexual shenanigans—still mostly from his leftist support base. And, in the 2016 election, the conservative (Republican) voting base was mostly oblivious to Donald Trump's equally egregious sexual proclivities. By this time Christian cultural standards were of zero import to the nation.

Until the 1990s, the Christian evangelist, Billy Graham was considered by Americans as more-or-less a national icon. He was friendly with Presidents Dwight Eisenhower, John F. Kennedy, Lyndon B. Johnson, Richard Nixon, Gerald Ford, Jimmy Carter, and Ronald Reagan, George H.W. Bush, Bill Clinton, and George W. Bush. However, the son of Billy Graham was never so delicately courted by

America's political elite. By the end, Franklin Graham was persona non grata in New York City despite his attempt to provide medical care to Covid-19 patients in Central Park. All eight venues reserved for Graham's UK evangelism campaign cancelled, arguing explicitly anti-Christian ethical values.[136]

Dr. James Dobson's Christian values were still supported by a large segment of the American population in the 1980s and 1990s. At its peak, the "Focus on the Family" message was carried over 7,000 radio stations and heard daily by 220 million people. Before it was all done however, the tide turned hard on the "good doctor." In 2010, Dobson was removed from the ministry he founded. His uncompromising stance on social issues proved to be utterly repudiated by the new cultural zeitgeist. Dobson's outreach was reduced to 300 radio stations while his replacement at Focus on the Family continued on 7,000 stations, committed to an agenda of much reduced cultural confrontation. Jim Daly explained the "refocus" to the secular media as: "My core theme is to demonstrate the love of God...to see those living outside God's will not as opponents to conquer but as people loved by God."[137]

Homosexuals found little support from the churches in the 1980s and 1990s, with the exception of a few Metropolitan Community Churches. But 40 years later, almost every denomination was bending over backwards to accommodate what the macro culture had wholeheartedly embraced—homosexual orientation, same-sex attraction, homosexual marriage, and gender-neutrality/confusion. The Christian churches would have a hard time coming to grips with the "negative view," which would entail more cultural confrontation, more carefully-calculated engagements, more separation and ostracization, and more persecution and cancel culture. The church would have to become explicitly counter cultural if it was to be distinctively Christian. Such conditions called for a robust faith.

A STARK DIVIDE—EAST & WEST, NORTH & SOUTH

Over the last decades of the decline of the West, Pew Research Center conducted a regular Global Attitudes Survey. This organization noted a global divide occurring specifically on views relating to homosexuality.

Only Eastern Europe exhibited a negative trend towards this sin, while South Africa, India, Turkey, South Korea, Japan, South America, and the United States registered significant public support for the sin. The most pro-homosexual countries were exclusively Western countries: first Sweden, then the Netherlands, Spain, France, the UK, Germany, and Australia. In just six years, the United States had increased its support for homosexuality by 12%.

Region	Popular Support for Homosexuality Median Percentage[138]
Western Europe	86%
Australia	81%
North America	79%
The Philippines	73%
Japan	68%
South Africa	54%
South America	52%
South Korea	44%
India	37%
China	22%[139]
Russia	14%
Africa (without South Africa)	10%
Indonesia	9%

Importantly, Pew Research reported that "Attitudes on this issue are strongly correlated with a country's wealth."[140] Only the richest and most decadent nations, having enjoyed God's outpouring of material blessings and technological advancement, most enthusiastically embraced self-destructive patterns. The Philippines and Japan were corrupted mostly by America, and South Africa by the Netherlands and Britain. Meanwhile, the South American countries had been fairly well corrupted by the influence of Western European colonialism by 2020. Only Africa, Russia, the Middle East, and certain Far Eastern nations were somewhat exempted from the terrible influence of an apostate, corrupted West in this area.

Given the historical record of nations which publicly endorsed socially-destructive conventions, the survival of Western Europe, Australia, North America, the Philippines, Japan, South Africa, and Brazil was very much in the balance. Despite efforts to correct the terribly destructive policies of the Soviets, Russia still retained the highest abortion rate of all the major powers. These same nations were saddled with serious birth implosions—never a good sign for the perpetuation of a civilization. As Western civilization died out, would God's temporal blessings of prosperity and power shift to China, India, Indonesia, and Africa in future years? At the end, among the younger generation (18-24 years old), 40% claimed "LGBT orientation" compared to 3.8% for their parents' generation (by the 2020 Gallup survey and George Barna). And, 70% of Americans supported Neronic marriages, up from 27% in 1996. What had destroyed Ancient Greece and Rome had destroyed the Christian West.[141]

The age of Western Christendom was over. The West fell. The Gentile branch was severed. They boasted, and then they were humbled.

> And at the end of the days I Nebuchadnezzar lifted up mine eyes unto heaven, and mine understanding returned unto me, and I blessed

the most High, and I praised and honoured him that liveth for ever, whose dominion is an everlasting dominion, and his kingdom is from generation to generation: and all the inhabitants of the earth are reputed as nothing: and he doeth according to his will in the army of heaven, and among the inhabitants of the earth: and none can stay his hand, or say unto him, What doest thou? (Daniel 4:34-35)

ADDENDUM: ALFRED THE GREAT'S DOOMS

"The Lord spoke these words to Moses, and said: 'I am the Lord your God. I led you out of the lands and out of the bondage of the Egyptians.'"

1. "Do not love other strange gods before Me!"

2. "Do not call out My Name in idleness! For you are not guiltless with Me, if you call out My Name in idleness."

3. "Mind that you hallow the rest-day! You must work six days; but on the seventh you must rest! For in six days Christ made Heavens and Earth, the seas, and all the shapen things in them; but He rested on the seventh day. Therefore, the Lord hallowed it."

4. "Honour your father and your mother whom the Lord gave you— so that you may live longer on Earth!"

5. "Do not slay!"

6. "Do not commit adultery!"

7. "Do not steal!"

8. "Do not witness falsely!"

9. "Do not unrighteously desire your neighbour's goods!"

10. "Do not make gold or silver gods for yourself!"

11. "These are the judgments which you must appoint. If anyone buys a Christian slave [or man in bondage], let him be bonded for six years—but the seventh, he must freely be unbought. With such clothes as he went in, with such must he go forth. If he himself had a wife [previously]—she must go out with him. However, if his overlord gave him a wife—she and her bairn [must] go to the overlord. If, however, the bondsman then says, 'I do not wish to go away from my overlord; nor from my wife; nor from my bairn; nor from my goods'—let his overlord then bring him to the door

of the church and drill his ear through with an awl, as a sign that he should be a bondsman ever since!" Exodus 21:2-6.

12. "Though anyone sells his daughter as a maidservant, let her not at all be a bondswoman like other women. Nor may he sell her to foreigners. But if he who bought her does not respect her—let her go free, [even] among foreigners. If, then, he [her overlord] allows his son to cohabit with her—let him give her marriage-gifts, and see to it that she receives clothes and the dowry which is the value of her maidenhood! Let him give her that! If he do none of these things to her—then she is free." See: Exodus 21:7f.

13. "The man who intentionally slays another man—let him suffer death [Genesis 9:5- 6]! He, however, who slay him out of necessity or unwillingly or involuntarily—as when God may have sent him into his power, and when he had not lain in wait for him— he is worthy of his living and lawful fine, if he [the involuntary manslaughterer] seeks asylum. But if any one presumptuously and wilfully slays his neighbour through guile—drag him from My altar, so that he should suffer death!" See: Numbers 35:11-33.

14. "He who smites his father or his mother—shall suffer death!"

15. "He who steals a Freeman and sells him, and it be proved against him, so that he cannot clear himself—let him suffer death!"

16. "If any one smites his neighbour with a stone or with his fist—if he [the one smitten] may go forth, even though only with the help of a staff: get him medicine; and do his work for him, while he himself cannot!" See: Exodus 21:12-16.

17. "He who smites his own bondservant or bondswoman—if he or she does not die the same day but still lives for two or three nights—he is not at all so guilty [of death]: for it was his own chattel. However, if he or she die the same day—put the guilt upon him [the overlord]!" See: Exodus 21:20-21.

18. "If anyone, while fighting, hurt a pregnant woman—let him pay a fine for the hurt, as the evaluators determine! If she die—let him pay soul with soul!" See: Exodus 21:22-23.

19. "If anyone puts out another's eye, let him give his own for it: tooth for tooth, hand for hand, foot for foot, burning for burning, wound for wound, stripe for stripe!" See: Ex. 21:24-25.

20. "If anyone smite out the eye of his manservant or his maidservant, so that he makes them one-eyed—for that, he must free them!" See: Exodus 21:26-27.

21. "If an ox gores a man or a woman so that they die—let the ox be stoned to death; but do not let its flesh be eaten! The owner is guiltless—if the ox gored two or three days earlier and the owner did not know about it. However, if he did know about it, and if he did not want to impound it—and if it then slew either a man or a woman—let it be destroyed with stones, and let the owner of the slain or the gored bondsman be paid whatever the Council finds to be right! If it gore a son or a daughter, it is worthy of the same judgment. However, if it gored a bondsman or bondsmen, let thirty shillings of silver be given to the overlord; and let the ox be destroyed with stones!" See: Exodus 21:28-32.

22. "If anyone digs a water-pit; or unties a tied-up animal, and does not tie it up again—let him pay for whatever falls therein; and let him have the dead one!" See: Exodus 21:33-34.

23. "If an ox wounds another man's ox so that it dies, let them sell the [live] ox and share its value—and, similarly, also the meat of the dead one! However, if the owner knew that the ox was goring, but did not wish to restrain it—let him give another ox for it, and keep all the meat for himself!" See: Exodus 21:35-36.

24. "If anyone steals another's ox, and slays or sells it—let him give two for it; and four sheep for one! If he does not have anything to give—let him himself be sold for the fee!" See: Exodus 22:1.

25. "If a thief breaks into a man's house at night, and he be slain there—he [the slayer] is not guilty of manslaughter! If he does this after sun-rise, he is guilty of manslaughter; and he himself shall then die—unless he slew out of necessity! If he [the thief] be caught red-handed with what he previously stole—let him pay twofold for it!" See: Exodus 22:2-4.

26. "If anyone harms another man's vineyard or his acres or any of his lands—let him pay the fine as men value it!" See: Exodus 22:5.

27. "If fire be kindled to burn right—let him who tindered the fire then pay a fine for the mischief!" Here, for "fine" Alfred uses the Anglo-Saxon word bot (compare the word 'booty'). See: Exodus 22:6.

28. "If anyone entrust livestock to his friend—if he [the friend] himself steals it, let him pay for it twofold! If he does not know who stole it, let him clear himself [from the accusation] that he committed a fraud! However, if it were quick [alias 'live'] cattle—and if he says that the army took it; or that it died of itself; and if he has a witness—he need not pay for it. If he, however, has no witness—and if he [the loser of the livestock] does not believe him [the custodian]—let him then swear!" See: Exodus 22:7-11.

29. "If anyone deceives an unwedded woman and sleeps with her, let him pay for her—and have her afterwards as his wife! However, if the woman's father does not want to let her go—let him [the seducer] give money, according to her dowry!" Cf. Exodus 22:16-17.

30. "Don't let women live who are wont to receive enchanters and conjurers and witches!" See: Exodus 22:18. Note: these sorcerers and practitioners of witchcraft were usually also murderers and/or kidnappers.

31. "Let him who has intercourse with cattle, suffer death!" See: Exodus 22:19.

32. "Also let him who offers sacrifices to the gods—except to God alone—suffer death!" See: Exodus 22:18-20...

33. "You must not vex strangers and those who come from afar—for you were strangers, long ago, in the land of the Egyptians!" See: Exodus 22:21.

34. "You must not scathe widows and step-children, nor harm them anywhere! However, if you do otherwise—they cry out to Me, and I hear them; and then I slay you with My sword. Thus I make your wives to be widows, and your bairns to be stepchildren!" See: Exodus 22:22-24.

35. "If you give money as a loan to your comrade who wants to dwell with you—do not pressure him as one in need; and do not oppress him with interest!" See: Exodus 22:25.

36. "If a man has nothing but a single garment with which to cover himself or to wear, and he gives it as a pledge—before the sun sets, give it back to him! If you do not do so—he calls out to Me; and I hear him. For I am very mild-hearted." See: Exodus 22:26-27.

37. "You may not revile your Lord; nor curse the overlord of the people!" See: Exodus 22:28.

38. "Your tithe-monies and your first-fruits of things that go, and things that grow—you must give to God!" See: Exodus 22:29-30.

39. "You may not eat at all of that meat which wild animals leave! Give it to the hounds!" See: Exodus 22:31.

40. "Do not listen to the words of a liar; nor permit his judgments; nor speak to anyone who gives testimony in his favour!" See: Exodus 23:1f.

41. "Do not, beyond your right reason, wend yourself to people who are unwise and unrighteous in their wishes, when they speak and cry out—nor to the learning of the most unwise! Do not permit them!" See: Exodus 23:2f.

42. "If another man's stray cattle come into your power—though it be your foe—make it known to him!" See: Exodus 22:4f.

43. "You must judge very evenly; do not give one judgment to the wealthy, [but] another to the poor! Nor give one judgment to the more beloved—and another to the more disliked!" See: Exodus 23:6.

44. "Always shun lies [alias 'Shun thou aye leasings']!"

45. "You must never slay a righteous [alias 'sooth-fast'] and unguilty man!"

46. "You must never accept bribes [alias 'meed-monies']! For they all too often blinden wise men's thoughts and turn their words aside." See: Exodus 23:7-8.

47. "Do not act in any way uncouthly toward the stranger from abroad [alias 'out-comer']; nor oppress him with any unrighteousness [alias 'uncouthly']!"

48. "Never swear by heathen gods; nor may you call out to them, in any way!" Exodus 23:9.[142]

THE RISE & FALL OF HUMANITY & CHARITY IN THE WEST

O LORD, our Lord, how excellent is thy name in all the earth! who hast set thy glory above the heavens. Out of the mouth of babes and sucklings hast thou ordained strength because of thine enemies, that thou mightest still the enemy and the avenger. When I consider thy heavens, the work of thy fingers, the moon and the stars, which thou hast ordained; What is man, that thou art mindful of him? and the son of man, that thou visitest him? For thou hast made him a little lower than the angels, and hast crowned him with glory and honour. (Psalm 8:1-5)

A right conception of God will necessarily produce a right conception of man. Conversely, a deficient understanding of man will produce a wrong understanding of God. So, an examination of Western society's anthropological view, as demonstrated by the value placed on human life and care for the poor and infirm, supplies another good metric for tracing the rise and fall of the Western world.

Certainly, life was cheap in the ancient world. Who knows how many babies the Spartans tossed off the cliff of Mount Taygetus? Archeologists have yet to count the millions of children sacrificed in the Tophets of Carthage. It was nothing for Alexander "the Great" to drag the still-living bodies of kings around the cities he conquered. Why shouldn't he have launched a spear through one of his most loyal generals in a drunken party? Did it come as any surprise that Chinese Emperor Qin Shi Huang buried 463 Confucian scholars in dirt up to their necks, so as to crush their heads under his chariot wheels? (Nothing has changed much in the politics of China in the past 2,200 years.) Even the most charitable of the Greek and Roman historians and philosophers recommended infanticide for deformed and sickly infants. The colosseums of the Roman Empire, filled to the brim with the blood of hapless victims over six centuries, are proof enough of the dehumanization advocated by humanist cultures constructed on man-centered philosophies. Through the wide dreary centuries, before Christ came, the advancement of any and all of human civilization was perpetually aborted as "a tribe was wiped off its ice field, and lights would go out in Rome."[1]

Although humanist man pretends to deify himself and form his own ethics and reality, he always returns to a more self-consistent position. At some point, the humanist must come back to the realization that he cannot be god. Utterly refusing to consider the Creator, the true and living God, he would rather settle on the position that these creatures sitting on the third rock from the sun must be nothing more than cosmic dust floating about in a meaningless universe. For a moment, he attempts to put ultimate value upon himself by deifying himself. Rather than accepting the ultimate value and existence of the Creator, he is forced to admit that neither he himself nor anyone else may retain any intrinsic value whatsoever. This is the mind of godless, atheistic humanism. Without God, man is always left with the words of Solomon in Ecclesiastes 3:

> For that which befalleth the sons of men befalleth beasts; even one
> thing befalleth them: as the one dieth, so dieth the other; yea, they
> have all one breath; so that a man hath no preeminence above a beast:
> for all is vanity. All go unto one place; all are of the dust, and all turn to
> dust again. (Ecclesiastes 3:19-20)

By His very appearance upon this earth and by His consistent
testimony, Jesus Christ underscored the value of the human soul. No
person was more qualified to speak on these things than the Creator
Himself. He spoke of an eternal heaven and hell. He warned with
the most sober words ever spoken, "And do not fear those who kill
the body but cannot kill the soul. But rather fear Him who is able to
destroy both soul and body in hell. Are not two sparrows sold for a
copper coin? And not one of them falls to the ground apart from your
Father's will. But the very hairs of your head are all numbered. Do
not fear therefore; you are of more value than many sparrows" (Matt.
10:28-31). The value of the human soul must always be fixed upon
the eternality of God, the ultimate value of God, and the ultimacy of
the existence of God. Thus, any true valuation of man can only come
through a sober reflection upon God in all of His excellencies. Any
right valuation of man will be measured by a right fear of God (Prov.
1:7).

Scripture teaches that man in his fallen state still retains the image
of God. By creating man in His own image, the Creator placed a certain
value upon man. This value must then be retained in both word and
deed, as Jesus' brother James instructed:

> Therewith bless we God, even the Father; and therewith curse we men,
> which are made after the similitude of God. Out of the same mouth
> proceedeth blessing and cursing. My brethren, these things ought not
> so to be. (James 3:9-10)

When man fails to realize the greatest value and the ultimate Good he will inevitably give way to a devaluation of everything, including man made in the image of God. Apart from God's common grace, this deception will lead to the ultimate devaluation, as witnessed at Auschwitz and the abortion clinics of the Western world.

Neoplatonism, Gnosticism, Manichaeism, and other heretical philosophies devalued the physical world in favor of the spiritual or immaterial world of ideas. However, when the Creator of the world entered the womb of the virgin, the death knell sounded for all philosophy that depreciates the material world. The Son of God demonstrated His love for man and a valuation of His material creation by taking upon Himself human flesh and rising bodily from the dead. Truly, Christ became one of us and "continueth to be, God and man in two distinct natures, and one person, forever."[2]

Another counter to the Christian faith came in the 7th Century when the Islamic worldview repudiated the notion that God should take on human flesh. "Can God also become a dog?," Muhammed's apologists intoned derisively. When the divine Personality humbled Himself and took the "form of a servant" (Phil. 2:7), He sent another message to the world. "For You have made him a little lower than the angels, and You have crowned him with glory and honor" (Ps. 8:5). His creation ordinance dignified man at the first, but Christ's coming crowned him with even more glory and honor.

Islam rejected this view of mankind. The Islamic worldview would put no limit on the number of stripes administered in beatings for civil offenses. The fellow creature becomes "vile" in the sight of his punishers, and neither women or children are exempted from the slaughter executed by Islamic jihad. These laws stand as direct violations of Deuteronomy 20:14 and 25:3.

The true and living God disallows "vile" treatment of mankind created in His own image. As the crown of God's creation, as one created to be a reflection of God Himself, man must be regarded with honor and treated with dignity and mercy. While this original nature was terribly marred by sin, man still retains some remnant of the image of God. Moreover, the mercy of God is evident in the visitation of the Creator Himself to redeem man from sin and bring about a renewed creation. More than anything else, Jesus Christ demonstrated an irrepressible compassion, always healing, always casting out demons, always raising the dead, always preaching the good news to the poor. With God there is mercy. With Jesus comes an outpouring of love, mercy, and grace upon the world. As those who reflect the image of Christ and follow in His footsteps, Christians bring His compassion and light to the world.

JESUS CHANGED THE WORLD

The Spirit of the Lord GOD is upon me; because the LORD hath anointed me to preach good tidings unto the meek; he hath sent me to bind up the brokenhearted, to proclaim liberty to the captives, and the opening of the prison to them that are bound; to proclaim the acceptable year of the LORD, and the day of vengeance of our God; to comfort all that mourn; to appoint unto them that mourn in Zion, to give unto them beauty for ashes, the oil of joy for mourning, the garment of praise for the spirit of heaviness; that they might be called trees of righteousness, the planting of the LORD, that he might be glorified. And they shall build the old wastes, they shall raise up the former desolations, and they shall repair the waste cities, the desolations of many generations…For as the earth bringeth forth her bud, and as the garden causeth the things that are sown in it to spring forth; so the Lord GOD will cause righteousness and praise to spring forth before all the nations. (Isaiah 61:1-4, 11)

These are the words Christ read at the outset of His ministry at the synagogue in His hometown of Nazareth. A new day had dawned upon the world.

Two thousand years ago, Jesus Christ brought something completely new into the world. He changed the world forever. Whatever happens, the world will never return to the way it was. Some have debated this point, but reality defies any other possibility. The Messiah has come, and the world will never be the same.

Almost immediately, a Christian morality pervaded pagan society. As already demonstrated, nearly every extant Christian record from the first centuries decried abortion and infanticide. This itself is an astounding fact, for Christ never spoke directly of the practice except to underscore His love for children throughout His ministry. From the beginning, Christ's message was "Repent, for the kingdom of heaven is at hand" (Matt. 4:17). Yet, His ministry was first dedicated to the "lost sheep of Israel." For the Jews, the message focused on their hypocrisy, superficiality, pride, self-righteousness, and rejection of the Messiah. Only later, after Pentecost, would His followers turn to the Gentile world with another message of repentance. For the Gentiles, the problem was gross idolatry, sexual sin, and infanticide.

MERCY CONQUERS OVER JUDGMENT

For he shall have judgment without mercy, that hath shewed no mercy; and mercy rejoiceth against judgment. (James 2:13)

In a Christian worldview, mercy conquers over judgment. Thus the greatest heroes are those who administer mercy. Contrariwise, the pagan worldview idealized the killer and the power-consolidator. Augustus Caesar gained his position by murdering three hundred senators and 2,000 lesser magistrates. After crossing the Rubicon in 49 BC, Julius Caesar kicked off five years of civil wars in which the population was reduced by 170,000 persons.[3] These were the ruthless heroes of the "great" City of Man, always glorified according to the number of their own citizens they slaughtered and their success in consolidating power. Is it any wonder that men still glory in the ancient

Greek and Roman world? In the mind of the modern humanist, there was still something heroic and "very great" about these larger-than-life classical heroes. He finds something in them to admire, as he steals one more adoring glance their way. With the recapitulation to humanism in the West, came the wide-eyed acceptance and glorification of the "nephilim" of the bygone age. William Blake (1757-1827) described the weird spell cast, in verse:

> The Strongest Poison ever known
> Came from Caesar's Laurel Crown
> Nought can Deform the Human Race
> Like to the Armour's iron brace.[4]

Poison, yes. But also a drug to the humanist soul.

This hero in the City of Man reappears, but only in fits and starts. Napoleon (1769-1821) revived the idea of the classical hero in his wars of the 19th Century. With over 4,000,000 casualties, the Napoleonic wars chalked up more deaths than any other European conflict over a period of two hundred years.

A thorough-going supporter of Robespierre and the French Revolution, Napoleon Bonaparte emerged as the most important figure reviving the god-like humanist nation state in the 19th Century. Out of this came a great many powerful humanist institutions, revolutions, wars, messiah complexes, and the assorted miseries of the 20th Century. More futile campaigns to build humanist utopias by sheer power would end in hundreds of millions of casualties. Among the communists and more consistent humanists, the most-admired messianic heroes always turned out to be thugs who followed in the footsteps of the Caesars, murdering their millions—Josef Stalin, Che Guevara, Mao Zedong, Pol Pot, Fidel Castro, and others. In the Islamic world also, the pious terrorist is granted the highest honor and regarded as most heroic. Before he died, the terrorist Osama bin

Laden enjoyed a higher popularity rating in Pakistan than the nation's president.[5] Jesus introduced a different hero to the world!

> Jesus knowing that the Father had given all things into his hands, and that he was come from God, and went to God; He riseth from supper, and laid aside his garments; and took a towel, and girded himself. After that he poureth water into a bason, and began to wash the disciples' feet, and to wipe them with the towel wherewith he was girded. (John 13:3-5)

After washing His disciples' feet, Christ was crucified for them, and He cleansed them with His blood. For Jesus, mercy conquers judgment. This is the great story of the cross. Therefore, mercy becomes the hero of the story. The one who doesn't deserve mercy receives it from the one who suffers in order to provide it. The hero is not the one who wins the competition for power but the one who surrenders position and possession to show love and mercy.

In the wars of the nations that ensued during the 19th and 20th Centuries, occasionally a story would surface contrasting these two opposing worldviews. In 1861, after the First Battle of Bull Run, General Thomas "Stonewall" Jackson became the instant hero of Virginia and the most famous name in the American South. On the evening following the battle, Jackson sat down to write a letter to his pastor back home in Lexington. As the pastor opened the letter weeks later, he was greatly interested to find out the backstory and details of the great battle fought at Bull Run. But, to his surprise, Jackson didn't write about the battle. Instead, the pastor read these words,

> My dear pastor, in my tent last night, after a fatiguing day's service, I remembered that I had failed to send you my contribution for our colored Sunday School. Enclosed you will find my check for that object, which please acknowledge at your earliest convenience and oblige yours faithfully, T. J. Jackson[6]

1.1 Alexander Solzhenitsyn
(1918-2008): "Men have
forgotten God."

1.2 Francis Schaeffer (1912-1984): "The Christian influence upon the whole of culture
has been lost."

1.3 Leonard Ravenhill (1907-1994): "America cannot fall—because she is already fallen!"

1.4 Pat Buchanan (1938-): "A cultural wasteland and a moral sewer that are not worth living in and not worth fighting for…"

1.5 Malcolm Muggeridge (1903-1990): "We see around us on every hand the decay of the institutions."

2.1 Augustine: "I believe that I might understand."

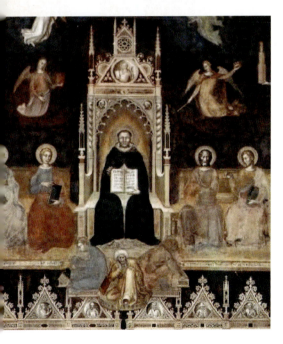

2.2 Thomas Aquinas in Andrea da Firenze's (d. 1377) famous painting. Pictured elevated above Aristotle, Cicero, Ptolemy, Euclid, and Pythagoras.

2.3 Dante Alighieri: "[Pagan Rome] a most holy see."

2.4 Immanuel Kant "freed man from biblical morality."

2.5 Anselm of Canterbury: "Thou canst not be saved but by the death of Christ."

2.6 Friedrich Nietzsche crossed the line of despair.

3.1 The Venerable Bede: "They preached the Word."

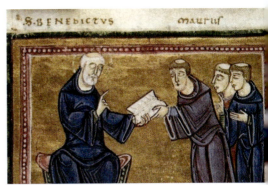

3.2 Benedict of Nursia formed the first discipleship centers.

3.3 Alcuin of York—Seeking "preachers of upright conduct" for Charlemagne.

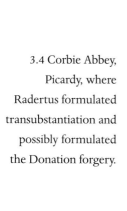

3.4 Corbie Abbey, Picardy, where Radertus formulated transubstantiation and possibly formulated the Donation forgery.

4.1 Pope Gregory VII (Hildebrand): Reformed the church by force and unbiblical means.

4.2 Peter Abelard (1079-1142) abandoned the plain meaning of Scripture, preferring the Aristotelian dialectic.

4.3 Peter Lombard institutionalized transubstantiation, and opposed the doctrine of Christ's substitutionary atonement.

4.4 Innocent III opposed the Magna Carta and advocated the inquisition.

5.1 Waldensian Crusade (c. 1487).

5.2 Pre-reformer John Wycliffe
(c. 1320-1384) saw the Donation
of Constantine as
"the beginnings of all evils" for
the church.

5.3 Bohemian Refomer Jan Hus (1369-1415) burned at the stake: "I shall die with joy today in the faith of the gospel which I have preached."

5.4 Reformer Martin Luther (1483-1546): "Nothing is more devilish than an unreformed university."

6.1 Increase Mather, The Last Puritan: fought a losing battle at Harvard.

6.2 Johann Gottfried Eichhorn (1752-1827): German Skeptic denied supernaturalism and miracles.

6.3 Benjamin Whichcote (1609-1683): first of the Cambridge Platonists.

6.4 The Romanticist-Dionysian Revolution takes over in the 21st century.

6.5 Charles Spurgeon (1834-1892): victim of the Downgrade Controversy.

7.1 Justinian I (ruled 527-565) formed Corpus Juris Civilis, the basis of Christian Civil Law.

7.2 Alfred the Great (849-899) encoded his laws using Exodus 21—the basis on which "English Common Law" was founded according to Winston Churchill.

7.3 The Santo Spirito Foundling Hospital (est. 1204), displays infanticide and the return to pagan practices in Rome.

7.6 Colorado Republican Governor John Love introduced abortion on demand in the United States (1967).

7.5 Jeremy Bentham (1748-1832)—English utilitarian political ethicist suggested the abandonment of Christian values (especially in relation to sexual perversion).

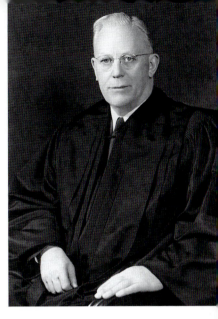

7.7 Chief Justice of the US Supreme Court, Earl Warren (1891-1974) responsible for removing Christianity from schools, and opening the way for mass distribution of pornography.

7.4 The French Revolution marked the triumph of a Satanic humanism in the Western world, and the beginning of mass revolutions and bloodshed for successive centuries.

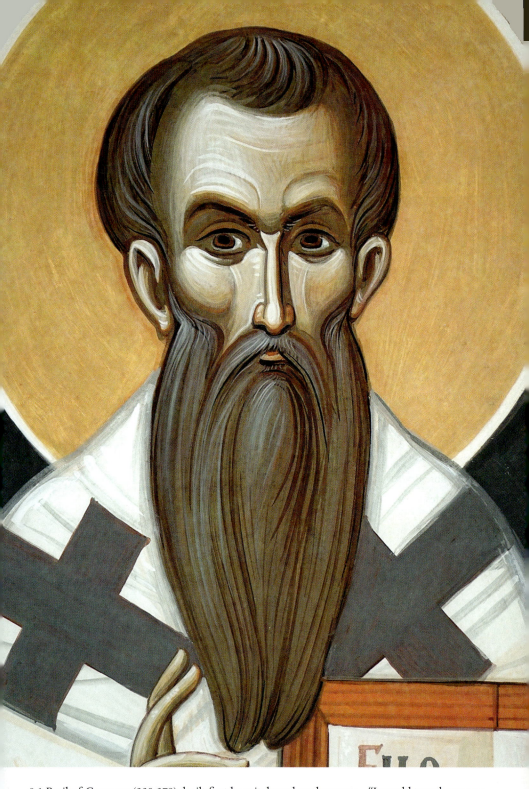

8.1 Basil of Caesarea (330-379), built first hospitals and orphanages—"I would tear down my barns to help the poor."

8.2 Jean-Jacques Rousseau (1712-1778): first opponent of private charity, and advocate of socialist state.

8.3 Dorothea Dix (1802-1887): crusader for socialism and opponent of private charity in America.

8.4 Theodore Roosevelt and Franklin D. Roosevelt are known for advocating socialism in the United States.

9.1 First eyeglasses appeared in monasteries (c. 1286).

9.2 Eilmer of Malmesbury and his glider (c. 1040).

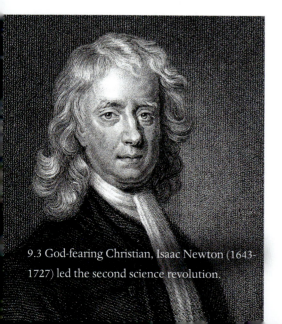

9.3 God-fearing Christian, Isaac Newton (1643-1727) led the second science revolution.

9.4 Roger Bacon (1219-1292), Franciscan friar, generally regarded as father of science in the Christian West.

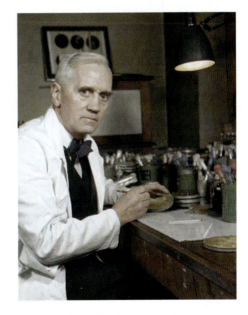

9.5 Major medical advancements over 200 years came by exclusively Christians. Edward Jenner (1796) developed smallpox vaccine, Louis Pasteur (1861) developed germ theory, Alexander Fleming (1928) discovered penicillin and antibiotics, and Charles Best (1922) discovered insulin treatment for diabetics. All God-fearing Christians.

9.6 Devoted Christians James Clerk Maxwell (1831-1879) and Michael Faraday (1791-1867) led the third and final revolution in the hard sciences.

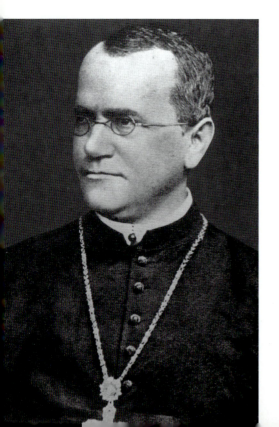

9.7 God-fearing Gregor Mendel (1822-1884) got genetics right. Charles Darwin (1809-1882) got it wrong, and becomes father of scientism and modern junk science.

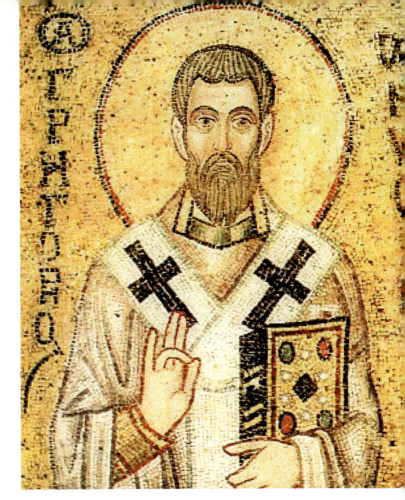

10.1 Gregory of Nyssa (c. 335-395): first major pastor to speak out against slavery.

10.2 Feudalism replaced slavery in the medieval period, as a rent-based economy.

10.3 Tomb of King Athelstan (894-939), first king of England, Christian, opposed slavery, instructing his lords: *"Every year…set at liberty someone that has for his crimes been condemned to slavery."*

10.4 Bishop Anselm of Canterbury issued declaration at English church council (1102): *"That none exercise that wicked trade, which has hitherto been practiced in England, of selling men like beasts."*

10.5 John Law (1671-1729), a felon and an economist from Scotland, introduced unbacked paper money into the West.

10.6 Salmon Chase, Abraham Lincoln's Secretary of the Treasury, introduced the first unbacked dollars in the US.

10.7 John Maynard Keynes (1883-1946), a homosexual economist, became the major advocate of a debt-based economy in the Western world.

11.1 Early Christian statuary often featured the shepherd retrieving a lost sheep.

11.3 Monks singing in medieval period. Ubaldus Hucbald (840-930) introduced Trinitarian, polyphonic music to the world.

11.2 The parting of Abraham and Lot (c. 430s). Early art avoided pictures of Jesus, but preferred Old Testament scenes.

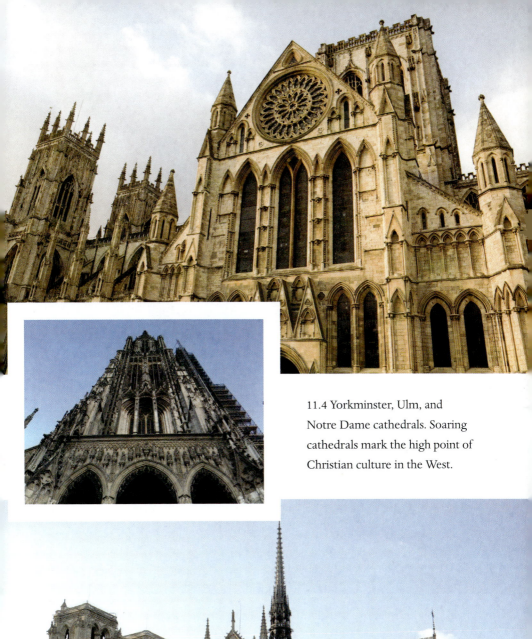

11.4 Yorkminster, Ulm, and Notre Dame cathedrals. Soaring cathedrals mark the high point of Christian culture in the West.

11.5 Reformation art: Vermeer's *Milk Maid* is realistic, humble, and non-assuming.

11.6 Vincent Van Gogh (1853-1890), the ultimate post-Christian artist depicted extreme emotion, disjointedness, meaninglessness, anguish, and despair.

11.7 Peter Paul Rubens' (1577-1640) self portrait. This Renaissance artist represented a full return to humanism, self-adulation, and paganism.

11.8 Ludwig van Beethoven (1770-1827) represented a return to thorough-going humanism and irrational romanticism: "I am that which is. I am all that is."

11.9 Johann Sebastian Bach (1685-1750) represented the height of Christian music in the West.

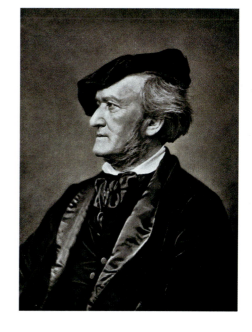

11.10 Christian apostate, and artist, Pablo Picasso (1881-1973), produced scenes of rape, strangulation, and torture, as well as intentional disorder, confusion, and disunity. These were the destroyers.

11.11 Leading the Dionysian revolution and the disintegration of Western culture, Richard Wagner (1813-1883): "True art is revolutionary."

11.12 The Norman Lear-produced *All in the Family* Sitcom featured revolutionary scenes for public consumption, encouraging public acceptance of abortion and homosexuality.

11.13 The celebration of the inane and the self-mockery of the post-modern: Andy Warhol's impression of the Campbell's Soup Can sold for $12 million in 2006.

11.14 Known for lyrics espousing blatant homosexuality and self-immolating nihilism, singer Lady Gaga was described as "the exhausted end of the sexual revolution."

12.1 The Signing of the Magna Carta at Runnymede (1215)—a major step towards liberty from tyranny in the Western world.

12.2 William Tell opposed the tyrants. The tyranny of empire was curtailed and Swiss independence came in 1315.

12.3 Robert the Bruce secured Scottish independence at Bannockburn (1314).

12.4 William the Silent gained Netherlands' independence from Spanish tyranny and the fearful inquisition (1598).

12.5 The tyrants, Stuart Kings James II and Charles II introduced slavery to North America by the shipload, and slaughtered 17,000 Covenanters on the highlands of Scotland.

12.6 Karl Marx (1818-1883). The ideologies of German philosophers Karl Marx and Friedrich Nietzsche, as well as the eugenics of Charles Darwin contributed most to the tyrannies of the 20th century (Adolf Hitler, Vladimir Lenin, etc.).

12.7 The father of "cancel culture," Antonio Francesco Gramsci (1891-1937), developed Marxist strategy to establish cultural hegemony.

12.8 Elaine Huguenin. First bonafide Christian persecution case lost at the US Supreme Court (2014).

13.1 Charlemagne's Lindisfarne, where Alcuin (c. 800) set out to prepare pastors for the Christian churches at the institute.

13.2 Thomas Aquinas (1225-1274) reintroduced Aristotle to the Western world, by bifurcating knowledge into two categories: that which was built up on human reason and that built on Scripture.

13.3 John Amos Comenius (1592-1672), attempted a Christian reformation in education.

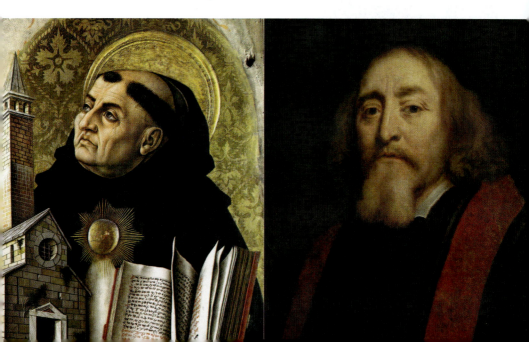

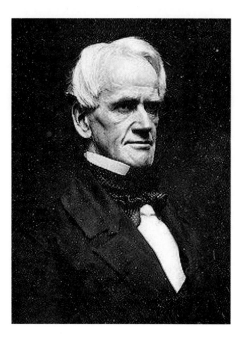

13.4 Horace Mann (1796-1859) advocated state control of education in the US, as a means of saving humanity.

13.5 With Jean-Jacques Rousseau, the Prussian Johann Gottlieb Fichte (1762-1814) advocated state control of education.

13.6 As president of Princeton University, Woodrow Wilson (1856-1924) was responsible for removing Bible classes, and advocated an evolutionary atheistic view of government and law.

13.7 Prominent atheist, humanist, and government school advocate, John Dewey (1859-1952) contributed the most to ending Christian education in the West.

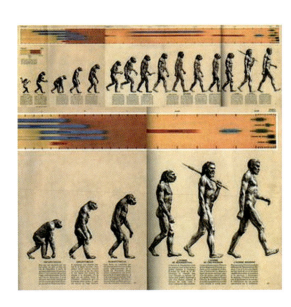

13.8 Fanciful imaginary drawings depicting what artists thought might be the evolution of man appeared in school textbooks throughout the 20th century. Such imaginary drawings relieved the need for any scientific evidence in the minds of billions in the modern world.

13.9 High school science teacher John Scopes was the subject of a mock trial over teaching evolution in public schools in 1925. Teaching a theistic creationism as an explanation for origins was banned in the public schools by another mock trial at the US Supreme Court in 1987 (*Edwards v. Aguillard*).

ALL GENDER RESTROOM

13.10 As humanism prevailed and gender confusion was advocated in the schools, bathrooms were opened to boys who were pretending to be girls and vice versa.

The Christian general had better things on his mind than war. His first concern was the children in his home church, whom he had been regularly instructing in the things of the Lord.

THE MIDDLE AGES

Following the arrival of Christianity, tribal wars continued through the Middle Ages. Fake Christian tribal leaders picked on other Christianized tribes. The pagan Vikings, Frisians, and Saxons launched assaults on Christian tribes. Degenerate and imperialistic power mongers like William the Conqueror initiated offensive wars to gain territory and develop their micro-empires. The Muslims pressed on with their vision to impose Islam on the world, evangelized by bloody wars, all the way to the heart of Europe. The caliphate reached Spain by AD 711. Ten years later, the horde had reached France, where Charles Martel halted the onslaught at the Battle of Tours in 732.

As should be expected where the remnants of fallen human nature remain, greed, pride, and competition continued disturbing relations within and between nations professing to follow Christ. No Christian nation would be devoid of apostates, turncoats, and hypocrites. Yet, we find the West submitting to biblical standards for warfare—some of which were outlined in Augustine's *jus bellum justum* (just war theory).

The poetic saga *Sir Gawain and the Green Knight* (c. 1390), described the hero not in terms of any murderous deeds of violence, but instead by the five virtues of "generosity, brotherhood, courtesy, a clean heart,...and the finest point, compassion—these five virtues marked him more than any man alive."[7] The hero of the story, Sir Gawain, placed all his faith "in the five wounds that Christ carried on the cross."[8] And the defining act of heroism comes as Gawain holds true to his word to the death, and proves himself a man of honor.

The treatment of women in warfare changed dramatically in the Christian age as well. Following Columba of Iona, Adomnán (AD 679-

704) took up the role of abbot, and he is best known for his draft of "The Law of the Innocents." This legal edict, for which he obtained signatures from ninety-one tribal leaders throughout the British Isles, banned the employment of any woman "in an assault or in a host or fight."[9] The compact instituted that:

> ...Women be not in any manner killed by men, through slaughter or any other death, either by poison, or in water, or in fire, or by any other beast, or in a pit, or by dogs, but that they shall die in their lawful bed... he who from this day forward shall put a woman to death and does not do penance according to the Law, shall not only perish in eternity, [but] be cursed for God and Adomnán.[10]

The same legislation also protected women from rape and other abuse. Such language stands as a remarkable example of the Christianization of public morality and civil law in the Western world. The reintroduction of women into the killing fields would have to wait for the post-Christian era, first with Norway in 1988 and then the United States in 2013.

Adomnán had personally witnessed the scenes of mangled bodies of female warriors lying dead on the fields of battle. One medieval source quoted in the *Law of the Innocents* recorded that "they beheld the battlefield and they saw nothing more touching and pitiful than the head of a woman in one place and the body in another, and her little babe upon the breasts of the corpse, a stream of milk upon one of its cheeks, and a stream of blood upon the other."[11]

To moderate war, the Council of Toulouges of 1027 issued "The Truce and Peace of God" prohibiting warring activities from Saturday evening until Monday morning. Later, in 1040, the truce was extended from Wednesday sunset to Monday morning upon the threat of excommunication. These restrictions held for several hundred years. Of course, men will always seek other outlets for violence, and so jousting became popular in medieval Europe for a time. The Council of Clermont (1130) banned jousting tournaments in hopes of limiting the senseless violence and false heroism of the day. The blunt-tipped "Lance of Peace" was added to the contests in 1292. But still, medieval sporting could never hope to match the brutality and the murderous character of the pagan gladiatorial competitions of Rome.

HEROISM IN THE POST-CHRISTIAN WORLD

Heroism in post-Christian civilizations was less and less interested in Christ's values. But neither were these Europeans and Americans all that interested in military men or empire builders. After the 1960s, the heroes of a dying civilization were typically play actors (movie stars) and pop music singers. Out of YouGov's list of the twenty most popular people in the United States, thirteen were movie stars and pop singers like Beyoncé, Will Smith, and Lady Gaga. The other seven were mostly "liberal" politicians who promised wonderful benefits for everybody.[12] Ranker replicated the list except for adding several movie producers, a few sports stars, and wealthy individuals who made a fortune in the technology industry.[13] Heroes of the ancient world would build kingdoms that lasted a few hundred years. Modern heroes lasted for a decade or so. They pretended to perform amazing feats of courage and skill on movie sets and basketball courts, and their "great" politicians were very generous with handing out other people's money, always promising great things which they would never deliver.

THE PAGAN WORLDVIEW ON CHARITY

If there was one thing which marked the pagan world, a single defining characteristic of the pre-Christ world, it is the absence of Christ-compassion. The survival-of-the-fittest motif is inescapable in a materialist, godless world. Whether barbarian or civilized, the pagan world was harsh, unforgiving, self-centered, and uncharitable. In the single case in which a mutual-benefit charity developed (as a primitive insurance program), Pliny still complained of the program to Emperor Trajan.[14] There were no orphanages; none were needed where there was a ready market for child slaves, and where infanticide was socially normative. Says one historian of the ancient world, the pagan "habit of selling young children, the innumerable expositions, the readiness of the poor to enroll themselves as gladiators, and the frequent famines, show how large was the measure of unrelieved distress."[15]

> And there was also a strife among them, which of them should be accounted the greatest. And [Jesus] said unto them, The kings of the Gentiles exercise lordship over them; and they that exercise authority upon them are called benefactors. But ye shall not be so: but he that is greatest among you, let him be as the younger; and he that is chief, as he that doth serve. (Luke 22:23-26)

Jesus here addressed a contemporary norm which formed the basic framework of Roman society. The Roman system of *liberalitas* ordered the exchange of gifts or the distribution of largess for the lower classes. Both Cicero and Seneca expended a great deal of eloquence on the subject of giving and receiving gifts. Primary among the values considered for offering gifts was that the recipient be a "worthy" and "deserving" person.[16] Then, with the gift came patronage (*clientela* or *amicitia*), in which the party receiving the gift would be beholden to the giver.

Despite its outward appearance of generosity and care toward inferiors, Roman *liberalitas* rarely embodied true love for neighbor in the Christian sense. For example, the wonderful liberals and their *liberalitas* did not stand in good stead when it came to caring for the diseased. Dionysius, pastor of Alexandria, reported during the epidemic of AD 251, "At the first onset of the disease, [the pagans] pushed the sufferers away and fled from their dearest, throwing them into the roads before they were dead and treated unburied corpses as dirt, hoping thereby to avert the spread and contagion of the fatal disease."[17] During a plague that struck Athens, Thucydides noted that the people "died with no one to look after them;...the bodies of the dying were heaped one on top of the other, and half-dead creatures could be seen staggering about in the streets or flocking around the fountains in their desire for water."[18]

With the coming of Christ, the standard of charity shifted dramatically. Cyprian (c. 200-258), pastor of the church in Carthage, praised God for the plague that visited North Africa. Such opportunities, he said, searched out "the mind of the human race; whether the well care for the sick, whether relatives dutifully love their kinsman as they should, whether masters show compassion for their ailing slaves, whether physicians do not desert the afflicted."[19] The resurrection gospel re-formed the mind of the Christian, such that Cyprian said, "we are learning not to fear death" in the care for the sick. Dionysius of Alexandria also expressed gratitude for the servants in his congregation, noting that "most of our brothers showed unbounded love and loyalty, never sparing themselves and thinking only of one another. Heedless of danger, they took charge of the sick, attending to their every need and ministering to them in Christ, and with them departed this life serenely happy; for they were infected by others with the disease, drawing on themselves the sickness of their neighbors and cheerfully accepting their pains. Many, in nursing and curing others, transferred their death to themselves and died in their stead...The best of our brothers lost their lives in this manner, a number of presbyters, deacons, and laymen winning high commendation so that death in this form, the result of great piety, and strong faith, seems in every way equal to martyrdom."[20]

A brief resurgence of paganism occurred under Julian the Apostate (330-363), who took Caesar's throne for two years. Significantly, the Pagan expressed irritation over the fact that Christian love had exposed the vacuity and cupidity of pagan *liberalitas*. Writing to the high priest of Galatia, Julian tried to cheerlead a little charity out of the pagan temple, and noted that "the impious Galileans [followers of Jesus of Galilee], in addition to their own, support ours, [and] it is shameful that our poor should be wanting our aid."[21]

After the formation of the New Testament Church, the apostles appointed deacons to look after the widows (both Jews and Greeks) for a "daily distribution" of food (Acts 6:1-7). In what seems unnatural and shocking to the modern world (and the ancient world), members of the church voluntarily sold their lands and homes to provide for the vital needs of others (Acts 4:33-35). It was a voluntary, sacrificial, and supernatural, Spirit-filled expression of love for brothers and sisters in the new-formed church. This "redistribution" was nothing like the forced, demonic-inspired, involuntary form of pseudo-charity later advocated by Karl Marx and others in the post-Christian era.

The Christian system of charity matured, and historian Paul Johnson called it "a miniature welfare state in an empire which for the most part lacked social services."[22] Tertullian (155-222) explained, "How these Christians love one another!...Every man once a month brings some modest coin, or whenever he wishes and only if he does wish, and if he can—for nobody is compelled; it is a voluntary offering. You might call them trust funds of piety. For they are not spent upon banquets nor drinking parties nor thank-less eating houses; but to feed the poor and to bury them, for boys and girls who lack property and parents, and then for slaves grown old, and shipwrecked mariners, and any who may be in the mines, islands, or prisons, provided that, for the sake of God's school, they become the beneficiaries of their confession."[23]

The Church's priority was to do good first and foremost "to the household of faith" (Gal. 6:10). The Christians took care of their own orphans, widows, prisoners, slaves, and shipwrecked mariners first, after which they would attend to the orphans and the destitute within the wider community.

The earliest constitutions of the Christian church handed down by the apostles in Antioch required church members to:

> ...maintain and clothe those that are in want from the righteous labor of the faithful. And such sums of money as are collected from them in the manner aforesaid, appoint to be laid out in the redemption of the saints, the deliverance of slaves, and of captives, and of prisoners, and of those that have been abused, and of those that have been condemned by tyrants to single combat and death on account of the name of Christ. For the Scripture says: "Deliver those that are led to death, and redeem those that are ready to be slain, do not spare."[24]

In the classic passage outlining the weekly Sunday worship, Justin Martyr included mention of this critical institution of the church:

> And there is a distribution to each, and a participation of that over which thanks have been given, and to those who are absent a portion is sent by the deacons. And they who are well to do, and willing, give what each thinks fit; and what is collected is deposited with the president, who succours the orphans and widows and those who, through sickness or any other cause, are in want, and those who are in bonds and the strangers sojourning among us, and in a word takes care of all who are in need.[25]

Earlier, Ignatius (c. 100) condemned the pagans and commended Christians in the same breath:

> But consider those who are of a different opinion with respect to the grace of Christ which has come unto us; how opposed they are to the will of God. They have no regard for love; no care for the widow or the orphan or the oppressed; of the bond or of the free; of the hungry or of the thirsty.[26]

Clement of Alexandria (150-215) also condemned the pagans for treating their children and elderly no better than birds and apes:

They do not receive the orphan child; but they expose children that are born at home, and they take up the young of birds, and prefer irrational to rational creatures; although they ought to undertake the maintenance of old people with a character for sobriety, who are fairer in mind than apes, and capable of uttering something better than nightingales; and to set before them that saying,…"Inasmuch as ye have done it unto the least of these My brethren, ye have done it unto Me."[27]

Another early church father summarized the primitive Christian faith in simple words in *The Shepherd of Hermas:*

First of all there is faith, then fear of the Lord, love, concord, words of righteousness, truth, patience…Then there are the following attendant on these: helping widows, looking after orphans and the needy, rescuing the servants of God from necessities, the being hospitable, for in hospitality good-doing finds a field.[28]

At the turn of the 3rd Century, Origen was adopted by a pious woman after his father was martyred. By AD 251, the church at Rome was made up of 78,000 members who provided support for 1,500 widows and infirm persons.[29] This would be akin to a local church of 500 members caring for about ten widows at a time.

Three Christian siblings from Cappadocia are recognized as the primary influence in the transformation of the European Gentile world through the love of Christ as expressed in charity. The elder sister, Macrina (AD 330-379), led the way. As the biographical accounts tell the story, somehow she received the Christian faith and rejected all pagan literature, preferring the Proverbs and the Psalms of the Scriptures instead.[30] She ate and slept with the household slaves, always on the floor and never on a bed. Meanwhile, her brother Basil attended the classical schools of Athens and returned home quoting the classics and arguing the philosophy of the Greeks. Macrina aired her concerns with him that he had become "puffed up beyond measure with the pride of oratory."[31] Basil received her chastening and followed her into the Christian faith. As famines spread through Cappadocia, Macrina would cruise the garbage dumps, searching for abandoned children still alive. She collected them and cared for them in her own home; later in life, organizing a spiritual discipleship center for women. Basil of Caesarea went on to build early orphanages (*orphanotrophia*) and the first hospital. His famous homily "I Will Tear Down My Barns," describes the severe conditions attending a local famine in the 4th Century: "[Parents will] turn their gaze to their own children, thinking that perhaps by bringing them to the slave-market they might find some respite from death. Consider now the violent struggle that takes place between the desperation arising from famine and a parent's fundamental instincts. Starvation on the one side threatens a horrible death, while nature resists, convincing the parents rather to die with their children."[32] Basil went on to exhort his congregation:

> When someone strips a man of his clothes we call him a thief. And one who might clothe the naked and does not—should you not be given the same name? The bread in your board [cupboard] belongs to the hungry; the cloak in your wardrobe belongs to the naked, the shoes you let rot belong to the barefoot; the money in your vaults belongs to the destitute. All these you might help and do not—to all these you are doing wrong.[33]

Gregory, yet another of the Cappadocian siblings, served as the pastor of Nyssa. He took it upon himself to go after the 4,000-year-old institution of slavery so deeply embedded in the socio-economy of the West and East. To own slaves, he said, was "to set one's own power above God's." No price in all the universe, Gregory insisted, "would constitute an adequate payment for the soul of a mortal."[34] Nobody listened to him, but future millennia of Christian influence in the Western world would prove him right.

This was only the beginning of a complete and radical transformation of Western society, institutionalizing and prioritizing the charitable care of widows, orphans, the infirm, and the elderly. Throughout the later Middle Ages, the Order of the Holy Ghost formed 800 homes for orphans. Contra the pagan vision of the "good death" or euthanasia for the elderly, Christians introduced *gerontocomia*—care for the elderly. In the 4th Century, Paulinus of Nola created a hospital for "the poor, the elderly, and the miserable."[35] Later, in the 15th Century, a physician and instructor at the University of Padua, Gabriele Zerbi (1445–1505), assembled an entire manual aimed at equipping the churches for care of the elderly.

By the 7th Century, the Christian church had in place a very well-integrated institution of care for the poor. In a letter penned about AD 600 in response to questions from the missionary Augustine of Canterbury, the Roman Bishop Gregory outlined the customary budget for local churches: 25% was allocated to the pastorate, 25% to clergy and missions, 25% to the building and supplies, and 25% of church offerings were to be used for widows and orphans.

THE CHRISTIAN HISTORY OF HOSPITALS

Basil of Caesarea built the first hospital in the West around 369, to include a complex of dwellings for doctors and nurses, workshops, and industrial schools.[36] The second hospital appeared in Rome around 390, financed by a Christian woman named Fabiola, an acquaintance of Jerome. These were the first known charitable hospitals in the world. Medical historian Fielding Garrison writes, "[There is] no certain evidence of any medical institution supported by voluntary contributions... till we come to Christian days."[37]

Chapter 36 of *The Rule of St. Benedict* (issued AD 500) emphasized care for the sick as a priority for the Christian church and life.

Care of the sick must rank above and before all else, so that they may truly be served as Christ, for he said: "I was sick and you visited me" (Matt 25:36), and, "What you did for one of these least brothers you did for me" (Matt 25:40).

In the early 9th Century, Charlemagne issued a capitulary requiring every monastery and cathedral in his dominion to maintain a hospital. By the turn of the millennium, there were an estimated 500 "purpose-built" hospitals in Europe staffed by ten to twenty monks, nuns, or canons.[38] The progress did not stop here. Over the next five hundred years, an additional thirteen hundred hospitals were built in towns and cities across England.[39] Well into the 1500s there were 37,000 Benedictine monasteries perpetuating Benedict's vision to provide care for the sick.[40] Psalms and masses were sung throughout the buildings during the daytime, and both spiritual as well as physical care was the order of the day. Quite different from medical schools in the post-Christian age, the medieval physicians studied music as part of their basic preparation for medical work.[41]

The crusades did more than kill people and fight for control over the holy land. The Order of Knights Hospitallers built its first hospital in Jerusalem in 1122. The institution was capable of handling 1,000 patients at a time. Others were built by the same order throughout Europe, and the Knights of Malta provided the first mental institute in Valencia, Spain in 1409. London had its first mental institute in 1369 for those "who suddenly fell into a frenzy." As Christianity spread into the Americas, the Spanish explorer Hernando Cortes established the "Jesus of Nazareth Hospital" in Mexico City in 1524.

Within the bleak pagan world of the Greeks, blind boys were sentenced to a life in the galley ships and blind girls were remanded into dens of prostitution. But Jesus turned on the lights, and Christians opened the first institution for the blind in Jerusalem in AD 630. Louis IX, king of France, entirely banned prostitution in his country and opened a care facility for the blind in Paris to serve 300 blind persons in 1254. This Christian king was also known to share his table with beggars.

Beginning in the 9th Century, Christian influence would scatter salt and light into the rest of the world. The Muslim world borrowed a little of the Christian Western standard of medical care. Around AD 800, with assistance from Nestorian Christian physicians like Jabril ibn Bukhtishu of Mesopotamia, the first general hospital was constructed in Baghdad, Iraq.

THE DEHUMANIZATION OF HUMANISM

Upon observing Mother Teresa in Calcutta, Malcolm Muggeridge, an atheist-journalist from the 20th-Century West, had to admit that "atheistic humanism had not inspired anyone to devote his or her life to serve the dying destitute of Calcutta."[42] Socialists and atheists were willing to throw "other people's money" at the problem and call themselves "benefactors" for their own glory. Yet only the servants of Jesus would find such value in the despised of the world as to throw away their own lives for the utterly destitute.

As Christian influence faded in Western culture, Christ's heart of compassion disappeared from once charitable institutions. Charity turned depersonalized and thus dehumanized by godless, materialist, socialist, and communist governments. The full intent of the kings of the Gentiles was to "lord it over them," as Jesus put it. "But not so among you," He added (Luke 22:25-26). Modern socialist systems existed for themselves, for power, for perpetual expansion, and for domination. Using the democratic election process, the Gentiles would trade the vote for public welfare, corrupting charity by the most insidious form of *Liberalitas quid pro quo*. Bureaucracies built in incentives to self-perpetuate and to grow with every opportunity—at the taxpayers' expense. These systems always depreciated the dignity of the recipient and the hapless taxpaying public—emptying all mutual honor, love, and gratitude from the heart. Such terms could never be used in connection with the state and national Health and Human Services bureaucracies. Over time, the state extended its funding and control into education, diet, welfare, medical decisions, euthanasia, transgender operations, and the administration of psychotropic drugs for children. And, as the state stepped in, the church and family stepped out, and parents increasingly surrendered responsibility and involvement in their children's lives. This contributed much to the disintegration of the nuclear family and the Fall of the West. On March 15, 2020, the mainline *Atlantic* magazine openly announced the fatal conclusion in the headline: "The Nuclear Family was a Mistake."[43]

MARXISM & THE DESTRUCTION OF CHARITY

Therefore My Father loves Me, because I lay down My life that I may take it again. No one takes it from Me, but I lay it down of Myself. I have power to lay it down, and I have power to take it again. This command I have received from My Father. (John 10:17-18)

In preparation for its fall, the Western world lost the Christian view of both law and love. As defined by Christ, love is voluntary and abides by the commandments of God. Marxism and similar ideologies bring about the destruction of charity through a rejection of God's law (by embracing stealing) and by a rejection of the voluntary nature of charity (in favor of state-ordered extortion). In a biblical framework, charity is always voluntary, often accountable (non-anonymous), and mostly local. The early church voluntarily sold property to provide for the needs of the poor in crisis. According to God's commandment, the Christians clearly recognized the legitimate private ownership of property. When Ananias lied about the sale price of his property, the Apostle Peter very explicitly reminded the man that the property was his own, and "after it was sold, was it not in your own control?" (Acts

5:4). There was no centralized apostolic bureaucracy put in place to designate the amount Ananias was required to contribute; charity was absolutely voluntary.

If there is one lesson to learn from the Old Testament, it is that we cannot love our neighbor without loving God and keeping His commandments. Christ would never separate the two. Repeatedly, He told His disciples, "If you love Me, keep My commandments" (John 14:15). Stealing for the sake of charity is a contradiction in terms. Paul elucidates in Romans 13: "For the commandments, 'You shall not commit adultery,' 'You shall not murder,' 'You shall not steal,' 'You shall not bear false witness,' 'You shall not covet,' and if there is any other commandment, are all summed up in this saying, namely, 'You shall love your neighbor as yourself.' Love does no harm to a neighbor; therefore love is the fulfillment of the law" (Rom. 13:9-10). Any other definition of love is not love—just the twisted love of Marx.

Democracy in the modern age shifted the focus from the church to the civil government as the primary if not the only meaningful social unit. Increasingly, man and his state turned into god on earth in the mind of the modern. Unrealistic expectations developed concerning what the state could do and the problems it could fix.

Primary among revolutionary thinkers was the French philosopher Jean-Jacques Rousseau (1712-1778), considered the father of the modern socialist state. Baptized a Calvinist in Geneva, young Rousseau was raised on Plutarch's *Lives of the Noble Greeks and Romans.* Upon leaving home, he converted to the Catholic faith and thereafter lived a profligate life of sexual promiscuity. Fittingly, Rousseau abandoned five of his children on the streets of Paris (upon their birth) and advocated a Platonic state in which the government would be responsible for the education and welfare of children. He was the grandfather of all modern government-based schooling. Most significant for the post-Christian decline that would follow, this father of all future socialists defined himself thusly, "No one ever had more talent for loving. I was born to be the best friend that ever existed...I am the friend of mankind, and men everywhere."[44] Here was the archetypal liberal of the modern age. Supremely hypocritical, dangerously utopian, and decked out with a meticulously-groomed appearance of benignity—the liberal throws away his own newborn child in the morning and argues for welfare and free school lunches for inner-city kids at legislative committee meetings in the afternoon.

Despite his overwhelming influence upon the entire modern world, Rousseau's contemporaries and modern historians are surprisingly severe in their descriptions of the character of the greatest philosopher of the modern age: "deceitful, vain as Satan, ungrateful, cruel, hypocritical and full of malice," "odious," "a monster of vanity and vileness," a "masochist, exhibitionist, neurasthenic, hypochondriac, onanist, latent homosexual...incapable of normal or parental affection, incipient paranoiac, narcissistic introvert...filled with guilt feelings, pathologically timid, a kleptomaniac, infantilist, irritable, and miserly."[45] What fitting descriptions for the man and the socialist institutions birthed out of his vision!

Rousseau's humanist vision forged in the French Revolution culminated in the Napoleonic Code, which strengthened the modern state at the expense of weakening the family. Homosexuality and convenience divorce were allowed, marriage was turned over to the control of the state, and education was brought under the central government (placed under the Department of the Interior). Napoleon's empire had spread across Europe by 1812, enveloping Spain, France, Belgium, Holland, parts of Germany, and Italy as far south as Rome). Other alliances were formed with Denmark, Sweden, Austria, and Russia.

Beginning with Jean-Jacques Rousseau and a disciple of Immanuel Kant in Germany named Johann Fichte (1762-1814), the new prophets of humanism would push hard for "free public education" supported by central government funds. In his "Addresses to the German Nation," Fichte promised salvation by state-funded education.

> The salvation which I promised to indicate consists in the fashioning of an entirely new self, which may have existed before perhaps in individuals as an exception, but never as a universal and national self, and in the education of the nation.[46]

Getting the jump on the later vision espoused by Karl Marx, Johann Fichte called for an education that would eliminate all class distinctions and create the national egalitarian state: "So there is nothing left for us but just to apply the new system to every German without exception, so that it is not the education of a single class, but the education of the nation.... All distinctions of classes,... will be completely removed and vanish. In this way there will grow up among us, not popular education, but real German national education."[47] Friedrich Immanuel Niethammer formed the first publicly funded high schools in 1808, and 118 such schools were in operation across Prussia by 1848.[48]

The German philosopher and Lutheran apostate Karl Marx entered the scene in the 1840s, preaching his message egalitarianism and forced redistribution of wealth: "From each according to his ability to each according to his needs." However, his *Communist Manifesto* provided little in terms of promise of welfare and charity for the people— except for "Free education for all children in public schools."[49] Boston had its first government-funded high school in 1821, and the State of Massachusetts introduced its first compulsory attendance law in 1852. By 1870, every state had followed suit with its own government-funded primary schools.

PRIVATE CHARITY THRIVES IN THE US

Private charity continued in the United States for a while in the early 19th Century as a plethora of charitable societies formed to meet just about every perceptible need. These included The Society for the Prevention of Pauperism (1817), The Society for Reformation for Juvenile Delinquents (1825), The Association for the Improvement of the Condition of the Poor and The Children's Aid Society (1843), as well as the American Red Cross (1871). George Williams formed the Young Men's Christian Association (YMCA) in 1844, which grew into a $2 billion organization over 180 years, spreading into 120 countries around the world. Meanwhile in London, William Booth formed the Salvation Army (1865), and branches were opened in America in the 1880s. Today, the US Salvation Army continues its work with an annual budget of about $4 billion.[50] Other offices continue in 130 nations around the world—a reflection of true Christ-like charity. Contributing over $300 billion a year to charity, in 2016 the United States was still the source of over 75% of the total world charity while supplying only about 25% of the Gross World Product. Adding in the UK and Canada, these Protestant nations accounted for 84% of the world's charitable contributions.[51]

Until the 1700s, families generally took care of their own mentally-challenged relatives. After that, asylums and institutions for the mentally unstable were begun. By 1774, there were sixteen such institutions in London alone. The Quakers built the first mental asylum in America in 1752, and The Asylum for the Relief of Persons Deprived of the Use of Their Reason was founded in 1813. The first asylum for the mentally-challenged in the state of Kentucky was initiated by voluntary donations in 1816 and completed by government funding in 1821.[52]

THE SEEDS OF CORRUPTION PLANTED—1828-1929

The pressure to displace Christian voluntarism and restore the ancient *liberalitas* of the pagans came on hard and strong in the United States in the 1820s. Against the wishes of Tennessee congressman Davy Crockett, the US House of Representatives approved a stipend for a certain Widow Brown in April of 1828. Crockett had instead suggested a more personal approach to charity: he recommended passing a hat around the room, allowing congressmen to contribute out of their own pockets, but gained no traction on the motion. Crocket's challenge illustrated the hypocritical love so characteristic of the "Gentiles." The Apostle warned about this in Romans 12:9: "Let love be without hypocrisy." When the congressmen were contributing other people's money, they were quite willing to support the poor widow. When asked to contribute out of their own pockets, however, their hypocritical "love" showed itself in its true colors. This first congressional action was a potent harbinger of what was to come.

Welfare champion and Unitarian adherent Dorothea Dix is remembered for her criticism of private charity and her push for state funding of mental asylums in Massachusetts, New Jersey, and North Carolina. Her efforts to secure federal funding of public welfare met with a veto from President Franklin Pierce in 1854. She was the prototype for modern socialists, unwilling to give up her own life, time, or money for the needy and helpless in society after the pattern of Macrina. Here was the new socialist—utopian, revolutionary, idealistic, pestiferous, not very charitable, yet very generous with other people's money.

Another prototype socialist, Jane Addams, known for her lesbian tendencies and cofounder of the American Civil Liberties Union, was particularly committed to public education, and state regulation on private industry. In 2 Timothy 3, Paul had warned of perilous times that would come, in which many would demonstrate a form of godliness, but deny its power. He also expressed a concern for women who would be captured by their own lusts and foolish ways:

> This know also, that in the last days perilous times shall come. For men shall be lovers of their own selves, covetous, boasters, proud, blasphemers, disobedient to parents, unthankful, unholy, Without natural affection, trucebreakers, false accusers, incontinent, fierce, despisers of those that are good, Traitors, heady, highminded, lovers of pleasures more than lovers of God; Having a form of godliness, but denying the power thereof: from such turn away. For of this sort are they which creep into houses, and lead captive silly women laden with sins, led away with divers lusts. (2 Timothy 3:1-6)

The hard work of 19th Century socialists paid off in the 20th Century as government welfare programs burgeoned in every major Western nation. Christian family, church charity, and privatized care for poor neighbors and relatives pretty much disappeared. Central governments took over education, healthcare, care of the elderly, food distributions, and housing for the poor. This was the most significant social shift in 1,700 years. Between 1880 and 2020, this new religion of modern *liberalitas* in the form of socialism had displaced the Christian faith.

WELFARE PROGRAMS INITIATED IN GERMANY

Not surprisingly, modern socialism experienced its first major burst at the turn of the 20th Century in Germany, the home base of Karl Marx, Adolf Hitler, the Forty-Eighters, and the National Socialists. For 5,900 years, great monarchs and empires seldom handled more than 3%-10% of the nation's income. The great state of Prussia still only controlled 4.9% of its people's income in 1850.[53] But henceforth, the power of the state would radically increase to accommodate this new *liberalitas*, known as *Solidarität* in German. In 1883, the Bismarck government introduced the Health Insurance of Workers Law followed up with the Old Age and Invalidity Insurance Law of 1889. The National Insurance Code integrated the nation's entire social welfare program into a single unit in 1911. Then came the Youth Welfare Act of 1922 and various unemployment programs in 1923.

Socialism arrived later for Americans. The 1912 presidential elections marked the turning point towards the *liberalitas* of the pre-Christian world. Theodore Roosevelt and Woodrow Wilson advocated equally socialistic agendas, with Roosevelt's agenda leaning a little more to the left. He wanted a minimum wage law, more powerful federal

Public Social Spending as a Share of the GDP, 1880-2016

Our World in Data based on OECD and Lindert (2004). Reference OurWorldInData.org/public-spending

regulatory agencies, and social welfare programs. Woodrow Wilson won the election and found a way to redistribute more wealth through the new graduated income tax brought by the 16th Amendment and the Federal Reserve central banking system. Following on President Wilson's heels, Franklin Delano Roosevelt responded to the Great Depression in the 1930s by adding a host of federal welfare programs and the Social Security system. Later, Lyndon B. Johnson's Great

Society programs added another 60% to the US Federal Government budget.

After the year 1900, the whole world turned to socialism—to the old pagan *liberalitas*. Ten percent (the tithe) had always proved sufficient to provide for charity in the past, but 20th Century leaders now chose to drive their economies deep into debt to provide public social welfare for those who would not or could not work. The above chart displaying the history of public social spending reveals in stark colors this dramatic worldview shift in the West. Between 1900 and the present, central governments increased their *liberalitas* from zero to as much as 30% of their respective national economies.

The fruit of Marxist "charity" was not pretty. The corruption of morals, marriage, fatherhood, family life, procreation, politics, medicine, and economy was thorough-going in Western nations. Free handouts offered to those in broken family situations served as an incentive to further immorality, irresponsibility, and social disintegration. European illegitimacy rates increased from 5% to 60%, and US rates increased from 6% to 40%.[54] The effects upon ethnic minorities were even more devastating. Among the African immigrant ethnic group, for example, the illegitimacy rate increased from 22% in 1960 to 77% by 2017,[55] and the abortion rate for this group was three times the national average.[56]

Throughout the socialist revolutions, repeatedly "liberal" Christian groups would trot out a kludged theological justification for the agenda. The liberal view was Christian apostasy. What follower of Christ would mistake the atoning, substitutionary, voluntary sacrifice of Christ for the social Gospel? Who would believe that the liberation theology of the Roman Catholics or the social justice movement of the liberal Protestants was anything more than Marxism? It wasn't God's love, and it certainly was not in accord with God's law. Compulsive charity was a farcical monstrosity, a despicable counterfeit of the love of God. These heresies and twisted caricatures of Christian doctrine remained well into the 21st Century.

The 19th Century humanist philosopher Friedrich Nietzsche attempted a complete return to the harsh pagan world of the Romans and Greeks when he announced that God was dead. Advocating a "Master Morality," he redefined "good" to be that which is strong-willed, powerful, and brutal. He repudiated the biblical value of charity, which he defined as, "The measure of a man's compassion for the lowly and the suffering comes to be the measure of the loftiness of his soul."[57] Nietzsche acted the part of a second Julian the Apostate, in hopes of resurrecting the old paganism. But, try as he might, he could not rid the world entirely of Jesus the Crucified.

Yet, the whole world condemned movie producer Harvey Weinstein when it was alleged he took advantage of more than 80 women. Nobody cared that he broke God's seventh commandment; it was merely the victimization of a perceived disempowered minority that bothered the masses. A million women aligned with the #MeToo movement and joined a march in Washington DC on January 21, 2017 (shortly after the election of Donald Trump). Such demonstrations revealed the faint remnants of Christian foundations somewhere under this post-Christian society. Nobody would have marched for the sexual degradation of women in Nero's Rome. Nobody would have marched through the streets of ancient Milan for some single victim of police abuse, memorializing Rodney King or George Floyd. Yet the alleged murder of a counterfeiter and drug addict in 2020 inspired millions to rush into the streets in some 2,000 cities around the world, complaining of police abuse. Historian Tom Holland remarks on Nietzsche's prophetic word, "God might be dead, but his shadow, immense and dreadful, continued to flicker even as his corpse lay cold. Feminist academics were no less in thrall to it, no less its acolytes, than were the most fire-breathing preachers. God could not be eluded simply by refusing to believe in his existence...Two thousand years on, and the discovery made by Christ's earliest followers—that to be a victim might be a source of power—could bring out millions onto the streets."[58]

In the ancient pagan world, it was commonly accepted that "every master is entitled to use his slave as he desires."[59] It was assumed that power would express itself sexually. Nero subjected even aristocratic women in Rome to the most degrading sexual behavior. Twenty centuries later, modern feminism and egalitarianism retained a flavor of charitableness in the mind of the post-Christian. Holland again notes that "because communism was [purportedly] the expression of a concern for the oppressed masses—[communists] rarely seem as diabolical to people today."[60] Racist Nazis and allegedly racist cops are regarded as a hundred times worse than the brutal communist with his bloody revolutions.

The #MeToo and Woke movements were no more than a faint reminder, a mere shadow, and a twisted caricature reminiscent of the old Christian ethic. The poverty class. The sexually abused. The power deprived. Victimhood. Intersectionality. Racial persecution. These became the new wrongs to be righted in all the wrong ways—usually by messiahs of revolution or the state. Faint shades of quickly-fading Christian virtue were visible, but the new morality was primarily composed of thick pharisaical hypocrisy, a complete abandonment of God's law, a preference for Marxist revolutions, the power-mongering of the ancient pagans, and an utter rejection of the self-sacrificial love of Christ. There was no true justice, no true mercy, and no genuine love in any of it. All was a pretense, an illusion, and a hypocritical façade.

The major post-Christian charities soon fell in line with this new ethic—protect the sexual minority and abandon God's law as the means by which we love God and neighbor. The YMCA endorsed the homosexual agenda in 2018;[61] United Way announced its first support for the homosexual lifestyle in 2010;[62] the Boy Scouts of America endorsed homosexuals and transvestites in 2015 and 2017;[63] and the Salvation Army announced their support for homosexuality, lesbianism, bisexuality, and transgenderism (LGBT) in 2019.[64]

> The sacrifice of the wicked is abomination:
> How much more, when he bringeth it with a wicked mind?
> (Proverbs 21:27)

Yet, well into the 21st Century, the West was still marked by its generosity. According to the World Giving Index of the Charities Aid Foundation, the ten stingiest nations in the world well represented the Middle East and the Christian East which had been subjected to communism: China, Greece, Yemen, Serbia, Palestine, Lithuania, Bulgaria, Montenegro, Croatia, and Russia.[65] In 2020, the United States was still the most generous nation in the world, followed by Myanmar, New Zealand, Australia, Ireland, Canada, the United Kingdom, the Netherlands, Sri Lanka, and Indonesia.[66] The world was still feeling the 2,000-year influence of Christ among Europeans and Americans. Paul's last words to the church at Ephesus (in modern-day Turkey) would continue to ring for millennia afterwards:

> I have shewed you all things, how that so labouring ye ought to support the weak, and to remember the words of the Lord Jesus, how he said, It is more blessed to give than to receive. (Acts 20:35)

THE FAILURE OF THE CHURCH

> Let not a widow be taken into the number under threescore years old, having been the wife of one man, Well reported of for good works; if she have brought up children, if she have lodged strangers, if she have washed the saints' feet, if she have relieved the afflicted, if she have diligently followed every good work. (1 Timothy 5:9-10)

As Western society embraced the Marxist conception and corruption of charity, the Christian church abdicated its responsibilities to the poor as outlined in 1 Timothy 5 and Acts 6. The sharp drop-off in average charitable contributions for church members clearly signaled the decline of the faith in the West. The biblical tithe set in the Old Testament was 10%. Under the New Covenant one would expect to find higher percentages of financial generosity. Yet, the first modern data available in the United States lists the average per-member annual giving (as a percentage of income) at 3.7% in 1923. This rate steadily declined for almost 100 years, registering at 2.12% in 2017.[67] Total church offerings (as a percentage of the Gross Domestic Product) declined from 1.1% to 0.7% between 1987 and 2014,[68] partly due to the drop-off in membership and partly to the reduction of average giving per member. With 75% of American adults still claiming formal church membership in 1924, total church charitable offerings exceeded 2.8% of the GDP. Given the decline to 0.7% over a hundred years, that amounted to a 75% decrease in the influence of the church in the Western socio-economy. Including non-ecclesiastical giving, total charitable gifts amounted to only 1.4% of the US GDP in 2017. By this time almost all church giving would support clergy and buildings, while governments were peeling off 20-30% of the GDP for social programs.

Recently, the Lilly Endowment found that churches spend 49% of their budgets on personnel, 23% on facilities, 11% on missions, 10% on programs, 6% on dues, and *nothing on widows and orphans.*[69] Similarly, the Church Budget Priorities Study conducted on 800 churches by *Christianity Today* in 2019 listed no category for the diaconate, the poor, or the widows in the church—*not a single dime.*[70] Only five percent of church budgets went to missions, and only four percent was allocated to domestic missions. In the modern socialist world where a forced, *liberalitas*-driven charitable system dominated, the Western church had become irrelevant to human society. The humanist state was now assuming the role of the church, and the church had abandoned the Acts 6 vision for the diaconate. A look at church budgets revealed a wide and glaring disparity between spending patterns within the modern church and that of the historical church during the Christian age.

	Church Budget in the Christian Age[71]	Church Budget in the Post-Christian Age[72]
Pastoral Salaries	25%	51%
Church Building/Supplies	25%	29%
Missions & Church Programs	25%	20%
The Poor and Widows	25%	0%

The Christian legacy of charity long established by Christian churches was now entirely displaced by the Marxist state. Funding of the medical industry was almost entirely in the hands of the state—by some studies it provided 67% of all expenditures.[73] Only 7% of overall healthcare spending in the US came by philanthropic means[74]—and almost nothing was provided by churches. Although practically all of the hospitals were established by the churches—Catholic, Lutheran, Presbyterian, Baptist, Seventh Day Adventist, etc., the state had seized almost total control by extensive regulation and funding. The Church was now socially and culturally irrelevant.

PERSECUTION IN THE NAME OF "LOVE"

He that justifieth the wicked, and he that condemneth the just,
Even they both are abomination to the LORD. (Proverbs 17:15)

Yet another twisted aberration of compassion appeared when governments forced benefits on families, even threatening imprisonment for those who refused to participate. Instead of availing themselves to the "free" Marxist programs, some Christian parents opted to homeschool or Christian school their children. Believers in the United States, Germany, Sweden and elsewhere faced arrest, fines, and imprisonment for exempting their children from the socialist schools. Similarly, the Chinese communists would routinely close Christian schools, and children of believers were forbidden by law to enter church buildings.[75]

Still more aberrant counterfeits of compassion and charity came in the 21st Century with the persecution of Christians who refused to embrace homosexuality or participate in celebratory events for transvestites and homosexuals. In the name of tolerance and charity, special rights were offered to those participating in sexual perversion and Christians were hauled into court, fined, and, in some cases, put out of business. These Christian believers preferred not to render complicit approval of sinful lifestyles by taking the food offered to idols at the "heathen ceremonies," according to the apostolic warning issued in 1 Corinthians 10:25-28. Some refused to support homosexuals with provisions and services for "weddings," "honeymoons," and "family" employment benefits. Christian employers were hesitant to allow a "flaunting" of sinful lifestyles in the workplace. In March 2019, the US Supreme Court refused to hear the Aloha Bed and Breakfast case in which Christian owners were reticent to accommodate lesbianism. Finally, on June 15, 2020, the US high court ruled that a Christian funeral home ministry should retain employment of a man who wanted to dress like a woman in the manner of Caesar Elagabalus (AD 204-222). Even for the Romans, the Caesar's perversions were too much to handle—he was killed, his dead body was dragged through the streets, and he was buried in a common grave. There were limits to the sexual anarchism permitted in Roman society.

But there were no limits to the perversion of charity and the hypocritical benefaction of the Gentiles (Luke 22:25). Abortion and born-alive infanticide was sold to the public under pretense of compassion for women who could not be inconvenienced with children. Single women were told that they were six times more likely to finish college and "succeed in life" if they would only abort the child. In the name of love, billions of children were killed and those opposing the practice were unloving to women. The "tender mercies of the wicked are cruel" (Prov. 12:10).

Modern *liberalitas* was more corrupted and more coerced than anything previously seen in human history. It was a perversion of love. It was opposed to true Christian charity, true love for God and His law, and real Christ-love for one's neighbor—sinner or saint.

Nonetheless, this super abundant offering of *liberalitas* in the United States and the other Western states was only temporary. British prime minister Margaret Thatcher had already warned, "Socialist governments traditionally do make a financial mess. They always run out of other people's money."[76] The softer socialism of the Confucianists always gives way to the harder treatment of the Legalists, as in the Chinese experience. Where Christ is not present, the nightmarish world of Nietzsche's Master Morality, the Stalinists, and the Nazis are ready and willing to fill the void. After more than 80 million abortions, irrecoverable birth implosions, and bankrupted governments, the US Social Security Trust Fund would fail by AD 2031.[77] False charity would always betray its true colors and real heart motive. Health-care rationing and forced euthanasia was inevitable. In the end, the rotting foundations and ruined character of a post-Christian culture was made manifest to the world.

> And because iniquity shall abound, the love of many shall wax cold. But he that shall endure unto the end, the same shall be saved. (Matthew 24:12-13)

IX

THE RISE & FALL
OF SCIENCE IN THE WEST

Some trust in chariots, and some in horses: but we will remember the
name of the LORD our God. They are brought down and fallen: but
we are risen, and stand upright. (Psalm 20:7-8)

At this point, the reader may already be convinced that the
Western world has failed morally, ecclesiastically, and socially. Yet
something still lingers of that humanist notion, some hope and faith
that somehow modern science has saved mankind and will save him
again. After all, how could the most technologically-advanced society
in all of human existence possibly fall? *Of all the things that have ever
failed mankind, how could science fail?* The question comes across as
rhetorical, but the answer may come as a surprise. Science has *already*
failed the modern world.

The purpose of science is to know the creation and the Creator,
to provide some relief for physical needs, and to assist in man's duty to
steward God's creation. Science must submit to God's law order and
the dominion mandate, or it will fail. Simply stated, the syllogism is
this: If science has come to the point of hurting instead of helping, it

has failed. That is what has occurred in the Western world. As human society turned against God and true knowledge, 20th Century science turned morally and socially destructive. Instead of saving Western culture and society, science merely hastened its demise.

Too quickly, Western science was conflated into a new religion called "scientism" which only pretended to ask the ultimate questions. In the Western mind, the scientist shifted roles from a servant of God to playing the part of god. The rise of the hard sciences and the rise of scientism came almost simultaneously, and then . . .the Fall.

THE "DARK AGES"

> Woe unto them that call evil good, and good evil; that put darkness for light, and light for darkness; that put bitter for sweet, and sweet for bitter! Woe unto them that are wise in their own eyes, and prudent in their own sight! Woe unto them that are mighty to drink wine, and men of strength to mingle strong drink: which justify the wicked for reward, and take away the righteousness of the righteous from him! (Isaiah 5:20-23)

Honest historians of both the Christian and non-Christian pedigree have come to question the popular historical narrative, mostly manufactured by Enlightenment philosophers, commonly called the "Dark Ages." The consensus of academics like Rodney Stark, Ernst Benz, Samuel Sambursky, Lynn White Jr., and Aldous Huxley is that the Dark Ages weren't really dark. While not all fans of the Christian faith, honest historians found it hard to deny reality.

The myth of the Dark Ages began at the revival of Greek humanism with Petrarch (1304-1374). This father of the Italian Renaissance closed his illustrious career with his work *Secretum*, in which he conducted imaginary dialogues with Augustine. In conversation with Petrarch, this pseudo-Augustine explains that his *True Religion* is made of "doctrine...drawn from philosophers, more especially from those of the Platonist and Socratic school. And, to keep nothing from you." He continues, "I may say that what especially moved me to undertake that work was a word of your favourite Cicero."[1] True knowledge ostensibly came from the ancient Greeks, and Christianity interrupted man's quest, in his view.

Thus, sufficiently enlightened by the pagans and disillusioned with the Christian faith (which had transformed Europe from AD 400 to 1300) Petrarch referred to these centuries as "the time of darkness." Later, Jean Jacques Rousseau, the chief apostate of the Enlightenment, described the Middle Ages as a "relapse into the barbarism of the earliest ages...a condition worse than ignorance."[2] Voltaire chimed in, describing the Christian Era as the period in which "barbarism, superstition, [and] ignorance covered the face of the world."[3] For, the modern humanist then Christ becomes darkness and humanism becomes light. Dark is light, and light is dark. For centuries, Protestant and Roman Catholic colleges and universities taught their students this view of history. The Christian Era was the Dark Ages—until the world had re-installed man on the divine throne. Nevertheless, the truth has a way of worming its way out. Historian and sociologist Rodney Stark pointed out that "serious historians have known for decades that this scheme is a complete fraud—'an indestructible fossil of self-congratulatory Renaissance humanism.'"[4]

To fully appreciate the development and achievements of Western civilization, one must consider its ecclesiastical, moral, educational, political, economic, and technological development and achievements at the same time. A civilization is everything about that society; and each element hinges on the other. For example, it is difficult to imagine the development of an economy without the accompanying political freedom. Down through the millennia, the Chinese hegemony would squelch innovation and economic freedom, repeatedly forcing the socio-economic system into stasis. A Christian epistemology, Christian education, Christian socio-economics, a Christian view of liberty, and a Christian view of science coordinated to transform human civilization over a thousand years. More than any other society, Christian civilization provided the highest motives to scientific inquiry and practical technological development for the betterment of mankind. Christians developed the most effective definition of science and method for scientific inquiry to bring about technological progress.

The difference between the pagan Greek and the Christian view of knowledge became immediately obvious in the first centuries of the Christian era. The Greeks and (to some extent), the Eastern Church were content to receive *illumination*, but the Christian West would settle for nothing less than *application*. In the words of Jesus' brother, it wasn't enough for Christ-followers to hear the Word; one must be a doer of the Word as well (Jas. 1:22-24). The knowing comes at least partially by the doing, as Jesus said: "he who does the truth comes to the light, that his deeds may be clearly seen, that they have been done in God" (John 3:21). The effect of this theory of knowledge on the scientist and the educator was most profound. Science without useful application was a distraction.

"Knowledge puffs up, but love edifies," says the Apostle Paul (1 Cor. 8:1). To the Christian mind, a science which does not serve, edify, or benefit mankind is repugnant and to be rejected. This is why true monasteries would not permit monks to sit, meditate, and hypothesize all day long. There was work to be done. As Benedict reminded his followers, "Idleness is an enemy of the soul."[5]

Moreover, the Christian man is ever aware of the creation mandate to take dominion over the earth and its resources. He should not tolerate the earth to rule over him. Also, the Christian commitment to abolish slavery, dating back to the earliest centuries of the church, produced an economic incentive for innovation. Thus, Christian monks and others sought ways to shed grunt labor or slave labor, enabling more viable and sustainable household economies (without the need for slaves). Not a Christian but still recognizing the contribution of the Christian West, renowned medieval historian, Lynn Townsend White calls these inventions a humanitarian endeavor:

> The humanitarian technology which our modern world has inherited from the Middle Ages was not rooted in economic necessity; for this 'necessity' is inherent in every society, yet has found inventive expression only in the Occident, nurtured in the activist or voluntarist tradition of Western theology. It is ideas which make necessity conscious. The labor-saving power-machines of the later Middle Ages were produced by the implicit theological assumption of the infinite worth of even the most degraded human personality, by an instinctive repugnance towards subjecting any man to a monotonous drudgery which seems less than human in that it requires the exercise neither of intelligence nor of choice.[6]

White goes on to laud these technological contributions as "the chief glory of the later Middle Ages."[7] These inventions, White insists, were not conditioned by economic necessity alone, as many cultures around the world faced the same problems but failed to respond with the initiative and inventiveness found in the West. Instead of looking to "necessity" as the mother of invention, White calls attention to the practical outworking of Christian theology, adding that, "it is ideas which make necessity conscious." It was the faith of the West—Christian ideas and convictions—which inspired technological advancements and cultural improvements. Beginning as early as the fifth Century, Christians in the West acted upon their God-given call to dominion. For 1,500 years, Christians engaged one long uninterrupted series of useful scientific and technological innovations—a list much too long to detail in this short synopsis.

HOW THE LORD GIVES WISDOM

If thou seekest her as silver, and searchest for her as for hid treasures;
Then shalt thou understand the fear of the LORD, and find the
knowledge of God. For the LORD giveth wisdom: out of his mouth
cometh knowledge and understanding. (Proverbs 2:4-6)

All true knowledge finds its source in God, and it is only by
God's grace that the minds of men comprehend any truth. Surely,
His grace was showered plentifully on the Christian West for at
least a millennium. The heavy iron plow, complete with the coulter
and moldboard for turning the soil, was first mentioned in AD 643
in northern Italy. Wheels were added, and eight pair of oxen were
employed for large plow jobs. This motivated cooperative farming
and the feudal (landlord)-based economic system. The improved
plough appeared in Denmark by AD 900. This technology revolution
in agriculture aided in increasing population density and improving
economic conditions across Europe.[8] Better horse collars engineered
for pulling and metal-based horseshoes were added by the 600s-700s.

For hundreds of years, Eastern cultures had employed windmills
to turn prayer wheels, hoping to mass-produce prayers for gods with
hearing problems. These are found in Tibet dating back into the 6th
Century. The nations would have to wait for useful applications of
such technology produced by Christians. Well into the 21st Century,
African and Indian women continued carrying drinking water on their
heads for long distances. Christian author Vishal Mangalwadi points
out that the untouchables in Indian cultures still carry containers of
excreta on their heads to this day.[9] And in some cultures, women still
use grindstones to process grains. All of this changed for Christians in
the West a thousand years ago.

Whereas there is evidence that the Greeks and Romans knew
something about watermills and built a few themselves, it was the

Christian West that mass-produced them. A Christian pastor and abbot, Gregory of Tours (AD 539-594), strongly advocated the use of watermills in monasteries, and by 1086 there were 5,624 such mills in England alone. The early biographer of Bernard of Clairvaux (1090-1153) notes these developments and offers thanks to God for "such machines [that] can alleviate the oppressive labors of both man and beast."[10]

Sometime around 1120, a Christian theologian and monk, Theophilus, was the first to publish an invention of the flywheel—a device which maintains momentum and conservation of power within a larger machine. Other inventions were soon to follow. The Chinese created a wheelbarrow of sorts, but the wheel was located under the center of the barrow—not very handy for human manual use. Once again, medieval Christians improved the design, applying the principle of leverage, moving the wheel to the far end of the barrel (around AD 1200). Medieval inventors also added brakes and swiveling front axles to wagons.

The first horizontal-access windmill in recorded history is found in Yorkshire, England around 1185. Throughout the long "Dark Ages," this technological advancement kept seawater pumped out of the Netherlands and Belgium. Also, the first chimneys appeared in European castles in the 1100s.

Tucked into a sermon given on February 23, 1306, Dominican monk Giordano of Pisa announced the invention of eyeglasses:

It is not yet twenty years since there was found the art of making eyeglasses, which make for good vision, one of the best arts and most necessary the world has. And it is so short a time that this new art, never before extant, was discovered.[11]

Nobody needed this wonderful invention more than monks whose job was to read and copy the Scriptures for long hours, by hand.

The identity of the inventor who so mastered the field of optics as to develop such a useful device as eyeglasses (in 1286) remains one of the great mysteries in the history of science.

Perhaps the most useful and influential invention of the Christian world came when a German metallurgist from Mainz, Johann Gutenberg (1398-1468), developed the modern printing process. This technological advancement included moveable metal type, allowing each letter to be reused on successive pages. Adding an oil-based ink and a high-quality screw press, Gutenberg produced 170 copies of the first printed Bible in 1455.

Vishal Mangalwadi points out that while the Indian yogis were practicing their levitation techniques through transcendental meditation, Christian monks were busy doing more useful things. A Benedictine monk from Wiltshire Abbey in Malmesbury, England charted the world's first recorded flight around 1030. The monk flew his glider off an 80-foot tower for a distance of six hundred feet, only breaking a leg or two in the process.[12] Nine hundred years later, it was two brothers, sons of a Christian pastor from Dayton, Ohio, who charted the first successful propelled takeoff and landing.

As for sea transportation, the Romans used galley ships powered by rowing (and a small sail), but it was the Christianized West that engineered the true sailing ship.

For millennia, the Chinese had used pyrotechnics for fireworks displays. However, the Europeans first applied gunpowder for armed defense in the 1320s. They also solicited church bell suppliers to cast iron into cannons, for equipping their armies and navies.

THE CHRISTIAN PHILOSOPHY OF SCIENCE

But be ye doers of the word, and not hearers only, deceiving your own selves. For if any be a hearer of the word, and not a doer, he is like unto a man beholding his natural face in a glass: for he beholdeth himself, and goeth his way, and straightway forgetteth what manner of man he was. (James 1:22-24)

Peter the Pilgrim (Petrus Peregrinus de Maricourt, c.1269) may be considered the archetypal Christian scientist who placed experience over argument and experimentation over theory. The Christian seeks knowledge from a position of humility and always resorts to "doing" the word. He must never idealize his own conceptions. Peter's work on magnetism was seminal in the development of modern science, while at the same time Roger Bacon (1214-1292) was busy formulating the Christian basis for Western science. Bacon's magnum opus *Opus Majus* was actually meant to be a defense of the Christian faith in the face of rising skepticism. Interacting with Aristotle, Bacon argued that science must be the handmaiden of theology. He concluded that logical arguments are not enough for the "verification of things." Testing and repeated observation is the only way to confirm or refute theoretical scientific claims. Roger Bacon conducted work in optics, conceptualized a telescope, and introduced gunpowder to the West. He also suggested the possibility of horseless carriages and airplanes to the world, in this remarkable passage:

> It is possible that a car shall be made which will move with inestimable speed, and the motion will be without the help of any living creature...
> It is possible that a device for flying shall be made such that a man sitting in the middle of it and turning a crank shall cause artificial wings to beat the air after the manner of a bird's flight.[13]

The Arabs and Chinese were good at theory, but Christians were committed to "doing the truth" so as to "come to the light." The technological applications provided by the medieval Christian world were essential to real progress in science.

Redeeming the time is a basic command of Scripture (Eph. 5:16), and nowhere was this injunction more important than with the

Christian discipleship centers covering the European continent. The office of reading psalms seven times a day demanded punctuality and reminders—which only a mechanical clock outfitted with a chime could provide. This was produced in the 1340s by an Italian clockmaker. The English mathematician Richard of Wallingford (1292-1336) improved the efficiency of a clock for the abbey church at St. Albans and wrote a helpful manual for future clockmakers. Besides perfecting the mechanical clock, this mathematical genius invented a very complex astronomical instrument called "the Albion" which could calculate the location of certain stars at any given time. Richard also developed the mechanical escapement, arguably the first major mechanical design in modern history—leading to a million other mechanical designs by which the whole world runs today. James Hannam explains the escapement as:

> a mechanism that allows a clock to keep time. Power is provided by a weight hung from a rope wrapped around a horizontal shaft. As gravity pulls on the weight, it tries to rotate the shaft. However, the shaft cannot turn freely because it is attached to a gear wheel whose teeth control its rate of rotation. The escapement itself is a weighted spinning crossbar that allows the gear wheel to turn by only one notch for each one of its rotations. Each time the gear moves on by one notch, there is one tick of the clock, and the weight-driven shaft can turn by a very small amount.[14]

Most readers would have a hard time grasping the description of such a complex device. Suffice it to say that this was an inventive breakthrough which could only have been conceived by a mechanical genius—especially when no one else had done it in 5,400 years of living history. It was Christians—practical men with an eye towards service and dominion—who would provide technology for billions of people around the world in the modern age. So much for the "Dark Ages."

Although the humanist Renaissance cultivated some popular

interest in alchemy and pagan forms of magic, real Christians rejected this pseudo-science and instead busied themselves with discovering the complexities of God's creation. Medieval chemists discovered hydrochloric, nitric, and sulfuric acids. Distillation of these substances by condensation was achieved somewhere in the 13th Century.

Leading the first revolution in the development of the hard sciences (before the period of humanist Renaissance), Oxford's Merton College produced a number of practical mathematicians and physicists, beginning with Thomas Bradwardine (1300-1349). Aristotle failed to apply the discipline of mathematics to establish the relationship of variables in physics. This Bradwardine set out to change, although unsuccessfully at first. Aristotle's law of motion turned out to be wrong, and it was left to Christians to correct the wrongheaded thinking of the Greeks.

Earlier, in the 6th Century, the Eastern Christian thinker John Philoponus (c. 570) laid the groundwork for Newton's First Law of Motion: An object in motion will stay in motion because of the initial force set to the object. Also, Philoponus corrected the Aristotelian misconception that a rock and a feather would fall at a rate proportional to their weights. Once again, Christians were willing to experiment and disprove Aristotle's "genius" hypotheses, rendering true progress to observational science. Bradwardine went so far as to say that both the feather and rock would fall at the same rate under ideal conditions (i.e., in a vacuum). Arguably, the world's first true physicist, Richard Swineshead (another Merton man), studied motion and came up with the mean speed theorem: "A moving [accelerating] body will travel in an equal period of time, a distance exactly equal to that which it would travel if it were moving continuously at its mean speed."[15] A French pastor and scientist, Nicole Oresme, would prove the theorem by graphical representation in the 1370s. Another important breakthrough, Oresme's discovery was the first use of mathematical graphing as an effective technique to study and describe a physical or natural law. Oresme plotted velocity against time on the graph. Although junior high students do this every day in the contemporary world, such leaps in human intuition as conducted by these Christian pastors and monks were seismic at the time. It would be another 300 years before another Christian, Isaac Newton, developed calculus—a method to determine the area under a curve of a given function, and the gradient of the function to calculate velocities and distances on the same graph.

And so, England's Merton College, Oxford took the forefront in the first of three scientific revolutions in the Western world. The world would have to wait for a theological Reformation and a spiritual awakening to receive further significant developments in science and technology. Before that came the wayward meanderings of an apostate Renaissance and its infatuation with astrology and alchemy (at least partially inspired by Islamic mystics).

FIGHTING OFF THE PSEUDO-SCIENCE OF ASTROLOGY & ALCHEMY

> Stand now with thine enchantments, and with the multitude of thy sorceries, wherein thou hast laboured from thy youth; if so be thou shalt be able to profit, if so be thou mayest prevail. Thou art wearied in the multitude of thy counsels. Let now the astrologers, the stargazers, the monthly prognosticators, stand up, and save thee from these things that shall come upon thee. Behold, they shall be as stubble; the fire shall burn them; they shall not deliver themselves from the power of the flame: there shall not be a coal to warm at, nor fire to sit before it. (Isaiah 47:12-14)

As far back as 700 BC, the Scriptures warned of astrology. The Christian church frowned on the practice from the outset. Yet, century upon century, the burnt fool's bandaged finger goes "wobbling back to the fire." Man gravitates to seeking power and secret knowledge (especially in *future-telling*) obtained from within the natural world and the human mind, with God entirely removed from the equation. For some years during the medieval period, only a thin line remained between astrology and astronomy, but generally the church held the distinction. Augustine of Hippo unequivocally rejected astrology, concluding his discussion on the subject in *City of God* in this way:

> Considering all this, the belief is justified that when astrologers miraculously give true replies, as they often do, this is due to the furtive prompting of evil spirits, whose aim is to plant in the minds of men these harmful beliefs about the control of destiny by the stars, and to confirm them. It is not due to any art of observing and studying the horoscope, for no such art exists.[16]

Astrology is based on the wrong metaphysic (view of reality) verging on fatalism and naturalism—as opposed to a sovereign God who rules over all things in the universe at His own discretion. Thomas Aquinas (1225-1274) agreed with Augustine, that "if anyone attempts from the stars to foretell future contingent or chance events, or to know with certitude the future activities of men, he is acting under a false and groundless presupposition, and opening himself to the intrusion of diabolic powers." Aquinas distinguished real science from astrology, further explaining that, "if a scientist uses his astronomic observation to forecast future events which are actually determined by physical laws, for instance, drought and rainfall, and so forth, then this is neither superstitious nor sinful."[17] Among the first of the medieval astrologers, one Cecco d'Ascoli (c. 1269-1327), went so far as to say events on earth were absolutely determined by the stars. When he doubled down, and connected the death of Christ to the position of the stars, the church responded. Ascoli was fined and forbidden from continuing his astrological business. The spiritual pull was too strong upon him, however, and he returned to the work. He was executed on September

16, 1327. The church had no tolerance for witchcraft or astrology. Science yes, astrology no. Only God could determine the future or tell the future with perfect certainty. To control every contingency and forecast every action to make a certain future condition is an infinite impossibility for any part of the created sphere, whether that be star, demon, or otherwise.

SCIENTISM—THE WORLDVIEW BATTLE BEGINS

The idols of the heathen are silver and gold, the work of men's hands. They have mouths, but they speak not; eyes have they, but they see not; They have ears, but they hear not; neither is there any breath in their mouths. They that make them are like unto them: so is every one that trusteth in them. (Psalm 135:15-18)

By the turn of the 13th Century, both Jews and Muslims were working hard to make room for Aristotle's naturalistic theories in Western thought. Averroes of Spain (1126-1198) and Maimonides of Spain (1135-1204) quickly adopted a humanist synthesis into their respective religious frameworks. Later, Thomas Aquinas followed suit. Aquinas' second stint at the University of Paris occurred between 1265 and 1268, where he began drawing a hard and fast line between sacred knowledge and that knowledge built up on human reason. Siger of Brabant entered the same university in 1266 and eagerly adopted Aristotle's foundational beliefs that matter was eternal and humans lacked eternal souls—thus introducing the naturalist, materialist worldview to the Christian West. Siger tried to keep his feet in both camps—Scripture and Aristotle—but the heterodoxy proved too much for the Bishop of the Parisian Church. Stephen Tempier produced a writ of 219 condemnations against Siger, chief of which was his thesis that God could be restricted by natural laws or that "God cannot do anything that is naturally impossible." This was the beginning of an enormous, 800-year tug-of-war between the naturalistic worldview and the Christian worldview, which holds to the very "godness" of God—His absolute sovereignty over His creatures and all their actions. The church's condemnation of Siger slowed the humanist, materialist view of scientism, while at the same time none of this discouraged investigation into the Creator's designs.

Such is the history of science. God-fearing Christians focused on the right things, while man-centered humanists were always caught in unprofitable digressions and intellectual cul-de-sacs. With the Italian Renaissance came the counter-productive diversions from true science and dominion work. The lapsed Christian world lurched into dabbling with magic, astrology, and the occult. A neo-pagan magician reintroduced Plato's writings, and one of his chief devotees, Gemistus Pletho (c. 1355-1452), fancied himself a "sun worshiper and a champion of paganism." Marsilio Ficino (1433-1499) became infatuated with an Egyptian seer, Hermes Trismegistus, and sought magical power to harness the sun and stars. Regrettably, in his spare time, Ficino translated the Platonic dialogues and produced his own Platonic theology called *Theologia platonica*. It was Christian-humanist synthesis at its worst and produced no good fruit. Here was the resuscitation of pagan occult, sprinkled with a little Platonic holy water for academic and ecclesiastical acceptance. As one historian put it, "magic now went mainstream. It was no longer the preserve of strange old women and renegade priests. Couched in the elegant Latin of the humanists, the Hermetic corpus was a license to reinvent astrology, alchemy, and other forms of occult knowledge."[18] This was the contribution of the humanist Renaissance, not Christianity.

The tentacles of the astrology beast extended well into the 16th Century, affecting the Roman Catholic mathematician Jerome Cardan, who assisted in developing the field of algebra. He referred to astrology as "the most lofty of the branches of knowledge because it deals with celestial things and with the future."[19] Cardan worked on "the horoscope of Christ," which got him in trouble with the church authorities (although he was never convicted).

Post-Christian historians have attempted to discern or to drive a wedge between the medieval church and science. This is nothing but a "pure fabrication," as Rodney Stark puts it. Some point to the execution of Giordano Bruno as an example of the ecclesiastical rejection of science. Bruno (1543-1600), however, was hardly a serious scientist; more a Hermetic sorcerer and a primordial science fiction novelist theorizing multiple universes. He was burned at the stake by order of the Inquisition and later considered a martyr of scientism or modern science-fiction cults.

PROTESTANTISM & THE SCIENTIFIC REVOLUTION

> Through faith we understand that the worlds were framed by the word of God, so that things which are seen were not made of things which do appear. (Hebrews 11:3)

The biblical doctrine of creation won out over the naturalist worldview of Aristotle in the scientific revolution taking place before and after the Reformation. Helpfully Reformation thinkers introduced a more realistic, pessimistic, and humble view of post-lapsarian human reason. The German reformer Martin Luther, for example, stated that, "it is impossible that nature could be understood by human reason after the fall of Adam."[20] John Calvin added that, by the Fall into sin, "the reason of our mind, wherever it may turn, is miserably subject to vanity."[21] The Scriptures also describe the mind of natural man as fundamentally perverted by the Fall.

> Walk not as other Gentiles walk, in the vanity of their mind, having the understanding darkened, being alienated from the life of God through the ignorance that is in them, because of the blindness of their heart... (Ephesians 4:17-18)

Lie not one to another, seeing that ye have put off the old man with his deeds; and have put on the new man, which is renewed in knowledge after the image of him that created him... (Colossians 3:9-10)

Given that man's mind had been so corrupted by the Fall, Protestants concluded this must include Aristotle's mind as well—extending to his worldview, categories, and conclusions. This drove Protestant science to a humbler reliance upon experimentation and repeatability rather than resting on the dubious conclusions of pagan philosophy. Roger Bacon had already outlined the basics of a Christian method of science known to this day as "the scientific method." He recommended testing and repetition, including observation, hypothesis, experimentation, and independent verification. Put in the modern vernacular used by the engineering community: "In God we trust. All others bring data." Theories of fallen human minds call for repeated observation, independent corroboration, and augmentation to assist the limitation of human sense. Extraordinary efforts were expended for developing adequate instrumentation to aid in observation, such as telescopes and microscopes.

Christians more than anyone had every reason to study God's world and to categorize the orders of His creation. After all, this was the command at creation: "Be fruitful and multiply; fill the earth and subdue it; have dominion over the fish of the sea, over the birds of the air, and over every living thing that moves on the earth" (Gen. 1:28). Adam took the task seriously and immediately provided names or categories for the animals.

Luther urged Christians to fulfill the creation mandate as an honorable endeavor—to work and discover for the glory of God. The Christian life must not consist of withdrawal from the physical world into a life of contemplation. It is meant to be lived in the physical world, where God's resources are used for the betterment of man's existence. Luther encouraged the believer to "use" these resources, "to build, to buy, to have dealings and hold intercourse with his fellows, to join them in all temporal affairs."[22]

Protestant Christians increasingly realized that God could be glorified in all of life, including scientific investigation. Johannes Kepler testified to his own motives: "I wished to be a theologian; for a long time I was troubled, but now see how God is also praised through my work in astronomy."[23] If the world were a "temple of God," Kepler concluded that a scientist serves as "the priest."[24]

Besides this, the Christian knows God's creation will be discoverable. He is motivated to the discovery process by the high anticipation of learning more about the Creator and rejoicing in His works. To the degree that man's conception of God is restored in his mind, he begins to notice the character of God in His works and to search for more out of it. The Christian believer begins to realize the genius, order, intentionality, wisdom, and discoverability of the world he lives in. As the early Christian discoverers put it, "nature was a book meant to be read." Thus the Christian mind is "renewed in knowledge according to the image of Him who created him" (Col. 3:10), rendering the believer much more useful in thinking God's thoughts after Him and "reverse engineering" His creation, as it were.

> The works of the LORD are great, sought out of all them that have pleasure therein. (Psalm 111:2)

Reality or the right conception of it fades in the minds of those who cannot accept God or those who remain doubtful concerning the "I Am"—the ultimate and absolute Existence. But Christians who are committed to a belief in the almighty, sovereign Creator, to His worship, and to His total governance over all are more likely to believe in the reality and discoverability of a physical creation.

> It is the glory of God to conceal a thing: but the honour of kings is to search out a matter. The heaven for height, and the earth for depth,

and the heart of kings is unsearchable. Take away the dross from the silver, and there shall come forth a vessel for the finer. (Proverbs 25:2-4)

Only in a Christian framework could science progress for still more reasons. Unlike other religious outlooks, the Christian takes as the most fundamental presupposition that God is good. Thus, if He would have us subdue the earth, it must be subdue-able. If it is the honor of kings to find out the things He has hidden in the world, these things must be discoverable to His glory and for our benefit. Moreover, we learn from 1 Corinthians 14:33 that God is not "the author of confusion." There is order and regulation in creation—a unity in the diversity of God's nature and His work. After all, He promised, "While the earth remains, seedtime and harvest, cold and heat, winter and summer, and day and night shall not cease" (Gen. 8:22). Scientific induction relies on the assumption of the regularity of nature, and only the Christian worldview can guarantee this paradigm. In a chance universe where all is governed by unintentional chaos or chance, how could a scientist hold to the assumption that the same natural laws that operate today will still be in operation tomorrow? Only by an incorrigible adherence to an internally consistent Christian paradigm of thinking can scientific endeavor make any concerted, sustainable progress.

O LORD, our Lord, how excellent is Your name in all the earth, who have set Your glory above the heavens! Out of the mouth of babes and nursing infants You have ordained strength, because of Your enemies, that You may silence the enemy and the avenger. When I consider Your heavens, the work of Your fingers, the moon and the stars, which You have ordained, what is man that You are mindful of him, and the son of man that You visit him? For You have made him a little lower than the angels, and You have crowned him with glory and honor. You have made him to have dominion over the works of Your hands; You have put all things under his feet, all sheep and oxen—even the beasts of the field, the birds of the air, and the fish of the sea that pass through the paths of the seas. O LORD, our Lord, how excellent is Your name in all the earth! (Psalm 8)

A right view of God and a right relative view of man in reference to God are crucial for right knowledge. The eighth psalm provides this for the Christian. The dignity of man is established by God, as is his place in creation. The psalm includes man's position in the universe between two doxologies expressing God's ultimate glory and praise. Given this position of dignity, man then is held responsible for taking dominion over the lower creation as God's vice-regent.

The pagan mind couldn't conceive of a Creator like this. Stark comments that, "none of the traditional Greek gods would have been capable of such a creation."[25] The eastern worldview also placed the physical world in the realm of "maya" or non-existence. Why would anyone want to explore what doesn't exist?

Having researched the biographies of fifty-two key scientists who birthed the second and most prolific scientific revolution, Stark found that all but one were professing Christians. Sixty percent were characterized "devout," and 35% were "conventionally religious."[26] Half were Protestant and half Catholic. Only one skeptic appeared in the crowd, defined as one who did not believe the world to be the work of a personal God. The collection of fifty-two "star" scientists lived between 1543 and 1680 and were responsible for the development of modern mathematics, physics, astronomy, biology, chemistry, and physiology.

Dr. Henry Morris listed forty-two modern scientific and mathematical disciplines which gave foundation for the hard sciences and modern technology—all developed by "Bible-believing scientists."[27] Where would the world be without bacteriology (Louis Pasteur), calculus (Isaac Newton), chemistry (Robert Boyle), computer science (Charles Babbage), dynamics (Isaac Newton), electrodynamics (James Clerk Maxwell), electromagnetics (Michael Faraday), electronics

(Ambrose Fleming), energetics and thermodynamics (Lord Kelvin), fluid mechanics (George Stokes), gas dynamics (Robert Boyle), genetics (Gregor Mendel), isotopic chemistry (William Ramsay), physical astronomy (Johannes Kepler), reversible thermodynamics (James Joule), statistical thermodynamics (James Clerk Maxwell), and systematic biology (Carolus Linnaeus)?

Every modern technological development and engineering field is inextricably linked to these "hard sciences." There would be no aeronautical engineering without Isaac Newton. Nor would there be any mechanical engineering, electrical engineering, civil engineering, chemical engineering, industrial engineering, or petroleum engineering without Isaac Newton, Robert Boyle, James Clerk Maxwell, Lord Kelvin, George Stokes, Michael Faraday, and James Joule—all devout Christians. There would be no refrigerators, ovens, washers and dryers, toasters, blenders, HVAC systems, computers, electronic devices, automobiles, trains, and airplanes without these scientific foundations laid by Christians.

The doxologies of the great scientists from this era are inspiring in themselves. Assembled into one place, such confessions could provide a helpful devotional aid for the pious. Robert Boyle found the ultimate purpose for his investigations of the universe in worship: "When, in a word, by the help of anatomical knives, and the light of chymical furnaces, I study the book of nature,...I find myself oftentimes reduced to exclaim with the Psalmist, 'How manifold are Thy works, O Lord! in wisdom hast Thou made them all!'"[28] Elsewhere, Boyle explained the chief motive behind practicing science (as a Christian). Such a statement represents the heartbeat of the entire scientific revolution following the Reformation:

> There are no men that seem to me to have nobler and sublimer aims, than those to which a true Christian is encouraged; since he aspires to no less things than to please and glorify God; to promote the good of

mankind and to improve, as far as is possible, his personal excellencies in this life; and to secure to himself for ever a glorious and happy condition in the next.[29]

After all his studies, the most famous scientist in history, Isaac Newton, concluded: "This most beautiful system of the sun, planets and comets, could only proceed from the counsel and dominion of an intelligent and powerful Being...This Being governs all things, not as the soul of the world, but as Lord over all; and on account of his dominion he is wont to be called Lord God...or Universal Ruler."[30]

The third of the great revolutions in the development of Western science occurred in the mid 19th Century, again spawned by devoted Christians—James Clerk Maxwell (1831-1879) and Michael Faraday (1791-1867). Science historians Nancy Forbes and Basil Mahon attempt an assessment of the enormous contribution of these men to the science and technology of our world: "It is almost impossible to overstate the scale of Faraday and Maxwell's achievement in bringing the concept of electromagnetic field into human thought. It united electricity, magnetism, and light into a single, compact theory; changed our way of life by bringing us radio, television, radar, satellite navigation, and mobile phones; inspired Einstein's special theory of relativity..."[31] The preeminent astrophysicist of the 20th Century, Albert Einstein, said the two scientists had opened up a new epoch in human knowledge about the universe, and told the world, "I stood on Maxwell's shoulders."[32] And, "There would be no modern physics without Maxwell's electromagnetic equations: I owe more to Maxwell than to anyone."[33]

Once again, the method of science conducted by Maxwell and Faraday centered on experiment, not theory—humility and worship of God, not pride. Historians Forbes and Mahon, wrap up their treatment of this final, paradigm-setting breakthrough in science with this summary of Maxwell and Faraday's approach: "The dialogue between experiment and theory that they conducted was one of the most fertile ever to occur in science, and it set a priceless precedent for twentieth-Century physics."[34]

Above all, James Clerk Maxwell lived and worked in the fear of God as clearly evidenced by His diary entries and prayers. This excerpt reveals a definitive Christian outlook, including two purposes for which a Christian engages in scientific inquiry:

> Almighty God, Who hast created man in Thine own image, and made him a living soul that he might seek after Thee, and have dominion over Thy creatures, teach us to study the works of Thy hands, that we may subdue the earth to our use, and strengthen the reason for Thy service.[35]

Michael Faraday, the singularly-gifted genius who discovered the semiconductor, (to whom all people living owe a debt for every computer and almost every piece of electronic equipment in the world), plainly stated that, "The book of nature which we have to read is written by the finger of God."[36] Faraday was raised in an extremely poor home, and his family was associated with an evangelical group called the Sandemanians. Writing to a friend in 1861, he urged the man to trust in Christ, "Since peace alone is the gift of God; and since it is He who gives it, why should we be afraid? His unspeakable gift in His beloved Son is the ground of no doubtful hope."[37] Toward the end of his life, a friend asked him what he thought his occupation would be in heaven. Faraday replied, "I shall be with Christ and that's enough for me."

THE ROOT SOURCE OF ALL SCIENTIFIC SUCCESS

> And when thy herds and thy flocks multiply, and thy silver and thy gold is multiplied, and all that thou hast is multiplied...And thou say in thine heart, My power and the might of mine hand hath gotten

me this wealth. But thou shalt remember the LORD thy God: for it is he that giveth thee power to get wealth, that he may establish his covenant which he sware unto thy fathers, as it is this day. And it shall be, if thou do at all forget the LORD thy God, and walk after other gods, and serve them, and worship them, I testify against you this day that ye shall surely perish. As the nations which the LORD destroyeth before your face, so shall ye perish; because ye would not be obedient unto the voice of the LORD your God. (Deuteronomy 8:13,17-20)

The Christian finds the ultimate reason for every success in scientific endeavor in God's goodness and common grace. Every good gift given by science and technology has enabled modern nations "to get wealth," and this comes from above. . . from "the Father of lights." (James 1:17). Significant scientific breakthroughs do not come easily, or often. We call it genius, but where might these flashes of inspiration come from? They cannot but proceed from an all-wise, good, and sovereign God who gives gifts to men. But when successful, powerful, and proud men forget God, the source of these gifts, they will begin to boast that, "My power and might has gotten me this wealth." In a nutshell, this scriptural passage tells the sad story of the rise and fall of science in the West.

What a severe shift occurred in the Western mind following Faraday's and Maxwell's deaths, and the completion of a 500-year, Christian-led scientific revolution! The American National Academy of Sciences membership consisted of 93% self-described atheists in 2010.[38] Only 33% of scientists claimed the remotest belief in God–a commitment held by 83% of the general population.[39] The religion of science became the religion of Christian skepticism. Christians who believed the Bible (especially the biblical account concerning origins) became the subjects of unrelenting mockery and scorn by the scientific and higher education communities. At this juncture, those Christian scientists from previous centuries who made up the heritage and foundations of Western science would have been similarly excoriated by these modern fools for their belief in the Genesis creation account and their commitment to the glory of the Creator.

Over 99% of contemporary universities taught the pseudo-science of macro-evolution[40]—the completely fantastical idea that inanimate matter turned into a human being over a period of four billion years by indeterminate, random chance. The theory was a mathematical impossibility. The pseudo-scientists offered no mechanism for such a farfetched idea except a meaningless non-mechanism like "punctuated equilibrium" or, as one leading atheist evolutionist suggested, an alien spaceship introducing life to the earth (another non-explanatory explanation). The process was never observed and never repeated in a laboratory, and the "missing links" in the fossil records were still missing after two hundred years of fruitless search.

Modern science was a return to the deification of theory in the mind of man, and a rejection of verification and experimentation. The proud humanist was too enamored with his own cheap hypothesis to bother with verification, and a science that would yield meaningful and practical value.

THE CHRISTIAN REVOLUTION IN THE DEVELOPMENT OF ASTRONOMY & PHYSICS

As already set forth, the idea that the church through history was at war with science is a pure fabrication. Galileo Galilei (1564-1642) was not persecuted for his scientific views, but rather censured because of his repudiation of the Scriptures in favor of an overweening confidence in the autonomous mind of man. When questioned about the usefulness of the Bible in regard to scientific research, Galileo's response elicited grave concerns from church authorities. "Within the universe of physics, mathematics are superior to the Bible,"[41] he said. The church wasn't rejecting three hundred years of scientific investigations into the universe. More troubling was Galileo's arrogant confidence in the ability of the fallen mind of man to discover truth unaided by Scripture. Historian and theologian Jean-Marc Berthoud concludes of Galileo, "The Bible at the outset was excluded from his scientific system."[42]

Christianity was never opposed to true science. From Augustine and Cassiodorus through the Middle Ages, Christians always rejected astrology, not astronomy. Well before Copernicus entered the scene, Nicole Oresme (1325-1382), pastor and rector at the University of Paris, had pretty well established the point that the earth turns on an axis in reference to a stationary light source (the sun) to produce sunset and sunrise each day. Nicholas of Cusa (1401-1464) postulated that the globe moved through space. Nicholas Copernicus (1473-1543) was the first to provide the heliocentric model, complete with mathematical calculations, although he failed to note the elliptical pattern of the revolutions. Johannes Kepler (1571-1630), a German Lutheran, would get it right with his description of the elliptical orbit. Finally, Isaac Newton (1642-1727) would render the right mathematical calculations for the regular movement of these heavenly bodies. None of this constituted a "Copernican Revolution," however. It was a constant, slow but steady development of thought over a period of 400 years. The formation of modern astronomy came by a team of Christian thinkers and observers. Rodney Stark summarizes: "the scholars involved in this long process were not rebel secularists. Not only were they devout Christians; they all were priests or monks—even bishops and cardinals."[43] The separation of church and science was a revisionist imposition placed upon history by biased historians who didn't care very much for Christ or His people.

Astronomy turned out to be only mildly helpful for practical dominion over the earth, but not nearly as much as might be expected from the $1.17 trillion spent on space exploration during the last half of the 20th Century. Rejecting God and the Christian worldview entirely, the National Aeronautics and Space Administration (NASA) explicitly stated the purpose of its exploration to be to "address fundamental questions about the history of the Earth, the solar system and the universe—and about our place in them."[44] There was little practical reason for such taxpayer-funded expense unless one assumes we live in a godless universe where man must find his own way in the chaos of indeterminism. Satellites have been helpful for telecommunications and global positioning, but space mining, searching for extraterrestrial life, and colonizing other planets were fruitless diversions.

THE HUMANIST ENLIGHTENMENT— A WORLDVIEW SHIFT

O Israel, return unto the LORD thy God; for thou hast fallen by thine iniquity. Take with you words, and turn to the LORD: say unto him, Take away all iniquity, and receive us graciously: so will we render the calves of our lips. Asshur shall not save us; we will not ride upon horses: neither will we say any more to the work of our hands, Ye are our gods: for in thee the fatherless findeth mercy. (Hosea 14:1-3)

The humanist Enlightenment of the 1700s left the world with a new religion, complete with a new plan of salvation for mankind, a new temple (the university), and new high priests—or, better, witchdoctors (scientists). Modern man came to trust in the oracles brought down by the science class above all else. Man's problem or "sin" (using religious language) was redefined as wrong social influences, psychoses and neuroses, ignorance, disease, pollution, and economic decline. And the saviors became psychiatrists, sociologists, social planners, evolutionists, philosopher-educators, technologists, sexologists, biologists, geneticists, environmentalists, political scientists, and economists—scientists all. These were Plato's philosopher-kings empowered by democracy—the combination of the total state and the techno-state.

It was the ultimate humanist alliance of technologists and political power.

The most radical change, coming into the Western mind through the scientific revolution was foundational and epistemological (covered in detail in chapter two of this volume). In the end, skeptics like David Hume undermined empirical thinking, denying it could provide any certainty concerning ultimate questions. Kant attempted a rescue, but the basis for any certain knowledge continued to erode. Absolute values, purpose, social objectives, and truth disappeared. Nonetheless, the masses seemed content to trust the white-coated scientists with their thin hypotheses and their stated probabilities to tell them what to do.

EMPIRICISM IN THE CHURCH

Jesus saith unto him, Thomas, because thou hast seen me, thou hast believed: blessed are they that have not seen, and yet have believed. (John 20:29)

The humanist Enlightenment begins with a lapse of faith. Well before Locke and Rousseau appeared on the scene, Protestants and Puritans were calling for empirical natural evidence to prove the existence of the supernatural. In 1666, Joseph Glanvill, fellow of the Royal Society, published his tome *Sadducismus Triumphatus* in a last-ditch attempt to prove the existence of the supernatural by empirical analysis of witchcraft and the demonic paranormal. At the point where belief in the supernatural (i.e. God's existence) hinges on the evidence of demonic existence, the faith has pretty much died. At the least, this sort of pitiful apologetic was indicative of the force of a humanist empiricism upon the minds of professing Christians. As the thinking played out, this reasoning would end with a logical impossibility: "If you cannot observe God, the Invisible and the Supernatural, then the invisible must not exist." Glanville insisted that "Reason and Reason alone" must prove the doctrines of religion. At last, four hundred years after Aquinas had separated sacred knowledge from that knowledge built up on human reason, sacred doctrine had become the handmaiden of human reason and the casualty of empirical science.

This lapse in faith certainly affected the last of the American Puritans as they obsessed over visitations from angels and sought direct communications with the spirit world. Increase Mather published *Angelographia* (1696) in an empirical attempt to "defend the very existence of the spiritual world" against the relentless attacks of "secularism and atheism."[45] Jesus told his disciples, "Blessed are those who have not seen and yet believe" (John 20:29), but the Enlightenment empiricists weren't seeking the blessing. Later in the 18th Century, this empirical worldview carried over to the ministry of Jonathan Edwards and others who would put greater value upon immediate spiritual experientialism in religion. Somehow, a religious experience with certain physical manifestations was thought to prove the supernatural and render authenticity to the faith. Paul's experience on the Damascus Road came to be seen as the essence of the Christian faith. Creedalism, daily obedience to God, abiding in Christ, walking with Christ, and church involvement were downplayed. "Seeing is believing" turned into "experiencing is believing" for Christians caught up in the empiricism of the day. They failed to realize that the spiritual cannot easily be portrayed in the physical and emotional world. This misconception would continue to plague evangelical Christianity in America for centuries.

THE RELIGION OF SCIENTISM

What developed out of the Enlightenment was the new religion of scientism. There is a difference between science and scientism. Science is a useful tool with its limitations. But scientism is a religion or a worldview, pretending to answer the ultimate questions and, more importantly, subvert the Christian faith. The first and primary task of this new religion of scientism was to theorize a universe independent of God. The doubtful and skeptical among the Christian world set themselves to describe this new world with new-found relish. Once again, this new "science" was more interested in the theory than observation and practice.

Christian philosopher J. P. Moreland defined modern scientism as "the view that the hard sciences—like physics, chemistry, biology, astronomy—provide the only genuine knowledge of reality...this scientific knowledge is vastly superior to what we can know from any other discipline."[46] Tom Sorrell described this epistemological perspective as "the belief that science (especially natural science), is... the most valuable part of human learning...the most authoritative, or serious, or beneficial."[47] However, scientism is dishonest. Science can offer no certainty, and all scientific data is interpreted through a worldview grid of secretive assumptions. All true science must presuppose certain truths already revealed by God, but the high priests of scientism would not want to admit this. Science must assume certain ethical values or objectives to function. For example, science assumes that laws governing mathematics and logic exist. Scientists must also assume there is an objective world to explore, as well as some law of regularity governing the natural world. To disprove scientism and to humble its adherents, J. P. Moreland helpfully provided a list of things science cannot explain: the origin of the universe, the origin of the fundamental laws of nature, the extreme fine-tuning of the universe, the origin of consciousness, and the existence of moral, rational, and aesthetic objective laws[48]—all of which are easily explained by the Christian worldview.

> Seest thou a man wise in his own conceit?
> There is more hope of a fool than of him. (Proverbs 26:12)

This new science operates by a robust hubris, a mass-popularization of its hypotheses (on matters like evolution), and an incipient inability to moderate the dogmatism with which it defends its positions. Recent Nobel Prize recipient Francois Jacob described this new paradigm for science:

> Contrary to what I once thought, scientific progress did not consist simply in observing, in accumulating experimental facts and drawing up a theory from them. It began with the invention of a possible world, or a fragment thereof, which was then compared by experimentation with the real world. And it was this constant dialogue between imagination and experiment that allowed one to form an increasingly fine-grained conception of what is called reality.[49]

THE "SCIENCE" OF CHARLES DARWIN

Charles Darwin takes the place as the most influential "scientist" of the humanist age, but not because he discovered the laws of motion, the gravitational constant, the ideal gas law equation, the smallpox vaccine, or any other useful science. His science consisted of a highly tenuous, unproven hypothesis. Yet, serious scientific sources would still refer to it as among "the best substantiated theories in the history of science." Darwin proposed that a single cell or simple organism evolved into the complexity of life seen today by a mechanism of genetic mutations and natural selection. The hypothesis suggested that new species developed by random mutations, and the survival of the better mutants was a function of adaptability to its environment (and its ability to reproduce).

Darwin hoped the fossil record would substantiate his hypothesis by offering thousands of intermediate forms, but 150 years of paleontology failed to yield the data. The speciation process was never observed and never substantiated in a laboratory. For forty years, Richard Lenski, an evolutionary biologist at Michigan State University, experimented with Darwin's theory in a laboratory hoping to develop new species from E-coli bacteria. To his credit, the scientist patiently cultured 60,000 generations of the germ, equivalent to 1,200,000 years of human evolution, hoping to find an advanced mutation. None of the twelve cultures tested gained any resistance to antibiotics, and this has been referred to as "the industry's longest evolution experiment dead end."

Though scientists have been able to increase the number of chromosomes in a flowering plant for example, evolutionary biologist Douglas Futuyma had to admit that such experiments do not "confer major new morphological characteristics...[and] does not cause the evolution of new genera" necessary to validate Darwin's hypothesis of the evolution of species.[50]

THE EVOLUTION & RACIST CONNECTION

> Then Peter opened his mouth, and said, Of a truth I perceive that God is no respecter of persons: but in every nation he that feareth him, and worketh righteousness, is accepted with him. (Acts 10:34-35)

Darwin's evolutionary theories were largely motivated by both atheist and racist worldviews completely antithetical to biblical Christianity. Modern racism and evolutionary constructs for human origins date back to the 18th-Century French Enlightenment. While Christians like Robert Boyle held to the biblical position that all humans were members of a single race descending from Adam and Eve, the French philosopher Voltaire (1694-1778) rejected a single human bloodline. These were the dangerous roots of the racist genocides which proceeded in the 20th Century. Voltaire's tone comes across sarcastic and sinister in his writings:

> It is a serious question among [Europeans] whether the Africans are descended from monkeys or whether the monkeys come from them.

> Our wise men have said that man was created in the image of God.
> Now here is a lovely image of the Divine Maker: a flat and black nose
> with little or hardly any intelligence.[51]

Racism and "white supremacy" dripped from the "enlightened" philosopher. Africans, Voltaire adds, have "only a few more ideas than animals, and only more facility to express them."Another Enlightenment "scientist," Lord Kames of Scotland (1696-1782), propounded the theory that God made different races of men in different geographical locations around the world. A German "scientist," Christoph Meiners (1747–1810), went further, claiming that some races rated better than others—comparing the "beautiful white race" with the "ugly black race." Such were the "Enlightenment" ideas which set the tone for Charles Darwin's theory in the post-Christian age. Known as the father of paleontology, Georges Cuvier was similarly biased by racism in his own work, claiming that, "The white race...[is] the most beautiful of all,...superior to others by its genius, courage, and activity."[52] It was this new evolutionary scientism and its attendant eugenicist theories that led to a terribly ill-conceived program of social engineering and two world wars for the 20th Century.

> Every one that is proud in heart is an abomination to the LORD:
> Though hand join in hand, he shall not be unpunished. (Proverbs
> 16:5)

CHARLES DARWIN & THE FALL

While the majority opinion in the West views Charles Darwin as the apex of Western science, history will remember him to be the Achilles heel—the beginning of the end of science in the West.

Returning to the question raised about astrology and alchemy in previous centuries once more, was the work of Charles Darwin useful at all? Or was it entirely counterproductive to true dominion work, real science, and genuinely helpful technology? Darwin's work in eugenics, origins, and genetics was highly subject to critique from the beginning. Isaac Newton's physics was helpful, and so was Robert Boyle's chemistry. There are literally hundreds of thousands of helpful inventions, technical aids and systems, medical treatments, and so on that follow from these scientists. But what good has come from Charles Darwin's theory of natural selection? How has this benefited mankind?

Some point to Darwin's contributions in the field of genetics, but this also is highly questionable. The side effects or long-term usefulness of the mRNA genetic vaccines are entirely unknown. The use of aborted fetuses to create certain vaccination lines, animal and human cloning, and human genome editing, are of questionable value and ethically problematic. The first GMO-grown salmon was released into the market for human consumption in 2020.[53] The jury is still out on the revolution in genetically-modified crops and organisms in agriculture. To what extent does man's manipulation of God's original design introduce complications into the ecosystems and human health? The pride of man in scientific work knew no bounds in the 20th and 21st centuries. Evidently, the market wasn't trusting the new genetics much, with the organic foods industry increasing from $15 billion per year to $100 billion per year between 1999 and 2018.

Of note also, Charles Darwin's contributions to the field of genetics were far less impressive than his contemporary, Gregor Mendel's (1822-1884). Darwin might have identified the genetic range of mutation in a species, but he was unable to identify "the mechanism of inheritance." Mendel, on the other hand, was less interested in theorizing on origins and much more focused upon solving "the most difficult problem in 19th Century biology" by "combining rigorous genetic experiments with quantitative, probabilistic predictions about their expected outcomes: in other words, using biological data to test a quantitative hypothesis."[54]

Darwin's worldview was so dependent upon a naturalistic hypothesis he so wanted to be true that he would not have risked investigation that could have disproven it. Besides, such a wide-sweeping and tenuous hypothesis would have taken at least 200 years of further investigation and testing (best case), to identify a mechanism with any degree of certainty. Obviously, he didn't have time for that. He was hoping for a mechanism by which genetic information might be added to organisms through succeeding generations. He had theorized that species could evolve into other species. Meanwhile by careful experimentations in his gardens, Mendel actually found out that individual characteristics within a species remained constant. The genetic information contained in the parents' genes might remain recessive for generations and then reappear, but genetic variations were limited within the species or the animal "kind." Each generation is produced by a reshuffling or "recombination" of genes already present. Mendel's findings would prove devastating to Darwin's farfetched hypothesis of evolution by natural selection.

Largely because of Darwin's overwhelming popularity, Mendel's real contributions to science were ignored until twenty years after his death in 1884. Mendel's belief in Christ was clearly attested to in a sermon probably preached in his later years (on Easter):

> As expected of pious Christians, the joy of victory is heard in the midst of an unjust world; victory and not disparagement, insult, persecution. With the day of the victory of Christ, Easter, the bonds are broken, death and sin laid [on Him], and the Redeemer of mankind rises strongly the human race from night time and fetters, in blessed heights ...[55]

In another sermon, Mendel drew a distinction between those who believe in Christ and infidels:

[After His resurrection] Jesus let the infidels and Jews aside, he appeared only to the chosen apostles, he was concerned only with the faithful believers. To these he taught, rebuked, and sanctified, in order to perfect them to perfect the saints. This not only made sin and death be taken away from us, but by the resurrection of the Son of God grace was also obtained.[56]

These are not the words of a skeptic, an atheist, or an agnostic. On the other hand, three years before he died, Darwin confessed in a letter to John Fordyce: "I think that generally (& more and more so as I grow older) but not always, that an agnostic would be the most correct description of my state of mind."[57]

REAL SCIENCE, USEFUL SCIENCE— GEORGE WASHINGTON CARVER[59]

Surely I am more brutish than any man, And have not the understanding of a man... There be three things which are too wonderful for me, yea, four which I know not... (Proverbs 30:2, 18)

Born a slave in Diamond, Missouri and starting out in life with nothing to his name, George Washington Carver (c. 1864-1943) carried on the vision of real Christian-based science well into the 20th Century. Mainly, his work focused on the practical and ever-useful field of agriculture. Considered idiosyncratic to the extreme, Carver maintained a robust spiritual life, lived and studied to give God the glory, and treated his students at Tuskegee Institute as more-or-less disciples with whom he would consummately share Scripture. Few scientists have ever enjoyed God's works of nature as much as George Washington Carver did. In many ways, he was the ideal Christian scientist and artist, utterly enamored by God's works—the beauty, goodness, usefulness, wisdom, and majesty reflected in them. Carver looked on nature as "unlimited broadcasting stations, through which

God speaks to us every day, every hour and every moment of our lives." At the same time, his science was imminently useful especially to cotton farmers in the South. He is best known for his research on the peanut, inventing 265 uses for the legume and 118 uses for sweet potatoes. Such useful science yielded hundreds of products for common use, including cosmetics, various household products, paints, glues, foods, beverages, and medicines. [58]

George Washington Carver's view of science was a clear affront to the contemporary approach. His national popularity took a hit on November 1924, as he addressed a crowd at the Marble Collegiate Church in New York City. In his simple style, Carver explained his philosophy of science: "God is going to reveal things to us that He never revealed before if we put our Hand in His…Without God to draw aside the curtain I would be helpless."[59] Forthwith, *The New York Times* published an article chastising the scientist for his piety, "Men of Science Never Talk That Way." The writer accused Carver of demonstrating "a complete lack of the scientific spirit."[60] The editorial went on to criticize Christianity, setting a divide between modern science and faith. Shortly thereafter, George wrote an article in response to the attack. He told the world, "I thoroughly understand that there are scientists to whom the world is merely the result of chemical forces or material electrons. I do not belong to this class."[61] He explained that scientific discovery was a combination of information and divine inspiration, quoting from Galatians 1:12, "For I neither received it from man, nor was I taught it, but it came through the revelation of Jesus Christ."

Unlike so many academics and scientists who give way to pride— as if they had obtained the knowledge of the universe by their own wisdom—George Washington Carver always maintained a humble approach to his scientific achievements. He would go so far as to say, "I didn't make these discoveries. God has only worked through me to reveal to his children some of his wonderful providences."[62]

His favorite story (told in a variety of ways to various audiences) is an exchange between himself and God regarding the mysteries of the peanut.

> One day I went into my laboratory and said, "Dear Mr. Creator, please tell me what the universe was made for." The Great Creator answered, "You want to know too much for that little mind of yours. Ask something more your size, little man." Then I asked, "Please, Mr. Creator, tell me what man was made for." Again the Great Creator replied, "You are still asking too much." So then I asked, "Please, Mr. Creator, will you tell me why the peanut was made?" "That's better," God answered, "what do you want to know about the peanut?"[63]

Christians in the West, and almost everyone else, would prefer the peanut butter produced by George Washington Carver over the doctrine of eugenics invented by Darwin, Galton, and others. Peanut butter was helpful. Eugenics was harmful.

CHRISTIANS APPLY SCIENCE TO USEFUL ENDS

A list of the most useful things in the world would probably include wristwatches, automobiles, electric motors, engines, refined oil, electronic telecommunication, welding, aluminum, eyeglasses, semiconductors, the light bulb, and airplanes. All were invented by Christians in the West who would apply science to good and useful ends.

Each year, watchmakers produce 1.2 billion wrist-worn timepieces—the most familiar piece of jewelry, possessed by practically every living person on earth. Here again the invention was the production of Christians. Peter Henlein (1485-1542) is credited as the first inventor of a watch, but only after spending years in a Christian monastery in Nuremberg, studying mathematics and clockmaking. Then it was the Calvinist jewelers of Geneva who perfected the art. Reforming fervor in Geneva in the 1540s resulted in anti-sumptuary laws limiting the use of jewelry, about the same time the Italian cities of Florence and Venice came up with long lists of rules regulating the wearing of pearls, gold necklaces, and the like. Not to be put out of business by the new regulations, jewelers of the Calvinist tradition in Geneva set to work perfecting the watch as a practical instrument for timekeeping. The world's first watchmaking guild appeared in Geneva around 1601. Calvinist-Huguenot refugees like Antoine Arlaud (1590-1641) dominated the business for a generation. Arlaud is know for creating the "Watch of the Risen Christ" as an emblem of the death of Christ and man's need for salvation.

Mechanical power produced by something besides animals and watermills would wait for Christian ingenuity in the Western world. That came by a Baptist lay preacher, Thomas Newcomen (1664-1729), who is credited with the first steam-powered device producing mechanical work for a practical application. Iron-mongering was his tent-making source of income while Newcomen served as an elder in his local church. His steam-powered pump offered a critical aid to the coal mining business in his district. Later James Watt would improve on the Newcomen engine. Virtually all cars and trucks, most marine vehicles, construction equipment, farming vehicles, and railroad locomotives used on every continent on earth rely on the rudimentary technology produced by this Baptist minister. Newcomen penned a letter to his wife on December 30, 1727, assuring her that he "greatly rejoice[s] to hear [their three children] were seriously enquiring the way to Sion with their faces thitherward. This," he wrote, "ought to be their Chiefest Concern." Hinting at his own ultimate life commitment, Newcomen pointed out to his wife, concerning a certain European prince, who: "In my Apprehension (notwithstanding the many sorrowful Reflections he may be supposed to make upon it) his Case is very desirable when set in Comparison with that fool mentioned by our Saviour (Luke 12) who when his Soul comes to be required of him, shall be found only to have been laying up Treasure to himself and is not rich towards God. For the former hath Time and Opportunity to provide himself of a far better and greater Treasure than what he hath lost, whilst the other is past all Hope in that Respect: the former hath nothing left to fear from the Rage of his Great Master than the killing of his Body, but Oh! what hath not the latter to fear from the Anger of an Incensed God, who had so often Offered himself unto him as his Portion in order to his Everlasting Happiness, but was neglected and slighted; and for what was the Gracious Offer declined? Even for the Gratification of Sinful Lusts, or for the enjoyment of Lying Vanities."

A devout Christian, Sir Humphrey Davies (1778-1829), the first inventor of the incandescent lightbulb, would write, "In everything belonging to the economy of nature, I find new reasons for wondering at the designs of Providence," and that "a firm faith in the doctrines of Christianity is more highly to be prized than any other ornament of the human mind." Thomas Edison would improve on the technology a century later.

Elihu Thomson (1853-1937), the inventor of the electric welding process, was also raised in a Christian home and taught the Bible by his father. Although he abandoned "organized religion" in his later years, Thomson still maintained a basic fear of God and a recognition of the Creator.

Blaise Pascal, another Christian, gave us the first barometer. The God-fearing Michael Faraday developed the first electric generator. Father of electrical engineering, Joseph Henry (1797-1878), produced the first electric motor when he discovered electromagnetic induction, as well as a simple telegraph using an electromagnetic relay. Chair of Natural History at Christian Princeton, Henry insisted on conducting science in the fear of God, "making it a regular practice to stop, to worship God, and then to pray for divine guidance at every important juncture of the experiment." His philosophy of science was clearly evident in his writings: "Let us labor like servants who are certainly and shortly to give an account of their stewardship, diligently seeking to know our duty, and faithfully and fearlessly strive to do it; constantly mindful of the fact that nothing but purity of heart is acceptable to God and that we are constantly in His presence, and known to Him are all our thoughts and intentions however they may be hid from our fellow men."

Another devout Christian, Samuel F. B. Morse (1791- 1872) blazed the trail for modern communication methods, perfecting the telegraph. Importantly, Morse's first electronic communication contained the words: "What hath God wrought!" The inventor's final attribution was to God. He said, "It is His work. 'Not unto us, but to Thy Name, O Lord, be all the praise.'"

Although distracted from the Christian faith later in life, the Wright brothers were given much impetus to the development of the first airplane by their pastor-father's inspiration and teaching. Of the 117 greatest "essential" inventions of all time, 91% are attributed to Western countries, 68% to Protestant countries in the West, 5% to Russia, and 4% to China and Japan. As Christians applied themselves to scientific inquiry and invention over the last five centuries, God's common grace was poured out upon Western nations and the whole world. Real science and genuinely helpful technology was almost exclusively the product of Western Christians—followers of the Carpenter from Nazareth. Every person on earth driving an automobile, donning a watch, availing of eyeglasses, or taking advantage of semiconductors for a thousand uses should thank a Christian every day of his life; or better yet, thank Christ for bringing light and life to the world.

Charles Martin Hall (1863-1914), the son of a Presbyterian missionary to Jamaica, mastered the incredibly complicated method of processing aluminum in 1886. The whole world is filled with Hall's aluminum, used to manufacture aircraft, automobiles, spacecraft, computers, containers, kitchen utensils, and window frames. Homeschooled by his mother, Hall figured out the process by using the furnace at his family home—with a little help from his sister. This was not Darwin's science. Here was another example of practical, dominion science at work, to this day accommodating billions of people with a supremely useful technology.

John D. Rockefeller (1839-1937) discovered a way to process oil for modern applications and became the richest man in the world. A Sunday School teacher at his local Baptist church, he said, "I believe the power to make money is a gift from God."[64] But, sadly, riches corrupted him, and he turned towards supporting "liberalism" later in life. However, Rockefeller's processing technology enabled the use of oil and gas for seven billion people around the world over the next Century. Without oil and gas, modern systems of transportation, agriculture, construction, energy production, and manufacturing would be non-existent. Christians, carrying on the heritage of the West, continued ushering in extremely useful and helpful inventions for the benefit of the whole world.

Well into the 20th Century Christians continued to invent and take serious dominion over God's earth and resources for the benefit of mankind. Before his death, R. G. LeTourneau (1888-1969) held 300 patents for his various inventions relating to earthmoving equipment and machine tools used for constructing roads, buildings, and homes. His company's designs and equipment were relied upon to provide 70% of the earthmoving work in World War II.[65] His inventions included the development of rubber tires for land movers, the bulldozer, earth scrapers, the tree crusher, the power log skidder, the airplane tow, the air crane, the electric wheel, and the first mobile offshore oil platform.

LeTourneau turned over most of his profits to Christian ministries (on a 90/10 split), including a Christian college named LeTourneau University. As he would say, "It's not how much of my money I give to

God, but how much of God's money I keep for myself."[66] He was not ashamed to say, "I have felt the love of our Lord Jesus Christ...He is my Lord and Savior."[67] Once again, it was Christians who discovered the most useful equipment for land development and construction—for the benefit of the whole world.

MEDICAL ADVANCEMENT

For all our days are passed away in thy wrath: we spend our years as a tale that is told. The days of our years are threescore years and ten; and if by reason of strength they be fourscore years, yet is their strength labour and sorrow; for it is soon cut off, and we fly away. Who knoweth the power of thine anger? even according to thy fear, so is thy wrath. (Psalm 90:9-11)

Moses' psalm places the average human lifespan between seventy and eighty years as far back as the 15th Century BC. Not much has changed through the ages. Metropolitan areas expanded just prior to the Bubonic plague coming to Europe, subjecting populations to the threat of pandemics. Disease quickly spread in the cities, impacting infant mortality rates. Covering sewers and processing waste was an important step towards implementing biblical principles in relation to civic health, sadly deficient among Western communities for centuries (Deut. 23:13). Up until 1875, US cities exceeding a population of 100,000 had no sewage treatment. Finally, by 1926, twenty US cities had installed sewage treatment plants. British inventors George Jennings (1851), Daniel Bostel (1875), and Thomas Crapper (1885) were the first to introduce the flushing toilet—a major advancement for modern sanitation practices.

And thou shalt have a paddle upon thy weapon; and it shall be, when thou wilt ease thyself abroad, thou shalt dig therewith, and shalt turn back and cover that which cometh from thee... (Deuteronomy 23:13)

About the same time, Christian doctors Joseph Lister (1827-1912) and Ignaz Semmelweis (1818-1865), with Louis Pasteur (1822-1895) identified germs as a root cause for disease and centered in on the importance of cleanliness and sterilization as basic medical practices. Pasteur is well known for his commitment to a Christian faith and his critique of the growing anti-supernatural skepticism of the day. His comment was: "Posterity will one day laugh at the foolishness of modern materialistic philosophers. The more I study nature, the more I stand amazed at the work of the Creator. I pray while I am engaged at my work in the laboratory."[68]

After these changes in sanitation standards, life expectancy in the US improved from 47 years to 78 years between 1900 and 2000 (roughly back to where Moses put it in Psalm 90).[69]

Not many significant medical breakthroughs would occur in the 20th Century. What may have been the most useful discovery in medical history once again came by a Christian researcher, Alexander Fleming (1881-1955). His discovery came about "accidentally," when he forgot to clean a petri dish in his laboratory. Upon returning two weeks later Fleming found a mold growing, and the staphylococcus bacteria in the dish was prevented from multiplying. Later the scientist commented on his discovery: "One sometimes finds what one is not looking for. When I woke up just after dawn on Sept. 28, 1928, I certainly didn't plan to revolutionize all medicine by discovering the world's first antibiotic, or bacteria killer. But I guess that was exactly what I did."[70] Fleming was not ashamed to testify of his Christian faith in the most explicit language possible: "My greatest discovery was that I needed God, and that I was nothing without him and that he loved me and showed his love by sending Jesus to save me." Reviewing the statistical breakdown of the causes for American deaths in 1910, it turns out that 20% of annual deaths were due to diseases that could have been fixed by antibiotics.[71] In the US alone, these treatments saved about 45 million lives over 75 years. Applying the same rates for the rest of the world, Alexander Fleming's discovery would have saved over 1 billion lives. No other medical discovery in Western history comes close to such contributions. At the turn of the 21st Century, the prestigious British Medical Journal conducted a survey of its professional reading base on "the greatest medical advance since 1840." Quite appropriately, clean water and sewage disposal topped the list, "followed closely by the discovery of antibiotics."[72]

The third most important medical advancement in the BMJ study was vaccinations—a medical breakthrough which has extensively curtailed the severity of viral pandemics worldwide. This also came by Christian influence. During the spring of 1721, a sailor introduced smallpox into the city of Boston, infecting about 5,000 people and killing 800. Famed pastor of Boston's North Church, Cotton Mather (son of Increase Mather) is credited as the first to promote inoculation during the epidemic. Admittedly, the treatment the pastor recommended was crude, where the pus from a person infected with smallpox is introduced into the punctured skin of another healthy individual. Despite the enthusiastic support of the ministers in Boston, there was little or no support to be had from the doctors in Massachusetts Bay. Nonetheless, the experiment was reasonably successful—of the 400 who received inoculation, only six died. Mortality for the rest of the city's population was one in six.

Another Christian would develop the safer vaccine later in 1796. Edward Jenner (1749-1826) noticed that milk maids who worked with cows in a dairy would not contract smallpox if they had the more mild disease of cowpox. The physician drew the first vaccine from cowpox and administered it successfully to an 8-year-old boy. It is estimated that about 10% of the English population died from viruses like the smallpox before the vaccine came along. Cotton Mather and Edward Jenner's invention of the vaccine would save about 500 million lives worldwide in the following centuries. Towards the end of his life, Dr. Jenner told a friend: "I am not surprised that men are not grateful to me; but I wonder that they are not grateful to God for the good which He has made me the instrument of conveying to my fellow creatures."[73] Edward Jenner would boil down his principles of scientific investigation to this: "The Sacred Scriptures form the only pillow on which the soul can find repose and refreshment...[and] the power and mercy of Providence is sublimely and awfully displayed in lightening and tempest...how beautifully is power here seasoned with mercy."[74]

The fourth most important discovery in medical science of the last two centuries was again the contribution of a Christian doctor in Toronto, Canada. Raised in Maine, Dr. Charles Best came upon the use of insulin while testing diabetic dogs in 1922. An active member of St. Andrews Presbyterian Church in Toronto, the doctor was called upon to read the Scriptures regularly and his biographer (son, Henry) reported his favorite hymns as "The Old Rugged Cross" and "Abide with Me."[75] In an interview with the British Medical Association conducted in 1959, Dr. Best clearly acknowledged the Creator.[76] Charles Best's work on insulin has saved at least 200 million lives worldwide.[77]

A comprehensive survey of the most significant medical discoveries would have to include the application of anesthesia to medical surgeries. James Young Simpson (1811-1870) takes his place in history as the first physician to use anesthesia for a patient in 1847. A devout Christian, this doctor also testified to his faith in an extended essay entitled "My Substitute":

> I saw...myself a sinner standing on the brink of ruin, deserving nought but hell. For one sin? No, for many, many sins committed against the unchanging laws of God. But again, I looked and saw Jesus, my Substitute, scourged in my stead, and dying on the cross for me. I looked, and wept, and was forgiven. And it seemed to me to be my duty to tell you of that Saviour, to see if you will not also 'look and live.'[78]

As he lay on his death bed, Simpson continued to affirm his faith in Christ to the very end according to transcriptions made by his nephew. Highly significant are the doctor's dying words: "I have mixed a great deal with men of all shades of opinion. I have heard men of science and philosophy raise doubts and objections to the gospel of Christ, but I have never for one moment had a doubt myself."[79] Upon his death, a crowd of 100,000 people lined the streets of Edinburgh to honor the man who first introduced anesthesia for patients subject to invasive medical treatments.

On November 8th of 1895, a German physics professor Wilhelm Conrad Roentgen made a remarkable discovery. In a laboratory, a floor below his living quarters, the scientist noticed something very strange happening. He had taken a tube similar to a fluorescent light bulb, removed all the air and filled it with a special gas. As he activated the tube, he noticed a greenish ray reflect on a distant crystal. Holding a book, a playing card, and a block of lead against the ray, he observed the density of the ray on the screen changing. But then, he picked up something quite strange—the image of the bones of his fingers holding the lead piece, reflected on the screen. He called the image an X-ray, for the unknown variable used in algebra.

In true form to the Christian method of science, Roentgen explained later the basis of his success in scientific inquiry. "I did not think; I investigated," he said.

Roentgen picked up the first Nobel prize for Physics for this extraordinary contribution to science and medicine. In another recent survey conducted by the Science Museum of London, the invention of the X-ray was voted the most important modern scientific discovery.[80] Alexander Fleming's penicillin discovery came in second in this poll. Roentgen's contribution turns up number seven on the list of the BMJ's most important medical advancements.

Raised in the Evangelical Church of the Netherlands where his grandfather had served as an elder, Roentgen continued in the faith through his professional life. On Sunday afternoons the scientist would read the Bible aloud to his wife, Bertha, and his primary biographer notes that his Bible reading only increased in later years. Robert Nitske concluded that, "Roentgen was a believing Protestant...convinced of an absolutely ordered existence of all things. Creation was not a haphazard or accidental occurrence, but a magnificent process of precise orderliness."[81]

After the discovery of X-ray imaging, MRI imaging would have to be the next most important discovery in modern medical science. At 4:45 am on July 3, 1977, an evangelical Christian scientist named Raymond Damadian completed his first MRI scan of a human heart and lung. In his college years, Damadian had turned away from his parents' evangelical faith by what he called the "atheism of evolution."[82] However, Damadian confessed that "through faith in Jesus alone, my soul was gloriously rescued by God."[83] He attributed his discovery in magnetic resonance as "the unfolding of God's plan for my life."[84] The scientist went on to say that all creation originates "in an eternal God and Creator of us all. And He has graciously seen fit to share much of His truth with us. But He has also allowed mankind to stumble upon that truth or to systematically uncover it through experimentation and experience. Apart from His willingness to share it, we would know virtually nothing at all."[85] Damadian was refused the Nobel Prize for his discovery, at least partially because he was (in his words), a "scientific heretic...refusing to pay homage to Darwin and his misguided theory of origins,"[86] holding rather to the "literal 6-day creation" account contained in Scripture. Over half a billion MRI scans are performed each decade saving tens of millions of lives.

Although the BMI poll identifying the greatest medical breakthroughs put the birth control pill in sixth place, one can hardly argue this has saved any lives in contrast with the billions of lives lost to its abortifacient effects. Suffice it to say that every *meaningful* advance in modern medicine came by committed Christians in Western nations. Without exception, they were God-fearing men, humble men, practical men, experimental men, and scientists who relied on God for special insight. This short survey offers irrefutable proof that Christ has indeed blessed the entire world in the field of medical science, especially during the 18th and 19th Centuries following the Protestant Reformation.

A 1994 study conducted on the 397 Greek and Roman men contained in the Oxford Classical Dictionary found the ancients living into their 70s.[87] Eliminating those who died by murder, suicide, and warfare, the average lifespan was seventy-two years. A comparison was then made to men who died between 1850 and 1949. The average lifespan of this group was seventy-one years of age. In 1951, life expectancy for mature men (15+ years of age) was sixty-eight, and by 1981 it had increased to seventy-two.[88] American males live to about age seventy-eight today. Would 20th Century medical technology accomplish all that much? Or should we be more concerned with the advancements of sewage treatment and other forms of disease prevention?

THE FAILURE OF MODERN MEDICINE & SCIENCE

The latter 20th Century produced few useful scientific discoveries. Instead of focusing on sensible research directed toward beneficial ends, scientists preferred to keep busy by hypothesizing on subatomic particles, four-dimensional space, searching for water on Mars, and identifying planets beyond our solar system.

Most of the science news conveyed through the major media during these years would either return to far-fetched attempts to find proof of human evolution or "environmental science." In 2000, major US newspapers averaged less than five articles per month on environmental issues, and twenty years later the same news outlets were carrying almost 200 articles per month on this "scientific" obsession.[89] By 2018, 69% of Americans surveyed said they were "worried about" climate change or global warming, up from 53% in 2013 and virtually 0% in 1995.[90] Of course these same people were not thinking in terms of the earth burning up in a fiery blaze ordained by Almighty God.

The tool of science may be used for developing accurate observations and descriptions, distinguishing one created thing from another, and identifying cause-effect natural relationships with stated statistical probabilities. That's it. To expect more from science or to pretend that science can accomplish more than this is pure fakery.

The problem afflicting modern science was essentially the incipient inability to moderate dogmatism, or to think in terms of gradations in certainty or probabilities. For modern man, scientific theory was the only epistemological authority left after he had abandoned God and His revelation. Thus, the modern scientific mind was incapable of distinguishing the difference between "sciences" represented by the following activities:

a. Dropping a ball 100 times and concluding with 99% probability that the force of gravity exists, or

b. Applying U-238 testing to a rock, assuming certain starting conditions and steady state for the decay rate over four billion years, and concluding with absolute certainty that the rock is four billion years old, or

c. Noticing a one degree increase in global temperature over one hundred years and concluding with absolute certainty that the change was human-caused, and detrimental to life on earth.

For the modern mind, testing, verification, and probabilities were no longer important considerations when "science" addressed matters of b and c. Although, some scientists were still interested in the science involved with a.

Even worse, scientists used computer models to prognosticate the future, eerily similar to how Renaissance astrologists read the stars to discern cause and effect relationships. Incredibly, the popular infatuation with global warming, significantly impacted public policy and national economy in every developed nation in the world—all of it inspired and directed by this computer modeling. Not experimentation. Not the Christian way. Not the humble way.

Computer modeling may have provided a little helpful forecasting for weathermen for extremely short term (24 hour) and localized application. But the faith placed in this new astrology, resisting verification and experimentation, was virtually unbounded now. After the climate change computer models were first released in the early 2000s, the average global temperature diverged more and more from the average annual temperatures projected by the models. The Cornwall Alliance updated the report on the models for Congress in the later 2010s—"On average, models simulate more than twice the warming observed over the period during which anthropogenic warming is supposed to have been the greatest (about the last 35 years). None simulate the complete absence of observed warming over approximately the last 20 years at Earth's surface and 17 to 27 years in the lower troposphere. Over 95 percent simulate more warming than observed."[91]

Process and design engineers who work in process optimization, experimental design, and statistical techniques for industrial applications know very well the difficulty of eliminating confounding factors in experimentation. It is hard enough to do this in a closed laboratory setting. How much more difficult would it be to determine the cause of global warming, without placing the earth into a laboratory setting? How could scientists possibly block the confounding factors of sunspots, solar flares, ocean currents, etc., when experimenting with increased or decreased levels of man-caused sources of warming? Since engineering companies look for a degree of financial benefit, they will pay close attention to the alpha and beta risks associated with changing the process or design on the basis of the experiment.[92] Yet, these risks are not assessed in the ivory towers of the techno-political power centers when determining policy on the basis of global warming. The blind arrogance and flagrant foolhardiness of modern scientists has resulted in the destruction of true science and the ruin of national economies.

Moreover, how might this new "scientific" religion possibly determine the ethical value of a warmer earth? These questions go well beyond the realm of science. Legitimate questions remain as to whether more carbon dioxide has contributed positively by adding more greenery to the earth's surface. How can science know for sure whether more greenery and less ice caps is better or worse for the earth? Again, this is not the business of science.

The "astrology" of computer modeling predicted the end of the world by 2100 via global warming, and 2.2 million US deaths by Covid-19 in 2020.[93] This precipitated the shutdown of the world economy, and a subsequent worldwide economic depression. The astrologers or computer-modeling scientists missed the mark by a mile. At the end of the year, the US ended up with about 20,000 deaths (as sole cause), or 220,000 deaths by co-morbid causes.[94]

JUNK SCIENCE

And even as they did not like to retain God in their knowledge, God gave them over to a reprobate mind, to do those things which are not convenient... (Romans 1:28)

As the field of science degraded in the universities, the modern world became enraptured with junk science not unlike the medieval infatuation with alchemy. The public was increasingly taken in by hucksters pawning off junk science. What developed was a mindless trust in every form of scientism, farfetched conspiracy theories, anecdotal evidence for just about any conclusion, and every other witchdoctor coming down the pike. As long as God's transcendent truth was ignored, practically any "scientist" with the title or credentials would be deemed believable. Failing to recognize the limitations of science, all bets were off for measuring the trustworthiness of the conclusions. Less and less were scientists interested in verification, probability, or testing far-fetched theories. This led to an increasingly irrational world, an insane world, and an unscientific world—indeed, to the very destruction of science itself.

Modern science became more faddish, more unreliable, and less meaningful as time went on. In the 1970s, the fad was the new ice age. This was followed by global warming in the 2000s. In previous decades, the problems were DDT, asbestos, acid rain, cholesterol, and so on. The fads came and went, but with each panic the world was left with more skepticism about science, truth, and reality itself. After awhile, people do lose confidence in the alchemists.

A rising skepticism and a naive credulity came simultaneously in the unravelling mind of the post-modern. On the one hand, nobody was to be trusted, but on occasion anybody could be trusted, that is, if the news appeared in social media. Such irrationality contributed to increasing levels of social chaos and disunity.

When considering the fields of dietetics, human sociology, and psychology, scientific inquiry concerning cause-effect relationships cannot possibly ascertain truth at any appreciable level of probability. For one thing, it is impossible to place one hundred humans in a closed environment for sixty years, block all confounding factors, and experiment with this food or that food to determine the best effects on longevity or anything else—in the long run. It would be far better to leave food, immunizations, medical treatment, vitamins, essential oils, sociological influences, etc., in the realm of Christian liberty—and reference Romans 14 from time to time. Moreover, the wide range of genetic differences among people might very well require a wide variety of diets, medical treatments, and sociological inputs as well. At the very least, the Christian requires honesty—a willingness to submit medical treatments to a regimen of testing (double-blind studies) to determine the helpfulness of one product or another. The true scientist, doctor, and pharmacologist would do well to moderate the "advertising" and dogmatic language used to promote a preferred treatment or cure, according to the degree of testing conducted, the testability, and the results obtained for the product. Some "cures" resisted all testing, relying more on the psychosomatic effect, and disallowing a "blind" test group in the experiment.

WILL SCIENCE KILL US?

As far as modern man refused to fear God (as the beginning of knowledge), his science would turn to "barking up the wrong tree," producing counter-productive results. Major developments in modern science during the latter half of the 20th Century included weapons of mass destruction, computer and information technology, and genetic engineering. The grand inventions topping the list for the 21st Century include the internet, the iPhone and mobile operating systems, social media, bitcoin, gene editing, augmented reality, the conception control patch, artificial intelligence, online streaming, ebook readers, and touchscreen glass. Would any of this really help man in the dominion task? Would these things free man to serve God or further enslave him? Would he use them for good or for ill—predominantly? And (we keep asking ourselves) what is this buying us? Is life really better off with all of this?

The 21st Century produced children born of three parents,[95] artificial insemination, surrogate wombs, millions of disposable "snowflake" children,[96] human-animal hybrids,[97] artificial wombs,[98] and innumerable other monstrosities. The overuse of antibiotics made the world more susceptible to highly resistant superbugs.[99] The natural was traded for the unnatural, children conceived outside of human relationship, and then institutionalized womb-to-tomb. There was no end to what Dr. Frankenstein would do, absent of the fear of God and all biblical morality. Would proud scientists set the world up for the most spectacular failure in all of human history?

But modern man had already lost a grip on the definition of that essential good. Since technology had enabled mass abortion, total conception control, easy pornography access at every moment of the day, gene-edited designer children who wouldn't bother us with their problems, "well-cultivated" relationships by social media, and ever fluctuating cryptocurrency values, did all this amount to an existential good? In the tech-savvy age, personality faded. Human relationships were increasingly tenuous, short-lived, shallow, broken, or non-existent. There was no time for genuine relationships, and no time for worshiping God either. Children, marriage, family, and community were no longer a blessing in the media-saturated life of self-worship, entertainment, escapism, convenience, distraction, and depersonalization. The good life was no longer seen as rooted in relationships, voluntary giving, self-denial, and service; for modern life with its big-government security and welfare, access to information, technology, and big insurance programs was geared to insulate us from all of that. What was the good life anyway?

In a rational moment, some were asking what man would do given the power and technology to destroy himself. If "the heart is deceitful above all things and desperately wicked" (Jer. 17:9), and modern man had already used medical technology to kill five to eight billion babies since 1960, what would he do with nuclear warheads and chemical warfare? What follows a century of teaching science sans the fear of

God in American high school and college classrooms? What comes of all this?

An assessment of the sum total effect of the entire conglomeration of modern technology upon human society would have found that there was enough to destroy humankind—or at least subjugate him. By a significant percentage, the majority of babies conceived in the 21st Century were killed by IUD technology, surgical abortion, RU-486, and other means. Conservatively, 68% of babies conceived annually in the US and 64% of babies conceived worldwide were terminated by these technologies.[100] *Man had become quite adept at mass-production killing.*

According to a Nielsen study in 2016, the average American adult spent 10 hours and 32 minutes on unproductive uses of media per day (an increase of 10% from the previous year). Most of the electronic usage was live television, time-shifted television, AM/FM radio, and smartphones.[101] That amounted to 65% of waking hours dedicated to entertainment as compared to 35% committed to productive labor. Media consumption for adults averaged only 156 minutes (2.5 hours) in 1960, and 258 minutes (4.25 hours) in 1980.[102] The shift to a counter-productive technology and a ruinous science occurred just after the turn of the 21st Century.

God created man, with the intent that he would take dominion over creation, but modern technology had taken dominion over man. Maybe Jacques Ellul had a point—forty years before the Fall:

> The human being who acts and thinks today is not situated as an independent subject with respect to a technological object. He is inside the technological system, he is himself modified by the technological factor. The human being who uses technology today is by the very fact the human being who serves it. And conversely, only the human being who serves technology is truly able to use it.[103]

And so it was . . . the science and technology intended to save man came to destroy him. This was a key force used to precipitate the Fall of the West.

> The pride of thine heart hath deceived thee, thou that dwellest in the clefts of the rock, whose habitation is high; that saith in his heart, Who shall bring me down to the ground? Though thou exalt thyself as the eagle, and though thou set thy nest among the stars, thence will I bring thee down, saith the LORD. (Obadiah 3)

X

THE RISE & FALL
OF THE WESTERN
ECONOMY

And it shall come to pass, if thou shalt hearken diligently unto the voice of the LORD thy God, to observe and to do all his commandments which I command thee this day, that the LORD thy God will set thee on high above all nations of the earth...The LORD shall command the blessing upon thee in thy storehouses, and in all that thou settest thine hand unto; and he shall bless thee in the land which the LORD thy God giveth thee. The LORD shall establish thee an holy people unto himself, as he hath sworn unto thee, if thou shalt keep the commandments of the LORD thy God, and walk in his ways. And all people of the earth shall see that thou art called by the name of the LORD; and they shall be afraid of thee. And the LORD shall make thee plenteous in goods, in the fruit of thy body, and in the fruit of thy cattle, and in the fruit of thy ground, in the land which the LORD sware unto thy fathers to give thee. The LORD shall open unto thee his good treasure, the heaven to give the rain unto thy land in his season, and to bless all the work of thine hand: and thou shalt lend unto many nations, and thou shalt not borrow. And the LORD shall make thee the head, and not the tail; and thou shalt be above only, and thou shalt not be beneath; if that thou hearken unto the commandments of the LORD thy God, which I command thee this day, to observe and to do them... (Deuteronomy 28:1, 8-13)

Thanks much to the contribution of Christian scientists and inventors, and good politics based in God's law and liberty, Europe and America were the dominant force in the world economy at the turn of the 19th Century. By the good graces of God, this continued until the year AD 2015. At the zenith of its productivity in AD 1990, the West produced 56% of the Gross World Product while only making up 19% of the world population. Western countries were producing three times per capita what the rest of the world produced. The decline began in the 1990s under the political leadership of post-Christian "progressives" like Bill Clinton (US), Tony Blair (UK), and Jean Chretien (Canada).

The Productivity of the West Compared to the Rest of the World[1]

Year	% GWP Produced in West (Europe and North America)	Productivity Ratio % GWP / % World Population
1820	36%	1.72
1870	58%	1.90
1900	67%	2.09
1960	66%	2.49
1980	58%	2.71
1990	56%	2.96
2000	50%	2.95
2015	37%	2.52

As the Fall of the West accelerated, the International Monetary Fund kept an eye on the balance sheets of national governments—

assets minus liabilities (or debts). America was bankrupt by 2016—in the red. The other most severely bankrupted nations were Japan, Germany, Austria, Portugal, the UK, and France. Solvent national governments with the highest net worth included China, Russia, South Korea, Australia, Indonesia, and Norway.

National Government Net Worth[2]

Nation	National Government Net Worth	Nation	National Government Net Worth
China	$8 trillion	Australia	$4 trillion
Russia	$6 trillion	Indonesia	$1.25 trillion
Korea	$4 trillion	Norway	$1.2 trillion

By another metric, charting the position of Western nations in the world economy, the date for the toppling of the West was AD 2015. In the space of forty years, the West contracted from controlling 100% of seven of the world's most prolific economies to controlling only 31%. The collapse accelerated quickly as illustrated by the following table[3]:

Place	1980	1990	2000	2010	2020
1st	US	US	US	US	China
2nd	Japan	Japan	China	China	US
3rd	Germany	Germany	Japan	India	India
4th	Italy	Italy	Germany	Japan	Japan
5th	Brazil	China	India	Germany	Germany
6th	France	France	France	Russia	Russia
7th	UK	Brazil	Russia	Brazil	Indonesia
Western Nations	7	6	4	4	3
Eastern Nations	0	1	3	3	4
West Control of Economy	100.0%	92.3%	76.1%	55.1%	30.8%

THE FALL OF THE WEST BY FAILURE OF ECONOMY

This world economic shift equated to a tip in the balance of world power with a realignment of military positions. In the words of Deuteronomy 28, the East had become the head and the West had become the tail. Times of severe humbling and tough judgment descended upon America and Europe with the rise of the East and the fall of the West.

The Western nations of Europe and North America had a two-hundred-year run at leading the world economy. Beyond any other influence, the boom came as a result of the inculcation of a Christian world and life view in nations most receptive of the Protestant Reformation. The humanist worldview predominated in the later 19th and 20th centuries to the demise of the West. This corrupted epistemology, meta-ethic, and teleology in the post-Christian mind could no longer hold up a civilization. The combined effect of the loss of faith, the weakness of the church, the breakdown of moral character, and the failure of science and technology undermined the Western economy. Yet, the long-term economic productivity of the Western world remains one of the best historical examples of God's blessings upon nations. Although Deuteronomy 28 was intended first for Israel, this passage does contain an underlying principle which may be used to interpret history. All material blessings come from God and, generally, nations are blessed "whose God is the LORD" (Ps. 33:12). Regardless of what view is taken of history or economics, all Christians should at least realize that God is the source of all blessings. *God blessed the West.*

In 1951, US General Douglas MacArthur sensed the nation's moral deterioration, forecasted an economic decline, and called for a spiritual reawakening. That never quite materialized.

In this day of gathering storms, as the moral deterioration of political power spreads its growing infection, it is essential that every spiritual force be mobilized to defend and preserve the religious base upon which this nation was founded. For it is that base which has been the motivating impulse to our moral and national growth. History fails to record a single instance in which nations subject to moral decay have not passed into political and economic decline. There has been either a spiritual reawakening to overcome the moral lapse, or a progressive deterioration leading to ultimate national disaster.[4]

THE RISE OF A CHRISTIAN ECONOMY

I beseech thee for my son Onesimus, whom I have begotten in my bonds...But without thy mind would I do nothing; that thy benefit should not be as it were of necessity, but willingly. For perhaps he therefore departed for a season, that thou shouldest receive him for ever; not now as a servant, but above a servant, a brother beloved, specially to me, but how much more unto thee, both in the flesh, and in the Lord? (Philemon 10, 14-16)

A Christian economy, as prescribed by Scripture, espouses the principles of family economy, decentralized economic power, the free market, moral self-government, and privatized charity. The rise of a Christian economy was very slow and gradual, metered by the degree to which hearts were changed, Christian morality and voluntary charity advanced, and political leaders bowed to the Lordship of Christ.

For Christian economy to flourish, the institution of slavery would have to end, but this would only happen when "Philemon" and others voluntarily released their slaves and treated them as "beloved brothers." Beginning with one voice crying in the wilderness (Gregory of Nyssa), the early Christian church took a stand against the 4,000-year-old institution. The fall of chattel slavery came only after a long, arduous battle fought over the course of five hundred years.

He saith unto them, Moses because of the hardness of your hearts suffered you to put away your wives: but from the beginning it was not so. (Matthew 19:8)

And ye shall hallow the fiftieth year, and proclaim liberty throughout all the land unto all the inhabitants thereof: it shall be a jubilee unto you; and ye shall return every man unto his possession, and ye shall return every man unto his family. (Leviticus 25:10)

Old Testament law regulated slavery and divorce. Both were frowned upon in early divine revelation though permitted for "the hardness of men's hearts." Every fiftieth year, the Israelites were required to release their slaves in the year of Jubilee. After Christ's coming, Christians almost universally realized a perpetual Jubilee. For He had said He came to "proclaim liberty to the captives" (Luke 4:18-19).

CHRIST PUTS AN END TO THE PAGAN SLAVE ECONOMY

Along with everything else he got wrong, Aristotle advocated for slavery as a perpetual human institution. "A slave," the philosopher said, "is a living tool, just as a tool is an inanimate slave. Therefore there can be no friendship with a slave as slave."[5] By Kyle Harper's careful study, during the late Roman Empire the slave population constituted ten percent of the Roman world.[6] Earlier, around the time of Christ, varying estimates put the Italian slave population between 20% and 30%.[7]

Christians changed this 4,000 year traditional economy. The Apostle Paul had placed high value on freedom from slavery in 1 Corinthians 7:21-23. "Ye are bought with a price; be not ye the servants of men." So from the outset, the Christian church was committed to emancipation for Christian brothers and sisters. An early summary of the apostolic traditions collected in the Syrian church, *The Apostolic*

Constitutions, prioritized manumission for the church offerings. Historians find many instances of Christians setting their slaves free in the early years of the church. Hermes, a prefect, released 1,250 slaves around AD 100, and another Roman prefect, Chromatius, set 1,400 slaves free about the year AD 290. St. Melania is said to have released 8,000 slaves, and Ovidius of Gaul another 5,000.[8] Augustine of Hippo and Patrick of Ireland are especially well known in church history for their opposition to the slave trade and support of manumission.

The Justinian Code of AD 535 abolished laws which had made it difficult to free slaves. As Muslims continued to support and fuel slave-based economies through the centuries, Christians were applying their efforts freeing Moorish slaves. Muhammed himself was a slaver. This clash of worldviews between Muslims and Christians continues to the present day.

Clovis II of the Franks (633-657) married a slave. After his death, his wife Bathilda fought the slave trade, dedicating the remainder of her life to redeeming slaves. Charlemagne (d. 814) also opposed slavery, taking seriously the exhortation from Abbot Smaragdus of Saint-Mihiel; "Most merciful king, forbid that there should be any slave in your kingdom."[9]

During the reign of King Athelstan of England, slavery was still imposed on those who had committed crimes, but this Christian king erred on the side of mercy, recommending that the nobles, "Every year …set at liberty someone that has for his crimes been condemned to slavery." And he tacked on the requirement that pardon for crimes take place according to the local pastor-bishop's "testimony" and approval.[10] As the Christian age reached its zenith in the West, the bishops of Worcester and Canterbury, Wulfstan (1008-1094) and Lanfranc (1010-1089) joined forces to shut down the slave trade in Bristol. William the Conqueror finally banned slavery completely after the Norman invasion of 1066.

Under the auspices of Bishop Anselm of Canterbury, an important English church council was held in London, AD 1102, addressing several key Christian moral issues. The council declared sodomy a sin requiring excommunication and the deprivation "of all lawful dignity,"[11] and as well reprobated all slave trade in England:

> ...that none exercise that wicked trade, which has hitherto been practiced in England, of selling men like beasts.[12]

THE FEUDAL SYSTEM

As Christ's influence spread across Europe, a feudalist or rent-based economy gradually replaced the age-old slave-based economy of the pagan world. Economic freedom was enhanced appreciably by imposing responsibility on the individual or the family to use land resources and capital for their own profit. By 1100, two classes had developed: 12% of the population were "free" renters, and 35% were "serf" renters.[13] "Free" renters paid a small fee to work their land, much as landowners pay property tax today. Serfs would have to spend x amount of time working in the landlord's fields, which limited the time they could spend working their own fields. All were given hereditary right to the land. The landowner (and the barons) took responsibility for protecting his renters, which usually involved building a castle and maintaining a defense force. A hierarchy developed of kings, barons, and lords. Eventually, the ratio of free-renters to serf-renters increased, and serfdom disappeared sometime in the 14th Century. Rodney Stark points out that the Black Death reduced the renting base, requiring landlords to award more for labor thereby empowering the lower classes. The serfs' position improved to free tenant, and they received better housing and access to oxen teams. During the Christian era, the means of production, profit, and wealth largely remained in the hands of those who worked the soil. Here was a heavily distributive economic system. Improved liberties and opportunities were made available in cities where freemen found increased division of labor, an expanding selection of trades, and much trading of goods and services. Between 1000 and 1230, a great number of cities and towns cropped up across Europe—125 towns in England alone. City charters typically referred to the establishment as a "free borough," and the residents were free to sell, rent out, and bequeath land as they saw fit. Once a serf worked and subsisted in a town for a year and a day, he would have achieved the status of a freeman. "Town air makes free" was the popular saying, and the Christian economy had opened up substantial opportunity for upward mobility. It was a first in human history. By 1215, London was the second largest town in Europe with a population around 50,000 (second only to Paris). Trade was booming, international wares of all sorts were available: "fine gems from the Nile, from China crimson silks; French wines; and sable, vair and miniver, from the far lands where Russ and Norselands dwell."[14] Visitors to London would have found 139 Christian churches, a mint, ready-cooked meals for easy purchase, theaters, taverns, magicians, beggars, mimes, and buffoons.

For centuries the major trade centers of Europe remained in Genoa, Florence, and Venice. Merchant and trade guilds were organized to maintain quality standards, training regimens, and information sharing. This kept the civil government out of the picture and enabled a measure of free enterprise. In some cities, the guilds paved the way for more democratic involvement in city governance. When the guilds gave way to excessive regulation by specifying the formulae of a scarlet dye, setting wages, or controlling prices, (as with the merchant weaver's guilds in Flanders), competing industries formed in other cities—and free enterprise continued to flourish. The decentralization of powers throughout the Christian era greatly stimulated the growth of the free market, something that did not happen with China for instance, where hegemonic control was a constant. As far back as 147 BC, Chinese

Han emperors had taken on the bad habit of seizing control of the successful iron and alcoholic beverage industries. Then again, in AD 23, Wang Mang seized ownership of the mining industry, instituted price controls, and levied an unprecedented 10% tax on all profit. And once more in AD 1018, Confucian socialists of the Song Dynasty grabbed control of the iron smelters and foundries, snuffing out what little industrial revolution had developed. Historian Roger Osborne described the economic history of China simply: *"Property is insecure. In this one phrase the whole history of Asia is contained."*[15]

IMPROVED EFFICIENCY & DIVISION OF LABOR

Some inventions are more revolutionary than others, because they open up opportunity for further division of labor, and free men and women from extreme drudgery—by orders of magnitude. In Western history, two inventions meet these criteria (besides those already mentioned in the previous chapter)—both delivered by Christians.

The first landmark invention appears in AD 1589 with the first knitting machine for the production of cloth or clothing. A Protestant pastor, Rev. William Lee, curate of Calverton in Nottinghamshire, takes credit for this breakthrough. The backstory of the invention is given by 19th Century historian, Gravenor Henson: "This gentleman [Rev. Lee], it is said, paid his addresses to a young woman in his neighbourhood, to whom, from some cause, his attentions were not agreeable; or, as with more probability it has been conjectured, she affected to treat him with negligence, to ascertain her power over his affections. Whenever he paid his visits, she always took care to be busily employed in knitting, and would pay no attention to his addresses."[16]

Queen Elizabeth rejected the Reverend Lee's application for a patent, and at first he was hesitant to seek interest in France, "where his life, from his religious opinions, might be continually endangered."[17] Nevertheless, he eventually took his invention to Paris but died before achieving any real success in marketing the product. Meanwhile, the pastor's apprentice (a miller named Aston) back in Nottinghamshire continued improving on the machine, and a new industry was born.

Another English inventor, John Kay (1704-1779), added the "flying shuttle," once more paving the way to a quick weave—something the world had never seen in 5,700 years. Then James Hargreaves added his genius to the process of cloth-making with the invention of the "spinning jenny" in 1770 (used for manufacturing yarn). Initially, the machine was built to produce eight spools of yarn at a time—increasing quickly to 120. Two centuries following the good pastor's breakthrough invention added improvements which vastly accelerated the process of making cloth.

THE SECOND LABOR SAVING INVENTION IN MODERN HISTORY

Cyrus McCormick, a devoted Christian of the Presbyterian tradition, put the finishing touches on the world's first automated "reaper" in 1831. The mechanical device, first pulled by horses, was a multi-generational vision in the making. His father had worked for twenty-eight years on various iterations of the automated reaper, but it was 22-year-old Cyrus who pulled off a workable design. By the year of his death, McCormick had sold 500,000 reapers, having achieved the most important advancement in agriculture since the optimization of the plow 1,500 years earlier. Men had been hand-cutting hay for 5,800 years of world history—until this Christian invention came along. The first mechanical reaper could do the work of twelve men, saving the farmer tremendous time and expense.[18] Subsequently, thousands of design iterations improving on McCormick's technology yielded reapers capable of covering 150-200 acres per day. Few inventions have enabled such efficiency and division of labor for the developing world. In the words of his biographer, "No other man so truly represented the dawn of the industrial era...[McCormick's reaper] made all other progress possible, by removing the fear of famine and the drudgery of farm labor."[19]

Biographer Herbert Casson recorded Cyrus McCormick's favorite Bible passage as Paul's doxology in Romans 8:31-36. The inventor would confess his complete dependence on the Lord in his work: "If it were not for the fact that Providence has seemed to assist me in our business, it has at times seemed that I would almost sink under the weight of responsibility hanging upon me; but I believe the Lord will help us out."[20] McCormick was raised on the Westminster Shorter Catechism and regular teaching of the Bible, and by his own attestation he affirmed the doctrine of the absolute sovereignty of God.[21]

> O the depth of the riches both of the wisdom and knowledge of God! how unsearchable are his judgments, and his ways past finding out! For who hath known the mind of the Lord? or who hath been his counsellor? Or who hath first given to him, and it shall be recompensed unto him again? For of him, and through him, and to him, are all things: to whom be glory for ever. Amen. (Romans 11:33-36)

GOD'S BLESSING ON A WESTERN ECONOMY

> The blessing of the LORD, it maketh rich, and he addeth no sorrow with it. (Proverbs 10:22)

The economic benefits attending the break-through developments in the hard sciences and technology in the West were extraordinary, completely unparalleled in all of world history. Never in Christian history was there to be found more external evidence of Christ's influence upon the material world. What followed the 18th Century was nothing less than a deluge of divine blessings poured out on the whole world. Previous economic boons in world history may have enriched an occasional sultan, emperor, or aristocracy. But these advancements came by the Christian West improved the median income for the average Joe, well beyond any social improvement offered by any other human initiative in history. These were universal and permanent improvements, sustaining through the winds of famine, war, and disease in the 20th Century. The following table illustrates the amazing effect of the Christian worldview upon science and economy over seven centuries.

Average Annual Income for Workers in the Western World (England)[22]

Date	Average Annual Income (Adjusted for Inflation)
AD 1300	$1,176
AD 1400	$1,740
AD 1500	$1,725
AD 1600	$1,714
AD 1700	$2,502
AD 1800	$3,372
AD 1900	$6,600
AD 2000	$37,500

For thousands of years the nations of the world made very little progress improving economic conditions for the average household, with average worker income hovering around $1,700 per year. Between AD 1600 and AD 1800, England and other Western nations finally succeeded in doubling average worker income and advancing society beyond bare sustenance farming. Such were the benefits of the Protestant Reformation and accompanying scientific contributions. Following the technological quantum leaps of the 19th Century in the West came another 10-fold increase in average worker income. Here reveals yet one more vivid demonstration of the explosive influence of Christ and His people upon the Western nations and the rest of the world economy.

The immediate effects of this economic blessing upon the character of the people and the national institutions, however, were almost universally detrimental. Regrettably, these economic blessings did not result in more gratitude to God, but instead unprecedented levels of religious skepticism, hubris, state worship and controls, and self-sufficiency. The 20th Century was the most economically prosperous era in human history, thanks to the outpouring of God's blessings and the contributions of Christian innovation and economy. For the first time in history the average household moved beyond subsistence living in Europe and America. But, it turned into the century of man-centered humanism. It was the century of blatant apostasy—God was removed from schools, and the most powerful courts in the world banned all thanksgiving to God and fear of God in the classrooms. It was the century of high technology, when man had finally come into his own with fond dreams of saving himself. It was the century of eugenics, conception control, mass abortion, and institutionalized sexual perversion for every Western nation. It was the proudest Century in human history. And it ended with the greatest fall of entire socio-economies and civilizations ever experienced in recorded history.

FIRST DEGRADE OF THE WESTERN ECONOMY

The religious decline in the Western church prior to the Reformation precipitated a terrible setback for the Christian economy, yielding tragic consequences in succeeding centuries. Seventy years before Martin Luther and 400 years after Anselm, Pope Nicholas V issued the *Dum Diversas* bull, reinstituting slavery in the West. The bull dates AD 1452, and reads:

> We grant you by these present documents, with our Apostolic Authority, full and free permission to invade, search out, capture, and subjugate the Saracens and pagans and any other unbelievers and enemies of Christ wherever they may be, as well as their kingdoms,

duchies, counties, principalities, and other property... and to reduce their persons into perpetual servitude.

Later, in 1548, Pope Paul III authorized the purchase of Muslim slaves in the papal states. Even more significant was the pope's issuance of a bull called the *Sublimis Deus,* intended as a Magna Carta for Native Americans, but later withdrawn due to political pressure coming from the slave trade sector. Early Protestantism opposed the Catholics on slavery, and the tug-of-war between revived humanism (in the Italian Renaissance) and the Reformation continued. John Calvin commented: "We must praise God for having banished such a very cruel brand of servitude."[23] Bondslavery, Calvin said, was a result of man's fall into sin, "all things being turned upside down."[24] In his commentary on Deuteronomy 24:7, Calvin affirmed the death penalty for man-stealing and selling into slavery.

Accommodated by Muslim influence, as well as a lapsed faith and a corrupt Roman Church, the rejuvenated slave-based economy appeared first in Portugal around AD 1441. The influence of Islam in Portugal and Spain dated back to the 8th Century, contributing to the reintroduction of Aristotle in the 12th Century, as well as slave-based economies of the 15th Century. Spain attempted to abolish slavery in 1542 but allowed its continuance in her Caribbean colonies until 1886.

The Dutch picked up the human trade in the early 1600s, no doubt a consequence of the Spanish influence over the Netherlands earlier in the 1500s. Regrettably, Dutch Reformed pastors failed to assemble a unified voice against the practice. Godefridus Udemans (1581-1649) was the first to address the subject in writing with something of a commendation. In his words: "It was only by God's mercy that some people were born free."[25] Udemans wrongly pointed out that Jesus came to free men from spiritual slavery, not physical slavery, completely ignoring the key New Testament passage addressing the matter—1 Corinthians 7:21-23. The Dutch argument was for a "kinder and gentler" slavery as opposed to what they called "the barbaric cruelty of the Spanish and Portuguese."[26] This position was further solidified by the treatise produced by Dutch Reformed pastor Jacobus Capitein (1717-1747) of the University of Leiden, whose *Dissertatio* argued that slavery was not opposed to the doctrine of Christian freedom.

Not to be outdone, the English jumped into the trade around 1564 when ship captain John Hawkins carried his first shipment of slaves into Santo Domingo and Columbia. The contest for empire building, mainly between Spain and England, would take place on the backs of slavery and mercantilism. The intent was always to enrich the mother country at the expense of freedom. Power-mongering and greed would increasingly fuel the fires of tyranny for the next five hundred years of Western history.

In 1654, an indentured servant who worked for an African immigrant in Virginia was sentenced to lifelong slavery in a civil court case. This was the beginning of chattel slavery in the American colonies. Roughly 4% of the slaves shipped to the Americas ended up in North America.[27]

The faith-lapsed Stuarts, King Charles II (ruled 1660-1685) and King James II (ruled 1685-1688), were largely responsible for fast-tracking the English slave trade in the American colonies. Formed in 1660, the Royal African Company was owned and operated by the royal family, who retained a monopoly over the English slave trade for 28 years. The company shipped 5,500 slaves into the American colonies by 1675. These slave-trading Catholic monarchs will also be remembered for the politically-inspired martyrdoms of 16,000 Christian Covenanters during the "Killing Time" in Scotland, as well as the "Great Ejection" of 3,000 English Puritan pastors in the 1680s. What other English kings could have competed with the apostasy, the debased perfidy, the moral corruption, and the vicious tyranny demonstrated by the Stuarts, sons of Charles I (each of whom produced a dozen or so illegitimate children)?

The saddest part of the story was the extensive capitulation of Christianity to the worldview of Aristotle and the Muslims. The supply chain for slaves was almost entirely fueled by Arab Muslims. Between 1500 and 1900, a total of 17 million African slaves were marketed and transported by Arab traders—12 million to the Americas and 5 million elsewhere.[28] The reintroduction of slavery cannot in any sense be considered the work of Jesus Christ. The credit belongs to Muhammed and Aristotle, and lapsed Christians.

THE DISTRIBUTION OF PROPERTY
IN EARLY AMERICA

By 1860, twelve percent of the American population was enslaved, including 43% of the lower Southern states.[29] Stemming from the initial wayward vision of the Catholic Stuarts, 93% of US slaves resided in Georgia, Maryland, Virginia, and the Carolinas in 1792.[30] Three percent collected in New York, and the other four percent in the seven states more committed to Puritanism and a stronger Reformation heritage. From the beginning, the New England Puritan settlements maintained a family-based economy, and largely avoided the slave-based economy cultivated in the South. The first public opposition to slavery in America came by a tract written by the Puritan, Samuel Sewall (1652-1730), where he condemned man-stealing as "an atrocious crime."

Instead of forming large plantations run by slave masters the Pilgrims envisioned decentralized household economies for the first settlements in America. After an ill-conceived plan to build an economy by working a communal farm together, the Pilgrims settled on an approach where, "every person [had] one acre allowed to him as to property, besides their homesteads, or garden plots."[31] Later, in 1627, each land allotment was increased to twenty acres per household. From its earliest beginnings, private property ownership was a fundamental value for the New England colonists. The Connecticut Settlement in 1636 was laid out (in Thomas Hooker's words), "that they should turn the wilderness into gardens and fields, that they should plant and cultivate the earth."[32] The colonists referred to themselves as the "free planters" and property owners were assigned to elect their own governors and sign off on the civil covenant. Historian Daniel Ford notes that "a thriving economy based on private property and private interest was then the greatest benefit of the public good at large. Consequently, the local towns [in New England] formed by an industrious people, an agreeable faith, and common respect for private property became an important feature of free and independent colonial life."[33] Because of this robust application of distributed property and free family economy, New England was far less involved with the slave market as compared with the Southern Colonies.

Noah Webster described this characteristic of a free America in his little pamphlet, *An Examination into the Leading Principles of the Federal Constitution*. In his words:

> Liberty of the press, trial by jury, the Habeas Corpus writ, even Magna Charta itself, although justly deemed the palladia of freedom, are all inferior considerations, when compared with a general distribution of real property among every class of people.[34]

> Wherever we cast our eyes, we see this truth, that *property* is the basis of *power;* and this, being established as a cardinal point, directs us to the means of preserving our freedom.[35]

Without this distribution of power and widely-accessible liberty for property ownership, Webster argued, all other rights were less secure. The American free economy would constitute a significant improvement over the feudalism of previous centuries as long as a powerful federal government could be kept at bay. This experiment in liberty, however, was short-lived.

THE CENTRALIZATION OF POWER & PROPERTY OWNERSHIP IN THE HUMANIST AGE

With the age of man and the conquest of secular humanism, came the centralization of power, a massive increase in the size of national governments, and what Hilaire Belloc called "an unfree majority of non-owners" and the "reestablishment of slavery"[36] in the West. Historian Allan Carlson notes that by 1912 one third of England was indigent, and 95% were dispossessed of land and capital. Belloc sees the rise of statism and power concentration occurring with Henry VIII seizing church lands—an act which certainly empowered the state and its most ardent supporters. While the major Eastern powers (China and Russia) turned to communism in the 20th Century, the West created an unhealthy liaison between the socialist state and the rising capitalist system. Centralization of control over the means of production at the hands of the state and the new aristocracy came on strong. The citizen voters surrendered ownership of land and other means of production, and all were educated in government schools to rely upon the state for everything, from daycare to transgender surgeries.

Belloc points out that this was a return to the "servile basis—the foundation [of economy] before the advent of the Christian faith, from which that faith slowly weaned it, and to which in the decay of that faith it naturally returns."[37] It was a comfortable slavery, however. Government-enforced policies like workers' compensation, unemployment insurance, minimum wage, medical insurance, socialist medicine, and so forth were intended to lock the masses into a "wage-earning servility."[38]

Mark well, Belloc was not advocating renting a home or

"purchasing" a home on a thirty-year mortgage. He called for distributed ownership of the means of production by which the worker earns his living. Belloc's main concern was the loss of the will to this freedom. He believed all "relics" of the freedom instinct were gone by the turn of the 20th Century.[39] With only a few exceptions, the trends he spoke of continued to worsen over the succeeding century. The sum total of economic freedom diminished everywhere in the world during the humanist age.

The inevitable result of these economic trends included the dissolution of the family, a wider and deeper integration of women into the workforce, the ever-increasing irrelevance of fatherhood, and the breakdown of the moral character for each successive generation.

Both the capitalists and communists played tug-of-war over incorporating women into the labor force. Neither were interested in sustaining the nuclear family or the family economy. As core to the *Communist Manifesto*, Karl Marx (1818-1883) wanted the instruments of communal production equally distributed "to women."[40] His was the makings of a social revolution. Well before the revolution gained traction, Marx laid out the agenda: "The first condition for the liberation of the wife is to bring the whole female sex into public industry and... this in turn demands the abolition of the monogamous family as the economic unit of society." When his detractors accused him of "abolishing the family," Marx argued that the capitalists were doing the same thing. His socialist co-conspirator, Friedrich Engels further insisted that "the liberation of the wife" from the husband and the family economy must include bringing "the whole female sex back into the public industry."[41] He clearly understood the implications of these new definitions for "freedom" and "equality":

> With the transfer of the means of production into common ownership, the single family ceases to be the economic unit of society. Private housekeeping is transformed into a social industry. The care and education of the children becomes a public affair; society looks after

all children alike, whether they are legitimate or not. This removes all the anxiety about the "consequences," which today is the most essential social—moral as well as economic—factor that prevents a girl from giving herself completely to the man she loves. Will not that suffice to bring about the gradual growth of unconstrained sexual intercourse...[42]

"Unconstrained sexual intercourse," the collapse of the family, the increase in illegitimacy, and mass abortion was the inevitable consequence of this new economy–all part of the social experiment attempted by the post-Christian world over a period of 150 years. The results were devastating for Russia, Europe, and America.

The increased participation of married women in the workforce may have been the most revolutionary and devastating economic development in the modern age. Married women (35-44 years of age) working outside the home in the United States increased from 2% to 75% between 1900 and 2000.[43] Not once does the participation trend shift direction until flatlining after the 2008 recession. Engel and Marx's agenda reached near-completion with 70% of American mothers with home-bound children moved into the labor force.[44] What would this do to the character of nations?

A few social commentators had the courage to suggest that the total absence of fathers and the almost total absence of mothers would harm children in the progressive age—that utopian vision of the socialist-capitalist world. At the twilight of Western civilization, Mary Eberstadt (2004), Christina Hoff-Sommers (2000), and a few others wrote some very unpopular books suggesting there might be a problem.

THE BREAKDOWN OF CHARACTER &
THE CONSEQUENCES OF SIN

Economics is a hotly debated topic and extremely worldview-dependent when arguing for certain policies, preferred objectives, and the social good. Applying the relativist outlook, the humanist cannot possibly identify the desired end, or determine with any certainty the economic policies which might yield that end. At the very root of it, the Christian worldview holds that only God can define the good life and prescribe how to achieve it. The Word of God therefore offers the gold standard for all economic wisdom. For example, the Bible does not condemn wealth disparities as a sinful condition.

> The LORD maketh poor, and maketh rich: he bringeth low, and lifteth up. (1 Samuel 2:7)

Ultimately, God is the source of all material blessings. Yet wealth is not a measure of a man's life. Contrary to materialistic thinking (whether coming from Karl Marx or anyone else), the Christian does not value a man's life according to an economic metric. However, the Bible does condemn stealing and the confiscation of property as a violation of God's commandments. Such acts are defined as unethical behavior. And the sins of greed, covetousness, and envy are soundly condemned. Legitimate wealth and riches come by humility, the fear of the Lord, and hard work. Get-rich-quick schemes and intentions are reprobated, and the potential snares attending wealth are pointed out throughout Scripture.

> By humility and the fear of the LORD are riches, and honour, and life. (Proverbs 22:4)

> He becometh poor that dealeth with a slack hand: but the hand of the diligent maketh rich. (Proverbs 10:4)

> Wealth gotten by vanity shall be diminished: but he that gathereth by

labour shall increase. (Proverbs 13:11)

An inheritance may be gotten hastily at the beginning; but the end thereof shall not be blessed. (Proverbs 20:21)

And he said unto them, Take heed, and beware of covetousness: for a man's life consisteth not in the abundance of the things which he possesseth. (Luke 12:15)

Godliness with contentment is great gain. For we brought nothing into this world, and it is certain we can carry nothing out. And having food and raiment let us be therewith content. But they that will be rich fall into temptation and a snare, and into many foolish and hurtful lusts, which drown men in destruction and perdition. (1 Timothy 6:6-9)

To the extent that nations and individuals follow these principles, they will find the good life and achieve the good end. In all economic assessments and studies, the Christian will hold to these principles as the fundamental metric. Also, Scripture describes a nation which comes under the judgment of God in certain economic terms:

Thou shalt plant vineyards, and dress them, but shalt neither drink of the wine, nor gather the grapes; for the worms shall eat them. Thou shalt have olive trees throughout all thy coasts, but thou shalt not anoint thyself with the oil; for thine olive shall cast his fruit. Thou shalt beget sons and daughters, but thou shalt not enjoy them; for they shall go into captivity. All thy trees and fruit of thy land shall the locust consume. The stranger that is within thee shall get up above thee very high; and thou shalt come down very low. He shall lend to thee, and thou shalt not lend to him: he shall be the head, and thou shalt be the tail. Moreover all these curses shall come upon thee, and shall pursue thee, and overtake thee, till thou be destroyed; because thou hearkenedst not unto the voice of the Lord thy God, to keep his commandments and his statutes which he commanded thee. (Deuteronomy 28:39-45)

Taken from a biblical perspective, debt is not necessarily a sin any more than disease or divorce is a sin. Yet, it is still seen as a negative evil—a consequence of living in a sinful world. Thus, the metrics for determining a good economy or a bad economy should be obvious. Work is an obligation for all. Employment is a positive. Debt is a negative. Losing children to the state is a negative. Slavery is a negative, and—under Christ—chattel slavery is wrong. Stealing or redistributing wealth is a violation of God's laws.

Verse 41 of Deuteronomy 28 quoted above, includes the dissolution of family and parental rights in the enumerated list of curses befalling the society that rejects God's commandments. As far as the family economy breaks down and sons and daughters are hired by, regulated by, or made part of the state, that society has come under some measure of God's judgement.

THE FAILURE OF THE FAMILY ECONOMY

Between 1820 and 1880, an enormous shift occurred in Western socio-economics. Whereas children had previously been employed in family economies (generally family farms or home businesses), the Industrial Revolution moved them into the corporate-capitalist economy. Subsequently, children were passed off to the socialist economy via child labor laws and school compulsory attendance laws throughout most modern nations. In the opening paragraphs of his classic autobiography written in 1888, missionary John G. Paton commented that the destruction of the family farm and the family economy in Scotland were tragedies that need not have happened. The loss to the nation, he lamented, was "vital, if not irreparable."[45]

At first, the Industrial Revolution introduced children into the large factories and mills. In 1788, about two-thirds of operators on 143 watermills in Britain were children.[46] By 1819, the numbers had dropped to 56%, then down to 42% by 1835.[47] The 20th Century introduced the age of adolescence, compulsory school attendance, minimum wage laws, college education, massive disposable income (compared to previous centuries), and an entertainment culture, all of which delayed maturity and initiation into the work force.

The following data illustrates child labor trends in the United States from 1880 to 1930 for children ten to fifteen years of age. Child labor continued to drop sharply from 1880 through 1930 as children were moved into government-provided educational institutions. Yet the participation of young boys and girls on family farms stayed strong through 1930, with 75% of young boys and 62% of young girls still involved. As the family farm disappeared over the next ninety years, barely 0.5% of America's children were involved in the family economy by the 21st Century. Between 1935 and 2017, the number of family farms dropped off from 7,000,000 to 2,000,000.[48] By 2015, the proportion of persons registering as self-employed had dropped to 10%, representing a steady decline from 19% in 1949 and 50% in 1900.[49] Household economy and the distributed system was all but gone.

Child Labor in the US—1880-1930[50]

	1880	1900	1930
Labor force participation rates of children 10 to 15 years old (percentages)			
Males	32.5	26.1	6.4
Females	12.2	6.4	2.9
Percentage of 10 to 15-year-olds in agricultural employment			
Males	69.9	67.6	74.5
Females	37.3	74.5	61.5

Note: 1880 figures are based on Carter and Sutch (1996). Other numbers are unadjusted from those reported by the Bureau of the Census.

A serious conundrum faced the post-Christian world. How would human society salvage maximum freedom without Christ (and

Christian faith and character) without slipping back into the slave-oriented economy of the pre-Christ world? Sans Christ, the world could only trade one form of slavery for another while pretending the new forms were better than the old. Slavery to the modern totalitarian state would win out in most cases.

Absent of true faith in God and the capacity for self-government among a substantial segment of the population, the character of the nation would fall. The salt loses its savor, and the lapse of faith in the church means a loss of influence upon the nation as a whole. The organized church in the West was irrelevant by the turn of the 20th Century. When the progressive (or regressive) church attempted to influence the culture, the faith was stripped of God's law and all that was left was a "social gospel." That was more of a cover for socialism, an advocacy program for big government solutions. The churches failed to disciple nations by teaching them to observe all that Christ had commanded (Matt. 28:20). By this time, Church attendance in the United States had little to do with the character of the nation. Rising divorce rates, illegitimacy rates, pornography addiction rates, drug addiction rates, and the lack of parental discipline would progressively undermine the character of the nation. Since a healthy economy and economic freedom are always dependent on the character of the nation, there was no economic plan that could save this civilization. Only Christ and His Gospel could have provided appreciable change for family life and society.

Karl Marx and the progressives of the 19th Century rejected child labor and the "disempowerment" of the employee class. And the socialist solution would take Western society "out of the frying pan into the fire." Radical socialists pushed for egalitarian pay, the elimination of property ownership, the abolishment of the family, and government-controlled education of children. Western Europe and

North America rather opted for a capitalist-socialist materialism—a slower, softer, and gentler path to slavery.

THE FALL OF THE WESTERN ECONOMY

The fall of the Western economy comes by the fall of the socialist-capitalist economy, and the fall of a monetary system, both of which were built up on humanist ideals, covetousness, and greed.

Marxist class envy and ethnic envy, encouraged by the social justice, the social gospel, and liberation theology movements among the Catholics and Protestants spread like a cancer through Western societies (not to mention African and South American nations). Proverbs 14:30, stated that envy "rots the bones," but systemic covetousness and envy rots out whole economies. By definition, Marxist ideologies have always been destructive to the character of nations. For one, the abolition of the family as proposed by Marx and advocated by government policies (pushing abortion, free sex and birth control, gender confusion, and every form of sexual anarchy) was a bad idea. The attempt on the part of the government to eliminate God, and then to replace God with government, must end in utter ruin. But then, the economic fallout and breakdown of character resulting from the redistribution of wealth schemes (or better called "institutionalized stealing"), would be impossible to repair for a century or two. Socialism didn't work for the Chinese during the Xin Dynasty, and the same can be said for the Western experiment (and every other nation in the world that copied the ill-conceived economy).

Taking the US as representative of other nations, in 1950, only 8% of the Gross National Product consisted of social welfare and social security expenditures.[51] About 12% of Americans received a check from the government. By the end, the super majority of Americans were taking welfare checks from federal and state governments. Seventy million American elderly (21% of the population) were supported by federal social security programs, and fifty-nine million Americans (18% of the population) were on welfare. Add to that President Biden's "advanced child tax credit program," which placed another 61 million children (and their parents) into government welfare in 2021. A family of ten children would have received $36,000 of welfare payments in 2021. In all, an estimated 73% of Americans received some form of government assistance. Heritage Foundation calculated that the average poor family received $76,400 in benefits in 2021—about the same as the median household income in the country.[52] Such wild redistribution schemes would only create more government dependency, upset worker supply for companies, and further wreck the economy. Socialism was the dry rot of modern society.

GAMBLING, GREED, &
THE COLLAPSE OF CAPITALISM

Meanwhile, the US stock markets as the best representative of Western capitalism turned into casinos, and a spirit of greed ruled among investors. During the final years of the Western economic boom, investors in the stock market would routinely run the price-earnings (P/E) ratio and the Wilshire 5000 to GDP ratios to record levels. Such metrics provided insight into the investor's interest in productivity and value.

For thirty years post-1992, the Standard and Poor P/E mostly hovered between 20 and 45, as compared to the seventy-year average of 13.5.[53] The Wilshire 5000/GDP reached 201%, against a historical average of 80%. This meant that investors were far less interested in the earnings and productivity of their investments. Such metrics indicate that Americans had shifted to a greed-and-gambling mode in which they were more committed to the capital gain of their investment by the quick sell, than they were to owning the means of production, real productivity, and annual earnings.

As this commitment to real productivity died out, Western civilization lost interest in re-investing for the future and stewarding a heritage for coming generations. The Age of Greed takes shape first in 1985 as the P/E exceeded 16 for the first time. On this metric, there were only two greedy years up until 1995 and then seventeen years of greed post 1995. The stocks were overpriced, but the market had turned into just another gambling casino for those who would still trade. For the decade following the Great Recession of 2008, the US economy eked out a miserable 2.0% per annum growth—the lowest recovery cycle rate in history, for a 27% expansion. Over the same period, wild-eyed market investors intoxicated with greed drove the stock indexes up by 500%. This extreme valuation of stock was at least in part due to stock buy-back programs, in which companies would borrow to purchase their own stock. By artificially inflating the value of the stock, companies hoped to rustle up more lemmings to participate in the buying frenzy. An insatiable greed would inevitably lead to stock market "crashes" and the great depression to follow.

The shift to the "Age of Greed" was also visible in the US gambling spree initiated during the mid-1970s. Initially consisting mainly of government-sponsored lotteries, this gambling binge began with total sales reaching only a few billion dollars annually. By 2020, the US economy was frittering away $120 billion per year in gambling losses, topping both China and Japan's numbers (averaging $80 billion together). An additional $90 billion annually was gambled away in other Western European countries and Australia. In total, the post-Christian West accounted for 72% of the world's gambling losses in any given year. The global gambling industry increased from $220 billion to $495 billion between 2002 and 2019.

ENSLAVEMENT TO DEBT

The rich rules over the poor, and the borrower is servant to the lender.
(Proverbs 22:7)

The whole world ran into debt in the 20th and 21st Centuries, but the debt binge was mainly inspired by Western nations. For centuries, during periods of relative peace, world debt would hover between 20% and 50% of the Gross World Product. Between 1970 and 2020, this ratio increased from 30% to 100%.[54] Contrary to the ancient biblical principle contained in Proverbs 22:7, debt was marketed as a preferred state for families, businesses, and governments during the Keynesian era. Enslavement was preferred. The pretense of wealth or economic health, and the pretense of social and sexual health was preferred over real health. Above all, biblical values were never to be considered as establishing ethical standards.

Private Debt to GDP hovered around 5% for the United States and most of Europe at the turn of the 19th Century. One hundred years later, private debt averaged around 80% of the GDP, and by the turn of the 21st Century, the ratio had increased to 175%. Meanwhile, non-financial business debt burgeoned from 38% of the GDP in 1962, to 63% of the GDP in 2004, scraping 85% of the GDP in 2021.

As illustrated in the accompanying chart, coming out of the War for Independence, the United States had faced a federal-debt-to-GDP ratio of 18%. By 1830, more principled presidents and legislatures managed to reduce that back down to 1-2% of the GDP. At the turn of the 20th Century, gross government debt in the US (local, state, and federal) amounted to 30% of the GDP. By 1980, the ratio had grown to 45%.[55] Largely due to the Keynesian policies of Presidents Ronald Reagan, George W. Bush, Barack Obama, and Donald Trump, this ratio expanded to an unprecedented 130% by 2020. To better understand the change in the national psyche and the revolutionary worldview that seized control of the nation after 1980, one needs only to follow the exponential increase in national debt spending. Between 1800 and 1900, the nation increased its debt ratio a full 17%. Between 1900 and 1980, the ratio increased by only 15%. Then, between 1980 and 2020, mostly "conservative" Republican administrations expanded the government debt to GDP ratio by the unprecedented increase of 90%. And, at the end, 73% of the total world government debt was subsumed by Western nations. These nations only made up 53% of the Gross World Product. Remarkably, the wealthiest nations in the world were the most indebted. . .and impoverished. This is how the debtor nations of the US, the UK, France, Germany, Italy, Spain, Canada, and Japan became the tail, and not the head in the world economy (to use biblical language).

Future historians will always remember the devolution of the Western economy by debt-spending following the election of Ronald Reagan in 1980. The root problem, however, was more than economic. At first came the ideas, the worldview shift, and the social and moral

U.S. Government Debt, 1790-2015

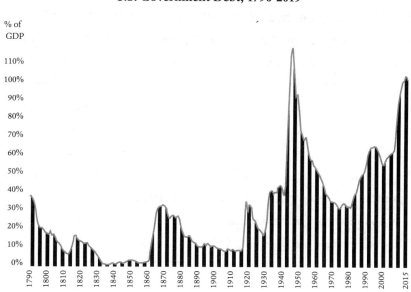

revolutions rotting out the foundations of the Western world. The economic policies were only the effects—the bad consequences of bad ideas which had already corrupted the Western mind. The reasons for the debt binge is better explained by the shift in monetary philosophy— the story of the rise and fall of money in the West.

A BRIEF REVIEW OF THE RISE & FALL OF MONEY

> How is the faithful city become an harlot! it was full of judgment; righteousness lodged in it; but now murderers. Thy silver is become dross, thy wine mixed with water... (Isaiah 1:21-22)

As referenced in this prophetic word against Jerusalem, the ancient pagan world thought nothing of debauching the money supply by adding tin to the silver coinage. Chinese banks began fractional reserve banking sometime around AD 1000 when they discovered that they could lend out more money than they held in reserve. By Trajan's reign in Rome (AD 117), the Augustus denarius (a coin originally containing 95% pure silver) had been debased to a silver content of 85%. A century later, the coin held only 50% of its original value, and by AD 270 the coin had fallen out of use, with only 0.5% silver left. This monetary debauchery has always been a charade, a sleight-of-hand device to accommodate the power state. Intending to benefit the ever-burgeoning state coffers, the charlatan-politicians responsible were still hoping nobody would notice or care until it was too late.

In the end, only a Christian civilization would care enough to insist upon honesty and uprightness in these dealings. The Christian King Charlemagne instated honest money and made sure his son maintained the course. Nonetheless, debasement of coins was still a problem through the centuries, especially with the Muslims. The Saracens started out with a Spanish coin of 65 grains in AD 600, measured out at 60 grains around 1150, finally dropping off to 13 grains by 1220. Christian law resisted the corruption for a thousand years. Should a moneyer fail to mint quality coins during the reign of King Henry I in England (ruled 1100-1135), he would lose his right hand, specifically on Christmas Day at the assize of Winchester.

But with the resurgence of humanist ideologies in the Italian Renaissance, came moral compromise in banking. The Medici banks lowered their reserve ratio under 50% (some say to 5 or 10%), and the banks were ruined by 1390.

Three hundred years later, a certain Johan Palmstruch introduced paper money via the Bank of Stockholm (around 1658), and then proceeded to issue excess loans on demand deposits. His paper money was supposed to have been exchangeable for gold or silver but, alas, Johan issued more notes than what he had in hard metals. For his pains, the banker was thrown in prison for the rest of his life.

The first serious debasement of money in the Christian West would have to wait until the rise of the revolutionary spirit in France. Most fittingly, the French Revolution planted the first seeds for the destruction of the Western socio-economy. Against the better advice of finance minister Jacques Necker, the frenzied French legislature issued $9.5 billion (or 45 billion livres) in worthless paper notes, reputedly backed by lands confiscated from the Church. This flagrant fiscal policy just about killed the French economy, only salvaged by Napoleon and the Napoleonic Wars. This was the beginning of an economic revolution which, by ebb and flow, would wash over the entire Western world for the greatest debauching in human history.

> With the exception only of the period of the gold standard, practically all governments of history have used their exclusive power to issue money in order to defraud and plunder the people. (Friedrich A. Hayek, Austrian economist, 1974 Nobel Prize-winner for economics)[56]

The modern concept of a national bank, a government-monopoly of printed money, and fractional reserves was the contribution of a contemptible man by the name of John Law (1671-1729). After killing a man in Scotland, Law fled to France, where he tested his far-fetched economic theories. Louis XIV had driven his economy into the ground and was desperate for a quick fix. Law proceeded to print up a batch of paper money only partially backed by silver. When depositors enmasse converged on the bank looking to change their paper notes back into gold coin, the government banned the sale of gold. Scores of people were killed in the ensuing riots. Law spent the remaining years of his life gambling away the last of his own earnings and died an indigent. Yet his economist-biographer reminds us, "John Law behaved very much like a man of the Twentieth Century who knew that the banking system did not need to be anchored by gold or silver... His theoretical economic writings...captured many key conceptual points which are very much part of modern monetary theorizing."[57] As it turns out, this would not be the first profligate economist to take the whole world in the wrong direction. The abject failure of John Law was no discouragement to future economists who wished to repeat these same policies on a much larger scale. As the Western economy faltered, the populace was still asking the question: Have we reached the pinnacle of human achievement in the third millennium, or is this the most spectacular moral, social, and economic failure in the history of mankind?

SEEDS OF DESTRUCTION PLANTED IN THE US

Byzantium in the East was successful at retaining honest money for about a thousand years; and the West was also blessed with hard money for about fifteen hundred years. Of all the themes which could be followed in the history of the West, the battle for honest money is one of the most illuminating. The hearts of men are revealed in the unfolding saga of banking and money.

The French revolutionary influence and the constituent spiritual forces working in America immediately following independence were monumental and irresistible. With grudging support from President George Washington, Alexander Hamilton forced the national bank upon the country in 1791—an ostensibly private entity. In 1816, the bank agreed to kick back $1.5 million annually to the federal government in exchange for a banking monopoly of sorts. For the President and Congress, the lure of these monies to further aggrandize a still-slender government was hard to resist. When the national bank and others would lend out more money than they held in deposits (in gold and silver coins), bank runs ensued in 1819 and 1837. Importing the revolutionary spirit into the states, a French atheist became the major investor in the Second Bank of the United States—and the wealthiest man in the US between 1810 and 1831. Stephen Girard also attempted to form the first secular, atheist public school in America, stipulating that no clergy enter school grounds and only secular curriculum be employed. President Andrew Jackson vetoed the rechartering of the US National Bank on July 10, 1832, arguably the most gutsy presidential action in the nation's history to that point.

The first "Continental Dollars" issued by the Continental Congress in 1776 were intended to be zero-interest bonds or IOUs, attached to a kind of weak promise they could be repaid later in hard money. Redemption dates were changed in 1779 and 1780, resulting in a devaluation of the bonds—a precursor to the dishonest system to come. President Abraham Lincoln's administration was the first to issue unbacked paper money (not convertible on demand at a fixed rate into any specie) via the National Banking Acts of 1863 and 1864, and the Legal Tender Act. This would constitute the first major turning point for the Western world—the end of a 1,500 year legacy of honest money.

Fifteen years later President Rutherford Hayes (1822-1893)

attempted to make good on the unbacked dollars, offering to exchange the "greenbacks" for gold or silver. In his words, "expediency and justice both demand an honest currency."[58] A devout Christian of Presbyterian background, President Hayes would organize Bible readings, hymn sings, and prayer meetings at the White House.

Honesty still a prime value to the man filling the highest office in the land, President Hayes did his best to clean up the spoils system (political favoritism) in a burgeoning bureaucracy, while returning the country to trustworthy weights and measures. However, the National Banking Act of 1863 had already created a national monopoly on bank notes (currency) by assigning a 10% tax on state bank-issued notes. By 1870, there were 1,638 national bank locations and only 325 state banks. However, some margin of competition was still allowed, and by 1913 the number of state banks had increased to 15,526 compared to only 9,500 national banks. Resisting any and all free market or decentralized banking solutions, powerful interests laid out a plan for complete centralized control of banking, lending, and issuance of money via the Federal Reserve System.

Established by the US Congress in 1913, the Federal Reserve was made up of twelve regional banks. A national board of directors would be appointed by the president of the United States, with each bank to be privately owned (at least on paper). This board would control the money supply and reserve requirements for commercial banks— at first setting the marginal reserve requirement at 20%. The ratio requirement was later reduced to 10%, and then to 0% on March 26, 2020.[59] By its sheer size and power, the Federal Reserve enabled the United States to take on unprecedented debt, with the intent of courting a high level of public trust and an appearance of stability for an extended period of time. This lasted for over a century.

WOE TO THAT MAN

Woe unto the world because of offences! for it must needs be that offences come; but woe to that man by whom the offence cometh! (Matthew 18:7)

In the words of Christ, great offenses must necessarily come into the world. In the case of the economic collapse of the Western world, the offense came by one man more than any other. John Maynard Keynes (1883-1946) stands out as the best single representative of the whole ruinous scene. His lifestyle and worldview exactly correlated with his economic theories, all of which were wholeheartedly adopted by Western society between 1980 and 2020.

Well into the 21st Century, John Maynard Keynes was still commemorated as "the greatest economic thinker of the 20th Century."[60] He helped establish the International Monetary Fund and the World Bank, and his policies have been incorporated into the largest economies in the world—including the United States, Japan, the UK, and China.

Both political parties, Democrat and Republican alike, embraced Keynesian economics in the United States. Although at first opposed to the idea, Franklin Delano Roosevelt accepted Keynes' theories by the time of his inauguration in 1933, declaring to the world that "our greatest primary task is to put people to work. This is no unsolvable problem if we face it wisely and courageously. It can be accomplished in part by direct recruiting by the government itself, treating the task as we would treat the emergency of a war…"[61] American President Richard Nixon announced to the world in 1971, "I am now a Keynesian in economics."[62] Virtually all economists agreed that President Ronald Reagan continued the legacy of John Maynard Keynes by accelerated debt spending in the 1980s.[63] After a brief respite in the 1990s, President George W. Bush revived Keynesian economics with more unprecedented debt spending in the 2000s.[64] Continuing the legacy in 2008, President Barack Obama was also characterized as an "unapologetic Keynesian."[65] According to his own admission, President Donald Trump's fiscal spending policies emulated John Maynard Keynes' philosophy of "priming the pump."[66] By this time, it was "Keynes on steroids."

APOSTASY OF THE HIGHEST ORDER

> But these, as natural brute beasts, made to be taken and destroyed, speak evil of the things that they understand not; and shall utterly perish in their own corruption...Having eyes full of adultery, and that cannot cease from sin; beguiling unstable souls: an heart they have exercised with covetous practices; cursed children: which have forsaken the right way, and are gone astray, following the way of Balaam the son of Bosor, who loved the wages of unrighteousness; (2 Peter 2:12, 14-15)

As in the case of the rest of the apostate philosophers or the modern "Nephilim" who destroyed the Western world, the Christian heritage of John Maynard Keynes was thick and full of significance. His maternal grandfather John Brown took the pastorate at John Bunyan's Meeting House at Bedford in 1864. It was the same church building in which the renowned Baptist John Bunyan had preached two hundred years earlier. John's mother Florence was raised in John Bunyan's manse, decorated in relics handed down from the author of the most famous Christian book published in the last half millennium. Pastor John Brown was seen as the nonconformist bishop overseeing surrounding churches, and Florence helped her mother teach Sunday school in the old meeting house on Sundays.

Similarly, John Maynard Keynes' father Neville also received a religious upbringing in which his father taught the boy he must be "like Jesus."[67] Neville's grandmother lived with the family in the home, where "she sat all day with a Bible on her knee, mouthing the words of the scriptures."[68] Neville got to know Florence while attending her father's preaching at Bunyan's old meeting house. They were married in 1882, and John Maynard was born on June 5, 1883.

Apostasy came first with Keynes' father. Neville was heavily influenced by Henry Sidgwick, his instructor at Cambridge University. The son of an Anglican bishop and the brother-in-law of the Archbishop of Canterbury, Sidgwick was best known for introducing Jeremy Bentham's utilitarian ethics into Cambridge. Keynes noted of Sidgwick: "He never did anything but wonder whether Christianity was true and prove that it wasn't..."[69] While the Downgrade controversy was gaining steam, the Keynes family was souring on their Baptist evangelical roots.

As early as six years old, John Maynard Keynes registered his strong distaste for God. Upon leaving church one Sunday morning, the boy uttered his opinion loud enough for all to hear him. "It's the prayers I dislike the most,"[70] he said. At fourteen years of age, John studied under a devout Christian headmaster at Eton, the Rev. Edmond Warre. But the preachers at chapel made him "squirm," and he called the messages "revolting."[71] Although he was officially confirmed to take communion at seventeen, Keynes never took the faith seriously. It was always a great delight for him "to puncture his friends' religious beliefs by refuting arguments for the existence of God."[72]

The British apostasy was in full swing by the turn of the 20th Century, as specially evidenced by the rise of homosexuality among the "educated class." John Maynard Keynes' first illicit liaison came about with the young son of an Anglican bishop—Dillwyn Knox. How the young "Christian" Brits could face down the 2,000-year moral praxis is explained by biographer Richard Davenport-Hines: "Keynes's classical education ensured that his limited susceptibility to guilt was nearer to Plato's than to a Christian's."[73] His second tryst at Eton followed with

Daniel Macmillan, elder brother of the future prime minister. The corruption of British society was fairly complete by this time.

At Cambridge, Keynes came under the influence of Oscar Browning, a professor who had been removed from Eton in 1875 for his inappropriate relations with the male students.[74] For some reason, Browning was promoted to a professorship at King's College in Cambridge where he advanced his foul influence, re-introducing Greek forms of education and sexuality into the university in the early 20th Century.

The extremely vile nature of Keynes' life following Eton turns out to be highly reminiscent of the biblical accounts of Sodom or Gibeah (Judges 20-21), yet very much unprecedented in the history of the Christian West. The details are publicly accessible but would too easily defile the reading audience to include them here.

These classically-educated men were self-conscious humanists. They saw themselves as above the law, exempt from all morals, and members of a social and intellectual class which might escape the judgment of almighty God. Well before the masses turned to wholesale sexual sin, homosexuality, adultery, and divorce (in the 1960s and 1970s), the *avant-garde* pushed the sexual boundaries and social mores as far out as anyone could. These were the academic elite. At Cambridge the young rebels referred to themselves as "The Apostles" of the new gospel of humanism—men who had pretty well "set themselves against the Lord and His Anointed" (Ps. 2:3). They called themselves "Pagan missionaries, looking towards dead cities [Sodom and Gomorrah] for a cult."[75] Somehow, they hoped they would find safety in numbers. Collecting all that hubris in one place gave them a sense of impenetrability to any god who might attempt to interfere with them.

John Maynard Keynes understood the risks of participating in flagrant sexual perversion, but times were changing in London in the early 20th Century. Oscar Wilde had defended his homosexual trysts in three separate court trials (by appealing to the love sonnets of William Shakespeare). Wilde was found guilty and sentenced to two years of hard labor on May 25, 1895. But young Keynes sinned flagrantly in this manner, assembling careful lists of his dozens of anonymous sexual encounters in his diary—sixty-five in 1909, another twenty-six in 1910, and thirty-nine in 1911. He frequented the darkest corners of London and did not stop short of pedophilia, recording his sordid behavior with "boys" and "youth."[76]

> If a man also lie with mankind, as he lieth with a woman, both of them have committed an abomination: they shall surely be put to death; their blood shall be upon them." (Leviticus 20:13)

More the social or sexual revolutionary than an economist, Keynes became something of an international prophet for the new age of humanism and Christian apostasy, leading the charge for the moral, social, cultural, and economic unravelling of the West. Addressing an audience of communists in 1925, Keynes encouraged a "progressive" view of conception control, feminism, the use of contraceptives, and the dismantling of family economies. Such words as these were common parlance in the 21st Century, but revolutionary in the 1920s. Keynes told his audience, "Conception control and the use of contraceptives, marriage laws, the treatment of sexual offences and abnormalities, the economic position of women,...in all these matters the existing state of the law and of orthodoxy is still medieval—altogether out of touch with civilised opinion and civilised practices."[77]

THE PHILOSOPHY OF JOHN MAYNARD KEYNES

After Eton, Keynes was happy to discard the utilitarian ethics of Jeremy Bentham in favor of the amoral philosophy of G. E. Moore. To argue for any kind of good outcome in the long run (as Bentham had suggested) would, Keynes thought, be an "accountant's nightmare." The thing he liked about Moore was that his worldview dispensed with morals altogether. In Keynes' words, "We accepted Moore's religion, so to speak, and discarded his morals. Indeed, in our opinion, one of the greatest advantages of his religion, was that it made morals unnecessary."[78] Biographer Robert Skidelsky connected Keynes' apostasy to Moore: "Keynes never needed a Jehovah, because he had never experienced despair. It was not his atheism, but his faithfulness to Moore's revelation, embedded in his life of a secular religious order, which kept him out of the Christian camp."[79]

For these 20th Century profligate philosophers, ethics became haphazard and degraded into "what seems good to me for the moment" or, worse yet, "what feels good to me for the moment." Entire institutions and economic systems would follow in the footsteps of the modern ethicists who admitted to no ethics at all.

In those days there was no king in Israel: every man did that which was right in his own eyes. (Judges 21:25)

THE ECONOMICS OF JOHN MAYNARD KEYNES

Unequal weights and unequal measures are both alike an abomination to the Lord." (Proverbs 20:10)

John Maynard Keynes, the homosexual, followed up on the economic philosophy of John Law, the murderer from Scotland. His was big-government economics, including total centralized control and monopoly of the money supply, fractional reserve banking, and fully unbacked currency. In his *Tract on Monetary Reform* released on December 11, 1923, Keynes called for an "inflation tax" in which "a government can transfer resources to itself without applying to Parliament (or Congress) for the money."[80] He repudiated the gold standard as a "barbarous relic."

John Maynard Keynes published his magnum opus in 1936, *The General Theory of Employment, Interest, and Money*, referred to by Murray Rothbard as "one of the most dazzlingly successful books of all time." Rothbard explained that this "revolutionary theory had conquered the economics profession and soon had transformed public policy, while old-fashioned economics was swept, unhonored and unsung, into the dustbin of history."[81]

Keynes considered his method of government manipulation of the money supply as a means to provide a hidden tax. In his classic work *The Economic Consequences of the Peace*, he admitted openly that:

> By a continuing process of inflation, governments can confiscate, secretly and unobserved, an important part of the wealth of their citizens.... There is no subtler, no surer means of overturning the existing basis of society than to debauch the currency. The process engages all the hidden forces of economic law on the side of destruction, and does it in a manner which not one man in a million is able to diagnose.[82]

Yet Keynes insisted on governmental control of the "aggregate amount of resources devoted to augmenting" the instruments of production and "the basic rate of reward"[83] for the investors. During economic downturns, he recommended government intervention and substantial increases in government spending—what he called "a comprehensive socialization of investment."[84]

According to Keynesian theories, governments would increase deficit spending by artificially lowering interest rates to stimulate more investment and consumption, which in turn was supposed to produce higher employment rates and more productivity. Trusting all power to central governments, Keynes charged the supreme controllers with saving national economies. They would kick start a stagnating economy using debt-spending, fractional reserve banking, and money generation. Such ultimate reliance on human governments would prove fatal. The homosexual economist wrongly assumed that consumerism offers the best motivation to work, and employment the best stimulant for the economy. The idolatry of consumerism only fed a spirit of selfishness and further moral decline, appealing to the lowest inclinations and motives of the human heart. Keynes' theory, fast-tracked and mass-produced across the globe, would destroy the character of a people and remove whatever common grace was still operable. As money flowed into consumption by consumers who were living for the moment, less money was available for re-investing into new hiring, tooling, and development. Savings was discouraged, while debt and consumer-driven lifestyles were encouraged. Lower interest rates, easy debt, big government spending programs, and money generation produced out-of-control inflation, which resulted in stagflation and a drop-off of longterm productive investing. Such was the worldview of a perverse economist who laid the groundwork for a worldwide economic conflagration a century later.

WHAT'S WRONG WITH THIS THINKING?

And for this cause God shall send them strong delusion, that they should believe a lie: that they all might be damned who believed not the truth, but had pleasure in unrighteousness. (2 Thessalonians 2:11-12)

John Maynard Keynes was wrong, mainly because he disagreed with God. His assumption that debt spending makes for a stronger nation flatly contradicted biblical instruction on debt and economics.

Deuteronomy 28:43-45 clearly testifies that nations subscribing to a debt-based economy over the long haul prove themselves to be under God's judgment. They become very low. Short-sighted economists who cannot see beyond the next twenty years or the next government administration may assume that conditions will improve and that human character will sustain with each generation of debt spending.

But, after the nations embracing these deceptions collapse, the world will once more realize that God's principles are true and right. And Kipling's "gods of the copybook headings" will "limp up to explain it once more."

Yet Keynes failed at another point. Economies are fundamentally built upon the character of the people, not the motive to spend and consume. If the overall character of the workers (in a corporation or nation) slumps, the productivity of the corporate body will inevitably contract. Somehow, this homosexual economist lacked the character to realize that the artificial capitalization of bureaucracies and corporations with more debt and increased consumer spending could not compensate for the lapse in the national character. No nation could survive the idolatry of mass consumerism, especially with unlimited access to debt-spending and conception control. The self-centered, lifestyle of the modern existentialist was further enabled by the breakdown of marriage and the family, and the rise of homosexuality and pornography. Living for oneself, seldom meant investing for the future. Little concern was paid towards productivity of labor or future returns. Devoted to living for the moment, the existentialist gives little thought to the long-term effects of his actions and fails to recognize the idolatry of his consumer-driven lifestyle. Such a morally corrupt worldview will inevitably lead to the destruction of a society, where the citizenry has given up.

As the character of a nation fails, the quality of products and services diminishes. Supply drops off, and prices increase. Even foods mass-produced under such a system lose nutritional value. Products won't last as long as they used to. Debt money produces less and less for both the employer and the consumer. With the diminishing concern for future generations and the decline of character, there is far less motivation to pay back the debt. And, the economy demands increasing levels of debt to stay afloat.

The weakening of an economy comes in direct proportion to the weakening of the character of a nation. But even more fundamentally, the weakening of an economy comes about by divine providence—an act of God. Economies break down when millions lose the motivation to work, or with the onset of mass illnesses, wars, and agricultural droughts and blights. All of these secondary causes are entirely under God's control. The secular economists, academics, and politicians who do not fear God can never solve these socio-economic conundrums by scientific solutions and centralized controls. They may (as God orders it) succeed in delaying a mega-depression for 30-40 years. But in such cases, social controllers are merely tools in God's hands to put off the inevitable and bring an even more severe lesson to bear upon the nations later.

THE FRUIT OF KEYNES

Divers weights, and divers measures, both of them are alike abomination to the Lord. (Proverbs 20:10)

At the behest of President Franklin D. Roosevelt, Congress remanded gold held by Federal Reserve banks into the U.S. Treasury via the Gold Reserve Act of January 30, 1934. FDR then arbitrarily increased the price of gold from $20.67 per ounce to $35.00 an ounce, thereby devaluing the dollar for the first time by fiat. Despite Winston Churchill's opposition, Britain capitulated to the Keynesian agenda on September 19, 1931 as the Bank of England abandoned the gold standard. Over the next eighty years, the value of gold increased to $2,000 per ounce—a result of the devaluation of the paper dollar by a hundred fold. To compare, Rome devalued its silver denarius to 5% of its original value over a period of three hundred years. The demise of the American dollar occurred over a period of eighty years—a much quicker moral and economic collapse this time. John Maynard Keynes' more sophisticated justifications for debauching the currency and artificially stimulating economies by deficit spending may have fooled the world for a century, but eventually "the gods of the copybook headings with terror and slaughter return." Whether it be ancient Persia, Greece, or Rome, or any other empire in the history of the world, the corruption of both sexuality and money (weights and measures) has meant the death knell of nations.

> Thou shalt not have in thy bag divers weights, a great and a small. Thou shalt not have in thine house divers measures, a great and a small. But thou shalt have a perfect and just weight, a perfect and just measure shalt thou have: that thy days may be lengthened in the land which the Lord thy God giveth thee. For all that do such things, and all that do unrighteously, are an abomination unto the Lord thy God. (Deuteronomy 25:13-16)

The international exchange rate for gold stayed at $35 per ounce until the Nixon Administration. After several inflationary adjustments, the US Congress finally removed the gold standard entirely in October 1976.

These monetary manipulations resulted in an extended peacetime debt crisis for the United States and the entire Western world. Between 1870 and 1976, America's peacetime total (public and private) debt to GDP ratio hovered between 140% and 160%. Following the removal of the last vestiges of the gold standard in 1976, the ratio rocketed upwards to 417%.

US Debt Explosion Follows Removal of Gold Standard

Year	Total Debt to GDP[85]	Government Debt to GD[86]
1870-1980	140% - 160%	20% -30%
1980	164%	31%
1990	230%	56%
2000	269%	55%
2008	363%	64%
2020	417%	130%

Taking its cues from Western nations after World War II, Japan adopted Keynesian policies on steroids, and the second largest economy in the world stumbled over and over again, and fell at the turn of the millennium.[87] Devoid of Christian foundations, the eastern nation remade into the Western image, fell quicker than the US and Europe. Between 1998 and 2016, Japan attempted seventeen stimulus spending bills, hedging bets on the Keynesian horse. Japan's debt-to-GDP ratio increased to 266%—the highest national debt in the world. To make matters worse, the Bank of Japan began purchasing government bonds through quantitative easing in 2013 and dallied with negative interest rates for awhile; and by 2021, the central bank held about 50% of Japan's debt. Faith in government monetary systems was slipping fast by this time. Quantitative easing was more or less the same thing as printing up money and then lending it to yourself. What investors in their right mind would have lent out their money to an entity that financed half its debt by printing money and lending to itself? All the while Japan courted the world's lowest birth rate (from the 1950s), and its population was shrinking at a rate of 600,000 citizens per year by AD 2020—a prime example of national burnout in the modern age.

When John Maynard Keynes was confronted with the question of what would happen with his debt-based economy in the long run, he responded, "In the long run, we are all dead."[88] What else would a childless, homosexual economist say, after he had passed $200 trillion of debt on to everyone else's grandchildren?

As judged by the annals of world governance, the general maxim for assessing world powers is this: the highest-populated nations retain the most power. When nations give up the will to bear children, they give up the will to carry on a civilization. At the turn of the 20th Century, seven out of ten of the most populated and most powerful countries in the world were Western nations. Russia was the third largest and the US was fourth largest in the world, followed by Germany, Austria-Hungary, Japan, the UK, France, and Italy. That was when Europe and America ruled the world. By 1950, only five out of the ten most populated countries in the world were Western nations. By the Fall of the West in the 2020s, only two out of the ten most populated nations claimed Western heritage—Russia and the United States. But Bolshevism, Marxism, the legalization of abortion, and the destruction of the family ruined Russia, imploding its birth rates ahead of the rest of the West. According to these forecasted trends, only two nations would remain in the list of the top 20 most populous and powerful nations in the world by 2050—the United States (4th place), and Russia (14th place). Germany would slip to a negligible 23rd place, the UK to 26th place, and France would barely beat out Niger and Mozambique at 28th place. The other 18 nations poised to control the world economy in the thirty year span of 2020 to 2050 hailed from south and east. Whether the United States, the only Western nation left of any size, could retain its national integrity, given the disintegration of values, the loss of its national heritage, and the multicultural disunity that prevailed, was another question altogether.

As the Fall approached, the world's wealthiest nations in Europe, North America, and Asia were doubling and tripling their debt-to-GDP ratios, while slicing their birth rates in half (and reducing the worker-to-retiree ratio by 60-70%). All of this took place during a period of relative peace, where no large wars would otherwise drain these nations' resources. Between 1950 and 2020, the global debt-to-GDP ratio expanded from 140% to 356%, (an increase from 260% during the Great Recession of 2008)[89]—the consequence of ten recessions and subsequent governmental responses. By this time, it was pretty well clear that Keynes' proposition that governments could "stabilize" the world economy and fend off further recessions was seen to be catastrophically flawed. Such were the metrics for a self-centered, myopic, existentialist worldview.

The reigning maxim was "Carpe diem"—live for today, and "to hell with the children and grandchildren." The United States had aborted 80-120 million babies since 1960 and had spent up the inheritance that might have been passed on to whatever grandchildren were left, leaving posterity with a huge debt and a worthless monetary system. Working from the same worldview, the grandchildren would proceed to euthanize the elderly and consume the last of the capital investments of previous generations.

The long run had finally arrived. The piper has invoiced. Was it really so prudent to have shoved aside the few cranks who opposed Keynesian policies over this one-hundred-year experiment? Was it possible the nations had been so badly and universally deceived? Murray Rothbard called Keynesian economics "the most successful and pernicious hoax in the history of economic thought."[90] Rothbard identified the root problem with Keynes to be his character, "...his overweening egotism, which assured him that he could handle all intellectual problems quickly and accurately and led him to scorn any general principles that might curb his unbridled ego. The second was his strong sense that he was born into, and destined to be a leader of Great Britain's ruling elite...The third element was his deep hatred and contempt for the values and virtues of the bourgeoisie, for conventional morality, for savings and thrift, and for the basic institutions of family life.[91]

US Employment Recovery—By Months Following Recessions

Recession	Months Required to Recover (with Stimulus)[92]
1973 recession	19 months
1981 recession	26 months
1990 recession	33 months
2001 recession	49 months
2008 recession	78 months
2020 recession	120+ months (est.)

The failure of Keynes' economic stimulus schemes became increasingly obvious with each successive recession. Each economic downturn was met with increasingly lower interest rates so as to trigger more debt, combined with outrageously-generous government debt-spending. With each iteration of the process for successive recessions, the stimulus produced less effect. The months required to recover employment numbers to their original peak following each recession always increased, as demonstrated in the adjoining table.

The US Gross Domestic product lagged badly after the turn of the millennium. Per annum growth averaging 3.83% between 1954 and 2001, dropping off to 2.58% average between 2001 and 2007. Following the 2008 recession, the nation's productivity slowed to 1.66% per year until the fall, at which time the average was scraping 0% and less.

As the last of the big dominoes toppled and the world economy jacked up on the Keynesian economic theory collapsed, the blame would fall on a homosexual pedophile, the grandson of the pastor from Bedford. In the words of the Prophet from Galilee: "By their fruits you shall know them" (Matt. 7:20). The highly vulnerable Western economy tumbled in AD 2020 and again in AD 2022, touching off a worldwide economic catastrophe, unprecedented in recent history. The world GDP contracted 4.4% in 2020, the largest contraction since accurate data was made available (over a period of 75 years). The major contributors were the UK (-9.9%), Spain (-8.7%), Japan (-5.7%), Germany (-4%), France (-3.9%), and the US (-3%)—Western countries.[93] For the fading economy of the United Kingdom, this was the largest contraction since the "Great Frost" of 1709. Meanwhile, the Eastern powerhouse, China ended the first Covid year with a 2.9% gain. America's exports slipped 13%, while China upticked its exports 3.6%.[94] China had surpassed the US economy on purchasing power parity in 2014. The Asia Times noted that, at this point, "China's grand strategy is to watch and wait while the US goes bankrupt."[95] The US trade deficit exploded from $0 in 1992 to $109 billion per month (or 5.2% of the GDP) in 2022.

After the 2008 worldwide recession, the US median household wealth never recovered from its 2006 peak of $210,000.[96] If anything, 2006 was the year marking the beginning of the end. Median household income could not keep up with real inflation rates, and household debt could not compensate for the reduced standard of living anymore. The ever-increasing prosperity trend of a half millennium, come by the grace of God and the economic and technological developments of the West, was over. The worship of man and money, the greed, the apostasy, and the debt-orgy had run its course.

Following the 2008 worldwide recession, the US Federal Reserve and the other national banks turned up the economic malfeasance of quantitative easing—creating money out of thin air to monetize irresponsible government debt-spending. Increasingly severe economic conditions "called for" increasingly aggressive Keynesian intervention, resulting in more trillion-dollar debt binges. Besides, with increasingly lower interest rates imposed by the Fed, who would invest in government bonds where the return rate averaged well under the inflation rate for fourteen years running (between 2008 and 2022)? This left central governments with only one option if they would save heavily leveraged economies from certain ruin—issue trillions of dollars by the central banks, purchase the bonds, and pretend that some of it will be paid back sometime in the future. This would only add more instability to the world economy, as nations pursued hard on the Keynesian theory to stimulate their dying economies.

Between 2008 and 2022, the four Western central banks combined (the US Federal Reserve, Bank of England, the European Central Bank, and the Bank of Japan) increased their QE holdings from $3.9 Trillion to $27 Trillion. The US Federal Reserve increased its balance sheet from $1 Trillion to over $9 Trillion (nine-fold), most of which occurred between 2020 and 2022. This meant that most of the debt was monetized by the Federal Reserve during the Covid-19 crisis, and almost none of it was purchased by foreign governments and private households. By 2021, the Federal Reserve held 21% of US debt. Such flagrant money-creation constituted the greatest government-inspired heist in human history. As should have been expected, the flagrant expansion of fiat money resulted in double-digit inflation, the devaluation of savings, the reduction of the median household income (adjusted for inflation), and severe economic recession. Institutionalized thievery at this magnitude could only cripple and corrupt a worldwide economy for a very long time.

The US Federal Reserve Board had finally reached the point it could no longer raise interest rates to beat inflation. In the 1980s, the Fed took the inflation-adjusted funds rate to a positive 9% to successfully beat down double digit inflation. Forty years later, the best the Fed could do was take the inflation-adjusted funds rate to negative 6-8% to beat the double-digit inflation created by the unhinged QE injections employed between 2008 and 2022. By this time, Fed policy was just a ridiculous playact. The Fed couldn't lower interest rates past 0% to stimulate more investment - not with inflation running in the double digits. Raising interest rates would only destroy the housing market during the largest housing bubble in American history, and bring on full bore recession. After a full century of high-level monetary chicanery, the pedophile economist was done. The central banks had run their course. It was the failure of government economic power and control. It was the collapse of financial market confidence in governments. It was the failure of a world economy controlled by economic planners. By their commitment to long term, indefinite debt-spending, and the monetization of their debt, these Western nations met the definition of wickedness given in Psalm 37:21: "The wicked borrows and does not repay, but the righteous shows mercy and gives." It was the Fall of the West.

> And after these things I saw another angel come down from heaven, having great power; and the earth was lightened with his glory. And he cried mightily with a strong voice, saying, Babylon the great is fallen, is fallen, and is become the habitation of devils, and the hold of every foul spirit, and a cage of every unclean and hateful bird. For all nations have drunk of the wine of the wrath of her fornication, and the kings of the earth have committed fornication with her, and the merchants of the earth are waxed rich through the abundance of her delicacies. And I heard another voice from heaven, saying, Come out of her, my people, that ye be not partakers of her sins, and that ye receive not of her plagues. For her sins have reached unto heaven, and God hath remembered her iniquities. Reward her even as she rewarded you, and double unto her double according to her works: in the cup which she hath filled fill to her double. How much she hath glorified herself, and lived deliciously, so much torment and sorrow give her: for she saith in her heart, I sit a queen, and am no widow, and shall see no sorrow. Therefore shall her plagues come in one day, death, and mourning, and famine; and she shall be utterly burned with fire: for strong is the Lord God who judgeth her. (Revelation 18:1-9)

XI

THE RISE & FALL OF
WESTERN CULTURE

And God saw every thing that he had made, and, behold, it was very
good. (Genesis 1:31)

Before considering the rise and fall of Western art and music, it
would be good to first identify a metric by which to distinguish
good art from the bad. This of course assumes that an *absolute good*
exists—an assumption vital to a biblical world and life view.

God is good. God knows what is good, and He provides us with the
definition. At creation, He declared His own works "very good." That
is the baseline datapoint. Therefore, to the extent that man expresses
God's wisdom, God's thoughts, and God's design and order by thought,
word, or visual art, such a production is good. To the extent that man
fails in his expression of these things, such a production is defective,
inferior, or bad.

Because of the Fall, man has perverted every such expression.
However, by common grace, man is able to reproduce a little of what
God has communicated by His design. Art as well as science is thus a
matter of discovery and not creativity.

Good art also expresses this content with clarity, a lucidity which
necessarily involves a mastery of the medium. Thus, both form and

content will be complementary. The complexity and the rich character of the art should enhance the clarity of the message. The many-ness should contribute to the oneness, in a Trinitarian conception of reality. Put another way, the complexity should enhance the simplicity or singleness of what is communicated. And, the most excellent cultural expression must be capable of communicating across maturity levels and over multiple generations of observers.

ART IN THE FALLEN WORLD

> For the wrath of God is revealed from heaven against all ungodliness and unrighteousness of men, who suppress the truth in unrighteousness, because what may be known of God is manifest in them, for God has shown it to them. For since the creation of the world His invisible attributes are clearly seen, being understood by the things that are made, even His eternal power and Godhead, so that they are without excuse, because, although they knew God, they did not glorify Him as God, nor were thankful, but became futile in their thoughts, and their foolish hearts were darkened. (Romans 1:18-21)

Jesus said, "Out of the abundance of the heart, the mouth speaks" (Luke 6:45). Therefore artistic expression will emanate from the heart, and issue according to its fundamental orientation. The natural inclination as described in Isaiah 53:6 "All we like sheep have gone astray. We have turned every one to his own way." Because natural man is wayward, the body of his art will reflect the trajectory of his heart. Romans 1 refers to a baseline of knowledge available to all persons. This includes God's "eternal power and Godhead," a knowledge accessible to man in his fallen state. The expression of a person's heart and art therefore begins with this base knowledge and then moves forward to "suppressing the truth in unrighteousness" (Rom. 1:18), after which come increasing levels of futility and darkness in heart and mind.

In the order of things, ideas and philosophy come first, then artistic expression. Philosophers identify and express the foundational viewpoint concerning man's reality and values, and the artist expresses what is believed as well as what is felt. It is impossible not to believe anything and, whether true or false, good or bad, the artist expresses the fundamental commitment of heart and mind. Art and music are immensely helpful means of communicating a worldview immediately without using long drawn-out explanations. Starting with a general understanding of the zeitgeist (spirit of the age) is helpful to assist a person in recognizing the message visible on the face of any artistic expression.

Because man exists both as an individual and in community, artistic and musical expressions will form in a social context. Artists seldom operate independently of other artists. Genres develop through the generations, and societies set their own cultural trajectories for better or worse. Macro movements and micro movements sometimes operate independently of each other and sometimes within each other. Artistic movements are best pictured as streams and rivers. And, on occasion, enormous cultural rivers form and flow into gigantic waterfalls. This macro-cultural trend is best described as the "zeitgeist", and the present chapter tells the story of the flow of Western art and music.

THE WATERFALL

Announcing the institution's vision and mission upon a billboard at the entrance to the Department of Modern Art at the University of British Columbia in Vancouver, were the words: *"We are the Destroyers."* Could the mission have been put more succinctly? There is no other way and no better way to express it. The cultural objective of the Western world is destruction, and the mission is pursued with the highest levels of self-consciousness and self-consistency within the dominant academic principalities.

The Google Ngram Viewer counts the occurrences of various

terms in contemporary literature by year. Not surprisingly, the search term "Johann Sebastian Bach" is found to have slipped in popularity by 58% between 1940 and 2020. "Beethoven" slipped 75% in popular usage over the same time frame. Meanwhile, Charles Darwin's popularity increased by 67%. Recent studies found that only 7% of the twenty-something crowd attends classical concerts, down from 14% for the twenty-something crowd forty years earlier.[1] Only 1% of album sales in 2018 represented the classical music genre (from the Christian Era), compared to 75% dedicated to the Rock/R&B genre and 9% to the Country/Rock genre. As late as 1930, at least 24% of recordings were still of the classical/operatic genres.[2] The cultural revolution playing out in the Western world was as important but even more conspicuous than the social revolutions of the 20th Century.

THE RISE OF CHRISTIAN ART
OUT OF THE ASHES OF PAGANISM

And God spake all these words, saying, I am the LORD thy God, which have brought thee out of the land of Egypt, out of the house of bondage.

Thou shalt have no other gods before me.

Thou shalt not make unto thee any graven image, or any likeness of any thing that is in heaven above, or that is in the earth beneath, or that is in the water under the earth. Thou shalt not bow down thyself to them, nor serve them: for I the LORD thy God am a jealous God, visiting the iniquity of the fathers upon the children unto the third and fourth generation of them that hate me; And shewing mercy unto thousands of them that love me, and keep my commandments. (Exodus 20:1-6)

To better understand the flow of Western culture, consider how Athanasius or Augustine might respond if he were transported into a 21st Century theater for a screening of *The Hunger Games* (2012). No doubt the church father would witness something strangely reminiscent of what he witnessed in the coliseums as a youth—except that these new games would have seemed more insipid, more of a play act. The post-Christian film genre was just a pitiful attempt to resurrect the paganism of a bygone era—human beings degrading themselves, but nothing like what the Romans did. But then Augustine would catch a faint whiff of a Christ presence. "Christ has been here," he would say. Still there was the unmistakable hesitation to kill. Self-sacrifice was yet seen as a value. Then, he would notice the Lord's name abused in the films, a clear indication of brazen apostasy. He would sense that Christ had departed. Yet, he must conclude that Christ still secures victory in the cultural wars of the millennium. What could possibly reverse the 2,000 year legacy of Christian influence over Western culture? The cultural transformation of the West was an act of God, epochal and irreversible.

As early as AD 325, Christians were removing statues from pagan temples in Alexandria, Egypt. Later, in AD 392, Christians were tearing down the Serapeum in lower Egypt erected by the Greeks centuries earlier. Most of the pagan statuary had been removed from Egypt by the 600s.

Augustine's *On Christian Teaching* (written AD 397) formed the "foundation of Christian culture" in the view of classical scholar James Halporn.[3] Augustine was careful to tear down pagan elements from cultural expressions, kicking loose the "theatrical trumpery" but encouraging the saints to make use of harps and other instruments "to lay hold upon spiritual things."[4] Pictures and statues he relegated to "superfluous devices of men" and encouraged Christians to explore the reasons for which they were made. He discouraged literature and artwork which promoted "fellowship with devils."[5] And music, he noted, is beneficial if it enhances our "understanding of holy Scripture."[6]

Ancient Greek and Roman statuary was idolatrous. Either it represented false gods or deified and idealized men and women, portraying them as sinless. Revealingly, the nude was an attempt to deny the Fall into sin—to idealize man without Christ, the Redeemer. The American post-Christian author Herman Melville speaking on classical statuary, epitomized the heart of the humanist ideal:

> How well in the Apollo is expressed the idea of the perfect man. Who could better it? Can art, not life, make the ideal? Here, in statuary, was the Utopia of the ancients expressed...[The moderns] did, indeed, invent the printing press, but all the best thoughts that it sends forth are from the ancients, whether it be law, physics or philosophy. The deeds of the ancients are noble, and so are their arts; and as the one is kept alive in the memory of man by the glowing words of their own historians and poets, so should the memory of the other be kept green in the minds of men by the careful preservation of their noble statuary.[7]

Whether the Greek god is turned into the ideal man or man is turned into a god, the statuary represented the wrong idea. These false worldviews both deified man and pretended to resurrect him from his fallen state. The ancient classical world was obviously far from ideal, as badly fallen from moral rectitude as anyone else in this fallen creation.

In their writings, early Church fathers grappled with the *purpose* of art and music. This was and continues to be core to the distinction between Christian and pagan art and music forms. What is music's primary purpose? Is is primarily intended for worship? Is it an expression of joy? Does it serve as a help to win wars and build empires? Or should music and entertainment be employed for emotional comfort, suppression of reality, diversion, or Bacchanalian enthusiasm?

Tertullian (AD 145-220) found the theater to be merely the expression of an idolatrous worldview:

> The path to the theater is from the temples and the altars, from

that miserable mess of incense and blood, to the tune of tibias and trumpets…Quite obviously Bacchus and Venus are the patrons of the arts of the stage.[8]

Tertullian concluded that "every show is an assembly of the wicked,"[9] applying Psalm 1 to any and all participation with it:

> Well, we never find it expressed with the same precision, "You shall not enter circus or theatre, you shall not look on combat or show;" as it is plainly laid down, "You shall not kill; you shall not worship an idol; you shall not commit adultery or fraud" (Exodus 20:14). But we find that that first word of David bears on this very sort of thing: "Blessed," he says, "is the man who has not gone into the assembly of the impious, nor stood in the way of sinners, nor sat in the seat of scorners."[10]

Clement of Alexandria warned against secular music which, he said, encourages "disorderly frivolities" and "corrupts men's morals, drawing to perturbation of mind, by the licentious and mischievous art."[11] The church father rejected the "frenzied and frantic," "the mournful, voluptuous, and licentious," "the florid and meretricious,"[12] all of which adjectives might well describe the Bacchanalian popular music of the modern age. Clement contrasted this with Christian music, which presents as grave and sober, soothing, and glorifying to God.[13] In concert with Colossians 3:15-17, Clement commended music as an expression of "thankful revelry"[14] to God for His good gifts—food, drink, love and marriage, etc. Paul too would say that thankfulness is the warp and woof of Christian living.

> And let the peace of God rule in your hearts, to the which also ye are called in one body; and be ye thankful. Let the word of Christ dwell in you richly in all wisdom; teaching and admonishing one another in psalms and hymns and spiritual songs, singing with grace in your hearts to the Lord. And whatsoever ye do in word or deed, do all in the name of the Lord Jesus, giving thanks to God and the Father by him. (Colossians 3:15-17)

Hymn singing was mentioned in a letter written by Pliny the Younger (AD 111), speaking of Christians assembling on a "fixed day before it was light, when they sang in alternate stanzas songs to Christ as to a god."[15] The first extra-biblical hymn is attributed to Ignatius (d. AD 107).

Without question, the backbone of Western music was always psalmody. This was far and away the most dominant feature for a thousand years. In the East, John Cassian (360-435) organized a daily psalm-singing regimen for morning and evening prayers to take place in discipleship centers—requiring the chanting of twelve psalms for each service. Cassian's main interest was that the disciples apply the intelligence of the mind, "aiming with all their might at this: 'I will sing with the spirit: I will sing also with the understanding.'"[16] He required 2-3 second breaks between each verse, for contemplation.

Although hymns (uninspired poems put to music) were commonly accepted in the early church, the misuse of them often became a stumbling block. Wayward sects and cults were particularly fond of using music to distract and deceive the uninformed. Thus, the Council of Laodicea (AD 365) issued a canon requiring that "No psalms composed by private individuals nor any uncanonical books may be read in the church, but only the Canonical Books of the Old and New Testaments."[17] Also, canon 19 prescribed that after every psalm was sung, "a lesson shall intervene." The early church was particularly careful not to allow music to displace the intellect or devalue the exhortations and teachings of the church.

Christians added much variety and creativity to music through the centuries. Antiphonal music (two groups singing alternately) was added around the time of Ambrose (340-397). The Milanese Pastor is well known for organizing congregational singing by using iambic dimeter, a simple two-foot poetic meter intended to keep everybody singing in unison. Gregory I introduced the Gregorian Chant (AD 600), and the first church operas appeared around AD 800. Basically, these were dramatized biblical stories with such themes as "The Visit to Christ's Sepulcher." Polyphonic music (singing in parts or harmony) came about by the musical genius of a Benedictine monk named Hucbald (840-930). Another monk, Guido of Arezzo (995-1050), produced the first written music using a staff of four lines and six notes. The scale would later be increased to eight notes.

Hucbald was the first to present a musical theory to the Western world in written form. His work was composed of two treatises, *Musica Enchiriadis* and *Scholia Enchiriadis*. Western music, as developed in the church, was thoroughly Christian in worldview, as the monk explained that through music we come "to know God and His everlasting divinity, and [we are] inexcusable if [we] do not glorify God and give Him thanks."[18]

The polyphonic "music" of the New Guinea Highlanders, the Aka Pygmies, and other pagan tribes was a simplistic drone sound devoid of decent harmony. The polytheists could not find harmony as reflected in a Trinitarian worldview. Polytheistic cultures found it impossible to employ many tones simultaneously to produce a unity with equal ultimacy. Only in a Christian mind and spirit could a Trinitarian culture be developed and sustained over any length of time. The One and the Many were integrated into polyphonic harmony primarily in the West. Science had developed over many centuries of continuous work (AD 1000-1820), and the arts followed a similar pattern. Suffice to say, Western art and music did not begin with Michelangelo or Bach.

The motet appeared in the 1200s, a composition intended for a professional choir—first introduced at Notre Dame in Paris. Typically, the words were based on Scripture and intended to be sung in the church. In the 14th Century came the madrigal—a polyphonic, continuous song without repetition of verses and without instrumental accompaniment. The form was removed from the sacred context and applied to secular music during the late Italian Renaissance. Some musical forms were developed as a special praise to God such as the oratorio, the first of which came in the 1560s. Yet tension developed during these later medieval years. Was the primary purpose of music to glorify man or to glorify God? Was the performance mainly for man or for God? Was music to express thanksgiving and praise, or was it intended for the pleasure, pride, and emotional comfort of man? The motive of the heart would affect the mode, and consequentially the message transmitted in the mode. The shift from a God-centered to man-centered culture is always extremely subtle.

> Whether therefore ye eat, or drink, or whatsoever ye do, do all to the glory of God. (1 Corinthians 10:31)

With the development of Western music within the church accompanying professionalization, a deficit of congregational involvement in worship and music materialized. As one historian put it, "At the threshold of the Reformation...many had lost sight of the beauty of this discipline of daily prayer. It was regarded as a heavy burden, barely held up by endowed choirs and a secularized clergy which had lost its spiritual fire."[19]

Generally, Reformation churches retained polyphonic music and, in many cases, instrumentation while setting aside the professional choir in favor of congregational singing. The challenge was and continues to be how to interest church members in the importance of music and musical training, not to mention active participation in public worship and prayer.

Throughout the medieval Christian age, a wonderful variety of musical instruments were invented to accommodate the demand for Christian music in the church. First, the rudimentary pipe organ was developed in the East and imported into the West by Pepin the Short (AD 757), and Charlemagne incorporated it into the church. The first large pipe organ was installed in a church in Halberstadt, Germany in 1361—400 years before the work of Johann Sebastian Bach. The violin appeared first in northern Italy around the 1530s. The first guitars were developed in medieval Spain in the 1100s. The cello came around 1500, and the piano was invented by Bartolomeo Cristofori in northern Italy about 1700. These are the most commonly-used musical instruments of our day—all developed or at least perfected for use in the Christian West.

Classical music or high art materializes over many centuries by unnumbered increments of applied skill and creative genius—one generation building upon the next. Western music in its highest form was never merely the product of isolated spurts of genius or less-helpful revolutionary excretions. Only by careful discipline, by due honor paid to the fathers and masters of past generations, and by steadfast commitment to the Christian faith and worldview over centuries could the high art of classical music have found its zenith with Johann Sebastian Bach and George Frideric Handel. Without the steady commitment of resources on the part of the community and church, such extensive development would have been impossible. As interest in high culture and music waned and funding dissipated, fewer artists were able to dedicate their lives to cultural expression. Despite the increase in wealth and division of labor among Western nations, little funding was made available for the positive development of culture. Financial commitments shifted to empty diversions, entertainment, and disposable forms of cultural expression.

EARLY CHRISTIAN STATUARY & ART

And thou shalt make two cherubims of gold, of beaten work shalt thou make them, in the two ends of the mercy seat. And make one cherub on the one end, and the other cherub on the other end: even of the mercy seat shall ye make the cherubims on the two ends thereof. And the cherubims shall stretch forth their wings on high, covering the mercy seat with their wings, and their faces shall look one to another; toward the mercy seat shall the faces of the cherubims be. (Exodus 25:18-20)

The first Christian statuettes appear in the early 300s, the most common of which depict the shepherd of Christ's parable in Luke 15 retrieving the lost sheep. The earliest version of the carving portrays the shepherd more fully clothed—signifying a preference for modesty against pagan shamelessness.

As early as the 430s, Christians had developed mosaic art constructed out of colored glass—as, for example, the panels displayed in the Santa Maria Maggiore Church. Most conspicuous was the absence of pictures of Christ; instead the mosaics focused on Old Testament scenes such as *The Parting of Abraham and Lot*. From the beginning, the church studiously avoided representations of Jesus. Images portraying the persons of the Trinity were forbidden by the church fathers, including Irenaeus, Clement of Alexandria, and Eusebius of Caesarea. The 36th canon issued by the Council of Elvira in AD 306 ordered that: "Pictures are not to be placed in churches, so that they do not become objects of worship and adoration."[20] This was to change later in the 4th Century.

Sensitive to the human tendency for idolatry and the inclination to displace the written Word by picture and statuary, the Western church pushed back hard against images. The East, on the other hand, welcomed icons in worship, and the iconoclastic reformations of AD 726-787 and AD 814-842 (ridding the church of images) dissipated quickly. The West steadfastly resisted statuary, and Charlemagne issued the *Libri Carolini* (c. 787) as a refutation of the Eastern church's approval for the veneration of images at the second Council of Nicaea.

The Christian Age is sometimes critiqued for its reticence to display the human element in art, especially during the 7th-11th centuries. Was this a rejection of nature in favor of the spiritual, or was it a caution against the worship of man and the worship of images? Through the early Medieval Period, artists refused to depict man in an idealized, godlike, disrobed, or athletic form. Rather, the preferred imagery was more realistic. Hardworking, plain, and even homely-looking men and women are presented fully clothed, plowing fields, worshiping, and engaging in acts of charity. Humble artists offered humble art, portraying humble people.

ARCHITECTURAL EXPRESSION & THE
APEX OF CHRISTIAN CULTURE

The height of Christian cultural expression is probably best witnessed in the towering cathedrals built across Europe during the Medieval Period. Much larger and more grandiose than castles built to the glory of man, these architectural wonders were built to the glory of God and for the worship of God. When originally constructed in 537, the Hagia Sophia of Constantinople was the largest building in the world—the prime exemplar of Byzantine architecture.

THE GREAT CHRISTIAN CATHEDRALS AT THE
HEIGHT OF CHRISTENDOM

The greatest advancements in Western architecture did not come in the classical period or even during the Renaissance (post AD 1300). As witnessed by the following list, Christian architecture exploded on the scene well before the revival of humanism and the re-commitment of the universities to the pagan Greek and Roman worldview.

Cathedral	Country	Size (sq. ft.)	Year Construction Began
Strasbourg	France	60,000	1015
Winchester	England	50,000	1079
Durham	England	40,000	1093
Saint Denis	France	40,000	1135
Chartes	France	52,000	1145
Notre Dame	France	55,000	1163
Bourges	France	60,000	1195
Reims	France	65,000	1211
Palma	Spain	66,000	1220
York Minster	England	60,000	1230
Ulm	Germany	83,000	1377
Florence	Italy	83,000	1296

Renaissance humanists would later smear this distinctively Christian architecture with the ugly pejorative "Gothic." In reality, the architecture had nothing to do with the primitive Goths from East Germany. It was Christian, beautifully balanced, coordinating unity with a spectacularly interesting diversity, in sharp contrast with the boring architecture of the unitarian world. The towering spires and arches pointing towards the heavens communicated the transcendence and majesty of God in worship, while the narrowly-constructed nave allowed for a sense of immanence. Contrary to popular imagination, this Christian architecture was far from dark, foreboding, and sinister. Expansive high windows introduced a tremendous amount of light into the building—representing the radiant light Christ brought into the world.

Such architectural advancements as the flying buttress and rib vaults reflected more of the genius of the medieval Christian mind.

Unlike the cheap tin buildings used for worship in the modern world, these colossal constructions were built to last for a thousand years. If the gates of hell could not prevail against the church, and if there was no end to the increase of this Kingdom, why not build to last for a thousand generations? Some of these cathedrals were 150-500 years in the making. Worldly empires would never have dedicated hundreds of years to building these works of meticulous genius and dedicated creativity. Dynasties and empires simply don't last that long. But, among Christians, the general sentiment was simply that Christ was worthy of more honor than all the kings of the earth in their palaces. These awe-inspiring architectural feats were meant to convey God's infinite majesty and glory and man's finitude. The grandeur of the buildings was wonderfully enhanced by biblically oriented frescoes, engravings, and stained-glass mosaics. Even the pillars were adorned with exquisitely carved frescoes and engravings—the Augsburg Cathedral, featuring scenes depicting the prophets of the Old Testament.

THE CLASSICAL REGRESSION

For so it was, that the children of Israel had sinned against the Lord their God, which had brought them up out of the land of Egypt, from under the hand of Pharaoh king of Egypt, and had feared other gods, and walked in the statutes of the heathen, whom the LORD cast out from before the children of Israel, and of the kings of Israel, which they had made. And the children of Israel did secretly those things that were not right against the LORD their God, and they built them high places in all their cities, from the tower of the watchmen to the fenced city.

And they set them up images and groves in every high hill, and under every green tree: and there they burnt incense in all the high places, as did the heathen whom the LORD carried away before them; and wrought wicked things to provoke the LORD to anger: for they served idols, whereof the LORD had said unto them, Ye shall not do this thing. (2 Kings 17:7-12)

The year was AD 1343. With the dawning of the Renaissance, an inordinate interest in ancient pagan culture and sexuality had returned to northern Italy. As Florence turned into a seedbed of prostitution and homosexuality, city workers of Siena, sixty miles to the south, had exhumed the nude statue of Venus. A thousand years earlier, the goddess of sex had been torn down by Christians and left for dead. Now her rediscovery ushered in a joyful celebration among the townsfolk, and the statue was hauled to the center of town and installed over the fountain in the piazza. In his historical survey, Lorenzo Ghiberti recorded that "she was paid great honour."[21] However, some five years later, the bubonic plague hit Tuscany and wiped out half the population of Siena. The townspeople could not help but notice that "from the moment we found the statue, evils have been ceaseless."[22] The town council made the determination to destroy the Venus. Forthwith, the goddess was smashed to pieces and her remains were buried outside the city.

A thousand years of Christian influence had not yet extinguished all light, even in Renaissance Italy. Somehow, this civilization was still sensitive to the moral problems with perverse sex. At this point, the Christian world was not ready to reinstate the promiscuous gods of the heathen, once so venerated for their incest, rape, and assorted perversions. Even Florence joined the campaign to stop the sexual anarchy in the year of the plague (1348), sentencing one, Agostino di Ercole, to execution for crimes delineated in Leviticus 20:13 and Romans 1:32.

The Italian Renaissance rejected the Christian worldview and, for good measure, the humanists discarded the Trinitarian architecture developed over the previous 400 years. Instead, the Renaissance introduced a non-complementary diversity, blending geometrical forms of circles and squares—as in the case of the Cathedral at Florence designed by Brunelleschi (1377-1446). The Italian humanists fixated upon the dome largely preferred by Muslims and Eastern churches. Christian thinker Francis Schaeffer explained that, "[Renaissance architecture] placed man in the center of this space, and space became subordinated to mathematical principles spun out of the mind of man."[23] Schaeffer also contrasts the Renaissance men all lauded with "swaggering autobiographies," with Christian architects and musicians of the previous 500 years who were mostly unknown and unrecognized. With the Renaissance men, portraits and self-portraits were also common—the predecessor of the selfie. The glorification of man marked the humanist Renaissance and every humanist institution since.

Beginning with Petrarch of Florence (c. 1350), a vast gulf appeared between anti-Christian Renaissance art and that which retained the Christian worldview. The French painter Fouquet (1416-1480) epitomized the anti-Christian character of the Renaissance with *The Red Virgin*, likening a partially disrobed mistress of the king to the Virgin Mary.

After Donatello (1386-1466) restored the classical nude, merging the idealized form with the biblical David, Michelangelo (1476-1565) followed suit with another David completely disconnected from the biblical story. His statuary was the revival of the idealized man, complete with disproportionately large hands—attributing an inordinate capacity and strength to man. Michelangelo's art was a complete synthesis with paganism. His almost universally-lauded artwork, decorating the Sistine Chapel, included both the Greek witch of Delphi and the prophet Jeremiah, equally presented as sources of wisdom. Disrobed men and women everywhere throughout this "chapel" pictured the idealized man, void of the problem of sin and shame, without the need of redemption. Considered by classicists the most perfect sculpture of the ancient world, "the Apollo," (featuring the Greek god), was installed in the Vatican's Belvedere Palace in the year AD 1511. The syncretism was complete, and an undiluted humanism had gained mastery over the Roman Church.

Leonardo da Vinci (1452-1519), oft touted as the ultimate genius and the very essence of "Renaissance Man," was consumed with knowing the universal, formulated by human reason—the one thing which would summarize all things. In his words, "Only observation is the key to understanding...All our knowledge has its origins in our perceptions." This would turn out to be nothing less than a cul-de-sac for human knowledge. Raised in Florence during the age of sexual profligacy, da Vinci was the subject of a civil trial in which he was accused of the crime of sodomy. Da Vinci's scientific musings never materialized in practical invention. However, his highly-developed art depicted more the pride of man or woman, as in the case of the *Mona Lisa*. Da Vinci's philosophy was summed up as: "Men of lofty genius accomplish the most when they work the least, for their minds are occupied with their ideas and the perfection of their conceptions, to which afterwards they give form."[24] Instead of thinking God's thoughts after Him and submitting to His will, the humanist man would attempt to invent knowledge for himself—and then fail miserably in the process. Da Vinci's *Jesus* was feminized and man-oriented in appearance.

Philosophically, the Renaissance migrated from the particulars advocated by Aristotle to the universal emphasized by Plato. Neither philosophy was helpful for the development of science and art in the West. Only a Trinitarian view would allow for an equal ultimacy in terms of man's acceptance of the universal principle in the idea realm and the individual particularities found in the realm of nature.

THE REFORMATION & THE APEX OF WESTERN ART

And the vineyard which thy right hand hath planted, and the branch that thou madest strong for thyself. It is burned with fire, it is cut down: they perish at the rebuke of thy countenance. Let thy hand be upon the man of thy right hand, upon the son of man whom thou madest strong for thyself. So will not we go back from thee: quicken us, and we will call upon thy name. Turn us again, O LORD God of hosts, cause thy face to shine; and we shall be saved. (Psalm 80:15-19)

The shameful portrayal of woman came with the Italian Renaissance as well. Titian of Venice (1490-1576) returned the nude Venus in pornographic form. This revival of pagan art with its sexual perversities was largely financed by Philip II—son of the Holy Roman emperor and well known for his advocacy of the Inquisition, and his persecution of Reformed Christians.

Quite distinct from the anti-Christian trends represented by the Italian Renaissance, Reformation art took a different turn. The two streams mixed at points, but the distinction was obvious and radical. Some Reformed artists had experienced veritable spiritual conversions from the apostasy of Renaissance humanism. By God's grace, the Reformation dammed up the flood waters of humanism until the Enlightenment of the 18th Century.

Reformation art in the Dutch and German traditions was humble. The subjects were clad, and the landscapes were presented in full color. Vermeer's (1632-1675) *Milk Maid* was humble and hardworking, while the *Mona Lisa* was not. Reformers were not afraid to present the world in its true colors, without sentimentality, without obfuscation, and without optimization. While they would never deny the fallen condition of the world, they still exhibited a humble and optimistic expectation of redemption. There was no depreciation of the physical world, as Dutch painters revealed wonderful, realistic, and extensive landscapes. If God had labeled His created reality as "very good," Albrecht Durer (1471-1528) thought it quite fitting to present a realistic view of the owl and rhinoceros.

Reforming elements were seen in the Van Eyck brothers' oil paintings. Significantly, Jan Van Eyck (1390-1441) was the chief popularizer of oil-based art, and the first to master the landscape, most beautifully portrayed in his magnum opus *The Adoration of the Lamb*. While the Italians abandoned faith, the renewed personal piety of the *devotio moderna* movement (initiated by Geert Groote and Thomas à Kempis) influenced an entire genre of devotional artistry in the low countries, including that of Jan van Eyck, Rogier van der Weyden, Petrus Christus, and Hans Memling. The Van Eyck brothers and Robert Campin, also of Belgium (1375-1444), were the pioneers in naturalism and observational realism, and predated the humanist artists Fouquet, Titian, Da Vinci, and the anti-Christian Renaissance to the south. It should be pointed out that these artists worked quite independently of the Italian Renaissance.

At the turn of the 16th Century, worldviews—or rather principalities and powers—were battling for preeminence over institutions and individuals. The struggle was epitomized in the life and work of Albrecht Durer (1471-1528) of Nuremberg, Germany. Durer began his artistic career solidly embedded in the Renaissance, churning out scores of nude scenes of witches, women, and men's bathhouses. Post-1505, however, a conversion and a reformation may have come upon the artist. *Folded Hands* appeared in 1508, followed by the *Apostle Paul* (1514), an extremely modest *Madonna and the Pear* (1512), the *Peasant Couple Dancing* (1514), and the *Four Apostles* (1525). The conversion was unmistakable. When Durer received the news that Martin Luther had been taken captive, his diary entry records wholehearted support for the reformer. Durer commends Luther for "chastis[ing] the unchristian papacy, which resists the liberation by Christ with its heavy burdens of human laws."[25] Included in the same diary entry is a prayer: "Oh Lord Jesus Christ, pray for your people, deliver us at the right time, preserve in us the right, true Christian faith, gather your widely scattered sheep by your voice, which is called the Word of God in Scripture." And, he says, "should we have lost this man [Luther], who has written more clearly than any other that has lived in the last 140 years, and to whom you have given such an evangelical spirit, we pray you, oh Heavenly Father, that you would give your Holy Spirit again to someone who would gather your holy Christian church so that we might live together again in a Christian manner and that because of our good works, all believers, as there are Turks, heathen, and Kalicutes, would desire after us of themselves, and would accept the Christian faith."[26]

The height of Dutch Baroque art was achieved a century after Durer with the work of Johannes Vermeer (1632-1675). As was the case with much Christian art in the post-Enlightenment era, Vermeer was ignored for centuries. Unlike Rembrandt Harmenszoon van Rijn (1606-1669), Vermeer did not commit adultery or conceive children out of wedlock. Although Rembrandt was raised in the Reformation tradition by parents who were members of the Dutch Reformed Church, he turned from the faith to pursue the humanist worldview of the Renaissance. His art reflected a Christian baseline and a humanist trajectory—a clear turning away from that heritage. Peter Paul Rubens (1577-1640), another Flemish artist, completed the crossover to paganism with an emphasis on sensuality, rape, and an obsession with mythological nudes. Unquestionably, the battle in the realm of principalities and powers was raging hard in the West through the 17th Century.

Even to the present day, most "Christian" surveys of the history of art fail to find the hard line between humanism and Christianity during the Renaissance. This irrepressible tendency to mold a synthesis in worldviews became the Achilles heel for the Christian liberal arts college, which would become the fountain of Western apostasy in the centuries that followed.

BACH & HANDEL—THE APEX OF WESTERN MUSIC

> Praise ye the LORD. Praise God in his sanctuary: praise him in the firmament of his power. Praise him for his mighty acts: praise him according to his excellent greatness. Praise him with the sound of the trumpet: praise him with the psaltery and harp. Praise him with the timbrel and dance: praise him with stringed instruments and organs. Praise him upon the loud cymbals: praise him upon the high sounding cymbals. Let every thing that hath breath praise the LORD. Praise ye the LORD. (Psalm 150)

Western music enjoyed a sustained period of development and continued an upward course for an additional 150 years after the Reformation, largely due to the respected place hymnody held within the church. Protestantism was much more suspect of Renaissance art, and none of the Lutheran or Reformed chapels would have tolerated Michelangelo's plethora of nudes. Music, however, was essential in the church—mandated in Old and New Testaments for godly life and worship. Moreover, the venues for mass access to secular music were limited to the courts of Europe, while sacred music was accessible in every church and chapel.

The test of great music is sustainability and recognizability over centuries. To this day, the most recognized songs, hymns, and anthems from previous centuries are anything but secular. Which hymns have been sung a billion times in a hundred languages over multiple centuries? Martin Luther's *A Mighty Fortress is Our God*, Charles Wesley's *Hark the Herald Angels Sing*, John Newton's *Amazing Grace*, and Augustus Toplady's *Rock of Ages* would head the list.

Hardly any cultural historian, believer or unbeliever, questions the position of Johann Sebastian Bach (1685-1750) in the progression of

Western music. Bach is still the uncontested master—the apex of a thousand years of Western Christian culture. Yet he did not appear as some isolated genius. He stands on the shoulders of those who went before him. His own family offers one micro-model of the development of the musical art. Fully fifty members of the Bach family were well-respected musicians. At fifty years of age, Bach himself drew up a family genealogy to honor his musical heritage. His great-great-great-grandfather Vitus Bach (1550-1619) was a convert to the Lutheran faith and a consummate musician. Vitus' son Johannes Bach (1580-1626) was the first professional musician in the family line. Bach's father Johann Ambrosias was a violinist, and four of his sons became professional musicians. The development of art is never the consequence of a few part-time hobbyists here and there. This can only happen by the dedication of 150 years of continuous work, fathers training sons and sons honoring their father's forms, and a realization of a higher purpose in the work.

Bach's commitment to Christ is indisputable. His compositions were typically autographed with the addition of abbreviations—J.J. (*Jesu juva* or "Help me, Jesus"), I.N.J. (*in nomine Jesu* or "In the Name of Jesus"), or S.D.G. (*soli Deo gloria,* or "Only to God be the Glory"). Demonstrating a longstanding commitment to worship music, the St. Thomas Lutheran Church of Leipzig provided financial support for Bach's work. And his production was prolific—over two hundred and fifty chorales, more than two hundred cantatas, organ preludes, suites, and sonatas, as well as many concertos for organ and violin. To this day, Bach is considered the father of "classical music" throughout the world, and he is still rated the greatest composer of all time.[27]

Born the same year as Bach, George Frideric Handel (1685-1759) was also raised in a devout Lutheran family, and as a lifelong celibate he dedicated his life to music. Handel moved to England in 1727 and turned into an English icon of culture. His life work yielded twenty-five oratorios, 42 operas, and over 120 cantatas. Composed in 1741 and completed in only twenty-four days, Handel's most popular work was *The Messiah*, in which he highlighted the Old Testament messianic prophecies pointing to the coming of Christ. He personally conducted the oratorio for English audiences at least thirty times, raising thousands of pounds for an orphanage and other charitable causes. Handel's biographer remarked, "*Messiah* has fed the hungry, clothed the naked, fostered the orphan...more than any other single musical production in this or any country."[28] From all reports, Handel was a man of deep personal piety. He could be found in deep meditation and even prostrate in the Anglican worship services of his church. His friend Sir John Hawkins tells of him: "Throughout his life [Handel] manifested a deep sense of religion. In conversation he would frequently declare the pleasure he felt in setting the Scriptures to music, and how contemplating the many sublime passages in the Psalms had contributed to his edification."[29]

THE STRUGGLE FOR CHRISTIAN CULTURE— MOZART & MENDELSSOHN

The musicians following in the Western classical tradition maintained some semblance of faith, including Franz Joseph Haydn (1732-1809) and Amadeus Mozart (1756-1791). Both Catholics, Haydn was humbler, more prolific, and lived longer. Like Bach, he signed off his scores with *soli Deo gloria* and *in nomini Jesu*. His most famous Oratorio, *The Creation*, was written for the purpose of "adoration and worship of the Creator." Mozart, on the other hand, played to the rising demand for sexual intrigue with outrageously popular operas like *Don Giovanni*.

Finally, Felix Mendelssohn is generally considered the great inheritor of Bach's legacy and the tapering end of Christian influence upon music in the Western world. Mendelssohn's parents were converted Jews, and he was raised a Reformed Christian—his worldview self-consciously Trinitarian to the core. Getting to the very soul of his art form, Mendelssohn explained, "the essence of beauty is unity in variety." He was particularly fastidious about retaining the true words of Scripture in his work: "I have time after time had to restore the precise text of the Bible. It is the best in the end."[30] Mendelssohn wrote several hymns as well, one of which follows:

> Let all men praise the Lord,
> In worship lowly bending;
> On His most Holy Word,
> Redeem'd from woe, depending.
> He gracious is and just,
> From childhood us doth lead;
> On Him we place our trust
> And hope, in time of need.
> Glory and praise to God,
> The Father, Son, be given,
> And to the Holy Ghost,
> On high enthron'd in Heaven.
> Praise to the Three-One God;
> With power'ful arm and strong,
> He changeth night to day;
> Praise Him with grateful song.

While the Western world was fast abandoning the Christian faith in politics, ethics, theology, and culture, God raises up a believing Jew to preserve the Christian cultural heritage. Was this a representative development in a full scale re-graft of the Jews, accompanying the apostasy of the Gentiles in the 19th and 20th centuries?

> For if thou wert cut out of the olive tree which is wild by nature, and wert grafted contrary to nature into a good olive tree: how much more shall these, which be the natural branches, be grafted into their own

olive tree? For I would not, brethren, that ye should be ignorant of this mystery, lest ye should be wise in your own conceits; that blindness in part is happened to Israel, until the fulness of the Gentiles be come in. And so all Israel shall be saved: as it is written, There shall come out of Sion the Deliverer, and shall turn away ungodliness from Jacob... (Romans 11:24-26)

THE FALL OF WESTERN CULTURE

Woe unto them that rise up early in the morning, that they may follow strong drink; that continue until night, till wine inflame them! And the harp, and the viol, the tabret, and pipe, and wine, are in their feasts: but they regard not the work of the LORD, neither consider the operation of his hands. Therefore my people are gone into captivity, because they have no knowledge: and their honourable men are famished, and their multitude dried up with thirst. Therefore hell hath enlarged herself, and opened her mouth without measure: and their glory, and their multitude, and their pomp, and he that rejoiceth, shall descend into it. And the mean man shall be brought down, and the mighty man shall be humbled, and the eyes of the lofty shall be humbled: but the LORD of hosts shall be exalted in judgment, and God that is holy shall be sanctified in righteousness. Then shall the lambs feed after their manner, and the waste places of the fat ones shall strangers eat. Woe unto them that draw iniquity with cords of vanity, and sin as it were with a cart rope... (Isaiah 5:11-18)

First came the philosophies of the Enlightenment, and afterwards, the fall of Western culture in the Protestant and Catholic West.

As man turned inward, the genius of the classical composer made way for the worship of man. There was no more *soli Deo gloria* for Ludwig van Beethoven. From henceforth, it was all to the glory of man. A friend, Bettina von Arnim, said of Beethoven, "He treated God as an equal."[31] Jean-Jacques Rousseau had presented himself as some sort of "divine genius," the "voice of a god, " and the market was ripe for it. Percy Shelley (1792-1822) the poet entered the scene, forging the way for the modern. He called himself "the unacknowledged legislator of the world."[32] And, he made no bones about the pure humanism of his philosophy—a complete return to the pagan Greek worldview: "We are all Greeks. Our laws, our literature, our religion, our arts have their root in Greece. But for Greece—Rome, the instructor, the conqueror, or the metropolis of our ancestors, would have spread no illumination with her arms."[33]

A new persona developed in the form of "the Bohemian" and the "uncontrollable, outrageous genius."[34] Romanticism came on the heels of the Enlightenment, a philosophy espoused or incarnated best by the English poet, Lord Byron (1788-1824). Romantics like Byron and Shelley were infatuated with evil, not so much with the intent to condemn it as to play with it. Rebellion and revolution against the established order was the new value. That vagabond who wandered in the wilderness East of Eden became the hero to emulate. Isolation from God and man became the life to live. "I stood among them, but not of them," pens Byron. The Romantics were existentialists before the word existed. They rejected marriage and family, climbed into themselves, and died. Theirs was a life of "continual self-pity,"[35] to use one author's expression. Another literary analyst sums up the Romantic as "champions of victimhood... homosexuals, lesbians...leftists, artists, and many, many others, see themselves as victims. The Romantics made of the peoples of the 20th Century a world of victims."[36]

The British poets led the way for the reintroduction of homosexuality into the modern world—first with William Shakespeare's sonnets and then with Algernon Charles Swinburne (1837-1909). The anti-Christian oracle handed down the false prophecy from the new "Temple of Delphi." Speaking of Christ, Swinburne intoned: "Thy kingdom shall pass, Galilean, thy dead shall go down to thee dead." Another English poet and playwright, Oscar Wilde (1854-1900), successfully broke through the moral boundaries in place for 1,500 years against homosexuality, at least for the *avant-garde*. Then an American poet, Walt Whitman (1819-1892), was the medium by which the gates were opened to the abomination of the Greeks in the United States. Widely considered the most important American poet of the Romantic era, Whitman embodied the American spirit. An uncontrollable Romanticism on steroids embraced pantheism, self-worship, sex-worship, and moral relativism.

As the age of modernity initiated in the early 19th Century, concert halls took on the appearance of temples, and composers and literary men were the high priestly class, as it were. The theater replaced the church, and the performance replaced the worship service. It was a time in which the conductors and composers like Rossini and Beethoven were "shouted for and sonnetted and feasted—and immortalized much more than...the emperors."[37]

John Martin (1789-1854), the most popular artist in Britain during the early modern era, used tremendous exaggeration in his art, magnifying man's conception of himself and his creations. Modern man had arrived at the zenith of his intelligence, civilization, abilities, and knowledge of the universe. His art reflected the "cult of gigantism."[38] The British Empire had developed into the most powerful institution of man on earth since Rome, and modern man had reached the height of optimism and pride in himself.

Above and beyond all others, it was Ludwig van Beethoven (1770-1827) who pioneered the Romantic era in music—which at base was just another expression of humanist autonomy. Beethoven kept his creedal statement under the glass top of his desk, leaving no doubt as to the operational worldview of the great composer: "I am that which is. I am all that is, that was, and that will be. No mortal man has lifted my veil. He is of himself alone, and it is to this aloneness that all things owe their being."[39] When a fellow composer showed Beethoven a piece of his work with the inscription: "Finished with the help of God," underneath it the romanticist scrawled the words "Oh man, help yourself!"[40] His opposition to God and his resignation to the "fates" takes form in a letter to a friend in which Beethoven wrote, "Already I have often cursed my Creator and my existence; [but] *Plutarch* has taught me *resignation*."[41] Pagan humanism had returned in full force to the Western world by AD 1820.

> Thus saith the LORD; Cursed be the man that trusteth in man, and maketh flesh his arm, and whose heart departeth from the LORD. For he shall be like the heath in the desert, and shall not see when good cometh; but shall inhabit the parched places in the wilderness, in a salt land and not inhabited. Blessed is the man that trusteth in the LORD, and whose hope the LORD is. (Jeremiah 17:5-7)

Towards the end of his life, Beethoven wrote a letter to a friend, noting that he was "resigned to what fate has ordained" and referenced the justice of God. His references to Christ were cynical to the end, and witnesses claim that his last words spoken after a visit from a Catholic priest for the administration of the sacrament were: "Applaud friends, the comedy is over." At the end, Beethoven raised himself up and held a clenched fist towards the heavens, in what Anselm Hüttenbrenner described as "a very serious, threatening expression," and then collapsed in the hands of his friend...dead at 56 years of age.[42]

The revolutionary character of Beethoven's emotion-driven music at first repelled the majority of his audiences. His 9th Symphony, performed first in Vienna on May 7, 1824, almost sparked a riot. When 90% of the audience left the Paris performance of Opus 131, Hector Berlioz stayed till the end and confessed, "I fell under the spell of the composer's genius...Here is music, then, which repels almost all those who hear it and which, among a few, produces sensations wholly out of the ordinary."[43] As the prototypical Romantic, Beethoven's "conversation was spattered with key words: *boundless, eternal, infinite, pure sensation, power, ecstasy, excitement, the spirit, the senses, enthusiasm,* and *incomprehensible.*"[44] During the Romantic Age, music became the new philosophy. Thoughtful predication and objective truth claims were no longer important. The feel and the experience of the music was now everything. Beethoven represented the first leading artist to tentatively cross over from reason to Romanticism, from the rational to the irrational. And the world followed.

The new artist was characterized as the Bohemian—living in purposeful squalor and flagrant immorality, scorning tradition and parental wisdom, abandoning the nuclear family, and valuing all that is eccentric and odd. Beethoven's room was described as "dreary, almost sordid...in the greatest disorder: music, money, clothes lay on the floor, linen in a heap on the unclean bed, the open grand piano covered in thick dust, and broken coffee cups lay on the table."[45] Relationships with family for this new breed were often ruined, and sexual sin became the standard.

The ruling assumption for the classical masters of the humanist bent was "complexity is genius," and the objective was complexity for the sake of complexity. The arduous outpouring of artistic energies in the expression of a false worldview was treated as commendable and worthy of the greatest accolades. However, this cultural expression had set the wrong trajectory, and the creative element began the long process of self-destruction.

THE BIRTH OF THE MODERN

The Lord knoweth how to deliver the godly out of temptations, and to reserve the unjust unto the day of judgment to be punished: but chiefly them that walk after the flesh in the lust of uncleanness, and despise government...Having eyes full of adultery, and that cannot cease from sin; beguiling unstable souls: an heart they have exercised with covetous practices; cursed children…For when they speak great swelling words of vanity, they allure through the lusts of the flesh, through much wantonness, those that were clean escaped from them who live in error. While they promise them liberty, they themselves are the servants of corruption: for of whom a man is overcome, of the same is he brought in bondage. For if after they have escaped the pollutions of the world through the knowledge of the Lord and Saviour Jesus Christ, they are again entangled therein, and overcome, the latter end is worse with them than the beginning. For it had been better for them not to have known the way of righteousness, than, after they have known it, to turn from the holy commandment delivered unto them. But it is happened unto them according to the true proverb, The dog is turned to his own vomit again; and the sow that was washed to her wallowing in the mire. (2 Peter 2:9-22)

The "Modern" emerged after AD 1820, best defined as that one committed to an abandonment of the past. More than this, it is the person who sets out to destroy all that came before. All must be destroyed before a re-creation is attempted. "True art," said the truly epistemologically self-conscious modern, Richard Wagner (1813-1883), "is revolutionary, because its very existence is opposed to the ruling spirit of the community."[46] To all intents and purposes, the modern was really the Christian apostate, committed to releasing himself and all society from 2,000 years of Christian ethics, art, education, law, and religion. All memories of the past were to be expunged. This was to be an extremely difficult process after the embedment of Christ into the consciousness and institutions of the West.

The Reformation influence on the musical arts had largely disappeared a hundred years after the death of Bach. Inspired especially by the works of Beethoven, Richard Wagner was primarily responsible for the re-introduction of Bacchus, the Greek god of unrestrained licentiousness and emotion, into the modern world of music and culture. His operas themed around the tension plaguing the conscience of the modern—the tension between restrained sexuality and unrestrained sexual autonomy. With his first production, *Das Liebesverbot (1836),* clearly sexual "freedom" wins out at the end of the cosmic opera, as the entire carnival erupts in the wild party spirit. Whereas Amadeus Mozart's last opera, *The Magic Flute (1800),* celebrated the triumph of "the light of reason" over religious superstition, Wagner's *Tristan and Isolde* (1865) lets loose sensual autonomy against the restraining influence of reason. Wagner followed through on his artistic vision, conducting three affairs with married women along the way.

Wagner viewed Christianity as stifling—the "negation of life," its dogma "not realizable."[47] The composer attempted total autonomy through music—the impulse of revolution and the original sin. For previous classical composers like Bach, heightened emotional intensity was still subordinated to the melody—but not so for Wagner. Unfettered emotion would abandon reason and require no logical defense. More than revolt against God, here was a revolt against reason and all truth claims. Wagner's music was hyper-sensual, emotion without resolution, and, as he put it: "a sybaritic [orgiastic] message to the sensuous feeling."[48] With Wagner, modern man found his liberation from both morality and melody. When the Fall had come, the melody was gone in the popular culture. The music was dead.

GOD FADES, REALITY FADES

And [Jesus] cometh to Bethsaida; and they bring a blind man unto him, and besought him to touch him. And he took the blind man by the hand, and led him out of the town; and when he had spit on his eyes, and put his hands upon him, he asked him if he saw ought. And he looked up, and said, I see men as trees, walking. After that he put his hands again upon his eyes, and made him look up: and he was restored, and saw every man clearly. (Mark 8:22-25)

As the true and living God faded away from Western consciousness, reality faded as well. With the abandonment of absolute truth (and any and all possibilities of identifying truth by reason or revelation) came the rejection of an absolute reality. Usually, spiritual reality fades first and man is reduced to a stark physical reality, as in the case of the realism of Francisco Goya (1746-1828). The artist said he would paint "only what I see." Thus, man was reduced to skin, blood, and bones, and there was no way to see love in the heart, hope in the eye, light in the soul, or God behind the scenes.

Following the disappearance of God in the empirical world of the strict realist came the disappearance of the world itself. When the world is reduced to whatever you can see and touch, the physical disappears also. An escape from God must necessarily result in escape from all reality.

Thus, the destruction of Western art happened by increments— first with impressionism. When a man comes alive spiritually, as Jesus restores his sight, at first he sees "men as trees walking." The deconstruction of Western culture is the reversal of this story of Jesus' miracle. When Western man wanders into the "country of the blind," as the old H. G. Wells story goes, he soon denies the existence of the very concept of sight—and reality itself. With others in the community of the blind, he puts out his own eyes so that he is unable to see the reality everyone claims does not exist. The process begins with the application of a little humanist spit in the eyes. Before the entire surgical process is completed, the man still sees men as trees walking. Such was the condition of 19th Century man as best expressed by impressionist art. It was a half-way house to the abandonment of reality and the insanity that came with it.

Impressionist art developed by a more involved philosophical explanation. By this time, the world was following the thinking of Immanuel Kant. The world is what you make of it. Empirical observation is first, and then the mind imposes categories upon the data. What you see is not necessarily real, but man must attempt to make something of it. Thus, impressionists were directing man to trust his more primal sensations and reconstruct reality as he sees it. Painting by patches and blotches, the artists were supposed to be receiving raw, uninterpreted data and transferring it to the canvas. This was a radical break from the past.

The impressionist art of Claude Monet (1840-1926) comes across as out of focus, vaguely connotative of something in our experience—a lily pond, a boulevard, a sailboat, or a ballerina. With this art, the observer is invited to "interpret" reality as he would like to, not as reality really is. For Edgar Degas, reality is presented in the art as random, chaotic, and accidental. Part of the picture in *Ballet Rehearsal* (1874) is cut off, and his lighting shows up in random locations throughout. Given his self-conscious commitment to humanist autonomy and his rejection of God, he would have to reject the possibility of reality and opt towards epistemological and cultural suicide.

Vincent van Gogh (1853-1890) offered an ideal portrait of the post-Christian apostate artist. Raised in a Dutch Reformed home, his grandfather and father both ministers, Van Gogh failed ministerial school and attempted missionary service until his twenty-seventh year. Rejecting God, and embracing complete humanist autonomy in his philosophy and art, Van Gogh confessed, "I can very well do without God both in my life and in my painting, but I cannot, suffering as I am, do without something which is greater than I, which is my life, the power to create."[49]

Apostasy was not an easy prospect for these men as they committed themselves to shed a thousand years of Christian heritage. Nietzsche was diagnosed clinically insane for the last seven years of his life, and cared for by his sister until his death. Jean-Paul Sartre admitted that his apostasy was "a cruel and long-range affair" in which he had to "collar the Holy Ghost in the cellar and [throw] him out." Van Gogh's was a similarly excruciatingly painful affair, and he was remanded to a mental institute, thereafter suffering multiple mental breakdowns. Finally, on July 27, 1890, the tortured apostate pulled out a revolver and shot himself in the chest. For over a century afterwards, Vincent van Gogh would be lauded as an insane martyr for the apostate Christian world.

Van Gogh's post-Christian art chronicles the apostasy—filled with anguish, hallucinations, and despair. His 2,100 works of art express varying degrees of madness. Quite distinct from impressionist art, the expressionist art of Van Gogh used lurid colors, disjointed spaces, exaggeration, and distortion to produce extreme, ungodly emotions. In more stark and honest tones, this art shouted a rejection of God's reality and by implication, God Himself. Expressionism induced a more explicit rejection of objective reality.

Van Gogh was a pioneer-cultural apostate. While he sold only a single painting in his lifetime, the post-Christian world enthusiastically embraced his work—turning it into the highest valued art of all time. As the decline of Western culture reached the breaking point, nine of Van Gogh's most popular paintings were reputedly worth $900 million (equivalent to 562,000 ounces of gold).

THE WEAK CHRISTIAN STRANDS REMAINING

The 19th Century did not completely capitulate to Christian apostasy, but clearly the battle for a Christian world and life view was on. For instance, William Holman Hunt (1827-1910) brought every detail of his paintings into sharp focus, striving for both spiritual and material realism. Cultural critic Erich Auerbach explained the Christian way in art: "[The reality of God] reaches so deeply into the everyday that the two realms of the sublime and the everyday are not only actually unseparated but basically inseparable."[50] Henry Tanner (1859-1937), son of a pastor in the African Methodist Episcopal Church, held on to some strands of realism, the extraordinary element in the ordinary, and certain biblical themes during the collapse of Western art.

Through the 19th and 20th centuries, humanist rebellion and autonomy produced varying strains within the Christian church. Sentimentalized art was one way to replace faith in the historical Christ and objective truth with a romanticized-spiritualized feeling. In the words of Dorothy Sayers, summarizing much of the Christian novels and art of the 19th Century: "We have very efficiently pared the claws of the Lion of Judah" and have turned Him "into a household pet for pale curates and pious old ladies."[51] This translated into "Jesus is my girlfriend" song lyrics, and a disoriented Christian piety in "worship music" at the turn of the 21st Century. Previous centuries of Christians would have found sentimentalized lyrics like "Softly and tenderly Jesus is calling," and "Oh Jesus thou art pleading in accents meek and low," as rather vapid, powerless, faithless, and strange. The Romantic Era increasingly used music and art to produce a religion devoid of content, a sentimentalized faith, and a preference for feeling over reason and faith.

The heavily sentimentalized "painter of light," Thomas Kinkade (1958-2012), died of "acute intoxication from alcohol and Valium," according to news reports. His girlfriend of eighteen months informed the news media that he had been "drinking all night." The self-described "devout Christian" artist was still married to another woman at the time of his death. Such was the state of Christian art by the dawn of the 21st Century.

A few Christians dabbled with post-Christian art forms, but the expressionist Georges Rouault (1871-1958) had to burn 300 pieces of his artwork at the end of his life. Or, as in the case of the pioneering contemporary Christian artist, Larry Norman (1947-2008), towards the end of his life, advised that all music be thrown out of the modern church *in toto*.

MODERN ART

Art is a reflection of worldview, and the predominant form in a society reflects the spirit of the age—the generally-accepted worldview of a society.

As modernity progressed, impressionism led to increasing levels of abstraction in art. As man attempted to define his own reality, he found less and less to define. He was less concerned with the visible world, and the abstractions became increasingly connotative of a pseudo-reality.

Something is made out of the rationalist tendencies of the cubist who treats art like a high school geometry project. Some say the cubists such as Pablo Picasso (1881-1973) were imposing their own order on the world, but of course, there was no order to it. Picasso's art was an intentional disorder, discombobulation, confusion, madness, and wild anarchy. Baptized into the Christian church and given ten names honoring Christian saints gone before, Picasso apostatized, professed atheism, and glorified violence in his "artistry," frequently picturing unbridled hostility against women—rape, strangulation, and torture. Peter Gay summarizes Picasso: "He imagined rapes with fair frequency, it seems with almost sadistic relish."[52] Picasso was essentially a pornographer. Not much more need be said of 20th Century art. *These were the destroyers.*

Following Picasso, the breakdown of Western culture proceeded with remarkable speed. Impressionism had a thirty year run (1870-1900)—immediately followed by futurism, cubism, and chaos. As the gauge for the progress of the Western zeitgeist, the *avant-garde* art forms marked the death of a culture before 1920. Commenting on the revolutionary nature and the complete deconstruction of culture in the 1960s, Christian historian/philosopher Francis Schaeffer described Marcel Duchamp's *Nude Descending a Staircase* (1912) thusly: "The chance and fragmented concept of what *is* led to the devaluation and absurdity of all things. All one was left with was a fragmented view of a life which is absurd in all its parts. . . Thus art itself was declared absurd."[53] From here, the institution-based *avant-garde* was self-consciously committed to the meaningless and suicidal. Jackson Pollock (1912-1956) dangled his paint cans over the floor, randomly slapping swaths of colors over the canvas. Igor Stravinsky's *Rite of Spring* (1913) was one mass of dissonance—chaos celebrated as something or other. After the complete abandonment of melody, the modern world embraced atonality or total dissonance, pioneered mainly by Arnold Schoenberg (1874-1951).

Where realism still existed in modern art, the message communicated was clearly nihilistic, brutal, and grotesque. The beauty of nature was rejected as something meaningless, and the artist's configuration of meaninglessness was preferred over nature. Meaningless though the art was professed to be, patrons paid millions to exempt themselves from God and His reality.

Between 1912 and 2012, modern art traded one form of absurdity for another, and another, and another. By 1976, the entire art world (including patrons and critics), according to Tom Wolfe, was reduced to 10,000 people out of a worldwide population of 6 billion.[54] Once the artist kills the art, nobody cares much about the art anymore. Once a person commits suicide, he fails to make much of a mark on humanity thereafter. Martyrs leave more of a legacy than suicides. While the public more or less ignored the *avant-garde*, another more pedestrian form of meaninglessness developed for mass consumption—pop art.

POPULAR ART & MUSIC IN THE MAINSTREAM

And the great dragon was cast out, that old serpent, called the Devil, and Satan, which deceiveth the whole world: he was cast out into the earth, and his angels were cast out with him. And I heard a loud voice saying in heaven, Now is come salvation, and strength, and the kingdom of our God, and the power of his Christ: for the accuser of our brethren is cast down, which accused them before our God day and night. And they overcame him by the blood of the Lamb, and by the word of their testimony; and they loved not their lives unto the death. (Revelation 12:9-11)

By the early 20th Century, the ideology of Friedrich Nietzsche, Richard Wagner, Charles Darwin, John Stuart Mill, and Pablo Picasso had mainly influenced the university elite and certain socio-economic and political institutions in the West. How to reach the rank and file was the next challenge for those working the project of cultural deconstruction. This was provided by a centrally-controlled system of electronic mass media.

Social revolutions combined with cultural revolutions to pave the way for the dry rot of popular culture, first making its entrance in the 1920s. Such revolutions could never come about without the dissolution of the family, the destruction of the family economy, the development of large age-segregated public schools, child labor laws, the dating culture absent of parental involvement, the replacement of fathers and grandfathers with socialist programs, feminist ideologies, easy divorce, and the inciting of teen rebellion by the Rousseau and Goethe Romanticist types throughout the 19th Century. By 1940, 75% of America's 10,000,000 teens (14 to 17 years old) were officially off the family farm and checked into large high schools, where they could be thoroughly discipled and enculturated into the "peer group." What may be called a paradigmatic anomaly unparalleled in human history, the teenager was born on October 12, 1944, when 30,000 frenzied teen girls descended on Times Square to meet their new teen idol—Frank Sinatra. Historian Bruce Blevin, described the scene as "a phenomenon of mass hysteria that is only seen two or three times in prior history."[55] The popular cultural revolutions of the 20th Century, whether it was Frank Sinatra in 1944, the Beatles Invasion of 1964, or Woodstock (1969), almost exclusively consisted of youth, ages 14-24 years. Teen culture as developed from 1820 to 1920, had institutionalized as blatantly rebellious, perpetually immature, flippant, sullen, defiant, immature, foolish, fixated on style and self image ("the cool"), contemptuous of adults, and shockingly revolutionary. Outrageous though it may sound, teen culture very much led popular culture for the breakdown of Western culture. Best described in Proverbs 30, it was a "generation that cursed its father, and did not bless its mother. . . pure in its own eyes, yet not washed from its own filthiness." Such was a generation "whose teeth were like swords and whose fangs like knives."

Popular culture was designedly disposable, diversionary, trivial, transient, sensual, and mass-produced and modern architecture, music, art, sculpture, and technology took on these traits. This was a power culture. Limited accessibility to radio and television station licenses contributed to the centralization of control over media. Expensive satellites would beam signals into every farmhouse in Iowa and every apartment building in Chicago. Tattoo parlors were as common in farm towns in South Dakota as in downtown Los Angeles. Standards of morality and cultural systems homogenized, beginning with the first radio station airing from Pittsburgh, Pennsylvania in October of 1920. Mass producing opera and live theater in 1782 for the corruption of the populace throughout the hill country of France would have been difficult if not impossible, but principalities found a solution to this dilemma for the 20th Century. The production and printing of film began with the 1902 opening of the first Tally Movie Theater in Los Angeles, California. The three to five cent admission fee was a bargain when compared with the average $2.00 admission to the opera. The average American attended the movie theater every other week in the

1930s. Overnight, a small number of film producers assumed almost total control over the national culture. Henceforth, the nation's morals and character would be ordered by Hollywood and the popular music and media industries. Mass media would lead the cultural apostasy and increasingly frame the worldview of the nations. With the advent of television in the 1940s, this centralized control and mass production of popular culture accelerated to a daily and hourly routine. The content for popular media was anything but Christian, excepting an occasional sentimental Christmas show. While some called this new media "secular," the term was imprecise. The content chiefly reflected the spirit of the age—an anti-Christian worldview of materialism, anti-supernaturalism, humanism, and existentialism. The ideology of Jean-Paul Sartre's existentialism was especially embraced by popular music, country music, television, and motion pictures. Pop culture was the choice means by which Western society would self-destruct.

A study conducted in 2012 looked at 464,411 recordings made between 1950 and 2010, and found the inane, the uncreative, and the artlessness increased. Harmonic complexity and timbral diversity decreased, while loudness increased to compensate.[56] In short, the primal screams erupting out of an unrestrained Romanticism in popular music achieved maximum volume. Dionysius was unleashed. The crude and the vulgar was celebrated, preferring the raw over the refined, and the authentic over artifice—or rather a preference for the authentic, unrestrained and unvarnished expression of the depravity of human nature. The words meant little or nothing, whether they were the lowest form of gutter speak or Christian lyrics. The mode communicated a complete irrationalism for the Post-modern ear.

The history of popular music could very well tell the story of the slow but steady disappearance of the melody. The most popular song in 1942 was "I'm Dreaming of a White Christmas." The melody was distinct. The most popular song of 1949 was "Ghost Riders in the

Sky," a melody with a moral, and a warning about hell. Then, came "Heartbreak Hotel" in 1956, a revolutionary change in music—a bluesy song, with more beat than melody. Elvis Presley's antics may have been taken as sexualized, but more essentially, the form was pure energy, and primitive. The Beatles' "I Want to Hold Your Hand" (most popular song of 1964), introduced the "jangle sound"—a term describing the discordant, harsh, and unpleasant. The tune was tantalizingly close to some sort of melody, except that the boy band from Liverpool sounded out of tune, dissonant, and obviously uncommitted to the tune itself. The sheer defiance in the form, the sexual tension, the preeminence of the rock and roll beat, took the world by storm.

Marvin Gaye's 1973 "Let's Get It On" sticks with a melody for three or four notes at a time, accommodating the sexual revolution of the day—punctuated with screeching, cheering, and howling. There was no melody left in 1984 with Prince's "When Dove's Cry." The "Funk" style, early predecessor to Hip-Hop, abandoned chord progressions and melody for pure high-energy, baseline rhythm. By the 2010s, the vocalists would hover around a single note, and we weren't sure if they were yelling, rapping, or singing. The melody was all gone. Human personality was dispensed with. The music was reduced to a monotonous Dembow rhythm, usually delivered in a heavily-synthesized, mechanical, techno sound. Any computer could program itself and run through the hypnotic loops.

Nothing in human history could compare with the sheer primal energy generated by this modern pop form. Charles A. Reich wrote approvingly of the revolutionary character of the rock and roll medium in his 1970 Manifesto, "Not even the turbulent fury of Beethoven's Ninth Symphony can compete for sheer energy with the Rolling Stones."[57] It was a music that "rocks the whole body." For Lord Byron (the epitome of the Romantic Apostasy), the great object of life was "Sensation—to feel that we exist," and the new idiom maximized on this objective.

If there was one composition that represented the modern and post-modern age better than anything else, it was the most requested rock song of all time—"Can't Get No Satisfaction." The hit, says songwriter, Mick Jagger, captured the "feeling of the times," which he concluded was "alienation."[58] The individualism of existentialism was inherently isolating, because autonomy (man seeking godhood for himself) must always lead to the destruction of community and loneliness.

Highly caffeinated, flesh-pulsating, adrenalin-pumping, sensual experience was all that was left. This wasn't "White Christmas" and "Battle of New Orleans" anymore. At the end, pop music was dehumanized, depersonalized, intensely isolating, highly sexualized, purposeless, and suicidal—and its consumers lived and breathed it out. If there were any melodies left, the tune wandered aimlessly here and there, conveying the randomness and meaninglessness of modern life without God. The lyrics were put in free verse, and the unity was lost for the chaos or the ultimacy of the particulars.

There was little opportunity to exempt oneself from this cultural zeitgeist. Within just ten years, rock had taken the place of what Kenneth Meyers referred to as the "dominant idiom" in Western society. The cultural expression was omnipresent—blasting from the stores, the restaurants, the churches, car radios, the movies, and homes. Only 2.9% of the nation's radio stations played the classical format, and another 2.7% played a folk gospel format. The rest of the stations were programmed for pop and rock—and nothing produced prior to the Beatles. Christian music followed precisely the same pop form, except for the 2.7% of radio stations holding to folk Gospel.

Sexual perversion predominated in popular music, with Elton John leading the way in the 1970s, followed by David Bowie, George Michael, and others. Cultural leaders in popular music influenced popular opinion first, before the US Supreme Court ruled on *Obergefell*.

The most outspoken advocates of homosexuality turned out to be Christian singers like Amy Grant and Carrie Underwood, and Country superstars like Garth Brooks (as early as 1992), Willie Nelson (2006), Kacey Musgraves (2013), and Dolly Parton (2014). Lady Gaga's "Born This Way" (2011), captured the prize for Guinness Book of World Record's fastest selling single of all time. Billions around the world resonated to the homosexual anthem—a fitting preparation for mass culture's acceptance of the "same sex marriage" fad solidifying worldwide between 2011 and 2020.

REVOLUTION IN THE VISUAL MEDIUM

While popular music took the forefront in the cultural revolution, the visual medium followed hard after it. The US Supreme Court decision *US v. Roth* (1957) opened the way for pornographer, Hugh Hefner, and then pornography was normalized with affirmations from television hosts Johnny Carson and Bob Hope in the early 1970s. Popular movies introduced pornographic eroticism in 1967 for universal consumption with the release of *Blue Movie*, directed by Andy Warhol (1928-1987), and *Last Tango in Paris* (1972).

The debut of *I Love Lucy* on October 1, 1962 presented the first divorced woman in an endearing role—Lucy shared a house with Vivian, a divorcee. Based on Irene Kampen's *Life Without George*, the popular television program with the same title, normalized divorce at least five years before Governor Ronald Reagan signed off on convenience divorce in the state of California. Cultural forces preempted political force, every time.

As early as 1972, The Mary Tyler Moore Show promoted the conception control pill for unmarried women, opening the way to widespread promiscuous sexuality over the next fifty years. Leading television producer, Norman Lear, made sure that Maude had an abortion (1972) and introduced homosexuality in a positive light to the rank and file in his sitcom, *All in the Family* (1971). Evidently, the television program was offensive even to the president of the United States, who was overheard, telling his staff, "I don't want to see this country go this way. You know what happened to the Greeks. Homosexuality destroyed them..."[59] Another sitcom, *Soap*, featured the first openly homosexual character in 1977.

The film industry also led the way to sexual nihilism with *Capote* and *Brokeback Mountain* (2005), both richly lauded with Academy and Golden Globe awards. The pro-homosexual film, *Dallas Buyer's Club* (2013) won awards as well, as did *Moonlight* in 2016. *Bohemian Rhapsody* gained highest awards in 2018. By the end of the 2010s, most of the Best Picture awards were going to movies featuring homosexuality.

For the final initiative in the mass corruption of Western culture, the zeitgeist set its sights on the children. The sexualization, (or better put—the "homosexualization"), of children came primarily through Disney, the premier producers of children's programming, and the $80 billion-per year leader in world entertainment. Disney was the zeitgeist at the end. For the tweens and teens, a 13-year-old outs himself as "homosexual" in 2017 on the Andi Mack program. A supporting character is endeared to the audience for his homosexuality in Disney's *Beauty and the Beast* in 2017. The first openly-lesbian supporting character is presented for 6-10-year-old children in *Onward* (2020), and male homosexuals were the main characters for the entertainment of 6-10-year-old children in *Out* (2020). As the final coup de grace, the most successful children's franchise of all history, Disney's *Toy Story* included a homosexually-charged scene for 5-10 year old children, with the June 2022 release of *Lightyear*. What was probably the most endearing children's animated film series of all time turned into "Introduction to Sodomy 101."

Paganism revived in the mainstream, featured prominently in blockbuster films like *Avengers Endgame* in 2019—a film celebrating human sacrifice, sorcery, and the heathen fates. This top grossing film (at $2.8 billion) involved a battle over the infinity stones between the gods of the new pantheon—a polytheistic worldview reviving the paganism of the pre-Christian world. To complete the reintroduction of paganism into the major motion picture industry, *Avengers-Eternals* (2021) included male homosexual sexual content.

With the advent of web-streamed visual media, there were no meaningful controls left for children plugged into their smartphones and iPads. Forty-one percent of teen programming for Netflix were rated TV-MA (suitable for "mature audiences"), and 55% of Netflix originals were rated TV-MA, meaning that children received generous doses of the most obscene language, graphic violence, graphic sexual activity, or any combination of these elements.

THE ULTIMATE ISOLATION OF MODERN MAN

June 29, 2007, marked another phase in the ongoing isolation of modern life—the introduction of the "smartphone." For the previous seventy years, families had participated in entertainment, whether by radio or television, as a family, in community. The iPhone and other portable devices revolutionized entertainment, providing for almost complete isolation for almost every person in the world. Prior to 2007 it would have been difficult for children to take in popular culture and ultimate depravities in isolation, but now the gateway to Pandora's box was made available to all. It would have been practically impossible for a 12-year-old child to carry a television set into the bathroom in 1997, and plug himself into the medium in isolation. Some reasonable accountability was available in every family. Now, the sensual or aesthetic experience was placed in individualized isolation, and the escape from reality and human relationships was almost total. To put the matter simply, there was no more reasonable protection for eleven-year-old children from the corruption of ten million bad websites and the corrupting influence of peers with access to all of it. Isolation by electronic forms would begin with children at two and three years of age, and the experiment would prove more destructive than anyone could imagine.

Between 2007 and 2014, access to smartphones for teens increased to 73%. Four years later, access had increased to 95%, with 45% claiming to be online "almost constantly."[60] The addiction to online isolation had doubled in just four years.

Now pornography was mainstream, and nobody was talking about burying the nude Venus in Siena, Italy anymore. A few social critics like the transgendered Camille Paglia couldn't help but notice that the West had descended into the "latrine of culture." The irony was thick. Apparently, there was a teaspoon of common grace left with one burned-out prophetess who noticed the artlessness, sexlessness, and self-destructiveness of popular culture. Paglia described the popular singer Lady Gaga as the "exhausted end of the sexual revolution."[61]

The lag between decadence and despair for the 19th Century artist was twenty to thirty years. By the 1980s, the lag shortened to five years for musicians like Kurt Cobain. Forty years later, there was mainly despair. Western culture had crossed over the line.

THE END OF POPULAR CULTURE

I have seen the wicked in great power, and spreading himself like a green bay tree. Yet he passed away, and, lo, he was not: yea, I sought him, but he could not be found. Mark the perfect man, and behold the upright: for the end of that man is peace. But the transgressors shall be destroyed together: the end of the wicked shall be cut off. But the salvation of the righteous is of the LORD: he is their strength in the time of trouble. And the LORD shall help them, and deliver them: he shall deliver them from the wicked, and save them, because they trust in him. (Psalm 37:35-40)

Intended from the first as a disposable commodity, pop culture was doomed for extinction. In 1977, the US popular music industry took in $70 per capita (adjusted for inflation). This peaked at $78 per capita in 1998, and then the bottom fell out. By 2015, the business had reduced to $21 per capita,[62] to include streaming services and all sales for recorded music. Annual movie box office sales followed a similar pattern, declining from 6 tickets per capita to 3 tickets per capita between 2000 and 2020.[63]—a huge reduction from 32 tickets per capita at the peak of Hollywood's influence in 1946.[64] Centralized forces dominated music and other media from the 1940s until 2000, thus far, and no further.

Nobody really cared that the 92nd Academy Awards ceremony gave Best Picture to a nihilist South Korean motion picture called *Parasite*—basically a film about popular culture eating out the innards of South Korean and Western life. Westerners were supposed to crowd into theaters to hear Koreans mispronounce the F-word—and explain to everyone the meaninglessness of life and the worthlessness of the film they were watching. It was one of the most unpopular of all academy-awarded films in history. Meanwhile, the 2020 Grammys lavished the green-haired, despondent, apparently suicidal Billie Eilish with five awards. Viewership had dropped in half over eight years. No wonder. Billie's big album sold 343,000 copies in 2019—hardly in the league with Michael Jackson's *Thriller* album which sold 65 million copies in the 1980s. Pop was dead, with faded stars receiving just 0.5% of the popularity the big stars had enjoyed in previous decades.

Whatever was left of the aesthetic, the meaningful, the edifying, and the intelligent was all but gone. What survived was the inane, the addictive, and the escapist. The US entertainment industry expanded from roughly $40 billion to $300 billion between 1970 and 2020. The bulk of the increase came from much-expanded television selections ($80 billion), gambling ($140 billion), pornography ($15 billion), and computer gaming ($30 billion). Almost none of this existed in 1970. The size of the illicit drug market was estimated at an additional $120 billion. Big businesses found ways to manufacture games and gaming to maximize the potential of addictions by psychological manipulation, to the benefit of market share. It was the first time in history that technology and complex computer algorithms were used to purposefully create addictions for a society in its death throes.

Such a universally-celebrated trivial and disposable culture could not last much longer. Andy Warhol's impression of a Campbell's Soup Can may have sold for $12 million in 2006, only to end up in landfills a few decades later. Like Lady Gaga's farcical concerts, the art was meant to mock the patrons, and to represent in itself the bankruptcy and meaninglessness of modernity.

At the Fall of the West, the sheer size of the pyre, the magnitude of the burning and the burnout, was beyond anything previously recorded in world history. The degree to which modern man, including much of the Christian world, had received the humanist-nihilist worldview was hard to fathom. The self-deception was deep. As already covered previously, statistical studies found that not much of the Christian worldview was left anymore in the minds of professing Christians. The Christian worldview had been extricated from the churches, schools, universities, media, entertainment, and cultural productions. The whole of Western cultural institutions had been corrupted by the anti-Christian zeitgeist defined by Sartre, Nietzsche, Darwin, Marx, and Kant.

WHAT SURVIVED

For analogy, the cultural mainland was nuked, but islands of culture could still thrive. Where Christians dragged the polytheistic fragmentation of the forms into the music of the church; where pure romanticized, primal emotionalism prevailed and where the pride of performance and the triviality of popular culture were preferred, none of it would survive what followed. During the previous five hundred years, there had been conditions under which some Christian synthesis with foreign worldviews still retained sustainable culture and faith. But during the cultural conflagration of the 21st Century, attempts on the part of Christians to synthesize in the zeitgeist amounted to nothing more than rank apostasy and pure suicide. Those Christian elements which clung to the wasted forms of a degraded culture could not possibly survive.

Yet, where Christian pastors discipled the next generation by the investment of thousands of hours in a biblical way of thinking over ten years in private homes, the church would survive and thrive. Wherever honor for historical, orthodox theology and practice existed; where the fear of the Lord was still regarded as the beginning of wisdom; and where the honor of fathers and mothers broke through by the grace of God, healthy culture would develop on the islands of culture. Where there was a holy reverence for God and honor for cultural forms of the past, some folk art survived.

Where a shallow, meaningless gospel was pasted over a meaningless post-modern worldview, nothing could survive. Where there was no hard and fast antithesis set against the philosophies of the world, "Sardis" was dead and dying. Where the men disappeared and only women and immature children were left to lead the church and culture, nothing could survive.

Yet, where the ideas of the godless public schools, public media, universities, apostate philosophers, Greeks, astrologers, and the wizards that peep and mutter were thrown out, and where true repentance and renewal of mind came about according to the radical teaching and straightforward preaching of the Holy Scriptures, something survived. Preaching and teaching come first, followed by repentance. Then some islands of culture developed. As the Lord tarried, Christians would plant the gardens in the ashes of Western civilization and build the next Christendom on its ruins. And, where the primary purpose of music and culture was to express gratitude and praise to God rather than to provide entertainment and superficial emotional comfort or to suppress reality, the islands would flourish.

> God is our refuge and strength, a very present help in trouble. Therefore will not we fear, though the earth be removed, and though the mountains be carried into the midst of the sea; though the waters thereof roar and be troubled, though the mountains shake with the swelling thereof. Selah.
>
> There is a river, the streams whereof shall make glad the city of God, the holy place of the tabernacles of the most High. God is in the midst of her; she shall not be moved: God shall help her, and that right early.
>
> The heathen raged, the kingdoms were moved: he uttered his voice, the earth melted. The LORD of hosts is with us; the God of Jacob is our refuge. Selah.
>
> Come, behold the works of the LORD, what desolations he hath made in the earth. He maketh wars to cease unto the end of the earth; he breaketh the bow, and cutteth the spear in sunder; he burneth the chariot in the fire.
>
> Be still, and know that I am God: I will be exalted among the heathen, I will be exalted in the earth. The LORD of hosts is with us; the God of Jacob is our refuge. Selah. (Psalm 46)

XII

THE RISE & FALL OF
WESTERN LIBERTIES

If the Son therefore shall make you free, ye shall be free indeed.
(John 8:36)

M an, left under the total dominion of evil spiritual powers in the world, will always turn out to be mean, treacherous, and cruel. The history of the ancient empires of men is a long tiresome account of the most unspeakable treacheries and cruelties. When examining the dark era predating the coming of Christ, the student of history loses count of the kings and emperors who killed their mothers, wives, and children, or the emperors killed off by their friends and relatives. Ancient records of the Assyrian Empire are stuffed with endless accounts of the flaying alive of victims, stabbings, body mutilations, burnings, and dismemberments. Sennacherib was murdered by his own sons. Before Alexander III (the Great) of Macedonia appears, Alexander II was murdered by his cousin Ptolemy, who was then killed by Perdiccas (Alexander's brother). Three years later, Philip II had to eliminate two of his half-brothers before he could secure his place on the Macedonian throne.

The history of the Roman Empire is one long account of murder, treachery, wicked intrigue, bloody pogroms, and revolutions. Caligula murdered his mother and brothers. Claudius killed thirty-five senators and some 300 knights. Nero murdered two wives, his mother, and his stepbrother. A paranoid and autocratic Domitian murdered senators, knights, and other officials…by the hundreds. He introduced exquisite forms of torture, and nobody was safe from his informants and police state tactics. There is nothing to see here that might commend the classical world, its ethics, or governments.

The world before the arrival of Christ was a living nightmare, accurately described by Paul in his letter to the 1st Century Romans:

> And even as they did not like to retain God in their knowledge, God gave them over to a reprobate mind, to do those things which are not convenient; being filled with all unrighteousness, fornication, wickedness, covetousness, maliciousness; full of envy, murder, debate, deceit, malignity; whisperers, backbiters, haters of God, despiteful, proud, boasters, inventors of evil things, disobedient to parents, without understanding, covenantbreakers, without natural affection, implacable, unmerciful: who knowing the judgment of God, that they which commit such things are worthy of death, not only do the same, but have pleasure in them that do them. (Romans 1:28-32)

SHORT-LIVED LIBERTY IN ROME

The Greek and Roman world was big on the word *liberty* but short on delivery. The experiment with the Roman Republic (509-50 BC) was one long series of revolutions, wars, mobs, massacres, and dictatorships. Junius Brutus, the first Republican revolutionary, murdered his own sons and brothers-in-law. The plebeians clambered for government welfare, urged on by tribunes like Tiberius Gracchus and Gaius his brother. These welfare programs were typically followed by more insurrections and dictatorships. Gaius Marius and Sulla murdered thousands of Romans in their respective coups. During Sulla's reign of terror, hit lists of those assigned for assassination were posted on the door of the Roman Forum. No one was safe. Whatever democracy existed in ancient Rome quickly disintegrated into tyranny, and the deification of the state under the Caesars.

The slow but steady consolidation of power with the dictators and then by Caesar was described as "tyranny" by Roman historians like Suetonius, who attempted a justification for the Caesar's murder in the Senate:

> Therefore the plots which had previously been formed separately, often by groups of two or three, were united in a general conspiracy, since even the populace no longer were pleased with present conditions, but both secretly and openly rebelled at his tyranny and cried out for defenders of their liberty.

While the Romans considered liberty from tyranny a value of sorts, fallen man could not retain the conditions wherein that liberty might prevail. Inevitably, the citizenry would seek security from the state by the empowerment of the state. Notably, the Roman tax was hardly comparable to the tyrannies that developed with the decline of the Christian West. Augustus' sales tax of half a percent was considered unreasonable at the time, and Tiberius' increase to one percent (in AD 31), was met with strong resistance. But the major source of taxation for the Roman state came by the surreptitious tax of inflation and the debauchment of currency. Ultimately, money empowers tyrants, a lesson learned by the Caesars and all modern socialist tyrannies after AD 1913.

TYRANNY IN THE EAST

The rest of the world followed the pattern of Roman tyranny as well. From the reign of the legendary Huang Di onward, the god state developed in China and a culture of hegemony became deeply engrained for millennia. The Shang Dynasty (1766-1122 BC) accepted the Canon of Shun with its provisos of body mutilations for criminal offenders, and then created a bureaucracy that far exceeded that of Egypt and Mesopotamia.

As though presenting themselves as substitutes for the Son of God who was to come centuries later, the Chinese kings used language only fitting for Jesus in reference to themselves. With the Zhou Dynasty (1027-249 BC) came a Book of Odes to the kings.

> King Wen ascends and descends,
> On the left and the right of God…
> His fame is without end…[1]

The emperor's intent to rule the world and claim ownership of all land appears in another hymn:

> All land under heaven belongs to the king
> And all people on all shores are subject to this king.[2]

Under this dynasty, the king would come to be described as the "Son of heaven," another none-too-subtle reference to the Son of God who was to come.

The Chinese totalitarian hegemony would take further shape under Duke Huan of Qi State (685-643 BC). Huan's government was the first to advocate the Chinese philosophy of "legalism," largely masterminded by the prime minister, Guan Zhong. "The Book of Master Guan" encoded his legal philosophy, in which he designated the king as the very source of law. Herein is the ultimately self-consistent humanist position asserting radial autonomy in opposition to transcendent law of the Creator God:

> The sovereign is the creator of law. The officials are the followers of
> the law, and the people are subjects of the law.[3]

Absolute power was therefore to be endowed upon whomever
happens to be king at the moment, and no Bill of Rights, Constitution,
Law of God, or any other legal restraint would limit the ruler's policies
and actions. Guan explained further in his book:

> The wise sovereign holds six powers: to grant life and to kill; to enrich
> and to impoverish; to promote and to demote.[4]

In 273 BC, the armies of Qin led by General Bai Qi fought and
won the battle of Huayang. No mercy was shown the surrendering
army—130,000 soldiers were decapitated. Thirteen years later, when
the Qin finally conquered the Zhao, they proceeded to bury 400,000
Zhao prisoners *alive*. Such was the severity of Eastern tyranny

Having consolidated power in this first Chinese empire, the
legalists went to work to organize the first massive socialist state in
history. Ownership of weapons was banned, and all swords and arrows
were collected at the capital. Wandering minstrels were replaced
with official state-sanctioned entertainers. Rich landowners and their
families were moved to the capital to remain under the watchful eye of
the central government. If one violated a major law, his entire family
was executed. Work camps were created for those violating minor state
regulations, and millions populated these gulags. There was plenty of
work to do for 700,000 state-owned slaves and workers, first with the
construction of Emperor Qin Shi Huang's ornate palace. Other state
projects included 4,000 miles of highways and thousands of miles of
canals, and 1,500 miles of the Great Wall in the north.

Under legalism, the emperor was endowed with godlike qualities,
and a state cult worship developed. Most essential for this state was

the eradication of any opposition to legalist ideology. The ruthless legalist-philosopher Li Si, assured the king, "Your Majesty…has firmly established for yourself a position of sole supremacy…And yet these independent schools [Confucianists and others], joining with each other, criticize the codes of laws and instructions. Hearing of the promulgation of a decree, they criticize it, each from the standpoint of his own school…If such license is not prohibited the sovereign power will decline above and partisan factions will form below. It would be well to prohibit this. Your servant suggests that all books in the imperial archives, save the memoirs of Qin, be burned."[5]

The infamous edict produced by Li Si became the prototype for future tyrannies the world over:

Memorial on the Burning of Books

Anyone owning classical books or treatises on philosophy must hand them in within thirty days. After thirty days anyone found in possession of such writings will be branded on the cheek and sent to work as a laborer on the northern wall or some other government project. The only exceptions are books on medicine, drugs, astrology, and agronomy.

Private schools will be forbidden. Those who wish to study law will do so under government officials.

Anyone indulging in political or philosophical discussion will be put to death, and his body exposed in public.

Scholars who use examples from antiquity to criticize the present, or who praise early dynasties in order to throw doubt on the policies of our own, most enlightened sovereign, will be executed, they and all their families.

Government officials who turn a blind eye to the above-mentioned crimes will be deemed guilty by virtue of the principle of collective responsibility, and will incur the same punishment as that inflicted for the offense itself.

What followed this edict was not to be soon forgotten in the annals of history. Emperor Qin Shi Huang personally tried the case of 463 Confucian scholars. They were assigned to five excruciating tortures, then buried to their necks in dirt, after which their heads were crushed under the emporor's chariots. The actions of Qin would hold a special significance and legal precedent for the future of Chinese governance. Up until and including the incident in Tiananmen Square 2,200 years, any and all dissent would be crushed by powerful governments in China (and later, North Korea) in a similar manner.

The world without Christ was marked by mass pogroms, genocide, and civil wars, routinely reducing national populations by 30-50%. China's Three Kingdoms War (AD 220-280) killed off 40 million, and the An Lushan pogrom took out another 36 million of the citizenry in the 8th Century.

Indian historian, Vishal Mangalwadi describes the tyranny of 17th Century Mogul emperor Shah Jahan. While building the Taj Mahal (a tomb for his dead wife), his people starved to death by the millions. To fund the building of this monstrosity, the Shah increased taxes to 50%-80% of the people's annual yield. More like a roaring lion and a raging bear, this wicked ruler's policies were ruinous for a helpless people, who were dealing with a weak monsoon season. The famine that decimated the land was described by Peter Mundy, a British traveler: "From Surat to this place all the highway was stowed with dead people, our noses never free from the stink of them...women were seen to roast their children...a man or a woman no sooner dead but they were cut in pieces to be eaten."[6] This was not a failure of either technology or intelligence on the part of the Indian people, as Mangalwadi points out. The regime could have built dams and canals to channel water for irrigation during droughts, or they could have provided storehouses to set aside food for the lean years. Historian Stanley Wolpert described the Shah's administration as a self-serving tyranny:

> Bullied and treated like children by their emperor, it was hardly surprising to find such "nobles" behaving in turn as petulant petty tyrants to their servants, bearers, soldiers, and peasants. The whole system was a pyramid of power designed to perpetuate its imperial pinnacle, whether through ruthless violence, extortion, harem intrigue, bribery, or sheer terror.[7]

This description perfectly outlines the system of government found within almost every pagan kingdom before Christ, from ancient Egypt to Rome.

THE NATURE OF POLITICAL LIBERTY

> For the transgression of a land many are the princes thereof. (Proverbs 28:2)

America's early leaders understood the Proverbs 28:2 principle, as encapsulated in Benjamin Franklin's famous quip: "Man will ultimately be governed by God or by tyrants." Robert Winthrop, speaker of the US House of Representatives, put it this way in 1849: "Men, in a word, must necessarily be controlled, either by a power within them, or by a power without them; either by the Word of God, or by the strong arm of man; either by the Bible, or by the bayonet."[8] That is, an immoral people must be and will be subjected to hard tyranny. This being the case, it is fruitless to complain about big government tyranny as long as the citizenry is countenancing gross immorality.

For this reason, liberties are not birthed in the political realm. Some degree of political liberty may be *preserved* by prudent and righteous leaders, but the seed of it is found in the hearts of men. With the rise and fall of public morality (as described in chapter seven of this work), one would absolutely expect to find a concomitant rise and fall of political liberty. Only by the Christian gospel and the conversion and discipleship of nations could any measurable political liberty exist on earth.

The modern libertarian defines liberty as the freedom to break God's commandments. Yet, this thinking runs counter to the biblical definition. To act sinfully by getting drunk, killing one's own children by abortion, or committing fornication, is to surrender liberty. Christ defined core liberty as freedom from sin in John 8. According to the teaching of Jesus, true liberty is freedom from sin.

> [The Jews] answered him, We be Abraham's seed, and were never in bondage to any man: how sayest thou, Ye shall be made free. Jesus answered them, Verily, verily, I say unto you, Whosoever committeth sin is the servant of sin. (John 8:33-34)

Inevitably, a nation fulfilling the libertine vision will be a nation enslaved by tyrants. This was the problem with Rome, and this is the problem with 21st Century Russia and the West in the post-Christian era.

THE WORST FORM OF TYRANNY

> And the dragon was wroth with the woman, and went to make war with the remnant of her seed, which keep the commandments of God, and have the testimony of Jesus Christ. (Revelation 12:17)

Scripture here describes the highest form of tyranny and evil governance as that which contributes to Christian persecution. It is the work of Satan himself. When a civil government sets itself to persecute the King of kings (and His people), the leaders operate outside the bounds of their God-given authority, and to that extent, they forfeit their right to govern. They may be rightly considered a tool of the devil—the very essence of all rebellion, anarchy, and wickedness. In such a state, all restraint of evil is lifted, and common grace is withheld. Christian persecution is nothing less than Satanic work, and any nation that oppresses the most righteous, the most godly, and the most peaceful of its citizens, is guilty of committing the highest crimes and most tyrannical evil of which man is capable.

Following the decline and fall of the Christian church in the West, and the concomitant removal of the Christian cultural influence, the dragon unleashed his forces with a vengeance against the worldwide church. Open Doors reported that 360 million Christians in 76 countries (40% of the world) experienced "high levels of persecution" in 2022. The world had not witnessed this level of persecution since the Roman persecutions 1,600 years earlier. Neither had there ever been such a universal opposition to Christ and His followers on the part of all major institutions, as well as such widespread, global proliferation of a persecuting force. Most concerning of all, for the purposes of this survey, persecution returned to the Western world against those Christians who decried sexual sins advanced by men like Nero and Herod. Universities, schools, corporate businesses, and political states almost universally endorsed homosexuality and transgenderism, and they persecuted Christians who refused support for these sins. This constituted the worst possible condition for human society on earth. It was a return to pagan Rome. It was the removal of almost all common grace from the Western world.

The first major persecution against Christians commenced around AD 64 under Caesar Nero. This was followed by nine additional state-ordered persecutions, including those under Decius (249-251), Valerian (253-260), and Diocletian (285-305). The last was the worst, Christian churches and homes were burned to the ground, copies of the Scriptures were destroyed, and thousands were martyred for the faith. All told, an estimated 2 million were killed—about a third of the Christian population in the empire. At no other time in history did the dragon exceed this proportion of Christians killed for their faith.

"Bloody" Mary killed about 300 Protestants, amounting to 0.01% of the population. The Killing Time in Scotland (1660s-1670s) produced an estimated 18,000 martyrs, about 1.5% of the population. Hundreds of thousands of Protestants were killed by the French during and after the St. Bartholomew's Day Massacre (1572), comprising about 15% of the population. This is tyranny at its worst.

THE RISE OF CHRISTIAN INFLUENCE
UPON THE NATIONS

> Give the king thy judgments, O God, and thy righteousness unto the king's son. He shall judge thy people with righteousness, and thy poor with judgment. The mountains shall bring peace to the people, and the little hills, by righteousness. He shall judge the poor of the people, he shall save the children of the needy, and shall break in pieces the oppressor…The kings of Tarshish and of the isles shall bring presents: the kings of Sheba and Seba shall offer gifts. Yea, all kings shall fall down before him: all nations shall serve him. (Psalm 72:1-4, 10-11)

Christian influence moderating the unbridled tyranny of Roman governance began with Constantine's conversion. Though not without occasional concessions and regressions, Western civilization witnessed a radical shift from paganism towards Christianity. Within 70 years, marked progress in cultural transformation comes by Christian pastors issuing reprimands to the emperors. Trouble started in the city of Thessalonica in April of AD 390 when a Roman military commander tried to arrest a popular charioteer athlete for a homosexual offense. The populace revolted, killing the commander. Instead of prosecuting the offending parties, Emperor Theodosius I ordered a military retaliation against the city, resulting in the slaughter of 7,000 citizens in cold blood. As historian Theodoret recorded:

> The anger of the Emperor rose to the highest pitch, and he gratified

his vindictive desire for vengeance by unsheathing the sword most unjustly and tyrannically against all, slaying the innocent and guilty alike. It is said seven thousand perished without any forms of law, and without even having judicial sentence passed upon them; but that, like ears of wheat in the time of harvest, they were alike cut down.[9]

This did not sit well with Ambrose of Milan, the pastor/bishop responsible for the spiritual oversight of the Emperor. Taking unprecedented action, Ambrose courageously called the emperor on the carpet for this tyrannical abuse of power, effectively banning him from the Lord's Table for eight months. Upon the emperor's promise to institute a thirty-day delay for all executions, and his public confession of sin before the congregation in Milan, he was restored to communion. It was the first time in Christian history in which the proper exercise of the church's spiritual authority was used to rein in the tyrannical exercise of civil power.

Through the initial centuries following the year of our Lord, the influence of Christ seeped into the economy, culture, and politics of the West and the East. Byzantium in the East had its problems, but Constantine left the "second Rome" with a gold and silver-backed currency. Resisting the temptation to devalue the coinage (as the Roman tyrants had done for the preceding eight hundred years), Byzantium survived for about a thousand years. Constantinople increased its population base to 600,000, at the same time old Rome declined to an occupancy of 50,000-100,000. Despite occasional perfidy at the highest levels of political office, honest money turned Byzantium into the commercial center of the world. Between 867 and 1057, this Christianized kingdom was among the most stable nations the world had ever known. Agriculture flourished, the economy doubled in size, and soldiers were able to defend the empire from the Islamic threats from the south. However, the papal crusaders proved counter-productive to the preservation of their Eastern brethren, especially when they diverted their energies to the sack of Constantinople in AD 1204. This, combined with internal moral and spiritual corruption, weakened the Eastern empire sufficiently, making way for the final invasion and capture of the city on May 29, 1453. Only 8,000 defenders were left to ward off the Sultan's army in the military campaign that lasted for seven weeks.

In the providence of God, Rome was devastated time and again by wave after wave of the deplorable barbarian tribes well into the 6th Century. The Vandals settled in North Africa. The West Goths invaded Spain. The Visigoths drove the Vandals out and then sacked Rome in AD 410 and 435. Theodoric the Great killed Odoacer the Ostrogoth in 493, regaining control of Rome for a time and attempting to revive "Roman civilization." Yet through it all, this period of tremendous political upheaval provided adequate opportunity for Christian missionary work to gain serious ground. When the Frankish King Clovis (481-511) entered Gaul, he was converted to orthodox Christianity and subsequently incorporated Christian law into his realm. The Merovingian kings permitted a decentralized system of governance in the feudal tradition, improving individual freedom for the populace. This was the political system passed down to Charles Martel (714-741) and his grandson, Charlemagne (768-814).

By this time, Christian political leaders had quit the bad habit of killing their relatives and political competitors, as commonly practiced among pagan rulers. A Christian population had come to realize that tyranny and unrestrained autocracy absent of the fear of the true and living God, was to be resisted. The Sachsenspiegel Saxon law book (compiled around AD 1220) required resistance to authority when necessary to uphold the law. This ancient code specifically addresses the case of the tyrant, in these words:

> A man must resist his king and his judge, if he does wrong, and must hinder him in every way, even if he be his relative and feudal lord. And

he does not thereby break his fealty.[10]

With the Ordinance of 817, the bishops of Charlemagne's kingdom laid out a formal procedure by which "tyrannical kings" might be penalized as follows:

> But if, what God avert and what we least of all wish, it should happen that any one of the brothers, on account of desire for earthly goods, which is the root of all evils, shall be either a divider or oppressor of the churches or the poor, or shall exercise tyranny, in which all cruelty consists: first, in secret, according to the precept of God, he shall be warned once, twice, and thrice, through faithful envoys, to amend; and if he refuse them, being summoned by one brother before the other he shall be admonished and punished with fraternal and paternal love. And if he shall altogether spurn this healthful admonition, by the common sentence of all it shall be decreed what is to be done concerning him; so that him whom a healthful admonition could not recall from his wicked ways, the imperial power and the common sentence of all may coerce.[11]

Thus, that Christian spirit submitted to the King of kings had tempered the autocratic tendency among kings and lords. Institutions preserving liberties would sink their roots deep into Anglo-Saxon soil, and the island-nation would serve as the deposit and safeguard of Christian liberties for a millennium. As Christ, the author of all liberties, would have it, the heritage of law and liberty was first left by King Alfred (849-899), his son, and grandson. Alfred's last words to his son record his commitment to self-government and opposition to all forms of oppression and tyranny:

> One can be no right ruling king under Christ himself unless he have learning, know the law, and understand the use of his writs, and be able by his own reading to inform himself how according to law to govern his land...My days are almost done. We must now part. I

shall to another world, and thou shalt be left alone in all my wealth. I pray thee…strive to be a father, and a lord to thy people. Be thou the children's [orphan's] father, and the widow's friend. Comfort thou the poor, and shelter the weak; and with all thy might, right that which is wrong. And son, govern thyself by law; then shall the Lord love thee, and God above all things shall be thy reward. Call thou upon him to advise thee in all thy need, and so shall he help thee, the better to compass that which thou wouldst.[12]

In the measured words of biographer Sir John Spelman, Alfred established for Englishmen "a fit and a reasonable liberty" by subjecting himself to the rule of law "and by subjecting them only to the equitable trial of a known and certain law." At the outset of the English nations, Alfred paved the way for English liberties, fashioning himself as a "sovereign of a free people."[13]

THE ENGLISH STRUGGLE AGAINST TYRANNY[14]

The struggle for liberty in a world of sin, avarice, malice, and power-hungry tyrants is never easy—and England became a principal battleground for centuries. Alfred's great-great-grandson King Ethelred the Unready lived up to his name—and the tyrant William the Conqueror invaded England in 1066.

Before the Norman invasion, the Anglo-Saxon property owners held title to their own lands. Alfred had provided liberty for the churches and monasteries to "remain secure, free and unburdened for ever from the claim of all king's taxes…" And he added to his charter, "if any one, which God forbid! swollen with the breath of pride, and led on by tyrannic power, shall endeavor to infringe and nullify this gift, let him know that he is anathematized by all the Christian church …"[15] Alfred's charters to his nobles secured property rights "forever", and, his contracts were typically appended with the stern warning: "to those who oppose or endeavour to infringe [this grant], be woe! and a portion with the traitor Iscariot!"[16]

Tyranny returned with the Normans, as the Conqueror assumed ownership of all lands, leasing them to his barons through feudal tenure in exchange for military service.[17] This constituted a major power grab and commenced a gigantic battle for freedom. William also instituted the first universal tax on property in Western history. In the years that followed, tyrannical kings would take undue advantage of this absolute control over the inheritance and estate of the family. Upon a landholder's death, for example, a king would sell off both the estate and the man's wife for his own gain, placing an unreasonable "relief price" on the estate.

The English did not submit to Norman tyranny without resistance. Attempts to revolt occurred under every monarchical rule from 1066 to 1215—including William I, William II, Henry I, Stephen, Henry II, and Richard I. Most of these revolts were led by disgruntled royalty, brothers and sons of the kings. As early as 1100, Henry I published a charter to which he attached fourteen campaign promises, covenanting to "abolish all the evil customs by which the kingdom of England has been unjustly oppressed."[18] But, alas, liberty did not run in the bloodlines of the Normans and Plantagenets.

BAD SEED

The throne quickly slipped away from the House of Normandy into the hands of the Plantagenets when William the Conqueror's son Henry I had no surviving heir, only 24 illegitimate children. After his death, civil war broke out between his nephew Stephen and daughter Matilda, resulting in Matilda's son Henry II taking the throne. A ruthless leader, Henry gained control of Wales and eastern Ireland as well as Brittany and Aquitaine in France. Henry did what tyrants do best, instituting his own version of a reign of terror. In an effort to subjugate Wales, he took the royal families of the nation, "cut off the noses and ears of the daughters... [and] blinded and castrated their brothers."[19] Henry's most infamous act was the murder of Archbishop Thomas Becket. Upon hearing that the archbishop had removed some unworthy priests and prelates from their positions, the king responded in uncontrolled rage, crying out: "What a pack of fools and cowards I have nourished in my house [speaking of his own men], that not one of them will avenge me of this turbulent priest!"[20] Four of his knights hurried off to Canterbury to do what fighting men do best—the archbishop was murdered in the cathedral on December 29, 1170.

KING JOHN

The sexual exploits of Henry's son, King John, are notorious even by modern standards. He divorced his first wife Isabel to marry another in 1200, and then sold her to Baron Geoffrey de Mandeville for 20,000 marks. Reports of John having violated wives and daughters of barons were common. After attempts to seduce Baron Eustace de Vesci's wife and a rape of Baron Robert Fitzwalter's daughter, these two men became his most ardent enemies. It is one thing for a king to confiscate a man's property and material belongings, but should he go after a man's wife or daughter, he invites a war that will never end.[21] Fitzwalter would champion the cause of the Magna Carta and lead the armies of the barons against the king. Perhaps William of Jumièges, an assistant to one of King John's commanders, said it best in his extensive survey of the various dukes of Normandy. John, he said, was "a very bad man, cruel and lecherous."[22]

Though John had inherited one of the largest and wealthiest kingdoms in Europe, he was incapable of holding it, for his immorality was only exceeded by his incompetence. However, if a man's success in governance is measured by the increase of his own net worth, John did well. He doubled the family's holdings between 1204 and 1215. By the time of the publication of the Magna Carta, he had amassed a total of fifty castles, palaces, houses, and hunting lodges. His extravagant lifestyle required a coterie of hundreds of assistants, bakers, butlers, cooks, carters, chamber clerks, chambermaids, footmen, scullions, grooms, and knights.

Social unrest throughout the England had reached the boiling point by 1205. Winston Churchill explained the cause of it: "By systematic abuse of his feudal prerogatives John drove the baronage to violent resistance."[23] In the fall of 1214, the nobles held a meeting in which they issued certain demands in the form of "The Charter of Privileges" to the king, and requested a second meeting for December or early January. The king agreed to meet on his own home turf (in London), and the nobles showed up armed to the teeth on January 8th, 1215. They pressed John to confirm the Charter of Privileges, introduced by Henry I over a hundred years earlier, to which they added a few of their own demands. The Magna Carta was slowly taking shape. John requested a delay until Easter, though at this point no one trusted him or his word. By Easter week, the opposition had assembled a respectable army consisting of 2,000 knights, forty barons, and five earls. Gathering at Stampton near Peterborough, the opposition marched towards Northampton, a royal dominion about sixty miles to the west. On May 5th, 1215, the barons formally renounced their fealty to John.

On June 15th, 1215, the parties assembled twenty miles to the east of London at a large meadow called Runnymede. This would be the birthplace of Western liberties, an eight-hundred-year stop gap to the ever-pressing demands of the tyrannical state. Through the past millennia the world had never seen such a declaration of liberties as this—a written constitution that would bind back the hands of the tyrant. Here was a line in the sand, a written compact or covenant to which kings and rulers would be bound for generations.

Always a staunch opponent to political liberties, the papacy soundly condemned the Magna Carta as "not only shameful and base, but also illegal and unjust."[24] The English nobles forthrightly ignored the pope and pledged their lives to secure the freedoms contained therein. Arguably the linchpin for the success of the Magna Carta, Archbishop of Canterbury, Stephen Langton, lent full support to its passage. Pope Innocent III suspended him from ecclesiastical functions and Langton was exiled for three years. But it was too late now to reverse the course of liberty.

By God's grace, the opponents to liberty were dead by the following year—both king and pope (passing on July 16 and October 19, 1216 respectively). Henceforth, the nobles continued to hold the monarchy to the charter and the rights contained in it. By 1217, the document was well-established in the realm. Between 1215 and 1315, the charter would be amended and reissued thirty-eight times. The Magna Carta introduced the concept of the first representative government in England, freedom for the church, rights of inheritance, limitation on monarchical taxation, legal rights in court proceedings, and restoration of lands and liberties unjustly taken from the Welsh. Especially important to securing individual rights under the law, comes this provision:

> No free man shall be seized or imprisoned, or stripped of his rights or possessions, or outlawed or exiled, or deprived of his standing in any other way, nor will we proceed with force against him, or send others to do so, except by the lawful judgment of his equals or by the law of the land. To no one will we sell, to no one deny or delay right or justice.

The first assembly of England's House of Commons came about in the year of our Lord 1258. Within forty years, the "Model Parliament" was made up of two knights from each shire and two representatives from each town as well as a collection of bishops and abbots.

LIBERTY & TYRANNY FACE OFF (AD 1290-1690)

Thus saith the LORD God, Behold, I will lift up mine hand to the Gentiles, and set up my standard to the people: and they shall bring thy sons in their arms, and thy daughters shall be carried upon their shoulders. And kings shall be thy nursing fathers, and their queens thy nursing mothers: they shall bow down to thee with their face toward the earth, and lick up the dust of thy feet; and thou shalt know that I am the LORD: for they shall not be ashamed that wait for me. Shall the prey be taken from the mighty, or the lawful captive delivered? But thus saith the LORD, Even the captives of the mighty shall be taken away, and the prey of the terrible shall be delivered: for I will contend with him that contendeth with thee, and I will save thy children. (Isaiah 49:22-25)

Ironically enough, the advancement of liberty in the world came by Christian nations in the West, but no thanks to the papacy or the Roman Church—arguably, the most ardent opponent to liberties through the struggle. By the grace of God, liberty survived, and the Protestant Church and nations most influenced by the Reformation became the depository for the Western heritage of liberty over a period of five hundred years.

Liberty survived in the Swiss cantons despite opposition from the Holy Roman Emperor Henry V, the bishop of Constance, and King Rudolph I. Against all odds, Swiss independence was secured by 1315.

Liberty from English tyranny was won for Scotland despite steadfast opposition from Pope Clement V, who proceeded to excommunicate Robert the Bruce. Always favoring independence over papal tyranny, the Scottish clergy ignored the pope and declared Robert "chosen before God and man as the rightful king of Scotland" in 1309. The Bruce won Scotland's independence at the Battle of Bannockburn in June 1314. And on April 6, 1320, the Scottish Parliament issued the Declaration of Arbroath, which prominently underscored the nations position as having been called to the Christian faith by "the King of kings and Lord of lords, our Lord Jesus Christ." The declaration closed with those "immortal" words:

> As long as a hundred of us remain alive, never will we on any condition
> be subjected to the lordship of the English. It is in truth not for glory,
> nor riches, nor honors that we are fighting, but for freedom alone,
> which no honest man gives up but with life itself.

For over half a millennium Scotland, Switzerland, and England would secure the deposit of Western liberty and safeguard national independence. In consequence, these nations would also become centers for Church Reformation in the 16th Century.

But still, the Italian papacy, combined forces with sundry tyrannical powers to oppose the developing political freedoms and the decentralized approach to governance that comes by a Christian world and life view. The inclination to concentrate power is basic to Gentile rule (Luke 22:25-27).

The Inquisition championed by Innocent III, ratcheted up the tyranny. This arbitrary rejection of God's law on the part of powerful tyrants was attended by anarchical elements doing the same thing. The Late Medieval Period witnessed the proliferation of eccentric cults, the rise of homosexuality, and an unhealthy fixation on witchcraft. Over-zealous efforts to thoroughly expunge the heterodox and grotesquely evil elements of society would end up tyrannizing the innocent in the process. In 1320, Jacques Fournier, later Pope Benedict XII, initiated an inquisition against the Waldensians. Pope Innocent VIII declared war on these well-meaning orthodox Christians in 1487, kicking off 33 separate military conflicts in the years that followed. To anyone who killed a Waldensian, the pope promised pardon of sins and the right to keep any property confiscated from the victim.

The Reformation was particularly concerned about the religious tyranny of the Roman church. For instance, the French reformer John

Calvin complained of tyranny ninety-four times in his *Institutes*, about as often as he spoke of predestination. In his famed speech given at the Diet of Worms, Martin Luther diagnosed the problem with the Church as an "unbelievable tyranny."

> No one can either deny or conceal this, for universal experience and world-wide grievances are witnesses to the fact that through the Pope's laws and through man-made teachings the consciences of the faithful have been most pitifully ensnared, troubled, and racked in torment, and also that their goods and possessions have been devoured (especially amongst this famous German nation) by unbelievable tyranny, and are to this day being devoured without end in shameful fashion; and that though they themselves by their own laws take care to provide that the Pope's laws and doctrines which are contrary to the Gospel or the teachings of the Fathers are to be considered as erroneous and reprobate. If then I recant these, the only effect will be to add strength to such tyranny, to open not the windows but the main doors to such blasphemy, which will thereupon stalk farther and more widely than it has hitherto dared…I stand convicted [convinced] by the Scriptures to which I have appealed, and my conscience is taken captive by God's word, I cannot and will not recant anything, for to act against our conscience is neither safe for us, nor open to us. On this I take my stand. I can do no other. God help me.[25]

The nub of the protest which energized the Protestant Reformation, at least from the viewpoint of Martin Luther at Worms, was the papist tyranny imposed on the consciences of men and women. It was a tyranny mostly spawned and cultivated in the Western *church*—not the state.

POLITICAL LIBERTY FOR THE LOW COUNTRIES

Nowhere did such tyranny bring about more misery than in the Low Countries beginning in the 1550s. The Spanish had sent the first Protestants to the stake in 1540, and Charles V and his son Philip II exported the Spanish Inquisition to the Netherlands a decade later. This terrible massacre of innocents pursued by the Habsburgs in the Netherlands claimed the lives of 18,000 men, women, and children (and this number only includes those that the Duke of Alva admitted to killing). This accounts for about 1% of the population, which would equate to the slaughter of 3,000,000 persons in 21st Century America.

Philip could hardly contain his enthusiasm for the work of the Inquisition in the Netherlands, fashioning it "much more pitiless" than that of Spain. It was truly a reign of terror, a hell on earth.

Men and women were broken on the wheel, racked, dragged by horses' tails; their sight was extinguished, their tongues torn out by the roots, their hands and feet twisted off and burned between red-hot irons; they were starved, drowned, hanged, burned and killed in every slow and agonizing way that the malicious inventiveness of priests could devise. Some were suspended by the feet and left to suffer in misery for days on end. Others were racked, torn and tongueless— their arms and legs were fastened together behind their backs and each was hooked by the middle of the body to an iron chain and then made to swing to and fro over a slow fire until entirely roasted.[26]

To fund his persecutions of the Dutch Protestants, the Duke of Alva levied an unprecedented 1% property tax and 10% sales tax— nothing by today's standards, but exorbitant for the lowlanders of the 16th Century. Mercifully, the nation's stedholder (governor), William the Silent, took the side of his people against the tyrants of Spain. For the cause of liberty, William lost his property, his personal wealth, his rightful political position, the lives of three of his brothers, his wife, and his son (kidnapped by Philip II) in the conflict that ensued (1568-1574). Mostly singlehandedly, he prosecuted a war against the Spanish tyrants—and won. In one final act of vindictive retaliation, Philip commissioned several assassins to take William's life. The second attempt was successful. As he lay in a pool of his own blood on the afternoon of July 15, 1584, William's sister asked him the simple question: "Do you die reconciled with your Savior, Jesus Christ?" He replied, "Yes," and he died.[27]

Liberty hung by a thread in Leyden in 1574 as the Silent directed the defense of the city from the Spaniards' armed force surrounding it. Finally, in the workings of God's good providence, the tidewaters flushed the Spanish armies out. The Netherlands announced independence on July 26, 1581.

William explained his motives for engaging the struggle in a letter to his brothers:

> To answer the points that you raise, you know quite well that it was never and is not now my intention to seek the slightest advantage for myself. I have only aspired and claimed to seek the country's freedom in the matters of religious conscience and government, in which the foreigners tried to oppress it. I therefore see nothing else to propose but that it be permitted to practice the Reformed religion according to the word of God, and that this whole country and state return to its ancient privileges and liberty. To achieve this the foreigners in the government and the army, especially the Spaniards, must be driven out.[28]

The Silent's Christian and Reformed commitments would make a mark for political and religious liberty over succeeding centuries. Without a free Holland, there would have been no Glorious Revolution and no accession for William and Mary in 1689. King William III of England was the great-grandson of William the Silent. The Stuart tyrannies most certainly would have continued, and religious freedom for Presbyterians and Puritans in England would have tarried for another time. Moreover, without a free Holland, it is hard to imagine the United States producing its own Declaration of Independence, the precedent of which is found in the Dutch Declaration of 1581.

Most significant of all the details relating to the Dutch battle for liberty is found in the city where the Dutch resistance made its last stand against the Spanish. Leyden turned into a haven of liberty for the English Pilgrims who faced persecution at the hands of James I—only thirty-two years hence. In the providence of God, the most dangerous place in Europe became the safest place on earth for those seeking liberty from tyrants, and all by the life sacrifice of a single man. Nobody had contributed more to that liberty than William the Silent, of Orange.

THE HUGUENOTS

> If the world hate you, ye know that it hated me before it hated you. If ye were of the world, the world would love his own: but because ye are not of the world, but I have chosen you out of the world, therefore the world hateth you. Remember the word that I said unto you, The servant is not greater than his lord. If they have persecuted me, they will also persecute you; if they have kept my saying, they will keep yours also. But all these things will they do unto you for my name's sake, because they know not him that sent me. If I had not come and spoken unto them, they had not had sin: but now they have no cloak for their sin. (the words of Jesus in John 15:18-22)

By sheer numbers, the third most persecuted people in all of Europe during the Reformation years were the French Huguenots. Although the battle was mostly lost in France, and though that nation could never claim any real contribution to Christian liberties, the Huguenots still left a treasury of faith and ideological contributions. For example, Francois Hotman's (1524-1590) classic work, *Francogallia,* rejected the monarchical absolutism of the day in favor of a more democratic representative assembly, over which the king could preside. Hotman barely escaped the St. Bartholomew's Day Massacre and is recognized as one of France's most distinguished jurists. The Genevan-French theologian Theodore Beza (1519-1605) offered his work, *The Right of Magistrates,* as yet another Protestant defense of interposition—

the obligation of the lower magistrate to operate as God's ministers, to defend the people's God-given liberties, not merely to act as the king's appointees or minions. Finally, Philippe du Plessis-Mornay (1549-1623) was probably the anonymous author of *Vindiciae Contra Tyrannos* (Defense of Liberty Against Tyrants) the most controversial of the 16th Century Huguenot works. Highly influential during the formation of the United States in the 1770s, the *Defense of Liberty* insisted that kings be subject to the laws of God contained in Scripture. The Huguenot author unreservedly limited the king's powers under God—for example, "...he shall not, of his own proper authority, impose any taxes, customs, or tributes, [and] he shall not make peace or war, nor determine of state affairs, without the advice of the council of state."[29] Moreover, the Huguenot insisted that the king be subject to a written or stated covenant, which, in modern terms, is effected when presidents are themselves made subject to written constitutions. He may not at his whim violate the covenant without censure. These were fighting words in the age of the "divine right" of kings:

> And, if under pretext of his royal dignity he become insolent, violating the laws, and neglect his public faith and promise given, then, by the privilege of the kingdom, he is judged, excommunicated, as execrable as Julian the apostate was by the primitive church: which excommunication is esteemed of that validity, that instead of praying for the king in their public orations, they pray against him, and the subjects are by the same right acquit from their oath of allegiance: as the vassal is exempted from obedience and obligation by oath to his lord who stands excommunicated; the which hath been determined and confirmed both by act of council and decree of state in the kingdom of Arragon.[30]

Upon his visit to Holland in 1572, Philippe de Mornay surveyed the devastation caused by the Spanish Inquisition and immediately joined forces with William the Silent. Between 1578 and 1582, Mornay served as a counselor to the stadholder of the Netherlands and prepared the way for Dutch independence.

TOWARDS THE GODLESS, DEMOCRATIC STATE

Throughout the Christian era, from Alfred (875) to William Bradford (1620), nations carved out liberties for their people by acknowledging God and His law. Covenants were agreed upon, under God and in submission to His law. The Magna Carta (1215) came "at the prompting of God," The Swiss Pact of Brunnen (1315) is prefaced, "In the Name of God Amen." The Scottish Declaration of Arbroath (1315) submits its case to "the Supreme and Judge." The English Pilgrims also prefaced the Mayflower Compact (1620) with "In the Name of God, Amen." The Dutch Declaration of Independence (1581) underscores the point that the monarchy is "constituted by God."

In contrast, the US Constitution begins not with "In the Name of God", but with "We the People." This marked a considerable shift in the definition of liberty in the Western world, linking back to the Dutch political philosopher Hugo Grotius (1583-1645). At the same time that Rembrandt was turning away from Reformation thinking and heritage, Grotius was apostatizing in the field of political philosophy. With his magnum opus, *De iure belli ac pacis,* Grotius philosophized on the state's right to power. From where does this power derive? Grotius concluded that, "the right of the state is the result of collective agreement"[31] in which individuals may voluntarily transfer a purely man-derived authority to a representative of the state.

This represented a sharp turn away from a Christian view and the beginning of the formation of the modern humanist state. Romans 13:1-4 clearly states that all authority comes from God (and not the people), and is delegated to man. Within civil societies, there may be a covenant or a written/unwritten understanding between men and before God, establishing the right to rule. God's law provides limits to the authority—whether that be monarchical or democratic in form. Thus, power may reside with a king or senate, by right of primogeniture or by democratic vote. Whatever form that power may take, the ruler is always subject to the covenant and always bound by laws of God. To the extent that he fails to rule by God's law, the ruler concedes his right to rule.

> Let every soul be subject unto the higher powers. For there is no power but of God: the powers that be are ordained of God. Whosoever therefore resisteth the power, resisteth the ordinance of God: and they that resist shall receive to themselves damnation. For rulers are not a terror to good works, but to the evil. Wilt thou then not be afraid of the power? do that which is good, and thou shalt have praise of the same: for he is the minister of God to thee for good. But if thou do that which is evil, be afraid; for he beareth not the sword in vain: for he is the minister of God, a revenger to execute wrath upon him that doeth evil. (Romans 13:1-4)

Hugo Grotius is best understood as the first fruits of the Protestant-humanist synthesis (both theologically and philosophically), paving the way for "the evolution of humanity," to borrow A. D. White's description. Grotius will be remembered for his Arminian opposition to the sovereignty of God, his advocacy of natural law (versus revealed law), and his reworking of the doctrine of the atonement (rejecting the idea that Jesus suffered the penalty due for our sins).

THE ENGLISH BATTLE FOR LIBERTY

While the Dutch were losing the Christian definitions for law and liberty, the English were having their own troubles with monarchs. For four hundred years, the kings of England elbowed for power over the appointment of church bishops and abbots via the Investiture Controversy. Amid these medieval power struggles, monarchs deeply resented the pope's control over their respective nations and the centralization of ecclesiastical power in Rome. At the same time, popes resisted civil and monarchical control of the church. The Reformation brought welcome political relief to monarchs by loosening the pope's stranglehold over the affairs of kingdoms. However, this disruption of ecclesiastical power also offered the opportunity for kings to expand their own power base.

The very-shrewd King Henry VIII of England turned the Reformation to his own ends, first to relieve himself of the pesky moral requirements to marital fidelity. Henry was concerned to get himself a male heir for the continuance of his dynasty, which his first wife, Catherine, could not provide. But the king also saw this an opportunity to disempower the church, shifting ecclesiastical economic capital (and the control of the church) over to the political state. By shedding papal authority, and pretending support for Reformation doctrine which had gained much popular support, Henry took advantage and seized control of church lands for the expansion of state powers. Between 1536 and 1541, at least 1,000 ecclesiastical properties, mostly monasteries and convents, were sold or reassigned to the gentry, for the benefit of the king's coffers. This wholesale confiscation of church properties and channels of revenue ushered in a time of unprecedented restructuring of church and state. The medieval church's care for the poor, wayfaring travelers, and the infirm was discontinued, making way for the modern socialist state. A quick review of contemporary church-state economics sheds light on these historical developments. Prior to the Reformation, the English churches were pulling in an estimated 320,000 pounds a year. The king's income was only an eighth of that—obviously causing Henry no end of consternation.[32] Thus, the dissolution of the monasteries would increase the king's income by an additional 180,000 pounds per year. Altogether, the fire sale of confiscated ecclesiastical booty yielded over 1,000,000 pounds, all of which Henry used to prosecute his wars with France.[33]

The ancient Roman Empire never taxed its citizens more than 13 HS (sestertius) per year or 5% of the people's income.[34] Absent the grasp of power-hungry monarchs and central governments, economic and political liberties flourished for centuries following the Magna Carta. During the Medieval Period, the state (or civil government) administered far less than 5% of the national income. At the same time, the church had control of 20-25% of the national income and usually managed the care of the poor and sick. With the rise of the secular state in later centuries, the church would be reduced to receiving 2% of the people's income, and the state would take 50%, leaving about 45% for the family and individual spheres. Here is seen the subtle power shift from the pope to the prince under Henry VIII, during the Protestant Reformation. For the first time since Roman days, the modern state was vastly empowered, this time at the expense of the church. Under Henry, the central government's expenditures increased from 1% of the GDP to 5%. Although the size of these governments were remarkable for their times, national power would increase by 10-100 fold under the influence of modern democracies. The monarchical tyranny pales in the face of modern socialist tyrannies.

To be counted a downside of the English Reformation was the dissolution of the balance of power between church and state, and the developing preeminence of the State. This led to the doctrine of the divine right of kings and ever-increasing, powerful, and cruel monarchies under Henry VIII, Mary, Elizabeth, James I, Charles I, Charles II, and James II.

Kings James I and Charles I strongly resisted the doctrine of the sovereignty of God, preferring the sovereignty of man—or, more specifically, the sovereignty of the state. In a speech given to Parliament in 1607, King James I went so far as to say: *"Rex est lex,"* asserting the king rather than God as the source of law. The Puritan emphasis on the sovereignty of God in His absolute control over all things and God's law as the highest standard for human ethics was a constant bother to the Stuart kings. Scottish pastor Samuel Rutherford (1600-1661) responded to the doctrine of the divine right of kings with his classic work *Lex Rex:* God's law is king. Tyrants don't like books restraining tyrants, and Rutherford's was no exception to that rule. The pastor was charged with "inveighing against monarchy and laying ground for rebellion," and his book was ordered to be burned. Any person not surrendering his copy of the tome was considered an enemy of the state. Though summoned to appear before the Parliament at Edinburgh on charges of high treason, Rutherford died before making it to his trial. His last words were: "Glory, glory, dwelleth in Emmanuel's Land."[35]

The quest for achieving the humanist god-state continued as absolutism transferred from the pope to the prince in the 16th and 17th centuries. The humanist Babel instinct to consolidate power would then shift from the prince to the people in the 18th Century. A simple outline of the historical trend towards humanism is sketched out below in terms of the Source of Law. If God is not the source of law, man will take that position instead.

> The Pope is Law—*Pope Lex* (1100-1550)
>
> The Prince is Law—*Rex Lex* (1550-1750)
>
> The People is Law—*Populi Lex* or *Vox populi vox dei* (1750-present)

Only two solutions offered themselves as correctives to the absolutism of the monarchy: Rutherford and the Enlightenment. Rutherford insisted that all kings must be "obliged and restricted by the laws of God."[36] All kings are assigned by God's law to appoint judges who are "men of wisdom, fearing God, hating covetousness."[37] He encouraged both houses of Parliament to "execute the moral law of God on their king."[38] Rutherford defined tyranny as that rule which was sinful, demonic in origin, and a departure from God's moral code:

> Tyranny being a work of Satan, is not from God, because sin, either

habitual or actual, is not from God: the power that is, must be from God; the magistrate, as magistrate, is good in nature of office, and the intrinsic end of his office, (Rom. xiii. 4) for he is the minister of God for thy good; and, therefore, a power ethical, politic, or moral, to oppress, is not from God, and is not a power, but a licentious deviation of a power; and is no more from God, but from sinful nature and the old serpent, than a license to sin.[39]

A second response to the divine right of kings came via the Enlightenment, primarily advocated by the French philosopher Jean-Jacques Rousseau's *Social Contract*—leaving God and His law completely out of the picture. The Western world largely ignored Rutherford, and the Enlightenment position won out by the 1780s in the modern secular, democratic state.

Whereas the early Puritans favored biblical law as the standard for human ethics and civil law, right-wing Enlightenment philosopher, John Locke (1632-1704), advocated natural law. He suggested that the Ten Commandments and Old Testament law were meant for Israel, and natural law could be ascertained apart from special revelation (God's Word). Meanwhile, for the left-wing Enlightenment philosopher Jean-Jacques Rousseau (1712-1778), God's law was completely out of the picture. Rousseau defined natural liberty as the ability to do whatever an individual wants to do—complete autonomy or liberty from God's law. However, he noted, the state is formed by the general will of the people, which may curtail individual liberties. Yet, the intent remains that man should "obey only himself." For Rousseau, the general will of the people is the source of law. From this forms the cry of the French Revolution and the position of the modern democratic state in almost every country around the world: *Vox populi vox dei*. "The voice of the people is the voice of god." This god would turn out to be much more of an onerous tyrant than anyone had expected.

THE TYRANNY OF EMPIRE

Already covered in a previous chapter, colonialism's slave-based economies developed largely out of the Spanish, Portuguese, and French empires. Through the 1600s and 1700s, these Catholic empires claimed 74% of the colonial slave economy. Britain contributed 22%, and about 4% of slaves ended up in the United States.[40]

The same Stuart English tyrants who championed the slave trade in North America contributed to the most extensive persecution of Christians in the English Reformation. Charles II and James II were responsible for the slaughter of at least 16,000 Scottish Covenanters and the ejection of 2,500 of England's greatest Puritan pastors. These persecutions far eclipsed the killings of Protestants and Pilgrims under "Bloody" Mary and her sister. While Charles II was a closet Catholic and tyrant in his own right, historian Thomas Macaulay referred to James' reign as a "tyranny which approached to insanity."[41] If there was a move back towards pagan Rome among the Protestants, it would have been under these tyrants. Finally, James was stopped in his tracks, at the interposition of William the Silent's great-grandson. The Glorious Revolution of William and Mary and the ousting of the Stuarts put the brakes on tyranny for a while in post-Reformation England.

Although the idea seems quite foreign to a post-Christian citizenry, free peoples have always been resistant to excessive taxation. Economist Walter Williams points out that the American colonists went to war with Britain over 67 cents of annual taxation, while at the turn of the 21st Century the American democracy was willing to submit to $6,000 of taxes per year. This unprecedented level of taxation represented a 9,000% increase over seventy-five years, adjusted for inflation.

> And when they were come to Capernaum, they that received tribute money came to Peter, and said, Doth not your master pay tribute? He saith, Yes. And when he was come into the house, Jesus prevented him,

saying, What thinkest thou, Simon? of whom do the kings of the earth take custom or tribute? of their own children, or of strangers?

Peter saith unto him, Of strangers. Jesus saith unto him, Then are the children free. Notwithstanding, lest we should offend them, go thou to the sea, and cast an hook, and take up the fish that first cometh up; and when thou hast opened his mouth, thou shalt find a piece of money: that take, and give unto them for me and thee. (Matthew 17:24-27)

Given the principle Christ offered here, it seems odd that democratic nations have been willing to impose upon themselves unprecedented levels of taxation. During the years of the developing Western empires, the kings looked for strangers to tax, and they found opportunity in the colonies. England imposed high tariffs on manufactured goods. Mercantilist policies required the colonies to trade only with the mother country, forcing the "strangers" to pay exorbitant prices for goods. At the same time, the British government would back up the monopoly by subsidizing exports to the colonies.

THE AMERICAN PUSHBACK

Art thou called being a servant? care not for it: but if thou mayest be made free, use it rather. For he that is called in the Lord, being a servant, is the Lord's freeman: likewise also he that is called, being free, is Christ's servant. Ye are bought with a price; be not ye the servants of men. (1 Corinthians 7:21-23)

In the outworkings of providence, only one circumstance slowed the push towards empire and concentrated political power after the Reformation—the independence of the American colonies.

England was taking full advantage of a prosperous America. Between 1700 and 1760, the nation's per capita income had doubled, and the English parliament seized the opportunity to grow state coffers. The Sugar Act of 1764 added import taxes to sugar, indigo, coffee, pimento, wine, and textiles. The Townsend Duties of 1767 raised these taxes on the colonies. The Tea Act of 1773 introduced a tax on tea shipped directly to the colonies from India. Then, the Prohibitory Act of 1775 banned all foreign trade with the colonies and legitimized the confiscation of colonial ships. The colonials took this as an act of war, "the final straw" as John Adams put it. Although all of these taxes were extremely minor when compared to modern taxation, the colonies were especially concerned with "taxation without representation." The colonials declared independence in the spirit of liberty espoused by Scotland, the Netherlands, and Switzerland in previous centuries. Considering themselves English citizens with a right to historical liberties, they appealed to the Magna Carta of 1215 and the 1689 British Bill of Rights.

The most popular song in America during the War for Independence was called "Chester":

> Let tyrants shake their iron rod,
> And slavery clank her galling chains,
> We fear them not, we trust in God,
> New England's God forever reigns.

Although Unitarianism, deism, and the humanist enlightenment had severely eroded the American faith, there were important exceptions to the trend at this pivotal moment in American history. The seminal leaders advocating independence in the 1760s and 1770s, Patrick Henry of Virginia and Samuel Adams of Massachusetts, were both known for their evangelical faith in Jesus Christ. Without these Christians committing their energies towards America's independence in the early years, it is doubtful there would have been any progress towards liberty and a check on the growth of imperial power. Until 1797, George Washington continued steadfast at the helm of the nation. The president's humility, reverence for God, and his evangelical faith in Christ is a matter of historical record. These early leaders of the Republic stand in stark contrast to the deism, the skepticism, and the humanist pride that characterized American leadership at the turn of the 19th Century.

During the American conflict, British parliamentarian Edmund Burke (1729-1797) explained why the "fierce spirit of liberty is stronger in the English Colonies probably than in any other people of the earth."[42] First and foremost, Americans were "descendants of Englishmen." Also, the religious faith of the people was another cause for this free spirit. Said Burke, it was the northern colonies which maintained great "averseness in the dissenting churches from all that looks like absolute government."[43] Burke pushed hard for Americans to elect their own representatives in accord with the principle of taxation with representation, in the spirit of the Magna Carta. He sympathized with the American cause and stood against the atheism of the French Revolution, which he called an "irrational, unprincipled, proscribing, confiscating, plundering, ferocious, bloody and tyrannical democracy."[44]

Due in large part to the contributions of Patrick Henry, Samuel Adams, and John Hancock, a Bill of Rights was added to the U.S. Constitution in 1791, securing liberties by written covenant for future posterity. It was the culmination of an eight-hundred-year struggle for Christian political and religious liberty in the Western world. The First Amendment secured the right to peaceably assemble, freedom to exercise religion, and freedom of speech.

> Congress shall make no law respecting an establishment of religion, or prohibiting the free exercise thereof; or abridging the freedom of speech, or of the press; or the right of the people peaceably to assemble, and to petition the government for a redress of grievances.

Persecution of Christian sects was no longer tolerated in this free country. The Second Amendment secured the right to keep and bear arms, placing a quiet but firm restraint on would-be tyrants waiting in the wings. For several hundred years, the doctrine of the balance of powers written into the U.S. Constitution, would secure tremendous liberty for the nation, maintaining decentralized states rights, and steering clear of the consolidation of power under a single branch of government. Yet tyranny would slip in under other forms in the post-Christian West.

THE DECAY OF LIBERTY IN THE POST-CHRISTIAN WEST

Political tyranny re-appeared in the Christian world because of the influence of a materialistic, atheistic worldview—the mindset of the post-Christian, anti-Christ apostasy. The exceedingly strident, atheistic, materialistic ideologies of Karl Marx and Friedrich Nietzsche first infected the Germans and the Russians. Both produced miserable tyrannies out of Nazi Germany and Bolshevik Russia and the Eastern bloc. The Nazis killed 21,000,000 innocent non-combatants—political enemies, handicapped persons, Jews, Christians, Slavs, Serbs, Germans, Czechs, Italians, Poles, French, Ukrainians, and others.[45] The Russian Bolsheviks killed another 100,000,000 innocent citizens in Russia, the Ukraine, and the Eastern Bloc. The post-Christian tyrannies outdid the ancient tyranny of Rome by a factor of 10 to 100 fold and exceeded the barbarity of the Catholic inquisitions by a factor of 1,000. Nothing in the history of Western tyrannies could possibly compare with the Christian apostasy of the 20th and 21st centuries.

THE BATTLE FOR LIBERTY IN THE UNITED STATES

Meanwhile, the United States did not fold as quickly to tyranny as did its European and Russian counterparts. The fight was a knock-down, drag-out affair. Nevertheless, all nationalistic sentimentalities and irrational jingoism aside, America was not the paradigm for liberty in the 18th and 19th centuries. The shameful legacy of Andrew Jackson's Trail of Tears, General Sheridan and Sherman's exterminations of Native Americans in Colorado and Montana, and the English slave trade buttressing the Southern economy must not be ignored. The persecution of the Christian missionary Samuel Worcester at the hands of the Georgia state government remains a shameful blot on the national character. However, this was just the beginning of the evils to come in the 20th Century.

The consolidation of the US central government occurred between the presidential administration of Woodrow Wilson (1913-1921) and the present day. It was a century in which the central government grew eighteen-fold (based on expenditures as a percentage of the gross domestic product). Debt spending kept the GDP artificially propped up under most of the administrations from FDR to the present, only exacerbating the economic problem. The US government made its largest consolidations of money and power (as measured by the total expenditures of the central government per GDP) under Abraham Lincoln, Woodrow Wilson, Franklin D. Roosevelt, George W. Bush, and Donald Trump, (as witnessed by the accompanying table).

Crisis was always the excuse for a greater consolidation of power. Either the populace would look to God or the government at these times—always a test of faith for a world that was turning away from God. Six major crises developed in the course of these two hundred years, all of which resulted in a consolidation of power in Washington DC. Some conservative groups would attribute the entire process to conspiracy, but that was not the primary driver. The problem lay in the hearts of the people who looked to government for salvation rather than to God. Abraham Lincoln's administration increased the size of government by six times under the pretext of the American "Civil War." While Presidents Grover Cleveland and Rutherford Hayes were successful at reducing government and the federal debt, President Woodrow Wilson advocated big government socialism and used World War I as a pretext to consolidate the size of the federal government by a factor of two. Mercifully, President Calvin Coolidge successfully stripped back federal powers in the 1920s contracting the federal budget by an unprecedented 60%. Only months following Coolidge's departure, the third major crisis for America hit with the Stock Market Crash, and the Depression that followed. Economic instability came about by greed and the massive increase in the nation's overall debt to GDP ratio, which had rapidly expanded from 160% of the GDP to 300% between 1920 and 1930. President Herbert Hoover's administration proceeded to quadruple the size of the central government.

Most Tyrannical Administrations Measured by Consolidation of the US Central Government

	Spending/GDP		Debt/GDP
President	**Before**	**After**[46]	**Debt Change**[47]
Abraham Lincoln (R)	2%	20% (5% in 1870)	2% - 32%
Woodrow Wilson (D)	2%	4%	8% - 32%
Herbert Hoover (R)	2%	8%	16% - 39%
Franklin D. Roosevelt/ Truman (D)	8%	18%	39% - 72%
Lyndon B. Johnson (D)	17%	20%	50% - 38%
Ronald Reagan (R)	21%	22%	35% - 55%
George W. Bush (R)	18%	24%	57% - 83%
Donald Trump (R)	20%	36%	105% - 130%

World War II became the pretext for another massive expansion of the federal government under Presidents Franklin D. Roosevelt and Harry S. Truman. The fifth crisis came with a massive recession in 2008, when President George W. Bush consolidated more government control of the economy and increased the spending-to-GDP ratio from 18% to 24%. And the final crisis came with the unprecedented worldwide depression of 2020, as President Donald Trump's administration expanded federal spending from 20% to 36% of the GDP. Total government spending for the United States (federal, state, and local) increased from 8% of the GDP in 1900 to 32% in 1970.[48] After a slight dip in the 1990s, total government expenditures increased to 38% by 2010, and scraped 50% in 2020 under President Donald Trump. The decades representing the largest growth in government were the 1930s, 1940s, 1980s, and 2010s (during the administrations of Hoover, F.D. Roosevelt, Reagan, Obama, and Trump).

Although the Republican Party was sometimes characterized as the smaller government party, altogether five Republican and four Democrat administrations contributed the most to the consolidation of Federal powers as measured by annual expenditures. Reagan's was the presidential administration which drove the debt up the furthest under peacetime conditions; and Donald Trump was the president who increased the spending-to-GDP ratio under peacetime conditions by the highest margin. Calvin Coolidge (serving 1923-1929) was the only president commanding a reduction of the federal debt in a hundred years, at the same time reducing government expenditures by a remarkable 60%.

Meanwhile, the central governments of Europe followed a similar trend, increasing control of their economies from an average of 2-4% in the early 20th Century to 37% per GDP in 2017. By this measure, worldwide tyranny increased ten-fold between 1880 and 2020.

The Steady Growth of Tyranny in the US by Decade

Decade	Average Total Government Expenditure (per GDP)[49]
1900s	7.2%
1910s	12.0%
1920s	11.9%
1930s	19.0%
1940s	31.4%
1950s	26.4%
1960s	28.0%
1970s	30.9%
1980s	34.2%
1990s	34.2%
2000s	34.2%
2010s	37.4%
2020s	45%

Spending as a percentage of the GDP is the simplest and most honest way to measure the relative size of tyranny and the consolidation of large centralized governments. Such large centralization of funding inevitably results in more tyranny, more wars, more control of individual lives, more regulation of business, and more bureaucratic nonsense. US regulatory agencies received $70 billion in 2020, up from $4 billion in 1960 (adjusted for inflation), while the federal register of regulations increased from 25,000 pages to 180,000 pages.[50] That's an increase in tyrannical federal controls by a factor of ten to twenty-fold.

The full picture of the spread of this modern democratic tyranny includes local, state, and provincial government spending. Total US government spending increased from 3% of the GDP in the mid-19th Century to 50% of the GDP in 2020.

On this metric, communist countries were less tyrannical than Western "capitalist" nations, averaging government expenditures of about 27% of the GDP. Russian governance was consuming 37% of the GDP, while twelve western European nations averaged 52%, and Asian countries (South Korea, Indonesia, Japan, etc.) averaged 26% of the GDP.[51] Thus, the most tyrannical nations in the world by sheer size of government and consolidation of power were Western nations— Europe, the United States, and Canada. Most of the Western European nations crossed the highly significant 50% mark around 1980, and the United States crossed over after the Fall. This was the point at which the "democratic" governments consumed the majority of the life of the private individual and the family in the West.

SOCIALISM

And when they were come, they say unto [Jesus], Master, we know that thou art true, and carest for no man: for thou regardest not the person of men, but teachest the way of God in truth: Is it lawful to give tribute to Caesar, or not? Shall we give, or shall we not give? But he, knowing their hypocrisy, said unto them, Why tempt ye me? bring me a penny, that I may see it. And they brought it. And he saith unto them, Whose is this image and superscription? And they said unto him, Caesar's. (Mark 12:14-16)

What the government funds, or what has already been surrendered to government control, will remain under the control of civil government. That appears to be the principle submitted by Christ in Mark 12. Since 1900, about 90% of education, health care, and nutrition for children has been surrendered to the civil government. This was a gradual process. The percentage of Americans dependent on the government for regular sustenance increased from 0% in 1940 to 53%

by 2015. The percent of healthcare funding provided by government increased from 13% in 1929 to 31% in 1965, and then topped 65% in 2013.[52] Total or predominate government control of the citizenry was well in place by 2020.

The chart on page 404 illustrates the massive social and political revolution that came about in the modern world as governments took control of family, education, healthcare, and everything else across the entire Western world. Whereas social endeavors had been a function of family and church for 1,600 years, all this economy was moved under state control in the 20th Century. Germany and Prussia being slightly ahead of the others, their average public social spending increased from 0.5% of the GDP to 25% of the GDP—a fifty-fold increase in one hundred years.

Except for a few "islands of freedom" such as homeschooling and Christian healthcare sharing, the rule became totalitarian government control over practically every aspect of social existence.

EXPRESSIONS OF ULTIMATE TYRANNY

And there came one of the seven angels which had the seven vials, and talked with me, saying unto me, Come hither; I will shew unto thee the judgment of the great whore that sitteth upon many waters: with whom the kings of the earth have committed fornication, and the inhabitants of the earth have been made drunk with the wine of her fornication. . . And the woman was arrayed in purple and scarlet colour, and decked with gold and precious stones and pearls, having a golden cup in her hand full of abominations and filthiness of her fornication: and upon her forehead was a name written, MYSTERY, BABYLON THE GREAT, THE MOTHER OF HARLOTS AND ABOMINATIONS OF THE EARTH. And I saw the woman drunken with the blood of the saints, and with the blood of the martyrs of Jesus: and when I saw her, I wondered with great admiration. (Revelation 17:1-6)

Whether this passage primarily describes Nero, the present era of aberrant-sexual tyranny, or some other era is not the concern here. The message is clear. This "Mother of Harlots" riding the beast will be promoting sexual sin and persecuting the saints of God. The final return of tyranny could only be completed in the Western world with the reincorporation of the "Neronic" agenda—the persecution of Christ and His body at the hands of the state.

Throughout the 1980s and 1990s, there were several isolated cases of Christian persecution in the West. These usually involved families attempting to homeschool without state license or families who were employing child discipline methods not sanctioned by the state. Occasionally, Christians were arrested for protesting abortion and participating in "civil disobedience."

However, the first bona fide cases of Christian persecution at the hands of "the harlot" came on the pretext of defending "homosexual rights." In 2019, the US Supreme Court refused to hear the appeal of a Christian-owned bed and breakfast, penalized by the State of Hawaii for not making accommodations for homosexual couples.[53] Several years earlier, the high court had also refused to side with Christian photographers in New Mexico who could not accommodate a "homosexual wedding" for reasons of conscience.[54] This was followed up in 2020 by the *Bostock v. Clayton County* decision in which a Christian-owned funeral home was forced to retain a male employee who wished to flaunt his transvestism in the workplace. By linking the US Title VII non-discrimination laws to sexual orientation and transgenderism, the US Supreme Court acted to violate the Christian conscience and reward those abominable sins of "the harlot riding on the beast." This watershed decision represented at least as much of a turn away from the Christian heritage as *Obergefell* (2015) and *Roe v. Wade* (1973).

Effectively, the high court had ruled that if a male employee in a Christian-owned company were to flagrantly violate God's law in the workplace by dressing like a woman, or by interrupting the social order by openly advertising certain sexual perversions, an employer may not fire that person. At the least, the court decision was a violation of private property rights—a contravention of the eighth commandment on the part of the civil magistrate. In addition, this was an abridgment of religious liberty, a forced violation of conscience, and a blatant advocacy for violations of the seventh commandment. This sort of mandate was nothing less than overt coercion of Christian-owned companies to promote the violations of God's laws by permitting employees to flaunt their preferred sexual perversions.

Importantly, a George W. Bush appointee (Justice John Roberts) and a Donald Trump appointee (Justice Neil Gorsuch) both joined the anti-Christian position to initiate persecution of Christian-owned businesses in the United States. Finally, after two thousand years, Nero had scored a major victory in the West.

THE EDUCATION BATTLEGROUND

Although most court cases involving street preachers and the exercise of free speech did not result in the persecution of Christians, the same could not be said for Christian colleges. In 2018, Trinity Western University's law school lost its national accreditation on appeal to the Canadian Supreme Court because of the school's biblical stance against the sin of homosexuality.[55] A similar assault on the Christian faith followed in the United States—the final Christian hold-out in the Western world. Certain state doctrines relating to feminism, transgenderism, and homosexuality were imposed on Christian colleges and universities receiving Title IX federal funds. First, the state imposed feminist ideologies on the colleges. Then the agenda was expanded to include sexual perversions. Only sixteen private colleges had exempted themselves from federal funds, representing only 1% of the Christian college enrollment (or about 6,500 Christian students over the entire country). By 2020, fully 99.96% of post-secondary students attended colleges funded and/or controlled by the ideologies of the state. Such policies pressed some Christian colleges to adjust their standards so as to accommodate homosexuality on their campuses.[56] Directly after his inauguration, US president Joe Biden signed an Executive Order requiring all federal agencies, including the Department of Education, to include sexual orientation and gender identity under the federal non-discrimination laws. The order extended to "children's access to restrooms, locker rooms, and school sports; access to health care; and workers whose dress does not conform to sex-based stereotypes."

Persecutions intensified in the workplace with what became known as "cancel culture." Following the pattern outlined by the Italian Marxist, Antonio Gramsci (1891-1937), the educational establishment formed a cultural hegemony which would pressure Christians and non-conformists into following the reigning zeitgeist. College professors and public school teachers were extremely vulnerable to losing their positions if they refused to use the "correct pronoun" for students who were pretending to change their gender.[57]

Christian churches who refused to comply with the new state definition of marriage and allowance for sexual orientation—whether homosexual, incestuous, bestial, or otherwise, were at risk.

THE NANNY STATE &
THE POLICE STATE CONVERGED

After the terrorist attacks on the World Trade Center buildings and the Pentagon on September 11, 2001, the US introduced the most draconian controls on transportation ever seen to that point. Full body scans and mandatory pat-downs became a way of life for travelers, quickly received by a people who used to be free.

Almost twenty years later, the Covid-19 scare produced the most obtrusive controls on human activity that the Western world had ever seen. Masks were mandated everywhere. Stay at home orders affected most US states, sometimes for months on end. Economies were shut down. Healthy people were quarantined by the billions in the West and around the world.

Between 1930 and 2020, socialist governments everywhere around the world had gathered up majority control of the medical economy. Over 60% of the medical needs of the nations were covered by government funds. Having assumed responsibility for the Intensive Care Units, the ventilators, the physicians, the drug treatments, the vaccines, and all the rest of the medical industry by funding and regulation, the national governments were now prepared to control everything during pandemics. This applied whether the death rate was 30% (as in the case of the Bubonic plague) or 0.005% in the case of the Covid-19 virus. If governments were responsible for offering or rationing treatment, then these powers would take responsibility for preventive measures as well, including forced immunizations. Most Western countries turned into police states, with very little resistance from the populace. Governments would only permit individuals to leave their homes for an hour a day. Police check points were put in place to monitor travelers. Businesses were fined up to $100,000 for breaching rules. For the first time in US history, churches were fined up to $350,000 for gathering to worship.[58] Pastors were arrested.[59] Churches were closed by the tens of thousands—directives upheld by Circuit Courts and the US Supreme Court.[60] Some churches went into hiding. Few Americans protested. By this time, the post-Christian world was fairly well adapted to this convergence of the nanny state and police state, a sort of velvet-gloved totalitarianism.

All in all, the Western nations had lost moral virtue and the will to be free. As the West rejected God and His law, the citizenry willingly submitted to the surveillance state, the revolutionary state, the socialist state, the nanny state, and the police state... but, not for long. The socialist state inevitably runs out of "other people's money," and the totalitarian state breaks down under its own weight. The scientific technocracy always miscalculates the right means and ends to the "perfect society." The revolutionary state is destructive at heart—always destructive of economy, family, morality, and that which is foundational to human society. Internal divisions, external pressures, and economic breakdown then lead to civil war, world war, or something else—a reset button for civilization.

> Come, behold the works of the LORD, what desolations he hath made in the earth. He maketh wars to cease unto the end of the earth; he breaketh the bow, and cutteth the spear in sunder; he burneth the chariot in the fire. Be still, and know that I am God: I will be exalted among the heathen, I will be exalted in the earth. The LORD of hosts is with us; the God of Jacob is our refuge. (Psalm 46:8-11)

THE RISE & FALL OF EDUCATION IN THE WEST

Cease, my son, to hear the instruction that causeth to err from the words of knowledge. (Proverbs 19:27)

The root cause of the Fall of the West was definitively a lapse of faith—a fundamental compromise of the church with the world's false ideas and false gods, primary of which was the man-god. But, the *catalyst* precipitating the Fall was academia and the institutionalization of anti-Christian worldviews. The battleground was always the hearts and minds of the next generation, and Christian parents and pastors were increasingly AWOL in the conflict, especially after AD 1700. As the Western Christian epoch came and went, Paul's warning recorded in Colossians 2:8 applied with ever-increasing relevance. Most of the Western church would be robbed of the faith through classical "philosophy" and "vain deceit" after the "basic principles of the world."

From the earliest days of the church to the present, the struggle between the wisdom of Christ and the wisdom of the world never ceased on the education battlefront. The early Christian church, family, and school required a good deal of weaning from the pagan institutions of learning. For instance, Macrina, the early 4th-Century Cappadocian, is remembered for warning her brother Basil concerning his overweening love of pagan philosophy and fables. Of note, modern classicists still center on Basil for his warmer endorsements of pagan literature.

Almost universally, the church fathers set a hard line of antithesis between the philosophies and writings of the Greeks and those of Christ. The early church manual, *Didascalia Apostolorum*, provides a helpful summary of the traditions and practices recommended by the apostles who labored in Antioch. In the section on children and education, this "Book of Church Order" warned against the schools of the heathen and particularly "the books of the heathen."

> Teach your sons handicrafts which are suitable and helpful to the fear of God, lest by means of idleness they serve voluptuousness, for not being educated by their parents, they wickedly do works like the heathen.[1]

> Keep far then from all the books of the heathen. For what hast thou to do with foreign words or with false laws or prophecies, which also easily cause young people to wander from the Faith? What then is wanting to thee in the Word of God that thou throwest thyself upon these myths of the heathen? If thou wishest to read the tales of the fathers, thou hast the Book of Kings, or of wise men and philosophers thou hast the Prophets, amongst whom thou wilt find more wisdom and scripture than amongst the wise men and the philosophers, because they are the words of God, of one only wise God; if thou desirest songs, thou hast the Psalms of David...[2]

Jerome,[3] well-known for translating the Scriptures into Latin, severely criticized classical literature offered in the schools of his day. His words are still worth paying attention to: "The food of the demons is the songs of poets, secular wisdom, the display of rhetorical language…they afford their readers nothing more than empty sound and the hubbub of words."[4]

Writing a "homeschooling" mom named Laeta, in reference to the question of education for her daughter, Jerome advised avoidance of worldly literature, and a rooting in the fear of God:

> Thus must a soul be educated which is to be a temple of God. It must learn to hear nothing and to say nothing but what belongs to the fear of God. It must have no understanding of unclean words, and no knowledge of the world's songs. Its tongue must be steeped while still tender in the sweetness of the psalms…Let her treasures be not silks or gems but manuscripts of the holy scriptures; and in these let her think less of gilding, and Babylonian parchment, and arabesque patterns, than of correctness and accurate punctuation. Let her begin by learning the psalter, and then let her gather rules of life out of the proverbs of Solomon. From the Preacher let her gain the habit of despising the world and its vanities. Let her follow the example set in Job of virtue and of patience. Then let her pass on to the gospels never to be laid aside when once they have been taken in hand. Let her also drink in with a willing heart the Acts of the Apostles and the Epistles. As soon as she has enriched the storehouse of her mind with these treasures, let her commit to memory the prophets, the heptateuch, the books of Kings and of Chronicles, the rolls also of Ezra and Esther. When she has done all these she may safely read the Song of Songs but not before: for, were she to read it at the beginning, she would fail to perceive that, though it is written in fleshly words, it is a marriage song of a spiritual bridal. And not understanding this she would suffer hurt from it. Let her avoid all apocryphal writings, and if she is led to read such not by the truth of the doctrines which they contain but out of respect for the miracles contained in them; let her understand that they are not really written by those to whom they are ascribed, that many faulty elements have been introduced into them, and that it requires infinite discretion to look for gold in the midst of

dirt. Cyprian's writings let her have always in her hands. The letters of Athanasius and the treatises of Hilary she may go through without fear of stumbling. Let her take pleasure in the works and wits of all in whose books a due regard for the faith is not neglected. But if she reads the works of others let it be rather to judge them than to follow them.[5]

Here was a radical break from the pagan world—a distinctively Christian approach to education. Of primary concern, taken up in these pastoral instructions, is the recommendation to completely avoid pagan literature. Jerome insisted that the homeschooled student must first be taught the Proverbs, the Psalms, and the rest of Scripture. After this, she should receive the great Christian writings available at that time, but never the pagan sources. Jerome's counsel served as the pattern for sustaining the faith and educating Christian children for 1,500 years. As the world reverted to pagan philosophies in the 20th Century, his instruction only became more relevant to the Christian remnant.

Tension between Athens and Jerusalem was very real in the mind of the early Christians growing up in a pagan world. Clearly, Christian academics had to be weaned from the vain philosophies, tainted methodologies, and enchanting stories of the Greeks. Church historian Justo Gonzalez offers this brief commentary on the struggle for Jerome:

> [Jerome] was an ardent admirer of classical learning, and felt that this love for an essentially pagan tradition was sinful. His inner turmoil on this score peaked when, during a serious illness, he dreamt that he was at the final judgment and was asked: "Who are you?' 'I am a Christian,' Jerome answered. But the Judge retorted: 'You lie. You are a Ciceronian." After that experience, Jerome resolved to devote himself fully to the study of scripture and of Christian literature. But he never ceased reading and imitating the style of the classical pagan authors.[6]

Especially important for this brief summary of early Christian thought on education are Augustine's comments in his *Confessions*. Speaking of a classical education which would have included the study of Homer and his peers, Augustine was clearly appalled that anybody would pay money for an education in the "classics":

> O torrent of hell, the sons of men are still cast into you and they pay fees for learning all these things!...These pagans attribute divine attributes to sinful men, that crimes might not be accounted crimes, and that whoever committed such crimes might appear to imitate the celestial gods![7]

Augustine further warned of what he called "courtly words" which carry unwholesome ideas: "Wisdom and folly both are like meats that are wholesome and unwholesome, and courtly or simple words are like town-made or rustic vessels—both kinds of food may be served in either kind of dish." The words, the turn of phrase, and syntax used by the great thinkers and writers share more than propositions. The form still conveys heart attitudes, affinities, carefully constructed systems of thought, and trajectories. Method and message should never be separated in the mind of teacher or student in the study of the classics.

In his extended essay on Christian pedagogy, Augustine rejects pagan literature—the "thousands of fables and fictions, in whose lies men take delight." He prefers music over the "theatrical trumpery" of the heathen. However, he maintains that manuals on grammar ("forms of letters") and foreign languages may be helpful even if explained by unbelievers. Yet, all devices must aid to the "understanding of Holy Scripture," which Augustine sees to be the preeminent business of education.[8] James W. Halporn detects a shift in Augustine's view of pedagogy, particularly evident in his treatise, *On Christian Teaching*: "If [Augustine] had once hoped to raise a Christian philosophy on scaffolding supplied by the disciplinary categories of pagan intellectual culture, by the time he undertook this work, he had come to believe in the theoretical autonomy of a Christian education centered on the Bible."[9]

CASSIODORUS

> Blessed is the man that walketh not in the counsel of the ungodly, nor standeth in the way of sinners, nor sitteth in the seat of the scornful. But his delight is in the law of the LORD; and in his law doth he meditate day and night. And he shall be like a tree planted by the rivers of water, that bringeth forth his fruit in his season; his leaf also shall not wither; and whatsoever he doeth shall prosper. (Psalm 1:1-3)

Cassiodorus (485-585) was another key figure in the development of a Christian pedagogy for the Christian age.[10] Serving as a Roman senator under the administration of the Ostrogoths, later in life he organized the monastery at Viverium. He is best known for his magnum opus on education: *Institutiones Divinarum et Saecularium Litterarum (Institutions of Divine and Secular Learning)*. Much of this work wrestles with the use of pagan learning, which he does not receive uncritically. Cassiodorus qualifies the use of it, in these words: "Secular writings should not be rejected. It is right however, as Divine Scripture says, to 'meditate on the law day and night,' because from time to time we gain from secular letters commendable knowledge of some matters, but from divine law we gain eternal life."[11]

Thus, while not entirely ignoring the corpus of pagan writings, Cassiodorus prioritized Scripture as the pervasive and preeminent content in education. Quoting Psalm 1, this father of Christian education was concerned that his students might sit in the seat of the Greek scorners and sinners. He recommended a quick "pass through" the secular letters,[12] acknowledging that the great philosophers were "unable to reach the source of wisdom and without the true light have been submerged in the blindness of ignorance."[13] He called his students to "remain in the law of God" so as not to be blinded by the ignorance of the pagans.[14] He insisted on maintaining the strict order of prioritizing Scripture above all other studies, "referring everything to the glory of the Creator."[15] For the young and the simple, Cassiodorus recommended the early grades focus on the Scriptures and the "holy Fathers."[16] Most importantly, the whole purpose of education for Cassiodorus was to understand divine law, and "to reach in the companionship of the Lord, true faith and holy works in which our life is eternal."[17]

Although in Book II of the *Institutions,* Cassiodorus commended the "methodological" studies of arithmetic, grammar, rhetoric, dialectic (logic), mathematics, music, geometry, and astronomy, he did not endorse the study of the poets, fables, and historical writings of the pagans. As for the study of history, he prioritized Augustine's *City of God* and the authors Eusebius, Josephus, Orosius, and Jerome. Only one mention is made of the pagan historian Livy, and that to remind Christians to use greater discretion when copying that author's "style."

EDUCATION IN LINDISFARNE

As the center of Christianity moved northward, the battle over education raged in Lindisfarne, England. Concerned that young students might be seduced into following the pagan superheroes, Alcuin of York wrote to Bishop Higbald in AD 797:

> What has Ingeld to do with Christ? The house is narrow, it cannot contain both. The king of the heavens will have nothing to do with the heathen and damned so-called kings. For the eternal King rules in the heavens, the lost heathen repines in hell.[18]

Alcuin's successor, at the Palace School, John Scotus (810-877), however, was more interested in reviving the pagan writers and submitted his argument against God's absolute Sovereignty to Platonic categories, in his debate with Gottschalk.

Commenting on pagan literature, Aldhelm of Malmesbury, England (639-709) asked the obvious question: "What advantage does it bring to the sacrament of the orthodox faith to sweat over reading and studying the polluted lewdness of Proserpine, or Hermione, the wanton offspring of Menelaus and Helen, or the Lupercalia and the votaries of Priapus [the ancient Roman gods]?"[19]

George Brown's book, *A Companion to Bede*, describes something of the discipleship programs used during the Christian centuries in England. The Venerable Bede strongly discouraged the reading of pagan literature. Brief mention is made of the poet Porphyry in *De Arte Metrica*, a neoplatonic philosopher of the 3rd Century. However, this was only to point out the variety of meters used in poetry, and Bede notes also about the poetry itself: "Because they were pagan, it was not permitted for us to touch them."[20] The curriculum used in Northumbria during the early years of the English church was mainly the Scriptures:

> In the abbey school the two main disciplines were grammar and biblical exegesis, with some study of time reckoning and a bit of natural history and geography as a complement to the Bible.[21]

> There was no apparent reason why the monastic curriculum should provide anything more than the study of grammar (for the reading of the Bible and liturgy and composition of hagiography, history, and hymns, and for the correct writing of manuscripts), computus (for the reckoning of the church calendar and history), and the practical arts of music performance (for chanting the texts of Office and the Mass), as well as physical arts such as husbandry, agriculture, and domestic management.[22]

These English Christian discipleship centers were highly suspicious of the vain philosophies and impractical knowledge endemic in pagan education. For a thousand years, the Christian mindset held a very uneasy relationship with the metaphysic, ethic, dialectic, and rhetoric of the ancient pagan world. Christian teachers could detect a defective worldview underlying these categories of learning. It was much safer to stick with arithmetic, music, geography, and grammar—subjects of more practical use and less likely to be contaminated with the wrong worldview.

THE DECLINE

> And these words, which I command thee this day, shall be in thine heart: and thou shalt teach them diligently unto thy children, and shalt talk of them when thou sittest in thine house, and when thou walkest by the way, and when thou liest down, and when thou risest up. And thou shalt bind them for a sign upon thine hand, and they shall be as frontlets between thine eyes. And thou shalt write them upon the posts of thy house, and on thy gates. (Deuteronomy 6:7-9)

The decline of Western education began in the cathedral schools and then continued into the universities over the succeeding 800 years. The root cause contributing to the disintegration of the Christian faith is no secret. *The new schools rejected the Scriptures as the core curriculum.* The scholastics were birthed out of the cathedral schools, where spiritual nurture and discipleship had fallen into less regard. For seven hundred years, the monasteries or discipleship centers had focused on the spiritual faith and character of the men being trained. They centered their instruction on Scripture, until the new schools shifted towards systematics and dialectics. These professional academies replaced disciplers with teachers, and disciples with students. Peter Leithart summarizes the differences between monk and school master: "Monks were rooted in a single place, while the masters of the schools were mobile...Monks were bound to obedience; masters made a living in a competitive environment, which encouraged innovation in order to win students. Monks were scholars of Scripture and used rhetoric and grammar as means for making Scripture plain; masters employed dialectic (logic) to resolve 'questions.'"[23] In AD 1109, abbot Rupert of Deutz, Germany complained of the new teaching gaining ground in the cathedral schools: "Whatever can be thought up apart from sacred scripture or fabricated out of argumentation is unreasonable and therefore pertains in no way to the praise or acknowledgment of the omnipotence of God."[24]

First of the scholastics and prime product of the cathedral school, Peter Abelard, arranged his teaching in the opposite direction of Anselm, confessing to his students: "I must understand in order to believe." This was a fundamental shift in epistemology. By this reasoning, that which cannot be thoroughly comprehended or worked out by human reason must be rejected out of hand. Scripture could only be trusted as far as it made sense to human reason. Christian historian Peter Leithart points to Abelard as the genesis of this newfound humanism whereby "theology became detached from exegesis, and eventually reason from faith, and philosophy from theology."[25] Abelard's new approach would govern the universities until the Reformation.

The lure of humanist autonomy and Greek philosophy was an irresistible spiritual force upon the Western mind. The long and drawn-out undermining of the Christian West in the new universities came with the rediscovery of Aristotle and his perceived "genius." Appropriately, the Arabian Muslims were the first to revive Aristotle in the 12th Century. From the outset, John of Salisbury (1115-1180) warned that the tongues of the universities "have become torches of war."[26] The Provincial Council of 1209 tried to stem the flood, forbidding the use of Aristotle in the university for three years. Pope Gregory IX issued a bull in 1229 affirming the provincial council, and cautioning that Aristotle's writings should not be read "until they have been examined and purged of every suspicion of error."[27] But the craving for a man-derived epistemology could not be assuaged by all the book banning and book burning in the world. Two years later, Aristotle was fully recognized at the University of Paris, by order of the pope. Pope Urban IV again put the brakes on Aristotle, but later endorsed the field of humanist philosophy in the universities. He called on Thomas Aquinas to synthesize the systems of thought contained in Greek philosophy with the Christian university. One contemporary historian testified: "About this time, Brother Thomas did and wrote much at the request of Urban...Professing in Rome, he gathered together nearly the whole of philosophy, both natural and moral, and wrote commentaries thereon; but chiefly upon the Ethics and the Metaphysics, which he treated in a novel and peculiar manner."[28] Then, in 1366, Aristotle was made required reading for all university students by order of Pope Urban V: the stated intent that "Aristotle shall be the universal teacher."[29] The Greeks were back.

Starting with the first university established in Bologna, Italy in AD 1088, the vision was replicated in Paris (1150), Cambridge (1209), Padua (1222), Orleans (1235), Coimbra (1288), Pisa (1343), Prague (1348), and Vienna (1365). The epistemological foundations of these institutions were corrupted from the beginning, offering a field in which human autonomy could operate, separate and independent of sacred doctrine. The foundation of Scripture was effectively removed from higher education between the 12th and 14th Centuries.

THE REFORMERS & THE UNIVERSITIES

The early reformers quickly identified the bankruptcy of humanist thought as the root rot of the Western church. Early in his reforming career, Martin Luther addressed himself first to the Aristotelian philosophy, dialectical method, and definitions infecting the university at Wittenberg. He recognized Aquinas as "the fountain and original soup of all heresy, error, and Gospel havoc, as his books bear witness."[30] In early 1517, the reformer committed himself to eliminating Aristotle's influence entirely from the school. Luther held nothing back in his imprecations for the philosopher:

> What will they not believe who have credited that ridiculous and injurious blasphemer Aristotle? His propositions are so absurd that an ass or a stone would cry out at them...My soul longs for nothing so ardently as to expose and publicly shame that Greek buffoon, who like a spectre has befooled the Church...If Aristotle had not lived in the flesh I should not hesitate to call him a devil. The greatest part of my cross is to be forced to see brothers with brilliant minds, born for useful studies, compelled to spend their lives and waste their labor in these follies. The universities do not cease to condemn good books and publish bad ones...[31]

By May of 1517, Luther was exalting over the downfall of Aristotle and the schoolmen at the university in another letter to John Lang: "Our theology and St. Augustine prosper and reign here, by God's help. Aristotle is gradually tottering to a fall from which he will hardly rise again, and the lectures on the [Peter Lombard's] *Sentences* are wonderfully disrelished. No professor can hope for students unless he offers courses in the new theology, that is on the Bible or St. Augustine or some other ecclesiastical authority."[32] Not long afterwards Thomas Aquinas's commentaries were also ejected from the university curriculum.

Two months before posting the 95 theses that initiated the Protestant Reformation, Luther published 97 theses opposing Aristotle's works and Scholastic theology.[33] Getting to the core of his issues with the universities and cathedral schools, Luther verges on a prophetic pronouncement with this:

> I would advise no one to send his child where the Holy Scriptures are not supreme. Every institution that does not unceasingly pursue

the study of God's word becomes corrupt...I greatly fear that the universities, unless they teach the Holy Scriptures diligently and impress them on the young students, are wide gates to hell.[34]

Despite Luther's serious concerns with Aquinas and Aristotle, the continental colleges and universities remained largely unreformed. This lapse would contribute greatly to the ongoing faith retrogression in the West.

Yet the reformers were still very much aware of the problems within these institutes of higher learning and complained of them. After three hundred years of autonomous human reason, cut loose from divine revelation, dominating Western universities, the English reformer William Tyndale (1494-1536) complained that:

In the universities, they have ordained that no man shall look in the Scriptures until he be noselled [nursed] in heathen learning eight or nine years and armed with false principles with which he is clean shut out of the understanding of Scripture.[35]

Tyndale was right, and this problem would continue to plague the Western world (and churches) without respite for eight hundred years.

Months before he died, the great Scottish reformer, John Knox (1514-1572), warned against the universities. Although the colleges were ostensibly established to support the church, he said they would end up oppressing it.[36] Addressing the church general assembly at Perth, Knox cautioned, "Above all things, preserve the Kirk from the bondage of the Universities...subject never the pulpit to their Judgment, neither yet exempt them from your Jurisdiction."[37] It was a fitting warning to every local church and denomination throughout the following centuries that would allow autonomous intellectual and academic institutions to subsist apart from the authority of pastors. These intellectual systems were far from the original discipleship vision cast by Christ, and the Apostle in 2 Timothy 2:2: "And the things that thou hast heard of me among many witnesses, the same commit thou to faithful men, who shall be able to teach others also."

A LASTING LEGACY: CHILDHOOD EDUCATION

Following the Reformation, a tremendous war broke out over who and what would frame the minds of the rising generation. If the Christian and secular humanist vision clashed anywhere. The major confrontation joined on the battlefield of education. In time, mighty principalities formed massive, centrally-controlled institutions, powered by trillions of dollars, for the purpose of shaping the worldview of billions of children.

While the Reformers had largely failed at reforming the universities, evangelical Protestants made some concerted contributions toward the education of children along the way. Since the Scriptures were to be made accessible in the common language of every plowboy (as envisioned by William Tyndale), it was incumbent upon churches and families that these plowboys could read. If he learned to read, Luther said, the boy "can rule his house all the better because of it, and besides, he is prepared for the office of preacher or pastor if he should be needed there."[38] The New England Puritans followed up with the Old Deluder Satan Act of 1647, intended to enable all children in the colonies to read the Scriptures:

> It being one chief project of that old deluder, Satan, to keep men from the knowledge of the Scriptures, as in former times keeping them in an unknown tongue, so in these later times by perswading from the use of tongues, that so at least the true sense and meaning of the Originall might be clowded by false glosses of Saint-seeming deceivers; and that Learning may not be buried in the graves of our fore-fathers in Church and Commonwealth, the Lord assisting our indeavors: it is therefore ordered by this Court and Authoritie therof; That every Township in this Jurisdiction, after the Lord hath increased them to the number of

fifty Housholders, shall then forthwith appoint one within their town to teach all such children as shall resort to him to write and read...[39]

Biblical instruction was fundamental to the education of children in early America, and the *New England Primer* opened with: "A. In Adam's fall, we sinned all."

EDUCATION REFORMER— JOHANN AMOS COMENIUS (1592-1672)

The most thoughtful and significant contributor to childhood education among the early Protestants came from the progeny of Jan Hus—the Moravian brethren. Persecuted and driven out of his mother country, Moravian Johann Amos Comenius was exiled to Poland, where he championed the cause of childhood education and formulated a Christian philosophy for future generations. He is widely hailed as the father of modern education—but on the Christian side of it. Here is yet another example of the two streams emanating from the Medieval Period—the man-centered and God-centered, the humanist Renaissance and the Reformation. Comenius was the major contender against the humanist fulminations of Jean-Jacques Rousseau.

First and foremost, Comenius rejected pagan books and non-Christian authors:

Should we not blush, therefore, when we confide the education of the sons of the King of kings, of the brothers of Christ and heirs of eternity, to the jesting Plautus, the lascivious Catullus, the impure Ovid, that impious mocker at God, Lucian, the obscene Martial, and the rest of the writers who are ignorant of the true God?[40]

If we wish our schools to be truly Christian schools, the crowd of Pagan writers must be removed from them...Our zeal in this matter is caused by our love of God and of man; for we see that the chief schools profess Christ in name only, but hold in highest esteem writers like Terence, Plautus, Cicero, Ovid, Catullus, and Tibullus. The result of this is that we know the world better than we know Christ, and that, though in a Christian country. Christians are hard to find. For with the most learned men, even with theologians, the upholders of divine wisdom, the external mask only is supplied by Christ, while the spirit that pervades them is drawn from Aristotle and the host of heathen writers. Now this is a terrible abuse of Christian liberty, a shameless profanation, and a course replete with danger.[41]

Significantly, Comenius' main beef with the humanists was their pride and self-confidence. He outright rejected Aquinas' false division of sacred and secular knowledge. Quoting Philip Melanchthon, the Moravian continues:

How much pride and haughtiness there is in Plato! It seems to me that a self-sufficient character must inevitably imbibe faulty instincts from the ambition that pervades his writings. The teaching of Aristotle is nothing but one long struggle to prove himself worthy of a good place among the writers on practical philosophy." Again it is said: If they do not teach theology rightly, at any rate they teach philosophy, and this cannot be learned from the sacred writings, that have been given us for our salvation. I answer: The Word of God most high is the fountain of wisdom...[42]

Although, the Moravian permitted the mature to read Cicero (or other unbelievers), this he held for rare cases:

I pass over the fact that those authors who are placed before Christian boys instead of the Bible (Terence, Cicero, Virgil, etc.), possess the very defects that are attributed to the Scriptures, since they are difficult and not suited to the young. It was not for boys that they wrote, but for men of mature judgment, accustomed to the theatre and the law-courts, and it therefore goes without saying that they can be of no advantage to any one else.[43]

Comenius took up the crusade for universal education for both sexes. His primary goal was that all children would constantly read "the Bible and other good books" so "they will learn to see, to praise, and to recognize God everywhere."[44] He summarized his philosophy with the simple statement: "Our schools, therefore, will then at length be Christian schools when they make us as like to Christ as is possible."[45]

Comenius also insisted on keeping knowledge, virtue (character), and piety (worship) "bound together by an adamantine chain."[46] For him, faith and virtue (or character) had to be preeminent throughout every educational program:

> Christian schools, therefore, should resound not with Plautus, not with Terence, not with Ovid, not with Aristotle, but with Moses, David, and Christ, and methods should be devised by which the Bible may be given to children dedicated to God (for all the children of Christians are holy) (I Cor. 7:14) as a means of learning their ABC; for thus they would grow familiar with it. For as language is made up of the sounds and the symbols of letters, thus is the whole structure of religion and piety formed out of the elements of Holy Scripture.[47]

He was particularly concerned to include life application of the Word—and not a bare knowledge of it—within all spheres of education:

> Faith, charity, and hope should be taught for practical use. From the very beginning it is necessary to form practical and not theoretical Christians, if we wish to form true Christians at all.[48]

Above all, Comenius wanted to be sure that all other courses were related to God and that the Scriptures were always held preeminent in the studies.

> Whatever is taught to the young in addition to the Scriptures (sciences, arts, languages, etc.) should be taught as purely subordinate subjects. In this way it will be made evident to the pupils that all that does not

643

relate to God and to the future life is nothing but vanity.[49]

Comenius erred in his soft handling of the doctrine of original sin and his emphasis on improvement by education rather than regeneration. His was an optimistic eschatology, fully expecting a radical renewal of mankind on earth aided by his regimen of education. He is to be commended for a strong faith in the triumph of Christ over sin and the eventual success of the kingdom of God. However, the humanists captured this same vision, purged it of all Christian elements, maintained a firm belief in the perfectibility of man and the innocence of children, and some to this day claim Comenius as their progenitor.

Comenius' influence was immediate, especially upon the English and American Puritans, including Samuel Hartlib, Oliver Cromwell, and John Winthrop, governor of the Massachusetts Bay Colony.

THE PURITANS' ACHILLES HEEL

For of this sort are they which creep into houses, and lead captive silly women laden with sins, led away with divers lusts, ever learning, and never able to come to the knowledge of the truth. Now as Jannes and Jambres withstood Moses, so do these also resist the truth: men of corrupt minds, reprobate concerning the faith. But they shall proceed no further: for their folly shall be manifest unto all men, as their's also was. But thou hast fully known my doctrine, manner of life, purpose, faith, longsuffering, charity, patience, persecutions, afflictions, which came unto me at Antioch, at Iconium, at Lystra; what persecutions I endured: but out of them all the Lord delivered me. (2 Timothy 3:6-11)

Once again, the university turned out to be the Achilles heel for the rather short-lived Puritan movement in England. Laurence Chaderton (1536-1640), founding master of Emmanuel College, Cambridge, was a convinced reformed theologian, a translator of the King James Version of the Bible, and a friend of William Perkins—probably the first bona fide Puritan author of the English Reformation. Chaderton refused to use the state-sanctioned prayer book and insisted on psalm singing as a daily routine at the college. This Puritan "training ground" barely lasted a generation—a flashback to the early discipleship centers, the monasteries of a previous age. Emmanuel College produced such Puritan luminaries as John Cotton, Thomas Hooker, Stephen Charnock, Thomas Watson, Thomas Brooks, and others.

Three years before Chaderton died, in April of 1637, Richard Holdsworth (1590-1649), was appointed master of Emmanuel College, and under Holdsworth's guidance, the college quickly took a sharp turn in its philosophy of education. The new master required readings in Cicero, Homer, Virgil, and Ovid, the licentious poet. For Holdsworth, Aristotle "reigned supreme," and the pagan's *Logic, Ethics, Physics,* and *Metaphysics* made up the third year curriculum at the college.[50] Eventually, Holdsworth joined the side of the Royalists and abandoned Reformed Puritanism altogether.

Nonetheless, Puritan pastors-in-training at the college were still required to read the Bible in a year with heavy doses of William Perkins, William Sibbes, and other Puritan greats. Historian Patrick Collinson draws attention to the danger of the two streams of thought contending over the minds of the young pastors:

> If Puritanism in its full theological development was a product of Emmanuel, so was the very different, antipathetic, theological and philosophical tendency known as the Cambridge Platonists.[51]

Training in Aristotelian thinking at Emmanuel College bore the strongest effect on the thinking of men like John Goodwin, who represented the last of the Puritans and the first of the Enlightenment pastors in England. Through the 1630s and 1640s the first of the latitudinarians were matriculating at Emmanuel: Benjamin Whichcote,

1633; Ralph Cudworth, 1639; Nathaniel Culverwell, 1642; Peter Sterry, 1636; John Worthington, 1642; and John Smith, 1636.

The first fruits of Holdsworth's work were discovered in Nathaniel Culverwell's (1619-1651) teaching, who remained at Emmanuel as a student and fellow from 1633 through 1651. With his landmark lecture series for the 1645-1646 academic year, Culverwell falls down prostrate at the altar of human reason, asserting that all moral law must be formed in the light of reason. He announced to the class that "there is nothing in the mysteries of the Gospel contrary to the light of Reason; nothing repugnant to this light that shines from the Candle of the Lord."[52] Generous references were made to Aristotle, Plato, Homer, Euripides, Ovid, Virgil, etc., in his lectures, always defending the pagans for their wisdom and sound reason. A man-centered academic pride oozed out of every corner of this series of lectures, which carried the patently immodest title of: "An Elegant Discourse of the Light of Nature." Says Culverwell, Plato and the other philosophers "discourse very admirably" concerning natural law. He attributes "first notions" to Pythagoras and renders to Plato "connate species" of knowledge.[53] Culverwell obviously failed to notice how the ancient Greeks and Romans had really "suppressed the truth in unrighteousness," as the Apostle rightly observed (Rom. 1:18).

HARVARD COLLEGE: THE NEXUS FOR THE DEGENERATION OF AMERICAN FAITH

Beware lest any man spoil you through [Greek] philosophy and vain deceit, after the tradition of men, after the rudiments of the world, and not after Christ. (Colossians 2:8)

Founded in 1636, Harvard College was named for Emmanuel College graduate (1635) and first donor, John Harvard. New England's first college set down for its charter mission: "the education of the

English and Indian youth of this country, in knowledge and godliness."[54] Listed among the rules and precepts for the school issued in 1646, was this spiritual object:

> Let every Student be plainly instructed, and earnestly pressed to consider well, the main end of his life and studies is, to know God and Jesus Christ which is eternal life (John 17:3) and therefore to lay Christ in the bottom, as the only foundation of all sound knowledge and Learning. And seeing the Lord only giveth wisdom, let every one seriously set himself by prayer in secret to seek it of him (Prov. 2:3).[55]

However, like many religious institutions, Harvard College quickly wandered from its biblical foundations—but not without struggle.

Sometimes regarded as the last of the American Puritans, Increase Mather (1639-1723), assumed the presidency of Harvard in 1685. At the precocious age of thirteen, Increase had attended Harvard College briefly, until his father removed him on account of unhealthy influences; instead, Increase was put into a mentorship under a local pastor. After a brief stint back in England, Increase accepted the pastorate at the North Church in Boston, serving in that capacity from 1661 until his death in 1723.

Immediately upon his appointment to the college presidency, Increase set out to address the problem that had afflicted Western education for 400 years—pagan Greek philosophy and its categories. Concerned that the seminary was undermining the Christian faith in America, he set his sights on replacing pagan Aristotelian ethics with biblical law. The Puritan diagnosed the problem as just this: "It is much to be lamented, that many Preachers in these days have hardly any other discourses in their Pulpits than what we may find in Seneca, Epictetus, Plutarch, or some such Heathen Moralist. Christ, the Holy Spirit, and (in a word), the Gospel is not in their Sermons."[56]

Not surprisingly, as the coursework turned back towards the

Greeks, drunkenness and other immoral conditions proliferated on campus. Increase then preached evangelical sermons at the college and cautioned the students against secular books which he said would "poison their young minds."[57] He also took an interest in the spiritual needs of the students and instituted one-on-one discipleship. Son Cotton Mather wrote that his father would "send for the Scholars one by one into the Library, and there consider with them about their [spiritual] State, and Quicken their Flight unto their Saviour,…and lay the Solemn Charges of God upon them to Turn [their lives] unto Him; …thus Dr. Mather did continually!"[58] Here was another attempt at the discipleship approach more akin to ancient discipleship centers and the method Jesus employed with His disciples. Increase openly criticized Greek philosophy and the Roman Catholic schools that defended "their Pagan Master Aristotle [and] his Principles."[59]

Mather's reforms did not go unnoticed by the intellectual elite and the institutional authorities of his day. In an attempt to maintain a more secular, political control over the college, professors from England were sent over to inspect Harvard's classes. When these "overseers" were barred from visiting the college, the Privy Council in England revoked Harvard's charter. What ensued was a tremendous power struggle among human agents and spiritual forces, fighting over control of the seminary and the training of American pastors for American churches. In retrospect, the spiritual struggles at Harvard must have been of much greater import than the spiritual problems at Salem. Undaunted by the forces marshaled against him, Mather suggested that the college board forfeit official accreditation from England, and he continued to disciple the students in the Scriptures on a one-on-one basis.[60]

While Mather worked reform at the school, two of his instructors, William Brattle and John Leverett, were quietly opposing his efforts. Both were outspoken humanists, once again favoring the sovereignty of man's will over the sovereignty of God against the Reformed emphasis on God's control over all things. And the two pushed hard to reintroduce Greek ethics back into the college's curriculum, providing Plato's philosophy equal standing with God's revealed law.[61] As the humanist Enlightenment came on like a storm, the latitudinarians got the upper hand, and humanism seized control of American schools, colleges, and churches. Finally, in 1701, Harvard College's board voted Increase Mather out of office, and shortly thereafter the old Puritan preached his most important message: "Ichabod: The Glory of the Lord Departing New England." The Jeremiad was one long lament. Chief among the pastor's concerns was that Harvard College had "become a Seminary for Degenerate Plants, who will with their Foolish hands pull down those Houses which their Fathers have been building for the Name of the Lord in this wilderness." He went on to say that, "A Learned man who has written the History of the Bohemian Brethren, observes that the Ruin of those Churches proceeded out of their College."[62] So it was that everywhere throughout the Western world, among both Catholics and Protestants alike, the ruin of the faith came through the university.

At last (AD 1707), the Massachusetts government chose the candidate most committed to the classical-humanist approach as president of Harvard—John Leverett. Within the next Century, the college would embrace Unitarianism, completely abandoning the biblical Trinitarian faith.

Harvard served as America's prototype for apostasy in academia, a process repeated ad nauseam over the next three hundred years—in Yale, Princeton, Dartmouth, Andover, etc. Always formed on Christian foundations for the purpose of Christian ministry, these universities were quickly undermined by humanist philosophies and ideologies, leading to the corruption both of the pastorate and local churches. Throughout Western history, humanist universities and seminaries would lead the way for apostasy in the Western church.

JEAN-JACQUES ROUSSEAU & JOHANN FICHTE

The two symbiotic and essential components of humanist education advocated by Jean-Jacques Rousseau, Johann Fichte (1762-1814), Friedrich Froebel (1782-1852), and G. Stanley Hall (1846-1924) were child-centricity and state control. If man would be god, man must be at the center. The individual was primary, but so was the state—the universal expression of man's self-definition and autonomy. For the humanist, either one serves well as god, while the true and living God is dismissed altogether.

The prototype apostate from Calvin's Geneva, Jean-Jacques Rousseau, had "more effect upon posterity than any other writer or thinker of that Eighteenth Century, in which writers were more influential than they had ever been before,"[63] as explained by modern historian, Will Durant. Paul Johnson also considered Rousseau "the first of the modern intellectuals, their archetype, and in many ways the most influential of them all."[64] Most significantly, Rousseau is generally recognized as the grandfather of modern secular and socialist education. Himself the father of modern public education, John Dewey praised Rousseau as "the greatest educational reformer of modern times."[65] Steeped in Greek philosophy from the beginning, Rousseau referred to Plato's Republic as "the finest treatise on education ever written."[66] Plato described his utopian society as that in which women would "bear children to the state," and where "no parent is to know his own child, nor any child his parent."[67] Durant summarizes Rousseau's revolutionary vision:

> Rousseau would have wanted a system of public instruction by the state…he prescribed a private instruction by an unmarried tutor, who would…withdraw the child as much as possible from parents and relatives…[68]

Rousseau insisted that, "A father. . . owes men to humanity, citizens to the state."[69] Playing an utmost significant role in the unfolding saga of the Fall of Western civilization is the tragic story of Rousseau's personal life. The apostate sage most responsible for the creation of modern political institutions and public education, is best known for throwing each of his five children onto the streets to die, upon their births. Above all, public education was designed as the vehicle to bring about a new social construct in the totalitarian state; and thus, in Rousseau's words, education must be treated as "the most important business of the state."[70]

Equally pernicious to his statist humanism, was Rousseau's advocacy of child-centered education. Presupposing that man is "born free" and innocent of all sinful tendencies, Rousseau configured the myth of the "noble savage" and the sacrosanct child. He demanded absolute autonomy for the child under instruction, encouraging the tutor to "give your scholar no verbal lessons," in the child-centered school.[71] And, he said, "The first impulses of nature are always right; there is no original sin in the human heart."[72] Thus, the source of law becomes the individual—the child, untainted by tradition, parents, revelatory law, and, most importantly, God. Humanism turns the individual into god and the source of his own moral law. The school becomes the temple to this deity.

Such fulminations were outrageously popular with 19th Century Western society, eager to reject the doctrine of man's depravity and much enamored by the idea of man's perfectibility, without God. The powerful attraction to Rousseau's ideas verged on the magical or demonic—almost the entire educational complex adopted the theories. The biblical view of the depravity of man, (the need for a divine salvation through the creation of a new man by the Son of God), fell on hard times. While some parents would reject the statist model, most private schools and homeschools still followed Rousseau's child-centric, humanist vision in the years to come.

Following up a generation later, the German pedagogue, Friedrich Froebel, philosophized that the child should "work out his own education" by play—guided, of course, by state-funded professionals. "The child is," Froebel gushed, "placed in the center of life, and of all life."[73] The son of a German Lutheran pastor, Froebel insisted that children were born innocent and sinless in the tradition of Pelagius; as well, advocated state-funded, universal kindergarten in accord with Rousseau's vision. Scores of 19th Century educators, including Marie Montessori, John Dewey, and Francis W. Parker, followed Froebel's child-centered, humanist philosophy of education.

SALVATION BY GOVERNMENT EDUCATION

Noah Webster (1758-1843) and William Holmes McGuffey's (1800-1873) Christian influence on primary education persisted in the United States for most of the 19th Century. Until the rise of the industrial complex and socialism, family farms, one-room schoolhouses, and homeschools anchored childhood education in the Scriptures and kept socialism at bay.

However, the abandonment of Reformation theology by the churches brought about a revolution in civil government and education for the country. A bright-eyed millennialism and the Pelagian-humanist conception of the nature of man combined for a toxic mixture in the modern public school. Horace Mann promised Americans that publicly-funded education "would save them from poverty and vice." He announced to the world that "The common school is the greatest discovery ever made by man!" In the same article, he assured everyone that "nine-tenths of the penal code would become obsolete" if the nation embraced state-regulated education.[74] A new American religion formed out of these 19th Century ideologies. Instead of looking to Jesus Christ as the means of salvation from sin and its effects, now moral improvement was to come by education and the funding and controls of civil government. Alas, two hundred years and trillions of dollars later, Mann's experiment and associated promises proved sadly lacking.

Henry Bernard (1811-1900) took up Horace Mann's crusade as chief editor of the *American Journal of Education*. Throughout the 1860s, American governance was instituting large elements of the socialist or Marxist agenda, and Bernard was appointed America's first commissioner of education (serving 1867-1870). He would refer to teachers as "the new priesthood," and the school as "the temple" or "the chief instrumentality" of the entire spiritual and intellectual nurture of a child.[75] In the minds of the academic elite, the state had replaced both the parent and the church at the helm of the child's paideia.

Achieving a total socialization and secularization of primary school education required the inculcation of the new worldview in the university. New humanist categories of thought and college majors were developed as modern man completely abandoned a biblical worldview. A new religion formed, providing a new description of man's problems and offering attendant solutions. These new "seminaries" for the new temples introduced degreed programs in psychology, sociology, and social learning theory. The new religion required entirely new systematics, course studies, and seminaries, put together mainly by G. Stanley Hall (1846-1924). A true visionary, Hall constructed his theories along the lines of Darwin's evolutionary model in hopes of producing what he called the "superman." He referred to his universities as "true shrines of this spirit and nurseries of these supermen,"[76] and he was certain that the government school was more "sacred...than the church."[77] The worldview was shifting in the Western world. With this new religion, man was perfectible on his own efforts, and the humanist state was the means of achieving it through the schools. Contemporary to Sigmund Freud and Carl Jung, Hall introduced thoroughly humanist (man-centered) systems of thought to the modern American university in the form of psychology and education majors. His students included the most influential progressives of the 20th Century—John Dewey and Woodrow Wilson.

What G. Stanley Hall initiated, his student John Dewey wrapped up. Both men were raised in Christian homes and apostatized from the faith while in university. John Dewey would become the most famous atheist in America and the architect of the *Humanist Manifesto*. For Dewey, the public school teacher was "the prophet of the true god, and the usher in of the true kingdom of this god."[78] Education was defined as that institution which regulates "the process of coming to share in the social consciousness."[79] Thus, secular education's objective was primarily sociological and socialist. This education was not concerned with an increase in the knowledge of the true God; or an increase in wisdom; or the worship of the Creator; or the seeking of His kingdom and His righteousness. The social unit of the community, the nation, the bureaucracy, and the ordering of the faceless masses of worldwide humanity were all that mattered in human existence. And the teacher's function was to help the student find his part in the mass of human consciousness without God. For most humanists, the state (or civil government) became the most palpable embodiment of this god essence.

THE CORRUPTION OF PRINCETON & YALE

Therefore thus saith the Lord GOD; Because ye have spoken vanity, and seen lies, therefore, behold, I am against you, saith the Lord GOD. And mine hand shall be upon the prophets that see vanity, and that divine lies: they shall not be in the assembly of my people, neither shall they be written in the writing of the house of Israel, neither shall they enter into the land of Israel; and ye shall know that I am the Lord GOD. (Ezekiel 13:8-9)

Succumbing to the influence of left-wing Enlightenment thinking of Rousseau and Voltaire seeping into the newly-formed United States of America, the colleges prostrated themselves at the altar of human reason. Reporting on his experience at Yale college in 1795, Lyman Beecher wrote: "The college church was almost extinct. Most of the students were skeptical, and rowdies were plenty. Wine and liquors were kept in many rooms; intemperance, profanity, gambling and licentiousness were common...That was the day of the infidelity of the Tom Paine school. Boys that dressed flax in the barn, as I used to, read Tom Paine and believed him;... most of the class before me were infidels and called each other Voltaire, Rousseau, D'Alembert, etc."[80]

About that time, Jonathan Edward's grandson Timothy Dwight became president of the college and a revival on campus sparked some healthy elements in America's Second Great Awakening. By the 1802-03 school year, about a third of the student body professed faith and joined the college church.

A Christian orthodoxy survived at Yale until the 1870s, when Horace Bushnell's weakened theology (questioning the doctrines of substitutionary atonement and the Trinity) was incorporated into the pedagogy. Signaling the end of its glory days, the school went on to invite the scandal-ridden Henry Ward Beecher to provide a series of lectures on "love." The irony was thick, given Beecher's reputation for loving the wrong women in the wrong way. As the 1880s rolled around, professors at the college were rejecting Jesus' miracles as well.

Charles Darwin's book *Origin of Species,* published on November 24, 1859, was seismic in its influence. It codified anti-supernatural humanism for the entire world. An irresistible juggernaut, the theory took the universities, seminaries, and churches by storm. Scarcely any public entity could stand against it by the early 20th Century. Usually considered a theological conservative, Princeton Seminary principal, B.B. Warfield, conceded to the juggernaut in 1888: "I do not think that there is any general statement in the Bible or any part of the account of creation, either as given in Gen. I & II or elsewhere alluded to, that need be opposed to evolution."[81] Princeton University presidents, James McCosh (served 1868-1888) and Francis Patton (served 1888-1902), were both theistic evolutionists. They accepted Darwin's theory of a long and gradual process of evolutionary development of man and animal over the course of billions of years. Who could stand against this? The force of the ideas, the spiritual powers, and the pride of the academic systems were just too strong. Hardly a single Christian in the academic field could find the faith or the strength to hold on to a biblical, young-earth creation perspective. Such was the state of the faith in the early 20th Century.

Princeton's degrade shifted into high gear when Woodrow Wilson replaced Francis Patton as college president. Wilson inherited rich Christian roots, his father serving as stated clerk for the Southern Presbyterian church (PCUS) from 1865 to 1898. Immediately, President Wilson put an end to the Bible instruction classes at the university.[82] Five years later, the lapsed Christian and his wife Ellen consulted a Ouija board hoping to conjure up James McCosh (who had been dead for thirteen years), on matters pertaining to Princeton politics.[83] Progressivism, liberalism, or better put, "the anti-Christian social agenda" was in full gear by 1908, with Woodrow Wilson at the helm. Drawing from Darwin's theory of evolution, Wilson argued in an essay entitled, The Constitutional Government of the United States, that evolutionary science be applied to political governance. "In our own day," Wilson remarked, "Whenever we discuss the structure or development of anything, whether in nature or in society, we consciously or unconsciously follow Mr. Darwin;. . . Living political constitutions must be Darwinian in structure and practice."[84]

Wilson's record at Princeton reveals the paradigm of Christian apostasy, and a national capitulation to full-blown skepticism and an anti-supernaturalist, materialist worldview, first by the Christian colleges and universities in the West. From the 13th Century to the present, Western universities led the way towards the apostasy, a worldview shift, moral degeneration, and political liberalization of the nations.

When the West fell, a full 99% of American universities were advocating an old-earth, macro-evolutionary theory regarding origins,[85] while 40% of the grassroots population still held to the young-earth creation account.[86] Five decades following Columbia College's incorporation of the nation's first homosexual campus group on April 19, 1967, 97% of colleges and universities were supporting the homosexual cause (as monitored by CampusPride.org).

Always, the modern university prided itself in leading the "progressive" cause. A UCLA Higher Education Research Institute survey found that 42% of college professors called themselves liberal in 1990, a ratio that increased to 60% twenty-five years later. The Econ Journal Watch surveyed 7,243 professors among forty prominent American colleges and universities and discovered the registered Democrat to Republican ratio at 11.5 to 1. For younger professors, the ratio was 23 to 1.[87]

A movement of Christian evangelical/conservative colleges made a weak attempt at resistance to the apostasy, but this too, largely failed. Representing only 4% of the total college population, the majority of these institutions relied on federal grants for their existence. Between 1970 and the 2020s, the feminist-homosexual juggernaut trampled these schools into the ground. Gender role distinctions were almost entirely discarded, and there was rapid capitulation to homosexual ideologies and gender confusion. The "spring" was pretty well polluted when Calvin University introduced their first "gay" student body president in AD 2020. Claire Murashima called herself "bisexual" and announced that "it's easy to be gay at Calvin in 2020," and "times have changed."[88]

The righteous had fallen down before the wicked in 2019 when the Council for Christian Colleges and Universities (CCCU) adopted the "Fairness for All" compromise—a legislative policy putting a stamp of approval on the persecution of Christian business owners who did not choose to promote homosexuality. The plan was to add sexual orientation and gender identity (SOGI) to federal nondiscrimination law, while exempting the Christian colleges from the same strictures. The CCCU list of "Christian" colleges included Pepperdine University, Azusa Pacific, Bethel College, Calvin College, Covenant College, Kings College, and Wheaton College. Only Masters College and Cedarville University pulled out before the fatal compromise was completed.

To further cripple the loyal opposition, Christian colleges were hopelessly beholden to the federal government grant and loan programs, all of which were tied to Title IX non-discrimination requirements extending to sex, gender, sexual orientation, and the rest. Only about one percent of evangelical colleges refused to take "Caesar's money" and remained free of Title IX restrictions. By one means or another, between AD 1020 and 2020, the Western educational complex had expunged the remnants of a Christian worldview from its universities and major institutions.

The brains behind the zeitgeist had pretty much dialed in a reproducible process for the advancement of the "progressive" agenda by the turn of the 21st Century. For a hundred years, "Red State" conservative parents would keep sending their children to the more progressive "Blue State" colleges, assuring a regular generational trajectory towards faith retrogression and the complete institutionalization of the anti-Christian zeitgeist. Successive generations of pastors, educators, and political leaders were processed through the universities where professors were six times more likely to be post-Christian or anti-Christian than the general populace. Churches would no longer set the direction for the nation, nor would they disciple the nations by framing a Christian worldview for the younger generation. Congregants were more likely to get their basic worldview from the media and the academy than from their pastors. All the while, the children were systematically indoctrinated for sixteen years by liberals, skeptics, atheists, and agnostics in government schools and universities.

THE FALL OF THE COLLEGE

> For the wrath of God is revealed from heaven against all ungodliness and unrighteousness of men, who hold the truth in unrighteousness; because that which may be known of God is manifest in them; for God hath shewed it unto them. For the invisible things of him from the creation of the world are clearly seen, being understood by the things that are made, even his eternal power and Godhead; so that they are without excuse: because that, when they knew God, they glorified him not as God, neither were thankful; but became vain in their imaginations, and their foolish heart was darkened. Professing themselves to be wise, they became fools... (Romans 1:18-22)

For a long time, even after the rejection of the Christian faith, the educational and scientific community continued to borrow from Christian presuppositions (at least on an inconsistent basis). Nonetheless, the slow but steady erosion of the Christian worldview in the Western world was removing the preconditions by which real knowledge is made possible. Increasing levels of relativistic thinking, incoherent reasoning, skepticism, emotionalism, irrationalism, and downright insanity governed the modern mind—even that which purported to be highly educated. In biblical language, "God gave them up to a debased mind" with that aberrant sexuality which was vigorously advocated by the colleges (Rom. 1:27-28).

The mental breakdown of the college resulted in exceedingly fragile "snowflakes," men and women who were incapable of engaging in critical thinking or a thoughtful exchange of ideas, while allowing for opposing opinions. Slight disagreements were interpreted as micro aggressions, and campuses would designate "safe spaces" for those too emotionally fragile to handle big ideas, Christian morality, and controversial discussions. Consequently, free speech zones on campuses withered away with each academic year. Colleges imposed policies banning antithetical opinions, particularly when it came to the sins of Sodom and Gomorrah. Groupthink, censorship, blacklisting, and cancel culture became the norm, shutting down all opportunities for some little kid to shout out something obvious in the emperor's-new-clothes procession.

Undergraduate college enrollment in the US (public and private) peaked at 18.1 million in 2010. By the spring of 2020, that number had collapsed to 14.7 million, and three months later the enrollment dipped another 20%—shrinking by some 30% in ten years.[89] During the same time frame, the total college debt load more than doubled—from $800 billion to $1.7 trillion,[90] contributing to the economic non-recovery from the 2008 worldwide recession. By July 2020, mainstream economists assured us that colleges were "never coming back"[91]—a fitting end to a thoroughly corrupt institution.

THE CORRUPTION OF PRIMARY SCHOOL EDUCATION

But whoso shall offend one of these little ones which believe in me, it were better for him that a millstone were hanged about his neck, and that he were drowned in the depth of the sea. (Matthew 18:6)

Near the end of his magnum opus, *City of God*, Augustine painted a picture for the "worst case scenario" for the future of the Christian church. Should the devil ever deceive the nations, Augustine foresaw a monumental challenge with salvaging "the little ones." However, the church father was still confident in the sustaining grace of God in the spiritual storm. He prophesied, as it were: "There shall be such resoluteness...in parents...that they shall conquer that strong one, even though unbound—that is, shall both vigilantly comprehend, and patiently bear up against him, though employing such wiles and putting forth such force as he never before used; and thus the children shall be snatched from him even though unbound."[92]

Though the present situation may not represent this worst case scenario, the mass apostasy of hundreds of millions of children raised in the Western church since 1880 should give pause to the remnant of Christian families. The influence of secular education (and mass media) in this apostasy simply cannot be underplayed.

Throughout most of the 19th Century and early 20th Century, Scripture was little more than wallpaper and memes on the headings of copybooks for school children. There was little real integration of God's Word and a Christian worldview into human knowledge and life, as was the standard in the monasteries of the early Middle Ages.

For the latter half of the 19th Century, the American "McGuffey Readers" were still referring to the Bible and encouraging the observance of the Sabbath. A generation later, the "Alice and Jerry" or "Dick and Jane" readers of the 1940s and 1950s had eliminated all references to God, the church, and Scripture. My parents remember one or two teachers praying in public school classrooms during their primary school years in the 1940s. Music hour for public schooled children allowed for a few hymns such as "O Worship the King" or "For the Beauty of the Earth" mixed in with Stephen Foster's "My Old Kentucky Home" and "Old Zip Coon." By this time, the schools paid tribute to cultural remnants of Christianity, but there was an absence of heart faith. The complete removal of the Bible and prayer from public school classrooms in the 1960s paved the way for the complete secularization of society and the widespread apostasy from the

Christian faith for the Gen X and millennial generations.

UNLEASHING THOROUGH-GOING HUMANISM IN THE SCHOOLS

The transgression of the wicked saith within my heart, that there is no fear of God before his eyes. For he flattereth himself in his own eyes, until his iniquity be found to be hateful. The words of his mouth are iniquity and deceit: he hath left off to be wise, and to do good. (Psalm 36:1-3)

After the US Supreme Court case, *Engel v. Vitale* (1963), the government-funded schools became more than a-Christian—they became anti-Christian and pro-homosexual. Harking back to the pagan Roman narrative of AD 60, the schools were turned over to Caesar Nero for the persecution of Christians and the aggressive promotion of homosexuality and gender confusion.

The 1963 prayer ban disallowed all reverence to God, worship of God, and thanksgiving to God in the classroom except for those teachers who would disobey the law and risk sanctions. In 1987, the Supreme Court ruled in *Edwards v. Aguillard* against teachers who wanted to present creationism in the classroom. The reasoning was that only a "secular" religion or worldview would be allowed henceforth in government schools, and any indication that a "supernatural being created mankind" was disallowed.[93] Henceforth, only that religion purporting to be "scientific" and presupposing the non-existence of God and non-involvement of God in origins was allowed by the secular, post-Christian states.

After God was dispensed with, every perversion was allowed in the schools—with a preference for that which was most outrageous and corrupting. In 2012, California became the first state to mandate instruction in homosexuality for children six to eighteen years of age. Nevada, Oregon, New Jersey, Colorado, and Illinois joined the program, and fifteen states required transgender education and accommodation for little boys pretending to be a girl, and vice versa.

For Britain's schools, Prime Minister Margaret Thatcher's government banned the promotion of homosexuality in 1986, a policy reversed in the year 2000. Eighteen years later, the Scottish government issued a mandate to incorporate homosexual training in all public schools by May 2021. England followed suit, and Wales committed to incorporating a full-orbed "LGBTQ+ sex education" by 2022. Public kindergartens and primary schools were almost universally concerned with gender confusion—encouraging, accommodating, advocating, and focusing upon gender autonomy for seven-year-old children. The insanity, or the reprobation of mind, was complete (Rom. 1:28).

In quick order, the sexualization and corruption of schools appeared strikingly homogenized across the United States, whether in liberal or conservative, urban or rural areas. High school literature programs were rife with nihilism, generous use of the "F" word (a perverse term used for rape), explicit sexual descriptions, and general obnoxiousness. A mother from the Scotland County, Missouri (population: 4,863) was horrified to discover her daughter's math lesson involved discussions of extreme sexual promiscuity. Said the mom, "This is something I imagine you would see on a coffee table in a brothel."[94] A substitute teacher in a conservative Utah town was hurried off school property when she made the "mistake" of telling the class homosexuality was wrong. Teachers were routinely fired for refusing to use a preferred pronoun for ten-year-old boys dressing like girls.[95] At points even the Christian church played along with the lie. In 2019, Southern Baptist Convention President J. D. Greear encouraged others to follow his practice of calling transgendered persons by their preferred pronouns.[96]

The confusion following this wholesale mental delusion knew no bounds. While the Fall was in full force, schoolgirls who wanted to compete in high school athletics were suing their schools over unfair physical advantage when too many transgendered boys (pretending to be girls) were gathering up the trophies while competing in girls sporting events. In Connecticut, two boys secured both first and second place in the girls track and field state championship.

> And for this cause God shall send them strong delusion, that they should believe a lie: that they all might be damned who believed not the truth, but had pleasure in unrighteousness. (2 Thessalonians 2:11-12)

CONCLUSION

Removing Scripture from the cathedral schools had produced very bad fruit in the 1100s. But the Western university built up on the metaphysics, ethics, and epistemology of human reason after AD 1250 produced even worse results, calling for a Reformation some three hundred years later. Yet the Reformation failed to reform the university in method or content—and the seeds of destruction were replanted with each new set of universities built in Europe and America over successive centuries.

Here and there, a fledgling remnant hung on to what they called "Bible Colleges" and Discipleship Centers during the last decades of the West. These returned to the Scripture as core, harking back to the old monasteries of Ireland and England. Rejecting the dead and dying systems, they found their precedent in the pattern of Christ who spent His time with twelve men in a boat and up on the mountain.

> God hath not cast away his people which he foreknew. Wot ye not what the scripture saith of Elias? how he maketh intercession to God against Israel saying, Lord, they have killed thy prophets, and digged down thine altars; and I am left alone, and they seek my life. But what saith the answer of God unto him? I have reserved to myself seven thousand men, who have not bowed the knee to the image of Baal. Even so then

at this present time also there is a remnant according to the election of grace. (Romans 11:2-5)

XIV

THE RISE & FALL
OF THE WEST

And this word, Yet once more, signifieth the removing of those things that are shaken, as of things that are made, that those things which cannot be shaken may remain. Wherefore we receiving a kingdom which cannot be moved, let us have grace, whereby we may serve God acceptably with reverence and godly fear: for our God is a consuming fire. (Hebrews 12:27-29)

The story of the West will be nothing less than epochal in the annals of world history. These works of God in time and space will be well worth studying for another thousand years into the future, should the world not end sooner. The Rise was spectacular, and so was the Fall. The phenomenon of Western civilization following the fall of pagan Rome was seismic, transforming the world for over a thousand years. The fall was a similarly seismic event effecting worldwide repercussions. Upon careful consideration of the entire story, however, an honest observer would have to conclude that the Rise was more spectacular than the Fall. The delta between Nero and Alfred was more phenomenal than the delta between Alfred and Joe Biden. Besides this, how could any

Christian overlook the tremendous spiritual and material blessings that cascaded into every corner of the world following the Reformation and the Christian-dominated, science-based, technological revolution?

Considering world history from a biblical perspective with a concerted eye kept on the development of the Christian church throughout, several significant, world-changing events stand out (following Christ's resurrection from the dead). These include Pentecost, the Fall of Jerusalem, the Fall of Rome, the Bubonic Plague, the Reformation, and the Fall of the West. These seismic events exceed in significance the exploration of the New World, the rise of empires, and the world wars of the 20th Century. For those who are immediately affected by them, these periods of massive social convulsions and spiritual upheavals might suggest the end of the world. The intensive and extensive transitions that follow, the revolutions and wars, the collapse of nations, and the shifting around of cultures and civilizations can touch off a pandemic of insecurity and fear. But, we can be assured that all plays out according to the plan of God, and all yields to the benefit of that "which cannot be moved." And, the Church of Christ continues on strong and secure, worshiping God "acceptably with reverence and godly fear" (Heb. 12:27-29).

The shock waves from the decline have reverberated for decades already. Honest and serious academic, social, and political leaders are already adjusting to this new paradigm, and ecclesiastical leaders are also waking up to the sober reality. An obscure little book published in 2017 called *The Death of Western Christianity* contained a preface written by the 103rd Archbishop of Canterbury. Reluctantly admitting to the thrust of the book, Lord George Carey wrote, "When I became vicar of St. Nicholas' Durham in 1975, I came across the diary of the church in 1925 and found that the Sunday school had numbered over 1,000 and when the Sunday school had its summer outing to places like Seaburn or Barnard Castle, the church hired a whole train. Fifty years later, however, in 1975, the Sunday school numbered less than 20. I could barely take in the scale of that decline."[1] The retired archbishop wholeheartedly endorsed the call to repentance and recommended a sober reflection on the "causes of the decline of the Western church."[2]

It was a petrifying moment for American evangelicalism, much talked about when it happened in 1991. The eccentric evangelist of the Jesus movement charged out of a Christian rock concert, hands in the air, crying out, "Ichabod! Ichabod!" The Hebrew expression is loosely translated, "The glory has departed." David Wilkerson's influence upon the Christian world had dissipated by then, but maybe he had a point. The Christian influence on the macro culture had almost completely dissipated. Liberal Christianity had already completed a total face plant, leaving the mainline denominations with no other recourse than to close church doors and die. Could the weakened, half-way house of Evangelical Protestantism survive the century?

Wilkerson, it turns out, was right. The glory had departed, though not exactly in the way he had thought. There wasn't much left of evangelicalism, except the show. Try as they might, the "shekinah glory" in the church could not be replicated by the worship band, the fog machine, and the primal screams. From this point forward, the world would no longer look to the West for spiritual, moral, diplomatic, political, or socio-economic leadership.

THE COLLAPSE OF WESTERN CIVILIZATION

Having dynamited its twenty-foot-deep Christian foundations over a period of 300 years, Western civilization finally crumbled, together with its socio-economic systems. Now obvious to the whole world (believers and unbelievers alike), the productivity of the West declined rapidly between 1960 and 2022, moving from contributing two thirds to a mere one third of the Gross World Product. The United States economy never recovered from the 2008 recession compensating only by more corporate and government debt spending. There was no recovery from the 2008 and 2020 recessions. Representing only 4% of the world population, the United States made up 52% of the gross world debt. The character of the nation had imploded on itself.

Birth implosions took their toll on the West, and nations slipped in both military presence and economic influence. By the year 2020, Europe's 65 million fighting-age men made up only 6.5% of the world's armed forces, down from 27% in 1914. Once Europe's most populous nation, the Republic of France had sunk into ignominy by the late 20th Century. Germany attempted world dominance and failed miserably, leading to two world wars in the process. Though the United States increased its population from 75 million to 300 million in the 20th Century, this nation's turn at world dominance lasted not quite a century.

America as a national entity fell apart after abandoning its Christian foundations, all while courting an unprecedented cultural diversity. The Babel principle of decentralization (on cultural lines) had to kick in at some point. Babel divided the world, and the Christian Pentecost was able to cross the cultural boundaries with a Word about the resurrected Christ spoken in all tongues. But, after the 1960s, the Holy Spirit left, and the US lost any unified cultural denominator upon which to build. Europe's demise followed the same course as masses of immigrants flooded in from Africa and Asia. Compensating for the loss of the will to have children and carry on a civilization, Western nations gladly reopened their borders to immigrants, mainly interested in dividing the spoil and taking advantage of whatever capital was left. However, this did nothing to restore a national unity, re-lay moral foundations, or maintain a workable cultural common denominator. The apostate West was not prepared to disciple the immigrant tribal groups into the Christian faith. If anything, most of the immigrants and their families were themselves ruined by the corrupted morals and toxic ideologies of the Western nations into which they assimilated. It was an aggregate loss of common grace and a breakdown of character for those seeking the good life in post-Christian nations.

> O God of earth and altar,
> Bow down and hear our cry,
> Our earthly rulers falter,
> Our people drift and die;
> The walls of gold entomb us,
> The swords of scorn divide,
> Take not thy thunder from us,
> But take away our pride.
> (G.K. Chesterton)

THE POST-CHRISTIAN ASHES OF A DEAD SOCIETY

So the last shall be first, and the first last: for many be called, but few chosen. (Matthew 20:16)

Visiting a public mall somewhere in America's heartland, we find ourselves surrounded by tattooed, body-mutilated, half-clothed natives—mostly of European derivation. The beaches of the Bahamas and Mexico are filled with rude, tattooed, bikini-clad Westerners, enjoying the service of modestly dressed, clean, and polite natives. Indigenous pastors in Asia and Africa often speak of opportunities to evangelize the US missionaries and mission teams visiting their churches. Some expatriates from the states stick around to hear the gospel preached by men of true faith. African pastors have taken the time to provide long-term discipleship for the American missionaries who were sent out by denominational mission agencies. In post-Christian London, over half of church attendees on any given Sunday are of African or Caribbean heritage.[3] Two-thirds of new church plants are "black" and "Pentecostal."[4] The ironies multiply—an application of that principle left to us by the Lord: "The first shall be last, and the last first."

American cities like Detroit, Cleveland, and Baltimore cultivate and support a single parent household rate of 70-80%,[5] and the US claims the highest rate of single parent households in the world (at 23%). It turns out that children have a better chance at a stable home in Africa in the 2020s given that Nigeria's single parent rate is only 4% and Uganda's is 10%.[6] Asian families are also doing far better than Western families. Single parent household rates in Vietnam and India hover around 4-5%.

WHAT DOES THE SPIRIT SAY TO THE CHURCHES?

> To him that overcometh will I grant to sit with me in my throne, even as I also overcame, and am set down with my Father in his throne. He that hath an ear, let him hear what the Spirit saith unto the churches. (Revelation 3:21-22)

Having completed this rapid and (admittedly) exhausting, if not exhaustive, two-thousand-year survey of the Rise and Fall of the West, the remnant is left asking the obvious question: "Where are we now?" Or, to use the words of the risen Christ recorded in Revelation 2 and 3: "What is the Spirit saying to the churches?" Of course, sufficient answers are always to be found in Scripture, but what is the specific word to the present situation? What now? Where are we now? *How shall we then live?* Particularly for those who will continue living in Europe and North America, it would be well to leave the reader with a strategy, an agenda, and hope.

Well before the fall of Jerusalem, the Apostle Paul registered the warning to the Roman Gentiles. He contrasted the apostasy of the Jews with what appears to be a prophetic reference to something similar occurring in the Gentile world (Rom. 11:20)—boasting and apostasy. Therefore, he urged his Gentile audience to an increase in humility, which was the afore stated objective for this particular work.

Given that the Jewish situation prior to AD 70 bears remarkable similarities to what is found in an apostate Christian world 2,000 years later, the words directed to the Jews by John the Baptist, Christ, and His Apostles must be equally relevant now as then. Those who would continue in the faith would do well to heed the hardest instructions and severest warnings from the Lord Jesus contained in the Gospels.

HYPOCRISY

Clearly, Jesus directed much of His teaching towards the blatant hypocrisy of 1st Century Judaism (especially prominent in the Gospels of Matthew and John). Likewise, the Baptist wasted no time shoving his listeners off the fence and calling them to repentance. The warnings found in the Book of Hebrews are also perfectly fitting for a Gentile world in apostasy.

In his epistles to the Galatians, Philippians, and Romans, the Apostle Paul warns constantly of a self-sourced righteousness and a works-based merit. The message is starkly relevant to the present situation. When asked, "Are you a good person?," or "Are you good enough for heaven?," the response inevitably comes back, "Sure! I'm a pretty good person." An age of rank apostasy calls for direct, clear, and unvarnished Gospel preaching on sin, the law of God, the holiness of God, the fear of God, the death and resurrection of the Son of God, repentance, and faith.

There comes a point in time at which gross hypocrisy cannot continue within the church. The Israelites were pressed to rid themselves of Achan and his family. The early church could not allow for the hypocrisy of Ananias and Sapphira. John the Baptist warned that the ax lay at the very root of the tree. Jesus promised the house would be "left desolate." True faith cannot tolerate hypocrisy for any extended length of time.

Whether the faith be reduced to a shallow nothing-nominalism, a hollowed-out sentimentality, an emotion-based romanticism, a powerless gospel, or an external legalism, the problem is the same. The faith is gutted of core and appears more as a white-washed sepulcher than a living body. The lapsed quickly become the non-affiliated and they don't see much need for attending "liberal" denominations even as a form of godliness. For those who wanted to sit on the fence for yet one more generation, there wasn't much of a fence left.

Truly, in more ways than one, "This is the day of salvation."

> For he saith, I have heard thee in a time accepted, and in the day of salvation have I succoured thee: behold, now is the accepted time; behold, now is the day of salvation. (2 Corinthians 6:2)

The distinction between real Christianity and its spurious counterfeits were more obvious than ever. If nothing else, the pornography download rates monitored by every internet server provider in the country told the story. Utah, Mississippi, and the other states boasting the highest church attendance rates made the top of the list. They had a form of godliness but denied the power thereof (2 Tim. 3:5).

Getting the religious language down and mouthing a few choruses on a Sunday morning is a poor substitute for faith in a God who raises the dead. A religion worthy of God must reflect the infinite power, wisdom, and love of God only evident in the true Son of God obtaining the victory for sinners by His death and resurrection. All other pseudo-Christian religions betray themselves by their powerlessness and spiritual vacuity.

The layers of hypocrisy and insincerity were slowly but surely peeled back and exposed. A constant stream of scandals in all segments of Christianity in the West over a century or so cleared out much of the refuse. Heresies and scandals abounded, "that they which are approved may be made manifest" (1 Cor. 11:19). The facades came down.

Church attendance fell, first in Europe and then in America beginning in 2010 and accelerating in the 2020s (especially after the Covid-19 crisis). As would be expected, pollsters found a steady decrease in the gap between the ratio of those who call themselves Christians and those attending church regularly. After about 300 years of propping up the mere appearance of Christian culture, the age of hypocrisy and insincerity had ended. Westerners weren't faking it much anymore, even with the pollsters.

Thus the order of the day for the remnant of faith was simply to "purge out the old leaven" and "keep the feast...with the unleavened bread of sincerity and truth" (1 Cor. 5:8). All hypocrisies and secret sins were uncovered and or confessed. The blood earnest heart cry emerged loud and clear: "Cleanse thou me from secret faults!...Search me oh God, and know my heart; try me, and know my thoughts! And see if there be any wicked way in me, and lead me in the way everlasting" (Ps. 139:23-24). It was not enough to destroy only "the vile and the refuse" with Saul who left the rest of the Amalekites alive (1 Sam. 15:9). This was not the time to dilute the import of God's law but rather to resurrect the true intent of it as Christ did in His ministry (Matt. 5:18ff; 15:1-8, etc.). This was no time to go after the external rotten fruits of abortion and homosexuality while ignoring the roots of self-centeredness, idolatry, pride, and ungratefulness within the heart. It was a time for transparency, brutal honesty, walking in the light, confessing real sins, and upholding the righteous law of God as the standard of right and wrong.

From the 17th Century onward, sectarian "conservatives" would settle for bare mental assent to a set of narrowly-configured doctrines and practices as some sort of cheap metric for sanctification or Christian piety. However, in the process, the "weightier matters of the law" such as real faith in God and His mighty works, love for God, fear of God, whole-hearted worship of God, self-denial, mercy, brotherly love, humility, and obedience were lost in the mix. Church leaders settled for their denominational preferences relating to certain baptismal practices, gifts of the Spirit, forms of church governance, translations of the Bible, or eschatological schemes as making for the "new and improved" church. Eventually, some "conservative" churches devolved further into emphases on methods, slogans, and narrow cultural contexts, as in the case of the "missional church," the "cowboy church," the "home church," the "liturgical church," the "homeschooling church" or the "emergent church." Such "movements" constituted a distraction at best—more grasping at straws and the loss of core faith. Inevitably, the denominational emphases were superficial and diverted people from the core faith, adding to the overall superficiality and hypocrisy of the Western church.

Meanwhile, the "liberal" side of the apostasy responded to the hypocrisy by a wholesale rejection of the faith, at every major part. For a while through the 20th and 21st centuries, lapsed churches and denominations threw it all out—the tithing of mint, anise, and cumin, *along with the weightier matters of the Word*. Instead of embracing the core gospel truths with a life-and-death, committed faith (beyond bare mental or verbal assent), these "liberal" churches would cast off all Christian distinctions and embrace every antithetical worldly philosophy and custom. Thus, apostasy came by both a sectarian "conservatism" and an ecumenical nothing burger "liberalism."

THESE THINGS WILL PASS

This Jesus hath God raised up, whereof we all are witnesses. Therefore being by the right hand of God exalted, and having received of the Father the promise of the Holy Ghost, he hath shed forth this, which ye now see and hear. For David is not ascended into the heavens: but he saith himself, The Lord said unto my Lord, Sit thou on my right hand, until I make thy foes thy footstool. Therefore let all the house of Israel know assuredly, that God hath made the same Jesus, whom ye have crucified, both Lord and Christ. (Acts 2:32-36)

All Christians accept one basic metaphysical reality. About 2,000 years ago, the Son of God came to earth; Jesus Christ died on the cross for sins, rose from the dead, ascended to the right hand of the Father, and sat down to reign until all enemies were brought under His footstool. For the Christian, this meta-reality is fundamental and preeminent over all other interpretive devices applied to human history.

The Roman persecutions ended. The form of chattel slavery re-instituted by the colonial powers ended in the US in 1865, and quite a few lives were lost in the process. "For He must reign, till He hath put all enemies under His feet" (1 Cor. 15:25).

The eugenicist vision advocated by Charles Darwin, Herbert Spencer, Adolf Hitler, Hirohito, Woodrow Wilson, Oliver Wendell Holmes, Theodore Roosevelt, and others was crushed when the atom bomb dropped on Hiroshima. The expense exceeded 60 million lives, but the eugenicist vision of the racists was buried in the bunker where Hitler committed suicide. Surely, the few Christians who opposed the vision must have felt themselves to have been in the minority in 1927 when the US Supreme Court took the wrong position on the matter. Not two decades later, the whole game had changed. Christians believe Christ rules over world events, and He is bringing His enemies under His footstool, one by one.

As sure as the King reigns, any and all forms of evil cannot continue indefinitely upon this earth. Of course, every person with true faith would agree with such a proposition. Certainly, every work will be brought into judgment at the end, and the devil will be cast into the lake of fire with the unbelieving and all liars (Rev. 20:10; 21:8).

Prior to Israel's inheriting the land of Canaan, Leviticus 18:28 tells of how the land "vomited out the nations that were before," on account of the sexual perversions listed in the same chapter. Herein lies another reason to anticipate a definite end to the present era. The earth itself wearies of it, and at some point, refuses to tolerate the flagrant violation of the created order. The analogy may be taken as either reification or personification. Either way, the principle is clear—the Creator has hardwired a "safety valve" into nature, limiting the reach and extent of sexual anarchy and moral corruption. All that to say, the wholesale killing by abortion and abortifacients, homosexuality, adultery, polyamory, and pornography simply cannot continue beyond a few decades from now. While God may have "winked at" the idolatries and perversions of the Sodomites, Persians, Greeks, and Romans for 300-400 years at a time, the Apostle said, Christ is on the throne now, and "He commands all men everywhere to repent" (Acts 17:30). He brings His enemies under His footstool. He continues to shake heaven and earth so that which cannot be shaken will remain. *The end of the present moral crisis must be soon.*

THE INTERNATIONALITY OF THE CHRISTIAN CHURCH

And what is the exceeding greatness of his power to us-ward who believe, according to the working of his mighty power, which he wrought in Christ, when he raised him from the dead, and set him at his own right hand in the heavenly places, far above all principality, and power, and might, and dominion, and every name that is named, not only in this world, but also in that which is to come: and hath put all things under his feet, and gave him to be the head over all things to the church... (Ephesians 1:19-22)

Herein lies the core metaphysical reality for Christians. The present seismic activity, the social upheaval, wars, disease, and economic cataclysm serve the purposes of the Lord, certainly. But all things must be for the benefit of the church.

Truly, His purposes for the Church are coming to pass in the real world, in real time and history. With the "casting away" of the Western world has come again "the reconciling of the world" and "life from the dead"—a recapitulation of the Romans 11:15 principle. The "every tribe and nation" vision of Revelation 5 and 7 was consummated in a greater way over the last century, more than any other time in history. Between 1800 and 1900, the percent of the world professing to be Christian increased from 23% to 34% and has held steady for the past hundred years. The number of Christians increased twelve-fold since 1800 (from 204 million to 2.4 billion).[7]

If there was a single distinguishing characteristic of the last two hundred years of kingdom history, this would be the gist of it. Whereas Europe and North America make up just 16% of the world's population, these continents constituted 81% of the world's Christian population in AD 1800.[8] This ratio declined to 38.4% by 2010,[9] leaving way for the "every tribe and nation" vision to materialize. Indubitably, the shift was intentional, completely dictated by the Lord of the church.

This historical reality is of major importance for all Christian mission strategies in this new era of human history now commencing. After the 20th Century, the center of Christianity moved into the jungles of Asia, the deserts of Africa, and the river valleys of South America. The internationality of the Christian church will be her strongest asset. By the second millennium after Christ, the median percentage of the professing Protestant/Catholic population in the nations of the earth was a surprising 68%, and the median percentage for self-identifying Protestants was 17%.[10] As Christianity's closest competitor, Islam's median percentage among the world's nations was only 6%[11]—indicating a much lower overall international penetration score. Although Hinduism claimed 1.2 billion adherents, its internationality median score was only 0.07%, a far cry from the outstanding accomplishment of the Christian faith. Provided a two-thousand-year test period, in the end Jesus Christ was a thousand times more successful at crossing ethnic borders than the promulgators of Hinduism.

Those with a passion for Christ and His kingdom must now more than ever consider this international aspect of the church. As the church in Macedonia was concerned for the Jerusalem church during a time of material famine, so the church in Uganda should be equally concerned about the church in London during this period of spiritual famine. Whether by prayer or other forms of ministry, churches from every nation must care for the worldwide body of Christ.

Meanwhile, the remnant in the West who have survived the onslaught of a destructive materialist ideology are better equipped to defend the church in Africa and Asia from the same destructive influences. The post-Christian Western nations have been eager to export their toxic ideas via media, Hollywood, financial institutions, international government agencies, family planning agencies, and educational institutions. That proud, man-centered, materialist juggernaut hammered away for at least 200 years on the forty-foot-deep Christian foundations laid down in the West. Most of the communist dictators in South America, Africa, and Asia, were trained in Western universities. The same agents worked their destructive agendas on the socio-economies of Japan and South Korea, but at a much quicker pace. Asian nations more readily adopted the earth-worshipping ideology of modern environmentalism and the destructive sciences of conception control and the electronic universe. Japan was one of the first nations to incorporate the vision of Margaret Sanger and Herbert Spencer into its social structures. As early as the 1950s, the Asian nation was killing over half its children by modern techniques—producing the most aggressive population implosion in the world by 2020.

At the Fall of the West, the remainder of the world had been fairly well "evangelized" in the secular humanist worldview. Nations throughout Asia, Africa, and South America had incorporated into their schools and universities the same destructive ideas which had corrupted the West.

Those Christians who have weathered the storm in the West were now obligated to equip their fellow believers to wage the same worldview war. It was time for Christians in the West to bring a reformation of the Christian worldview and Christian education to the whole world. The Scriptures had been translated into 704 languages—96.7% of the world's population had access to the Scriptures in their native languages.[12] The world had been reached with a basic gospel message. But, the problem now was that the whole world was consumed with the ideologies and media which destroyed Western society. Second and Third World nations had embraced the mistaken impression that this materialistic, post-Christian worldview is what brought the blessings of economic prosperity to the West. Just the opposite was the case, as has been argued in this book. Many of these nations had been drawn to the West and Western education because of the material prosperity and scientific know-how with which God had blessed the Christian nations of the United States and the United Kingdom in earlier years.

The time had come to bring a full-orbed Christian worldview and discipleship to the whole world—to be brought by those Western Christians who had faithfully engaged the war of ideas, especially in the field of education. This faithful remnant would be cultivated by a true renewal of the mind, a God-given repentance, and faithful discipleship in the Law, the Gospels, the Proverbs, the Psalms, and all of the Word of God.

MORE DIASPORA

As for Saul, he made havock of the church, entering into every house, and haling men and women committed them to prison. Therefore they that were scattered abroad went every where preaching the word. (Acts 8:3-4)

Because the Lord Jesus Christ is ruling over all things for the church (Eph. 1:22), we can be sure every persecution and diaspora (or dispersion/exile of believers) has greatly benefited the mission— the discipleship of the nations for Him. The major diasporas that had contributed much to the overall health of the worldwide church through the centuries include the persecution in Jerusalem (at the beginning), the Protestant exile into North America (Pilgrims, Puritans, Huguenots, and Scottish Covenanters), and the more recent Korean persecutions which resulted in a remarkable worldwide missionary work. When (not if) wars, economic cataclysm, anarchical riots, or persecutions come, this will bring about more diaspora for the health of the global church. The Lord never allows the church to become too comfortable and dormant, but He will always animate His people to the furtherance of the mission here, there, and around the world.

For now, the collection of an ethnic Christian population in a single location for the establishment of a Pilgrim-like commonwealth appears to be nothing more than a pipe dream. The first task will be the long-term restoration of healthy Christian families, faithful family discipleship, functional family economies, and a healthy Christian church fully engaged in faithful preaching, evangelism, and discipleship.

GOSPEL OPPORTUNITIES COME
BY THE HUMBLING OF THE NATIONS

Above all else, the collapse of Western civilization, or the "shaking of heaven and earth once more," would benefit the church and its gospel outreach. One thing is certain, there is never much hope for a proud audience. No person and no nation will ever receive the gospel without a serious humbling of one kind or another. John Bunyan's pilgrim pathway is entered through the wicket gate, and travelers must stoop down very low to enter it.

When nations are brought to repentance and the church to a thorough-going reformation, God will find a way to first bring His humbling judgments upon them.

Humbled cities cease their pride events. All 300 "gay pride" parades were canceled worldwide in 2020. When half of Siena was wiped out by the Bubonic Plague in 1357, the city council smashed the nude Venus to pieces. Before Martin Luther and Jan Hus entered the scene, John Wycliff appeared as the "prophet" crying in the wilderness. God's severe judgment came upon the world just before Wycliff's reformation commenced. The Black Death of 1347 left a very deep, somber temper in Europe and upon the young graduate from Merton College, Oxford. Historian Robert Vaughn comments that Wycliffe came through it with "very gloomy views in regard to the condition and prospects of the human race."[13] In utter shock and humble reverence for the God who would bring such judgment upon the earth, Wycliff penned his first treatise in 1356—headlined with the foreboding title: *The Last Age of the Church*. Such crushing humility gives birth to the fear of God and faith, followed quickly by courage to reform in the face of the most formidable opposition on earth. First comes the shaking, and a complacent, proud world utterly consumed in man-centered prideful institutions is turned on its head. Then the reformer is born, humbled, sobered, and made willing to risk his life—at one point standing virtually alone against all the powers of the civilized world, the powers both of state and church. And then—reformation.

For gospel progress man must always first lose faith in man and the other false gods of the heathen. Surely, modern man perceived himself to have arrived at the apex of faith in himself (especially regarding his science, economy, and government). Never was man more proud of himself, at least for those who would not acknowledge the source of the scientific advancements produced by Christians between the 16th and 20th centuries. Those who praise Darwin and Rousseau but would never thank the God of Maxwell, Faraday, Newton, Boyle, and Cyrus McCormick would attribute everything to man and nothing to God.

Invariably, pride and decadence accompany times of prosperity for all human society. Throughout history, these conditions marked the precursor to the breakdown of an occasional city-state like Sodom or Tyre and Sidon, but this time it would be a worldwide collapse.

Coming back to the study on average income for workers from AD 1300 to AD 2000 (contained in chapter 10), significant prosperity did not come until the 20th Century. For almost 500 years (or, more accurately, 5,800 years), the average household income remained fairly constant. The average income doubled in the 19th Century, at which period the ideological seeds of man-centered humanism were planted. Then during the 20th Century, the average household income improved by a factor of ten. This was the century of Christian apostasy and the ascendance of the man-god. It was the century of high-volume manufacturing, computers, mass communication, globalization, conception control, abortion, big government tyranny, Hollywood, pop stars, godless schools, and homosexual "marriage." It was the Century in which man did not need God (or any and all of the transcendent gods) anymore. Modern man had finally achieved enough money and medical technology to escape into a pretend reality, and delay his death for a few more years.

> There they were in great fear where no fear was. For God has scattered the bones of them that encamp against you. (Psalm 53:5)

The total abandonment of the fear of God in every mainstream cultural, political, scientific, and educational institution was completed well before the Fall. Man-centered pride and flagrant, gross violation of God's law took hold in the 20th Century. Beginning with the Soviet Union in 1917, the campaign to mass produce abortion continued for a hundred years. Finally, the humanist vision was realized *in toto* on

March 18, 2020, when New Zealand became the last Western nation to officially legalize convenience abortion. Five days later, God shut down the world economy in tandem with the Covid-19 pandemic, and a worldwide depression followed. *And then there was great fear where there was no fear.*

Man must lose faith in man first if he will ever turn back to God. The false gods must disappoint first that true repentance and faith may follow. The gods of money, civil government, medical technology, pseudo-science, and economic manipulation must fall down in the house of Dagon before the presence of the true and living God.

When man comes to realize he cannot save himself, he cannot save his economy, and he certainly cannot save himself from death, then perhaps he will look to God and His Christ—the Resurrection and the Life.

HUMILITY

If my people, which are called by my name, shall humble themselves, and pray, and seek my face, and turn from their wicked ways, then will I hear from heaven, and will forgive their sin, and will heal their land. (2 Chronicles 7:14)

These words for the Old Testament may very well apply to the 21st Century Western church. During the years of decline, the tendency among many conservatives and Christians was to shift the blame for the ruin of civilization from themselves to just about everything else. Some conservatives blamed the immigrants or the Muslims. There were conspiracy-theorists who blamed the Jews. The temptation was always to point to symptoms instead of the root cause. Liberals blamed the slave owners and capitalists. Conservatives blamed the media and the universities. Republicans blamed Democrats, and vice versa—further dividing the nation in loud, angry disagreement, usually over secondary issues like immigration and quarantine laws. All were consumed in pride, unwilling to be humbled before God.

Not many realized the root problem was to be found in the breakdown of faith and the Christian church. Not many admitted to pride, especially as the American president promised to "Make America Great" again and again and used the words "pride" and "proud" with nauseating frequency in almost every speech. The other party was busy organizing "gay pride" marches in almost every major city in the world. Everybody was proud of something or other, and almost nobody was interested in humility before God or the fear of God.

While entire socio-economic systems collapsed, churches were advertising "awesome" praise and worship, hilarious comedy performances, and "Holy Grounds" coffee bars. During the final years in the decline of the West, the wider evangelical church found the beatitudes of Jesus a little odd: "Blessed are they that mourn. Blessed are the poor in spirit. Blessed are the meek." Such words hardly fit contemporary music with a hyped-up back beat. There wasn't much mourning in the churches, and even less comfort.

Every now and then, somebody came along who understood the problem. When G. K. Chesterton (together with other leading figures of the day), was asked by the *London Times,* "What is the problem with the world?," Chesterton's answer was simple:

Dear Editor:

I am

Sincerely yours, G. K. Chesterton

The root problem was not with the institutions, the university, the seminary, or the political state. The problem was first to be found in the heart of God's people called by His Name. It was to be found in the church with the individual Christian, with the Christian father or husband. Human pride and the lapse of faith first infected the pastors who would not preach the hard words—"what the Spirit says to the churches." Western Christians boasted "against the branches" (Rom.

1:18). Unbelief swept through the universities, the seminaries, and the churches, and the West refused to continue in God's goodness. So it was cut off.

Like the Jews of old, what the Western churches thought was faith turned out to be pride in a heritage. What they thought was conservatism was only an external adherence to mere cultural expressions of a core belief system which had been long abandoned.

It was a sad irony at this moment in history that Western Christians had nothing left of which they could be proud, even if pride was a virtue. Mainline denominations had embraced the perversions of Nero, who for millennia was regarded by both Christian and pagan historians as the arch villain of history. Evangelicals were increasingly ambivalent on gender roles and gender dysphoria (feminism, homosexuality, and transgenderism). Their denominations were consumed with division and debates on intersectionality, critical race theory, racial justice, and socialism—the very demonic confusion disrupting the rest of the world. Well did Isaiah prophecy of them: "From the sole of the foot even unto the head there is no soundness in it; but wounds, and bruises, and putrefying sores: they have not been closed, neither bound up, neither mollified with ointment" (Isa. 1:6). Arguably, the condition of Western Christianity in the 21st Century was worse than 1st Century Judaism at the fall of Jerusalem. Missionary contributions from the West throughout the 20th and 21st centuries were increasingly counter-productive to the kingdom of God. In short, the West had boasted against the branches too much. Apostasy gained serious ground after 1700. The British Empire was too proud. The Americans were too proud. And, generally, so were the churches.

By the 21st Century, whatever remnant was left to read these words would know the thing to do, certainly: humble themselves, repent, and do the first works.

REFORMATION OF CHURCH

For the time is come that judgment must begin at the house of God: and if it first begin at us, what shall the end be of them that obey not the gospel of God? (1 Peter 4:17)

If "post-Christian" is defined as a decline of Christian influence upon the wider culture and civil realm, then the term was fitting for the West at the turn of the 21st century. The church lost its saltiness, and for that reason it was the duty of the church to get it back. Before the evangelical church would set out to evangelize the world, or call the world to repentance, or disciple the world in the things Jesus had commanded, the church would have to consider itself first. It would be better to pause and consider what was wrong with the doctrine and practice of the church. The focus would have to shift to church reform because "judgment begins at the household of God." Considering once more Christ's warnings to the churches in John's Revelation, the message to Sardis was best applied to the mainline Western church (dead and dying), the Laodicean message to the evangelical church (lukewarm), and Ephesus best pictured the conservative Reformed churches (losing their first love).

Before reforming, however, the syncretized church would have to first give up faith in the world and "come out from among them and be separate." Whether it be those Christians enamored with the pre-Christian classical world, or those captured by the post-Christian apostate world, either way, a sharper antithesis between the world and Christ was in order. A clearer conception of the enemy's modus operandi and doctrine was needed, to better discern how man-centered thinking had infiltrated the church. The reformed church would need to return to the *semper-reformanda* (always-reforming) agenda. The proud, fractured church would need to repent, return to humility and unity on the essentials, and put an end to endemic denominationalism. The faithless church would have to repent of externalism, emotionalism, superficial experientialism, antinomianism, watered-down evangelism, prayerlessness, defeatism, escapism, fear of the enemy, fear of the future, fear of circumstances, or fear of physical harm. Wherever there was reliance on the man, church music, and methodology, there would need to be a return to faith in the power of God and a return to simple, faithful preaching of the hard message and the good message.

The consumeristic, programmed church would have to return to long term, relationship-based discipleship and the preaching of the Word. The hard hearts of men would need softening, to receive the Word, meditate upon it, and work it out in daily life. Families would have to remove their children from humanistic indoctrination centers, and insist upon a Christian discipleship for their children, in the nurture of the Lord Jesus Christ. Churches and congregants would have to give up on humanist psychology and humanist psychological categories, and return to receiving the Word preached, one-on-one exhortation, and submission to one another in the fear of God. The anonymous mega-church, or whatever it was, would have to institute church membership and bring church discipline on those persisting in unrepentant sexual sin, illegitimate divorce, divisiveness, and other egregious sin.

Where Christians were once entertained by "Christian comedy" while the world went to hell, and reduced their confessions to glib cliches and shallow choruses, there would have to be a return to heart-deep sobriety, a fear of God, predominant psalm singing, and a life of repentance.

Where an artificial bifurcation of mind and heart, the spiritual and the secular, sacred knowledge and the knowledge built up on human reason, persisted, these Christians would see the hypocrisy of such commitments, and repent. Love for God must be thorough-going.

Where the Holy Spirit was grieved, quenched, and absented, repentance was due—especially where preaching/prophesying was despised, and the body life was molested by unloving gossip, slander, evil thoughts, quarrelsomeness, and divisiveness. Where generational apostasy prevailed, churches might enter the upper room again, and cry out for another outpouring of the Holy Spirit, that once more their sons and daughters would "prophesy" (speak the Word of God) and the hearts of the children would turn to the parents and parents to the children. Faithful pastors would reject any dilution of the law of God, of the message concerning sin, the gospel (Christ saving us from that sin), and the holiness of God. Loving the world and hating one's brother would have to be replaced by a repudiation of the world's ideas and a true love for the brethren. This rule would form the basis for a healthy ecumenicity. And where the church ceased to be an evangelistic light to the community, the people of God would call out for Holy Spirit filling and bold witnessing in the face of rejection and imminent persecution.

TRUE ECUMENICITY

I therefore, the prisoner of the Lord, beseech you that ye walk worthy of the vocation wherewith ye are called, with all lowliness and meekness, with longsuffering, forbearing one another in love; endeavouring to keep the unity of the Spirit in the bond of peace. There is one body, and one Spirit, even as ye are called in one hope of your calling; one Lord, one faith, one baptism, one God and Father of all, who is above all, and through all, and in you all. (Ephesians 4:1-6)

Another shameful aspect of the Christian apostasy of the 19th and 20th Centuries was the fragmentation and denominationalism of the church. Too much was rooted in pride, exclusivism, competition, the inability to distinguish between gnats and camels, and other fleshly elements. However, the international character of the Christian church and the huge increase in indigenous missions has shifted the entire question away from the cultural, the traditional, the denominational, and the focus on externals.

The unity of the church was always a concern, but especially so during the decline and fall of the West, and persecutions that accompany. Here was another opportunity to repent and go back and do the first works. This is the primary heart cry in Christ's prayer contained in John 17—"...that they may be one as We are one."

Wrong-headed forms of unity came about by the World Council of Churches and other initiatives in the 20th Century. The association of apostates did little to identify the true church and nurture real unity. To unite around opposition to God and His law, and His Anointed, is a false unity. Unity by extinguishing important epistemological, metaphysical, and ethical differences between the world's system and Christ would only mix more sheep and goats. Some evangelicals attempted unity around meaningless, nice-sounding words, which only introduced more confusion into the picture.

But true unity in the church is much less organizational and liturgical than it is ideological. The unity centers around the faith and the Object of this faith—one Lord, one Sovereign God and Father, and one Gospel. The unity must also form around united opposition against *fundamental* worldly thinking—man-centered ideologies.

Yet, the enemy had obfuscated the fundamental truths. By the end, the true church could hardly be identified by denominational labels. The aged creeds and confessions were helpful and necessary, but hardly addressed the antithesis which had corrupted the church for 300 years, since the Enlightenment.

Would the churches ever find a simple statement to further preserve the integrity of the body across denominations and national boundaries? Could such a statement be fundamental enough to nurture a unity, preserve substantial truth, and equip God's people against the antithesis? Would an ecumenical council agree on such basic statements as:

1. God is sovereign. Of God and through God are all things. (Rom. 11:36)

2. Salvation is of the Lord. God saves us. We do not save ourselves, and human powers and governments cannot save us. (Jon. 2:9)

3. God, not man, is the source of truth and ethics. God's Word is absolutely trustworthy, and man's word is not. Homosexual inclinations and actions are sin, because God says they are sin. (Isa. 8:19-20)

4. Sin is the transgression or opposition to God's law in thought, word, and deed. God's law determines right and wrong—not manmade paradigms such as Marxism, feminism, social justice, critical race theory, or any other manmade categorical system of ethical thought. (1 John 3:4)

5. Jesus Christ came to save us from our sins. He died on the cross and rose again from the dead and sits on the right hand of God the Father. (1 Cor. 15:20-28)

REPENTING OF ISOLATION & CHARACTERISTICALLY SHALLOW & SHORT-TERM RELATIONSHIPS

By this shall all men know that ye are my disciples, if ye have love one to another. (John 13:35)

If the church means anything in the post-Christian age, that is characterized by a brutal isolation, the body of Christ on earth must demonstrate the deepest love and commitment to one another, unlike anything the world has ever seen. By this mainly the world will know that these are Christ's followers. While the post-Christian church wanted to be identified more by missionary support, short-term ineffective mission trips, charitable work in the community, orphanages on foreign fields, and putting a dent in the sex slave trade, this was far from the focal point the Lord gave to His people. Mainly, Jesus wants

His people to forgive their brothers, do good to the household of God, wean their widows off the state, and maintain deep and meaningful long-term, edifying relationships in the local body. In an age addicted to isolation—texting, earbuds, web surfing, social media, and computer games—Jesus presents a different life of relationship and 1 Corinthians 13 agape love in the context of the local community. The true church and real believers are always called back to this life. Consequently, the post-modern wasteland of short-term relationships made up of incessant church hopping, megachurch involvement, *short-term* small groups, and the consumer church mentality could never sustain. The remnant church would have to emulate the early church, by a steadfast continuance in the Apostle's doctrine and *fellowship*.

WHAT SHALL WE THEN DO?

Francis Schaeffer's famous book issued in 1976 entitled *How Shall We Then Live?* left his readers with the same question. After chronicling the decline and suggesting a rather dystopian trajectory for Western culture, Schaeffer failed to answer the question for evangelicals who were hoping for an agenda of sorts. The question Schaeffer posed is still vital, and the answer even more so.

The obvious answer to the question comes in the Lord's last words to His disciples before His ascension: "Disciple the nations…teaching them to observe whatsoever I have commanded you" (Matt. 28:19-20). What then would He say now? Surely, Christ would keep to His original orders. He would say, "Nations will come and go, empires will rise and fall, but you, stay on task."

Only the discipleship of the nations could ever salvage and rebuild community, family, education, cultural sanity, economies, and civilization out of the multicultural chaos, tribalism, loss of character, irrational thinking, tyranny, and moral anarchy left in the ashes of Western civilization.

After monitoring fifty years of the decline of Western Christianity,

George Gallup Jr. addressed the Gordon-Conwell Theological Seminary in 2004, challenging future church leaders to the hard work of discipleship:

> Someone has to challenge people to be true disciples of Christ. Someone has to ask the hard questions. If we don't talk about the whole dimension of sin, repentance, grace and forgiveness, what is the faith all about? What are we doing?…Without true discipleship, the church can simply turn into a social services agency.[14]

In his book *The Death of Western Christianity*, Patrick Sookhdeo points to a dearth of Scripture as a fundamental cause of the Fall. The 20-minute pep talk following the "praise and worship" experience wasn't going to cut it anymore. The Sunday evening service was canceled a long time ago. One denomination discovered a fall off of Sunday evening service among their churches from 56% to 24% over a 15-year period (1992-2007).[15] Where the early church gathered for hearing the Apostles' doctrine on a daily basis, this practice all but disappeared in Western churches.

> Behold the days come, saith the Lord GOD, that I will send a famine in the land, not a famine of bread, nor a thirst for water, but of hearing the words of the LORD: and they shall wander from sea to sea and from the north even to the east, they shall run to and fro to seek the word of the LORD, and shall not find it. In that day shall the fair virgins and young men faint for thirst. (Amos 8:11-13)

KEEPING THE COMMANDMENTS OF GOD

> …teaching them to observe all things whatsoever I have commanded you. (Matthew 28:20)

Another crucial point not to be missed was Christ's injunction to teach the commandments of God. The very word "commandment" or "law" was almost universally taken as repulsive to the evangelical church or what some called the "Gospel-centered" church. However, those who were still true to the faith in the Book of Revelation were both "keeping the faith of Jesus Christ *and* keeping the commandments of God" (Rev. 14:12).

Thus, for any ostensibly reforming Christian movement, it would be well to look out for this. Are these voices reverting back to more discussions concerning natural law and humanist categories, and do they refuse that which is still in stone?

Apocalyptic cults and assorted zealots spoke loudly of their commitment to the commandments, but their focus migrated back to the externals—food laws, festivals, liturgies, and the like. At core, there was little to be found of loving God with heart, soul, mind, and strength. The Ten Commandments were largely missed, while the sepulchers were white-washed. With some, the bold proclamation of the Gospel was dismissed while the emphasis settled on the role of the civil government in executing those guilty of gross sin. Some "conservatives" dedicated ministries towards hating the deeds of the evolutionists and communists, but they were never lost in wonder, love, and praise in the worship of God and the appreciation of His works of creation and redemption. They did well with regulating Sabbath observance and tithing their mint, anise, and cumin, but missed the weightier matters of the law—justice, mercy, and faith (Matt. 23:23). The substance was lost in the mix.

True discipleship includes a unity of faith and repentance, Gospel and obedience, keeping and doing the commandments of God. Thus, discipleship is no mere academic concern. The university lecturer or Sunday School teacher may be content to spew out propositions and leave it there. But the discipler is vitally interested in follow through, obedience, and the faith and life of the disciple.

REFORMATION OF EDUCATION

The fear of the LORD is the beginning of knowledge: but fools despise wisdom and instruction. (Proverbs 1:7)

Following up on Luther, Tyndale, and Knox's complaints about the universities, the next Reformation would seek a more thorough-going reform in Christian epistemology and education. This would have to include a return to the "first works," before the cathedral schools and the universities removed the Scriptures as preeminent in the discipleship of each successive generation. Reforming efforts require one thing above all else—the Word of God must serve as "a frontlet" before the eyes of the people. This calls for a complete integration of Scripture into every subject and an absolute rejection of Aquinas' dualistic view of knowledge.

True reformers would study the divine teacher Himself and see very marked differences between the teaching method and content of Aristotle and that of Christ. They would review the *Didascalia Apostolorum*, the writings of Jerome, Augustine, Bede, Alcuin, and Comenius to carefully reconstruct this most critical element of modern life. Without radical reform in modern education at school and home, the next generation and the next would be lost. Returning to 19th-Century child-centered humanism would never do. Returning to 4th-Century Greek classical learning would only end in disaster. Returning to Aquinas and Lombard would only recapitulate the destructive pattern in the Western experience.

What would the remnant do upon the collapse of an entire civilization and a world economy? Faced with a cataclysm of unprecedented proportions, anyone with a modicum of wisdom would seek the wisdom of God contained in the Book of Proverbs and throughout the Word. Only God's wisdom will do for the inculcation of knowledge, wisdom, and understanding for a young man or young woman (Prov. 1:1-7). An entire curriculum centered on this Word would be the obvious go-to source for every Christian family. The Christian reformer would set a higher priority on this Word than upon math and grammar. The schools which refused to put God's wisdom at the core of their curriculum should be rejected out of hand by any thoughtful person, especially during the fall of a civilization.

A reformation of education demands there be no more hard and fast separation between education and discipleship, as if these were two distinct activities. Henceforth, no Christian should refer to himself as a Latin or math teacher. All teachers are called to disciple in faith and life, and Latin and math provide the context for these lessons. This separation of heart and head, knowledge and life, Sunday and Monday, or worship and education can no longer be countenanced in the Christian mind.

The Scriptures must remain preeminent now in the school—as a frontlet before the eyes of our children. The pagan classics must be dispensed with, and first priority given to the Christian writings of the church fathers, the reformers, and those who were saved out of paganism (not those returning to paganism).

For a hundred years, secularists convinced Christians that education could remain in an area of neutrality as long as the progressives were in charge of it. All that knowledge built up on human reason was supposed to be neutral facts, interpreted and presented in an entirely unbiased and neutral fashion. Over the years, increasing numbers of Christians began to sense they had been hoodwinked. Was this comprehensive sex education neutral? Was the 1619 Project a neutral assessment of facts, completely independent of any preconceived presuppositional framework, ethical, metaphysical, or otherwise? Could all this evidence of transitional forms from Piltdown Man to Lucy and the Neanderthal, presented to us with all the dogma of a cult leader, be just neutral facts after all? Christians could sense the wool flapping against their eyes.

Once and for all, Christian churches and parents would have to settle the matter that education is not neutral, and no child from a Christian home should be set at the feet of teachers who hold to a wrong worldview in the science or history class. It was a hard lesson learned over a hundred million apostasies for two centuries.

THE FAILURE OF CONSERVATISM

> And unto the angel of the church in Sardis write; These things saith he that hath the seven Spirits of God, and the seven stars; I know thy works, that thou hast a name that thou livest, and art dead. Be watchful, and strengthen the things which remain, that are ready to die: for I have not found thy works perfect before God. Remember therefore how thou hast received and heard, and hold fast, and repent. If therefore thou shalt not watch, I will come on thee as a thief, and thou shalt not know what hour I will come upon thee. (Revelation 3:1-3)

A comprehensive survey of the contributors and causes of the Fall of the West leaves us with another key lesson. Attempts to reform by conservatism failed repeatedly. If abortion was an essential moral element of the Fall, President Ronald Reagan provided two good US Supreme Court justices and two bad ones. George H. W. Bush provided one good justice and one bad. George W. Bush also nominated one good justice and one bad. Highly symbolic of the rottenness at the core, conservative hero, Governor Ronald Reagan, introduced the first abortion law to America in 1967 and the first convenience divorce law in 1969. Without the political and financial support of the Bush dynasty—Senator Prescott Bush, Congressman/President George H. W. Bush, and President George W. Bush—the largest abortion provider in America (Planned Parenthood) would never have turned into a multi-billion dollar behemoth. If there was one lesson to learn out of conservatism it was that lukewarm faith will always fail. Only a real fear of God and commitment to His law constitute true wisdom and bring genuine political reform (2 Sam. 23:1-4). Saul preserved the wrong king and the wrong sheep after his battle with the Amalekites, and he lost the kingdom for it. Attempts to conserve the wrong things or to give up principle by compromise always end in more failure.

At the Fall of the West, a cadre of Roman Catholic and Eastern Orthodox writers rushed in to explain how to save the West. Too often, the offered solution was a return to Rome or Constantinople—or, worse yet, Athens. They failed to realize that Rome and Istanbul were powerless to engage the humanist antithesis. Perhaps they missed the significance of the worldview conflicts...and the signs. God burned down Notre Dame Cathedral in 2019. In the fall of 2020, Pope Francis announced that "homosexuals have a right to a family," and encouraged the acceptance of homosexual relationships in the church. The word "Ichabod" appeared on the Eastern church as the Hagia Sophia was turned into a mosque on July 24, 2020.

Attempts to revive Homer in education (Augustine's "torrent from hell"),[16] or Aristotle (Luther's "devil incarnate"), have proven to be supremely counterproductive time and again since the days of Boethius and Aquinas. To repeat the error, hoping for different results meets the definition of insanity. A return to the pagans with their philosophies, pride, culture, and methodologies would yield nothing but more dismal failure, especially now at the end of the West.

One last desperate return to Aquinas with his philosophy "built up on human reason," after nearly 800 years of that destructive epistemology, could not possibly save the West. A return to the icons of the Eastern Church could not possibly salvage the Western Church. Why not prefer the ideas and teachings of the church fathers over their icons? Why not read the Christian classics rather than nurture some sentimental idealization of the authors? Only a return to Christ and the preaching of His true Gospel-Word would salvage anything in the ashes of Western civilization.

PRESERVING OR CONSERVING THE WRONG THINGS

Whether in the political or religious realm, conservatives were too superficial—more interested in conserving the icons and the external cultural carcass of bygone Christian movements. The conservatives failed to find any solid roots in core Christian principle, biblical theology, true Christian faith and character, the life of self-denial and care for the poor, and the right trajectory of thought with Augustine or Basil. Instead, the fixation was on the turn of a phrase, the beauty of linguistic construct, and the last few pagan excretions these Christian converts were shaking off. They were more interested in Basil's support for the classics than his sister's warnings and his later record of serving the poor. The thesis-antithesis of Christian thought versus pagan thought was largely ignored. Only the points of syncretism were retained. Precious little interest remained in the devotional thought, deep piety, profound faith, and love for God expressed in the writings of the old saints—Augustine, Athanasius, à Kempis, and Anselm. A stultifying, academic aloofness was all that was left in the study.

On his visit to Athens, the Apostle Paul wasn't out to survey the idolatry of the city with an aesthetic admiration for the fine workmanship and artistry demonstrated in the statuary. He wasn't interested in purchasing a souvenir for display in his study. Plainly, these were idols to be cast down, and Paul's spirit was deeply grieved at the spiritual bankruptcy and epistemological blindness of the city. He quoted a pagan poet, not to find common ground in foundational worldviews but only to point out the internal inconsistencies and self-deception operating when the truth is suppressed in unrighteousness (Rom. 1:18).

At best, the conservatism of the Republican party, pagan classical education, and the return to icons and ancient liturgies was all too superficial—too little too late. At worst, it was more recapitulation to all that had produced the Fall of the West.

MONASTERIES OF THE NEW DARK AGE

In 1996, a cleric from the conservative Roman Catholic tradition, Father Joseph Fessio, referred to homeschooling families as the monasteries of the new dark age.[17] Over the next two decades, the homeschooling movement in America tripled in numbers. The proportion of homeschoolers dedicated to the Christian faith was shrinking, however, along with the rest of the population. A survey conducted in 2016 by Generations.org found that homeschooled graduates from Christian homes were almost three times less likely to abandon the faith compared to their counterparts raised in Christian homes who attended public and private schools. Given that committed Christians made up about half of the homeschool population (of 5 million), there was the potential for the sustenance of the remnant in the next generation. Yet a reformation in family life without a concomitant reformation in the church would yield little lasting fruit.

SEPARATISM & ISLANDS OF CULTURE

Be ye not unequally yoked together with unbelievers: for what fellowship hath righteousness with unrighteousness? and what communion hath light with darkness? And what concord hath Christ with Belial? or what part hath he that believeth with an infidel? And what agreement hath the temple of God with idols? for ye are the temple of the living God; as God hath said, I will dwell in them, and walk in them; and I will be their God, and they shall be my people. Wherefore come out from among them, and be ye separate, saith the Lord, and touch not the unclean thing; and I will receive you. And will be a Father unto you, and ye shall be my sons and daughters, saith the Lord Almighty. (2 Corinthians 6:14-18)

As Christianity took the minority position in Western society and other developed nations around the world as a cultural force, necessarily there came a shift in the Puritan-Separatist continuum. During the decline of Christian faith and life in the West, and the associated disintegration of cultural influence, Christian sects argued over the question of involvement in culture. Should Christians abandon the macro-culture entirely? Should they apply a different ethic, a natural law scheme (rather than biblical law) to political engagement? What followed was a rain of polemics and assorted movements among Christian groups advocating more or less Puritan-type efforts to impact politics and the macro-culture. Nevertheless, the failure of the church to disciple the nations and the decline of faith in the West rendered these questions fairly moot. The opportunities for cultural impact were fading fast.

The question of separation versus engaging the macro culture is never easily answered. Individual Christians choose various avenues in which to channel their influence and efforts. Generally, politics is one of the least effective ways to impact the wider culture. While most of these questions are strategic in nature and a matter of individual calling, Christians are still responsible for discipling the nations, avoiding ethical synthesis, and holding to the commandments of God as the standard for ethics in every case.

The question of involvement became increasingly difficult for Christians laboring in public institutions that were dedicated to undermining Christian culture, persecuting the faith, and opposing God's law at every point. Should Christians teach in the public schools where the fear of God is disallowed and the teachers are immediately dismissed if they bring the gospel of Christ to the students? Should Christians put more effort into stopping abortion-promoting politics or should they engage other approaches to dealing with the problem of child killing? Should Christians be more concerned with reforming Hollywood, or would they do better to work outside of Hollywood with their filmmaking? Should Christian political groups and government officials focus more resources on religious liberty issues or pro-life issues? Or, put another way, would Christians remain in a defensive political posture and generally avoid the offensive posture on matters like abortion or homosexuality? Or, put more bluntly, should Christians let the ungodly kill their children while doing everything they can to preserve their own? Would the Christian church take a strong stance against the use of abortifacients for its membership (to the point of excommunication)? Would Christians support personhood legislation requiring legal sanctions for those who knowingly use abortifacient contraceptive devices? This author has taken both stances, serving as a sponsor for a personhood amendment in Colorado and authoring a resolution for denominational opposition to the use of abortifacients. The former approach turned out to be somewhat more effective than the latter.

Millions of Christian families opted for homeschooling or private Christian schooling, which entailed abandonment of the public school to its further demise. However, from the perspective of "the Puritans," to remove the salt is to do more damage to the macro-culture. An appreciable portion of conservative Christianity moved towards this separatism—separating from the macro-culture in one of the most fundamental ways possible. It was a social reformation and a cultural reformation—a true separation from the mainland onto these "islands of culture," metaphorically speaking. As these islands developed, fewer genuine Christians were drawn towards secular universities, the military, and politics. As the entertainment and media culture became more self-consciously and consistently anti-Christian, the believers pulled out en masse. Not many would want to tip into joining an Amish sect, but the trend was certainly towards separation.

However, the separation of Christians became far less noticeable with the general chaos and decline accompanying the Fall of Western civilization. It wasn't as if the new separatists were wearing blue trousers and black hats and sporting the Amish beard. The purpose of this survey is not to dial in the right mix of Separatism and Puritanism but only to challenge Christians to consider the present historical context and make wise decisions concerning the use of their time and resources. This calls for heart-level honesty. Is the Christian public school teacher contributing mainly to the promotion of the wrong worldview and failing miserably at bringing the gospel and true Christian discipleship to the classroom? In aggregate, has the salt lost its saltiness? Has compromise and synthesis resulted from involvement in the world's systems? Does involvement in the public schools and all the peer group contact this entails really aid in bringing a child up in the teaching and admonition of the Lord? Or, are parents risking the millstone treatment for causing children to stumble upon the bad worldviews and bad peer groups?

Will Christians participate in the cultural corruption and then be swept up in the demise of the West? Or, will they "come out from among them and be separate?" Will the nations further degrade by the removal of salt and light? Will internet pornography and other nihilist, isolating forms employed by modern man go the way of the gladiatorial competitions? Will the church regain saltiness, and then salt the earth once more? Or will the Christian church reform itself, while producing little appreciable effect on the dying culture around her? It is at this point that one's eschatology might be used for interpreting present historical trends and set the agenda for the immediate future. Ultimately, it doesn't matter what the apocalyptic prophets say. No man knows the time or season. Man proposes, but God disposes.

> Then Peter opened his mouth, and said, Of a truth I perceive that God is no respecter of persons: but in every nation he that feareth him, and worketh righteousness, is accepted with him. The word which God sent unto the children of Israel, preaching peace by Jesus Christ: (he is Lord of all:)...(Acts 10:34-36)

In the meantime, the Christian will bring all to the feet of Jesus, Lord and King. All Christians must now engage in a full-orbed reformation and repentance as a way of life. This reformation must take place in education, science and technology, media, culture, family life, business, and church. Whether or not the reformation will be confined to cultural islands is in God's hands. In the meantime, we will be thankful for all the gardens planted and every plant germinating out of the ashes.

> And they that shall be of thee shall build the old waste places: thou shalt raise up the foundations of many generations; and thou shalt be called, The repairer of the breach, the restorer of paths to dwell in. (Isaiah 58:12)

NOTES

CHAPTER I—THE FALL

1   Source data taken from "Our World In Data." https://ourworldindata.org/economic-growth#all-charts-preview. Also, referenced Angus Maddison, Contours of the World Economy, 1–2030 AD.

2   "Country List Government Debt to GDP," Trading Economics, https://tradingeconomics.com/country-list/government-debt-to-gdp.

3   "Net lending/borrowing (also referred as overall balance) % of GDP," International Monetary Fund, https://www.imf.org/external/datamapper/GGXWDN_G01_GDP_PT@FM/ADVEC/FM_EMG/FM_LIDC.

4   Ibid. This represents the net resources that the total economy makes available to the rest of the world (if it is positive) or receives from the rest of the world (if it is negative). In other words, when the variable is positive (meaning that it shows a financing capacity), it should be called net lending (+); when it is negative (meaning that it shows a borrowing need), it should be called net borrowing (−).

5   "All Sectors; Debt Securities and Loans; Liability, Level / Gross Domestic Product," St. Louis Fed, https://fred.stlouisfed.org/graph/?g=WRM.

6   "Fertility rate, total (births per woman) - European Union," World Bank, https://data.worldbank.org/indicator/SP.DYN.TFRT.IN?locations=EU.

7   Volant Sabrina, Pison Gilles, and Héran François, "French fertility is the highest in Europe. Because of its immigrants?" Population & Societies, 2019/7 (No 568), https://www.cairn-int.info/article-E_POP-SOC_568_0001--french-fertility-is-the-highest-in.htm.

8   Andrew Kolodny, "The magnitude of America's opioid epidemic, in six charts," Quartz, November 6, 2017, https://qz.com/1112727/the-magnitude-of-americas-opioid-epidemic-in-six-charts/.

9   "DEA Statistics Show Explosive Rise in Children Taking Ritalin and Adderall," Drug Enquirer, April 4, 2018, https://www.drugenquirer.com/news/rise-childhood-adhd-medications.html.

10   Alexia Fernandez Campbell, "Why Are So Many Millennials Having Children Out of Wedlock?" The Atlantic, July 18, 2016, https://www.theatlantic.com/business/archive/2016/07/why-are-so-many-millennials-having-children-out-of-wedlock/491753/.

11   "Millennials: The Me Me Me Generation," Time, May 20, 2013, https://time.com/247/millennials-the-me-me-me-generation

12   "Distribution of suicide rates (per 100,000), by gender and age, 2000," World Health Organization, 2002, https://www.who.int/mental_health/prevention/suicide/suicidecharts/en/.

13   A. W. Geiger and Lauren Kent, "Number of women leaders around the world has grown, but they're still a small group," Pew Research Center, March 8, 2017, https://www.pewresearch.org/fact-tank/2017/03/08/women-leaders-around-the-world/.

14   Anna Brown, "Despite gains, women remain underrepresented among U.S. political and business leaders," Pew Research Center, March 20, 2017, https://www.pewresearch.org/fact-tank/2017/03/20/despite-gains-women-remain-underrepresented-among-u-s-political-and-business-leaders/.

15   Mitra Toossi and Teresa L. Morisi, "Women In The Workforce Before, During, And After The Great Recession," U.S. Bureau of Labor Statistics, July 2017, https://www.bls.gov/spotlight/2017/women-in-the-workforce-before-during-and-after-the-great-recession/pdf/women-in-the-workforce-before-during-and-after-the-great-recession.pdf.

16   David Brooks, "The Nuclear Family Was a Mistake," *The Atlantic*, March 2020, https://www.theatlantic.com/magazine/archive/2020/03/the-nuclear-family-was-a-mistake/605536/.

17   https://www.cfr.org/article/womens-power-index. https://www.imf.org/external/datamapper/NGDPD-PC@WEO/OEMDC/ADVEC/WEOWORLD/FRA/NOR/SWE/CHE/FIN/ZAF/USA/ISL/BRA/CHN/RUS/CRI/NIC/CZE/HUN

18   "Madden NFL 20," Electronic Arts, https://www.ea.com/games/madden-nfl/madden-nfl-20/compete.

19   "EA SPORTS Madden NFL 19 Bowl Breaks Record as Most-Watched Live Tournament in Madden History – Drini Crowned Madden NFL 19 Champion," Business Wire, May 3, 2019, https://apnews.com/Business%20Wire/18d79ef7b9cd4e9dbf7d0088c629093c.

20   Katherine Schaeffer, "Most U.S. teens who use cellphones do it to pass time, connect with others, learn new things," Pew Research Center, August 23, 2019, https://www.pewresearch.org/fact-tank/2019/08/23/most-u-s-teens-who-use-cellphones-do-it-to-pass-time-connect-with-others-learn-new-things/.

21   "Pornography Statistics," Covenant Eyes, https://www.covenanteyes.com/pornstats/.

22   Tom W. Smith, An Analysis of the Use of Public Opinion Data by the Attorney General's Commission on Pornography (University of Chicago, 1986), "Current Porn Statistics," The Road to Grace, https://www.roadtograce.net/current-porn-statistics/.

23   http://www.wiu.edu/cas/history/wihr/pdfs/Spring%202019%20Runquist%20final%20draft.pdf https://news.gallup.com/poll/389792/lgbt-identification-ticks-up.aspx

24   Robin Gelburd, "STDs on the Rise: The Evidence of Insurance Claims," U.S. News & World Report, February 11, 2020, https://www.usnews.com/news/healthiest-communities/articles/2020-02-11/stds-on-the-rise-the-evidence-of-insurance-claims.

25   "Incidence, Prevalence, and Cost of Sexually Transmitted Infections in the United States," CDC Fact Sheet, https://www.cdc.gov/std/stats/sti-estimates-fact-sheet-feb-2013.pdf.

26   "Global HIV & AIDS statistics—2019 fact sheet," Joint United Nations Programme on HIV and AIDS, https://www.unaids.org/en/resources/fact-sheet.

27   "New Study Reveals Shocking Rates of Attempted Suicide Among Trans Adolescents," Human Rights Campaign, September 12, 2018, https://www.hrc.org/news/new-study-reveals-shocking-rates-of-attempted-suicide-among-trans-adolescen.

28   Cornelius Van Til, *Common Grace and the Gospel* (Phillipsburg, NJ: Presbyterian & Reformed, 1972), 82-83.

29   Joseph B. Stanford and Rafael Mikolajcyzk, "Mechanisms of action of intrauterine devices: Update and estimation of postfertilization effects," American Journal of Obstetrics and Gynecology, January 2003, https://www.researchgate.net/publication/10974531_Mechanisms_of_action_of_intrauterine_devices_Update_and_estimation_of_postfertilization_effects.

30   "Religion and Family Planning Tables," Guttmacher Institute, https://www.guttmacher.org/religion-and-family-planning-tables.

31   "Poll shows a dramatic generational divide in white evangelical attitudes on gay marriage," The Washington Post, June 27, 2017, https://www.washingtonpost.com/news/acts-of-faith/wp/2017/06/27/there-is-now-a-dramatic-generational-divide-over-white-evangelical-attitudes-on-gay-marriage/.

32   The PCA subsequently pulled out of the NAE in June 2022.

33   George Orwell, "Notes on the Way," in *Time and Tide* (London, 1940).

34   C. S. Lewis, *The Abolition of Man* (New York: Harper Collins, 1974), 18.

35   A. A. Hodge, *Popular Lectures on Theological Themes* (Philadelphia: Presbyterian Board of Publication, 1887), 283-84.

36   Charles H. Spurgeon, "Israel and Britain. A Note of Warning" (sermon preached June 7, 1885)

37   Ibid.

38   Ibid.

39   J. Gresham Machen, *Christianity and Liberalism* (New York: Macmillan, 1923), 14.

40   J. Gresham Machen, *Education, Christianity and the State* (Jefferson, MD: The Trinity Foundation, 1987), 136.

41   Ibid., 138.

42   Ibid, 141.

43   Gordon Clark, *A Christian Philosophy of Education* (Unicoi, TN: The Trinity Foundation, 2000), 138.

44   Letter to Reinhold Niebuhr, June, 1939.

45   Dietrich Bonhoeffer, Letters and Papers, DBWE 8:362.

46   Ibid.

47   https://billygraham.org/story/billy-graham-my-heart-aches-for-america/

48   Peter Marshall, *Trial by Fire*, March 11, 1944.

49   Francis Schaeffer, *The Complete Works of Francis A. Schaeffer: A Christian Worldview* (Wheaton, IL: Crossway, 1984), 4:310.

50   Ibid., 4:314.

51   Ibid., 4:319.

52   Ibid., 4:211.

53   Ibid., 5:423.

54   Ibid., 5:401.

55   Ibid., 1:235.

56   Ibid., 1:318.

57   R.J. Rushdoony, *The One and the Many* (Fairfax, VA: Thoburn Press, 1978), 370.

58   Ibid., 374.

59   R. J. Rushdoony, *To Be as God: A Study of Modern Thought Since the Marquis de Sade* (Vallecito, CA: Ross House, 2003), 150.

60   Jacques Ellul, *The New Demons* (New York: Seabury, 1975), 23.

61   Ibid., 28.

62   Jacques Ellul, *The Technological Bluff* (Grand Rapids: Eerdmans, 1990), 412.

63   Malcolm Muggeridge, *The End of Christendom* (Grand Rapids, 1980), 56.

64   Eugene Rose, *Nihilism: The Root of the Revolution of the Modern Age* (Platina, CA: St. Herman of Alaska Brotherhood, 2001).

65   "Acceptance Address by Mr. Aleksandr Solzhenitsyn," Templeton Prize, May 10, 1983, https://www.templetonprize.org/laureate-sub/solzhenitsyn-acceptance-speech/.

66   Ibid.

67   Aleksandr Solzhenitsyn, "A World Split Apart," The Aleksandr Solzhenitsyn Center, June 8, 1978, https://www.solzhenitsyncenter.org/a-world-split-apart.

68   Ibid.

69   G. K. Chesterton, *Heretics* (New York: John Lane Company, 1905), 107.

70   *The Quotable Chesterton*, ed. Kevin Belmonte (Nashville: Thomas Nelson, 2011), 174.

71   Ibid., 174.

72   Ibid., 172.

73   Paul Johnson, *Intellectuals* (Harper and Rowe, 1988), 342.

74   Benjamin Wiker, *10 Books That Screwed Up the World And 5 Others That Didn't Help* (Regnery, 2008), 227.

75   Gary Wilkerson, *David Wilkerson: The Cross and the Switchblade, and the Man Who Believed* (Grand Rapids: Zondervan, 2014).

76   David Wilkerson, *The Vision* (Old Tappan, NJ: Pyramid Publications for Fleming H. Revell Company, 1974), 27.

77   David Wilkerson, "The Self Destruction of America," February 25, 1993. https://worldchallenge.org/newsletter/1993/the-self-destruction-of-america.

78   Leonard Ravenhill, *Why Revival Tarries* (Bloomington, MN: Bethany, 1959), 91.

79   Quoted in James Davison Hunter, *Culture Wars: The Struggle to Define America* (New York: Basic Books, 1991), 8.

80   T. S. Eliot, *The Waste Land* (1922).

81   T. S. Eliot, *The Definition of Culture* (1948).

82   Rudyard Kipling, *The Gods of the Copybook Headings* (1919), http://www.kiplingsociety.co.uk/poems_copybook.htm.

83   Rudyard Kipling, *The Storm Cone* (1932), http://www.kiplingsociety.co.uk/poems_stormcone.htm.

84 "American Pie," Songfacts, https://www.songfacts.com/facts/don-mclean/american-pie.

85 Ibid.

86 Melissa Roberto, "'American Pie' singer Don McLean says music no longer exists because of 'nihilistic society,'" Fox News, April 11, 2020, https://www.foxnews.com/entertainment/american-pie-singer-don-mclean-music-no-longer-exists-nihilistic-society.

87 Merle Haggard, *Are the Good Times Really Over?* (1981)

88 Pat Buchanan, *The Death of the West* (New York: St. Martin's Press, 2001), 6.

89 Ibid, 34.

90 Friedrich Hayek, Letter to Editor, *The Times* (4 April 1981), 13.

91 Friedrich Hayek, *The Road to Serfdom* (Chicago: University of Chicago Press, 1944), Introduction.

92 https://www.lewrockwell.com/2020/11/paul-craig-roberts/the-west-has-thrown-itself-into-the-waste-basket-of-history/

93 https://www.businessinsider.com/david-stockman-america-is-doomed-2013-3

94 https://internationalman.com/articles/david-stockman-on-the-coming-financial-panic-and-the-2020-election/

95 Ibid.

96 Dr. Martyn Lloyd-Jones, "When God Turns Away," https://www.mljtrust.org/sermons-online/acts-7-42-43/when-god-turns-away/.

97 Dr. Martyn Lloyd-Jones, "Why Do the Heathen Rage?" https://www.mljtrust.org/sermons-online/psalms-2-1-12/why-do-the-heathen-rage/.

98 Ibid.

99 Neil Postman, *Amusing Ourselves to Death* (New York: Penguin, 1986), 155-156.

100 Herbert Schlossberg, *Idols for Destruction* (Wheaton, IL: Crossway, 1990), 295.

101 Ibid., 297.

102 Joel Belz, "Mistimed Message: But my warning about peace and prosperity, I think, still holds," *World Magazine*, December 9, 2017.

CHAPTER II—THE RISE & FALL OF THE CHRISTIAN ETHOS

1 Francis Schaeffer, *How Should We Then Live?* (Nashville: Lifeway, 2005), 21

2 Augustine, *City of God, in Nicene and Post-Nicene Fathers, Volume 2*, ed. Phillip Schaff, Alexander Roberts, James Donaldson, et. al. (Peabody, MA: Hendrickson, 1996), 395.

3 Eusebius, *Vita Constantini*, 2.45.

4 Athanasius, *On the Incarnation,* 8.55.

5 Quoted in J. N. D. Kelly, *Early Christian Doctrines* (Peabody, MA: Prince Press, 2003), 42.

6 John Chrysostom, *Homily,* Colossians 9.

7 Cornelius Van Til, *The Defense of the Faith* (Phillipsburg: Presbyterian & Reformed Publishing, 1955), 43.

8 The Council of Ephesus, Session I, https://www.newadvent.org/fathers/3810.htm.

9 *Martyrdom of Polycarp*, 14.

10 Clement of Rome, *1 Clement*, 27.110.

11 Justin Martyr, *Dialogue with Trypho*, 29.

12 Justin Martyr, *The First Apology of Justin*, 44.

13 Augustine, *City of God, in Nicene and Post-Nicene Fathers, Volume 2*, ed. Phillip Schaff, Alexander Roberts, James Donaldson, et. al. (Peabody: Hendrickson, 1996), 38.

14 Ibid., 82.

15 Augustine, *Confessions*, Book 4 (Outler translation).

16 Augustine, *City of God*, 5.1.

17 Augustine, "On the Predestination of the Saints," in *A Select Library of the Nicene and Post-Nicene Fathers* (NAPF), vol. 5, ed. Philip Schaff (Grand Rapids: Eerdmans, 1997), ch. 37, 516.

18 Anselm, *Anselm, of Canterbury: The Major Works* (Oxford: Oxford University Press, 1998), 450.

19 *Beowulf,* trans. Seamus Heaney, 11.3053-3057.

20   Ibid., 477-478.

21   Ibid., 977-978.

22   Ibid., 700-701.

23   Ibid., 1057-1058.

24   Quoted in Bede, *Ecclesiastical History of the English People*, 4.24.

25   Quoted in Douglas Jones and Douglas Wilson, *Angels in the Architecture* (Moscow, ID: Canon Press, 1998).

26   Bede, *The Age of Bede, Life of Cuthbert* (London: Penguin, 2004), 63.

27   Ibid., 57.

28   Rimbert, *Life of Anskar, the Apostle of the North*, Fordham University, https://sourcebooks.fordham.edu/basis/anskar.asp#lifeans.

29   Quoted in James Buchanan, *The Doctrine of Justification* (Edinburgh: Banner of Truth, 1997), 96-97.

30   William Langland, *Piers Plowman*, trans. J.F. Goodridge (London: Penguin Classics, 1966), 228-229.

31   *The Didache*, 1.3-4 (Kirsopp Lake translation).

32   Ibid., 2.

33   *Epistle of Polycarp to the Philippians*, 4.

34   Augustine, *On the Spirit and the Letter*, 36, https://www.newadvent.org/fathers/1502.htm.

35   John Chrysostom, Homily XXI, in *Nicene and Post-Nicene Fathers, Series 1*, ed. Phillip Schaff, Alexander Roberts, James Donaldson, et. al. (Peabody, MA: Hendrickson, 1996), 13:153-157.

36   "Anicius Manlius Severinus Boethius," Stanford Encyclopedia of Philosophy, revised July 19, 2016, https://plato.stanford.edu/entries/boethius/.

37   Eleanor Shipley Duckett, *Alcuin: Friend of Charlemagne, His World and His Work* (New York: Macmillan, 1951), 89.

38   Quoted in Ibid., 272.

39   Ibid., 103.

40   Ibid., 99.

41   Ibid., 111.

42   Mary Alberi, "'The Better Paths of Wisdom': Alcuin's Monastic 'True Philosophy' and the Worldly Court," *Speculum*, Vol. 76, No. 4 (2001), 898, JSTOR, www.jstor.org/stable/2903614.

43   Ibid., 899.

44   John Scottus Eriugena, *Treatise on Divine Predestination*, 3.3.

45   Paul Cavill, *Anglo-Saxon Christianity: Exploring the Earliest Roots of Christian Spirituality in England* (London: HarperCollins, 1999), 57.

46   Thomas Cahill, *How the Irish Saved Civilization* (New York: Doubleday, 1995), 158.

47   George Hardin Brown, *A Companion to Bede* (Suffolk: The Boydell Press, 2009), 20.

48   Anselm, *Proslogion*, ch. 1.

49   Bart D. Ehrman, *The Triumph of Christianity: How a Forbidden Religion Swept the World* (New York: Simon & Schuster).

50   "Great Writings, did you know?" *Christian History Magazine* #116, https://christianhistoryinstitute.org/magazine/article/did-you-know-great-writings/.

51   Thomas Aquinas, *Summa Theologica*, q. 1, a. 1, trans. Fathers of the English Dominican Province.

52   Thomas Aquinas, *Summa Theologica* (Allen, TX: Christian Classics, 1948), Ia q. 1 art. 2 ad. 1.

53   John M. Frame, *A History of Western Philosophy and Theology* (Phillipsburg, NJ: Presbyterian and Reformed Publishing, 2015), 146.

54   Ibid.

55   Nancy Pearcey, *Total Truth: Liberating Christianity from Its Cultural Captivity* (Wheaton, IL: Crossway, 2005), 80.

56   Philip Schaff, *History of the Christian Church*, 5:288.

57   Ibid.

58   Dante, *The Banquet*, 4.6.

59   Ibid.

60   Dante, *De Monarchia* II, xiii, 222.

61   *The Latin Works of Dante* (New York: Simon & Schuster, 2018), 4.

62   Dante, *The Divine Comedy: Paradiso*, Canto IV, lines 139-142.

63   Ibid., Canto XVIII, lines 14-15.

64   Dante, *The Divine Comedy: Purgatorio*, Canto XXX, line 39.

65   Ibid., Canto II, line 77ff.

66   Quoted in Gordon Rupp, P. Watson, *Luther and Erasmus: Free Will and Salvation* (Philadelphia: Westminster Press, 1969), 49.

67   Ibid., 68.

68   John Locke, *The Reasonableness of Christianity* (1695)

69   "Christian Wolff," Stanford University of Philosophy, revised September 30, 2019, https://plato.stanford.edu/entries/wolff-christian/.

70   Immanuel Kant, *Groundwork of the Metaphysic of Morals* (New York: Harper and Row, 1964), 116, 123.

71   Ibid., 16.

72   Kant, "The Science of Right," Introduction.

73   Norman Kemp Smith, translator, *Immanuel Kant's Critique of Pure Reason* (London: Macmillan, 1934), 16.

74   Königlichen Preußischen Akademie der Wissenschaften, ed., *Kants gesammelte Schriften* (Berlin: Georg Reimer, 1910), 6:72-73.

75   C.S. Lewis, *God in the Dock* (Grand Rapids: Eerdmans, 1970), 244.

76   "Hume on Religion," Stanford Encyclopedia of Philosophy, revised March 27, 2017, https://plato.stanford.edu/entries/hume-religion/.

77   Ralph Waldo Emerson, *Nature: An Essay*, Section 1.

78   John Dewey, *The Influence of Darwin on Philosophy* (New York: Henry Holt & Co., 1910), 1.

79   Charles Darwin, *The Descent of Man* (New York: D. Appleton & Co., 1971), 1:193.

80   Friederich Nietzsche, *Thus Spoke Zarthustra*, in *The Philosophy of Nietzsche* (New York: Modern Library, n.d.), 64.

81   Jean-Paul Sartre, *Existentialism and Human Emotions*, chapter 1.

82   Ibid.

83   Salvian the Presbyter, *The Governance of God*, 7.1

84   Andrew Sullivan, "The World Is Better Than Ever. Why Are We Miserable?" *New York Intelligencer*, March 9, 2018, https://nymag.com/intelligencer/2018/03/sullivan-things-are-better-than-ever-why-are-we-miserable.html.

85   Ibid.

CHAPTER III—THE RISE OF THE WESTERN CHURCH

1   Quoted in Rodney Stark, *The Triumph of Christianity: How the Jesus Movement Became the World's Largest Religion* (New York: Harper One, 2012), 198.

2   Bede, *Ecclesiastical History of the English People* (London: Penguin, 1990), 133.

3   Ibid., 134.

4   Ibid., 147.

5   Ibid., 175.

6   Ibid., 172.

7   Ibid., 194.

8   Ibid., 197.

9   Ibid., 209.

10   Ibid., 245.

11   Ibid., 284.

12   Ibid., 303.

13   Ibid., 341.

14   Ibid., 342.

15   Edward L. Smither, *Missionary Monks: An Introduction to the History and Theology of Missionary Monasticism* (Eugene, OR: Wipf and Stock, 2016), 109.

16   Eleanor Shipley Duckett, *Alcuin, Friend of Charlemagne: His World and his Work* (New York: Macmillan Company, 1951), 103.

17   Quoted in Augustus Neander, *Light in the Dark Places* (New York: Lane & Scott, 1851), 82.

18   Ibid.

19   Ibid.

20   Benedict, *Rule of Saint Benedict*, Prologue.

21   Benedict, *Rule*, Chapter 7.

22   Columba Stewart, *Prayer and Community: The Benedictine Tradition* (Maryknoll, NY: Orbis Books, 1998), 48.

23   Cahill, *How the Irish Saved Civilization*, 183.

24   Ibid., 39.

25   Patricia Wittberg, *The Rise and Decline of Catholic Religious Orders: A Social Movement Perspective* (Albany: State University of New York Press, 1994), 33.

26   "2018-2018 Annual Data Tables," The Association of Theological Schools, https://www.ats.edu/uploads/resources/institutional-data/annual-data-tables/2017-2018-annual-data-tables.pdf.

27   R. W. Southern, *Western Society and the Church in the Middle Ages* (London: Penguin, 1970), 254.

28   Philip Freeman, *St. Patrick of Ireland* (New York: Simon and Schuster, 2004), 62.

29   Quoted in Ibid., 177.

30   Quoted in Ibid., 186.

31   Quoted in Ibid., 189.

32   Quoted in Ibid., 192.

33   Quoted in Ibid.

34   Ibid., 179.

35   Quoted in Ibid., 170.

36   Ibid., 161-164.

37   Quoted in Schaff, *History of the Christian Church*, 4:24.

38   Freeman, 190.

39   Ceylan Yeginsu, "Legal Abortions Begin in Northern Ireland," *New York Times*, April 10, 2020, https://www.nytimes.com/2020/04/10/world/europe/northern-ireland-abortion-uk.html; "First same-sex marriage takes place in Northern Ireland," *The Guardian*, February 11, 2020, https://www.theguardian.com/uk-news/2020/feb/11/first-same-sex-marriage-northern-ireland-belfast-robyn-peoples-sharni-edwards.

40   Quoted in Freeman, *St. Patrick*, 160.

41   John V. Kelleher, "The *Táin* and the Annals," *Ériu* 22 (1971), 107-29, esp. 125-27; Kathleen Hughes, *The Church in Early Irish Society*, 161-66; Tomas O Fiaich, "The Church of Armagh Under Lay Control," *Seanchus Ard Mhacha* 5 (1969), 82-100. See also Donnchadh Ó Corráin, ed., *Irish Antiquity* (Cork, 1980), 314-17.

42   Paul Gallagher, "The Irish Monastery Movement," *The New Federalist*, March 1995, http://american_almanac.tripod.com/monks.htm.

43   Bede, *Ecclesiastical History*, 3.27.

44   W. L. Alexander, *Iona: The Druids Isle* (Nashville: Redford, 1875), 135-136.

45   Cahill, *How the Irish Saved Civilization*, 206-207.

46   Duncan McCallum, *The History of the Culdees* (Edinburgh: John Menzies, 1855), 99.

47   Jean Henri Merle d'Aubigné, *History of the Reformation of the Sixteenth Century* (New York: H.W. Hagemann, 1894), 5:35.

48   Quoted in John Brown, *The Exclusive Claims of Puseyite Episcopalians to the Christian Ministry Indefensible* (Philadelphia: Presbyterian Board of Publication, 1844), 252.

49   "Pope Adrian's Bull 'Laudabiliter' and Note upon It," in Eleanor Hull, *A History of Ireland and Her People*, https://www.libraryireland.com/HullHistory/Appendix1a.php#1.

50   Neander, *Light in the Dark Places*, 77.

51   Quoted in John Jamieson, *An Historical Account of the Ancient Culdees of Iona* (Edinburgh: John Ballantyne and Company, 1811), 226.

52   Quoted in Schaff, *History of the Christian Church*, 4:106.

53   "Donation of Constantine," *Catholic Encyclopedia*, https://www.catholic.com/encyclopedia/donation-of-constantine.

54   Schaff, *History of the Christian Church*, 4:130.

55   Ibid., 4:135.

56   Ibid., 4:136.

57   Quoted in Henry Chadwick, *The Early Church* (London: Penguin, 1967), 44.

58   Quoted in Bede, *Ecclesiastical History*, 121-122.

59 Ibid., 170.

60 Ibid.

61 Ibid., 137.

62 John Mason Neale, tr., *Mediaeval Hymns and Sequences* (London: Masters, 1867), 43.

63 Ibid., 43-45.

64 "100 best Christian books," Church Times, https://ct100books.hymnsam.co.uk/.

65 Jerry Newcombe, "Newsmax's 25 All-Time Greatest Christian Books," *Newsmax*, November 1, 2017, https://www.newsmax.com/bestlists/greatest-christian-books-list/2017/11/01/id/823347/.

66 Augustine, *On the Predestination of the Saints*, 7.

67 Augustine, *Enchiridion of Faith, Hope, and Love*, 102.

68 Eusebius, *Ecclesiastical History*, 5.16.7.

69 Quoted in Augustine, *On the Grace of Christ, and On Original Sin*, 1.26.

70 Schaff, *History of the Christian Church*, 4:212.

71 Ibid., 4:215.

72 *Didache*, 10.

73 Augustine, *Letters*, 98.9.

74 Schaff, *History of the Christian Church*, 4:240.

75 Ibid.

CHAPTER IV—THE DECLINE
OF THE MEDIEVAL CHURCH

1 "Against the Execrable Bull of the Antichrist," Martin Luther's Reply to the Papal Bull of Leo X, in Roland H. Bainton, *Here I Stand: A Life of Marting Luther* (Nashville: Abingdon Press, 1950), 162.

2 Martin Luther, *To the Christian Nobility of the German Nation Respecting the Reformation of the Christian Estate*. https://oll.libertyfund.org/titles/luther-first-principles-of-the-reformation-1883/simple#lf0224_head_012

3 Schaff, *History of the Christian Church*, Volume IV, 131.

4 Peter Damian, *The Book of Gomorrah: An Eleventh-Century Treatise Against Clerical Homosexual Practices*, trans. Pierre J. Payer (Ontario: Wilfrid Laurier University Press, 1982), chapter 1.

5 Ibid.

6 Ibid.

7 "First Lateran Council 1123 A.D." *Papal Encyclicals Online*, https://www.papalencyclicals.net/councils/ecum09.htm.

8 Quoted in Schaff, *History of the Christian Church*, 5:15.

9 Anselm, *Monologion*, 22.

10 *Abelard, Sic et Non.*

11 Quoted in Ruth Tucker, *Parade of Faith: A Biographical History of the Christian Church*, 167.

12 Peter Abelard, *Stanford Encyclopedia of Philosophy*, https://plato.stanford.edu/entries/abelard/.

13 Schaff, *History of the Christian Church*, 5:259.

14 Ibid.

15 Quoted in *Evangelical Dictionary of Theology*, ed. Walter Elwell (Grand Rapids: Baker Academic, 2011), 1296. Peter Lombard, *Sentences*, Book III, Dist. 26. John Calvin referred to such statements as "gross stupidity" in his *Institutes*, Book III, chapter 2, para. 43.

16 Lombard failed to distinguish between the freedom from compulsion and the freedom from a necessary cause, sovereignly ordained by God.

17 Lombard, *infra*, chapter iii. sec. 10, chap vii, sec. 9.

18 Lombard, *Sentences*, Book II, Dist. 21.

19 Quoted in Schaff, *History of the Christian Church*, 5:17.

20 Ibid.

21 Ibid., 5:78.

22 Ibid., 5:173.

23 Ibid., 5:79.

24 "The Canons of the Fourth Lateran Council, 1215," Medieval Sourcebook, Fordham University, https://sourcebooks.fordham.edu/basis/lateran4.asp.

25 Ibid.

26 Milan Loos, *Dualist Heresy in the Middle Ages* (Prague: Academia & Martinus Nijhoff, 1974), 50ff.

27 Ibid., 32ff.

28 Schaff, *History of the Christian Church,* Volume V, 202.

29 "Ad Extirpanda," https://www.documentacatholicaomnia.eu/01p/1252-05-15,_SS_Innocentius_IV._Bulla_'Ad_Extirpanda',_EN.pdf.

30 Quoted in W.A. Sibly and M.D. Sibly, trans., *The Chronicle of William of Puylaurens* (Woodbridge, UK: Boydell Press, 2003), 128.

31 Quoted in Jacques Madaule, *The Albigensian Crusade* (London: Burns and Oates, 1967), 159.

32 Ibid., 160.

33 Ibid., 95.

34 Quoted in Schaff, *History of the Christian Church,* Volume VI, 24.

35 Quoted in Ibid., 241-242.

36 Augustine, *City of God,* 21.13.

37 *The Correspondence of Pope Gregory VII, Selected Letters from the Registrum,* trans. Ephraim Emerton (New York: Columbia University Press, 1990), 148.

CHAPTER V—THE REFORMATION
OF THE WESTERN CHURCH

1 "Global Christianity – Christian Traditions," Pew Research Center, December 19, 2011, https://www.pewforum.org/2011/12/19/global-christianity-traditions/.

2 Quoted in https://www.hwalibrary.com/media/acthesis/PDF/Org_Plain_Truth_about_the_Waldensians_DCB.pdf

3 Ibid.

4 Ibid.

5 Ibid.

6 Ibid.

7 Kenneth A. Strand, "John Calvin and the Brethren of the Common Life," in *Andrews University Seminary Studies, Volume XIII, Number* 1 (Spring 1975), 67-78, https://digitalcommons.andrews.edu/cgi/viewcontent.cgi?article=1309&context=auss.

8 Quoted in Schaff, *History of the Christian Church,* 5:146.

9 William Langland, *Piers Plowman* (London: Penguin, 2006), 247.

10 Schaff, *History of the Christian Church,* 6:153.

11 Ibid., 6:324.

12 Thomas Fuller, *The Church History of Britain From the Birth of Jesus Christ Until the Year 1648,* Vol. 1 (London: Thomas Tegg, 1842).

13 Summarized in Schaff, *History of the Christian Church,* 6:156.

14 Quoted in "John Huss: Pre-Reformation Reformer," *Christianity Today,* https://www.christianitytoday.com/history/people/martyrs/john-huss.html.

15 Schaff, *History of the Christian Church,* 7:100.

16 John Foxe, *Actes and Monuments of These Latter and Perillous Dayes* (London: John Day, 1563), 570.

17 Martin Luther, *Of the Bondage of the Will,* trans. Henry Cole, section CLXVIII.

18 E. Gordon Rupp, P. Watson, *Luther And Erasmus: Free Will And Salvation* (Philadelphia: The Westminster Press, 1969), 68.

19 Luther, *Of the Bondage of the Will,* section IX.

20 Ibid., section XXIV.

21 Martin Luther, "Open Letter to the Christian Nobility of the German Nation Concerning the Reform of the Christian Estate (1520)," trans. C. M. Jacobs, https://web.stanford.edu/~jsabol/certainty/readings/Luther-ChristianNobility.pdf.

22 John Dillenberger, *Martin Luther: Selections from His Writings* (New York: Anchor Books, 1969), 403, 485.

23 Quoted in Schaff, *History of the Christian Church,* 8:192.

24 Ibid.

25 Quoted in Ibid., 195.

26 John Calvin, *The Necessity of Reforming the Church,* https://www.monergism.com/thethreshold/sdg/calvin_necessityreform.html.

27 Ibid.

28 Ibid.

29   Joel R. Beeke and Randall J. Pederson, *Meet the Puritans* (Grand Rapids: Reformation Heritage Books, 2007), xvii.

30   Ibid., 475.

CHAPTER VI—THE DIASPORA & FALL
OF THE WESTERN CHURCH

1   "Christianity in its Global Context, 1970–2020," *Gordon-Conwell Theological Seminary*, June 2013, https://archive.gordonconwell.edu/ockenga/research/documents/ChristianityinitsGlobalContext.pdf.

2   Mark A. Noll, *A History of Christianity in the United States and Canada* (Grand Rapids: Eerdmans), 47.

3   John Demos, *A Little Commonwealth: Family Life in Plymouth Colony* (New York: Oxford University Press, 2000), 13.

4   Noll, *History of Christianity*, 80.

5   James Deetz and Patricia Scott Deetz, *Times of Their Lives: Life, Love and Death in Plymouth Colony* (New York: Anchor Books, 2001), 146-148.

6   Rodney Stark, *The Triumph of Christianity* (New York: Harper Collins, 2011), 353.

7   "95 Percent Of Americans Had Premarital Sex," *Associated Press*, KLTV, December 20, 2006, https://www.kltv.com/story/5838784/95-percent-of-americans-had-premarital-sex/.

8   Michael G. Hall, *The Last American Puritan: The Life of Increase Mather, 1639-1723* (Wesleyan University Press, 1988), 284.

9   Ibid., 285.

10   Herbert Wallace Schneider, *The Puritan Mind* (Ann Arbor: University of Michigan Press, 1964), 101.

11   Thomas Prince, Sermon: "The People of New England Put in Mind of the Righteous Acts of the Lord to Them and Their Fathers, and Reasoned with Concerning Them"

12   Quoted in Perry Miller, *Errand into the Wilderness* (Harvard University Press, 1956), 175.

13   Ibid, 176.

14   Ibid, 182.

15   Charles Hodge, *The Constitutional History of the Presbyterian Church in the United States of America*, 2 vols. (Philadelphia: Presbyterian Board of Publication, 1851), 2:83.

16   Quoted in David McCullough, *John Adams* (New York: Simon and Schuster, 2001), 41.

17   Ibid, 46.

18   Ibid, 47.

19   Phillip Doddridge, *A Plain and Serious Address to the Master of the Family on the Important Subject of Family Religion* (Eben. Watson: London, 1777), 27.

20   Ibid.

21   Matthew Henry, "Sermon Concerning Family Religion" (Bible and Three Crowns: London, 1704), 19.

22   American Antiquarian Society, Oct. 1961, "The Autobiography of Increase Mather," 315.

23   Edmund Morgan, *The Puritan Family* (New York: Harper and Row, 1966), 185.

24   Jonathan Edwards, 1741, "The Importance of Revival Among Heads of Families"

25   Jonathan Edwards, 1750, "Farewell Sermon"

26   Ibid.

27   J.A. Alexander, *Family Worship* (1847), 1.

28   Ibid, 13.

29   Ibid, 250.

30   Ibid, 258.

31   W. H. Carslaw, D.D., *Exiles of the Covenant* (Paisley Alexander Gardner by Appointment to the late Queen Victoria, 1908), Chapter 1.

32   John Owen, *On the Nature and Causes of Apostasy*, To the Reader.

33   Ibid.

34   Ibid., chapter XIII.

35   John Goodwin, *Redemption Redeemed: Wherein the Most Glorious Work of the Redemption of the World by Jesus Christ* (London, 1651), 68-69.

36   Ibid., 51.

37   Ibid., 71.

38   "Cambridge Platonists," *Encyclopedia Britannica*, https://www.britannica.com/topic/Cambridge-Platonists.

39   Quoted in Hannah D'Anne Comodeca, "No 'Spoke in the Wheel': the German Evangelical Church and the Nazi State," (2014), 42-43, https://shareok.org/bitstream/handle/11244/14778/Comodeca_ok-state_0664M_13314.pdf?sequence=1.

40   "European court rules against German homeschooling family," *DW News*, https://www.dw.com/en/european-court-rules-against-german-homeschooling-family/a-47021333; "US grants homeschooling German family political asylum," *The Guardian*, January 27, 2010, https://www.theguardian.com/world/2010/jan/27/german-home-schooling-family-asylum.

41   "More than 220,000 people left the Protestant Church of Germany in 2018," *Evangelical Focus*, June 26, 2020, https://evangelicalfocus.com/europe/6752/germany.

42   James I. Packer, *Your Father Loves You* (Carol Stream, IL: Harold Shaw Publishers, 1986), May 30.

43   Arnold Dallimore, *George Whitefield: The Life and Times of the Great Evangelist of the 18th Century Revival* (Edinburgh: Banner of Truth, 1970), 1:23.

44   Luke Tyerman, *The Life and Times of John Wesley* (London, 1880), 1:217.

45   George Whitefield, *George Whitefield's Journals* (Edinburgh: Banner of Truth, 1986), 83.

46   Ibid.

47   Dallimore, *George Whitefield*, 1:140.

48   Ibid., 1:587.

49   Stephen Mansfield, *Forgotten Founding Father: The Heroic Legacy of George Whitefield* (Cumberland House, 2001), 101.

50   John Newton, *The Works of John Newton*, Volume 1, Letter XXXIX (Philadelphia, 1839), 196.

51   Ibid., 197.

52   Ibid.

53   Ibid.

54   Ibid.

55   Ibid., 198.

56   "Church attendance in Scotland falls from 12% to 7% in fifteen years," *Evangelical Focus*, April 28, 201, https://evangelicalfocus.com/europe/2514/church-attendance-in-scotland-falls-from-12-to-7-in-fifteen-years.

57   Libby Brooks, "Scotland to embed LGBTI teaching across curriculum," *The Guardian*, November 9, 2018, https://www.theguardian.com/education/2018/nov/09/scotland-first-country-approve-lgbti-school-lessons.

58   David Laing, ed., *The Works of John Knox*, Volume VI (Edinburgh: James Thin, 1895), 619.

59   Iain Murray, *A Scottish Christian Heritage* (Edinburgh: Banner of Truth, 2006), 80.

60   Ibid.

61   Ibid., 84.

62   Ibid., 97, 98.

63   Dr. and Mrs. Howard Taylor, *Hudson Taylor in the Early Years: The Growth of a Soul* (Singapore: OMF International, 1998), 1:349.

64   Thomas Phillips, *The Welsh Revival* (Banner of Truth, 1996), 7.

65   Ibid., 9.

66   Ibid., 119ff.

67   Charles Finney, "How to Change Your Heart," https://www.gospeltruth.net/1836SOIS/02sois_how2change_hear.htm.

68   Quoted in Iain Murray, *Revival and Revivalism* (Edinburgh: Banner of Truth, 1994), 246.

69   Charles G. Finney, *Finney's Systematic Theology* (Bloomington, MN: Bethany, 1976), 217.

70   Ibid., 209.

71   Quoted in Iain Murray, *Evangelicalism Divided* (Edinburgh: Banner of Truth, 2000), 69.

72   Bradley White, "How Many Americans are Evangelical Christians? Born-Again Christians?" Patheos, March 28, 2013, *https://www.patheos.com/blogs/blackwhiteandgray/2013/03/how-many-americans-are-evangelical-christians-born-again-christians/*.

73   "In U.S., Decline of Christianity Continues at Rapid Pace," Pew Research Center, October 17, 2019, https://www.pewforum.org/2019/10/17/in-u-s-decline-of-christianity-continues-at-rapid-pace/.

74   "Attitudes on Same Sex Marriage," Pew Research Center, www.pewforum.org/fact-sheet/changing-attitudes-on-gay-marriage

75   "List of Christian denominations by number of members," Wikipedia, https://wikipedia.org/wiki/List_of_Christian_denominations_by_number_of_members.

76   "Global Christianity—A Report on the Size and Distribution of the World's Christian Population," The Pew

Forum on Religion and Public Life, December 2011, https://www.pewforum.org/2011/12/19/global-christianity-exec/.

77 Samuel Waldron, *Baptist Roots in America* (Simpson: Boomton, NJ, 1991), 7.

78 Robert Shindler, "The Down Grade," in *The Sword and the Trowel* (March 1887), 123.

79 Ibid., 125.

80 Ibid.

81 Robert Shindler, "The Down Grade," in *The Sword and the Trowel* (April 1887), 168.

82 Ibid., 170.

83 *The Sword and the Trowel* (April 1887), 195. For a more complete record of the Downgrade, see the articles located at https://archive.spurgeon.org/downgrd.php.

84 Charles Spurgeon, "Another Word Concerning the Down-Grade," in *The Sword and the Trowel* (August 1887), 398.

85 Ibid., 399.

86 Ibid.

87 John F. MacArthur Jr., *Ashamed of the Gospel* (Wheaton: Crossway, 1992), 36.

88 Susannah Spurgeon, C.H. *Spurgeon's Autobiography*, Vol. 4, 1878-1892 (Chicago: Fleming Revell, 1900), 255.

89 Jeffrey Cox, *The English Churches in a Secular Society: Lambeth, 1870–1930* (New York: Oxford University Press, 1982).

90 "Churchgoing in the UK," BBC News, http://news.bbc.co.uk/2/shared/bsp/hi/pdfs/03_04_07_tearfund-church.pdf.

91 "Christianity in the UK," Faith Survey, https://faithsurvey.co.uk/uk-christianity.html; "Attendance at Church of England services continues to decline," *Christian Today*, October 12, 2020, https://christiantoday.com/article/attendance.at.church.of.england.services.continues.to.decline/135727.htm.

92 Ibid.

93 Ian Paul, "What state is the Church of England in?" Psephizo, October 23, 2019, https://www.psephizo.com/life-ministry/what-state-is-the-church-of-england-in/.

94 Guy P. Duffield and Nathaniel M. Van Cleave, *Foundations of Pentecostal Theology* (Los Angeles: Foursquare Media, 1983), 347.

95 https://www.pewresearch.org/fact-tank/2018/03/19/share-of-married-adults-varies-widely-across-u-s-religious-groups/ft_18-03-19_marriagereligion/.

96 "American Worldview Inventory 2020," Arizona Christian University Cultural Research Center, https://www.arizonachristian.edu/wp-content/uploads/2020/10/CRC_AWVI2020_Release11_Digital_04_20201006.pdf.

97 "No. 1253: Nigeria's Anglican Church breaks away over homosexuality rift," https://www.laits.utexas.edu/africa/ads/1253.html.

98 Orthodox Presbyterian Church General Assembly Ecumenical Standing Committee Report, 2014.

99 Gerard O'Connell, "Pope Francis to parents of L.G.B.T. children: 'God loves your children as they are,'" *America Magazine*, https://www.americamagazine.org/faith/2020/09/17/pope-francis-parents-lgbt-children-god-loves-your-children-they-are.

100 Derek Wilson, *Out of the Storm: The Life and Legacy of Martin Luther* (London: Hutchinson, 2007), 282.

101 Steve Orr and Kevin McCoy, "Buffalo diocese files for bankruptcy protection over hundreds of child sex abuse claims," USA Today, February 28, 2020, https://www.usatoday.com/story/news/nation/2020/02/28/buffalo-diocese-follows-rochester-diocese-into-bankruptcy-court-child-sexual-abuse/4901913002/.

102 Caroline O'Doherty, "Call to name and shame abusive clergy," Irish Examiner, August 21, 2018, https://www.irishexaminer.com/breakingnews/ireland/call-to-name-and-shame-abusive-clergy-863481.html.

103 Patrick Parkinson, "Child Sexual Abuse in the Catholic Church: The Australian Experience," Berkley Center, September 25, 2019, https://berkleycenter.georgetown.edu/responses/child-sexual-abuse-in-the-catholic-church-the-australian-experience.

104 Richard Fitzgibbons & Dale O'Leary, "Sexual Abuse of Minors by Catholic Clergy," The Linacre Quarterly, 2011, https://www.tandfonline.com/doi/pdf/10.1179/002436311803888276.

105 Parkinson, "Child Sexual Abuse in the Catholic Church."

106 Brian Smith, "Let Us Prey: Big Trouble at First Baptist Church," Chicago, December 11, 2012, https://www.chicagomag.com/Chicago-Magazine/January-2013/Let-Us-Prey-Big-Trouble-at-First-Baptist-Church/.

107 Robert Downen, Lise Olsen, and John Tedesco, "Abuse of Faith: 20 years, 700 victims: Southern Baptist sexual abuse spreads as leaders resist reforms," Houston Chronicle, February 10, 2019, https://www.houstonchronicle.com/news/investigations/article/Southern-Baptist-sexual-abuse-spreads-as-leaders-13588038.php.

108 "For a Lot of American Teens, Religion Is a Regular Part of the Public School Day," Pew Research Center, October 3, 2019, https://www.pewforum.org/2019/10/03/for-a-lot-of-american-teens-religion-is-a-regular-part-of-the-public-school-day/.

109 https://blogs.lcms.org/2019/convention-confesses-god-created-the-world-in-six-natural-days/

110 "Christian Traditions," Pew Research Center, December 19, 2011, https://www.pewforum.org/2011/12/19/global-christianity-traditions/.

111 "In U.S., Decline of Christianity Continues at Rapid Pace," Pew Research Center, October 17, 2019, https://www.pewforum.org/2019/10/17/in-u-s-decline-of-christianity-continues-at-rapid-pace/; Ryan P. Burge, "Evangelicals Show No Decline, Despite Trump and Nones," Christianity Today, March 21, 2019, https://www.christianitytoday.com/news/2019/march/evangelical-nones-mainline-us-general-social-survey-gss.html.

112 Jeffrey M. Jones, "U.S. Church Membership Down Sharply in Past Two Decades," Gallup, April 18, 2019, https://news.gallup.com/poll/248837/church-membership-down-sharply-past-two-decades.aspx.

113 "Religion," Gallup, https://news.gallup.com/poll/1690/religion.aspx.

114 "CRC Survey Shows Dangerously Low Percentage of Americans Hold Biblical Worldview," Cultural Research Center, March 24, 2020, https://www.arizonachristian.edu/wp-content/uploads/2020/04/CRC-AWVI-2020-Release_01-Worldview-in-America.pdf.

115 "Is the Bible True? CRC Study Shows America's Distrust of the Bible Undermines Its Worldview," Cultural Research Center, April 7, 2020, https://www.arizonachristian.edu/wp-content/uploads/2020/04/CRC-AWVI-2020-Release-02_Faith-and-Worldview-1.pdf.

116 https://www.barna.com/research/changing-state-of-the-church, https://www.barna.com/research/watching-online-church

117 https://www.washingtonpost.com/politics/supreme-court-wont-review-new-mexico-gay-commitment-ceremony-photo-case/2014/04/07/f9246cb2-bc3a-11e3-9a05-c739f29ccb08_story.html

118 https://www.cnn.com/2017/02/16/us/washington-florist-same-sex-wedding-discrimination-lawsuit/index.html

119 https://www.huffpost.com/entry/sweet-cakes-by-melissa-bankrupt-_n_5916226

120 Samuel Smith, "Number of Clergywomen Has Exponentially Increased Over Last 2 Decades, Study Says," Christian Post, October 11, 2018, https://www.christianpost.com/news/number-of-clergywomen-has-exponentially-increased-over-last-2-decades-study-says.html.

121 "Christian Bestsellers, May 2020," Christian Book Expo, https://christianbookexpo.com/bestseller/all.php?id=0520.

122 "ECPA Milestone Sales Award program," Christian Book Expo, https://christianbookexpo.com/salesawards/.

123 Rachel Hollis, Girl Wash Your Face (Nashville: Thomas Nelson, 2018), chapter 19.

124 Scott Thumma and Warren Bird, "Recent Shifts in America's Largest Protestant Churches: Megachurches 2015 Report," Leadership Network, https://leadnet.org/megachurch/.

CHAPTER VII—THE RISE & FALL
OF A CHRISTIAN CIVILIZATION

1 Plato, The Republic, in Plato in Twelve Volumes, translated by Paul Shorey (Cambridge, MA: Harvard University Press, 1969). 5.461.

2 Aristotle, Politics, 7.14.10.

3 Quoted in Will and Ariel Durant, Life of Greece (New York: Simon & Schuster, 1939), 568.

4 Quoted in Ibid.

5 Seneca, De Consolatione ad Helviam, 15.3.

6 "Augustan laws on sexuality," University of Oregon, https://pages.uoregon.edu/klio/tx/re/aug-law.htm.

7 Chris Scarre, Chronicle of the Roman Emperors (London: Thames and Hudson, 2015), 35ff.

8 Tacitus, Histories, 1.1.2.

9 Charles Merivale, A History of the Romans Under the Empire (London: Longmans, Green & Co., 1904), 6:453.

10 Ellen Curtin, "7 Blood-Soaked Facts about the Colosseum," Dark Rome, January 14, 2020, https://darkrome.com/blog/Rome/7-bloody-colosseum-facts#:~:text=A%20high%20death%20toll,walls%20of%20this%20particular%20amphitheater.

11 Plutarch, Moralia, 2.171D.

12 Cicero, De Legibus, 3.8.

13 Seneca, De Ira, 1.15.

14 This section has been adapted from Kevin Swanson, Keep the Faith Volume: On Family and Sexuality (Parker, CO: Generations with Vision, 2014), 61-72.

15 Justin Martyr, Dialogue with Trypho, 134.

16 Tertullian, To His Wife.

17 Epistle of Barnabas, 19.

18 Didache, 2.

19 Justin Martyr, *First Apology*, 27. Translated by Marcus Dods and George Reith. From *Ante-Nicene Fathers*, Vol. 1. Edited by Alexander Roberts, James Donaldson, and A. Cleveland Coxe. (Buffalo, NY: Christian Literature Publishing Co., 1885.).

20 "The Apocalypse of Peter," *The Apocryphal New Testament*, trans. M.R. James (Oxford: Clarendon Press, 1924).

21 Athenagoras, "A Plea for the Christians," in Schaff, *The Ante-Nicene Fathers*, 2:147.

22 Tertullian, "The Apology," *The Ante-Nicene Fathers*, 3:25.

23 Quoted in Michael J. Gorman, *Abortion in the Early Church*, 52-53.

24 Minucius Flexis, "The Octavius," *The Ante-Nicene Fathers*, 4:192.

25 "The Council of Elvira, ca. 306," The Catholic University of America, http://legalhistorysources.com/Canon%20Law/ElviraCanons.htm.

26 "The Canons of the Council of Ancyra," New Advent, http://www.newadvent.org/fathers/3802.htm.

27 Hugh Connolly, *The Irish Penitentials* (Dublin: Four Courts Press, 1995), 120. "The Canons of the Council of Trullo," New Advent, http://www.newadvent.org/cathen/04311b.htm.

28 "The Canons of the Council of Trullo," Canon 91.

29 Adapted from *Keep the Faith: On Family and Sexuality*, 82-94.

30 Phillip Schaff, Alexander Roberts, James Donaldson, et al., eds., *The Ante-Nicene Fathers* (Peabody: Hendrickson, 1996), 2:275.

31 Ibid., 276.

32 Ibid., 277.

33 Ibid.

34 Clement, *The Instructor*, Book 6, quoted in ibid., 251.

35 Ibid., 282.

36 Clement of Alexandria, *The Instructor*, 2.10.

37 Schaff, Roberts, Donaldson, eds., *The Ante-Nicene Fathers*, 7:463.

38 Ibid.

39 Cyprian, *Letters*, 1.8.

40 Cyprian, *Letters*, 1.9.

41 Augustine, *Confessions*, 3.8.15, AD 400.

42 Augustine, *The City of God*, Book XVI, chapter 30, in Philip Schaff, ed., *Select Library of the Nicene and Post-Nicene Fathers of the Christian Church*, Vol. 2, trans. J. F. Shaw (1887).

43 Augustine, *Letters, Vol. V*, trans. Sister Wilfrid Parsons (New York: Fathers of the Church, Inc., 1956), Letter 211, 50.

44 Ludwig Bieler, ed., *The Irish Penitentials* (Dublin: Institute for Advanced Studies, 1975), 69.

45 Adapted from *Keep the Faith: On Family and Sexuality*, 94-98.

46 Peter Damian, *Book of Gomorrah*, Trans. Pierre J. Payer (Wilfrid Laurier University Press, 1982), 50.

47 Bieler, *Irish Penitentials*, 97.

48 Louis Crompton, *Homosexuality and Civilization* (Cambridge, MA: Harvard University Press, 2003), 155.

49 Damian, *Book of Gomorrah*, 9.

50 Ibid., 63.

51 Ibid., 65.

52 Ibid., 60.

53 Ibid., 41.

54 Ibid., 80, 83.

55 Ibid., 82.

56 Ibid., 33.

57 Ibid., 34.

58 Ibid.

59 Ibid., 96.

60 "Third Lateran Council – 1179 A.D.," Canon 11, *Papal Encyclicals Online*, https://www.papalencyclicals.net/councils/ecum11.htm.

61 Augustine, *A Treatise Concerning the Correction of the Donatists*, in *The Nicene and Post-Nicene Fathers, Series 1*, 4:640-641.

62 *Imperatoris Theodosii Codex*, 9.7.3, http://ancientrome.ru/ius/library/codex/theod/liber09.htm#7.

63 Justinian, *Institutes of Justinian*, Book IV, xviii, 2.

64   Justinian, *Codex Justiniani*, nov. 77 and 141.

65   "Letter of Alcuin to Charlemagne," http://media.bloomsbury.com/rep/files/primary-source-35-alcuin.pdf.

66   "Capitulary of Charlemagne Issued in the Year 802," The Avalon Project, Yale Law School, https://avalon.law.yale.edu/medieval/capitula.asp.

67   Ibid, para 32,33.

68   Ibid, para. 32.

69   Asser, *Asser's Life of King Alfred*, paragraph 24.

70   Ibid., paragraph 87.

71   *The Whole Works of King Alfred the Great* (London: T. Bosworth, 1858), 1:196-198.

72   Quoted in F. N. Lee, *King Alfred the Great and Our Common Law* (Morrisville, NC: Lulu Press, 2005), 13.

73   Winston Churchill, *A History of the English-Speaking Peoples* (Skyhorse Publishing, 1998), 50.

74   Quoted in Tom Holland, *Athelstan: The Making of England* (New York: Penguin, 2016), 69.

75   John Johnson, ed., *Collection of all the Ecclesiastical Laws, Canons, Answers, or Rescripts...of the Church of England* (London: Robert Knaplock, 1720), 342, quoted in Holland, *Athelstan*.

76   Ibid., 344.

77   Ibid.

78   Ibid., 71.

79   Quoted in "Anglo-Saxon Law—Extracts From Early Laws of the English," The Avalon Project, Yale Law School, *https://avalon.law.yale.edu/medieval/saxlaw.asp.*

80   A. J. Robertson, ed. and trans., *The Laws of the Kings of England from Edmund to Henry I* (Cambridge: Cambridge University Press, 1925), 175f.

81   John of Salisbury, *Policraticus*, trans. Carey J. Nederman (Cambridge University Press, 2007), 36; https://archive.org/stream/JohnOfSalisburyPolicraticusJohnOfSalisbury.

82   Ibid., 42.

83   Samuel Rutherford, *Lex Rex, or The Law and the Prince* (Edinburgh: Robert Ogle, 1843), 57.

84   Edward Gibbon, *The History of the Decline and Fall of the Roman Empire* (London: Jones & Co., 1828), 6:255.

85   Damian, *Book of Gomorrah*, preface.

86   Ibid., 21.

87   Diana Bullen Presciutti, *Visual Cultures of Foundling Care in Renaissance Italy* (Abingdon, UK: Routledge, 2016), 118.

88   Ibid., 120.

89   *Malleus Maleficarum*, book 2, chapter 13.

90   Martin Luther, *Luther's Works: Lectures on Genesis*, Vol. 3 (St. Louis, MO: Concordia Publishing House, 1986), 251-252.

91   Otto Scott, *James I: The Fool as King* (Vallecito, CA: Ross House Books, 1976).

92   David Coleman and John Salt, *The British Population: Patterns, Trends, and Processes* (Oxford: Oxford University Press, 1992), 44.

93   William Acton, *Observations on Illegitimacy* (London, Statistical Society of London, 1859).

94   Daniel Defoe, *The Family Instructor*, 1715.

95   John G. Paton, *Missionary Patriarch: The True Story of John G. Paton* (San Antonio: Vision Forum, 2001), 4.

96   Acton, *Observations on Illegitimacy*.

97   "Offences Against the Person Acts 1861," *Uk National Archives*, https://www.legislation.gov.uk/ukpga/Vict/24-25/100/section/58.

98   Jeremy Bentham, *Offenses Against Oneself: Paederasty.*

99   Scott Van Voorhis, "What Cities Have the Largest Percentage of LGBT Residents?" *The Street*, May 31, 2018, https://www.thestreet.com/personal-finance/cities-with-largest-percentage-of-lgbt-residents-14605660.

100   "The Global Divide on Homosexuality Persists," Pew Research Center, https://www.pewresearch.org/global/2020/06/25/global-divide-on-homosexuality-persists/.

101   Johan van Slooten, "Homophobia Among Hindus in Holland," Radio Netherlands Worldwide, *http://www.rnw.nl/english/article/homophobia-among-hindus-holland.*

102   William Bradford, *Of Plymouth Plantation: Bradford's History of the Plymouth Settlement, 1608-1650* (San Antonio: Vision Forum, 1998), 21.

103   James Deetz & Patricia S. Deetz, *The Times of Their Lives: Life, Love, and Death in Plymouth Colony* (New York: Anchor Books, 2001), 134, 140.

104   John Winthrop, *The History of New England from 1630 to 1649*, ed. James Savage (Boston: Little, Brown, & Co., 1853), 2:32; as reprinted in Oakes, 273.

105   Hall, *The Last American Puritan*, 122.

106   Ibid., 195.

107   Ibid., 356.

108   Ibid., 330.

109   *The American Law Register,* May 1907, 279, University of Pennsylvania, https://scholarship.law.upenn.edu/cgi/viewcontent.cgi?article=6713&context=penn_law_review.

110   Oliver Wendell Holmes dissenting opinion in *Southern Pacific Company v. Jensen,* 244 U.S. 205 (1917), 222.

111   Francis Biddle, *Justice Holmes, Natural Law, and the Supreme Court* (New York: Macmillan, 1960), 49.

112   Letter from Oliver Wendell Holmes Jr. to Harold Laski, September 15, 1929 in Richard A. Posner, ed., *The Essential Holmes: Selections from the Letters, Speeches, Judicial Opinions, and Other Writings of Oliver Wendell Holmes, Jr.* (University of Chicago Press, 1992), 116.

113   Ibid.

114   Benjamin Cardozo, *The Nature of the Judicial Process* (New Haven: Yale University Press, 1921), 173.

115   John Dewey, *The Influence of Darwin on Philosophy and Other Essays* (New York: Henry Holt and Company, 1910), 1-2, 11-12, 16.

116   Earl Warren, *Trop v. Dulles* (1958)

117   Fyodor Dostoyevsky, *The Brothers Karamazov,* Part 4, Book 11, Chapter 4.

118   Darcel Rockett, "'I was absorbed in pornography for hours and hours': How porn is affecting kids," *Chicago Tribune,* April 3, 2018, *https://www.chicagotribune.com/lifestyles/parenting/sc-fam-porn-addiction-in-youth-0417-story.html*.

119   Katherine Schaeffer, "Most U.S. teens who use cellphones do it to pass time, connect with others, learn new things," Pew Research Center, August 23, 2019, https://www.pewresearch.org/fact-tank/2019/08/23/most-us-teens-who-use-cellphones-do-it-to-pass-time-connect-with-others-learn-new-things/.

120   "Pornography Statistics," Covenant Eyes, https://www.covenanteyes.com/pornstats/.

121   Tom W. Smith, *An Analysis of the Use of Public Opinion Data by the Attorney General's Commission on Pornography* (University of Chicago, 1986), http://gss.norc.org/Documents/reports/methodological-reports/MR048.pdf; https://www.roadtograce.net/current-porn-statistics/.

122   Frank Olito, "How the divorce rate has changed over the last 150 years," *Insider,* January 30, 2019, https://www.insider.com/divorce-rate-changes-over-time-2019-1.

123   Benjamin Gurrentz, "For Young Adults, Cohabitation is Up, Marriage is Down," United States Census Bureau, November 15, 2018, https://www.census.gov/library/stories/2018/11/cohabitaiton-is-up-marriage-is-down-for-young-adults.html#:~:text=Among%20those%20ages%2018%2D24,12%20percent%2010%20years%20ago.

124   Ibid.

125   Alexia Fernández Campbell, "Why Are So Many Millennials Having Children Out of Wedlock?" *The Atlantic,* July 18, 2016, https://www.theatlantic.com/business/archive/2016/07/why-are-so-many-millennials-having-children-out-of-wedlock/491753/.

126   "Family Structure Still Matters," *The Centre for Social Justice,* https://www.centreforsocialjustice.org.uk/core/wp-content/uploads/2020/08/CSJJ8372-Family-structure-Report-200807.pdf.

127   https://ourworldindata.org/marriages-and-divorce.

128   https://www.cdc.gov/nchs/data/series/sr_21/sr21_024.pdf ; https://ourworldindata.org/marriages-and-divorce.

129   "The World's Abortion Laws," Center for Reproductive Rights, https://reproductiverights.org/worldabortionlaws.

130   Ibid.

131   Frank Newport, "In U.S., Estimate of LGBT Population Rises to 4.5%," Gallup, May 22, 2018, https://news.gallup.com/poll/234863/estimate-lgbt-population-rises.aspx

132   Bertrand Barere, *Memoirs of Bertrand Barere* Vol. 2 (London: H.S. Nichols, 1896), 310.

133   Maximilien Robespierre, "Justification of the Use of Terror," Fordham University Modern History Sourcebook, https://sourcebooks.fordham.edu/mod/robespierre-terror.asp.

134   Megan Brenan, "Record-Low 54% in U.S. Say Death Penalty Morally Acceptable," Gallup, June 23, 2020, https://news.gallup.com/poll/312929/record-low-say-death-penalty-morally-acceptable.aspx

135   https://themasculinist.com/the-masculinist-13-the-lost-world-of-american-evangelicalism

136   https://www.courier-tribune.com/story/lifestyle/faith/2020/02/26/uk-cities-cancel-franklin-graham-tour-stops-citing-lgbtq-views/41800101

137   https://gazette.com/life/focus-on-the-family-turns-40-with-jim-daly-saying-the-good-word-is-shalom/article_8f56d288-acea-5e1b-a93f-52d83c9b0c9e.html

138   "The Global Divide on Homosexuality Persists," Pew Research Center, June 24, 2020,

https://www.pewresearch.org/global/2020/06/25/global-divide-on-homosexuality-persists/pg_2020-06-25_global-views-homosexuality_0-04/.

139   "Mapping out a spectrum of the Chinese public's discrimination toward the LGBT community: results from a national survey," BMC, May 12, 2020, https://bmcpublichealth.biomedcentral.com/articles/10.1186/s12889-020-08834-y

140   "The Global Divide on Homosexuality Persists," Pew Research Center, June 24, 2020, https://www.pewresearch.org/global/2020/06/25/global-divide-on-homosexuality-persists/pg_2020-06-25_global-views-homosexuality_0-04/.

141   https://news.gallup.com/poll/329708/lgbt-identification-rises-latest-estimate.aspx

142   F.N. Lee, 17-23; also reference Alfred, *The Whole Works*, Vol. 3 (London: Bosworth & Harrison, 1858), 118-124.

CHAPTER VIII—THE RISE & FALL
OF HUMANITY AND CHARITY IN THE WEST

1   See Rudyard Kipling, "The Gods of the Copybook Headings."

2   Westminster Shorter Catechism, Question 21.

3   Plutarch, *Caesar*, 55.

4   William Blake, "Auguries of Innocence."

5   Peter Bergen, "Poll: Bin Laden tops Musharraf in Pakistan," CNN, *https://www.cnn.com/2007/POLITICS/09/11/poll.pakistanis/index.html*.

6   Quoted in William C. Chase, *Story of Stonewall Jackson* (Atlanta: D.E. Luther Publishing, 1901), 249.

7   *Sir Gawain and the Green Knight,* trans. Paul Deane (1999), 28.

8   Ibid.

9   *The Law of the Innocents*, paragraph 52, in Cain Adamnain, *An Old-Irish Treatise on the Law of Adamnan*, https://sourcebooks.fordham.edu/source/CainAdamnain.asp.

10   Ibid., paragraph 33.

11   Ibid., paragraph 7.

12   "The most famous people in America," YouGov, https://today.yougov.com/ratings/entertainment/fame/people/all.

13   "The Most Influential Contemporary Americans," Ranker, June 14, 2019, *https://www.ranker.com/crowdranked-list/the-most-influential-contemporary-americans.*

14   *Letters of Pliny*, 10.92.

15   W. E. H. Lecky, *History of European Morals: From Augustus to Charlemagne* (New York: Appleton, 1927), 2:78.

16   Cicero, *De Officiis*, 2.20.

17   Eusebius, *Ecclesiastical History*, 7.22.

18   Thucydides, *The History of the Peloponnesian War*, 2.47, 2.51.

19   Cyprian, *Mortality*, chapters 15-20.

20   Eusebius, *Ecclesiastical History*, 7.22.

21   Quoted in Ayer, *A Sourcebook for Ancient Church History* (New York: Scribner, 1913, 1941), 332-333.

22   Paul Johnson, *History of Christianity* (New York: Atheneum, 1987), 75.

23   Tertullian, *Apology*, 39:5-6, trans. T. R. Glover.

24   "Constitutions of the Holy Apostles," 4.9., in Alexander Roberts and James Donaldson, eds., *Ante-Nicene Fathers, Volume 1,* (New York: Charles Scribner's Sons, 1905).

25   Justin Martyr, *First Apology*, 67, in Roberts, Donaldson, and Coxe, eds., *Ante-Nicene Fathers, Vol. 1,* translated by Marcus Dods and George Reith (Buffalo, NY: Christian Literature Publishing Co., 1885).

26   Ignatius, *Epistle to the Smyrnaeans*.

27   Clement of Alexandria, *Paedagogus*, 3.4, in *Ante-Nicene Fathers*, 2:279.

28   *Shepherd of Hermas*, Eighth Mandate.

29   Stark, *Triumph of Christianity*, 111, 163.

30   Gregory of Nyssa, *Life of St. Macrina*, http://www.tertullian.org/fathers/gregory_macrina_1_life.htm.

31   Ibid.

32   Basil, Homily 6, "I Will Pull Down My Barns."

33   Ibid.

34   Gregory of Nyssa, *Homilies on Ecclesiastes*, 4:1.

35   Paulinus of Nola, Poem XX.

36   Fielding H. Garrison, *Introduction to the History of Medicine* (Philadelphia: W. B. Saunders, 1914), 118.

37   Ibid.

38   D. A. Furniss, "The monastic contribution to mediaeval medical care: Aspects of an earlier welfare state," *Journal of the Royal College of General Practitioners*, April 1968; 15(4), 244; http://europepmc.org/backend/ptpm-crender.fcgi?accid=PMC2236411&blobtype=pdf.

39   "The Form and Function of Medieval Hospitals - Professor Carole Rawcliffe," YouTube, August 31, 2011, https://www.youtube.com/watch?v=R-to4mRVzAI&feature=emb_title.

40   C. F. V. Smout, *The Story of the Progress of Medicine* (Bristol: John Wright and Sons, 1964), 40.

41   Carole Rawcliffe, "The Form and Function of Medieval Hospitals," lecture given at the Tudor Health Reform Symposium, June 22, 2011, at Gresham College, https://www.medievalists.net/2011/08/the-form-and-function-of-medieval-hospitals/.

42   Quoted in Vishal Mangalwadi, *The Book that Made Your World: How the Bible Created the Soul of Western Civilization* (Nashville: Thomas Nelson, 2011), 75.

43   David Brooks, "The Nuclear Family Was a Mistake," *The Atlantic*, March 2020, https://www.theatlantic.com/magazine/archive/2020/03/the-nuclear-family-was-a-mistake/605536/.

44   Quoted in Paul Johnson, *Intellectuals* (New York: Harper and Row, 1988), 10-11.

45   Ibid., 26.

46   Johann Gottlieb Fichte, *Addresses to the German Nation*, trans. R. F. Jones and G. H. Turnball (La Salle, IL: Open Court Publishing Company, 1922), 12-13.

47   Ibid., 15.

48   Thomas Nipperdey, *Germany from Napoleon to Bismarck: 1800-1866*, trans. Daniel Nolan (NJ: Princeton University Press, 2014), 401.

49   Karl Marx, *Communist Manifesto*, Tenth Plank.

50   "Charity Review: Salvation Army," Give.org, https://www.give.org/charity-reviews/national/religious/salvation-army-national-corporation-in-alexandria-va-1221.

51   "Gross Domestic Philanthropy: An international analysis of GDP, tax and giving," Charities Aid Foundation, January 2016, https://www.cafonline.org/docs/default-source/about-us-policy-and-campaigns/gross-domestic-philanthropy-feb-2016.pdf.

52   "Eastern Kentucky Lunatic Asylum," Kentucky Historic Institutions, *https://kyhi.org/asylums/eastern-state-hospital/*.

53   Thomas Nipperdey, *Germany from Napoleon to Bismarck* (Princeton: Princeton University Press, 2014), 281

54   Riley Griffin, "Almost Half of U.S. Births Happen Outside Marriage, Signaling Cultural Shift," Bloomberg, October 17, 2018, https://www.bloomberg.com/news/articles/2018-10-17/almost-half-of-u-s-births-happen-outside-marriage-signaling-cultural-shift.

55   Paul Bedard, "77% black births to single moms, 49% for Hispanic immigrants," *Washington Examiner,* May 5, 2017, https://www.washingtonexaminer.com/77-black-births-to-single-moms-49-for-hispanic-immigrants.

56   "Abortion: The overlooked tragedy for black Americans," *Arizona Capitol Times*, February 25, 2020, https://azcapitoltimes.com/news/2020/02/25/abortion-the-overlooked-tragedy-for-black-americans/.

57   Quoted in Tom Holland, *Dominion: How the Christian Revolution Remade the World* (New York: Basic Books, 2019), 532.

58   Ibid., 532.

59   Musonius Rufus, *Lectures and Fragments*, lecture XII.

60   Holland, *Dominion*, 540.

61   Marian Conway, "YMCA Launches LGBTQ Inclusion Campaign with Support of Three Foundations," *Nonprofit Quarterly*, May 31, 2018, https://nonprofitquarterly.org/ymca-launches-lgbtq-inclusion-campaign-support-foundations/.

62   United Way Worldwide 2010 Annual Report, https://unway.3cdn.net/65baa8073da0505c36_mlbrwvl93.pdf.

63   "Boy Scouts of America Lifts Ban on Gay Adult Leaders," *Philanthropy News Digest*, July 29, 2015, https://philanthropynewsdigest.org/news/boy-scouts-of-america-lifts-ban-on-gay-adult-leaders; Emanuella Grinberg, "Boy Scouts open membership to transgender boys," CNN, January 31, 2017, https://www.cnn.com/2017/01/30/us/boy-scouts-transgender-membership/index.html.

64   "LGBTQ Support," Salvation Army, *https://www.salvationarmyusa.org/usn/the-lgbtq-community-and-the-salvation-army/*.

65   Charities Aid Foundation World Giving Index, October 2019, https://www.cafonline.org/docs/default-source/about-us-publications/caf_wgi_10th_edition_report_2712a_web_101019.pdf.

66   Ibid.

67   "Giving USA: Americans Donated an Estimated $358.38 Billion to Charity in 2014; Highest Total in Report's 60-year History," The Giving Institute, June 16, 2015, https://www.givinginstitute.org/page/GUSA2015Release; Alina Tugend, "Donations to Religious Institutions Fall as Values Change," *New York Times*, November 3,

2016, https://www.nytimes.com/2016/11/06/giving/donations-to-religious-institutions-fall-as-va ues-change. html.

68   The State of Church Giving Through 2017 (Empty Tomb, 2019), 36; Katherine Burgess, "Report: Church giving reaches Depression-era lows," *Washington Post*, October 24, 2013, https://www.washington post.com/national/on-faith/report-church-giving-reaches-depression-era-record-lows/2013/10/24/b2721a56-3ce9-11e3-b0e7-716179a2c2c7_story.html.

69   "Major national study of religious congregations' finances to be funded by $1.67 million Lilly Endowment grant," Lilly Family School of Philanthropy, November 13, 2017, https://philanthropy.iupui.edu/news-events/news-item/major-national-study-of-religious-congregations%E2%80%99-finances-to-be-funded-by-$1.67-mil lion-lilly-endowment-grant.html?id=245; Paul Maxwell, "How Churches Really Spend Their Money: 20 Fascinating Data Points [A New Study]," Tithe.ly, November 25, 2019, https://get.tithe.ly/blog/how-church

       es-really-spend-their-money-20-fascinating-data-points-a-new-study.

70   Matthew Branaugh, "A Peek Inside How Churches Spend Their Money: The trends from the past 20 years," *Christianity Today's* Church Law & Tax, March 5, 2019, https://www.churchlawandtax.com/web/2019/march/how-churches-spend-money.html.

71   Letter from Gregory to Augustine in Bede, *Ecclesiastical History*, 1.27.

72   Major national study of religious congregations' finances to be funded by $1.67 million Lilly Endowment grant," Lilly Family School of Philanthropy, November 13, 2017. Approximate numbers taken from several recent studies of church financing surveying 1,000+ churches.

73   Jackie Syrop, "Federal Government Funds Two-Thirds of Healthcare Costs, Study Finds," *American Journal of Public Health*, February 2, 1016, https://www.ajmc.com/view/federal-government-funds-two-thirds-of-health-care-costs-study-finds-.

74   Yoku Shaw-Taylor, "Nongovernment Philanthropic Spending on Public Health in the United States," *American Journal of Public Health*, January 2016, https://www.ncbi.nlm.nih.gov/pmc/articles/PMC4695957/.

75   China bans children–and their teachers–from churches," World Watch Monitor, September 8, 2017, https://

       www.worldwatchmonitor.org/2017/09/china-bans-children-and-their-teachers-from-churches/.

76   Margaret Thatcher, TV Interview for Thames TV, *This Week*, February 5, 1976, https://www.margaretthatcher.org/document/102953.

77   "A Summary of the 2020 Annual Reports," Social Security and Medicare Boards of Trustees, https://www.ssa.gov/OACT/TRSUM/index.html.

CHAPTER IX—THE RISE & FALL OF SCIENCE IN THE WEST

1   *Petrarch's Secret: Or, The Soul's Conflict With Passion*, trans. William Draper (London: Chatto & Windus, 1911), 44.

2   Jean-Jacques Rousseau, *Discourse on the Sciences and the Arts*, Part 1, quoted in Stark, *The Triumph of Christianity*, 237.

3   Stark, *The Triumph of Christianity*, 237.

4   Ibid., 238-239. Quote is from C. Warren Hollister, "The Phases of European History and the Non-existence of the Middle Ages," Pacific Historical Review, 61:1-22.

5   *The Rule of Benedict*, chapter 48.

6   Lynn White Jr., *Medieval Religion and Technology: Collected Essays* (Berkeley: University of California Press, 1978), 22.

7   Ibid.

8   Thomas Barnebeck Andersen, Peter Sandholt Jensen, Christian Stejner Skovsgaard, "The Heavy Plough and the Agricultural Revolution in Medieval Europe" (Department of Business and Economics, University of Southern Denmark, 2013).

9   Mangalwadi, *The Book that Made Your World*, 95.

10   White, *Medieval Religion and Technology*, 245.

11   Quoted in Vincent Ilardi, *Renaissance Vision from Spectacles to Telescopes* (American Philosophical Society, 2007), 5.

12   Mangalwadi, *The Book that Made Your World*, 108.

13   Roger Bacon, *Roger Bacon's Letter Concerning the Marvelous Power of Art and of Nature and Concerning the Nullity of Magic*, trans. Tenney L. Davis (Easton, PA: Chemical Publishing Company, 1923), 26-27.

14   James Hannam, *The Genesis of Science: How the Christian Middle Ages Launched the Scientific Revolution* (Regnery

Publishing, 2011), 158.

15 Marshall Clagett, *The Science of Mechanics in the Middle Ages* (Madison: University of Wisconsin Press, 1959), 271.

16 Augustine, *De Civitate Dei*, V.7, trans. W. M. Green (London: Heinemann and Harvard University Press, 1963), 163.

17 Thomas Aquinas, *Summa Theologiae*, vol. 40, Thomas O'Meara and Michael Duffy, eds. (London: Blackfriars, 1968), 55 (2.95.5).

18 Hannam, *Genesis of Science*, 233.

19 Quoted in ibid., 238.

20 Martin Luther, *Through the Year with Martin Luther* (Peabody, MA: Hendrickson, 2007), 212.

21 John Calvin, *Institutes of the Christian Religion*, 2.2.25.

22 Quoted in Peter Harrison, "How Protestantism influenced the making of modern science," Aeon Essays, December 2, 2019, https://aeon.co/essays/how-protestantism-influenced-the-making-of-modern-science.

23 Johannes Kepler, *Gesammelte Werke*, 20 Vols. (Munich: C. H. Beck, 1937-45), 8:40.

24 Johannes Kepler, *Mysterium Cosmographicum*, trans. Alistair M. Duncan (Norwalk, CT: Abaris, 1999), 53.

25 Stark, *The Triumph of Christianity*, 286.

26 Rodney Stark, *For the Glory of God: How Monotheism Led to Reformations, Science, Witch-Hunts, and the End of Slavery* (Princeton: Princeton University Press, 2003), 162.

27 Henry Morris, *The Biblical Basis for Modern Science* (Green Forest, AR: Master Books, 2002), 463-464.

28 Isaac Newton, *The Principia* (New York: George P. Putnam, 1850), 504.

29 Robert Boyle, *Seraphick Love* (Ann Arbor: University Microfilms International, 1981).

30 Robert Boyle, *The Christian Virtuoso* (London: Edward Jones, 1690), chapter 2.

31 Nancy Forbes and Basil Mahon, *Faraday, Maxwell, and the Electromagnetic Field* (New York: Prometheus Books, 2014), 17.

32 Ibid.

33 Quoted in Andrew Robinson, *Einstein on the Run* (New Haven: Yale University Press, 2019), 11.

34 Nancy Forbes and Basil Mahon, *Faraday, Maxwell, and the Electromagnetic Field* (New York: Prometheus Books, 2014), 17. Ibid.

35 Quoted in Frankjo Stvarnik, *Portraits of the Great Bible-Believing Scientists* (Victoria: Freisen Press, 2018), 290.

36 Michael Faraday, *Experimental Researches in Chemistry and Physics* (London: Taylor and Francis, 1859), 471.

37 Michael Faraday's letter to Auguste de la Rive, 1861.

38 "The Atheist-Dominated National Academy of Sciences," Human Events, June 17, 2010, https://humanevents.com/2010/06/17/the-atheistdominated-national-academy-of-sciences/.

39 "Scientists and Belief," Pew Research Center, November 5, 2009, https://www.pewforum.org/2009/11/05/scientists-and-belief/.

40 Forty-two out of 4,300 colleges in the United States teach the biblical creation account. "Colleges and Universities," Answers in Genesis, https://answersingenesis.org/colleges/colleges-and-universities/.

41 Quoted in Jean-Marc Berthoud, *Pierre Viret the Theologian: Reformation Theology and Contemporary Application* (Psalm 78 Ministries, 2019), 151.

42 Ibid.

43 Rodney Stark, *How the West Won: The Neglected Story of the Triumph of Modernity* (Wilmington, DE: ISI Books, 2014), 179.

44 "Why We Explore," NASA, https://www.nasa.gov/exploration/whyweexplore/why_we_explore_main.html#.XvecppNKg0o.

45 Hall, *The Last American Puritan*, 273.

46 J. P. Moreland, *Scientism and Secularism: Learning to Respond to a Dangerous Ideology* (Wheaton, IL: Crossway, 2018), 26.

47 Tom Sorrell, *Scientism: Philosophy and the Infatuation with Science* (London: Routledge, 1991), 1.

48 Moreland, *Scientism and Secularism*, 135-157.

49 Francois Jacob, *The Statue Within: An Autobiography* (Basic Books, New York, 1988), 224-225.

50 Douglas Futuyma, *Evolution* (Sunderland, MA: Sinauer Associates, 2005), 398.

51 Quoted in William B. Cohen, *The French Encounter with Africans: White Response to Blacks, 1530-1880* (Indiana

University Press, 2003), 88.

52   Ibid., 94.

53   Rachel Sapin, "AquaBounty CEO: GM farmed salmon will hit the market this year," *IntraFish*, March 11, 2020, https://www.intrafish.com/finance/aquabounty-ceo-gm-farmed-salmon-will-hit-the-market-this-year/2-1-770894.

54   Brian Charlesworth and Deborah Charlesworth, "Darwin and Genetics," *Genetics*, Volume 183, Issue 3, 757-766, https://www.genetics.org/content/183/3/757.

55   *Folia Mendeliana*, Volume 6 (1971), Moravian Museum, 254..

56   Ibid.

57   Letter of Charles Darwin to John Fordyce, May 7, 1879, in "Darwin Correspondence Project," https://www.darwinproject.ac.uk/letter/DCP-LETT-12041.xml.

58   Parts of this section have been adapted from the book by Kevin Swanson, Joshua Schwisow, Daniel Noor, et al., *American Faith: 27 Sketches from Winthrop to Wilkerson* (Parker, CO: Generations, 2019), 447-449.

59   Quoted in Christina Vella, *George Washington Carver: A Life* (Baton Rouge: Louisiana State University Press, 2015), 195.

60   Ibid.

61   Quoted in John Perry, *George Washington Carver* (Nashville: Thomas Nelson, 2011), 107.

62   Quoted in Ibid., 94.

63   Quoted in John Perry, *Unshakable Faith: Booker T. Washington & George Washington Carver* (Sisters, OR: Multnomah, 1999), 337-338.

64   Dennis Karwatka, "Technology's Past: R. G. LeTourneau and His Massive Earth-Moving Equipment," *Tech Directions* (2006), 65.

65   David Cloud, "Christian Inventor R. G. LeTourneau," Way of Life Literature, February 20, 2019, https://www.wayoflife.org/reports/christian_inventor_rg_letourneau.html; quotes are taken from R. G. LeTourneau, *Mover of Men and Mountains* (Chicago: Moody Press, 1967).

66   Ibid.

67   Ibid.

68   Quoted in James J. Walsh, *Makers of Modern Medicine* (New York: Fordham University Press, 1915), 318.

69   "U.S. Life Expectancy Statistics Chart by States," Disabled World, May 10, 2017, https://www.disabled-world.com/calculators-charts/states.php.

70   https://www.pbs.org/newshour/health/the-real-story-behind-the-worlds-first-antibiotic

71   https://www.cdc.gov/nchs/data/vsushistorical/mortstatbl_1910.pdf

72   BMJ, 2007, Jan. 20, Accessed in November, 2020 at https://www.ncbi.nlm.nih.gov/pmc/articles/PMC1779856/

73   Nolie Mumey, *Edward Jenner; 1949. Vaccination: Bicentenary of the Birth of Edward Jenner*, Volume 1 (Range Press), 37.

74   John Barron, *The Life of Edward Jenner, MD, Vol. II* (Cambridge University Press) 446-447.

75   Henry B.M. Best, 16, 430.

76   https://www.youtube.com/watch?v=W0j1nrP_rLo, 11:25-11:35.

77   Also, Dr. Best's co-inventor, Sir Frederick Banting was raised a Christian Methodist, on the Bible and Bunyan's *Pilgrim's Progress*. His parents had aimed for him to be a Methodist minister, but Banting chose to take up medicine instead at the University of Toronto (though lapsed from the faith before his death).

78   Quoted in Sinclair B. Ferguson, *Love Came Down at Christmas: Daily Readings for Advent* (The Good Book Company, 2019), 153.

79   Quoted in Ibid., 153.

80   W. Robert Nitske, *The Life of Wilhelm Conrad Rontgen, Discoverer of the X-ray* (University of Arizona Press, 1971), 287.

81   Ibid., 287.

82   Jeff Kinley with Dr. Raymond Damadian, *Gifted Mind: The Dr. Raymond Damadian Story, Inventor of the MRI* (Green Forest, AR: Masters Books, 2015), 90.

83   Ibid., 33.

84   Ibid., 164.

85   Ibid.

86   Ibid., 153.

87   Amanda Ruggeri, "Do we really live longer than our ancestors?" BBC, October 2, 2018, https://www.bbc.com/future/article/20181002-how-long-did-ancient-people-live-life-span-versus-longevity.

88   J. P. Griffin, "Changing life expectancy throughout history," *Journal of the Royal Society of Medicine*, December 1, 2008, 101(12); 577, https://www.ncbi.nlm.nih.gov/pmc/articles/PMC2625386/.

89   Laura Guertin, "Tracking media attention to climate change and global warming, by MeCCO," AGU Blogosphere, September 28, 2019, https://blogs.agu.org/geoedtrek/2019/09/28/tracking-media-attention-to-climate-change-and-global-warming-by-mecco/.

90   Abel Gustafson, Parrish Bergquist, Anthony Leiserowitz, et al., "A Growing Majority of Americans Think Global Warming is Happening and are Worried," Climate Change Communication, Yale, February 21, 2019, https://climatecommunication.yale.edu/publications/a-growing-majority-of-americans-think-global-warming-is-happening-and-are-worried/.

91   "An Open Letter on Climate Change to the People, their Local Representatives, the State Legislatures and Governors, the Congress, and the President of the United States of America," Cornwall Alliance, https://cornwallalliance.org/landmark-documents/an-open-letter-on-climate-change-to-the-people-their-local-representatives-the-state-legislatures-and-governors-the-congress-and-the-president-of-the-united-states-of-america/.

92   α (Alpha) is the probability of Type I error in any hypothesis test–incorrectly rejecting the null hypothesis. β (Beta) is the probability of Type II error in any hypothesis test–incorrectly failing to reject the null hypothesis.

93   https://www.cato.org/blog/how-one-model-simulated-22-million-us-deaths-Covid-19

94   https://nbc25news.com/news/local/cdc-94-of-Covid-19-deaths-had-underlying-medical-conditions

95   https://www.newscientist.com/article/2107219-exclusive-worlds-first-baby-born-with-new-3-parent-technique/

96   https://www.nytimes.com/2015/06/18/us/embryos-egg-donors-difficult-issues.html

97   http://www.wnd.com/2016/08/obama-gives-green-light-to-make-human-animal-hybrid-monsters/

98   https://www.theverge.com/2017/4/25/15421734/artificial-womb-fetus-biobag-uterus-lamb-sheep-birth-premie-preterm-infant

99   http://www.cnn.com/2017/01/16/health/cre-superbug-disease-study/index.html

100   The Stanford Study (Mechanisms of Action of Intrauterine Devices) indicated that an average of 0.8 post-fertilization babies were lost per woman by the IUD per annum on five different IUDs tested, and 14% of American women 15-44 years of age use the IUD. Therefore 6,750,000 babies are now being killed by its use per year (an increase from 960,000 babies in 2000). According to the same measure, 217,000,000 babies are killed each year worldwide through the use of the IUD alone. See Joseph B. Stanford and Rafael Mikolajczyk, "Mechanisms of action of intrauterine devices: Update and estimation of postfertilization effects," American Journal of Obstetrics and Gynecology, 187(6):1699-708, January 2003, https://www.researchgate.net/publication/10974531_Mechanisms_of_action_of_intrauterine_devices_Update_and_estimation_of_postfertilization_effects; Kai J. Buhling, Nikki B. Zite, Pamela Lotke, et al., "Worldwide use of intrauterine contraception: a review," Contraception, Volume 89, Issue 3, March 2014, pages 162-173, https://www.sciencedirect.com/science/article/pii/S0010782413007336#:~:text=Globally%2C%2014.3%25%20of%20women%20of,%2C%20it%20is%20%3E%2040%25.

101   The Nielson Total Audience Report, Q1 2016, https://www.nielsen.com/wp-content/uploads/sites/3/2019/04/total-audience-report-q1-2016.pdf.

102   Theodore Caplow, Howard M. Bahr, John Modell, et al., Recent Social Trends in the United States: 1960-1990 (McGill-Queen's University Press, 1991), 405-406.

103   Jacques Ellul, *The Technological System* (New York, 1980), 325.

CHAPTER X—THE RISE & FALL
OF THE WESTERN ECONOMY

1   Source data taken from Max Roser, "Economic Growth," Our World in Data, 2013, https://ourworldindata.org/economic-growth#all-charts-preview; Angus Maddison, *Contours of the World Economy, 1-2030 AD: Essays in Macro-Economic History* (Oxford University Press, 2007).

2   "Managing Public Wealth," International Monetary Fund, October 2018, https://www.imf.org/en/Publications/FM/Issues/2018/10/04/fiscal-monitor-october-2018;
China data taken from Frank Tang, "China has enough state assets to deal with its debt mountain, official think tank says," *South China Morning Post*, August 25, 2017, https://www.scmp.com/news/china/economy/article/2108344/china-has-enough-state-assets-deal-its-debt-mountain-official.

3   GDP figures taken from data collected by the International Monetary Fund, https://howmuch.net/articles/worlds-biggest-economies-over-time

4   Douglas MacArthur, "Speech delivered to Salvation Army," December 12, 1951.

5   Aristotle, *Nichomachean Ethics*, 8.11.

6   Kyle Harper, *Slavery in the Late Roman World, AD 275-425* (Cambridge University Press, 2011), 59.

7   Mark Cartwright, "Slavery in the Roman World," *Ancient History Encyclopedia*, November 1, 2013, https://www.ancient.eu/article/629/slavery-in-the-roman-world/. Walter Scheidel, *Escape from Rome: The Failure of Empire and the Road to Prosperity* (Princeton University Press, 2019), 74.

8   W. E. H. Lecky, *History of European Morals from Augustus to Charlemagne, Volume 2* (New York, 1897), 69.

9   Quoted in Rodney Stark, *How the West Won*, 124.

10   John Johnson, *Collection of all the Ecclesiastical Laws, Canons, Answers, or Rescripts of the Church of England, Volume One* (London, 1720), 341.

11   Council of London 1102, St. Peter's Church on the West Side of London, Canon 28.

12   Ibid., Canon 27.

13   McGarry, *Medieval History and Civilization* (New York, 1976), 242.

14   William Fitzstephen, *The Life and Death of Thomas Becket* (1961).

15   Roger Osborne, *Civilization: A New History of the Western World* (New York: Pegasus Books, 2006), 60.

16   Gravenor Henson, *The Civil, Political, and Mechanical History of the Framework-Knitters in Europe and America, Volume One* (Richard Sutton, 1831), 38.

17   Ibid., 50.

18   McCormick guaranteed 12-15 acres per day, as compared to a good hand reaper pulling in one acre a day.

19   Herbert Casson, *Cyrus Hall McCormick: His Life and Work* (Chicago, 1909), v, 190.

20   Ibid., 160.

21   Ibid., 158.

22   Table uses 1.5 Pound to Dollar conversion rate, inflation adjusted numbers. Reference: https://academic.oup.com/ej/article/129/623/2867/5490321 and https://ourworldindata.org/grapher/gdp-per-capita-in-the-uk-since-1270.

23   John Calvin, Sermon on 1 Timothy 6:1-2.

24   John Calvin, Sermon on Ephesians 6:5-9.

25   D. L. Noorlander, *Heaven's Wrath: The Protestant Reformation and the Dutch West India Company* (Cornell University Press, 2019), 169.

26   Ibid.

27   Kwame Anthony Appiah and Henry Louis Gates, *Africana: The Encyclopedia of the African and African American Experience* (Oxford: Oxford University Press, 1999).

28   "Focus on the slave trade," *BBC News*, September 3, 2001, http://news.bbc.co.uk/2/hi/africa/1523100.stm.

29   "Data Analysis: African Americans on the Eve of the Civil War," Bowdoin, https://www.bowdoin.edu/~prael/lesson/tables.htm.

30   Jenny Bourne, "Slavery in the United States," Economic History Association, https://eh.net/encyclopedia/slavery-in-the-united-states/.

31   Nathaniel Morton, *New England's Memorial* (1727), 72.

32   Ibid., 57.

33   Daniel Ford, *The Legacy of Liberty and Property in the American Colonization and the Founding of a Nation* (Lex Rex, 2010), 99.

34   Noah Webster, *An Examination into the Leading Principles of the Federal Constitution* (Prichard and Hall, 1787), 47-48.

35   Ibid., 46.

36   Hilaire Belloc, *The Servile State*, quoted in Allan C. Carlson, *Third Ways: How Bulgarian Greens, Swedish Housewives, and Beer-swilling Englishmen Created Family-centered Economies—and why They Disappeared* (ISI Books, 2007), 12.

37   Ibid., 16.

38   Ibid., 15.

39   Ibid.

40   *Communist Manifesto*, 1848.

41   Frederick Engels, *Origins of the Family, Private Property, and the State* (1884), https://www.marxists.org/archive/marx/works/1884/origin-family/ch02d.htm.

42   Ibid.

43   1890 to 1970, Goldin (1990) from U.S. Population Census; 1965 to 2004, March Current Population Survey (CPS), in Claudia Goldin, "The Quiet Revolution That Transformed Women's Employment, Education, and

Family," https://scholar.harvard.edu/files/goldin/files/the_quiet_revolution_that_transformed_womens_employment_education_and_family.pdf.

44   Mark Dewolf, "12 Stats About Women Working," U.S. Department of Labor Blog, March 1, 2017, https://blog.dol.gov/2017/03/01/12-stats-about-working-women.

45   John G. Paton, *Missionary Patriarch: The True Story of John G. Paton* (San Antonio: Vision Forum, 2001), 4.

46   Douglas Galbi, *Child Labor and the Division of Labor in the Early English Cotton Mills* (1994), https://www.galbithink.org/child.htm.

47   Ibid.

48   Raj Patel and Jim Goodman, "A Green New Deal for Agriculture," *Jacobin*, https://jacobinmag.com/2019/04/green-new-deal-agriculture-farm-workers.

49   Steven F. Hipple and Laurel A. Hammond, "Self-employment in the United States," U.S. Bureau of Labor Statistics, March 2016, https://www.bls.gov/spotlight/2016/self-employment-in-the-united-states/home.htm#:~:text=The%20self%2Demployment%20rate%20has%20trended%20down%20over%20the%20past%20two%20decades&text=In%201994%2C%20the%20self%2Demployment,8.7%20percent%20to%206.4%20percent; Justin Fox, "Where Are All the Self-Employed Workers?" *Harvard Business Review*, February 7, 2014, https://hbr.org/2014/02/where-are-all-the-self-employed-workers; Don McNay, "Are You Ready to Jump Into the World of Self-Employment?" *HuffPost*, August 10, 2011, https://www.huffpost.com/entry/are-you-ready-to-jump-int_b_922926.

50   Susan B. Carter and Richard C. Sutch, "Fixing the Facts: Editing of the 1880 U.S. Census of Occupations with Implications for Long-Term Labor Force Trends and the Sociology of Official Statistics," *Historical Methods* 29 (1996): 5-24; Robert Whaples, "Child Labor in the United States," Economic History Association, https://eh.net/encyclopedia/child-labor-in-the-united-states/.

51   https://www.ssa.gov/policy/docs/ssb/v39n1/v39n1p3.pdf

52   https://www.heritage.org/welfare/report/largest-welfare-increase-us-history-will-boost-government-support-76400-poor-family

54   https://www.imf.org/external/pubs/ft/fandd/2011/03/pdf/picture.pdf\

58   Friedrich A. Hayek, *Collected Works of F.A. Hayek*, Vol. 6 (Chicago: University of Chicago Press, 1999), 120.

59   Antoin E. Murphy, *John Law, Economic Theorist and Policy Maker* (Clarendon Press, 1997), 1.

60   Charles R. Williams, *The Life of Rutherford Birchard Hayes*, Vol. 2 (Boston: Houghton Mifflin, 1914), 120.

61   https://www.federalreserve.gov/monetarypolicy/reservereq.htm

62   Vince Cable and York Membery, "Karl Marx to John Maynard Keynes: Ten of the greatest economists by Vince Cable," *Daily Mail Online*, July 16, 2011, http://www.dailymail.co.uk/home/moslive/article-2014647/Karl-Marx-John-Maynard-Keynes-Ten-greatest-economists-Vince-Cable.html.

63   Evan Puschak, "FDR's evolution in thinking on Keynsian economics," MSNBC, August 13, 2013, http://www.msnbc.com/the-last-word/fdrs-evolution-thinking-keynsian.

64   Zygmund Dobbs, "Sugar Keynes," *The Review of the NEWS*, June 23, 1971, http://www.keynesatharvard.org/book/Sugar_Keynes.html.

65   Murray N. Rothbard, "The Myths of Reaganomics," Mises Institute, June 9, 2014, https://mises.org/library/myths-reaganomics.

66   Mark Thornton, "Hoover, Bush, and Great Depressions," Mises Institute, January 11, 2011, https://mises.org/library/hoover-bush-and-great-depressions.

67   Eric Alterman, "The Second Death of John Maynard Keynes," *The Nation*, September 19, 2011, https://www.thenation.com/article/second-death-john-maynard-keynes/.

68   Noah Smith, "Even Trump Is a Keynesian," *Bloomberg*, November 18, 2016, https://www.bloomberg.com/opinion/articles/2016-11-18/even-trump-is-a-keynesian; "Transcript: Interview with Donald Trump," *The Economist*, May 11, 2017, https://www.economist.com/united-states/2017/05/11/transcript-interview-with-donald-trump.

69   Robert Skidelsky, *John Maynard Keynes: Hopes Betrayed, 1883-1920* (Penguin Books, 1994), 6.

70   Ibid.

71   Ibid., 26.

72   Ibid., 42.

73   Ibid., 52.

74   Ibid., 55.

75   Richard Davenport-Hines, *Universal Man: the Lives of John Maynard Keynes* (Basic Books, 2015), 204.

76   Deborah McDonald, *The Prince, His Tutor, and the Ripper: The Evidence Linking James Kenneth Stephen to the Whitechapel Murders* (Jefferson, NC: McFarland and Company, 2007), 22ff.

77   Davenport-Hines, *Universal Man*, 217.

78   Ibid., 215, 245.

79   Ibid., 243.

80   Gilles Dostaler, *Keynes and His Battles*, trans. Niall B. Mann (Cheltenham, UK: Elger, 2007), 21.

81   Skidelsky, *John Maynard Keynes*, 517.

82   Ibid., 334.

83   Murray Rothbard, *Keynes the Man* (Mises Institute, 2010), 37.

84   John Maynard Keynes, *The Economic Consequences of Peace.*

85   John Maynard Keynes, *The General Theory of Employment, Interest and Money* (Macmillan, 1936), 378.

86   Ibid., 378.

87   https://fred.stlouisfed.org/series/TCMDO

86   https://fred.stlouisfed.org/series/GFDEGDQ188S

87   Kyung Lah, "Japan: Economy slips to third in world," CNN, February 14, 2011, http://edition.cnn.com/2011/BUSINESS/02/13/japan.economy.third/index.html.

88   John Maynard Keynes, A Tract on Monetary Reform

89   Katina Stefanova, "Are Collapsing Chinese Equities Just the Tip of the Iceberg?- Interview with a Tudor PM," Forbes, January 10, 2016, https://www.forbes.com/sites/katinastefanova/2016/01/10/how-collapsing-chinese-equities-impact-the-us-and-the-world-interview-with-a-former-pm-at-tudor/#521d3ac54173; reference https://www.axios.com/global-debt-gdp-898959ed-f96a-4c4d-85a3-5d3cc419631f.html.

90   Quoted in Llewellyn H. Rockwell, Jr, "Keynes Must Die," May 24, 2016, https://www.garynorth.com/public/15232.cfm.

91   Ibid.

92   https://www.ceicdata.com/en/indicator/united-states/unemployment-rate

93   https://www.statista.com/chart/18095/quarterly-gdp-growth-predicted-growth-selected-industrialized-nations-oecd/

94   https://www.reuters.com/article/us-china-economy-trade/chinas-export-growth-beats-expectations-on-resilient-global-demand-idUSKBN29J094; https://www.forbes.com/sites/kenroberts/2021/02/05/us-deficit-a-record-905-billion-in-2020-but-miraculously-trade-off-only-9/?sh=7b54f8be6aeb

95   https://asiatimes.com/2021/03/fed-is-financing-largest-us-deficit-since-wwii/

96   https://www.stlouisfed.org/open-vault/2020/december/has-wealth-inequality-changed-over-time-key-statistics

CHAPTER XI—THE RISE AND FALL
OF WESTERN CULTURE

1   Victor Tseng, "Why Classical Music Matters," Teasnag Blog, December 10, 2013, http://www.teasnag.org/why-classical-music-matters/.

2   Peter Martland, *Recording History: The British Record Industry, 1888-1931* (Scarecrow Press, 2013), 309.

3   Cassiodorus, *Institutions of Divine and Secular Learning and On the Soul*, trans. James W. Halporn (Liverpool, 2004), 32.

4   Augustine, *On Christian Teaching*, Book 2.

5   Ibid.

6   Ibid.

7   Quoted in *Detroit Free Press*, January 14, 1858.

8   Tertullian, *On Spectacles*, chapter 10.

9   Ibid., chapter 3.

10   Ibid., chapter 3.

11   Clement of Alexandria, *Instructor*, II.4.

12   Ibid.

13   Clement of Alexandria, *Stromata*, VI.

14   Clement of Alexandria, *Instructor*, II.4.

15   *Letters of Pliny*, 10.96.

16   John Cassian, *Nicene and Post-Nicene Fathers*, 10:209.

17   Synod of Laodicea, canon 59, http://www.allholyspirit.ne.goarch.org/about-orthodoxy/canon/ecf37synod_of_laodicea_historical_int-5ab.html.

18   Richard L. Holladay, "The *Musica Enchiriadis* and *Scholia Enchiriadis: A Commentary*," Doctoral dissertation, Ohio State University, 1977, https://etd.ohiolink.edu/!etd.send_file?accession=osu1392116314&disposition=inline.

19   Hughes Oliphant Old, "Daily Prayer in the Reformed Church of Strasbourg, 1525-1530," *Worship* 52, no. 2 (March 1978), 121-138.

20   Council of Elvira (AD 306), http://faculty.cua.edu/pennington/Canon Law/ElviraCanons.htm.

21   Quoted in Holland, *Dominion*, 278.

22   Ibid.

23   Francis A. Schaeffer, *How Should We Then Live?* (Crossway, 1983), 62.

24   Letter of Leonard da Vinci to Duke Ludovico of Milan.

25   Quoted in Schaeffer, *How Should We Then Live?* 95-96.

26   Quoted in ibid.

27   "The 50 Greatest Composers of All Time," *BBC Music Magazine,* January 30, 2020, https://www.classical-music.com/features/composers/50-greatest-composers-all-time/.

28   Quoted in Patrick Kavanaugh, *Spiritual Lives of the Great Composers* (Zondervan, 1996), 31.

29   Ibid., 32.

30   W. F. Alexander, ed., *Selected Letters of Mendelssohn* (London: Swan Sonnenschein and Co., 1894), 96.

31   Quoted in Paul Johnson, *The Birth of the Modern*, 117.

32   Ibid.

33   Percy Shelley, Preface to "Hellas."

34   Johnson, 125.

35   Edwin T. Bowden, *The Dungeon of the Heart* (New York, 1961), 69.

36   R. J. Rushdoony, *To Be as God: A Study of Modern Thought Since the Marquis de Sade* (Ross House Books, 2003), 76.

37   Quoted in Johnson, *Birth of the Modern*, 126.

38   A term used by Johnson in ibid., 163.

39   Gary D. Evans, "Beethoven's Final Months," March 25, 2019, https://www.ringnebula.com/music/beet/B_1827.htm.

40   Elliot Forbes, ed., *Thayer's Life of Beethoven, Volume 1* (Princeton University Press, 1967), 584.

41   Ibid., 284.

42   The most accurate account of Beethoven's death is recorded in Alexander Wheelock Thayer, *The Life of Ludwig von Beethoven Volume III*, Trans. Henry Edward Krehbiel (The Beethoven Association, 1921) 306-307.

43   Quoted in Jacques Barzun, Berlioz and the Romantic Century, Volume 1 (New York, 1969), 99.

44   Johnson, *Birth of the Modern*, 120.

45   Quoted in Ibid., 124.

46   Richard Wagner, *Prose Works*, Volume 1, trans. William Ashton Ellis (New York, 1966), 52.

47   Ibid., 59.

48   Ibid., 288.

49   William Gaunt, *The Life and Work of Vincent Van Gogh* (Columbus: Ohio State University, 1949), 70.

50   Erich Auerbach, *Mimesis: The Representation of Reality in Western Thought* (Princeton University Press, 2003), 22-23.

51   Quoted in Nancy Pearcey, *Saving Leonardo: A Call to Resist the Secular Assault on Mind, Morals, and Meaning* (Crossway, 2010), 271.

52   Peter Gay, *Modernism: The Lure of Heresy* (New York, 2008), 161.

53   Schaeffer, *How Should We Then Live?* 189-190.

54   Tom Wolfe, *The Painted World* (New York, 1976), 26.

55   Quoted in Jon Savage, *Teenage: The Creation of Youth Culture* (New York: Viking, 2007), 442.

56   https://slate.com/culture/2012/07/pop-music-is-getting-louder-and-dumber-says-one-study-heres-what-they-miss.html

57   Charles A. Reich, *The Greening of America* (New York: Random House, 1970), 245

58   https://americansongwriter.com/behind-the-song-i-cant-get-no-satisfaction/

59   "Richard Nixon Tapes: Archie Bunker & Homosexuality," Youtube, https://www.youtube.com/watch?v=TivVcfSBVSM.

60   Monica Anderson and Jingjing Jiang, "Teens, Social Media & Technology 2018," Pew Research Center, May 31, 2018, https://www.pewresearch.org/internet/2018/05/31/teens-social-media-technology-2018/.

61   Camille Paglia, "Lady Gaga and the death of sex," *Sunday Times*, September 12, 2010, https://www.thetimes.co.uk/article/lady-gaga-and-the-death-of-sex-lnzbcd70zj3.

62   Nick Routley, "Visualizing 40 Years of Music Industry Sales," Visual Capitalist, October 6, 2018, https://www.

visualcapitalist.com/music-industry-sales/.

63   "Number of movie tickets sold in the U.S. and Canada from 1980 to 2019," Statista, 2020, https://www.statista.com/statistics/187073/tickets-sold-at-the-north-american-box-office-since-1980/.

64   "The American Film Industry in the Early 1950s," Encyclopedia.com, https://www.encyclopedia.com/arts/culture-magazines/american-film-industry-early-1950s.

CHAPTER XII—THE RISE & FALL OF WESTERN LIBERTIES

1   "Wen Wang," trans. James Legge, Chinese Text Project, https://ctext.org/book-of-poetry/wen-wang.

2   Ibid.

3   Quoted in Steven W. Mosher, *Bully of Asia: Why China's Dream is the New Threat to World Order* (Washington DC: Regnery, 2017), 36.

4   Ibid., 37.

5   Quoted in Ibid., 44-45; also contains quote of *Memorial on the Burning of Books.*

6   Quoted in Phillip Mason, *The Men Who Ruled India* (Calcutta: Rupa, 1992), 12.

7   Quoted in Vishal Mangalwadi, *The Book that Made Your World*, 113.

8   Quoted in *Robert Winthrop, Addresses and Speeches on Various Occasions* (Boston: Little, Brown & Co., 1852), 172.

9   Theodoret, *Ecclesiastical History*, 5.17.

10   Fritz Kern, *Kingship and Law in the Middle Ages* (New Jersey: The Lawbook Exchange, 2005), 84.

11   "The Ordinance of Louis the Pius: Division of the Empire of the Year 817," The Avalon Project, Yale Law School, https://avalon.law.yale.edu/medieval/verdun.asp.

12   Sir John Spelman, *The Life of Alfred the Great* (London, 1709), 129-131.

13   Ibid., 96.

14   The story of the Magna Carta also appears in: Kevin Swanson, *The Story of Freedom* (Parker: CO, Generations, 2019), 68ff. Used by Permission.

15   Alfred, *The Whole Works of King Alfred the Great*, Volume 1 (Bosworth & Harrison, 1858), 387.

16   Ibid., 394.

17   David Carpenter, *The Struggle for Mastery: The Penguin History of Britain: 1066-1284* (New York: Penguin, 2004), 84.

18   Coronation Charter of Henry I in Derek Baker, ed., *England in the Early Middle Ages* (Dallas: Academia, 1993), 123.

19   Danny Danziger and John Gillingham, *1215: The Year of Magna Carta* (Simon and Schuster, 2003), 217.

20   Winston Churchill, *A History of the English-Speaking Peoples* (New York: Skyhorse Publishing, 2011), 87.

21   Danziger and Gillingham, *1215*, 92.

22   Ibid., 93.

23   Churchill, *History of the English-Speaking Peoples*, 103.

24   Danziger and Gillingham, 1215, 253.

25   H. C. Bettenson, ed., *Documents of the Christian Church* (Oxford University Press, 1967), 200-201.

26   Eugene Montague Macdonald, *A Short History of the Inquisition: What It Was and What It Did* (New York, 1915), 202.

27   C. V. Wedgwood, *William the Silent* (London, 1944), 250.

28   Quoted in Herbert H. Rowen, ed., *The Low Countries in Early Modern Times* (London: Macmillan, 1972), 45-46.

29   Kevin Gowen, ed., *Vindiciae Contra Tyrannos: A Defense of Liberty Against Tyrants*, https://reformed.org/documents/vindiciae/index.html.

30   Ibid.

31   Hugo Grotius, *De iure belli ac pacis*, chapter 8.

32   J. J. Scarisbrick, *Henry VIII* (University of California Press, 1969), 361.

33   John Clifford Solomon, "The Dissolution of the Monasteries: An Economic Study," Master of Arts thesis, Virginia Polytechnic Institute and State University, 1982, 54, https://vtechworks.lib.vt.edu/bitstream/handle/10919/80202/LD5655.V855_1982.S646.pdf?sequ.

34   Keith Hopkins, "The Political Economy of the Roman Empire" (Cambridge University, 1980).

35   Samuel Rutherford, *Lex, Rex, or The Law and the Prince* (Portage Publications, 2009), xxv.

36   Ibid., 401.

37   Ibid., 353.

38   Ibid., 310.

39   Ibid., 62.

40 Neil A. Frankel, "The Atlantic Slave Trade and Slavery in America," http://www.slaverysite.com/Body/facts%20and%20figures.htm.

41 Thomas Babington Macaulay, *The History of England from the Accession of James the Second*. Popular Edition in Two Volumes. (London: Longmans, 1889), 239.

42 Edmund Burke, *On Conciliation with America*, 1775, https://wisc.pb.unizin.org/ps601/chapter/edmund-burke-on-conciliation-with-america/

43 Ibid.

44 Clark, J. C. D., ed. *Reflections on the Revolution in France. A Critical Edition*. (Stanford University Press, 2001) 66-67.

45 R. J. Rummel, *Democide: Nazi Genocide and Mass Murder*, https://www.hawaii.edu/powerkills/NAZIS.CHAP1.HTM.

46 "Federal Net Outlays as Percent of Gross Domestic Product," FRED, https://fred.stlouisfed.org/series/FYONGDA188S.

47 "US Debt to GDP," Longtermtrends, https://www.longtermtrends.net/us-debt-to-gdp/.

48 https://taxfoundation.org/short-history-government-taxing-and-spending-united-states/
https://www.usgovernmentspending.com/total_spending_chart

49 Ibid.

50 Data obtained from Regulatory Studies Center, Columbian College of Arts & Sciences, https://regulatorystudies.columbian.gwu.edu/reg-stats.

51 Esteban Ortiz-Ospina, "Government Spending," OurWorldinData.org, 2016, https://ourworldindata.org/government-spending.

52 David U. Himmelstein, MD and Steffie Woolhandler, MD, MPH, "The Current and Projected Taxpayer Shares of US Health Costs," *US National Library of Medicine*, March 2016, https://www.ncbi.nlm.nih.gov/pmc/articles/PMC4880216/.

53 "Supreme Court rejects Hawaii B&B that refused to serve lesbian couple," NBC News, March 18, 2019, https://www.nbcnews.com/feature/nbc-out/supreme-court-rejects-hawaii-b-b-refused-serve-lesbian-couple-n984376.

54 Robert Barnes, "Supreme Court declines case of photographer who denied service to gay couple," Washington Post, April 7, 2014, https://www.washingtonpost.com/politics/supreme-court-wont-review-new-mexico-gay-commitment-ceremony-photo-case/2014/04/07/f9246cb2-bc3a-11e3-9a05-c739f29ccb08_story.html.

55 Elizabeth Redden, "A Win for LGBTQ Rights, or a Loss for Religious Freedom?" Inside Higher Ed, June 18, 2018, https://www.insidehighered.com/news/2018/06/18/canadian-supreme-court-upholds-denial-accreditation-proposed-christian-law-school.

56 Samuel Smith, "Faith-Based Pepperdine University Vows to Fully Comply With Obama's Title IX Interpretation," Christian Post, August 2, 2016, https://www.christianpost.com/news/pepperdine-university-vows-fully-comply-obamas-title-ix-interpretation.html.

57 Evan Gerstmann, "Teacher Sues After Getting Fired For Refusing To Refer To Transgender Student With Male Pronouns," Forbes, October 3, 2019, https://www.forbes.com/sites/evangerstmann/2019/10/03/virginia-school-district-fires-teacher-who-wouldnt-refer-to-transgender-student-using-male-pronouns/#5b5f437d-6ed5.

58 "SJ Church Faces $350K Fine, Court Order After Hosting Weekly Indoor Services," NBC Bay Area, October 30, 2020, https://www.nbcbayarea.com/news/local/sj-church-faces-steep-fine-court-order-after-hosting-weekly-indoor-services/2388877/.

59 Tamara Lush and Chris O'Meara, "Florida megachurch pastor arrested for holding services, defying social distancing orders," USA Today, March 31, 2020, https://www.usatoday.com/story/news/nation/2020/03/31/coronavirus-florida-megachurch-pastor-arrested-church-amid-orders/5093160002/.

60 Maura Dolan, "U.S. appeals court upholds California's coronavirus restrictions on churches," *Los Angeles Times*, October 1, 2020, https://www.latimes.com/california/story/2020-10-01/california-appeals-court-churches-coronavirus; Ian Millhiser, "The Supreme Court's surprising decision on churches and the pandemic, explained," Vox, July 25, 2020, https://www.vox.com/2020/7/25/21338216/supreme-court-churches-pandemic-covid-samuel-alito-brett-kavanaugh-calvary-chapel.

CHAPTER XIII—THE RISE & FALL
OF EDUCATION IN THE WEST

1 Margaret Dunlop Gibson, *The Didascalia Apostolorum in English* (Cambridge: C.J. Clay & Sons, 1903), 101.

2 Ibid., 5.

3 The following section has been adapted from Kevin Swanson, *Keep the Faith: On Education* (Parker, CO: Generations, 2016), 22-33.

4 *The Letters of St. Jerome*, Volume I, trans. Charles Christopher Mierow (New York: Paulist Press, 1963), 117.

5   Ibid., 190-194.

6   Justo L. Gonzalez, *The Story of Christianity, Volume 1: The Early Church to the Dawn of the Reformation* (New York: Harper Collins, 1984), 201-202.

7   Augustine, *Confessions,* trans. Albert C. Outler (Peabody, MA: Hendrickson, 2004), 1:16, 5.6.

8   Augustine, *On Christian Teaching,* 2:28,38,39,40, Nicene and Post-Nicene Fathers, Volume 2 (Peabody, MA: Hendrickson, 2004).

9   James W. Halporn "Introduction" in Cassiodorus, *Institutions of Divine and Secular Learning,* 32.

10   The following section has been adapted from Swanson, *Keep the Faith: On Education,* 43-50.

11   Cassiodorus, *Institutions of Divine and Secular Learning,* 230.

12   Ibid., 160.

13   Ibid.

14   Ibid.

15   Ibid., 230.

16   Ibid., 159.

17   Ibid.

18   Paul Cavill, *Anglo-Saxon Christianity: Exploring the Earliest Roots of Christian Spirituality in England* (London: HarperCollins, 1999), 57.

19   Thomas Cahill, *How the Irish Saved Civilization* (New York: Doubleday, 1995), 159.

20   George Hardin Brown, *A Companion to Bede* (Suffolk: Boydell Press, 2009), 20.

21   Ibid., 21.

22   Ibid., 19.

23   Peter Leithart, "Medieval Theology and the Roots of Modernity," *Revolutions in Worldview: Understanding the Flow in Western Thought* (Phillipsburg, NJ: Presbyterian and Reformed, 2007), 147.

24   M. D. Chenu, *Nature, Man and Society in the Twelfth Century: Essays on New Theological Perspectives in the Latin West* (University of Toronto Press, 1997), 272.

25   Peter Leithart, "Medieval Theology and the Roots of Modernity," 155.

26   Quoted in Brother Azarias, *Aristotle and the Christian Church* (New York: William H. Sadler, 1888), 50.

27   Quoted in Rufus M. Jones, *Studies in Mystical Religion* (Eugene, OR: Wipf and Stock, originally published 1909), 185.

28   Quoted in Azarias, *Aristotle and the Christian Church,* 70.

29   Ibid., 75.

30   Schaff, *History of the Christian Church,* 5:288.

31   Martin Luther, Letter to John Lang, February 8, 1517. Quoted in *The Life and Letters of Martin Luther,* Ed. Preserved Smith, (Houghton Mifflin, 1914), 26.

32   Ibid., 26.

33   Ibid., 25.

34   *Luther's Works, American Edition* (AE), Volume 44 (Fortress Press, 1966), 207.

35   Quoted in David Daniell, *William Tyndale: A Biography* (New Haven: Yale University Press, 1994), 37.

36   John Knox, *The Works of John Knox,* Volume VI (Banner of Truth, 2014), 630.

37   Ibid., 619.

38   Martin Luther, "A Sermon on Keeping Children in School," in *Luther's Works,* Vol. 46 (Philadelphia: Fortress Press, 1967), 213-257.

39   "Old Deluder Satan Law of 1647," Mass.gov, https://www.mass.gov/files/documents/2016/08/ob/deludersatan.pdf.

40   John Amos Comenius, *The Great Didactic,* trans. M. W. Keatinge (London: A. & C. Black, 1907), 236.

41   Ibid., 231.

42   Ibid., 240-241.

43   Ibid., 248.

44   Ibid., 69.

45   Ibid., 74.

46   Ibid.

47   Ibid., 224-225.

48   Ibid, 225.

49   Ibid., 226.

50 S. Bryn Roberts, *Puritanism and the Pursuit of Happiness: The Ministry and Theology of Ralph Venning* (Boydell & Brewer Ltd, 2015), 31.

51 Patrick Collinson, "The English Revolution," in Sarah Bendall, Christopher Brooke, & Patrick Collinson, *A History of Emmanuel College, Cambridge* (Suffolk, UK: Boydell Press, 1999), 256.

52 Nathaniel Culverwell, *An elegant and learned discourse of the light of nature, with several other treatises, Volume 1* (Oxford: Tho. Williams, 1669), 7.

53 Ibid., 53.

54 "The Harvard Charter of 1650," Harvard Library, March 31, 1650, https://emeritus.library.harvard.edu/university-archives/using-the-collections/online-resources/charter-of-1650.

55 "Shield and 'Veritas' History," Harvard GSAS Christian Community, http://www.hcs.harvard.edu/~gsascf/shield-and-veritas-history/.

56 Michael G. Hall, *The Last American Puritan*, 199.

57 Ibid., 272.

58 Ibid.

59 Ibid., 167.

60 Ibid., 304.

61 Ibid., 285.

62 Increase Mather, *Ichabod: Or, A discourse, shewing what cause there is to fear that the glory of the Lord is departing from New-England*, 1702, https://quod.lib.umich.edu/e/evans/N00897.0001.001?view=toc.

63 Will and Ariel Durant, *Rousseau and Revolution* (New York: Simon & Schuster, 1967), 3.

64 Paul Johnson, *Intellectuals* (New York: HarperCollins, 2009), 2.

65 Arthur Huebsch, "Jean-Jacques Rousseau and John Dewey: A Comparative Study and a Critical Estimate of their Philosophies, and their Educational and Related Theories and Practices," Doctoral dissertation, New York University School of Education, 1930.

66 Jean-Jacques Rousseau, *Emile*, Book 1, trans. Barbara Foxley, Project Gutenberg, https://www.gutenberg.org/ebooks/5427.

67 Plato, *The Republic*, Book 5, trans. Benjamin Jowett, Project Gutenberg, https://www.gutenberg.org/ebooks/55201/.

68 Durant, *Rousseau and Revolution*, 179.

69 Rousseau, *Emile*, Book 1.

70 Quoted in Guillemette Johnston and Allan Johnston, *Journal of the Philosophy of Education*, Vol. 3, Spring 2018, Fordham University, 161.

71 Rousseau, *Emile*, Book 2.

72 Ibid.

73 Friedrich Froebel, *Froebel's Chief Writings on Education* (London: Edward Arnold, 1912), 180.

74 Horace Mann, *The Common School Journal*, Volume III (January 1, 1841), 15.

75 Quoted in R.J. Rushdoony, *The Messianic Character of American Education* (Vallecito, CA: Ross House Publishers, 1963), 42

76 Granville Stanley Hall, *Life and Confessions of a Psychologist* (New York: D. Appleton, 1923), 540.

77 G. Stanley Hall, "Discussion" in *The Journal of Proceedings and Addresses of the National Educational Association* (New York: The Association, 1891), 99.

78 John Dewey, *My Pedagogic Creed*, 1897.

79 Ibid.

80 Quoted in Leonard Woolsey Bacon, *A History of American Christianity* (New York: Scribner, 1897), 138.

81 Noll, *A History of Christianity*, 371.

82 Gary North, *Crossed Fingers: How the Liberals Captured the Presbyterian Church* (Tyler, Texas: Institute for Christian Economics, 1996), 186-187.

83 William Barksdale Maynard, *Woodrow Wilson: Princeton to the Presidency* (New Haven, CT: Yale University, 2008), 147.

84 Woodrow Wilson, *The Constitutional Government of the United States* (New York: Columbia University Press, [1908] 1961), 54-57.

85 Only forty small colleges would maintain a young-earth perspective by the year 2020. "Colleges and Universities," Answers in Genesis, https://answersingenesis.org/colleges/colleges-and-universities/.

86 Megan Brenan, "40% of Americans Believe in Creationism," Gallup, July 26, 2019, https://news.gallup.com/poll/261680/americans-believe-creationism.aspx.

87   Colleen Flaherty, "Evidence of 'Liberal Academe,'" Inside Higher Ed, October 3, 2016, https://www.inside-highered.com/news/2016/10/03/voter-registration-data-show-democrats-outnumber-republicans-among-so-cial-scientists.

88   calvinchimes.org/2020/10/16/I-am-Calvin-universitys-first-openly-gay-student-body-president.

89   "Term Enrollment Estimates: Spring 2020," National Student Clearinghouse Research Center, https://nscre-searchcenter.org/wp-content/uploads/CTEE_Report_Spring_2020.pdf; "Total undergraduate fall enrollment in degree-granting postsecondary institutions, by attendance status, sex of student, and control and level of institution: Selected years, 1970 through 2028," Digest of Education Statistics, https://nces.ed.gov/pro-grams/digest/d18/tables/dt18_303.70.asp; James S. Bikales and Kevin R. Chen, "Over 20 Percent of Harvard Undergrads Do Not Intend to Enroll in Fall 2020," Harvard Crimson, August 7, 2020, thecrimson.com/arti-cle/2020/8/7/harvard-coronavirus-fall-enrollment-numbers/.

90   Megan DeMatteo, "Should Gen Z be taking on more student loan debt? The decision's getting 'harder and harder,' says an economist," CNBC.com, August 28, 2020, https://www.cnbc.com/select/are-student-loans-worth-it/.

91   Stephen McBride, "Why College Is Never Coming Back," Forbes, July 21, 2020, https://www.forbes.com/sites/stephenmcbride1/2020/07/21/why-college-is-never-coming-back/#7e72000924b7.

92   Augustine, City of God, Nicene and Post-Nicene Fathers, Vol. 2 (Peabody, MA: Hendrickson, 2004), 429.

93   Edwards v. Aguillard, 482 U.S. 578 (1987), US Supreme Court Center, https://supreme.justia.com/cases/feder-al/us/482/578/.

94   Claire Chretien, "Perverted school lesson describes woman who 'had sex with 21 men and 3 women,'" LifeSite-News, May 2, 2017, https://www.lifesitenews.com/news/missouri-high-school-word-problem-prudence-had-sex-with-21-men-and-3-w.

95   Evan Gerstmann, "Teacher Sues After Getting Fired For Refusing To Refer To Transgender Student With Male Pronouns," Forbes, October 3, 2019, https://www.forbes.com/sites/evangerstmann/2019/10/03/virginia-school-district-fires-teacher-who-wouldnt-refer-to-transgender-student-using-male-pronouns/#350cdd9f6ed5; Jonathan Petre, "I called a trans boy a girl by mistake ... and it may cost me my job as a teacher: Maths tutor suspended after praising pupil using the wrong gender," Daily Mail, November 11, 2017, https://www.daily-mail.co.uk/news/article-5073511/Teacher-suspended-praising-pupil-using-wrong-gender.html.

96   Samuel Smith, "SBC Pres. JD Greear says he'll refer to trans individuals by their preferred pronouns," Christian Post, November 26, 2019, https://www.christianpost.com/news/sbc-president-jd-greear-says-he-will-refer-to-transgender-individuals-by-their-preferred-pronouns.html.

CHAPTER XIV—THE RISE & FALL OF THE WEST

1   Patrick Sookhdeo, The Death of Western Christianity: Drinking from the Poisoned Wells of the Cultural Revolution (McLean, VA: Isaac Publishing, 2017).

2   Ibid.

3   "Black and ethnic minority Christians lead London Church growth," The Evangelical Alliance, July 25, 2013, https://www.eauk.org/church/one-people-commission/stories/black-and-ethnic-christians-lead-london-church-growth.cfm.

4   Ibid.

5   "Top 101 cities with the highest percentage of single-parent households, population 50,000+," City-Data.com, 2020, https://www.city-data.com/top2/h7.html.

6   Stephanie Kramer, "U.S. has world's highest rate of children living in single-parent households," Pew Research Center, December 12, 2019, https://www.pewresearch.org/fact-tank/2019/12/12/u-s-children-more-likely-than-children-in-other-countries-to-live-with-just-one-parent/.

7   "Statistics and Forecasts for World Religions: 1800-2025," Christianity in View, http://christianityinview.com/religion-statistics.html.

8   "Estimated world population, 1800-1950," University of Botswana History Department, 2000, http://www.thuto.org/ubh/ub/h202/wpop1.htm.

9   "Global Christianity—A Report on the Size and Distribution of the World's Christian Population," Pew Re-search Center, December 19, 2011, https://www.pewforum.org/2011/12/19/global-christianity-exec/.

10   Data analyzed from "The Global Religious Landscape: Christians," Pew Research Center, December 18,. 2012, https://www.pewforum.org/2012/12/18/global-religious-landscape-christians/.

11   Data analyzed from "The Global Religious Landscape: Muslims," Pew Research Center, December 18,. 2012, https://www.pewforum.org/2012/12/18/global-religious-landscape-muslim/.

12   https://www.wycliffe.net/resources/statistics/

13   John Wyclife, Tracts and Treatises of John de Wycliffe (London: Blackburn and Pardon, 1845), Trans. Robert Vaughn, Part 1.

14   Quoted in Sookhdeo, The Death of Western Christianity, 154.

15   https://www.christianCentury.org/article/2010-09/sunday-night-services-fading-tradition

16   Augustine, *Confessions*, Book 1.

17   Fr. Joseph Fessio, "The Family: Monastery of the New Dark Ages," Antrim Parish, September 23, 2013, http://www.antrimparish.com/2013/09/the-family-monastery-of-the-new-dark-ages/.

IMAGE CREDITS

1-1	Wikimedia Commons		6-5	Wikimedia Commons
1-2	Wikimedia Commons		7-1	iStock.com
1-3	Wikimedia Commons		7-2	iStock.com
1-4	Wikimedia Commons		7-3	Published in Renaissance
1-5	Wikimedia Commons			Quarterly 2011, Diana
2-1	Wikimedia Commons			Bullen Presciutti
2-2	Wikimedia Commons		7-4	Wikimedia Commons
2-3	iStock.com		7-5	iStock.com
2-4	iStock.com		7-6	Wikimedia Commons
2-5	Wikimedia Commons		7-7	Wikimedia Commons
2-6	iStock.com		8-1	Wikimedia Commons
3-1	Wikimedia Commons		8-2	Wikimedia Commons
3-2	Wikimedia Commons		8-3	Wikimedia Commons
3-3	Wikimedia Commons		8-4	Wikimedia Commons
3-4	Wikimedia Commons		9-1	British Library, Harley MS 2971 f.
4-1	iStock.com			109v, Book of Hours, c. 1450-1460
4-2	Wikimedia Commons		9-2	Wikimedia Commons
4-3	iStock.com		9-3	Wikimedia Commons
4-4	iStock.com		9-4	iStock.com
5-1	iStock.com		9-5	Wikimedia Commons
5-2	iStock.com		9-6	Wikimedia Commons,
5-3	iStock.com			iStock.com
5-4	Wikimedia Commons		9-7	Wikimedia Commons,
6-1	iStock.com			iStock.com
6-2	Wikimedia Commons		10-1	Wikimedia Commons
6-3	Wikimedia Common s		10-2	Wikimedia Commons
6-4	Unsplash.com, Rachel Coyne.		10-3	Wikimedia Commons

10-4	Wikimedia Commons	11-14	Wikimedia Commons
10-5	iStock.com	12-1	iStock.com
10-6	Wikimedia Commons	12-2	WililamTell.nl
10-7	Wikimedia Commons	12-3	sco.wikipedia.org
11-1	Wikimedia Commons	12-4	Wikimedia Commons
11-2	Wikimedia Commons	12-5	Public Domain, Public Domain
11-3	British Library, Stowe Breviary, Stowe MS12	12-6	Public Domain
		12-7	Wikimedia Commons
11-4	Wikimedia Commons, iStock.com	12-8	adfmedia.org
		13-1	Wikimedia Commons
		13-2	Wikimedia Commons
11-5	Wikimedia Commons	13-3	Wikimedia Commons
11-6	Wikimedia Commons	13-4	Wikimedia Commons
11-7	iStock.com	13-5	WIkimedia Commons
11-8	Wikimedia Commons	13-6	Wikimedia Commons
11-9	Wikimedia Commons	13-7	Wikimedia Commons
11-10	Wikimedia Commons	13-8	Rudolph Zallinger's "The March of Progress"
11-11	iStock.com		
11-12	Wikimedia Commons	13-9	Wikimedia Commons
11-13	Wikimedia Commons	13-10	iStock.com

GENERAL INDEX

A

à Kempis, Thomas 208, 255, 546, 700
Abelard, Peter 15, 177-178, 181, 636, 714
Abington School District v. Schempp 352
Abortifacients 21, 33, 34, 35, 37, 44-46, 124, 365, 460, 676, 703
Abortion 29-37, 44-45, 61, 93, 124, 218, 279, 283, 285, 288, 304, 309-315, 320, 337, 348, 358-359, 365-366, 370, 380, 382, 405, 411-412, 467-468, 484, 497, 519, 570, 587, 622 675, 678, 684-685, 698, 702-703, 713, 720, 722, 724
Acton, William 342-343
Adams
        Jay 287
        John 237, 257, 613-614
        Samuel 613, 614
Addams, Jane 402
Adomnàn 385-386
Adultery 93-94, 155, 292, 304, 305, 310, 311, 314, 316, 317, 320, 321, 325, 327, 332, 336, 342, 346, 347, 371, 398, 508, 510, 533, 547, 556, 678
Adventism 265, 410
Ælfric of Eynsham 200
Æthelwulf 328
Aethelflaed 329
Africa 14–15, 29, 37, 71, 79, 130, 161, 203, 230, 232, 257, 276, 280, 281, 289, 358, 359, 363, 368-370, 389, 405, 418, 444, 445, 486, 487, 497, 562, 591, 670-672, 679, 680, 718, 729
        South Africa 37, 230, 276, 281, 289, 363, 368-370
Agnosticism 114, 448, 659
Agobard 166
Aidan 132, 135, 136, 149, 157
Alcohol 32, 480, 562
Alcuin of York 87, 96, 97, 137, 148, 166, 231, 326, 633, 696, 711, 712, 721
Aldhelm of Malmesbury 98, 634
Alexander
        II (Macedonia) 579
        V (Pope) 212
        VI (Pope) 198
        J.A. 242
        James W. 179
        The Coppersmith 15
        The Great 341 359, 378, 579
Alexandria 85, 99, 151, 152, 165, 313, 315, 325, 388, 389, 391, 531, 533, 538
Alfred the Great 148, 327-331, 334-335, 344, 370ff, 592, 593, 605, 667
Alighieri, Dante 106-108, 359
All in the Family 571

Alleine Joseph 255

Allen A.A. 277

Ambrose of Milan 167, 534, 590

Ames, William 224

Amsterdam 47, 344-346

Anabaptists 226, 227 247, 267

Anarchy 42, 61, 84, 190, 247, 361, 497, 542, 563, 587, 678, 693

Anselm

       Hüttenbrenner 555

       Of Canterbury 88, 91, 98, 116, 176-182, 218, 478, 484, 636, 700, 710, 711, 714

Anskar 91, 132-133, 137, 711

Antichrist 72, 121, 164, 171, 172, 714

Antinomianism 69, 94, 190, 272, 284, 296, 689

Antioch 152, 231, 391, 628, 644

Antithesis 116, 576, 628, 688, 691, 699, 700

Apologetics 96, 101, 162, 259, 288, 440 508

Apostate 15, 18, 22, 30, 43, 70, 79, 104 115, 118, 121, 122, 128, 260, 281, 282, 301, 330, 341, 360, 366, 369, 385, 389 400, 406, 415, 424, 508, 557, 560, 561, 576, 604, 650, 651, 670, 673, 688, 691

Apostles Creed 81, 137, 156, 214, 274

Apple (company) 40

Aquinas, Thomas 15, 100-106, 111, 116, 117, 125, 182, 199, 425, 426, 441, 637-639, 642, 696, 699

Arianism 75–76, 153, 157, 256

Aristotle 70, 92–96, 178, 210–211, 227, 289, 404, 406–407, 410, 412, 456, 465–467, 516, 604–606, 610–611, 613–614, 616, 661, 664, 711, 726

Arius 83, 85, 185,

Arnaud-Amalric 193

Arnim, Bettina von 552

Arnot, Frederick Stanley 230, 259

Art 109, 197, 305, 313, 419, 527-575

Artaxerxes III 309, 579

Asaph 22

Astrology 86, 424-427, 438, 445, 463, 464, 576, 584

Astronomy 80, 82, 85, 133, 210, 271, 530, 630, 700, 710

Athanasius 71, 73, 76, 125, 202, 258, 502, 597, 665

Atheism 18, 49, 56, 57, 70, 86, 114, 119, 120, 245, 254, 264, 269, 271, 280, 286, 303, 346, 357, 361, 378, 396, 436, 437, 441, 444, 448, 460, 505, 512, 563, 614, 615, 654, 659

Athelstan 329-331, 334, 477, 721

Athens 99, 308, 344, 389, 392, 630, 699, 700

Augustine of Canterbury 132, 137, 149, 394, 725

Augustine of Hippo 17, 79, 80, 86-88, 93, 96, 98-100, 106, 108, 112, 138, 139, 140, 147, 161, 162, 167-169, 177, 178, 180, 182, 199, 218, 319 325, 344, 385, 414, 425, 438, 477, 530, 531, 631, 633, 638, 660, 696, 699, 700, 710, 711, 714, 715, 725, 726, 731, 735, 737, 738

Australia 37, 278, 280, 288, 355, 363, 368-370, 408, 473, 499, 718

Austria 363, 399, 473, 519

Autonomy 41, 53, 68, 104, 116, 120, 124, 176, 190, 220, 248-250, 280, 283, 284, 307, 338, 344-346, 359, 554, 558, 560, 562, 582, 610, 632, 636, 637, 650, 651, 663

Averroes of Spain 426

Avignon Papacy 195, 196, 203, 209, 216, 361

Aztecs 30, 307

Azusa Street Revival 275-276

B

Babbage Charles 432

Baby Boomers 35-36, 360

Baptists 205, 224, 225, 227, 232, 237, 241, 254, 263, 264, 266-173, 286, 296, 297, 410, 451, 454, 508, 509, 663

Bach

       Johann Ambrosias 549

       Johann Sebastian 530, 535, 537, 548-550, 557, 558, 561

       Johannes 549

       Vitus 549

Bacon, Roger 421, 429, 725

Bakker, Jim, 278

Barnabas 311, 719

Barnhouse, Donald 263

Barrow, Henry 223

Barth, Karl 252

Basil of Caesarea 321, 392-394, 628, 700, 723

Battenberg, Jan van 247

Bavaria 132, 133

Baxter, Richard 238, 255

Beatrice 107, 108

Becket, Thomas 595, 729

Bede 87, 90, 96, 98, 135-137, 147, 157, 200, 321, 634, 696, 711-713, 725, 735

Beecher

  Henry Ward 655

  Lyman 655

Beeke, Joel 223, 224, 263, 716

Beethoven, Ludwig van 530, 552, 554-557, 568, 732

Belgium 35, 47, 132, 141, 364, 399, 419, 548

Belloc, Hilaire 489, 490, 729

Belz, Joel 69

Benedict of Nursia, Benedictine Order 138-141, 147, 286, 395, 416, 420, 535, 713

Bentham, Jeremy 15, 119, 249, 344, 509, 511, 721

Benz, Ernst 414

Berkeley, George 15, 117, 119

Berlioz, Hector 555

Bernard

  Henry 653

  Of Clairvaux 141, 148, 178-180, 419

Berthoud, Jean-Marc 438

Best, Charles 458

Bestiality 317, 320, 624

Beyoncé 387

Beza, Theodore 604

Bible 111, 140, 200, 201, 211, 214, 21, 219, 238, 252, 270, 274, 289, 290, 352, 420, 432, 436-438, 452, 460, 482, 492, 506, 509, 551, 586, 632, 634, 638, 642, 643, 645, 656, 661, 664, 676, 716, 719 724, 726, 727

Biddle, Francis 350

Biden, Joseph 355, 498, 624, 667

Bin Laden, Osama 383-384

Bingham, Hiram 230

Birth Rates/Implosion 28, 29, 33, 35, 37, 41, 70, 216, 255, 259, 304, 364, 370, 412, 518, 519, 670, 707

Bjorn (King) 133

Black Death 455, 478, 542, 625, 668, 683

Blake, William, 383, 723

Bluetooth, Harald 133, 331

Boethius 95, 96, 699

Bogomil,189

Bohemia 132, 133, 174, 200, 21-213, 553, 556,

571, 659

Bolingbroke 249

Bolsheviks 342, 347, 582

Bonaparte, Napoleon, 363, 383, 399, 503

Bonar

  Andrew 261

  Horatius 261

Boniface 132, 133

  IV 146, 156

  VIII 195

Bork, Robert, 69

Bostel, Daniel, 455

Bostock v. Clayton 62, 366, 622

Boy Scouts of America 408

Boyle, Robert 432, 433, 444, 446, 684

Bradford, William 346, 605, 721

Bradwardine, Thomas 423

Brainard, David 230, 241

Brattle, William 15, 234, 648

Brecht, Bertolt 348

Brewster, William 224

Briggs, Charles 273, 274

Britton, Nan 349

Brooks, Thomas 289, 645

Brown

  George 634

  John 508

Browning, Oscar 510

Brunelleschi 543

Bruno, Giordano 428

Brussels 47, 216

Brutus, Junius 580

Bubonic Plague - See Black Death

Bucer, Martin 208

Buchanan, Pat 66, 710

Buck v. Bell 351

Bukhtishu, Jabril ibn 396

Bulgaria 189, 408,

Bunyan, John 508, 509, 682

Burke, Edmund 614, 734

Burkett, Larry 292

Burns, William C. 230, 259, 261

Bush

  George H.W. 365, 367, 698

  George W. 367, 500, 507, 616-618, 623, 698

  Prescott 698

Bushnell, Horace 655

Byron Lord, 48, 553, 568

C

Caedmon 89

Caesar 77, 84, 304, 305, 307, 349, 581, 620, 658,

    Augustus 78, 382

    Caligula 306, 326, 580

    Carus 306

    Claudius 580

    Commodus 306, 326

    Decius 588

    Diocletian 326, 588

    Domitian 580

    Elagabalus 306, 326, 411

    Hadrian 306

    Julian the Apostate, 389

    Julius 78, 309, 382

    Nero 41, 46, 306, 335, 326, 364, 406, 407, 588, 662

    Titus 306

    Valerian 588

Cahill, Thomas, 148, 711, 713, 735

Cain, Paul 278

Calusa Tribe 30, 307

Calvary Chapel 289

Calvin, John 88, 100, 109, 167, 183, 205, 208, 217, 220-222, 225 232, 236, 260, 262, 263, 267, 268, 289, 398, 428, 450, 451, 485, 600, 617, 618, 650, 714, 715, 726, 729

Calvin College 657, 658

Cambridge University 224, 248, 509, 510, 637, 644, 645, 717

Campin, Robert 548

Campus Crusade for Christ 289

Camus, Albert 121

Canada 35, 37, 47, 230, 266, 280, 282, 318, 401, 408, 458, 472, 501, 620

Canute 331, 332, 334

Capitein, Jacobus 486

Cardan, Jerome 427

Carey

    George 668

    William 230

Carlson, Allan 489, 729

Carslaw, W.H. 243

Carson, Johnny 570

Carthage, Carthaginians 77, 79, 165, 309, 317, 337, 378, 389

Carver, George Washington 448-450

Carzodo, Benjamin 350

Catholicism 26, 45, 60, 81, 137, 152, 182, 192-194, 203, 204, 212, 216, 248, 260, 264, 279, 282, 285, 286, 290, 340, 398, 405, 410, 415, 427, 432, 485-487, 497, 550, 552, 555, 611, 615, 648, 649, 679, 699, 701

Case, George 270

Cassian, John 534

Cassiodorus 96, 140, 438, 632, 633

Casson, Herbert 482

Castro, Fidel 383

Centralization of Power 134, 151, 175, 183, 228, 479 489, 566, 607, 619, 670

    Decentralization 228, 479, 670

Chad (Missionary) 135-136

Chaderton, Laurence 644-645

Chalmers, Thomas 260-261

Charlemagne 96, 97, 101, 137, 148, 152, 166, 231, 326, 327, 334, 395, 477, 502, 536, 538, 591, 592, 711, 712, 721, 723, 729

Charles

    I 225, 341, 487, 608

    II 15, 259, 486, 608

    V 220

Charnock, Stephen 645

Chauncy, Charles 249

Chesterton, G.K. 59, 60, 671, 686, 709

China 165, 229, 231, 261, 289, 389, 370, 378, 408, 453, 473, 479, 480, 489, 499, 507, 522, 582, 585, 725, 728, 731

Christendom 138, 292, 314, 370, 539, 577, 709

Christological Heresies 84, 165

Christiano, Rich 288

Christus, Petrus 546

Chromatius 477

Chrysostom, John 82, 94, 710, 711

Church Attendance 44, 233, 241, 257, 258, 273, 282, 290, 291, 496, 674, 675, 717, 718

Churchill, Winston 329, 516, 596, 721, 733

Cicero 96, 106, 237, 309, 388, 415, 630, 642, 645, 719, 723

City of God 17, 79, 79, 86, 96, 99, 161, 162, 319, 425, 633, 660

Civil War (England) 225, 594

Civil War (Rome) 382

Civil War (US) 348
Clark, Gordon 52, 287, 709
Clement
    Of Alexandria 313, 315, 316, 391,
533, 510
    Of Rome 85, 710
    Of Scotland (Franks) 150
    V (Pope) 598
Cleveland, Grover 617
Clinton, Bill 366, 367, 472
Clovis 591
    II 477
Cluniac Reform 141
Cobain, Kurt 21, 573
Cohabitation 44, 279, 356, 722
College 21, 36, 46, 141, 214, 215, 217, 224,
233, 234, 237, 249, 261, 262, 289, 412, 415,
423, 424, 454, 467, 495, 548, 623, 624, 639,
644, 645, 646-664, 683
Collins, Anthony 249
Colman 135, 149, 214
Colorado 61, 358, 364, 365, 616, 662, 703
Columbanus 132, 146, 147, 149
Columbia (Country) 35, 486
Columbia College 657
Comenius, Johann Amos 641-644, 696, 735
Commandments 17, 23, 28, 39, 62, 93, 94,
155, 164, 166, 198, 208, 214, 294, 301, 312,
327, 329, 354, 397, 398, 406, 471, 472, 492-
494, 530, 567, 587, 610, 623, 694, 695, 702,
Communion of Church 81, 82, 167, 186,
206, 233-235, 268, 280, 320, 509, 590, 701
Communism-Marxism 247, 280, 295, 397,
405, 407, 408, 489, 519, 692
Communist Manifesto 400, 490
Comstock, Anthony 348
Conception Control 21, 19, 34, 35, 44, 45,
246, 283, 304, 363, 365, 366, 466, 467, 484,
511, 515, 554, 570, 680, 684
Confessions and Creeds 441, 691
    Chalcedonian 158
    Nicene 158
    First London Baptist 267
    Philadelphia Baptist 234
    Second London Baptist 267
    Westminster 225, 267
Confessions
    Augustine 86, 161, 319,

    Patrick 142-143
Confucius 113, 378, 412, 480, 584, 585
Congreve, William, 342
Conservatism 60, 65, 66, 141, 166, 236, 268,
271, 275, 285, 287, 288, 297, 304 305, 340,
367, 419, 468, 501, 616, 655, 657, 658, 663,
675, 676, 685, 687, 688, 695, 698-703
Constantine 42, 79, 80, 85, 153, 589, 590
Constantius II 85
Coolidge, Calvin, 617-618
Copernicus, Nicholas, 438
Coronavirus (Covid-19) 21, 358, 367, 464,
522, 523, 624, 625, 675, 685, 728
Corruption 40, 60, 69, 71, 86, 104, 152, 154,
155, 171, 172, 182, 185, 191, 196, 199, 210,
216, 220, 243, 281, 306, 335, 336, 341, 344,
352-354, 360, 402, 405, 409, 486, 503, 508,
510, 517, 557, 566, 571, 573, 591, 649, 654,
660, 663, 678, 704
Corruption Perception Index 216
Cortes, Hernando 395
Cotton, John 224, 645
Council for Christian Colleges and
Universities 21, 658
Councils
    At Langres 88
    At Quierzy 88
    At Rheims 336
    At Savonniere 88
    At Soissons 150
    At Valence 88
    Ecumenical Seventh 166
    Lateran
        First 173
        Third 197, 324
        Fourth 168, 181, 185-
188, 205, 210
    Of Ancyra 314, 320
    Of Carthage 165
    Of Chalcedon 83
    Of Charon 150
    Of Clermont 387
    Of Constance 210, 212
    Of Elvira 166, 313, 314, 320, 538,
720, 732
    Of Ephesus 84, 710
    Of Florence 199
    Of Laodicea 534

Of Nicaea 83, 165, 173, 538
Of Orange 88
Of Paris 324
Of Toledo 322
Of Toulouges 386
Of Trullo 314
Privy 648
Provincial 636
Covenanters 43, 243, 259, 486, 611, 682
Coverdale, Miles, 216
Cranmer, Thomas, 224
Crapper, Thomas, 455
Crawford, Florence, 276
Creation 41, 85, 142, 143, 146, 160, 282, 287, 288, 360, 363, 366, 413, 416, 423, 428, 429, 430-432437, 460, 468, 527, 528, 656, 657, 659, 662
Cristofori, Bartolomeo 537
Critical Race Theory 296, 687, 692
Crockett, Davy 402
Cromwell
    Oliver 225, 247, 644
    Thomas 339
Crouch, Paul 278
Crusades 212, 395
Cudworth, Ralph 248, 646
Culdees 131, 132, 146, 147, 149, 713
Cults 163, 166, 189, 190, 247, 265, 266, 347, 362, 428, 534, 599, 695
Cultural Revolutions 18, 44, 65, 66, 302, 348, 361, 530, 537, 565, 566, 570
Culverwell, Nathaniel 646
Cuthbert 90
Cuvier, Georges 445
Cyprian of Carthage 317, 318, 389, 630, 720
Cyril the Deacon 79
Cyril and Methodius 77, 132, 200, 211, 212

D
D'Ascoli, Cecco 425
Da Vinci, Leonardo 544, 546
Dallimore, Arnold 256
Daly, Jim 367
Damadian, Raymond 460
Damascene, Hieromonk 58
Damian, Peter 173, 322, 323, 336, 714, 720, 721
Darby, John Nelson 268

Darius (King) 309, 579
Dark Ages 52, 414, 415, 419, 422
Darwin, Charles 69, 120, 121, 249, 270, 274, 346, 349, 351, 443-450, 454, 460, 530, 565, 575, 653, 655, 656, 677, 683, 712, 722, 727
Davenport-Hines, Richard 509
De Borbone, Stephanus 206
De Bruys, Peter 205
De Maricourt, Petrus Peregrinus (Peter the Pilgrim) 421
Debt 27-29, 36, 69, 70, 106, 258, 364, 405, 435, 473, 494, 500, 501, 502, 506-508, 513-524, 616-618, 660, 670, 707, 727
Debt-to-GDP Ratio 27, 28, 500, 501, 517-520, 616-618
Deen, Patrick 126
Defoe, Daniel 342
Degas, Edgar 560
Deism 117, 228, 248, 249, 613, 614
Denmark 132, 133, 184, 280, 331, 363, 399, 418,
Depersonalization 39, 40, 59, 277, 352, 363, 396, 467, 569
Der Weyden, Rogier van 546
Descartes, René 15, 112, 114, 117, 178
Dewey, John, 15, 39, 56, 120, 121, 123, 250, 287, 350, 650, 652, 654, 712, 722, 736
Di, Huang 582, 583
Diaspora 204, 227-299, 681-682
Didache 93, 167, 311, 711, 714, 719
Didascalia Apostolorum 167, 628, 696, 734
Diogenes 118
Dionysius (Greek Mythology) 294, 298, 567
Dionysius of Alexandria 388, 389
Discernment 19, 163, 229, 688
Discipleship 96, 130, 131, 134, 138, 140, 147, 148, 151, 156, 169-171, 192, 208, 235, 239, 242, 269, 282, 289, 293, 393, 422, 534, 587, 634, 639, 645, 648, 664, 671, 681, 682, 689, 693, 694, 695, 696, 697, 704
Disney 354, 571
Dispensationalism 268
Divorce 21, 44, 52, 60, 233, 277, 279, 281, 283, 309, 320, 340, 345-347, 355-357, 363, 365, 399, 476, 494, 496, 510, 565, 570, 595, 689, 698, 722
Dix, Dorothea 402
Dobson, James 367

Donatello 338, 543

Donation of Pepin 152

Donation of Constantine 152, 153, 167, 168, 175, 206, 210, 335, 401, 713

Donatism 161

Driscoll, Mark 293

Drugs 33, 123, 124, 313, 315, 365, 397, 584

Drunkenness 31, 254, 347, 378, 648

Dualism 112, 267, 272, 569

Duchamp, Marcel 564

Duff

    Alexander 230, 259, 260

    Samuel 230

Durant, Will 650, 719, 736

Durer, Albrecht 546, 547

Dwight, Timothy 118, 655

E

Eberstadt, Mary 491

Economy 28, 37, 43, 56, 57, 69, 72, 84, 302, 342, 393, 405, 409, 415, 416, 452, 463, 464, 471-525, 565, 590, 607, 611, 616, 618, 621, 625, 626, 669, 683-685, 696, 707

Ecumenicity 264, 676, 690, 691

Education 34, 49, 51, 52, 56, 71, 84, 95, 97, 105, 111, 141, 218, 249, 259, 269, 282, 283, 284, 287, 288, 302, 343, 351, 355, 362, 397-403, 415, 516, 436, 491, 495, 496, 509, 510, 557, 620, 621, 623, 624, 627-665, 680, 681, 684, 693, 696-700, 705, 708, 709, 717, 729

Edward

    Lord Herbert 117

    King of Wessex, 330

    I 175

    II 175, 341, 348,

    VI 222

Edwards, Jonathan 224, 235, 236, 241, 255, 260, 441, 655

Edwards v. Aguillard 662

Effeminacy 297, 303, 315, 317

Egalitarianism 69, 120, 281, 295, 400, 407, 496

Eichhorn, Johann Gottfried 251

Eilish, Billie 354, 574

Einstein, Albert 434

Eisenhower, Dwight D. 352, 358, 365, 367

Eliot

    John 229, 230

T.S. 62, 709

Elizabeth I, Queen 76, 222, 224, 339, 340, 480, 608

Ellis, Havelock 346

Ellul, Jacques 56, 57, 69, 468, 709, 728

Emerson, Ralph Waldo 120, 249, 350, 712

Emmanuel College 224, 644-646

Emmys 353

Empiricism 234, 440, 441

Engel v. Vitale 352, 365, 662

Engels, Friedrich 247, 251, 490

England 50, 53, 96, 98, 117, 132, 133, 136, 147-149, 172, 174-176, 180, 184, 185, 193, 195, 210, 211, 213, 217, 221, 222-225, 228, 230-233, 236-241, 243, 244, 247, 249, 253-255, 257, 263, 267-273, 280, 282, 289, 293, 327-333, 339-343, 346, 347, 358, 363, 395, 419, 420, 424, 477, 476, 479, 483, 486-489, 503, 516, 523, 540, 549, 593-597, 599, 602, 606, 607, 611-613, 633, 634, 640, 641, 644-649, 663, 664

Enlightenment 58, 59, 80, 104, 109, 111-113, 116-118, 217, 228, 231, 233-237, 243, 244, 247, 248, 250, 259, 265, 342, 343, 353, 357, 361, 414, 415, 439-441, 444, 445, 463, 545, 547, 552, 553, 584, 609, 610, 613, 645, 649, 655, 691

Epistemology 43, 56, 82, 84, 100-103, 113, 117, 128, 140, 177, 178, 199, 234, 236, 246, 288, 294, 302, 415, 440, 442, 462, 474, 557, 560, 636, 637, 664, 691, 696, 699, 700,

Erasmus, Desiderius Roterodamus 108, 218, 712

Ericson, Leif 229

Eriugena, John Scotus 89, 97, 633

Escapism 38, 124, 467, 689

Eschatology 14, 72, 265, 361, 644, 676, 704

Ethelbert of York 96

Ethelred the Unready 593

Ethics 20, 31, 49, 52, 78, 81, 94, 101, 102, 109-114, 119, 120, 124, 125, 161, 211, 219, 225, 228, 234, 245, 248, 251, 252, 279, 283, 284, 290, 297, 316, 318, 344, 346, 350, 367, 378, 407, 442, 446, 474, 492, 500, 509, 511, 512, 551, 557, 580, 609, 610, 635, 637, 645, 647, 649, 664, 691, 692, 697, 702

Euclid 106

Eugenics 21, 120, 274, 349, 351, 358, 445,

446, 450, 484, 677
Eulogius of Alexandria 151
Euripides 646
Eusebius of Caesarea 164, 167, 538, 633
Euthanasia 35, 36, 69, 394, 397, 412, 520
Evolution 116, 252, 273, 274, 280, 282, 287, 288, 346, 351, 352, 436, 437, 439, 443-447, 460, 461, 653, 656, 657, 695

F
Fabiola 394
Faith 14, 15, 18, 26, 33, 42, 44, 45, 46, 50, 63, 64, 71, 76, 78-82, 84, 85, 88, 90-96, 98, 102, 104, 108, 112, 114-119, 128, 131, 133-138, 142-147, 156-164, 167-191, 194, 201, 204-208, 211-216, 219-277, 282, 283, 289, 290, 293-299, 311, 322, 324-331, 362, 364, 368, 380, 384, 385, 389-393, 398, 403, 409, 413-415, 417, 421, 428 440, 441, 442, 448, 449, 452, 453, 456, 458-460, 463, 474, 485, 486, 488, 489, 496, 502, 509, 512, 518, 537, 546, 547, 549-551, 562, 576, 588, 592, 599, 600, 603, 604, 613, 614, 616, 623, 627, 628, 630, 633-636, 639, 640, 643, 644, 646, 647, 649, 654-656, 658, 659, 662, 670, 671, 673-679, 681-691, 694, 695, 697-702
Family, Family Economy 25, 30, 31, 36, 37, 46, 56, 135, 147, 238-242, 281-284, 289, 292, 304, 305, 309, 310, 342, 343, 353, 355, 356, 367, 397, 399, 403, 405, 411, 467, 475, 476, 478, 486, 487, 488, 490, 491, 494, 495-498, 511, 515, 519, 521, 553, 556, 565, 572, 620, 621, 626, 628, 652, 680, 682, 693, 697, 701, 705
Fantasy 38,39
Faraday, Michael 432-436, 452, 684, 726
Fatalism 86, 177, 425
Fatherhood 37, 289, 405, 490
Fear of God 13, 17, 46, 47, 48, 51, 93, 136, 139, 143, 206, 207, 239, 311, 326, 327, 333, 364, 365, 379, 392, 418, 427, 435, 444, 452, 456, 461, 466, 467, 484, 492, 516, 576, 591, 609, 628, 629, 662, 667, 668, 673, 675, 683, 684, 686, 689, 696, 698, 702, 704
Feminism 280, 281, 283, 292, 295, 297, 303, 315-317, 346, 406, 407, 511, 544, 565, 623, 657, 687, 692
Fessio, Joseph 701

Feudalism 194, 329, 418, 478, 479, 489, 591, 594, 596
Feuerbach, Ludwig 119, 251
Fichte, Johann 399, 400, 650
Ficino, Marsilio 106, 427
Finland 99, 131, 132, 133, 280
Finney, Charles 284, 717
Firenze, Andrea 106
Fitzwalter, Robert 595
Frame, John 103
Fleming
      Alexander 456, 457, 459
      Ambrose 433
Floyd, George 406
Focus on the Family 367
Forbes, Nancy 434, 726
Ford
      Daniel 488
      Gerald 367
Fordyce, John 448
Fouquet, Jean 543, 546
Fournier, Jacques. See Pope Benedict XII
France 47, 70, 132, 141, 148, 154, 169, 172, 174, 175, 183, 184, 193-195, 205, 207, 209, 217, 220, 335, 356, 361, 363, 364, 368, 385, 395, 399, 473, 480, 501, 503, 504, 519, 522, 540, 566, 594, 603, 608, 670
Francis I 353
Francke, August Hermann 113, 230
Franklin, Benjamin 256, 257, 586
Frederick III (Frederick the Wise) 218
French Huguenots 43, 217, 361, 603, 682
French Revolution 21, 343, 360-363, 383, 398, 399, 423, 503, 505, 610, 611, 614
Freud, Sigmund 121, 286, 654
Fritzgerald, F. Scott 358
Froebel, Friedrich 650, 652
Fulgentius of Ruspe 168
Futuyma, Douglas 444, 726

G
Galilei, Galileo 437, 438
Gall of Switzerland 147
Gallup
      George 694
      Polls 364, 370, 708, 719, 722, 723, 736
Galton, Francis 450

Gambling 498, 499, 504, 574, 655
Gardiner, Allen 230
Garrison, Fielding 394
Gaul 131-133, 156, 165, 477, 591
Gay, Peter 563, 732
Gender Dysphoria 41, 687
Germany 35, 47, 50-53, 85, 113, 117, 132, 133, 149, 165, 168, 171, 174, 175, 190, 208, 212-218, 228, 230, 231, 250-252, 271, 285, 294, 339, 349, 357, 364, 368, 399, 400, 403, 411, 420, 428, 438, 445, 459, 473, 501, 519, 522, 537, 540, 545, 546, 600, 615, 621, 636, 652, 670
Ghiberti, Lorenzo 542
Gibbon, Edward 48, 304, 336, 721
Giordano of Pisa 419, 428,
Girard, Stephen 505
Glanvil, Joseph 440, 441
Gnosticism 82, 114, 163, 164, 380, 424, 448, 463, 659
van Gogh, Vincent 560, 561
Goldman, Emma 121, 348
Gonzalez, Justo 630
Goodwin
          John 15, 245, 248, 264, 645, 716
          Thomas 224
Gorm, King of Denmark 133
Gorsuch, Neil 623
Gospel 50, 51, 77, 90, 91, 96, 103, 118, 131, 133, 134-137, 139, 142, 146, 148, 156, 164, 170, 180, 196, 197, 200, 203-205, 213-216, 219, 223, 227, 229, 230, 244, 245, 259-261, 263, 270, 271, 283, 284, 296, 297, 303, 310, 325, 331, 335, 342, 345, 389, 405, 459, 496, 497, 510, 569, 576, 587, 600, 629, 637, 646, 647, 671, 673, 674, 676, 681-683, 688, 690, 691, 695, 699, 702, 704
Gottschalk of Orbais 87, 88, 97, 168, 169, 190, 192, 218, 245, 633
Goya, Francisco 559
Gracchus, Tiberius 580
Graham
          Billy 53, 263, 264, 367, 709
          Franklin 367
Gramsci, Antonio Francesco 624
Great Awakening 213, 231, 235, 238, 241, 255, 257, 343, 655
Great Depression 349, 404, 499, 730

Great Ejection 216, 243, 486, 611
Greear, J.D. 663
Greece 27, 70, 78, 302, 303, 304, 344, 356, 370, 408, 517, 553, 719
Greek Philosophy 30, 78, 83, 94, 95, 97, 100, 105, 170, 211, 237, 303, 392, 532, 544, 553, 628, 636, 637, 646-650
Greed 27, 34, 69, 167, 185, 215, 303, 385, 486, 492, 497, 498, 499, 505, 507, 514, 523, 617
Greenwood John 223
Gregory
          Of Nyssa 393, 475
          Of Tours 419
Griswold v. State of Connecticut 365
Groote, Geert 208, 546
Grotius, Hugo 606, 606, 733
Guevara, Che 383
Guido of Arezzo 536
Guiscard, Robert 174
Gurnall, William 289
Gutenberg, Johann 420
Guthrie, James 259

H
Haggard
          Merle 65
          Ted 178, 293
Hall
          Charles Martin 453
          G. Stanley 650, 653, 654, 738
Halporn, James W. 531, 631
Ham, Ken 288
Hamilton
          Alexander 505
          James 261
Hancock, John 614
Handel, George Frideric 537, 548-550
Hannam, James 422
Harding, Warren G. 349
Harfarge, Harald 309
Hargreaves, James 481
Harper, Kyle 476
Harris, Joshua 293
Hart, Gary 366
Hartlib, Samuel 644
Harvard College/University 21, 59, 217, 234, 237, 249, 349, 646-649, 716, 719, 720, 726, 730, 736, 737

Hatmaker, Jen 202

Haven, Jens 230

Hawkins, John Sir 486, 550

Haydn, Joseph 550

Hayek, Friedrich 66, 67, 503, 710, 730

Hayes, Rutherford 505, 617

Haynes, Lemuel 118

Hedonism 60

Hefner, Hugh 570

Hegel, G.W.F 39, 56, 115, 116, 120

Hegemony 415, 582, 624

Heidegger, Martin 121, 123, 125

Heliopolis 79

Helwys, Thomas 267

Henry

    I 177, 503, 594-596

    II 150, 594

    IV 174, 183

    V 598

    VI 184

    VIII 222, 339, 340, 489, 607, 608

    Joseph 419

    Of Lausanne 205

    Of Uppsala 131-133

    Matthew 238, 270

    Patrick 257, 259, 613, 614

Henson, Gravenor 480

Heraclitus 104

Heresy 82-85, 103, 134, 142, 155, 156, 161, 163, 165-167, 188-190, 206, 207, 244, 245, 270, 285, 406, 608, 637, 643, 674, 714

Herigar (Sweden) 91

Hermes (Roman Prefect) 477

Herod (King) 588

Herrmann, Wilhelm 51

Heterodoxy 117, 228, 233, 234, 252, 269, 426, 599

Hierarchy 84, 141, 148, 154, 335, 478

Higbald 97, 633

Hincmar of Reims 15, 168, 169 245, 264

Hinduism 127, 279, 345, 679, 680

Hinn, Benny 278

Hirohito, Michinomiya 677

Hitler, Adolf 21, 116, 121, 228, 252, 403, 677

HIV / AIDS 41

Hobbes, Thomas 15

Hodge

    A.A. 49, 708

Charles 236, 716

Hoff-Sommers, Christina 491

Holdsworth, Richard 645, 646

Holland (country) See Netherlands

Holland, Tom 406

Hollis, Rachel 293, 719

Hollywood 61, 567, 574, 680, 684, 702

Holocaust 34, 35

Homer 90, 99, 631, 645, 646, 699

Holmes, Oliver Wendell 349, 350, 351, 677

Homeschooling 252, 287, 411, 454, 621, 622, 629, 630, 651, 652, 676, 701, 703, 717

Homosexuality 21, 29, 30, 40, 41, 45, 46, 49-52, 59-62, 77, 119, 195, 216, 229, 254, 258, 265, 280-286, 291, 292, 296, 303, 304, 306, 307, 310, 315-325, 337-369, 399, 407, 408, 411, 478, 509-515, 519, 522, 542, 544, 553, 554, 570-572, 588, 589, 599, 622-624, 657, 658, 660, 662, 663, 675, 678, 684, 687, 692, 699, 703, 714, 718, 720-723, 732

Honorius 79

    III 195

Hooker, Thomas 224, 488, 645

Hoover, Herbert 617, 618

Hope, Bob 570

Horden, John 230

Horic (Denmark King) 133

Horton, Johnny 354

Hotman, Francois 603

Houston, Frank 278

Huang, Qin Shi 378, 583, 585

Hucbald 535

Human Sacrifice 307, 77, 79, 131, 197, 309, 378, 572

Humanism 17, 18, 21, 31, 57, 62, 71, 77, 78, 80, 83, 84, 88, 95, 97, 100-110, 113, 114, 116, 120, 121, 125, 126, 140, 151, 177, 178 182, 189, 192, 196, 199, 214, 216, 217, 228, 229, 231, 233, 237, 244-249, 251, 253, 265, 269, 273, 274, 282-287, 290, 296, 297, 303, 304, 307, 338, 341, 342, 346, 351, 357, 359, 361, 363, 378, 383, 396, 399, 400, 406, 410, 413-415, 422, 423, 426, 427, 437, 439, 440, 443, 474, 484, 485, 489, 490, 492, 497, 503, 510, 511, 532, 539, 540, 542-547, 553-556, 559, 560, 562, 567, 575, 582, 605, 606, 609, 613, 614, 636, 637, 640, 641, 642, 644, 648-655, 662, 680, 684, 689, 695, 696, 699

Humanist Manifesto 21, 283, 654
Hume, David 117-119, 440
Humility 14, 64, 83, 95, 136, 140, 142, 143, 147, 157, 162, 179, 205, 218, 221, 269, 278, 348, 370, 380, 421, 428, 429, 434, 442, 449, 461, 463, 492, 539, 545, 550, 552, 614, 672, 676, 683, 685, 686, 688
Hunt
    John 230
    William Holman 561
Hus, Jan 211-213, 683
Hüttenbrenner, Anselm 555
Huxley, Aldous 69, 414
Hybels, Bill 293
Hymns 89, 90, 147, 158, 160, 179, 208, 257, 458, 506, 533, 534, 548, 551, 582, 634, 661, 714
Hypocrisy 34, 93, 172, 196, 243, 269, 338, 382, 385, 399, 402, 407, 411, 620, 673-676, 689
Hypothesis 121, 251, 287, 288, 298, 416, 423, 429, 437, 440, 443, 444, 447, 461

I
Iceland 77, 99, 122, 280, 363, 364
Ichabod 242, 649, 669, 699
Idolatry 69, 79, 80, 91, 110, 145, 157, 166, 189, 292, 297, 315, 324, 329, 330, 382, 411, 426, 514, 515, 532, 533, 538, 542, 565, 675, 678, 700, 701, 710
Ignatius 391, 534, 723
Impressionism 559, 563
Infanticide 30, 31, 33, 36, 77, 80, 93, 131, 304, 309, 310, 311, 313, 314, 315, 325, 337, 359, 378, 382, 388, 411
Inflation 66, 69, 483, 512-514, 517, 523, 524, 574, 581, 611, 619
Inter-Varsity Christian Fellowship 289
Internet 33, 39, 40, 68, 353, 354, 466, 674, 704
Investiture Controversy 174, 177, 183, 606
iPhones 39, 68, 352, 353, 434, 468, 572, 573
Ireland 34, 99, 132, 133, 142, 143, 146-150, 172, 197, 231, 281, 285, 330, 358, 363, 364, 408, 477, 594, 664, 713, 718
Irrationalism 56, 127, 294, 361, 567, 659
Isidore
    Of Pelusium 133
    Of Seville 87, 96
Islam 85, 276, 279, 345, 380, 383, 385, 424, 426, 477, 485, 487, 502, 543, 590, 636, 679, 685
Islands of Culture 289, 575-577, 621, 701-705
Israel (Modern) 47
Issachar 19
Italy 27, 47, 70, 85, 99, 119, 153, 172-174, 195, 266, 276, 335, 336, 338, 339, 342, 399, 418, 473, 501, 519, 537, 540, 542, 573, 637
IUD 34, 44, 45, 468, 728

J
Jackson
    Andrew 505, 616
    Michael 574
    Thomas "Stonewall" 384
Jahan, Shah 585
Japan 27, 47, 266, 273, 349, 356, 358, 368-370, 453, 473, 499, 501, 507. 518, 519, 522, 523, 620, 680
James
    I (Aragon) 201
    I (England) 224, 225, 339, 603, 608
    II (England) 259, 341, 486, 608, 611
Jehovah's Witness 266
Jenner, Edward 457, 458
Jennings, George 455
Jerome 147, 394, 427, 628-630, 633, 696
Jerusalem, Fall of 13, 18, 25, 50, 70, 668
Jews 13, 130, 197, 234, 235, 262, 277, 382, 390, 426, 448, 551, 587, 615, 672, 673, 685, 687
John
    (King) 184, 209, 595-597
    Of Salisbury 333, 334, 636, 721
Johnson
    Lyndon B. 367, 404, 617
    Paul 60, 390, 650, 709, 723, 724, 732, 736
Jonah 26, 91, 148
Jones, Humphrey 262
Josephus 633
Joule, James 433
Judas Iscariot 15, 594
Judgment of God 17, 22, 25, 26, 50, 56, 61, 69, 81, 88, 89, 127, 139, 144, 161-163, 183,

199, 204, 217, 241, 259, 307, 316, 323, 326, 328, 332, 334, 335, 354, 365, 382 384, 474, 482, 493, 502, 510, 514, 552, 556, 580, 621, 630, 677, 683, 688

Judson, Adoniram 230

Juggernaut 49, 274, 655, 657, 680

Julian the Apostate 79, 330, 389, 390, 406, 604

Jung, Carl 121, 654,

Junius, Johannes 198

Justinian I 325

Justinian Code 477, 720

K

Kalley, Robert Reid 230

Kames of Scotland 445

Kampen, Irene 570

Kant, Immanuel 15, 113-116, 120, 122, 399, 440, 560, 575, 712

Kay, John 481

Keach, Benjamin 267

Kendrick, Stephen 288

Kennedy, John F. 367

Kepler, Johannes 430, 433, 438

Kevin of Glendalough 146

Keynes

      John Maynard 15, 29, 66, 67, 69, 500, 507-523

      Neville 508-509

Keynesian Economics 67, 69, 500, 507, 508, 513, 516, 518, 520-523

Kuhlman, Kathryn 276, 278

Killian 132, 133, 149, 214

Kinkade, Thomas 562

King, Rodney 406

Kipling, Rudyard 63, 64, 515, 709, 723

Kirkland, Samuel 230

Knox

      Dilwyn 509

      John 109, 217, 222, 259, 639, 696, 717

L

Lady Gaga, 387, 570, 573, 575

Lanfranc, 176, 477

Lang, John, 638

Langdell, Christopher Columbus, 349, 350

Langton, Stephen, 185, 597

Lateran IV, 186

Latimer, Hugh, 224

Latitudinarian, 21, 216, 234, 245, 247–249, 645, 649

Law, John, 504, 512

Lawrence v. Texas, 363, 366

Le Peletier, Louis-Michel de Saint-Fargeau, 362

Leadership, 21, 37, 46, 71, 148, 149, 189, 249, 252, 261, 268, 274, 276, 278, 292, 293, 329, 363, 364, 472, 614, 669

Lear, Norman, 570

Lee, William, 480

Legalism, 272, 582, 583, 674

Leibnitz, 112, 117

Leithart, Peter, 635, 636

Lenski, Richard, 443

LeTourneau, R.G., 454

Leverett, John, 15, 234, 648, 649

Lewis, C.S, 49, 69, 118

Liberalism, 52, 257, 273, 274, 454, 656, 676

Liberty, 51, 65, 104, 115, 155, 184, 185, 220, 221, 247, 268, 284, 302, 333, 334, 381, 416, 465, 476, 477, 488, 489, 557, 580, 581, 586, 587, 592–594, 597–606, 610, 613–616, 623, 642, 703

Lincoln, Abraham, 347, 505, 616, 617

Lindisfarne, 97, 633

Lindsey, Theophilus, 135, 249

Linnaeus, Carolus, 433

Lister, Joseph, 456

Livingstone, David, 230, 259

Livy, 633

Lloyd-Jones, Martyn, 68, 69, 263

Locke, John, 15, 117, 118, 120, 236, 248, 440, 610

Logic, 97, 100–102, 178, 182, 211, 214, 253, 351, 421, 440, 442, 633, 636, 645

Lombard, Peter, 15, 85, 152, 181–183, 264, 638, 696

London, 47, 50, 67, 223, 225, 254, 256, 257, 267, 341, 342, 395, 401, 459, 478, 479, 510, 511, 596, 671, 680, 686

Lord Kelvin, 433

Louis

      IX, 193, 194, 395

      XIV, 362, 504

Love, John, 358, 365

Lucretius, 113
Luther, Martin, 19, 103, 171, 172, 208, 213–221, 253, 285, 323, 338, 428, 429, 484, 546–548, 600, 637–640, 683, 696, 699
Luxembourg, 35, 364
Lydia, 130, 131, 133, 180

M

M'Cheyne, Robert Murray, 261
MacArthur
Douglas, 474
John, 263, 272, 292
Macaulay, Thomas, 611
MacDonald, James, 293
Machen, J. Gresham, 21, 51, 52, 278
Mackay, Alexander, 230, 259
Macmillan, Daniel, 510
Macrina, 392, 393, 402, 628
Madaule, Jacques, 194
Magna Carta, 175, 184, 185, 209, 334, 485, 488, 595–597, 605, 608, 613, 614
Mahon, Basil, 434
Maimonides of Spain, 426
Malmesbury, 98, 99, 420, 634
Mandeville
        Bernard de, 248
        Geoffrey de, 595
Mang, Wang, 480
Mangalwadi, 418, 420, 585
Manichaeism, 380
Mann, Horace, 652, 653
Marbury, William, 21
Marcionism, 164
Marius, Gaius, 581
Marlowe, Christopher, 340, 341, 348
Marozia, 154, 335, 336
Mars Hill, 308
Marshall, Peter, 54
Martel, Charles, 385, 591
Martin, John, 554
Martyn, Henry, 230
Martyr, 79, 85, 93, 133, 137, 158, 194, 222, 243, 259, 271, 305, 389, 392, 428, 486, 564, 588, 589, 621
Martyr, Justin, 85, 158, 310, 311, 315, 391
Marx, Karl, 15, 69, 104, 115, 116, 119, 120, 250, 251, 390, 398, 400, 403, 490, 491, 492, 496–497, 575, 615, 624

Marxism, 280, 295, 397, 405, 519, 692
Mary I (Bloody Mary), 222, 224, 340, 589, 608, 611
Mason, George, 268
Materialism, 51, 104, 120, 280, 361, 567
Mather
Cotton, 457, 648
Increase, 234, 235, 237, 240, 347, 441, 457, 647–649
Richard, 224, 239
Maxwell, James Clerk, 230, 432–436, 684
Mayhew
Jonathan, 249
Thomas, 229
McCormick, Cyrus, 481, 482, 684
McCosh, James, 656
McGee, J. Vernon, 263
McGuffy, William Holmes, 652
McLean, Don, 65
McIlheny, Chuck, 62
McPherson, Aimee Semple, 276, 277
Media, 33, 39, 40, 46, 68, 72, 120, 124, 161, 285, 286, 288, 290, 353, 367, 461, 465–468, 562, 565–567, 572, 574–576, 659, 661, 679–681, 685, 693, 703, 705
Meiners, Christoph, 445
Melanchthon, Philip, 642
Melania, 477
Melville, Herman, 532
Memling, Hans, 546
Mendel, Gregor, 433, 446, 447
Mendelssohn, Felix, 550, 551
Mercer, Lucy, 349
Mercy of God, 14, 42, 128, 136, 143, 174, 213, 240, 260, 323, 381, 382, 384, 458, 485
Merivale, Charles, 306
Metaphysics, 75, 94–96, 101, 102, 113, 161, 163, 246, 350, 351, 425, 635, 637, 645, 677, 678, 691, 697
Methodius, 77, 132, 200, 211, 212
Michelangelo, 109, 535, 543, 548
Mill, John Stuart, 119, 249, 344, 565
Millennials, 36, 290, 345, 360
Milne
John, 261
William, 230
Modernism, 52, 228, 268
Moffat, Robert, 230, 259

Monarchy, 210, 225, 243, 341, 342, 597, 605, 609

Monet, Claude, 560

Money, 19, 21, 57, 64, 185, 215, 374, 375, 387, 391, 393, 396, 402, 412, 454, 455, 502–506, 512–515, 517, 518, 523, 524, 556, 581, 590, 611, 612, 616, 626, 631, 658, 684, 685

Monism, 120

Monophysite, 165

Monotheism, 79 85, 248

Montanism, 164

Montessori, Marie, 652

Moody, Dwight L., 228, 264, 348

Moore, G.E., 511, 512

Morality, 44, 54, 94, 114, 120, 192, 257, 259, 303, 304, 309, 310, 315, 326, 336, 342, 345, 348, 359, 360, 365, 382, 386, 406, 407, 412, 467, 475, 520, 521, 558, 566, 586, 626, 660

Immorality, 30, 60, 77, 173, 196, 313, 320, 321, 339, 342, 359, 361, 364, 365, 405, 556, 586, 595

Moravia, 132, 133, 211

Moravian Brethren, 213, 214, 230, 241, 255, 641, 642

Moreland, J.P., 442

Morgan

    David, 262

    Edmund, 241

    G. Campbell, 263

Mormonism, 46, 128, 266

Mornay, Philippe de Plessis, 604, 605

Morris, Henry, 288, 432

Morrison, Robert, 230

Morse, Samuel F.B., 453

Moses, 200, 251, 317, 329, 370, 455, 456, 476, 643, 644

Mother Teresa, 396

Movies, 569–571

Mozart, Wolfgang Amadeus, 550, 558

MRI, 460

Mueller, George, 342

Muggeridge, Malcolm, 57, 396

Muhammed, 380, 477, 487

Mundy, Peter, 585

Murahsima, Claire, 657

Murray, Iain, 259, 260

Music, 38, 44, 65, 102, 205, 282, 283, 293–295, 348, 354, 387, 395, 527, 529–537, 543, 548–550, 554–558, 562–564, 566–570, 573–575, 631, 633–635, 661, 686, 689

Muslims, 85, 279, 345, 385, 396, 426, 477, 485, 487, 502, 543, 636, 685

Mussolini, Benito, 121

N

NASA, 439

National Association of Evangelicals, 46, 287, 691

Naturalism, 69, 425, 546

Navigators, 289

Naylor, James, 247

Nazis, 34, 252, 407, 412, 615

Necker, Jacques, 503

Nelson, Justus, 230

Nephilim, 383, 508

Nestorianism, 84, 130, 229, 299, 396, 754

Nestorius, 84, 165

Netflix, 572

Netherlands, 35, 47, 132, 133, 136, 208, 217, 224, 228, 231, 345, 346, 356 363, 368, 369, 408, 419, 459, 485, 601, 602, 605, 613

Nettleton, Asahel, 118

New England, 224, 232, 233, 238–241, 268, 347, 487, 488, 613, 640–641, 646, 649

New Orleans, 47, 354, 569

New York City, 47, 348, 367, 449, 473

New Zealand, 34, 280, 358, 363, 408, 685

Newton

    Isaac, 114, 423, 424, 432–434, 438, 446, 684

    John, 257, 258, 260, 548

Nicholas of Cusa, 438

Niemoller, Martin, 252

Niethammer, Friedrich Immanuel, 400

Nietzsche Friedrich, 21, 39, 104, 115, 121–123, 286, 406, 412, 560, 565, 575, 615

Nihilism, 32, 49, 52, 57, 65, 104, 123, 364, 564, 571 574, 575, 663, 704

Nitske, Robert, 460

Nixon, Richard, 358, 367, 507, 517

Noble, Perry, 293

Noll, Mark, 233

Nondiscrimination Laws, 46, 658

Norman, Larry, 562

North America, 27, 29, 44, 46, 230, 232, 280, 359, 363, 369, 370, 472, 474, 486, 497, 519,

611, 679, 682
Northumbria, 90, 132, 135, 149, 157, 330, 634
Nuclear Family, 37, 355, 397, 490, 556

O
Obama, Barack, 21, 500, 508, 618
Obergefell v. Hodges, 21, 62, 68, 363, 366, 569, 622
Octavius, 78
Odoacer the Ostrogoth, 591
Oftfor, 136
Olivetan, Pierre, 205
Oresme, Nicole, 423, 424, 438
Origen, 148, 392
Origin of Species, 21, 351, 655
Orosius, 633
Orthodoxy, 51, 146, 158, 161, 163, 166, 177, 186, 194, 228, 247, 249, 250, 252, 269, 295, 298, 312, 511, 655
Orwell, George, 48
Osborne, Roger, 480
Osmund, 176
Ovid, 477, 641–643, 645, 646
Ovidius of Gaul, 477
Owen, John, 244, 260, 289

P
Packer, J.I., 253, 263
Paganism, 18, 76, 79, 82, 170, 245, 284, 301, 330, 353, 359, 389, 406, 427, 530, 531, 543, 547, 571, 572, 589, 697
Paglia, Camille, 573
Palmstruch, Johan, 503
Pantheism, 120, 554
Papacy, 141, 151–153, 172, 173, 175, 176, 191, 195–197, 199, 209, 216, 218, 335, 336, 338, 546, 596, 598, 599
Parham, Charles Fox, 275, 277
Parker
        Daniel, 268
        Francis W., 652
Parmenides, 104
Parricide, 36, 77
Pascal, Blaise, 452
Passivus, 323
Pasteur, Louis, 432, 456
Paton, John G., 230, 259, 342, 494

Patrick
        Darrin, 293
        Of Ireland, 142, 143, 146–148, 197, 295, 477
Patton, Francis, 656
Paul the Apostle, 42, 43, 130, 131, 135, 146, 148, 156, 186, 197, 250, 279, 283, 303, 307, 311, 315, 321, 360, 390, 398, 402, 408, 416, 441, 476, 482, 485, 533, 546, 580, 672, 673, 700
Paulinus, 132, 135, 394
Paulk, Earl, 278
Pearcey, Nancy, 103
Pederson, Randall, 223
Pelagianism, 161, 165
Semi-Pelagianism, 166, 169, 268
Pelagius, 142, 189, 264, 652
Penry, John, 223
Pentecostalism, 60, 261, 266, 275–279, 289, 671
Pepin, 152, 536
Perdiccas, 579
Perkins, William, 224, 645
Persecution, 41, 46, 62, 85, 164, 176, 188, 190, 193, 213, 217, 224, 231, 232, 241, 244, 268, 276, 291, 340, 361, 366, 368, 407, 410, 411, 447, 545, 587, 588, 601, 603, 611, 615, 616, 622–624, 644, 658, 662, 677, 682, 690, 691
Persia, 30, 165, 306, 307, 309, 517, 579, 678
Personality, 32, 39, 40, 165, 184, 380, 417, 467, 568
Perversion, 31, 44, 47, 68, 124, 146, 173, 285, 307, 315, 336, 338, 342, 345, 352, 353, 360, 362, 411, 412, 484, 510, 542, 569, 623, 662, 677, 678, 687
Pessimism, 31, 32, 110, 126
Peter the Apostle, 75, 129, 146, 151, 153, 154, 183, 325, 397
Petrarch, Francisco, 196, 414, 415, 543
Pew Research, 266, 368, 369
Philip II, 545, 580, 601
Phillips
        Carrie, 349
        Thomas, 263
Philoponus, 423
Philosophy, 18, 30, 39, 56, 60, 78, 81, 83, 94, 95, 97, 98, 100–103, 105, 106, 111–114, 116,

120, 121, 123, 125, 161, 170, 211, 217, 237, 265, 303, 351, 380, 392, 420, 429, 449, 452, 459, 502, 508, 511, 512, 528, 532, 544, 553, 556, 560, 582, 584, 605, 627, 628, 631, 636, 637, 641–643, 645–650, 652, 676, 699

Picasso, Pablo, 563, 565

Pierce, Franklin, 347, 402

Pilgrims, 43, 217, 224, 232, 346, 355, 487, 603, 605, 611, 682

Pink, A.W., 272

Pinker, Steven, 126

Piper, John, 263, 272

Plato, 78, 104, 106, 234, 248, 304, 398, 415, 427, 439, 509, 544, 633, 642, 645, 646, 649, 650

Platz, Elizabeth, 280

Pletho, Gemistus, 427

Pliny, 96, 388, 534

Pol Pot, 383

Politics, 45, 66, 84, 120, 195, 209, 274, 351, 378, 405, 472, 551, 590, 656, 702, 703

Pollock, Jackson, 564

Polybius, 304

Polycarp, 85, 93, 131, 271

Polygamy, 131, 247, 254, 283, 309, 310

Polytheism, 79, 97

Pompeii, 309, 353, 354

Pope, 149, 153, 172, 175, 176, 191, 193, 197, 209, 210, 213, 216, 218, 220, 228, 336, 339, 340, 439, 597, 600, 607–609

    Adrian IV, 150

    Alexander

        V, 212

        VI, 196

    Benedict IX, 359

    Clement V, 598

    Francis, 282, 699

    Gregory

        The Great, 96

        IX, 636

        VII, 174, 183, 184, 187, 200, 201

    Hildebrand, 173, 174, 183, 184

        XI, 209

    Innocent

        II, 178

        III, 15, 184, 187, 188, 193–195, 207, 597, 599

        IV, 191–192

        VIII, 196, 207, 282, 599

    John

        VIII, 200

        X, 335

        XII, 154, 282, 336

        XXIII, 359

    Julius II, 282

    Leo

        III, 152

        IX, 322

        X, 171, 215, 285

    Nicholas

        I, 154, 169, 172, 183, 335

        V, 484

    Paul III, 485

    Sergius III, 154, 335

    Stephen II, 152

    Urban

        IV, 637

        V, 637

Popoff, Peter, 278

Popular Culture, 88, 123, 342, 348, 558, 565–567, 572–574, 576

Population, 27, 34, 40, 42, 45, 60, 68, 76, 147, 172, 175, 190, 256, 273, 275, 287, 289–292, 304, 345, 347, 356, 359, 364, 367, 382, 418, 436, 455, 457, 473, 476, 478, 479, 487, 496–498, 518, 542, 564, 585, 588–591, 601, 657, 663, 670, 679–682, 701

Pornography, 33, 40, 60, 124, 283, 305, 306, 352–354, 362, 363, 365, 467, 496, 515, 570, 573, 574, 674, 678, 704

Porphyry, 98, 634

Porter, Cole, 348

Portugal, 27, 70, 473, 485

Post-

    Christian, 16, 30, 53, 54, 56, 89, 94, 105, 109, 115, 128, 141, 164, 283, 284, 286, 288, 301, 318, 325, 345–347, 360, 386, 387, 390, 395, 398, 406, 407, 410, 428, 445, 472, 474, 491, 495, 499, 531, 532, 560–562, 587, 611, 615, 625, 658, 662, 671, 680, 681, 688, 692

    Modern, 38, 39, 125, 282, 465. 567, 569, 576, 693

Postman, Neil, 68, 69

Pragmatism, 56, 123

Prayer, 31, 42, 87, 131, 136, 137, 139, 140, 144, 166, 176, 179, 190, 205, 207, 208, 214, 234, 239, 240, 253, 255, 257, 258, 262, 263, 271, 275, 277, 294, 295, 298, 352, 418, 435, 452, 456, 506, 509, 534, 536, 547, 593, 604, 645, 647, 661, 662, 680, 685, 689, 691

Predestination, 87, 88, 162, 600

Pride, 13, 30, 47, 53, 83, 93, 101, 112, 114, 126, 134, 143, 149, 151, 152, 163, 182, 184, 186, 189, 195, 199, 207, 233, 236, 237, 242, 243, 250, 269, 285, 296, 317, 344, 352, 382, 393, 434, 446, 449, 469, 536, 544, 554, 593, 614, 642, 646, 656, 657, 671, 675, 683, 684, 686, 687, 690, 699

Pride March, 47, 406, 686

Prison Ministry, 255

Pro-life, 288, 311, 312, 314, 337, 703

Prophets, 14, 15, 26, 44, 46, 48–50, 52–54, 56–63, 65, 67–70, 129, 133, 140, 144, 145, 155, 156, 163, 164, 196, 201, 203, 204, 208, 213, 244, 278, 292, 310, 346, 399, 406, 502, 511, 522, 541, 543, 573, 628, 629, 638, 654, 664, 672, 683, 704

Protestantism, 26, 76, 103, 109, 113, 150, 162, 166, 176, 183, 199, 203, 204, 211, 213–218, 222, 224, 225, 227–230, 233, 234, 243, 245, 247–250, 252, 257, 259, 260, 263, 266–269, 274, 280, 282, 283, 285, 286, 289, 295, 298, 340, 341, 343, 349, 401, 405, 428–430, 432, 440, 453, 460, 474, 480, 483, 485, 497, 548, 552, 589, 598, 600, 601, 604, 606, 611, 638, 640, 641, 649, 669, 679, 682

Providence of God, 22, 41, 65, 85–87, 109, 161, 176, 185, 204, 211, 241, 259, 313, 348, 349, 449, 452, 458, 482, 516, 591, 602, 603, 612

Psychology, 102, 105, 121, 286, 346, 465, 653, 654, 689

Ptolemy, 106, 579

Public School System, 41, 52, 287, 290, 352, 355, 365, 400, 505, 565, 576, 624, 652, 654, 661, 663, 702–704

Puritanism, 217, 222–225, 232–236, 238–241, 243, 244, 246, 248, 260, 263, 267, 269, 270, 289, 341, 343, 346, 347, 355, 400, 441, 486, 487, 602, 609–611, 640, 644, 645, 647, 649, 682, 702–704

Pythagoras, 106, 646

Q

Qi, Bai, 583

Queen Elizabeth, 76, 480

Quran, 127

R

Rabanus, 167

Racism, 252, 296, 444, 445

Radbertus, Paschasius, 15, 153, 167, 168, 181

Radbod of Frisia, 113

Radhost Mountain, 77

Radigast (god), 77

Ramsay, Willam, 433

Rand, Ayn, 121

Rastislav, 133

Ratramnus, 167

Ravenhill, Leonard, 61, 289

Raymond VI, 185, 193–195

Reagan, Ronald, 21, 67, 355, 358, 365, 367, 500, 501, 507, 570, 617, 618, 698

Recession, 27, 491, 499, 520–524, 618, 660, 669, 670

Reformation, 42, 88, 94, 99, 100, 105, 109, 141, 150, 169, 176, 183, 199, 203, 204, 208, 211, 213–218, 220–222, 224, 225, 227–230, 231, 232, 242–244, 250, 252, 253, 255, 259, 263, 268, 272, 285, 288, 298, 299, 334, 340–342, 361, 401, 424, 428, 433, 461, 474, 483–485, 487, 536, 538, 545–548, 557, 598–600, 603, 605, 607, 608, 611, 612, 636, 638, 640, 641, 645, 652, 664, 668, 681, 683, 688, 696, 697, 701, 703, 705

Relativism, 39, 49, 123, 125, 128, 282, 492, 554, 659

Rembrandt, Harmenszoon van Rijn, 547, 605

Renaissance, 88, 90, 99, 104–109, 119, 196, 217, 228, 237, 248, 303, 338, 339, 341, 342, 414, 415, 422–424, 427, 485, 503, 536, 540, 542–548, 641

Renn, Aaron, 366

Renwick, James, 259

Repentance, 18, 45, 54, 90, 212, 215, 216, 233, 253, 264, 278, 307, 320, 323, 342, 382, 576, 669, 673, 681, 683, 685, 688, 689, 690, 694, 695, 705

Revelation, 20, 51, 58, 83, 102, 103, 105, 111, 112, 113, 115–117, 118, 119, 127, 128, 161, 166, 236, 249, 251, 270, 276, 287, 290, 449, 462, 476, 512, 559, 610, 639, 688, 695

Revival, 33, 61, 71, 109, 228, 233, 235, 236, 244, 253–255, 257–265, 268, 272, 277, 288, 289, 297–299, 343, 348, 414, 539, 543, 545, 655

    Azusa Street, 275, 276

    Evangelical, 255, 257, 343

    New York Businessmen, 348

    Welsh, 262

Revoice Conference, 296–298

Revolution

    Cultural, 18, 65, 66, 302, 361, 530, 565, 566, 570

    Dionysian, 294, 298

    French, 21, 343, 361, 383, 399, 503, 505, 610, 614

    Industrial, 480, 494

    Musical, 44

    Sexual, 44, 61, 285, 286, 348, 354, 511, 568, 573

Richard

    I, 594

    Of Wallingford, 422

Ridley, Nicholas, 224

Robert the Bruce, 149, 175, 598

Roberts

    John, 623

    Paul Craig, 67

Robespierre, 362, 383

Robinson

    Gene, 21, 281

    Ida, 276

Rockefeller, John D., 454

Roe v. Wade, 21, 358, 366, 622

Roentgen, Wilhelm Conrad, 459, 460

Romanticism, 104, 112, 294, 295, 361, 553, 554, 556, 567, 674

Rome, 13, 17, 18, 34, 38, 41, 63, 65, 70, 77, 78, 80, 85, 106, 125, 131, 132, 138, 141, 149–154, 156, 162, 171, 172, 174, 176, 180 195, 196, 209, 210, 215, 216, 219, 231, 262, 285, 306, 314, 325, 336, 337, 342, 344, 370, 378, 387, 392, 394, 399, 406, 407, 502, 516, 517, 553, 554, 581, 586, 587, 588, 590, 591, 607, 611, 615, 637, 667, 668, 699

Roosevelt

    Eleanor, 349

    Franklin D., 349, 404, 507, 516, 616, 618

    Theodore, 349, 351, 404, 677

Rose, Eugine David, 57, 58

Rossini, Gioachino, 554

Roth v. US, 352, 365, 570

Rothbard, 513, 520, 521

Rouault, Georges, 562

Rousseau, Jean-Jacques, 15, 48, 112, 114, 361, 362, 398, 399, 415, 440, 552, 565, 610, 641, 650–652, 655, 683

Rubens, Peter Paul, 547

Rudolph I, 598

Rufus, William, 176

Rupert of Deutz, 132, 636

Rushdoony, R.J., 56, 287

Russia, 52, 58, 59, 99, 165, 276, 357, 369, 370, 399, 400, 403, 408, 453, 473, 489, 491, 519, 587, 615, 620, 621

Rutherford, Samuel, 191, 334, 609, 610

S

Sadoleto, Jacopo, 220

Sadomasochism, 354

Salvation, 22, 81, 82, 87, 89–92, 99, 100, 101, 107, 108, 116, 118, 128, 137, 146, 156, 157, 165, 169, 174, 177, 182, 199, 207, 218, 220, 221, 228, 241, 254, 260, 264, 265, 267, 270, 297, 316, 400, 439, 451, 565, 573, 616, 642, 651, 652, 674, 692

Salvation Army, 401, 408

Salvian, 125

Sambursky, Samuel, 414

San Francisco, 62, 345

Sanger, Margaret, 29, 358, 363, 680

Sardis, 16, 221, 222, 298, 576, 688, 698

Sartre, Jean-Paul, 15, 29, 39, 56, 121, 123–125, 560, 567, 575

Satanism, 197

Sayers, Dorothy, 562

Schaeffer, Francis, 46, 54–56, 69, 77, 105, 112, 287, 543, 564, 693

Schaff, 154, 172, 179, 184

Schlossberg, Herbert, 68, 69

Schmelen, Johann, 230

Schoenberg, Arnold, 564

Schopenhauer, Arthur, 119

Science, 34, 38, 39, 43, 56, 84, 86, 96, 100, 102, 104, 120, 121, 236, 242, 302, 350, 413, 414, 420, 421, 423–425, 427–429, 431–439, 441, 442–455, 458–469, 474, 483, 527, 535, 544, 656, 668, 683, 698, 705

    Fiction, 38, 39, 428

    Junk, 464

Scientism, 112 414, 426–428, 441, 442, 445, 465

Scofield. C.I., 268

Scott

    Dred, 21

    Otto, 341

Scougal, Henry, 255

Secular Education, 49, 51, 141, 287, 654, 661

Semmelweis, Ignaz, 456

Sennacherib, 579

Separatism, 206, 222–224, 272, 701–704

Serbia, 47, 364, 408

Sewall, Samuel, 487

Sexuality, 39, 40, 51, 59, 77, 119, 216, 280, 281, 283, 306, 315, 339, 341, 352, 363, 510, 517, 542, 558, 570, 659

Seymour, William J., 275

Shaftesbury, 249

Shakespeare, William, 340, 341, 511, 553

Shaw, George Bernard, 48, 346

Shelley, Percy, 48, 553

Shindler, Robert, 269, 270

Si, Li, 584

Sibbes

    Richard, 224

    William, 645

Sidgwick, Henry, 509

Siger of Brabant, 426, 427

Sigmund, 121, 286, 654

Silent Generation, 36

Simon the Sorcerer, 15, 278

Simony, 173, 213

Simpson, James Young, 458, 459

Sixtus IV, 196

Skepticism, 50, 51, 114, 118, 125, 228, 247, 251, 253, 264, 303, 421, 436, 456, 465, 484, 614, 656, 659

Skidelsky, Robert, 512

Skinner, B.F., 286

Slavery, 55, 61, 77, 143, 331, 347, 393, 416,

475–477, 484–487, 489, 494, 496, 497, 613, 677

Slessor, Mary, 259

Smallpox, 443, 457

Smaragdus, 477

Smartphones, 40, 352, 353, 468, 572, 573

Smeaton, George, 261

Smith

    Chuck, 289

    John, 646

    Will, 387

Social Media, 33, 39, 68, 465–467, 693

Social Security, 35, 404, 412, 497, 498

Socialism, 52, 257, 274, 284, 357, 362, 396, 398, 399, 402–405, 409, 411, 412, 480, 489–491, 494, 496–498, 565, 581, 583, 607, 608, 617, 620, 625, 626, 650, 652–654, 687

Society, 18, 32–34, 37, 39, 49, 55, 56, 62, 65, 69, 79, 83, 120, 122, 193, 236, 237, 241, 280, 302–305, 316, 322, 324, 326, 338, 342, 344, 345, 347, 352–356, 360, 377, 382, 388, 394, 401, 402, 405, 406, 409–411, 413–417, 440, 451, 468, 483, 490, 491, 494–496, 498, 507, 510, 513, 515, 557, 563, 567, 569, 575, 588, 599, 626, 650, 651, 656, 661, 671, 681, 684, 701

Socinianism, 247, 269, 279

Sociology, 120, 415, 439, 465, 466, 653, 654

Socrates, 118, 341

Sodom, 26, 29, 30, 49, 50, 53, 258, 316, 317, 319, 338, 347, 510, 660, 684

Sodomy, 30, 254, 278, 285, 317, 319, 321–324, 336, 359, 363, 366, 478, 544, 571

SOGI, 46, 658

Solzhenitsyn, Alexandr Isayevich, 58, 59, 69, 104

Sookhdeo, Patrick, 694

Sorrell, Tom, 442

Sovereignty of God, 82, 85, 86, 88, 89, 96, 97, 109, 118, 128, 134, 150, 151, 162, 168, 169, 177, 181, 182, 192, 218, 225, 241, 245, 246, 248, 260, 264, 265, 269, 271, 272, 277, 290, 328, 341, 427, 482, 606, 608, 609, 633, 648

Sozzini, Fausto, 15, 247

Spain, 47, 70, 85, 99, 132, 174, 184, 201, 313, 368, 385, 395, 399, 426, 485, 486, 501, 522, 537, 540, 591, 601

Spanish Flu, 41

Spelman, John, 593

Spencer, Herbert, 677, 680

Spilsbury, John, 267

Spinoza, Baruch, 117

Sports, 38, 387, 624

Sproul, R.C., 263

Spurgeon, Charles, 49, 50, 257, 269, 271–273

St. Andrew's Seven, 231, 260, 261

Stalin, Josef, 383, 412

Stanton, Cady, 346

Stark, Rodney, 414, 415, 428, 432, 438, 478

Staupitz, Johann von, 206

STD, 41

Steinbeck, John, 37, 358

Stephen, 594

Sterry, Peter, 646

Stock Market, 498, 499, 617

Stockman, David, 67

Stokes, George, 433

Stott, John, 263

Stravinsky, Igor, 564

Stuart, Mary, 341

Studd, C.T., 230

Suicide, 21, 32, 35, 37, 39, 41, 48, 125, 305, 348, 354, 461, 560, 564, 576, 677

Sulla, 581

Sullivan, Andrew, 126

Supreme Court, 21, 69, 291, 350, 351, 358, 363, 365, 366, 411, 569, 570, 622, 623, 625, 662, 677, 698

Swaggart, Jimmy, 278

Sweden, 91, 132, 133, 228, 280, 356, 363, 364, 368, 399, 411

Swinburne, Algernon Charles, 553

Swineshead, Richard, 423

Switzerland, 35, 132, 147, 174, 205, 217, 228, 231, 363, 599, 613

Synod

        Of Chiersy, 168

        Of France, 169

        Of the Grove of Victory, 321

        Irish, 314

        At Lent, 183

        At Mainz, 168

        Of Toulouse, 192

        Of Whitby, 149

Synthesis, 116, 134, 249, 282, 426, 427, 543, 547, 576, 606, 702, 704

T

Tacitus, 306

Tanner, Henry, 562

Taylor, Hudson, 230, 261

Tchividjian, Tullian, 293

Technology, 31, 34, 57, 68, 112, 126, 242, 348, 352, 387, 417, 418, 422, 424, 432, 434, 436, 446, 451–454, 461, 466–468, 474, 481, 482, 484, 566, 575, 585, 684, 685, 705

Templeton Address, 58

Tertullian, 259, 310, 313, 390, 532, 533

Tetzel, Johann, 215

Thatcher, Margaret, 412, 663

Theodora, 335, 336

Theodoric the Great, 591

Theodosius I, 85, 325, 344, 589

Theology, 20, 81, 97, 100, 102, 103, 106, 108, 111, 113, 140, 142, 151, 161, 162, 167, 178, 181, 182, 192, 208, 210, 219, 223, 225, 229, 246, 251, 252, 268, 284, 297, 346, 347, 405, 417, 421, 497, 551, 576, 636, 638, 642, 652, 655, 700

Theophilus, 419

Theophylact I, 335, 336

Thesis, 26, 116, 215, 426, 700

Thompson, Thomas, 230

Thoreau, Henry David, 120

Tiberius, 306, 580, 581

Tillotson, John, 248

Tindal, Matthew, 117, 248

Titian of Venice, 545, 546

Titus, 251, 306

Toland, John, 117, 248

Toplady, Augustus, 548

Totalitarianism, 67, 84, 496, 582, 621, 625, 626, 651

Tower of Babel, 48, 151, 609, 670

Tozer, A.W., 263

Trajan, 388, 502

Transgenderism, 21, 280, 315, 353–355, 359, 397, 408, 489, 573, 588, 622, 623, 663, 664, 687

Transubstantiation, 154, 185, 205, 210, 212, 219, 221

Trinity, 83, 95, 99, 118, 134, 143, 146, 150, 156, 157, 169, 206, 245, 246, 325, 538, 623, 655

Trismegistus, 427

Trudpert, 133
Truman, Harry S., 617, 618
Trump, Donald J., 367, 406, 500, 508, 616–618, 623
Tryggvason, 310
Tyndale, William, 190, 216, 639, 640, 696
Tyranny, 42, 51, 54, 84, 173, 176, 184, 190, 191, 197 210, 247, 323, 486, 581–583, 585–587, 589, 591–594, 598–600, 608–611, 615, 618, 619, 621, 622, 684, 693
Tyre, 26, 684

U
Udemans, Godefridus, 485
Ukraine, 47, 357, 615
Ultimacy of God, 78, 84, 85, 88, 99, 112, 379, 535, 544, 569
Unitarianism, 33, 117, 166, 228, 247–249, 253, 269, 347, 402, 540, 613, 649
United Kingdom, 335, 364, 408, 522, 681
United States, 27, 28, 37, 44, 45, 47, 67, 70, 71, 141, 150, 230, 232, 237, 266, 274, 281, 285, 287–289, 291, 345, 347, 355, 356, 358, 359, 365, 366, 368, 386, 387, 401, 402, 408, 409, 411, 412, 491, 495, 496, 500, 505–507, 517, 519, 520, 554, 571, 602, 604, 611, 615, 618, 620, 623, 652, 655, 656, 663, 669, 670, 681
Utah, 21, 663, 674
Utopian, 60, 339, 402, 491, 650

V
Vaccine, 443, 446, 457, 625
Valens, 85
Valerian, 588
Van Eyck, Jan, 546
Van Til, Cornelius, 43, 83, 287
Vanbrugh, John, 342
Vermeer, Johannes, 545, 547
Video Games, 38
Vikings, 329, 331, 385
Virgil, 90, 96, 106, 642, 645, 646
Voltaire, 48, 361, 362, 415, 444, 445, 655

W
Wagner, Richard, 294, 557, 558, 565
Wala, 322
Waldo, Peter, 205, 211, 221, 296

Waltrip, Burroughs, 264
Ware, Henry, 249
Warhol, Andy, 570, 575
Warre, Edmond, 509
Warren
    Earl, 352, 365
    Rick, 292
Washington, George, 257, 449, 450, 505, 613
Watson, Thomas, 645
Webster, Noah, 488, 652
Wedlock, 36, 37, 342, 356, 547
Weinstein, Harvey, 406
Wellhausen, Julius, 251
Wells, H.G., 559
Wesley
    Charles, 225, 256, 548
    John, 213, 255
West, Mae, 348
Whichcote, Benjamin, 25, 245, 248, 645
Whitcomb, John C., 288
White
    A.D., 606
    Lynne Townsend, 414, 417
    Paula, 278
    Randy, 278
Whitefield, George, 213, 255–257
Whitgift, John, 222
Wiker, Benjamin, 60
Wilberforce, William, 257
Wilde, Oscar, 60, 346, 511, 554
Wilkerson, David, 60, 61, 289, 669
William
    I, 594
    II, 594
    III, 602
    The Conqueror, 174, 176, 385, 477, 593, 594
    The Silent, 601–603, 605, 611
Williams
    George, 401
    Henry, 230
    John, 230
    Of Jumièges, 595
    Roger, 224, 268
    Walter, 611
Willibrord, 132, 136
Wilson
    Joseph Ruggles, 274

Woodrow, 274, 349, 404, 616, 617, 654, 656, 677

Winthrop
John, 224, 239, 644
Robert, 586

Wisdom, 14, 48, 80, 90, 96, 97, 108, 114, 144, 161, 217, 234, 237, 319, 418, 430, 433, 448, 449, 482, 492, 527, 533, 543, 556, 576, 609, 627, 628, 631, 632, 642, 646, 647, 654, 674, 696, 699

Witchcraft, 131, 197, 198, 330, 363, 374, 426, 440, 599

Wittenberg, 91, 106, 215, 216, 637

Wolfe, Tom, 114, 564

Wolff, Christian, 25, 113

Wollstonecraft, Mary, 346

Wolpert, Stanley, 586

Woodhull, Victoria, 346

Woolston, Thomas, 248

Worcester, Samuel, 616

World War, 54, 70, 121, 358, 445, 626
I, 617
II, 34, 70, 349, 352, 454, 518, 618

Worldview
Anti-Christian, 26, 285, 567, 627
Christian, 26, 71, 82, 90, 95, 99, 100, 101, 216, 285, 290, 327, 382, 427, 431, 439, 442, 483, 492, 542, 543, 567, 575, 627, 658, 659, 661, 681
Post-Christian, 681

Worship, 63, 77–80, 84, 87, 91, 131, 157, 166, 179, 184, 199, 205, 217, 220, 221, 238, 239, 242, 262, 273, 276, 289, 294, 295, 298, 329, 330, 362, 391, 427, 430, 433, 434, 436, 452, 467, 484, 523, 532, 533, 536, 538–541, 548–552, 554, 562, 583, 625, 643, 654, 662, 668, 669, 675, 680, 686, 694, 695, 697

Worthington, John, 646

Wulfstan, 477

Wycliff, John, 208–212, 218, 221, 249, 271, 683

X

X-ray, 459, 460

Xenoglossia, 275

Xerxes
I, 309, 579
II, 309, 579

Y

Yale University, 249, 649, 654, 655

YMCA, 401, 407

Z

Zebri, Gabriele, 394

Zedong, Mao, 383

Zeitgeist, 43, 49, 54, 277, 286–288, 292, 367, 529, 563, 569, 571, 575, 576, 624, 658

Zeus, 303

Zhong, Guan, 582

Ziegenbalg, Bartholomaus, 230

Zinzendorf, Nicolaus von, 230

Zoroaster, 106

SCRIPTURE INDEX

Genesis

1:28	429
1:31	527
3:1-5	124-125
8:2	431
9:5-6	372
11:4	151

Exodus

20-22	329
20:1-6	530
21:2-6	372
21:7	372
21:12-16	372
21:20-21	373
21:22-23	373
21:24-25	373
21:26-27	373
21:28-32	373
21:33-34	373
21:35-36	374
22:1	374
22:2-4	374
22:4	375
22:5	374
22:6	374
22:7-11	374
22:16-17	374
22:18	374
22:18-20	375
22:19	375
22:21	375
22:22-24	375
22:25	375
22:26-27	375
22:28	375
22:29-30	375
22:31	375
23:1	375
23:2	376
23:6	376
23:7-8	376
23:9	376
25:18-20	537-538

Leviticus

18	306
18:28	677
20:13	322, 347, 511
25:10	476

Numbers

23:19	127
35:11-33	372

Deuteronomy

4:2-4	198
6:4-9	200
6:6-8	111
6:7	111
6:7-9	635
6:7-9	238
8:13	435-436
8:17	236
8:17-20	435-436
20:14	380
23:13	455
24:7	485
25:3	380
25:13-16	517
28:1	471-472
28:8-13	471-472
28:39-45	493
28:41	494
28:43-47	28
28:53	33
29:29	82

Judges

20-21	510
21:25	512

1 Samuel

2:6	97
2:7	492
15:9	675
22:1-2	288

2 Samuel

23:1-4	699

2 Kings

17:7-12	541-542

1 Chronicles

12:32	19

2 Chronicles

7:14	685
24:19	48

Job

1:21	246

Psalms

1:1-3	632
2:1-3	104
2:3	510
2:4-5	47
8	431-432
8:1-5	377
8:5	380
11:4-7	308
12:6	127, 282
14:1-4	121-122
19:1	111
19:2	111
19:7	111
20:7-8	413
33:12	71
36:1-3	662
37:21	523
37:35-40	573
46	577
46:8-11	626
53:5	684
72:1-4	589
72:9-11	324
72:10-11	589
78:1-8	22-23
78:8-11	22
80:4-7	227
80:14-19	214
80:15-19	545
85:4-6	254
85:6	26
90:9-11	455
100:5	128
111:2	430
115:1-8	110
119:138	128
135:15-18	426
139:23-24	675
147:5	127
150	548

Proverbs

1:1-7	697

1:7	379, 696
2:3	647
2:4-6	418
4:18-19	38
8:36	35, 127
10:4	492
10:22	482
12:10	412
13:11	492-493
14:30	497
16:5	445
16:18	13, 47
17:15	410
19:27	627
20:10	512, 516
20:21	493
21:27	408
22:4	492
22:7	500
25:2-4	430-431
25:26	46
26:12	442
28:2	586
28:15-17	339
30:2	448
30:18	448

Ecclesiastes

1:9-11	17
3:19-20	379
7:17	33
7:29	117
12:13-14	17

Isaiah

1:5-9	29
1:21-22	502
2:2-3	93
3:12	36, 293
5:11-18	552
5:20-23	414
8:19-20	692
9:1-2	204
9:6-7	204
42:1-4	334
47:12-14	424
49:22-25	598
53:6	528

58:12	705
59:19-21	73
60:1-6	170
61:1-4	381
61:11	381

Jeremiah

6:14	14
17:5-7	555
17:9	467
23:16	201

Lamentations

5:16-22	25

Ezekiel

13:8-9	654
18:20	296

Daniel

4:34-35	370

Hosea

14:1-3	439

Joel

2:28-32	225-226

Amos

8:11-13	694

Obadiah

3	469

Jonah

2:9	91, 146, 692

Matthew

1:21	284
4:13-16	310
4:17	382
5:17-19	164
5:18	675
5:44-45	42
7:16	278, 298
7:20	521
11:21-24	26

13:24-30	187
13:41	188
15:1-8	200, 675
16:4	235
16:13-18	129
17:24-27	612
18:6	660
18:7	507
19:4	200
19:8	476
20:16	671
20:25-28	183
23:23	695
24:12-13	412
24:14-15	196
25:36	395
25:40	395
28:18-20	235, 279
28:19-20	130, 693
28:20	148, 496, 694

Mark

8:22-25	558-559
12:14-16	620
13:13	213

Luke

4:18-19	476
6:45	528
10:26	200
12	451
12:15	493
12:48	30
13:1-5	18
14:33-35	44
21:26	127
21:34-36	31
22:23-26	388
22:25	411
22:25-26	151, 396
22:25-27	599
22:42	277

John

1:1	161
3:21	416
8:33-34	587
8:36	579

9:25	299
10:17-18	397
13:3-5	384
13:35	692
14:15	398
15:4-5	207-208
15:9-10	207-208
15:18-22	603
16:1-3	168, 191
17	691
17:3	647
17:17	20
17:20-23	234
20:29	277, 440, 441

Acts

2:1-11	261-262
2:32-36	75, 676-677
3:19	253
3:19-21	203
4:32-34	275
4:33-35	390
5:4	398
6:1-7	390
7:51-52	48
8:1-4	231
8:3-4	681
10:34-35	444
10:34-36	704
14:15-17	43
15	329
15:5	94
15:19-20	94
16:12-15	131
17:30	678
17:30-31	308
19:13-16	197
20:28-30	171, 250
20:28-32	279-280
20:35	408

Romans

1	306
1:18	102, 528, 646, 686-687, 700
1:18-21	528
1:18-22	659

1:19	102
1:21-22	123
1:26	307
1:27	307
1:27-28	659
1:28	32, 464, 663
1:28-32	580
1:32	307, 322
2:3-4	307
2:14	43
3:2	26
3:4	128
3:20	284
6:23	31
8:6-7	182
8:31-36	482
9:2	13, 26
9:6	14
11:1-5	204-205
11:2-5	664-665
11:12	14
11:15	679
11:18-20	13
11:20	672
11:20-21	364
11:22	14
11:24-26	551-552
11:31-36	14
11:32	14
11:33	14
11:33-36	161, 217, 482
11:36	692
13:1-4	606
13:9	94
13:9-10	398
14	466
16:17	188

1 Corinthians

1:22	235, 237, 277
1:22-23	234
3:12	295
5	321
5:1-5	321
5:8	675
6:9-10	315, 321
6:9-11	297
6:11	297

7:14	643
7:21-23	476, 486, 612
8:1	416
10:11	15
10:11-13	41-42
10:16-17	186
10:18-19	285
10:25-28	411
10:31	536
11:19	674
12:26	26
13	693
14:15	294
14:33	431
15:1-4	156
15:20-28	692
15:25	72, 677

2 Corinthians

6:2	674
6:14-18	701
10:4-6	45
11:13-15	189

Galatians

1:8-9	245
1:12	449
3:8	229
3:13-14	229
6:10	390

Ephesians

1:19-22	678
1:22	682
2:10-14	295
2:12	125
4:1-6	690
4:17-18	77, 428
4:17-24	302-303
4:19	34
5:3-5	324
5:11-13	318
5:16	421
5:18	279
6:4	94

Philippians

1:9-11	278

2:7	380
2:12-13	297

Colossians

2:8	103, 646
2:16	94
3:9-10	429
3:10	430
3:15-17	533
3:16	283

1 Thessalonians

4:10	295

2 Thessalonians

2:3-4	184, 283
2:3	190
2:7	190
2:11-12	514, 664
2:11-13	128
3:6-13	235

1 Timothy

1:4	266
1:4-5	294
1:18-19	181
3:8-9	167, 185
4:1-2	243
4:1-3	172
5:9-10	408
6:4	265
6:6-9	493

2 Timothy

2:1-2	138
2:2	639-640
3:1	43
3:1-5	295
3:5	674
3:1-6	403
3:6-11	644
3:13	43
3:16-17	284
4:1-3	283
4:2	135

Titus

1:14	266
1:15	182
3:9	266

Philemon

10	475
14-16	475

Hebrews

6:18	127
11:1	277
11:3	428
11:32-38	208-209
12:27-29	667, 668

James

1:5-8	114
1:17	436
1:22-24	416, 420-421
2:13	382
2:17	298
3:9-10	379
4:9-10	14

1 Peter

4:17	45, 688
4:17-18	335
5:6	14

2 Peter

1:19-21	105
2:1	155
2:1-3	163
2:9-22	556-557
2:12	508
2:12-22	155
2:14-15	508
2:18-20	104-105
2:20	43
2:20-22	301

1 John

1:4	128
2:1	295
3:4	692
3:20	127

4:1-3	163-164

Jude
3	177

Revelation
2:14	188
2:18-22	292
3:1-5	221-222
3:1-3	298, 698
3:2-3	16
3:3	286
3:15-18	254
3:21-22	672
5	679
7	679
9:1-3	360
12:9-11	564-565
12:17	587
14:12	94, 695
17:1-6	621
17:3-6	305-306
18:1-9	524
19:11-16	98-99
20:10	677
21:8	677